RAF Bomber Command Profiles

75(NZ) Squadron

RAF Bomber Command Profiles

75(NZ) Squadron

Chris Ward and Chris Newey

www.aviationbooks.org

First published 2018 by Aviation Books Ltd., Merthyr Tydfil, UK.

This second edition published 2023 by Aviation Books Ltd.

Copyright 2018 and 2023 © Chris Ward.

The right of Chris Ward to be identified as Author of this work is asserted by him in accordance with the Copyright, Designs and Patents Act 1988.

The original Operational Record Book of 75(NZ) Squadron, all RAF Stations and the Bomber Command Night Raid Reports are Crown Copyright and stored in microfiche and digital format by the National Archives. All Crown Copyright material in this work is reproduced under the terms and conditions of Open Government Licence 3.0.

All rights reserved. No part of this publication may be reproduced, stored in a retrieval system, transmitted in any form or by any means, electronic, mechanical or photocopied, recorded or otherwise, without the written permission of the copyright owners.

This squadron profile has been researched, compiled and written by its author, who has made every effort to ensure the accuracy of the information contained in it. The author will not be liable for any damages caused, or alleged to be caused, by any information contained in this book. E. & O.E.

Cover design: Topics - The Creative Partnership www.topicsdesign.co.uk

A CIP catalogue reference for this book is available from the British Library.

ISBN 9781915335173

Also by Chris Ward from Bomber Command Books:

Casualty of War: Letters Home from Flight Lieutenant Bill Astell DFC

Dambuster Deering: The Life and Death of an Unsung Hero

Dambusters: The Complete WWII History of 617 Squadron
(with Andy Lee and Andreas Wachtel)

Other RAF Bomber Command Profiles:

10 Squadron (with Ian MacMillan)
35 (Madras Presidency) Squadron
44 (Rhodesia) Squadron
49 Squadron
50 Squadron
57 Squadron
83 Squadron
101 Squadron
102 Squadron
103 Squadron (with David Fell)
106 Squadron (with Herman Bijlard)
115 Squadron
138 Squadron (with Piotr Hodyra)
207 Squadron (with Raymond Glynne-Owen)
300 Squadron (with Grzegorz Korcz)
301, 304 and 305 Squadrons (with Grzegorz Korcz)
460 Squadron RAAF
467 Squadron RAAF
514 Squadron (with Simon Hepworth)
617 Squadron
619 Squadron

Contents

Introduction	9
Dedication	11
Narrative History	13
April 1940	15
May 1940	18
June 1940	25
July 1940	31
August 1940	37
September 1940	43
October 1940	49
November 1940	54
December 1940	58
January 1941	83
February 1941	85
March 1941	88
April 1941	91
May 1941	96
June 1941	99
July 1941	103
August 1941	110
September 1941	114
October 1941	118
November 1941	122
December 1941	125
January 1942	158
February 1942	159
March 1942	162
April 1942	166
May 1942	173
June 1942	177
July 1942	183

August 1942	189
September 1942	195
October 1942	203
November 1942	208
December 1942	211
January 1943	248
February 1943	251
March 1943	258
April 1943	266
May 1943	273
June 1943	281
July 1943	288
August 1943	296
September 1943	307
October 1943	315
November 1943	320
December 1943	325
January 1944	357
February 1944	361
March 1944	364
April 1944	373
May 1944	380
June 1944	385
July 1944	391
August 1944	398
September 1944	406
October 1944	411
November 1944	419
December 1944	425
January 1945	476
February 1945	482
March 1945	488
April 1945	496

Roll of Honour	530
Stations	557
Commanding Officers	557
Flight Commanders	557
Aircraft	559
Operational Record	559
Aircraft Histories	560
Key to Abbreviations	573

Introduction

RAF Bomber Command Squadron Profiles first appeared in the late nineties, and proved to be very popular with enthusiasts of RAF Bomber Command during the Second World War. They became a useful research tool, particularly for those whose family members had served and were no longer around. The original purpose was to provide a point of reference for all of the gallant men and women who had fought the war, either in the air, or on the ground in a support capacity, and for whom no written history of their unit or station existed. I wanted to provide them with something they could hold up, point to and say, "this was my unit, this is what I did in the war". Many veterans were reticent to talk about their time on bombers, partly because of modesty, but perhaps mostly because the majority of those with whom they came into contact had no notion of what it was to be a "Bomber Boy", to face the prospect of death every time they took to the air, whether during training or on operations. Only those who shared the experience really understood what it was to go to war in bombers, which is why reunions were so important. As they approached the end of their lives, many veterans began to speak openly for the first time about their life in wartime Bomber Command, and most were hurt by the callous treatment they received at the hands of successive governments with regard to the lack of recognition of their contribution to victory. It is sad that this recognition in the form of a national memorial and the granting of a campaign medal came too late for the majority. Now this inspirational, noble generation, the like of which will probably never grace this earth again, has all but departed from us, and the world will be a poorer place as a result.

RAF Bomber Command Squadron Profiles are back. The basic format remains, but, where needed, additional information has been provided. Squadron Profiles do not claim to be comprehensive histories, but rather detailed overviews of the activities of the squadron. There is insufficient space to mention as many names as one would like, but all aircraft losses are accompanied by the name of the pilot. Fundamentally, the narrative section is an account of Bomber Command's war from the perspective of the bomber group under which the individual squadron served, and the deeds of the squadron are interwoven into this story. Information has been drawn from official records, such as group, squadron and station ORBs, and from the many, like me, amateur enthusiasts, who dedicate much of their time to researching individual units, and become unrivalled authorities on them. I am grateful for their generous contributions, and their names will appear in the appropriate Profiles. The statistics quoted in this series are taken from The Bomber Command War Diaries, that indispensable tome written by Martin Middlebrook and Chris Everitt, and I am indebted to Martin for his kind permission to use them.

Finally, let me apologise in advance for the inevitable errors, for no matter how hard I and other authors try to write "nothing but the truth", there is no such thing as a definitive account of history, and there will always be room for disagreement and debate. Official records are notoriously unreliable tools, and yet we have little choice but to put our faith in them. It is not my intention to misrepresent any person or Bomber Command unit, and I ask my readers to understand the enormity of the task I have undertaken. It is relatively easy to become an authority on single units or even a bomber group, but I chose to write about them all, idiot that I am, which means 128 squadrons serving operationally in Bomber Command at some time between the 3rd of September 1939 and the 8th of May 1945. I am dealing with eight bomber groups, in which some 120,000 airmen served, and I am juggling around 28,000 aircraft serial numbers, code letters and details of provenance and fate. I ask not for your sympathy, it was, after all, my choice, but rather your understanding if you should find something with which you disagree. My thanks to you, my readers, for making the original series of RAF Bomber Command Squadron Profiles so popular, and I hope you receive this new incarnation equally enthusiastically.

This is an updated edition of the original book, written in 2018, for which I was greatly assisted by the Royal New Zealand Air Force Association and the New Zealand Bomber Command Association, for whose support I am most grateful. In particular, Peter Wheeler made the photo archive available to me, and Chris Newey was on hand to answer my frequent requests for information. Gentlemen, I salute you both! I wish to recognise this valued co-operation by including Chris Newey's name on the front cover. Chris was uncomfortable with having his name featured, because he draws on the research of others, in particular, the invaluable collection of information about the squadron that Simon Sommerville has assembled and databased. This is something we all do of necessity, and as long as due credit is given, honour is satisfied. Chris was my main point of contact, and as such, his name appears as the representative of all those in New Zealand and the UK whose research has added to our knowledge of this magnificent squadron. My thanks also, as always, to my gang members, Andreas Wachtel, Steve Smith, Greg Korcz and photo editor, Clare Bennett for their unstinting support, without which my Profiles would be the poorer. Finally, my appreciation to my publisher, Simon Hepworth of Mention the War Publications, for his belief in my work, untiring efforts to promote it, and for the stress I put him through to bring my books to publication.

Chris Ward. Skegness, Lincolnshire. February 2023.

Dedication

This wartime history of 75(NZ) Squadron is dedicated to the memory of Jack "Wakey" Wakefield, who served as a gunner during the Wellington era in 1940 and 41. Jack completed thirty operations with the squadron, including nine with the Fotheringham crew, whose Wimpy carried the famous "Soda Syphon spitting bombs" nose art. While instructing at an O.T.U. in 1942, he was recalled to action to participate in the three "Thousand Bomber" raids and ended his operational career in the Middle-Eastern theatre between late 1942 and the summer of 1943, completing a further thirty sorties mainly on anti-submarine patrols. He typified the 75(NZ) Squadron spirit and maintained an interest in the squadron until passing away on Armistice Day 2022 at the age of 101.

Narrative History

The seeds of 75(NZ) Squadron, which would go on to become one of the most prolific units in Bomber Command during the Second World War, were sown in 1937, when the New Zealand government placed an order for thirty Wellingtons and sent New Zealand personnel to the UK for training and to ferry the aircraft home. New Zealand government representatives in England took ceremonial delivery of the first Wellington from Vickers on the 4th of May 1939 and training began at Marham that month under the command of Squadron Leader Maurice William Buckley, MBE, RNZAF. On the 1st of June 1939, the New Zealand Squadron was formed, and personnel assembled for the 1st New Zealand Mobile Flight, the first of five planned ferry flights. The Flight drew its personnel from among its countrymen serving in RAF units, RNZAF personnel arriving from New Zealand, and a small number of RAF technicians "on loan".

On the day of the declaration of war, Sunday, the 3rd of September 1939, Bomber Command was represented by 3, 4 and 5 Groups as its main offensive arm, equipped respectively with Wellingtons, Whitleys and Hampdens, while 2 Group operated Blenheim light bombers. 1 Group had been sent to France with its Fairey Battles on the 1st and 2nd of September to operate as the Advanced Air Striking Force (AASF) and would remain there until the fall of France in June. The New Zealanders expressed a wish to remain in the UK and to participate in the conflict, and the New Zealand government magnanimously agreed to waive its entitlement to the Wellingtons ordered and placed its personnel at the disposal of the RAF. Rather than distribute these airmen among existing units, it was decided to retain what was by now known as the New Zealand Flight in its present form and raise it to full squadron status. In the meantime, however, a number of moves took place, to Harwell in September, Stradishall in January 1940, and Feltwell on the 16th of February.

The formation of a New Zealand squadron had the support of Air Chief-Marshal Sir Edgar Ludlow-Hewitt, Air Officer Commanding-in-Chief of Bomber Command, and Air Vice-Marshal Jack Baldwin, Air Officer Commanding 3 Group, however authorities back in New Zealand were concerned that the resources required would detract from the RNZAF's own training needs. After much debate and communication back and forth, the New Zealand Government advised on the 1st of March that it had approved the formation of a New Zealand Squadron within the Royal Air Force, to be formed round the existing New Zealand Flight. At the time, a 75 Squadron already existed in 3 Group as a Group Pool training unit, and was based at Stradishall, equipped with Ansons and Wellingtons. At the start of hostilities, each group had been instructed to take one squadron out of the line to undertake the vital task of training fresh crews to feed into the operational squadrons, and 75 Squadron had been selected. The declaration of war brought a move to Harwell, where it relinquished its Ansons. The establishment of Operational Training Units (O.T.U.) to replace Group Pool units resulted in 75 Squadron's absorption into 15 O.T.U. on the 4th of April 1940, freeing the 75 number plate to be passed on, on that day, to the New Zealand Flight and the letters NZ added.

In fact, the unit had carried out its first wartime operational sorties three weeks earlier on the 10th of March 1940, a daylight reconnaissance over the North Sea, "Operational Exercise No.1, Special Sweep as ordered". Two Wellingtons, P9207 "C" captained by S/L Cyril Eyton "Cyrus" Kay OBE RNZAF and P9212 "F" by F/O John Noel Collins RNZAF, had taken off from Feltwell at 13.50, proceeded to a point in the North Sea then separated to practice navigation and wireless. The weather was poor, but they spotted and identified several convoy ships and returned safely after two hours and twenty minutes of flying. On the 13th, a second Special Sweep was made. Wellingtons P9207, captained by F/L Aubrey Arthur Ninnis Breckon RNZAF, and P9212 by F/O John Adams RNZAF, took off from Feltwell at 13.55, with low cloud soon forcing the two to operate separately. A convoy and other ships were seen, photographs were taken, and Adams challenged two destroyers with the letter of the day. The crews flew home to base in low cloud and rain, landing at 14.20 and 14.15 respectively. No doubt relieved at finally having the chance to take part in this war, Breckon's second pilot, Fred "Popeye" Lucas, placed a circled number "1" alongside the entry in his logbook. Two days later the same two aircraft carried out a third sweep as part of "Operational Exercise No.7", F/O Collins captaining P9207 and F/O Adams in P9212. The two took off at 10.30, and while a botched wireless fix meant that they missed the destroyer they were looking for, they managed to stay together and returned to base at 14.40. A fourth operational sweep took place on the 19th of two hours duration involving the crews of F/Os Coleman and Williams in Wellingtons P9207 "C" and P9212 "F" respectively.

Next up were three leafleting (nickelling) sorties to northern Germany on the night of the 27/28th of March, S/L "Cyrus" Kay OBE departing Feltwell in P9206 at 22.30, to be followed at ten-minute intervals by F/O Collins in P9207 and F/O Adams in P9212. Once safely airborne, each then set course independently for a position some thirty-five miles off the Frisian Island of Schiermonnikoog, from where they headed for Dorum on the German coast, located between the Weser and Elbe estuaries. Their brief was to dispense leaflets over one of three regions from Lüneburg (F/O Adams), the most northerly, to Brunswick (S/L Kay), the most southerly, with Uelzen (F/O Collins) in between. Navigation was by dead-reckoning (DR) and astro-fixes, and S/L Kay and crew were most successful in this regard, which was fortuitous after their W/T transmitter burned out. The main problem was the extreme cold at minus 28°, which caused astrodomes to freeze over. Nickels were duly delivered from between 7,000 and 10,000 feet, although one crew ventured over the island of Hooge, off the west coast of the Schleswig-Holstein peninsula, and carried out a drop from 14,000 feet. All three returned safely after flights lasting between nine hours and nine hours fifty minutes. It is interesting to note, that at this stage of the war, before the new aircrew ranking system was introduced, servicemen of aircraftsman rank (AC 1 or 2) qualified as aircrew.

On the 20th of March, the imminent establishment of the new squadron was acknowledged when it played host to a visit from the Air Officer Commanding-in-Chief of Bomber Command, the Air Office Commanding 3 Group, the New Zealand High Commissioner, the New Zealand Liaison Officer with the Air Department, and several New Zealanders from other squadrons for a morale-boosting march past, inspection and presentation of decorations, including six DFMs. The newspapers back home reported: "In company with Air Chief-Marshal Sir Edgar Ludlow-Hewitt, the High Commissioner for New Zealand, Mr W. J. Jordan, inspected a large number of airmen in a hangar at an East Anglian bomber station, including New Zealand officers and men who recently carried out their first operation - a sweep over the North Sea. At Sir Edgar's request, Mr Jordan presented the DFM recently awarded to Corporal C. B. G. Knight, whose coolness and courage in maintaining wireless communication under intense enemy fire contributed to the success of the operation over Schilling Roads and Frisian Islands on December 14."

Twenty-seven-year-old Cpl Colin Knight, from Tolaga Bay, was one of the six wireless specialists sent from New Zealand in December 1938 to train on Wellingtons in preparation for the NZ Squadron ferry flights back to New Zealand. Four of the six had been posted to Marham in July 1939 to take part in the first Flight. Knight, however, was still with 99 Squadron and wireless operator in S/L (later AVM) Andrew "Square" McKee's crew when he earned his DFM in the Schilling Roads action. He was the first member of the RNZAF to be decorated in the Second World War and was posted to 75(NZ) Squadron a few months later. Sadly, the sixth wireless specialist, Cpl Jack Langridge, never made it to Feltwell and was killed in action with 149 Squadron on the 12th of April 1940, aged twenty-one. He was the first RNZAF casualty of the war.

April 1940

75 (New Zealand) Squadron came into being officially on the 4th of April, although it was by no means at full operational strength. It was allocated "AA" aircraft codes and inherited six front-line Mk 1A Wellingtons from the NZ Flight (P9205, P9206, P9207, P9209, P9210, P9212; "A" – "E"), and two or three of the original Mk1s, by now rarely flown. S/L Buckley, who was already forty-four years old, and prior to his posting to the NZ Flight, had been a flight commander with 38 Squadron on Wellingtons, was promoted to wing commander rank, and would remain in command of the squadron for a further seven months.

With the establishment of the new Squadron, and the need to form a second flight to bring it up to full operational strength, Buckley continued training new pilots through to September. A fatherly figure, "Buck" or "Old Buck" was highly respected by his men, as reported in a 1941 newspaper article: "We may not have hit our target, we may have got lost, or everything may have gone off well, or we may have been badly knocked about," said one of the pilots. "Whatever has happened, 'Old Buck' always gives us a good welcome and makes us feel that we've done a good job. He always says to us 'Good show, good show." He had flown with the Royal Naval Air Service in the First World War, been involved in several pioneering flights as a civil aviator in New Zealand, joined the New Zealand Permanent Air Force (NZPAF) in 1926 as an instructor, risen to base commander and the rank of squadron leader, and awarded the MBE for his services to the newly-established RNZAF.

Cyril Eyton Kay, OBE was promoted to squadron leader rank and installed as flight commander. He had been Buckley's second in command and Navigation Officer in the New Zealand Flight, having had considerable experience in long ocean flights. In 1930, while serving with the RAF as a navigation specialist, he and fellow New Zealander, F/O Harold Piper, flew a tiny Desoutter monoplane from Croydon to Darwin in an attempt to break the England-to-Australia record. In 1934 he competed with S/L Jim Hewitt in the 1934 MacRobertson centenary air race from England to Australia, and later that year, again with Hewitt, made the first flight from England to New Zealand, the pair becoming the first New Zealanders to cross the Tasman Sea by air. Kay joined the NZPAF in 1935 and became chief navigation instructor at Wigram Flying School. He was also highly respected by his men and followed closely Buckley's 'fatherly" style of command.

Much confusion has arisen around the designation of 75(NZ) Squadron, but it is not uncommon, even today, for a squadron number to be passed from a defunct unit to a new or reformed squadron, completely changing its identity. For that reason, the original 75 Squadron, the ancestry of which goes back to its initial formation on the 1st of October 1916 as a home defence unit, will correctly be treated as the forerunner of 75(NZ) Squadron.

The first sorties conducted as a properly established squadron took place on the day of its formation, and involved three Wellingtons, which were dispatched at 08.24 to carry out a special sweep in accordance with 3 Group Operations Order No 8. In the event, they were recalled ninety minutes later because of adverse weather conditions. The crews of F/L Breckon, F/O Neville Williams, F/O W.H. Bill Coleman and P/O W.M.C. Bill Williams were briefed on the 6th for a second "nickelling" trip to northern Germany that night. They were to dispense their propaganda leaflets over an area from Bremen in the north to Minden in the south, taking in Verden, Nienburg and Petershagen, and took-off between 19.12 and 19.25. Weather conditions were excellent, and all four crews carried out their assigned tasks without incident, before returning safely home in the early hours of the 7th. The experience gained in these operations was invaluable and would stand the crews in good stead for the future.

In 1919, Italian air-war strategist, General Giulio Douhet, had propounded the idea that future wars would be fought between giant armadas of self-defending bombers, flying directly over the front lines in daylight to target the economic centres of the enemy and destroy its will and capability to continue the fight. This theory gained advocates in a number of countries, in Britain with Arthur Harris, in America with Billy Mitchell and in Germany with Walther Wever. Fortunately for the conduct of WWII, Wever would lose his life in a flying accident in 1935 and the development of the Luftwaffe be put in the hands of army minded strategists, who saw bombing as a tactical extension of artillery. This would prove to be an inspired decision in a short war, and Blitzkrieg would be highly successful in rolling up France and the Low Countries. However, an extended conflict required a strategic bomber force, and by the time Germany realized that fact, it was already too late to catch up. The main flaw in the Douhet theory concerned the suggested ability of bombers to get through in sufficient numbers in daylight to reach the target. At the outbreak of war, only the Whitley crews of 4 Group were trained to fly at night, and they had been conducting long-range leafleting sorties since the start, learning about navigation over a blacked-out hostile country and how to deal with the challenges presented by extreme cold and icing conditions. During a shipping sweep by 3 Group in the Schillig Roads on the 14th of December, five of twelve Wellingtons were lost, and twelve out of twenty-two on the 18th. The losses had been blamed initially on poor formation-keeping, but the truth eventually dawned that unescorted daylight operations were not viable in the face of a highly trained and motivated enemy fighter force. The air planners were compelled to take stock, and this resulted in operations by all but 2 Group becoming a predominantly nocturnal activity.

On the 9th, German forces marched unopposed into Denmark, and simultaneously landed airborne troops in Norway, forcing the British and French to respond. This brought an end to the six months of shadow-boxing dubbed by the American press as the "Phoney War" and goaded the government into ordering landings by British troops around Narvik in the north of Norway. The extreme range would prohibit direct support by Bomber Command, and its contribution to the campaign would be through attacks on the airfields at Stavanger and Oslo in the south, along with the harassment of enemy supply ships in coastal shipping lanes. 75(NZ) Squadron's first involvement came on the 10th, when F/L Breckon and crew flew up to Wick on temporary detachment to 18 Coastal Command Group, from where they were to fly a reconnaissance sortie along the Norwegian coast to Narvik in a Wellington with long range tanks. The sortie began early on the 12th and lasted over fourteen hours, during which time some atrocious weather was encountered, and two thousand miles were covered.

With no automatic pilot fitted, Breckon and his second pilot, P/O Harkness, had manually flown the aircraft for fourteen-and-a-half-hours. It was one of the longest flights undertaken by a Wellington bomber, and an RAF record at the time. F/L Aubrey Breckon had been a newspaper photographer before the war, as was his father, and worked for the New Zealand Herald and the Auckland Weekly News. He gained his commercial pilot's licence in 1931, and became an aerial photography specialist, before joining the RAF and becoming a founding member of the New Zealand Flight. Meanwhile, four crews were briefed to join forces with eight from 37 Squadron to search for the enemy battlecruiser Scharnhorst, which was reported to be off the Norwegian coast between Kristiansand and Stavanger. This magnificent vessel, which entered service in January 1939, displaced 38,700 tons fully loaded, and boasted a length of 771 feet, with an armament of nine eleven-inch guns arranged in three triple turrets. S/L Kay, F/O Collins, F/O Adams and P/O Bill Williams took off between 09.10 and 09.15 and headed north-east into extremely adverse weather conditions in the target area. This prevented the quartet from making contact with the enemy warship and split up the formation. All returned independently to base to land safely between 14.20 and 15.15. During an engagement in June 1940, in which Scharnhorst sank the aircraft carrier, HMS Glorious, she was damaged by a torpedo from the sinking destroyer, HMS Acasta, and would spend the next six months under repair at the Krupp-Germania shipyard in Kiel.

On the night of the 13/14th, 5 Group carried out the first mine-laying operation of the war, in what represented the initial tentative steps in a new departure for Bomber Command operations, which would prove to be hugely successful and by war's end would have sunk or damaged more enemy vessels than the Royal Navy. The laying of parachute mines by air was given the code-name "gardening" and the entire enemy-held coastline from the Pyrenees in the south-west to the Baltic port of Königsberg in the north-east, and even the northern Italian coast, would be divided into gardens, each with a horticultural or marine biological name. The process of delivery was known as planting and the mines were referred to as vegetables, and it would not be long before the other groups joined in to help create a spiders' web of mines in chains across all of the sea-lanes employed by the enemy. That said, it would be a further two years before 75(NZ) Squadron became involved in this profitable endeavour.

The first bombing operation undertaken by 75(NZ) Squadron involved the crews of F/Os Adams, Collins and Neville Williams, who took-off between 18.00 and 18.10 on the 17th to attack Stavanger aerodrome in company with twenty-seven other 3 Group Wellingtons. F/O Adams had to return early with a smoking fuse panel, and was back on the ground after two hours, leaving his colleagues to press on and remain in sight of each other for a further 150 miles before losing contact. F/O Williams reached the target at 21.06, four minutes ahead of F/O Collins, and observed a parachute flare from a preceding aircraft. He flew in from the sea on a west-to-east heading, but his bomb-aimer failed to pick up the aiming point in time, and a second run had to be made from east to west. The bombs, two of which were delayed-action, were released at 21.18 in a shallow dive from 6,500 down to 6,000 feet, and two were seen to detonate, one on the intersection of the runways and the other at the end of the east-west runway, with the delayed action bombs somewhere between. F/O Collins found the target to be clearly visible from 5,000 feet, aided also by a flare, and bombed at 21.15, while being held in a searchlight and fired upon by flak, which prevented him from observing the results. An interesting addendum to the raid report provided the following statistics: flight duration seven hours, distance covered 1,053 statute miles, petrol consumed 527 gallons, miles per gallon two, oil consumption eleven gallons, oil consumption per hour six pints per engine.

Three pilots were posted in from 214 Squadron at Stradishall on the 20th, P/Os Best, Humphreys and Pownall, and six gunners would arrive from No 1 Aircrew Artillery School at Manby on the 22nd. In the meantime, F/Os Adams and Coleman and P/O Bill Williams were put on three-hours standby on the 21st for an operation against Aalborg aerodrome in northern Jutland. They eventually took off in a five-minute slot from 18.30, and located the target three hours later, aided by the perfect conditions of clear skies and bright moonlight, and also the airfield boundary lights, which were extinguished as the Wellingtons approached. F/O Adams dived from 10,000 to 7,000 feet and dropped his bombs in a stick from north to south, all the time held in searchlights and fired upon by intense light and heavy flak. After enduring this unwanted attention for about five minutes, he escaped into the darkness to head home, while F/O Coleman was experiencing a similarly torrid time, delivering his bombs from 6,200 feet in a run from south-west to north-east. P/O Williams made his first run from west to east, but the bomb-aimer failed to pick up the aiming point in time, and they were forced to make a turn over the town and carry out a second run from north to south at 8,500 feet. Somehow, all three Wellingtons made it back home, and only one displayed a slight graze from flak.

There were no further operations to negotiate during the month, during which period ten brand new Wellington Mk 1Cs arrived, R3156 – R3159, R3165 – R3169, and R3172, some directly from Vickers Weybridge, some via 115 and 214 Squadrons, along with one used example, L7784, a Mk 1A from fellow Feltwell residents, 37 Squadron.

F/L Breckon and his crew made a second reconnaissance flight from Wick on the 21st, this one to photograph and observe Trondheim, the adjoining frozen lake, and the aerodrome at Vaernes, which was now occupied by the Germans. While the flight was successful in providing information that led to a Fleet Air Arm attack on the lake later in the day, it was also somewhat 'hairy' and a burst of flak in front of the aircraft smashed the windscreen, injuring Breckon in the eye. Luckily, he had goggles on hand and was able to complete the nine-and-a-half-hour round-trip. During the course of the month the squadron operated on four occasions and dispatched thirteen sorties, not counting those by F/L Breckon.

May 1940

Before any operations could take place in May, another new Wellington arrived from Vickers, and an old one from 148 Squadron. F/L Wilfred Collett was posted in from 149 Squadron on the 5th to assume acting squadron leader rank and flight commander status. Wilfred Ira Collett, from Gisborne, New Zealand, had learned to fly at the Hawke's Bay Aero Club, where one of his instructors was Ted Olson, who would later become 75(NZ) Squadron's commanding officer. Collett sailed to England in 1933 and joined the RAF in June 1934, serving in Egypt, the Middle East, Cyprus, and the north-west frontier of India. Since the day that war broke out, he had flown operations with 149 Squadron, but apparently, had been in line to join 75(NZ) Squadron for some time, having trained with the NZ Flight in October 1939.

F/Os Coleman, Collins and Neville Williams took off in a ten-minute slot from 19.05 on the 7th to attack Stavanger aerodrome. They crossed the North Sea at 3,500 feet, and a hundred miles out from the Norwegian coast encountered a layer of ten-tenths low cloud lying on the surface of the water. As they approached landfall, the tops of mountains poked through, and, as there seemed to be no chance of carrying out an attack, they carried out a wide sweep to confirm the futility of continuing the sortie. A course was set for home, and all were safely back on the ground by 02.10. This was the final offensive action for the squadron in support of the ill-fated Norwegian campaign, and despite the gallant efforts of all the services, it had been a lost cause from the start and was heading towards its inevitable conclusion when events closer to home grabbed the world's attention.

At dawn on the 10th of May, German forces began their advance into the Low Countries, and it was at this point that the gloves came off for good, and the destruction of the Battle and Blenheim squadrons of the Advanced Air Striking Force (AASF) and 2 Group began. It was also the day on which Winston Churchill was handed the thankless task of leading Britain to almost inevitable defeat. The Fairey Battle squadrons of the AASF had mostly been in France since the day before the declaration of war in September 1939 and were kept on the ground as the German Blitzkrieg overwhelmed Belgium, Holland and Luxembourg in a matter of days. Rather than being allowed to impede the enemy advance, they were forced to wait until the German forces had dug in and set up formidable defences before being allowed to attack them. The result was the slaughter of the obsolete and cumbersome Battles at the hands of marauding and agile BF109s and Me110s and the lethal light flak batteries guarding the canal and river crossing points. By the 15th, the Battle squadrons had effectively been knocked out of the fight, and within a month, most would be withdrawn to England. The heavy squadrons of Bomber Command would play their part by attacking communications behind enemy lines, and eventually industrial targets in the Ruhr, but so overwhelming was the German tide, that they would also be called upon to attack troop concentrations and armoured columns at the front.

As one of 3 Group's front-line Wellington units, 75(NZ) Squadron was thrust into the battle on that first fateful night, when three of its aircraft joined thirty-three other Wellingtons from the group to attack the airfield at Waalhaven in Rotterdam. F/O Neville Williams took off at 22.50, to be followed ten minutes later by F/O Collins and at 23.35 by P/O Bill Williams, each carrying a load of twelve 250 pounders. The skies were clear, but the absence of a moon created extreme darkness, and F/O Williams was experiencing difficulty in finding the target until an aircraft ahead dropped a flare. He delivered a stick of six bombs from 2,000 feet and observed them detonating at twenty-yard intervals among airfield buildings, while a second stick fell across the airfield. The other two crews also attacked successfully, with some strafing of aerodrome buildings by F/O Collins, and all arrived home safely.

Two nights later, the squadron provided three more crews for a small-scale raid on the aerodrome at Uerdingen, situated on the west bank of the Rhine on the eastern side of Krefeld in the Ruhr. S/L Kay, F/L Breckon and F/O Coleman took off at 21.10, again carrying a dozen 250 pounders each, half of them fitted with delay fuses of three, six, eight and twelve hours in equal numbers. They found the target without difficulty, aided by a weak moon and a light on the aerodrome. S/L Kay dropped a stick of nine bombs from 10,000 feet at 22.55, finding that three had "hung-up" because of a fault with the electrical-release system. He was unable to observe the burst of his bombs through taking evasive action to avoid the many searchlights. F/L Breckon let his load go in a single stick from 11,000 feet at 23.10, while F/O Coleman dropped four bombs on the primary target from 10,000 feet, followed by four on a line of transport moving south-west from the target, and the remainder on a second transport column moving westwards.

The night of the 15/16th brought the first strategic bombing raids of the war, which involved ninety-nine Wellingtons, Hampdens and Whitleys in attacks on factories at Dortmund and synthetic oil refineries at Sterkrade-Holten and Castrop-Rauxel in the Ruhr. 75(NZ) Squadron provided three crews for the Ruhr-Chemie oil plant at Sterkrade, a northern district of Oberhausen in the central Ruhr, and three others to attack a bridge at Turnhout in north-eastern Belgium. F/L Breckon, F/O Neville Williams and P/O Trevor Owen Freeman RNZAF were briefed for the former and took off between 21.25 and 21.50, while F/Os Coleman, Collins and Lucas departed at 21.40 for the latter. It was Freeman's first operation as skipper and the start of a successful operational career. They set course for their respective targets loaded with a dozen 250 pounders each but ran into adverse weather conditions with electrical storms and extremely poor visibility, particularly over the Ruhr, where industrial haze would be a constant thorn in the flesh of Bomber Command until 1943. It was not an outstandingly successful night, and five of the six 75(NZ) Squadron crews failed to locate their target. The exception was F/O Collins, who delivered a stick of twelve bombs from 4,000 feet onto a bridge across the canal at Turnhout and saw them burst over a hundred-yard stretch from the canal northwards. Of the others, one crew jettisoned its bombs into the sea and four brought theirs home.

There was a busy night of operations on the 17/18th, which saw the launch of 130 sorties to multiple targets in Germany and Belgium. 75(NZ) Squadron briefed six crews for individual attacks on a variety of objectives, the identity of which is not always apparent because of the target coding system in use in 1940. S/L Kay was first away from Feltwell at 21.10 in P9206, bound for Belgium to bomb road and rail bridges over the Maas. At his first aiming point he delivered two sticks of three bombs each, observing strikes on the central base of the structure, and at the second he dropped a stick of six without observing the results. P/O Freeman took off next at 21.50 in R3158 AA-J with the Rheinpreussen (Meerbeck) synthetic oil plant at Moers/Homberg as his primary target, located on the western bank of the Rhine opposite Duisburg. On return he would claim a successful attack, and report also bombing a road convoy at Valkenswaard in central Belgium on the way home and observing six hits. F/Os Coleman and Collins took off at 22.15 and 22.30 in R3159 (AA-K) and R3157 (AA-H) respectively, but both failed to locate their primary objectives. The former had been assigned to the marshalling yards at Cologne-Eifeltor, and it is believed, the Union Rheinische Braunkohlen-Kraftstoff A G oil refinery at Wesseling to the south of the city, while the latter had the Ruhr-Chemie refinery at Sterkrade-Holten as his destination. F/O Neville Williams departed Feltwell at 22.45 in R3156 (AA-G), and made his way also to the Ruhr, where he was supposed to bomb marshalling yards, but attacked nearby blast furnaces as alternatives and was unable to observe results because of intense searchlight activity. On the way home he bombed a mechanized unit at an undisclosed location from 1,500 feet and claimed direct hits. Finally, F/L Breckon became airborne at 22.50 in P9209 (AA-B), and headed, it is believed, for the oil refinery at Wesseling, which he located with great difficulty in conditions of low cloud and bombed without observing the results. All returned safely to home airspace, where they were diverted to other airfields because of fog at Feltwell.

Seven of the squadron's crews attended briefings on the 19th and learned that they were to be sent against German troop communications in France and Belgium that night in company with elements of 37 Squadron. S/L Kay's target was at Givet in north-eastern France, almost on the border with Belgium, while F/L Breckon and F/O Lucas went for Fumay and F/Os Coleman and Collins for Haybes, both locations about a dozen miles to the south on the banks of the River Meuse in the Ardennes. F/O Neville Williams and P/O Freeman were assigned to Seneffe in Belgium, situated ten miles north-west of Charleroi. The target areas appear to have been provided as general locations of enemy activity in a fluid, ever-changing situation on the ground, and crews would need to be alert to opportunities as they searched the vast area of the Ardennes Forest. They took off between 21.15 and 21.45, each carrying six 250 pounders and six containers of 4lb incendiaries, and all reached their respective target areas. While running in on his target, P/O Freeman came under fire from machine-guns, which hit R3158 AA-J, shooting away the bonded cable for the bomb-release system. It also wounded the second pilot, P/O Charles Pownall, in the right shoulder, forcing them to turn for home. S/L Kay dropped three 250 pounders on a railway junction located three miles south of Charville-Mezieres, and three more on a railway line north of Deville, before delivering his incendiaries into woods a mile east of Montherme. F/O Lucas attacked a large, mechanized column at Fumay with three 250 pounders, and the rear gunner then sprayed it with his .303s. A second target was attacked with six containers of incendiaries, before the three remaining 250 pounders were dropped on a road and railway bridge at Nivelles, between Charleroi and Brussels. F/O N Williams bombed woods five miles west of Vouziers and later a convoy of transport wagons, many of which were seen to catch fire. F/O Coleman reported dropping incendiaries in a wood half a mile from Haybes, and also attacking a bridge, observing hits on the road alongside. F/L Breckon observed hits on both of his targets, at Fumay and Tubize, before returning safely with the others to make his report, while the ground crews got to work applying patches to four of the Wellingtons that had returned with bullet holes.

In an attempt to stem the tide of the German advance to the front, the Command was ordered on the night of the 21/22nd to attack railway communications between Cologne and Euskirchen, and particularly at Aachen, closer to the frontiers with Holland and Belgium, where two major marshalling yards, Aachen-West and Rothe Erde, were situated. Feltwell would launch eighteen Wellingtons, six of them representing 75(NZ) Squadron, while two others were made ready to attack enemy ground forces at Dinant in Belgium, close to the scene of the activity of two nights earlier. The Aachen element was to be led by S/L Collett, who would be undertaking his first sortie since his posting and would be backed up by F/L Breckon, with F/Os Coleman, Lucas and N. Williams and P/O W.M.C. Williams the other participants. They took off between 21.15 and 21.40, as did F/Os Adams and Collins, bound for Belgium, and each Wellington carried in its bomb bay twelve 250 pounders. S/L Collett failed to locate the target and brought his bombs home, but the rest of the Aachen brigade carried out an attack, F/L Breckon and F/O Coleman each delivering their full bomb loads onto the marshalling yards and observing direct hits. The remaining three crews also made bombing runs, now in the face of intense searchlight activity, which prevented them from observing the results. P/O Williams retained six bombs, which he delivered in three sticks of two onto a power station south-east of Maastricht and observed two of them to burst on a railway siding close by. Meanwhile, P/O Adams attacked a road and rail bridge at Dinant, before returning safely to report near-misses, and this left only F/O Collins unaccounted for. R3157, AA-H, was hit by flak shortly before reaching its target, a bridge at Dinant, and suffered an engine and wing fire, which proved to be terminal. F/O Collins headed the stricken Wellington back towards Allied territory and managed to keep it airborne for seventy miles, during which time the other four members of the crew took to their parachutes and fell into the arms of their captors. Sadly, F/O Collins RNZAF was still on board when the crash came north of Tournai in Belgium, while his second pilot, P/O Francis De Labouchere-Sparling, was killed by ground fire, probably during his parachute descent.

John Collins was aged twenty-three, and the first RNZAF pilot to be killed whilst serving abroad in WW2. His promotion to flight lieutenant rank was notified after he was listed as missing. Collins came from Christchurch, New Zealand, where he had attended Christ's College. He joined the RAF in 1938 and was one of the original pilots selected for the NZ Flight, transferring to the RNZAF on a five-year short-service commission. Observer, Sgt G. Thorpe, wireless operator AC John "Stan" Brooks, and rear gunner, P/O Leonard Hockey, (all RAF) became the squadron's first PoWs. Many years later, Stan Brooks became Secretary of the Friends of the 75 Squadron Association UK. As the squadron had not yet attained full strength, F/O Collins had been one of those frequently called upon to operate, and his loss was keenly felt. In actual fact, during the course of the 21st, sufficient new arrivals of personnel would allow the official formation of an A and B Flight on the 29th, under S/Ls Kay and Collett respectively, thus ending the squadron's status as a single flight outfit. After the loss of Collins, the 23rd provided a happier occasion, the wedding of F/L Aubrey Breckon to Dana (nee Waugh) at St Mary's Church Feltwell. The ceremony was performed by S/L the Reverend Arthur Kayll, the Feltwell Station Chaplain, Breckon's best man was F/O Neville Williams, and the bride was given away by S/L "Cyrus" Kay. After the ceremony a reception was held at the Feltwell officers' mess, and photos show "Buck" and a full muster of his pilots in attendance.

Both flight commanders were in action on the night of the 23/24th, when road and railway communications in Belgium were the targets. The squadron dispatched five Wellingtons to the Yvoy and Profondeville region, south of Namur, and they took off between 21.15 and 21.45, with F/Os Adams, Coleman and Lucas the other pilots on duty. On arrival in the target area, they encountered varying amounts of cloud and ground mist, and an effective blackout contributed to the difficulty in identifying ground detail. S/L Kay carried out two shallow-dive runs on a bridge, delivering six 250 pounders on each, but searchlight dazzle prevented him from observing precise details, other than a number of bursts near the objective. F/O Adams emerged through the cloud base on estimated time of arrival (e.t.a) and found himself to be surrounded by a dozen searchlights co-operating with light flak batteries. He dropped two sticks of three 250 pounders and three sticks of two among them, causing the searchlights to be extinguished and remain so. S/L Collett dropped his entire load in a single stick onto the Gembloux to Brussels railway line, while F/O Lucas did likewise on a crossroads in a diving attack. F/O Coleman did not locate his primary target but came across a convoy of around fifty vehicles on the road between Gembloux and Wavre, at which he aimed a stick of six bombs, before unloading the others onto a searchlight battery on the outskirts of Namur.

The squadron made ready eight Wellingtons for operations on the night of the 25/26th, briefing six crews for attacks on enemy troop positions in the battle area, and two to carry out a one-hour-forty-minute reconnaissance of the ground between Courtrai (Kortrijk) and Brussels. F/O Adams and F/L Breckon were assigned to the latter task, and took off at 21.30 and 22.45 respectively, each carrying the standard bomb load for use against targets of opportunity. F/O Adams saw no troop movements in his patrol area and released his bombs onto a railway junction at Enghien, fifteen miles or so south-west of Brussels, observing eight direct hits. F/L Breckon also saw nothing of interest while patrolling, and dropped his load in two sticks, one on a main road at Opphasselt and the other on a rail junction at Ninove. The remaining six Kiwi Wellingtons took off after 23.00, but one (believed to be S/L Collett) was forced to return early after developing engine trouble at the English coast. The others pressed on to find the target area in less-than-ideal weather conditions, which prevented F/O Lucas and P/O Bill Williams from locating their specific aiming points. The former spotted a motorized convoy crossing a road junction and attacked it with the full contents of his bomb bay, while the latter dropped half of his on the Courtrai to Audenarde road and the other half on the Audenarde to Ghent road just north of Eyne. S/L Kaye found his target by means of a parachute flare, and started many fires, and F/O N. Williams located his at 00.59, before bombing it from 8,500 feet and returning safely to report also starting many fires.

As the remnant of the British Expeditionary Force (BEF) assembled on the beaches of Dunkerque on the 26th, trapped within the shrinking semi-circle of territory and with its equipment littering the verges and ditches of the approach roads, the forlorn battle to save France continued overhead. Seven 75(NZ) Squadron Wellingtons were made ready for operations that night against enemy troop positions, and took off between 23.00 and 00.45, with S/L Collett the senior pilot on duty. He, P/O Freeman and P/O Lucas had been briefed to attack a target at Roeselare, some thirty miles east-south-east of Dunkerque, while F/L Breckon and F/Os Adams, Coleman and N. Williams bombed a similar one at Menin, a few miles further to the west. The visibility in the target areas was poor, with broken cloud extending from 1,000 to 12,000 feet, and intermittent thunder and rainstorms. As a result, only one crew at each location was able to positively identify the aiming point and carry out an attack. P/O Freeman made two diving runs from 2,500 feet, dropping six 250 pounders on each, and observing bursts. F/O Williams, who, unusually, was carrying a load of six 500 pounders, spotted his target from 5,000 feet and delivered a single bomb, before climbing 500 feet to drop two more, and finally descending to 4,000 feet to let go the last three. He returned to claim hits on the centre of the target, which caused many lights to be extinguished.

On the 29th, W/C Maurice Buckley marked the official establishment of the second flight, and achievement of full squadron status in a letter, listing and praising "the original NCO's and airmen who formed the New Zealand Flight at Marham almost a year ago". On the last night of the month, the squadron despatched its best effort to date of nine aircraft to attack German positions around the Belgian town of Nieuwpoort, situated on the coast between Ostend to the north-east and Dunkerque to the south-west. S/Ls Collett and Kay were the senior pilots on duty as they took off between 22.25 and 01.00, seven of them carrying seven 500 pounders each, while F/O Coleman and P/O Bill Williams each had fourteen 250 pounders in their bomb racks. It was another poor night for observation, but many lights were seen along the beach, with artillery fire in the region of Gravelines and numerous fires around Dunkerque. S/L Collett and P/O Williams failed to locate the target, and the former brought his bombs home, while the latter covered the dozen miles up the coast to Ostend and dropped all fourteen 250 pounders in a single stick, observing many direct hits. F/O Coleman delivered his 250 pounders in three sticks of four, five and five, and watched the first one set off a violent explosion and many fires. The second and third sticks fell nearby, but it was not possible to accurately assess the results. F/O Lucas glimpsed lights on a road south-east of the town and attacked them with all seven 500 pounders in a single stick. A large fire sprang up followed by red and white flashes, possibly caused by exploding ammunition. S/L Kay dropped a single 500 pounder from 4,500 feet and watched it detonate in the town, and released the remaining hardware in two sticks of three, observing a fire as a result. P/O Freeman carried out a straight-and-level run from 3,000 feet, and saw bursts in the town, before dropping a single 500 pounder on the Nieuwpoort to Ostend road. F/O Adams went for the main road junction on the eastern side of the town, while F/O Williams was unable to see the results of his efforts from 3,500 feet because of smoke drifting across the target. The same lack of visibility persuaded F/L Breckon to turn his attention upon a searchlight and flak battery two miles south of Poperinge, five miles west of Menin.

All returned safely home from a gallant attempt to stem the German tide, but it had been futile in the face of an organised and superior enemy, and it was now time for the Royal Navy to lift 338,000 battle-weary soldiers off the beaches, aided by the armada of little ships, and return them to England's shores to lick their wounds and bide their time. During the course of the month the squadron took part in fourteen operations, dispatching sixty-five sorties for the loss of one aircraft and crew.

June 1940

The new month began for the Command with a busy night of operations on the 3/4th, during which a record number of 142 sorties was dispatched to wide-ranging targets in Germany. Eighteen Wellingtons were made ready at Feltwell, eight of them belonging to 75(NZ) Squadron, and they took off between 21.25 and 22.30 with S/Ls Collett and Kay the senior pilots on duty. Their destination was the Rhenania-Ossag synthetic oil refinery in the Reisholz district to the south of Düsseldorf city centre, and all reached the southern Ruhr area to encounter the usual industrial haze. P/O Freeman was just five miles short of the target when engine problems forced him to turn back, and on the way home he dropped part of his load on a searchlight concentration at Krefeld, and a container of incendiaries on what appeared to be a factory at Venlo in Holland. F/L Breckon dropped a stick of nine bombs in a straight-and-level run from 11,000 feet and claimed a number of direct hits, and F/O Neville Williams delivered two sticks from 9,000 feet, observing only the splash of incendiaries two hundred yards west of the target. S/L Kay found the target without difficulty and delivered his load in a single stick from 9,000 feet, but was prevented by searchlight dazzle from seeing its fall. F/O Adams dropped a stick of five 250 pounders on the primary target from 12,000 feet, before being aided by the light from a parachute flare to find a nearby wharf to receive the remainder of his load. S/L Collett found the target already burning and straddled it, his incendiaries adding to the intensity of the flames. F/O Coleman claimed his near-misses started a new fire and that a dull, red fire near the eastern boundary was emitting clouds of black smoke. P/O Bill Williams attempted to drop his bombs in a stick from 10,000 feet, but they failed to release, forcing him to make a second run to deliver them in a salvo. Direct hits were observed, followed by an explosion and a large fire, which could be seen for some time into the return flight.

Two nights later the targets were a crossroads and marshalling yards at Cambrai in north-eastern France. Seven crews were briefed, and they took off between 21.50 and 22.55, with the flight commanders again the senior pilots on duty. They found conditions in the target area to be very hazy and parachute flares were employed by some to aid target identification. S/L Kay attacked the main road running north-east out of the town, dropping bombs from 9,000 feet onto the road itself and two junctions, but was unable to assess the results. F/O Adams went for the same target by the light from flares, making two runs in a shallow dive from 10,000 to 7,500 feet and observing bomb bursts on the main crossroads. F/O N. Williams was unable to locate his briefed target and bombed searchlights and a motorized convoy as alternatives. S/L Collett ran across the marshalling yards at 9,000 feet and delivered six 500 pounders in a slow stick, but was prevented by haze from observing their fall. F/O Coleman attacked the same target, also releasing his bombs in a slow stick, which he estimated to have straddled the aiming point. P/O Bill Williams misidentified the target and aimed his load at railway installations and a factory at Douai, ten miles to the north. Finally, P/O Freeman attacked the main roads to Paris and Abbeville to the south-west of Cambrai but was unable to report on the outcome.

Eight of the squadron's crews attended briefing on the 7th to learn that they would be involved again in the lost cause to prevent France from being overrun. Three target areas were divided among seven of the crews, who were given a roving commission to attack targets of opportunity around St Valery, Abbeville and Pont-Remy with eight 250 and two 500 pounders each. S/L Kay joined others from 9 and 37 Squadrons to attack special targets in woods at

Baileux and Boulers, both situated south-east of the town of Chimay in Belgium, and his Wellington was loaded with five 250 pounders and six containers of incendiaries. Seven of the Wellingtons departed Feltwell between 21.35 and 22.50, but F/O Adams's take-off was delayed until 23.55 by an air raid alarm, and by the time he reached the St-Valery target area on the coast at the mouth of the Somme, some eight miles north-west of Abbeville, the ground had become obscured by fog. Despite searching for a break for fifteen minutes, he was thwarted by the conditions and brought his bombs home. S/L Kay found his target in the light from long-burning parachute flares and dropped his 250 pounders on road junctions, before delivering the incendiaries into the woods, which were then machine-gunned from 1,500 feet. F/L Breckon, F/O Neville Williams and P/O Freeman were the others assigned to St-Valery and the first-mentioned delivered his bombs in a stick from 9,000 feet, aiming at a bridge over the Somme and observing a cluster of bursts on the bridgehead junction. P/O Freeman opted to make two diving approaches from 3,800 down to 1,200 feet and saw a direct hit on the bridge. F/O Williams dropped two 250 pounders in a dive from 5,000 to 3,000 feet, before aiming three more each on the airfield at Abbeville and the Abbeville to Hesdin road. S/L Collett's assigned target was at Abbeville, but he dropped four bombs on Pont-Remy first, before attacking a mechanized convoy on the Abbeville to Auxi-le-Chateau road. P/O Bill Williams was unable to locate the bridge at Pont-Remy because of heavy smoke and haze, so made three bombing runs across the town of Abbeville at 6,000 feet, dropping two bombs each time, before turning his attention upon the nearby aerodrome, where he delivered the rest of his load and observed bursts on the landing ground.

Briefings on the 9th prepared seven of the squadron's crews for further operations against enemy ground forces, and this night would see them back over the Ardennes with orders to set fire to the woods, and, thereby, destroy the enemy equipment hidden beneath the branches. The 75(NZ) Squadron crews were assigned to area 2 in company with elements of 9 and 37 Squadrons, and this encompassed the towns of Fumay, Gespunsart, Nouzonville and Recroi, which were to be attacked with bombs and incendiaries. Alternative targets of Hirson and Charleville-Mezieres were provided for any spare bombs in case of poor visibility over the primaries. They took off between 21.45 and 23.00 and found the target area to be free of cloud but partially obscured by smoke and haze. S/L Collett dropped four containers of incendiaries around Recroi and started forest fires, and four 250 pounders on the town, where they were seen to burst. S/L Kay found himself further east over Revin after deploying a parachute flare and established his position by the River Meuse. He dropped two 250 pounders on a road from 5,000 feet, before setting fire to nearby woods and scoring a near-miss on the town of Recroi, and finally, strafing vehicles on a road two miles west of Turnhout on the way to the coast. F/O Coleman bombed Charleville with four 250 pounders, starting two large, dull, red, circular fires, and set off four fires in nearby woods with incendiaries. P/O Bill Williams used his incendiaries to start a large fire in woods between Montherme and Braux and dropped a stick of four 250 pounders on Mezieres. F/O Neville Williams employed both incendiaries and bombs on woods in the Recroi and Revin areas and was rewarded with a number of small fires and explosions, before a large, blue flash was followed by a large, yellow one. Two bombs were then dropped from 9,000 feet on Recroi, the result of which could not be determined because of searchlight dazzle. P/O Freeman bombed a heavily-defended part of Charleville and extinguished searchlights, then delivered incendiaries onto a wooded area near the river, causing numerous fires and explosions. F/O Adams reported dive-bombing woods with incendiaries and bombing the town of Mezieres with 250 pounders, one of which hung up and had to be brought home.

It had been planned to employ the new fire-raising weapon "Razzle" against Germany's Black Forest on the night of the 10/11th, but the operation was cancelled after Italy declared war on the 10th. This prompted an order for elements of 3 Group to move to a base at Salon, near Toulon in southern France for operations against Italy under the orders of the Officer Commanding 71 Wing, who was under the operational control of the A-O-C 3 Group. Six Wellingtons each from 37 and 75(NZ) Squadron were made ready for departure on the 11th, the latter containing the crews of S/L Kay, F/Os Adams, Coleman and Williams and P/Os Freeman and Williams. That night, after 3 Group's participation in the Black Forest operation had been cancelled again, S/L Collett and F/O Lucas departed Feltwell at 22.00 for fire-raising duties of their own in the Ardennes Forest in the vicinity of Fumay. Each was carrying three 250 pounders and six containers of 25lb conventional incendiaries as they set off in adverse weather conditions that would remain constant throughout the operation. S/L Collett's incendiaries started fires and seemed to cause an ammunition dump to explode, and one of his 250 pounders scored a direct hit on a searchlight. F/O Lucas bombed on e.t.a, and his incendiaries started fires visible from twenty miles into the return journey.

The six crews sent to France on the 11th returned frustrated on the 13th, after prospective raids on Italian targets were cancelled. Their attempt to take off from Salon had been thwarted by several armed French military vehicles blocking the small grass airfield, after local authorities had decided that an attack launched from their airfield might invite reprisals. The combined 75(NZ) and 37 Squadron force would be replaced by elements of 99 and 149 Squadrons on the 15th, and an attack on Genoa would be attempted that night, ineffectively, as events were to prove.

Operations on the night of the 13/14th continued the attempts to block enemy communications and harass troop movements by sustained attacks on road centres at specified locations, most of which were in the Normandy region in an arc north-west to north-east of Paris. There were also to be further fire-raising attacks on specified areas of forest. The towns specified in the 3 Group ORB were at Pont-de-L'Arche, Les Anderlys, Gisors, Beauvais, Creil and Sissonne, and the forests at St-Gobain, Nouvion and St-Michel in the Pas-de-Calais. 3 Group contributed sixty-five Wellingtons on this night, seven of them representing 75(NZ) Squadron, which took off for their respective targets between 21.40 and 22.40 with S/L Collett the senior pilot on duty and F/O Samuel Miles Mackenzie Watson, a New Zealander in the RAF, flying as crew captain for the first time. The weather conditions over enemy territory were once more unhelpful, and three crews failed to locate their primary targets. F/O Watson bombed the airfield at Calais as an alternative and saw bursts but could not assess the results because of intense searchlight activity. P/O Bill Williams dropped all of his bombs on the docks at Boulogne after carrying out a shallow dive to 6,000 feet, while F/O Lucas bombed the approaches to Le Touquet. The remaining four crews managed to locate their objectives, S/L Collett unable to observe the fall of his bombs because of haze and F/L Breckon also watched his six 500 pounders fall from 10,000 feet and burst on the target, but without any indication as to their effectiveness. F/O Neville Williams dropped three 500 pounders onto a road junction at the eastern end of the undisclosed town to which he had been assigned, and F/O Adams was about to attack his briefed town when he spotted a convoy of around twelve vehicles and switched his attention to them. He carried out a shallow dive and released four 500 pounders from 6,000 feet, scoring three direct hits. The fourth bomb hit the road ahead of the first vehicle, and two more were added to that without the results being observed.

F/O Coleman and four crews from 37 Squadron joined forces with nineteen others from 3 Group on the night of the 14/15th to attempt to set fire to the Black Forest in south-western Germany, where, it was believed, concentrations of troops, dumps and depots existed. The crews from each station were given a specific map reference to attack with "Razzle", and F/O Coleman was assigned to a stretch of forest between Achern and Oberkirch, right on the western fringe, just east of Strasbourg. He took off in R3159 AA-K at 21.45 carrying six 250 pounders and ten 25lb incendiaries and found the route out to be mostly covered by ten-tenths cloud, with icing conditions existing between 7,000 and 13,000 feet. Navigation was by DR, with two-thirds of the flight being undertaken on instruments, despite which, he arrived in the target area and descended to 4,000 feet to deliver the incendiaries. Torrential rain had left the vegetation sodden, and the incendiaries seemed to become extinguished very quickly. He climbed to 8,000 feet to deliver the bombs singly and in a salvo and returned home safely to land at 04.40. The experiment with Razzle (also referred to as "deckers") would continue for a number of months, before it was consigned to the "it was worth a try" file, never to be resurrected.

It was back to the Ruhr for seven of the New Zealanders on the night of the 17/18th to attack the Rheinpreussen oil plant at Moers/Homberg near Duisburg. F/L Breckon was the senior pilot on duty as they took off between 21.50 and 22.40 and climbed into favourable weather conditions. These held firm all the way to the target, where a little ground haze was encountered. F/L Breckon carried out a bombing run at 10,500 feet from south-west to north-east, dropping a stick of nine 250 pounders and a container of incendiaries. F/O Watson made a dummy run at 14,500 feet, before delivering four 500 pounders and making a third pass to unload his incendiaries. P/O Bill Williams dropped his entire load in one go from 10,000 feet, while F/O Coleman approached from the north-west and watched his bombs and incendiaries straddle a road and railway track just short of the planned aiming point. F/O Lucas favoured a shallow-dive attack and released his load in a single stick from 7,500 feet, observing the middle bomb to hit a road immediately to the east of the aiming point and the rest to fall within the target area. F/O Adams adopted the same shallow-dive tactic and dropped his hardware in two runs, the first four 250 pounders hitting a railway line west of the target and the second four straddling the target, although the incendiaries fell short. A navigation error caused F/O Neville Williams to drop five bombs on a river west of Düsseldorf, after which, he flew on to Homberg to release the remainder.

3 Group prepared thirty-nine Wellingtons for operations on the night of the 19/20th against a variety of industrial and communications targets in Germany. 75(NZ) Squadron briefed eight crews, two to participate in an attack on the Erftwerk aluminium smelting works at Grevenbroich, situated on the south-western corner of the Ruhr, and six others to bomb the locks on the Mittelland Canal at Minden, between Hannover and Osnabrück. S/Ls Collett and Kay were the senior pilots on duty, and with further to travel, departed Feltwell first at 21.50, while F/Os Coleman and Watson took off at 22.30. The weather conditions were good as the main element flew out in loose formation, and there was even moonlight to aid navigation and target identification. S/L Kay dropped his load from 5,000 feet after a shallow-dive approach,

and P/O Freeman attempted a similar tactic with the intention of delivering his 500 pounders from 2,000 feet in a run from north to south. He was forced to break-off, however, after coming within range of intense light flak and made a second straight-and-level run from 7,000 feet. The recently-promoted F/L Adams dropped his bombs after a shallow dive from 8,000 down to 5,000 feet, and he saw bursts on the western bank alongside the lock gates. S/L Collett and F/L Breckon were unable to assess the results of their efforts, and a similar story was reported by F/O Lucas, who dived from 10,400 down to 7,500 feet to release his load in a stick onto a clearly-visible objective. Meanwhile, 130 miles to the south-west, F/O Watson had failed to locate the aluminium foundry and tried instead to hit a road and rail bridge at Düsseldorf, an endeavour in which he was unsuccessful, and reported his bombs falling on what might have been locks on the Rhine. F/O Coleman followed a parallel road and railway from Cologne to attack the target from south-east to north-west and released the bombs in a stick after a shallow dive, followed by the incendiaries. He observed six bursts between the road and the railway and was persuaded by grey smoke to report "every possibility of a hit".

S/L Kay was awarded a DFC on the 21st in recognition of his outstanding service thus far, and he was in action again when the squadron next went to war on the night of the 24/25th. This was to be 3 Group's largest effort in a single night to date, for which its aircraft were to be sent against enemy aircraft stationed at airfields in France and aircraft factories, oil plants and marshalling yards at a variety of locations from the Ruhr to Bremen in north-western Germany. 75(NZ) Squadron briefed eight crews, six to attack an aircraft factory at Kassel, some eighty miles to the east of the Ruhr, and two for an oil plant at Dortmund. There were three main oil-related targets in Dortmund, the Hoesch-Westfalenhütte A G, the Hoesch-Benzin GmbH in the Wambel district and the Zeche Hansa coking plant, while both Henschel and Fieseler had aircraft production sites in Kassel, the latter building Messerschmitt and Focke-Wulf aircraft under licence. The Fieseler company would also be responsible for the design and construction of the V-1 flying bomb that would be unleashed on London in the summer of 1944 and become known as the "Doodlebug" or "Buzzbomb".

S/Ls Collett and Kay were the senior pilots on duty as they took off for Kassel with F/L Breckon, F/O Lucas and P/Os Freeman and Williams between 21.35 and 21.50, to be followed by F/Os Coleman and Watson at 22.25 bound for Dortmund. Weather conditions of thick cloud, rainstorms and ground haze provided difficulties for target location and identification, but most crews found their respective target areas to deliver their hardware. S/L Collett was unable to assess the results of his attack, and it was the same for F/O Lucas, who dropped his 250 pounders in a stick after a shallow dive. P/O Williams was unable to find the exact location of the factory and dropped his bombs in a stick from east to west across the south of the city. S/L Kay followed the river and an autobahn to the target and dropped his bombs in a stick from a shallow dive on a south-west to north-east heading. F/L Breckon was unable to identify the primary target and returned home north of the Ruhr, dropping his entire load in a salvo from 12,000 feet onto the important marshalling yards at Hamm on the way. P/O Freeman was also unable to locate the factory and let some bombs go on a flak battery at Kassel, before adopting a course towards the north-west and dropping the remainder of the bombs on aerodrome buildings at Lippstadt, east of Hamm, and the incendiaries on a flak battery on the outskirts of Münster. Meanwhile, at Dortmund, F/O Watson found the general area of the target but not the oil plant itself, and dropped his bombs in a single stick from 9,500 feet. F/O Coleman released a flare in an attempt to illuminate the primary target, but it went out before the bombing run was completed, and his attention was attracted by the glow from a nearby blast furnace, which he attacked at 00.35 from 9,000 feet, without observing the results.

Germany was also the destination for eight of the squadron's crews on the night of the 26/27th, when they were divided among three targets. S/L Collett, F/O Lucas and P/O Bill Williams were briefed to attack marshalling yards at Osnabrück, while F/Os Coleman and Watson went for an airfield at Dortmund, and S/L Kay, F/L Breckon and P/O Freeman attended to another set of marshalling yards at Schwerte, south-east of Dortmund. The first-named trio was airborne by 21.40, followed thirty minutes later by the duo, and the second trio departed between 22.15 and 22.30. All were carrying ten 250 pounders, one with a six-hour delay fuse and another with a twelve-hour delay, plus a case of 4lb incendiaries. The weather outbound was unhelpful, with ice-bearing cloud and thunderstorms, and cloud and haze over western Germany added to the problems of target identification. S/L Collett was unable to assess the result of his efforts because of ground haze, but F/O Lucas watched three large fires break out at the western end of the yards after dropping his bombs in a stick. P/O Williams saw his bombs burst on the aiming point after a straight-and-level run from east to west and claimed that his incendiaries fell among buildings causing multiple fires, punctuated by many explosions and gushes of white flame. F/O Watson let his bombs go from 3,000 feet onto a railway bridge one mile east of Völlinghausen, fifteen miles to the east of Dortmund, and observed debris flying high into the air. F/O Coleman, assigned to the same aerodrome target, dropped his load in a single salvo onto the south-eastern corner, causing numerous small fires. It seems that only F/L Breckon located the Osnabrück marshalling yards and bombed them in a close stick from 12,000 feet, the rear gunner confirming them to burst in the target area and cause fires. The ORB talks of S/L Kay dropping his bombs onto an aerodrome rather than the yards to which he had been assigned. He released them in a single stick during a straight-and-level run and observed some to hit the airfield and others to burst among buildings. P/O Freeman was unable to locate his primary target because of thunderstorms and unloaded his bomb bay onto Schiphol aerodrome on the way home, after diving from 9,000 down to 2,500 feet. They fell in a line across the airfield from west-north-west to east-south-east, and three were seen to burst before searchlight dazzle blinded the crew to further observations.

Eight of the squadron's crews assembled in the briefing room on the 28th to learn that they were to attack a chemicals factory at Cologne in concert with four others from 37 Squadron. F/Ls Adams and Breckon were the senior pilots on duty as they departed Feltwell in two sections of four at 21.45 and 22.25 and encountered ground haze on arriving over the south-western corner of the Ruhr, particularly in the Rhine area. The intense searchlight activity and balloons at 10,000 feet over Cologne caused problems of identification, and F/L Breckon and first-time skipper, P/O Donald Joseph Harkness RAF, of the first section were unable to positively locate the primary target. They both turned back and headed for the alternative target of Waalhaven aerodrome at Rotterdam, where the former released his bombs in a stick, observing nine bursts, six of them within the target boundaries, and the latter followed suit from 10,000 feet, also watching some strike home. F/L Adams carried out a shallow dive attack on the chemicals factory, releasing his bombs from 5,000 feet without observing their fall. However, a large explosion shortly after their release suggested that some, at least, had found the mark. P/O Freeman searched for ninety minutes before locating the briefed aiming point and watched the first four bombs burst, setting off explosions and four fires, one green, one orange and two white. In the second section, F/O Neville Williams carried out a thorough search before dropping his bombs on a blast-furnace two miles east of Cologne's centre. Some bursts were seen within a hundred yards or so of the target, but with daylight approaching, he decided not to hang around to assess the results of his efforts. F/O Coleman managed to orient himself by pinpointing on a small lake and wooded area to the west of the target. He dropped his bombs in a stick from 11,000 feet but was prevented by searchlight dazzle from observing the outcome. F/O Lucas found the searchlights useful in momentarily lighting up the target, which enabled him to carry out a dive attack and drop his bombs in a stick. The rear gunner confirmed several small explosions as they retreated westwards. P/O Bill Williams searched for twenty minutes before releasing an illuminator flare, which lit up the River Rhine and directed him towards the aiming point. He dropped his bombs in a stick on a straight-and-level run from north to south at 11,000 feet and watched them all burst. All returned safely home, fog at Feltwell forcing three crews to divert to Wyton, and at debriefing, most reported heavy flak at Antwerp and over the Ruhr, along with intense searchlight activity.

The last night of the month saw six crews taking off at 21.45 to carry out fire-raising attacks, presumably with "Razzle", on a forest south of Frankfurt. S/Ls Wilfred Collett and "Cyrus" Kay were the senior pilots on duty, with F/Ls John Adams and Aubrey Breckon, F/O Bill Coleman and P/Os Trevor Freeman and Bill Williams making up the numbers. P/O Williams was back at Feltwell within two and a half hours after an oil pipe burst at 22.40 over the North Sea and flooded the rear turret. The others pressed on in good weather conditions to reach the target area, where bombs were dropped at half-mile intervals in circles from 9,000 to 11,000 feet. They initially caused fires, which did not seem to spread and could be seen to diminish as the retreating crews watched them recede behind them. Further attempts to burn Germany's woodland would be carried out, but, following the fall of France earlier in the month, attention now turned to the expected German invasion of Britain.

The thirteen nights of operations during the month brought a total of eighty-five sorties without loss, and there had now been 120 sorties since the squadron's one and only failure to return.

July 1940

The new month began operationally for 75(NZ) Squadron with briefings on the 2nd for an attack on the Rhenania-Ossag oil refinery at Düsseldorf/Reisholz that night. F/Os Coleman, Watson and Neville Williams and P/Os Harkness and Bill Williams departed Feltwell between 21.45 and 22.15, only to encounter adverse weather conditions in the target area, which prevented them from attacking the primary objective. F/O Coleman and P/O Harkness returned with their bombs, the latter having penetrated some fifty miles into enemy territory. He attempted to bomb searchlights at Gilze-Rijen aerodrome in southern Holland on the way home, but only one fell away after an electrical fault caused his battery to fail. Meanwhile, F/O Watson dropped his bombs in a stick on a building in the docks area of Rotterdam from 3,500 feet, observing gushes of flame and blue sparks. P/O Williams experienced great difficulty in locating anything to bomb, but eventually came upon the port of Zeebrugge, which he attacked in a shallow dive. Three 250 pounders hung up, but the remaining six caused many explosions and set off fires. F/O N Williams dropped his load in two sticks at 02.15 in the vicinity of Neuss, situated across the Rhine opposite Düsseldorf, and from 11,000 feet the crew registered four bursts and reported the incendiaries to have caused fires.

3 Group stations were ordered to put crews on invasion standby from sunset on the 3rd until 11.45 on the 4th in accordance with instructions issued on the 30th of June, and this practice would continue for as long as the threat existed. Five 75(NZ) Squadron crews attended briefings on the 4th, to be told that F/Ls Adams and Breckon and F/O N Williams were to attack the Blohm & Voss Flugzeugbau aircraft factory at Wenzendorf, south-west of Hamburg, while F/O Watson and P/O Harkness went for the marshalling yards at Osnabrück. They took off between 21.40 and 22.00 and reached their respective target areas in fair weather conditions but with poor visibility hampering identification of ground detail. F/L Adams experienced difficulties because of ground haze, and having been constantly harassed by searchlights, decided to make his way to Emden as an alternative target. He had clearly been forced well off track by the searchlights and was north-west of Hamburg when he came across Wedel aerodrome on the north bank of the Elbe and decided to drop his bombs there. F/O Williams found Wilhelmshaven docks as an alternative objective and delivered three 500 pounders from 11,000 feet at 01.12, observing them to burst in the Emsstrasse harbour area and set off a white glow. Only F/L Breckon located and attacked the Blohm & Voss factory, delivering a close stick from east to west from 11,000 feet, before flying back over it to observe the resulting fires. P/O Harkness failed to locate his primary target at Osnabrück, and, on finding the secondary target of Schiphol aerodrome to be obscured by cloud, decided to bring his bombs home. F/O Watson had the marshalling yards in his sights as he dropped his load in a single stick from 9,500 feet and returned to report several fires.

S/L Collett was the senior pilot on duty as five 75(NZ) Squadron Wellingtons departed Feltwell between 21.40 and 22.15 on the 6th, bound for the U-Boot construction yards at Bremen. The Deutsche Schiff und Maschinenbau A G shipyards, abbreviated to Deschimag, had been formed in the mid-twenties as a co-operation of eight shipyards to compete with the Blohm & Voss and Bremer Vulkan yards. The largest was the A G Weser company, which, after six of the others had fallen by the wayside before the outbreak of war, was partnered only by the Seebeckwerft, and in 1941 would become part of the Krupp empire, when that organisation was handed a controlling interest. They made their way out in very poor weather conditions, which prevented three crews from carrying out an attack, and in truth, the night was unfit for operations. F/L Breckon reached the Dutch coast in thick cloud navigating by DR, but his blind-flying instruments started to play up and ice began to form on the wings, persuading him to turn back. He adopted a different route in an attempt to break free of the evil conditions, but despite climbing to 11,000 feet and descending to 4,000 feet, he failed to emerge from cloud until reaching the English coast, and he was the first to land back at 00.55. S/L Collett brought his bombs back after failing to see the ground, and he was next to land at 03.00. P/O W Williams reached the target area at 00.20 having flown all the way from the English coast in ten-tenths cloud. He stooged around for forty minutes searching in vain for a break, then set off to try to find Wilhelmshaven, failing also, before returning home with his bombs at 03.50. F/O Coleman lost his trailing aerial to a lightning strike but managed to find the target through a rare gap in the clouds and dropped his bombs in a single salvo from 8,000 feet at 00.30, without observing any results. F/O Lucas carried out a dive attack from 12,000 down to 8,500 feet but returned to report no possibility of observing the results.

The 3 Group plan for the night of the 8/9th was to send aircraft against the Bismarck, which was believed to be in Hamburg, the oil plant at Homberg and marshalling yards at Hamm and Essen. Six 75(NZ) Squadron crews were briefed for the Rheinpreussen Meerbeck oil plant at

Homberg and took off between 21.40 and 21.55 with S/L Collett the senior pilot on duty. The weather over England was reasonable but deteriorated over enemy territory, adversely affecting the crews' ability to fulfil their briefs. The Kiwi crews reached the target area to find ten-tenths cloud at 6,000 feet and no possibility of locating the primary target. They went instead for the alternatives, which were airfields in Holland, and P/O Freeman managed to pinpoint on Schiphol, which he bombed after diving from 9,000 down to 4,000 feet. Three bursts were observed on the concrete runways and one just off, before he had to take evasive action to escape the attentions of intense searchlight and flak activity. P/O Gordie (or Geordie) Keith Larney RAF, who was undertaking his first sortie as crew captain, attacked Waalhaven airfield at Rotterdam at 00.55 and observed a stick of bombs bursting close to hangars. S/L Collett and F/O Coleman also carried out an attack on Waalhaven but saw no results from their efforts. F/O Watson flew south after passing over Moers and came across Lohausen airfield at Düsseldorf, upon which he released his bombs in a single stick from 13,000 feet, observing them to fall a hundred yards from the western perimeter. It is believed that F/O Lucas also attacked Lohausen after shallow-diving from 9,000 to 7,500 feet. He returned safely to report that his incendiaries had caused numerous fires, which sent thick columns of black smoke rising skyward and also set off explosions, which continued for fifteen minutes.

A welcome break of five days allowed the crews some respite before their next operation, which took place on the night of the 14/15th. F/O Watson and P/Os Freeman, Harkness and Larney were briefed for an oil refinery in Hamburg, while three others went for marshalling yards, S/L Breckon at Hamm and F/O Lucas and P/O Bill Williams at Soest, a few miles further to the east and north of the Möhnesee and its one-day-to-be-famous dam. There were at least four oil plants in the Hamburg area, coded A5, A7, A8 located on the northern bank of the River Elbe to the west of the city centre, and A10, the Rhenania-Ossag refinery at Harburg on the southern bank. The weather conditions were fine as they took off between 21.45 and 22.10, all but one carrying eight 250 pounders and incendiaries. They arrived at their respective target areas to find ground haze but generally good visibility, despite which, P/O Larney failed to pick up the aiming point in time and found himself heading westwards along the south bank of the Elbe. He came upon some marshalling yards at Stade, which he bombed from 9,000 feet and missed by a hundred yards. P/O Harkness did identify his aiming point and delivered his bombs in a stick after a shallow dive from 10,000 down to 8,000 feet. Searchlight glare and evasive action prevented him from observing the results, and it was a similar story for P/O Freeman, who carried out his attack from 15,000 feet and had his incendiaries and one bomb hang up. F/O Watson was also at 15,000 feet when he released his four 500 pounders in a single stick and saw two fall short and produce sheets of flame, while the last two burst within the target area. F/L Breckon dropped his load on Hamm marshalling yards from 12,000 feet and started two large fires which remained visible for forty miles into the return trip. F/O Lucas landed five 250 pounders in the town of Soest and three in the marshalling yards, causing fires visible from fifty miles away. P/O Williams dived through a layer of cloud at 10,000 feet and identified the target by the light of a parachute flare. He levelled out at 9,000 feet and delivered his bombs from west to east at 00.30, before stooging around for a further forty minutes, watching the fires rage fiercely and a new one start at 00.55.

Six crews were called to briefing on the 18th to learn that their target that night was to be an aircraft park at Rotenburg, situated some twenty miles north-east of Bremen. S/L Kay was the senior pilot on duty as they departed Feltwell between 21.15 and 21.40 and headed out over the North Sea to encounter ten-tenths cloud at 12,000 feet and a thunderstorm at the Dutch coast, which interfered with instruments and created navigation problems. F/L Breckon found the target with difficulty, despite improving visibility, and eventually dropped a close stick of 250 pounders onto hangars and the aerodrome, observing four bursts which started six fires. S/L Kay ran across the target at 9,000 feet and dropped his bombs in three sticks, the rear gunner reporting the first two bombs of the first stick to have struck hangars. The other bombs were also seen to burst, but nothing could be determined of the outcome. P/O Freeman searched for two hours but failed to locate the target, and dropped his bombs ineffectively on a northern stretch of the Dortmund-Ems Canal on his way back to the Dutch frontier. F/L Adams could not locate Rotenburg and dropped six delay-fused 250 pounders on an aerodrome at Bomlitz, some thirty miles south-east of Bremen, before heading north-east the few miles to Soltau, where two stationary trains were bombed in a marshalling yard. Both attacks were carried out from 3,000 feet after a steep dive, and the fires resulting from the latter could be seen from forty miles away. He described the conditions as perfect, and three Me110s took advantage of the visibility to dive upon him, only to sheer off without attacking to avoid being hit by friendly ground fire. F/O Coleman could not make a positive identification at Rotenburg and chose to bomb an aerodrome at Ütersen on the east bank of the Elbe, north-west of Hamburg. F/O Lucas managed to a hit a road junction at an undisclosed location with a single 250 pounder, and his incendiaries caused three yellow fires among buildings.

The squadron equalled its best operational effort to date when despatching nine Wellingtons to two synthetic oil refineries in Gelsenkirchen on the night of 20/21st. The German synthetic oil industry relied on two main production methods, the Bergius process, which involved the hydrogenation of highly volatile bituminous coal to manufacture high-grade petroleum products like aviation fuel, and the Fischer-Tropsch process, which produced lower-grade diesel-type fuels for vehicle, Tank, U-Boot and shipping requirements. F/O Williams and P/Os Harkness and Larney were briefed for the Hydrierwerke-Scholven coal-liquefaction plant at Scholven-Buer in Gelsenkirchen's north-western suburbs, while F/Ls Adams and Breckon, F/Os Lucas and Watson and P/Os Freeman and Bill Williams were assigned to the Gelsenkirchener Bergwerke A G Plant in the district of Horst, known to the Germans as Gelsenberg A G and to Bomber Command as Nordstern. They took off between 21.35 and 22.00 and headed for the Lincolnshire coast in good weather conditions, which would persist throughout. P/O Larney dropped a stick of three 250 pounders on Eindhoven aerodrome at 23.35 while outbound, before continuing on to deliver the remainder of his load onto the assigned target at 00.25. F/O Williams made two runs at 5,000 feet, beginning at 00.33, and delivered a stick of five bombs on each occasion onto fires started by another crew's incendiaries. P/O Harkness failed to identify the primary and flew on eastwards for a handful of miles to eventually bomb a railway junction at Kamen from 9,500 feet. F/L Breckon waited for the cloud to disperse over the Nordstern plant, before making a number of dummy runs and finally depositing his bomb load onto the north-eastern corner of the site. F/O Lucas saw his incendiaries burst on the southern extremities of the target but could not make out the fall of his bombs because of cloud. P/O Williams ran across the aiming point from north-east to south-west at 10,800 feet, and saw three hits on the northern side, but the remaining bombs appeared to fall short. P/O Freeman carried out his attack from 14,000 feet, while F/L Adams was at 11,000, and found the target easy to locate in the light of the moon. After leaving the target area, three "Heinkel 113's" (probably BF109s) attacked Wellington L7797, AA-F over Wesel, and the Neville Williams crew claimed one, possibly two enemy aircraft destroyed. Williams managed to get the Wellington home safely despite it being "riddled with bullets". From this action the squadron won its first immediate decorations, F/O Neville Williams awarded the DFC, while navigator, Sgt Donald Mackay RAF, and rear gunner, Sgt Lewis White RAF, were each awarded a DFM. R3165 AA-L failed to return with the crew of F/O Watson, and this represented only the squadron's second loss from over two hundred sorties. The cause of the loss and the precise crash site is not known, but heavy flak was experienced over Wesel and the entire Ruhr region and fighters had been seen, and the likelihood is that the Wellington came down in the target area. F/O Watson had been Mentioned in Dispatches, and he died alongside his experienced crew, the two gunners members of the RNZAF, and all would be missed by the Feltwell community.

"Sam" Watson had been born in Auckland, New Zealand and had attended King's College. He learned to fly while studying law at Cambridge University in England and as a member of the Wellington Territorial Squadron and Wellington Aero Club back in New Zealand. He had joined the RAF in October 1939. His crew was a mix of RAF and RNZAF, the four New Zealanders, P/O Edward Cameron, RAF (second pilot), F/Sgt Ronald Anderson, RNZAF (wireless operator), Sgt John Owen, RNZAF (rear gunner), and a Scot, Sgt Gordon Cumming, RAFVR (observer).

The third loss came with the very next operations, which involved another nine of the squadron's Wellingtons on the night of the 25/26th. According to the 3 Group ORB, crews were briefed for two targets, but the squadron ORB suggests three. S/L Kay and F/L Adams are shown as being assigned to attack an aircraft factory at Kassel, either the Fieseler or Henschel works, while S/L Collett, F/Os Coleman and Lucas and P/O Bill Williams were briefed for the Gothaer Waggonfabrik aircraft works at Gotha, some fifty miles to the south-east. The remaining three crews, those of P/Os Gow, Hogg and Larney were to attend to the marshalling yards at Hamm. P/Os Ian Ronald Gow and Richard John Kitchener Hogg, both RAF, were first-time captains of their own crews, the latter to become known on the squadron as "Hogg of Hamm" due to his frequent visits to the city. In addition to the normal bomb load, each aircraft carried five bundles of nickels to be dispensed over enemy territory. They took off between 21.10 and 22.00, but P/O Hogg was back home two-and-a-half hours later after an electrical problem forced him to abandon his sortie. F/L Adams was prevented by poor visibility from identifying the primary target at Kassel, so found a nearby aerodrome to bomb from 12,000 feet before heading home. On the way out, S/L Kay dropped a single 250 pounder on an aerodrome at Lippstadt, twenty miles east of Hamm, before delivering a stick of bombs and a small bomb canister (SBC) onto the Kassel factory from 7,000 feet during a run from south-east to north-west. The incendiaries caused large, red, green and orange fires among buildings, the explosions from which lit up the aircraft. P/O Williams was thwarted at Gotha by six-tenths low cloud at 2,000 feet, but back-tracked to Kassel, where he carried out a shallow dive from 10,000 to 8,000 feet to deliver his bombs in a stick onto the aircraft factory there. S/L Collett saw no results at Gotha because of ground haze and intense searchlight and flak activity. F/O Lucas dived from 11,000 down to 8,000 feet to release his bombs in a single stick but saw no results in the face of searchlight glare and gun flashes. Meanwhile, P/O Gow jettisoned his bombs live while evading anti-aircraft fire at Hamm, where P/O Larney could not identify the marshalling yards because of ground haze. On his way home he dropped a stick of three 250 pounders on an aerodrome at Duisburg, and six more plus incendiaries on the flarepath at Eindhoven. Following receipt of a Mayday call from the Wireless Operator, the return of R3235 was awaited in vain, and the experienced, ever-present F/O "Bill" Coleman DFC, RNZAF and his crew, which included a RNZAF rear-gunner, were posted missing. News eventually came through that the Wellington had crashed into the Ijsselmeer, the inland sea near Amsterdam, without survivors, and this was another crew whose loss would be keenly felt.

"Bill" Coleman came from Devonport, New Zealand, but attended school in Christchurch and learned to fly with the Christchurch Gliding Club and later the Auckland Aero Club. He sailed to England and joined the RAF in 1937, serving with 97 and 166 Squadrons before being selected as a foundation pilot for the NZ Flight. His crew included two fellow Kiwis, P/O Frank Twain Poole, RAF (second pilot), Sgt William Annan, RNZAF (rear gunner), and three Englishmen, Sgt Norman Wilson Brown, RAF (observer), Sgt William Eric Nevill, RAF (wireless operator) and Sgt John Dowds, RAF (mid-upper gunner). Although not gazetted until September, Coleman was awarded the DFC, and his long-term navigator (observer) Sgt Brown, the DFM.

When the operations orders came though on the 28th, nine 75(NZ) Squadron crews were called to the briefing room to learn of four targets for that night. F/Os Lucas and Neville Williams and P/Os Harkness and Larney found themselves assigned to an oil refinery in Hamburg, P/Os Gow and Hogg to the Meerbeck plant at Moers/Homberg and F/L Adams and P/O Freeman to yet another, the Chemwerke-Steinkohle refinery at Bergkamen in the north-eastern Ruhr, while F/O Williams attended to the marshalling yards at Hamm. They would be operating, as usual, in concert with aircraft from 37 Squadron and nickelling again formed part of their brief. They took off between 21.35 and 21.50 on a night of adverse weather conditions, characterized by ten-tenths cloud and ground haze in the target areas. At Hamburg, P/O Harkness delivered his bombs in a single stick from 11,000 feet but was prevented by the cloud and searchlights from observing the results. P/O Larney was similarly unable to comment on the outcome of his efforts, but F/O Lucas was able to determine that his bombs, dropped in a stick from 15,000 feet, had fallen across the docks on the north side of the Elbe. P/O Williams was unable to identify the aiming point through eight-tenths cloud at 9,000 feet, and instead, dropped four 500 pounders onto the aerodrome at Stade on the left bank of the Elbe. The hangar lights were extinguished, but the gooseneck flares remained lit, inviting P/O Williams to dive to 1,000 feet to allow his gunners to shoot up the area during two circuits. P/Os Gow and Hogg failed to identify Homberg, but the latter found two unidentified Ruhr blast-furnaces, which he straddled with his bombs, while the incendiaries started a fire. The former found no worthwhile target for his bombs and returned them to store. F/L John Adams was unable to identify the Bergkamen refinery because of haze and decided to seek out an aerodrome on the Dutch coast to bomb as an alternative. While searching, R3171 AA-E developed a problem with its port engine, which persuaded the crew to jettison the bombs, send out an SOS signal and set course for Manston in Kent. On arrival at the English coast, however, the engine picked up and a safe landing was carried out at Feltwell. P/O Freeman and crew experienced the same difficulties with target identification and found a blast-furnace to attack fifteen miles to the west, which would have been in the Herne/Castrop-Rauxel area of the Ruhr. Continuing homeward, he came across an aerodrome at Wesel with an illuminated flarepath, which he bombed just as an aircraft was landing. Meanwhile, F/O Williams had located Hamm and dropped his bombs in two sticks, observing just one burst estimated to be about four miles south of the town.

During the course of the month the squadron dispatched sixty-one sorties to eighteen targets, and posted missing two Wellingtons and crews.

August 1940

As the Battle of Britain gained momentum overhead during August and invasion fever continued to grip the nation, Bomber Command maintained its pressure on the Ruhr with a special emphasis on the oil industry, while also attacking airfields in Holland almost on a daily basis. The first night of operations for the Kiwis came on the 3/4th, when the Nordstern oil plant at Gelsenkirchen was the primary target for nine of its Wellingtons, with S/L Collett the senior pilot on duty. They took off between 21.15 and 21.30 and all reached the target area to find thick ground haze, which hampered their ability to identify the aiming point. P/O Hogg and F/Os Lucas and Neville Williams were the only ones to report bombing the primary target, the last-mentioned delivering a stick of five 250 pounders and an SBC from 12,000 feet at 00.15 after searching for forty-five minutes. On the way back he found a line of six blast furnaces on the eastern side of Gladbeck, which he attacked with a stick of four 250 pounders also from 12,000 feet. F/L Breckon was almost at the target when engine trouble struck, and he dispensed leaflets as he turned back towards the west, before dropping his bombs on Schiphol aerodrome from 12,500 feet. P/O Gow dropped his bombs on a flarepath to the west of Duisburg, while F/L Adams came upon marshalling yards at Haltern, situated on the northern-eastern rim of the Ruhr, which he deemed to be a worthy recipient for his hardware. He unloaded the contents of his bomb bay in a single stick and the ensuing explosions convinced him that substantial damage had resulted. P/O Freeman attacked Schiphol aerodrome from 4,000 feet in the face of an intense searchlight and flak response, which prevented him from observing the outcome. P/O Harkness found an aerodrome at Buer on the outskirts of Gelsenkirchen, which he bombed from 10,000 feet.

Weather conditions for returning crews were difficult in the extreme, with the cloud base as low as 300 feet, and some had to be diverted. Badly shot up and low on fuel, R3176 arrived back over the Suffolk coast with a dead engine, and it was during an attempted forced-landing at Mildenhall that the Wellington smacked into a ridge at Barton Mills at 04.20, inflicting injuries upon S/L Collett to which he would succumb later that day and injuring the other members of the crew, some of whom required hospitalisation. S/L Wilf Collett was twenty-eight, and his funeral procession was the first of many from the squadron to end at St Nicholas Churchyard at Feltwell.

Around the time that F/O Fred "Popeye" Lucas, F/O John Adams and P/O Bill Williams received promotions, the first two to flight lieutenant rank and the last-mentioned to flying officer, one of the squadron's most treasured legends was born. Poor weather meant flying was scrubbed, and as promotions required celebrating, a long, noisy and drunken party got underway in the Feltwell officers' mess. By the next morning, a mysterious set of black footprints had appeared across the ceiling of an ante room, down the wall, and out through a ventilator … It was one of Popeye's party tricks, in which his mates hoisted him above their heads, lying on his back on a small table, the soles of his bare feet blackened with shoe polish, to 'walk' foot-print by foot-print across the ceiling. Air Chief Marshall Sir Arthur Tedder apparently visited the station soon afterwards, and despite official displeasure over the incident, wrote in the visitors' book, "These footprints to remain for all time!" They were varnished over and were still there when Popeye visited Feltwell thirty-six years later! Another of his party tricks involved demonstrations of rotating his false teeth without removing them from his mouth, something he called "toothabatics", and most likely the origin of his nickname! The Popeye legend was further enhanced when his regular "Wimpy", R3169 AA-P, which would carry him and his crew through twenty-one operations, was painted up with "Popeye" nose art. Interestingly, other 75(NZ) Squadron Wellingtons bore nose art from the "Popeye" cartoon strip, including a "J. Wellington Wimpy", and a "Jeep".

The night of the 6/7th brought further operations against Germany's synthetic oil industry, for which eight 75(NZ) Squadron Wellingtons were made ready. S/L Kay was the senior pilot on duty, and he was briefed for the Moers/Homberg plant along with P/Os Hogg and Larney, while F/L Lucas joined F/O Neville Williams and his newly-promoted namesake and P/O Gow to attack the Rhenania-Ossag refinery at Düsseldorf/Reisholz. They departed Feltwell between 21.20 and 21.45 and encountered extremely adverse weather conditions over enemy territory, which prevented all but S/L Kay from locating a primary target. He attacked the Homberg site with two sticks of bombs delivered in a straight-and-level run from 10,000 feet and saw bursts and fires. Dutch and German airfields became suitable alternatives for the others, and attacks were carried out at Wesel, Schiphol, Ypenburg and Eindhoven. F/O Bill Williams found three field batteries on the western outskirts of Hamborn (Duisburg), which he attacked with four 250 pounders and incendiaries from 12,500 feet, before bringing the rest of his load home. P/O Larney and F/O Neville Williams, who was about to receive confirmation of his DFC, found no suitable targets for their bombs, and returned them to store.

Nine Wellingtons were made ready on the 9th, eight of them in response to an operations order to attack an aluminium plant at Ichendorf. The location of this target is in doubt because the only traceable locations bearing that name are in Bavaria and close to the Czech frontier, but it is believed to be either in one of the Ruhr cities or in the Hamm area, and possibly related to the Herringen aluminium foundry in that town. This belief is based on the other operations carried out by 3 Group squadrons on this night, which were against marshalling yards at Hamm and nearby Soest and the fact that the ORB takes the trouble to record the weather conditions for the Ruhr. The Kiwi brigade departed Feltwell between 21.00 and 21.20 led by S/L Aubrey Breckon, who had been promoted to succeed the late S/L Collett as B Flight commander. The primary target was located by F/L Lucas, both F/O Williams and P/Os Freeman, Harkness and Larney, and attacks were carried out in one or two runs from heights ranging from 9,000 to 14,000 feet over a period either side of 23.00. Returning crews described vivid flashes, large explosions and fires, but detail was difficult to ascertain because of the haze. S/L Breckon was outbound when flying over Eindhoven aerodrome, which was lit up and providing an irresistible target. He dropped a stick of bombs and incendiaries, which set off fires and caused the lights to be extinguished. F/L Adams was unable to locate the primary target and bombed Gilze-Rijen aerodrome from 5,000 feet as an alternative. The final departure on this night had been that of first-time captain P/O Eric Vernon Best RAF and crew at 21.40, flying what was to become their regular aircraft, L7857, AA-C "Dopey". Best had previously flown as second pilot with "Cyrus" Kay. They had been handed Gilze-Rijen aerodrome as a freshman target but failed to locate it after searching for ninety minutes over ten-tenths cloud down to 2,000 feet, and they brought their bombs home.

Following a few days' rest, eighteen crews assembled in the Feltwell briefing room, nine from each squadron, to learn of their destinations for that night. P/O Freeman and crew were handed a special duty, which would require of them a round-trip of five minutes short of nine hours. They took off well ahead of the others at 19.55 and set course for Denmark and beyond to carry out a photo-reconnaissance of the docks in the port-city of Stettin, situated on a waterway some thirty miles to the south-south-east of the Baltic port of Swinemünde. The remaining eight 75(NZ) Squadron crews were divided between an aircraft components factory at Frankfurt and the aluminium foundry at Grevenbroich and took off between 20.50 and 21.20 with S/L Breckon the senior pilot on duty. The weather was once more unhelpful, ten-tenths cloud hanging over most of north-western Germany, and those southbound for Frankfurt found similar conditions with a cloud base at 600 feet. F/L Adams searched the general area but failed to find the primary target, or indeed any suitable alternative and brought his bombs home. F/O N Williams experienced similar difficulties and headed home, dropping three 250 pounders and one SBC on a road and rail junction at Dorsel, some twenty miles short of the Belgian frontier. S/L Breckon believed he had aimed his bombs at the primary target and saw four bursts, while F/O W Williams was thwarted in his endeavours by cloud at 7,000 feet and settled for dispensing nickels over Frankfurt. On his way home he found nothing in either Germany or Holland worthy of his bombs and returned them to store. On his way to Germany, P/O Larney dropped a stick of three bombs on a flarepath at Vught in southern Holland at 22.20, before finding the primary target hidden beneath ten-tenths cloud and back-tracking to bomb the marshalling yards at Roermond, deep in south-eastern Holland at 23.35. P/O Best believed his bombs straddled the aluminium works, but haze made it difficult to be certain, and P/O Hogg dropped his in the target area at 23.30, observing a large fire develop as he retreated westwards. P/O Harkness cited low cloud and haze as the reason for his failure to locate the target, and his bombs were brought home.

The 15th was the day selected by the Luftwaffe as "Adlertag", Eagle Day, which was intended to be the opening salvo in the destruction of the RAF's ability to defend Britain. It began the most intense four weeks of the Battle of Britain, the outcome of which might determine the course of the war. The squadron set a new record on this night with the dispatch of ten Wellingtons to attack the Lünen aluminium works to the north of Dortmund. They took off between 20.45 and 21.20 with S/L Kay the senior pilot on duty and last to leave the ground and reached the target area to find four-tenths cloud and excellent visibility. On the way, they had been forced to run the gauntlet of searchlights and flak right across the Ruhr and dodge the many balloons tethered at 12,000 feet over Amsterdam and Dortmund. F/L Lucas made two bombing runs at 11,000 feet, the explosions from which lit up the aircraft, and F/O W Williams carried out three runs from west to east at 9,000 feet. P/O Hogg claimed that his bombs started a fire that remained visible for a considerable distance into the homeward flight, and S/L Kay, who delivered his load in a single stick from 10,000 feet, also reported setting off fires. P/O Larney commented on the smoke from the small fires resulting from his bombs, while P/O Best observed his burst across the target following his run from south to north at 10,000 feet. P/O Freeman made three runs, the first and last at 8,700 feet with a dummy run in between, and he was certain that his bombs had struck home, reporting a large column of white smoke as evidence. F/L Adams described his run at 11,000 feet as perfect, while F/O N Williams carried out the highest attack, from 12,500 feet at 23.36, and three bursts were observed by the rear gunner to the east of the target. P/O Harkness was the only one to experience difficulty in identifying the target and dropped his bombs from 9,000 feet onto a railway junction in the town.

Meanwhile, back at Feltwell, a night flying practice had come to a messy end, when at 21.35, S/L Breckon's pupil pilot had overshot the aerodrome in Wellington P9210, AA-Y, and crashed. No injuries were recorded, and the aircraft was deemed 'not to be causing an obstruction' for the returning aircraft. As the war went on, such accidents often went un-recorded in the Operations Record Book, and maintenance staff regularly performed minor miracles to return these aircraft to operational standard.

Ten crews were called to briefing on the 17th to learn of operations that night against three targets, the oil refinery at Zeitz-Tröglitz, one of a number of oil-related sites in an arc from north to south to the west of Leipzig, the aircraft park at Eschwege and the marshalling yards at Hamm. F/Ls Adams and Lucas were the senior pilots on duty as they took off between 20.25 and 21.00, but the former was back on the ground after forty minutes with a W/T electrical fault. Ten-tenths cloud hung over most of the route, with the exception of the Ruhr, and heavy, accurate flak was experienced between Utrecht and Münster by those heading for eastern Germany. F/O N Williams was unable to locate the target because of the cloud, and having insufficient fuel to carry out a search, jettisoned his bombs at a DR position about sixty miles west of Zeitz. F/O W Williams was also thwarted by the cloud and haze, and after searching in vain for thirty minutes, back-tracked to Soest, where he attacked the marshalling yards in a shallow dive from 8,000 to 7,000 feet at 01.10. P/O Freeman was similarly compromised by the cloud and dropped his bombs on what appeared to be an aerodrome. This left just F/L Lucas and P/O Harkness to attack the oil plant, and they arrived to find fires already burning following attacks by aircraft from 9, 37 and 214 Squadrons. P/O Harkness reported further fires after his bombs found the mark and oil storage tanks were seen to explode and send columns of thick, black smoke high into the air. F/O Lucas carried out a straight-and-level run at 9,000 feet and reported that two large explosions in factory buildings resulted from his stick of five 250 pounders.

Meanwhile, P/Os Larney and Best had located their target at Eschwege, the former delivering his bombs at 23.50 and reporting fires visible for a considerable distance into the homeward journey. The latter dropped his bombs on the aerodrome and the incendiaries on buildings, setting off thirteen distinct explosions, followed by others as the Wellington withdrew to the west. At Hamm, low cloud and ground haze caused some difficulties and P/O Curtis spent thirty minutes searching, aided by flares dropped by other aircraft, before making a shallow dive attack from the south and observing a stick of bombs to fall on the northern end of the yards. P/O Richard Melville Curtis RAF was on his first operation as captain, having flown previously as second pilot to "Popeye" Lucas. P/O Hogg returned to report his bombs falling onto the tracks inside the yards.

There were three targets on offer again for the ten 75(NZ) Squadron crews who attended briefing on the 19th. S/L Breckon was to lead F/Ls Adams and Lucas, F/Os Williams, Williams and Freeman to Kiel to attack the cruiser Gneisenau at berth, while P/Os Harkness, Hogg and Larney targeted the Deurag-Nerag synthetic oil refinery at Misburg to the north-east of Hannover and P/O Curtis went for the marshalling yards at Osnabrück. They departed Feltwell between 21.00 and 21.20 and headed into ten-tenths cloud for most of the route out, and this prevented all of the Kiel-bound crews from locating the warship. They were also subjected to intense flak and searchlight activity over northern Germany and the Frisian Islands. S/L Breckon and F/L Lucas dropped their bombs on a subterranean oil storage facility on the bank of the Kiel Canal to the north of the town, while F/O Freeman, having made four runs in search of the Gneisenau, dived from 13,000 down to 8,000 feet to attack the buildings on the edge of the fitting-out basin some eleven hundred yards away. F/O N Williams arrived over the target area at 15,000 feet and searched for thirty minutes before delivering the contents of his bomb bay onto the canal bank. F/O W Williams searched for an hour before heading back and releasing his load from 8,000 feet over the aerodrome on the island of Wangerooge at 02.00. F/L Adams attacked De Kooy airfield on the Den Helder peninsula, with six 250 pounders from 5,000 feet and observed a few bursts. The Misburg trio fared equally badly and ended up attacking aerodromes at De Kooy, Wunstorf and Diepholz as alternatives. P/O Curtis was the only one to positively identify his target at Osnabrück and bombed it from 11,000 feet during a run from east to west.

The night of the 24/25th brought a new record number of sorties for the Kiwis, when eleven were dispatched between 20.45 and 21.15, eight to attack the A161-coded oil production site located on the River Main in the Offenbach district to the south-east of Frankfurt city centre and three the marshalling yards at Hamm. F/L Adams was ninety minutes out and over enemy territory when engine trouble forced him to turn back, leaving the others to press on to their respective targets in extremely adverse weather conditions, which would render most efforts ineffective. At Hamm, P/O Curtis dropped his bombs in the general target area, aiming at the flashes from a flak battery, but saw no results, while F/O N Williams and P/O Gilmour found nothing and brought their bombs home. F/L Lucas ran across his Frankfurt primary target at 11,000 feet to deliver first his incendiaries, before making a second run to drop his 250 pounders, which set off a few fires. The remaining crews attacked alternative targets, P/O Larney finding a railway junction and landing ground at Koblenz as a suitable recipient for his bomb load. S/L Breckon picked out Knapsack power station near Cologne, while F/O W Williams, after failing to locate either the oil plant or a nearby chemicals factory, dropped his bombs on the aerodrome at Limburg in Belgium after diving to 5,000 feet. P/O Hogg found a hole in the cloud and employing an island in the River Main as a reference point, bombed the chemicals factory assigned as an alternative objective. P/O Freeman flew down a searchlight beam at an undisclosed location and surprised its crew with a 500 pounder, before diving from 4,000 down to 2,000 feet to attack two ships in Ijmuiden docks. P/O Harkness descended to 1,100 feet and targeted a factory on the bank of a river to the east of Hanau. It was a disappointing night's work, but at least all crews returned safely.

In retaliation for the inadvertent bombing of London on the night of the 24/25th, the War Cabinet sanctioned the first raid of the war on Berlin by around fifty mostly 5 Group Hampdens to take place on the 25th. The weather conditions were unhelpful, preventing most crews from locating their intended targets, and local sources confirmed that most of the bombing had missed the city to the south. The only building destroyed was a summerhouse, but it was an unsettling experience for the Nazi leadership and gave further lie to Göring's boast that no enemy aircraft would fly over the Reich.

Twenty-three crews assembled in the briefing room at Feltwell on the 26th, ten representing 75(NZ) Squadron, who were told that six of them were to target the previously attacked aircraft component factory at Frankfurt, while three others went for Germany's largest inland port at Duisburg-Ruhrort and the freshman crew of P/O Nicholas Richard Peel RAF (formerly second pilot to F/L Breckon), the Brussels aerodrome at Evere. They took off between 20.30 and 21.00 with F/Ls Adams and Lucas the senior pilots on duty, both assigned to Frankfurt with F/O N Williams and P/Os Harkness, Hogg and Larney. F/L Adams was greeted by an intense searchlight and flak response as he ran in, and opted to bomb the alternative target, the Chemische Fabrik Griesheim-Elektron, a subsidiary of the infamous I G Farben company, situated to the south of the city. Four bursts were observed, but the crew was too busy taking evasive action to assess the outcome. P/O Harkness was another to select this as an alternative target and released his bombs from 12,000 feet, observing greenish flashes but no fires. The remaining four crews attacked the primary target without observing any detail because of the intensity of the defences. Meanwhile, over the Ruhr, P/O Curtis was thwarted by the ten-tenths low cloud and returned his bombs to store. Another freshman, P/O Douglas Veale Gilmour RAF, who had previously operated as second pilot in F/O W Williams' crew, experienced similar difficulties and bombed the airfield at Arnhem from 6,000 feet as a last-resort, before strafing the buildings from 2,000 feet. P/O Best found the general target area but not a precise aiming point, and attacked five flak positions between Duisburg and Essen instead. P/O Peel did not locate Evere aerodrome but found a recipient for his bombs at Flushing aerodrome on the island of Walcheren.

The above-mentioned I G Farben company, literally translated as I G Dyestuffs, or to give it its full name, Interessengemeinschaft (Common Interest Group) Farbenindustrie A G, would become infamous for its widespread use of slave labour at all of its sites, and even built production sites close to concentration camps. Among its founder members were Hoechst, Bayer, Agfa and BASF (Badische Anilin und Soda Fabrik), the last-mentioned the one which led the development and production of its chemical products. It was another subsidiary of the group that produced the Zyklon B gas employed in the extermination of Jewish people during the Holocaust.

The busy month continued for the Kiwis with four more targets on the night of the 29/30th. Five crews were briefed for the Kohleöl-Anlage oil plant at Bottrop in the Ruhr, three for a fuel dump at St-Nazaire, located, it is believed on the aerodrome, two for the aerodrome at Evere and one for the marshalling yards at Soest. They took off between 20.30 and 21.00 with S/L Breckon the senior pilot on duty and bound for Soest, while the Bottrop element consisted of P/Os Best, Curtis, Gilmour, Hogg and Larney, and for a change, they encountered reasonable weather conditions outbound. However, cloud obscured the target area, and P/Os Larney and Gilmour were unable to identify the oil plant, the former attacking Wesel aerodrome and the latter dropping his bombs on a marshalling yard or railway junction to the west. P/Os Best and Hogg carried out their attacks without observing any results, while P/O Curtis spent fifty-five minutes waiting for the cloud to clear, and then dropped a stick of bombs, which started five or six large fires that were seen to be still burning as he withdrew westwards. F/Ls Adams and Lucas and F/O N Williams, meanwhile, were enjoying clear skies over St-Nazaire and no opposition, which enabled them to select their method of attack at two aiming points. F/L Adams conducted a shallow dive from east to west to release his bombs in a stick from 8,000 feet. F/L Lucas carried out a high-level first pass, dropping three 250 pounders onto the western extremity of the eastern aiming point, before diving from 8,500 down to 4,000 feet to deliver the rest onto the southern edge. F/O Williams arrived at the target at 00.35, and also made two runs, delivering bombs from 8,000 and then 4,000 feet, observing bursts but no results. S/L Breckon saw five bursts across the marshalling yards at Soest, and the incendiaries started fires that resulted in explosions and bright flashes. Freshman, P/O Charles Aylmer Pownall, RAF/RNZAF, was on his way home by this time, having attacked the aerodrome at Evere from north-west to south-east at 23.00. The other freshman that night, P/O Duncan Harold McArthur RAF (previously P/O Freeman's second pilot) had found Evere covered by ten-tenths cloud between 1,500 and 4,000 feet, and ultimately came upon Waalhaven aerodrome at Rotterdam by following a river and finding hangar lights on. He dropped his bombs and observed bursts but could not assess the outcome.

The squadron had been assigned to twenty targets during the month and dispatched ninety-seven sorties for the loss of a single Wellington and the death of S/L Collett.

September 1940

While the Battle of Britain was reaching a crescendo overhead and invasion fever gripped the nation, the overriding priority for the Command in September would be the destruction of the invasion craft assembling in ports along the occupied coast. 75(NZ) Squadron was in action immediately at the start of the new month, briefing eleven crews on the 1st for operations against the Misburg oil refinery near Hannover, a Junkers aircraft factory at Mockau near Leipzig, a power station/fuel store at Kassel, the marshalling yards at Soest on the northern rim of the Ruhr and Soesterberg aerodrome in Holland. S/L Breckon was to be the senior pilot on duty, and he was assigned to Mockau with P/O Curtis, while F/L Lucas and P/Os McArthur and Pownall went to Soest, and P/Os Gilmour, Hogg and Peel to Misburg. This left P/Os Best and Harkness to attack the Kassel target and the freshman crew of P/O Frank Henderson Denton RAF to attend to Soesterberg aerodrome. Denton, a Kiwi, had already flown twenty-one operations as second pilot with John Adams, and would go on to fly many more with the squadron.

They departed Feltwell between 20.20 and 21.00 and headed into cloudy skies, which began to clear a little as they flew eastwards across enemy territory. S/L Breckon was over southern Holland when an engine began to falter, and he took the opportunity to drop a stick of three bombs on Eindhoven aerodrome from 12,000 feet at 22.46, observing large explosions. P/O Peel failed to find the target at Misburg and brought his bombs back, passing over an airfield, which he took to be Feltwell. It was, in fact, East Wretham, a satellite of Honington, which gave him permission to land, something which in the hazy conditions and in an unfamiliar circuit, was easier said than done. He aborted the first attempt to land, and with dwindling fuel reserves, went round again. This time he lost sight of the flare-path as he turned in and was suddenly confronted by a line of trees, which he clipped, sending R3159 AA-K crashing into a field short of the runway, where it caught fire. The crew managed to scramble clear with only minor injuries, before the bomb load went up and totally destroyed the Wellington.

P/O Denton, meanwhile, could not locate Soesterberg, despite descending to 500 feet in a vain attempt to break cloud, and he, too, brought his bombs home. P/O Gilmour located the Misburg refinery at 23.40 and bombed it five minutes later without observing any results in the poor visibility and a similar account was offered by P/O Hogg on his return. F/L Lucas made a straight-and-level run at 11,000 feet and witnessed three terrific explosions resulting from the impact of his 250 pounders and incendiaries. P/Os McArthur and Pownall also carried out attacks at this target, but cloud prevented an observation of results. P/Os Best and Harkness failed to find their target at Kassel and returned their bombs to store. P/O Curtis brought back a much more encouraging report of his attack on the aircraft factory at Mockau, which he located after dropping a flare to illuminate the ground. He carried out a bombing run on a south-westerly heading at 11,000 feet, setting off a line of seven or eight fires, which were still burning as he turned away.

On the 3rd of September, S/L Cyrus Kay and F/O Neville Williams received their DFCs from the King at Buckingham Palace. F/O Neville Williams (later F/L and MiD) was born at Frankton Junction, New Zealand and educated at the New Plymouth Boys' High School. He learned to fly at the Western Federated Flying Club and was granted a short service commission with the RAF in 1937. Sadly, he would be lost on the night of 10/11th May 1941, aged twenty-six, together with his navigator, F/O Donald Mackay, DFM, RAF, who had followed him to 7 Squadron, the unit reformed in August 1940 to introduce the new Short Stirling to operational service.

The Command had not yet abandoned its quest to burn down Germany's forests, and the start of September brought further attempts to set fire to the Black Forest in the south-west, the Thuringian Forest south of Gotha in east-central Germany and the Forét de Neuhof south of Strasbourg. 75(NZ) Squadron was invited to contribute eight crews to the cause on the night of the 4/5th, and they took off between 20.15 and 20.40 with F/L Lucas the senior pilot on duty. He was bound for Thuringia with P/Os Curtis and Gilmour, while P/Os Best, Larney, McArthur and Pownall headed for the Black Forest and F/O Freeman for Strasbourg. This left P/O Denton to try his luck at Chartres aerodrome in northern France, which he found and bombed, observing two bursts among the hangars and six on the landing ground. F/L Lucas made a level attack from 11,500 feet, dropping an incendiary bomb every twelve seconds, until a line of fire eight miles long was visible and remained so for twenty minutes into the return journey. P/O Curtis ran across the target from north-west to south-east, creating over a hundred fires in a six-mile area, the glow from which could be seen for twenty miles. P/O Gilmour released his bombs in groups of four at eleven second intervals running from the Swiss border northwards and observed them burning under the trees as he turned away. It was a similar story for the three crews at the Black Forest, where P/O McArthur delivered most of his incendiaries in a stick across the northern corner, before dropping half a container onto the aerodrome at Luneville from 6,000 feet on his way home across France, setting off fires that could be seen for forty miles. At Strasbourg, P/O Freeman dropped his incendiaries into a circular area with a radius of about three miles, but a photograph taken after twenty minutes showed that the fires were failing to catch and lasted only for ten or fifteen minutes.

Six of the squadron's crews were briefed on the 7th for a return to the Black Forest, while P/O Larney was assigned to the Hydrierwerke-Scholven oil plant at Gelsenkirchen, P/O Hogg to the Krupp complex at Essen and P/O Pownall to the marshalling yards at Krefeld. They took off between 20.15 and 21.40 and headed for their respective targets in cloudy skies, which would hamper any attempts to make accurate observations. P/O Larney saw his bombs burst short of the target, and P/O Hogg observed a row of five fires following the release of his 250 pounders in a stick. P/O Pownall failed to locate the marshalling yards and dropped his bombs onto a nearby aerodrome as a last-resort target, observing them to burst four hundred yards short of the flare-path. All but one of the remaining participants in the night's activities were bound for south-western Germany, and on arrival, P/O McArthur dropped five cans of incendiaries, which started fires. One can failed to release, and this was dropped onto Colmar aerodrome across the frontier in France, setting on fire a wooden hangar, two enemy aircraft inside it and two others on the tarmac. P/O Denton could not locate the target and brought his bombs home. P/O Best delivered his bombs at twelve-second intervals from 10,000 feet, setting off moderately large fires, and although P/O Gilmour saw his incendiaries also burning among the trees, he believed that the flames did not spread. P/O Harkness came down to 2,000 feet and watched the incendiaries from the first container straddle a railway line north of Mulhouse on the French side of the frontier and start a fire in a large building. The remainder of his bomb load was dropped into the forest area but failed to cause fires to develop. Sgt Robert Frederick Noden RAF was operating as crew captain for the first time, and although the ORB is unclear on the matter, the likelihood is that he was assigned to the freshman targets of enemy aerodromes. He attacked Gilze-Rijen first with three bombs and then Oostvoorne, west of Rotterdam with two, which exploded on the flare-path.

As the Battle of Britain reached its zenith, the Germans continued to amass barges in the Channel ports in preparation for the intended invasion, and these had been a focus of attention for Bomber Command, more or less, since the fall of France. Before 75(NZ) Squadron entered this campaign, F/L Boffee was posted in from 214 Squadron and would be promoted to acting squadron leader rank to succeed S/L Breckon as B Flight commander on the 9th. F/L Norman Maxwell "Max" Boffee RAF had served with the original 75 Squadron before the war. Seven crews were called to briefing on the 10th, when P/Os Curtis, Gilmore, Harkness, McArthur and Pownall learned that they were to attack the harbour at Ostend, while P/Os Hogg and Larney attended to the docks at Flushing on the island of Walcheren in the Scheldt estuary. They departed Feltwell between 22.15 and 01.40 and arrived in their respective target areas to encounter ten-tenths cloud and thick haze covering the coastal region. P/Os Gilmour, McArthur and Pownall failed to locate the target under cloud that extended from 12,000 down to 700 feet and brought their bombs home. P/Os Curtis and Harkness took off three hours after the others and found Ostend by descending to 4,000 feet and dropping flares to illuminate the ground. P/O Curtis delivered his bombs from 3,500 feet and was too busy taking violent evasive action to notice their fall. P/O Harkness dived from 4,000 to 1,000 feet, and his attention was also firmly focused on escaping the searchlights and flak. P/O Hogg observed his bombs to burst across the docks at Flushing, and although P/O Larney also carried out an attack, he saw nothing of the results.

Nine of the squadron's crews assembled in the briefing room on the 12th to be told that P/Os Best, Curtis, Harkness, Hogg and Larney were to attack the docks at Emden, while P/Os McArthur and Gilmour attended to the marshalling yards at Schwerte on the south-eastern fringe of the Ruhr, and P/Os Pownall and Denton those at Soest. They took off between 19.30 and 20.15 to head into challenging weather conditions of ten-tenths ice-bearing cloud and thunderstorms, which prevented P/Os Best and Harkness from locating Emden. They returned their bombs to store, while P/O Larney dropped his, but had no clue where they fell and the same story was told by P/O Hogg and crew on their return, after they delivered the contents of their bomb bay from 6,000 feet. P/O Curtis found the general target area but had no chance of being more precise and aimed his bombs at the flashes from flak batteries.

Conditions were no better over the Ruhr and P/O Gilmour unloaded the contents of his bomb bay at 1,000 feet over De Kooy aerodrome after failing to locate Soest. P/O McArthur carried out an attack at Schwerte but had nothing to report at debriefing. P/O Pownall dropped his 250 pounders on flak concentrations along the twenty-five-mile corridor between Soest and Dortmund, while P/O Denton failed to locate Soest and made his way back towards the Scheldt, where he came upon the port of Flushing. He descended to 150 feet, from where he could pick out the docks and wharves, and in the face of withering flak and machine-gun fire, scored direct hits on a building, which happened to be an ammunition store. Heavy explosions lifted the Wellington 600 feet, from where a large fire could be seen, but because of the poor visibility, no details could be ascertained. Flak shells punched a three-foot diameter hole in each wing and damaged the tailplane and rudder, and the unoccupied front turret was riddled with machine-gun bullets. The return journey in the veteran Mk 1A P9212 AA-C was conducted in an unstable aircraft, which, according to an SOS message, was expected to go down over the sea but managed to make it home, where P/O Denton was awarded an immediate DFC. Frank Henderson Denton was born in Greymouth, New Zealand and educated at Greymouth Technical High School. He learned to fly with the Greymouth Aero Club, later joining the Civil Reserve of Pilots. He was selected for a short service commission in 1939 and received preliminary training at RNZAF Wigram before leaving for England to join the RAF at the end of 1939. Denton would return to Feltwell in 1942 for a second tour, this time as a flight commander.

The target for eight 75(NZ) Squadron crews on the night of the 14/15th was the docks at Antwerp, while P/Os Curtis and Larney were briefed for the marshalling yards at Soest. The main element was to be divided into two sections, the first consisting of S/L Boffee, P/Os Denton, McArthur and Pownall and Sgt Noden, who took off at 19.45. P/O Curtis followed them away at 19.55 bound for Soest and P/O Larney departed for the same destination two hours later. Finally, P/Os Best, Harkness and Gilmour set off on their journey to Belgium in a five-minute slot from 23.15. The weather over Belgium in the early stages at least was favourable, but those heading into Germany were greeted by ice-bearing cloud, which forced P/O Curtis to turn back and drop his bombs from 7,000 feet onto hangars on De Kooy aerodrome. Numerous fires sprang up, accompanied by major and minor explosions, which suggested an ammunition dump had been hit. P/O Larney was also defeated by ten-tenths cloud and delivered his bomb load onto a railway junction at Aarhus (believed to be Utrecht). At Antwerp, S/L Boffee dropped a stick of eight 250 pounders on the east docks, causing three explosions and followed it up with a stick of seven and an SBC of incendiaries on the new docks. P/O Gilmour carried out an attack but could not assess the outcome because of ground haze. Sgt Noden reported that he had started two fires in the dock basin, which gave rise to yellow explosions at irregular intervals. P/O Best watched all of his bombs find the mark but could not claim any fires as a result. P/O Harkness found himself over Bergen-op-Zoom in south-western Holland following a navigational error and dropped some of his bombs on the nearby coast, before heading south and locating the primary target on which to deposit the remainder. P/O McArthur claimed direct hits on docks and barges in a basin to the north of the town, and P/O Pownall hit the main dock area, leaving a burgeoning fire with orange-coloured flames in his wake. P/O Denton delivered a stick of nine 250 pounders onto the north-western docks and a second stick on the south docks nearer the town, but was too busy with evasive action to observe the result.

The Battle of Britain reached its climax on the 15th, and although skirmishes would continue into October, the decision had already been taken by Hitler to abandon Einsatz Seelöwe, Operation Sealion, and prepare instead for an assault on Russia in the coming summer. This was, of course, not appreciated by the British authorities and the campaign against invasion craft continued. The 17th brought Bomber Command's greatest commitment of aircraft to date in a single night of 197, approximately two-thirds of them assigned to invasion craft in the occupied ports. Le Havre was the destination for seven Kiwi crews on the night of the 18/19th, while P/O Curtis and P/O Best were briefed to attack railway yards at Ehrang and Brussels respectively. Typically for the period, the attacks were spread out over many hours and the first departures from Feltwell were those of two RAF freshmen, P/O Michael Ryves Braun at 18.40 and Sgt Richard Noel Stubbs ten minutes later. P/Os Curtis and Best took off an hour after that, to be followed at 20.05 by P/Os McArthur and John Edward Stewart Morton RAF (another freshman) and at 22.00 by P/O Gilmour and Sgt Noden, with P/O Harkness last away at 22.30. They flew out in cloud ranging from three to ten-tenths and although the conditions in the target areas were generally good, cloud did present an impediment to accurate bombing. P/O Braun reported a fire resulting from his bombs, but could not be specific, while Sgt Stubbs and P/O McArthur saw nothing of their efforts. P/O Morton claimed to have extinguished three searchlights with a 500 pounder but was unable to comment on the effects of his 250 pounders. The crews arriving later found better visibility and P/Os Gilmour and Harkness each delivered their loads in a single stick, the former from just under 7,000 feet, and both observed them to burst diagonally across the outer docks. P/O Harkness observed a fire on the quayside with two red glows, but P/O Gilmour was too busy with evasive action to make any assessment. Sgt Noden dropped one stick from east to west and observed bursts on the central jetty, which developed into two fires, one of which produced around eight intermittent yellow explosions. At Ehrang, P/O Curtis delivered his load from 9,000 feet, upon which fires erupted and a number of explosions followed, one of them of particular brilliance throwing lighted debris into the air. P/O Best reported that all of his bombs found the mark at the Brussels yards, and that fires were still burning forty-five minutes later.

The ports at Calais, Flushing and Ostend were the targets for 3 Group aircraft on the night of the 20/21st, and it was for the last-mentioned that nine 75(NZ) Squadron Wellingtons were made ready, including one for the freshman crew of P/O Maurice Henry Hankins RAF. They took off between 20.58 and 22.10 with no senior pilots on duty and arrived in the target area to find patchy cloud but generally good conditions. All but one returned safely to report accurate bombing of the docks area in the face of a spirited flak defence and fires visible for some distance into the return journey. P/O Denton observed a barge concentration in the Ostend-Bruges Canal and a U or E-Boot signalling in Morse code off the Belgian coast. P/O McArthur reported seeing an aircraft shot down from 3,000 feet north of the docks at 22.35, and T2463 AA-E subsequently failed to return to Feltwell. It was established later that there had been no survivors from the crew of P/O Braun RAF, who were operating with the squadron for just the second time. Braun was only nineteen and included in his crew was F/O Neville Williams' wireless operator/gunner, Sgt Lewis Adam White, DFM RAF, who was himself only twenty. S/L Kay was posted to Honington on the 23rd and F/L Francis George Levett Bain RAF arrived from 99 Squadron at Newmarket at the same time to succeed him on promotion as A Flight commander. Bain was already a veteran, having gained his commission as a pilot officer in 1930.

At this stage of the war there was no set number of operations before a crew could be declared tour-expired, and it was left to higher authority to decide when a crew or individuals had done enough. By now, most of "the old gang" had left the squadron for a "rest" period as instructors, but "Popeye" Lucas had heard that a big attack on Berlin was coming up. He was determined to go to the "Big City" and had asked to stay on. Finally, on the 23rd, the big night arrived and in a departure from normal practice, 129 aircraft took off for just the one destination, where, somewhat optimistically, eighteen separate aiming points were to be attacked, seven railway yards, six electrical power stations, three gasworks and two aero-engine and aircraft component factories. The 3 Group element of forty-five Wellingtons was assigned to gas works and power stations, and it was for the latter that eight of ten 75(NZ) Squadron crews were briefed, while P/O Gow and P/O Morton were handed the freshman target of Le Havre. F/L "Popeye" Lucas was the senior pilot on duty, and this would prove to be the thirty-seventh and final operation of his first tour. P/O Gow departed first, at 19.10, followed at 19.25 by P/O Morton, and they would return five hours later to report bomb bursts across the wharves and basins and four fires in the docks area accompanied by minor explosions. The others departed Feltwell between 21.30 and 22.05 and all proceeded according to plan until the hydraulics system failed in L7848 AA-C "Cuthbert" two hours into the outward flight and the undercarriage flopped down. This reduced the airspeed to around ninety mph, a situation made worse by icing conditions in cloud. P/O Curtis had no option other than to jettison the bomb load somewhere near Osnabrück and turn back. There is some confusion over P/O Denton's sortie, the squadron ORB reporting that he penetrated the defence zone first at Hannover and then at Bremen, some seventy miles to the north-west, before dive-bombing the marshalling yards in the centre of Hamburg, scoring direct hits on track and buildings and leaving one large building gutted by fire. The likely sequence of events is that he was driven off course by the Hannover defences, turned back, only to stumble into those at Bremen and found himself near Hamburg with an opportunity too good to turn down.

At Berlin, pinpointing was made easier for those crews identifying lakes to the west of the city, but all had to be aware of barrage balloons tethered at between 9,000 and 14,000 feet. P/O Harkness failed to locate his briefed aiming point because of cloud, ground haze and searchlights and selected an alternative target within the city, probably a power station under attack by other elements. P/O Larney experienced similar difficulties and dropped his bombs on Neuruppin aerodrome some thirty miles north-west of the capital. F/L Lucas made two runs at 12,000 feet, dropping a stick on each, while P/O Best let his load go in a single stick from the same level. All returned safely to report difficulty in assessing the results of their efforts, but Sgt Noden claimed a large fire, which was still visible for twenty minutes into the return journey. Looking at the bigger picture, however, a few fires aside, attacks on precision targets at this stage of the war were beyond the means of crews with the available bombing and navigation aids at their disposal. "Popeye" finished his last big trip rather ignominiously with a diversion to Marham because of unexploded bombs on the Feltwell airfield and a near ground loop due to a chunk of the port tyre having been sliced off by a piece of flak. This night did bring a record number of sorties, amounting to 209, the first time that the figure of two hundred had been exceeded, and only three aircraft failed to return.

Feltwell was the only 3 Group station to operate on the night of the 26/27th, when dispatching eight Wellingtons from each squadron to Le Havre. The Kiwis took off between 19.00 and

20.20 with S/L Boffee the senior pilot on duty and flew out in seven to ten-tenths cloud, which would persist throughout the operation. F/O Peter James Robert Kitchin RAF, who was operating with the squadron for the first time since his arrival from 15 O.T.U at Harwell on the 22nd, failed to locate the primary target and bombed Lisieux aerodrome a few miles to the south as a last-resort target. The others all released their 500 and 250 pounders in the general target area, some observing bursts, while others were unable to report anything of significance in the way of an assessment.

Eighty-eight crews were briefed for numerous targets on the night of the 29/30th, 3 Group focussing its attention on aluminium works and marshalling yards. 75(NZ) Squadron made ready ten Wellingtons and briefed eight crews for the distant Bitterfeld aluminium works north of Leipzig, while P/O Morton learned that he was to attack the Ehrang marshalling yards and Sgt Stubbs those at Osnabrück. They took off between 19.30 and 20.05 and flew out in generally cloudy conditions, which would cause difficulties for those penetrating deep into eastern Germany. P/O Morton failed to locate the Ehrang yards situated close to the Luxembourg frontier and dropped his bombs onto a similar target at Koblenz, some seventy miles to the north-east. Sgt Stubbs enjoyed better luck at Osnabrück, where he dropped his bombs in a single stick onto the tracks and started a large fire visible for thirty miles into the return journey. P/O Harkness was thwarted by ten-tenths cloud and looked for an alternative target on the way home. He found what he was looking for in Delmenhorst aerodrome near Bremen, upon which he delivered his 500 and 250 pounders, before dumping his incendiaries on De Kooy aerodrome on the Dutch coast at Den Helder. P/O Larney experienced similar difficulties in identifying the target and dropped his load onto an aerodrome at Nordhorn, on Germany's border with Holland. P/O Gilmour found an alternative target at Magdeburg, while F/L Colin Leslie Gilbert RAF, operating with the squadron for the first time, somehow found himself over Mannheim in southern Germany, presumably through taking a route home across France and Belgium and dropped a stick of eight 250 pounders on the marshalling yards there. The others bombed the primary target through cloud, and all made it back safely to home airspace. P/O Denton and crew arrived at the Devon coast short of fuel and prevented by fog from seeing the ground. The only sensible option was to abandon R3168 (probably AA-O), which they did safely, leaving the Wellington to crash on Exmoor at 05.00. Sadly, the rear gunner, F/O Edward Arthur Jelley RAF, struck a house as he came down and was killed, while some of the others sustained slight injuries and suffered shock.

The squadron was assigned to thirty separate targets during the month, dispatching a hundred sorties for the loss of three Wellingtons and one crew.

October 1940

The month of October was significant as the one that saw the first arrivals of New Zealand-trained pilots. Until now, their needs had been met from the ranks of the RAF, even though several of these had been New Zealanders. At the outbreak of war, pilot training had been a priority for the RNZAF, but as predicted at the time, this would not happen quickly enough to ensure that 75(NZ) Squadron maintained an all-Kiwi compliment. Now that they had started to arrive, however, they would have to serve their apprenticeships and gain operational experience as second pilots and it would be another three months before the first of the new RNZAF pilots would captain their own crews. Happily, the 3 Group ORB relinquished the use of target codes towards the end of September and began to refer to targets exclusively by name. Sadly, the squadron ORB persisted with codes, now with no means to identify them through cross-reference with the group record.

October's operations from Feltwell began on the night of the 2/3rd, when it was the only 3 Group station in action. Ten 75(NZ) Squadron Wellingtons were made ready, along with a dozen from 149 Squadron, to attack the Bottrop-Welheim oil plant and the marshalling yards at Hamm and Soest. P/Os Gow and Morton were briefed for the yards at Soest, and took off first at 19.20, closely followed by the crews of F/O Kitchin, P/Os Curtis and Gilmour and Sgt Noden as the first of two elements bound for Bottrop. S/L Bain, who was the senior pilot on duty for the first time since his posting, led the second element of F/L Gilbert and P/Os Best and McArthur, who departed at 21.30 on what was to be a night of wasted effort. They headed into adverse weather conditions of ten-tenths low cloud with sleet and snowstorms, which would prevent them from delivering accurate attacks. P/O Gow brought his bombs home after failing to locate his primary target or a suitable SEMO (self-evident military objective) alternative, and P/O Morton found an aerodrome (name misspelled and untraceable) for a stick of his bombs. Not one of the earlier Bottrop element managed to locate their target and each found an alternative, the aerodromes at Texel, De Kooy and Wesel and an unidentified objective in Essen. Those following on two hours later were able to carry out an attack, but none observed the outcome and the reflection of fire in the clouds was the only assessment possible.

Sir Charles Portal was promoted to become Chief of the Air Staff on the 5th, and he was replaced as C-in-C Bomber Command by Sir Richard Peirse, whose tenure would be dogged by poor performances and comparatively heavy losses, partly as a result of the unrealistic expectations of his superiors. A forecast of adverse weather on the 5th led to a scaling-down of 3 Group's planned operations for that night and ultimately only S/L Bain and P/O Gow represented the group, setting off at 18.30 to attack the docks at Flushing and Rotterdam respectively. S/L Bain watched his bombs fall about two hundred feet from the basin he had aimed for, but a succession of explosions over the ensuing fifteen minutes suggested that a bomb dump had been hit. P/O Gow observed his bombs to burst on the dockside to the south-west of the town and start a fire among buildings.

The main target for the squadron on the night of the 8/9th was an oil refinery in Hamburg, for which eight crews were briefed, while S/L Bain was assigned to the extensive Kalk marshalling yards on the eastern bank of the Rhine in the centre of Cologne and P/O Gow to those two miles to the south in the Gremberg district. The eight crews briefed for Hamburg took off in two sections of four, the first at 18.45 led by F/L Gilbert and the second thirty minutes later led by S/L Boffee. They found favourable conditions for the outward flight and over the targets, where the skies were relatively free of cloud and attacks were carried out from 10,000 to 11,500 feet. Explosions and fires were observed and there were claims of near misses, but searchlight and flak activity made it difficult to assess the raid. P/O Best dropped two bombs on the aerodrome at Oldenburg on the way home. At Cologne, P/O Gow reported three explosions in the centre of the incendiaries falling into the railway yards and S/L Bain claimed extensive and brilliant red fires visible for up to seventy miles, although the ORB records that he attacked an aerodrome rather than the primary target, which the 3 Group ORB identified as Ostheim, located just to the east of the Kalk yards. P/Os Curtis and Gilmour were posted to 20 O.T.U during the week, presumably having been declared tour-expired.

A heavy night of activity on the 10/11th saw 157 sorties launched to thirteen targets in Germany and the occupied countries. Ten 75(NZ) Squadron Wellingtons were made ready, five to be sent against the oil refinery at Reisholz and four the Nordstern plant at Gelsenkirchen, while P/O Rex Martyn Sanderson RAF was handed the freshman target of Eindhoven aerodrome for his maiden sortie with the squadron as skipper of his own crew, having flown two operations as second pilot with P/O Eric Best and ten with P/O Dick Curtis. He took off first, at 22.45, and for whatever reason, despite fine weather conditions, failed to locate the primary target and attacked the docks at Antwerp instead. His bombs were seen to fall short and start fires, which soon burned out. The Gelsenkirchen-bound quartet departed Feltwell shortly before 23.00 and all reached the target to carry out their attacks. P/O McArthur in T2736 AA-A reported his first two bombs causing large orange flashes and the next four vivid blue flashes, suggesting he had hit an electrical power station. On the way home he engaged an enemy aircraft, a Heinkel He111, which was seen to crash and burn three miles north-west of Steenbergen in south-western Holland. From this action, twenty-year-old P/O Duncan McArthur was awarded an immediate DFC, and his front gunner, nineteen-year-old Sgt John "Jack" Mylod, RAF, an immediate DFM. F/L Gilbert landed his bombs at the northern end of the works causing four fires, which joined up into a single large conflagration. P/O Best's bombs set off vivid green explosions, but his incendiaries hung up and these were released over railway sidings at Rheinberg. He reported a dozen fires visible from fifty miles into the return journey. P/O Morton released his entire bomb load in a single stick from 12,000 feet onto the alternative target of Wesel marshalling yards but failed to observe any results. The Reisholz quintet was the last to take to the air at 23.30, with S/Ls Bain and Boffee the senior pilots on duty. Thick ground haze and searchlight glare provided difficult conditions in which to identify the target, but all five crews claimed to have bombed in the target area, setting off explosions and large fires. They all returned safely but were unable to provide a detailed assessment of their efforts at debriefing.

The squadron briefed eight crews on the 14th, five to attack the oil refinery at Böhlen, south of Leipzig, while three freshman crews were to be blooded at Le Havre. With a long round-trip ahead of them, the Böhlen section took off first at 19.00 led by S/L Boffee, while P/Os James Fleming, Maurice Hankins and Geoffrey Wright departed an hour later for the shorter hop across the Channel. They encountered heavy cloud as far as the south coast, at which point the skies cleared to leave good visibility. P/O Fleming dropped his bombs in a single stick across the north side of N°1 basin and started a large fire, while P/Os Hankins and Wright landed theirs between N°s 2 and 3 basins and confirmed the fire. Meanwhile, in eastern Germany, F/L Gilbert saw his bombs burst along the length of the oil refinery from south to north and set off three fires that burned with an orange-red flame. The fires spread suddenly and rapidly, and an enormous explosion followed, which sent showers of sparks high into the air. Sgt Stubbs did not attack the primary target but dropped his bombs in a stick across a railway line at Hannover, leaving large white explosions in his wake. S/L Boffee reached the target area but was unable to locate either the primary or secondary objective and bombed the railway station at Lingen from 14,000 feet on the way home. F/O Kitchin observed all his bombs to burst on the target, setting off two explosions after thirty seconds and an enormous one ninety seconds later still. Two large fires sent columns of white smoke up to 6,000 feet as he turned away, dispensing fire-raising bomblets over the Ruhr on his way home. Sgt Noden delivered his load in a single stick and reported a heavy cloud of smoke hanging over the target.

An attempt to catch important elements of the Kriegsmarine at berth in Kiel and Bremen was launched on the night of the 16/17th. Gneisenau was believed to be at Kiel and Scharnhorst and Bismarck at Bremen, and it was to the former that Feltwell dispatched nine Wellingtons from each squadron, with S/Ls Bain and Boffee the senior Kiwi pilots on duty. They were airborne between 18.20 and 18.52, each carrying a load of 500lb semi-armour-piercing (SAP) bombs. It was a night of adverse weather conditions, particularly over England, but all arrived in the target area to encounter low cloud and carried out their attacks. S/L Boffee reported observing Gneisenau moored to the floating dock and F/O Kitchin managed to straddle it with a stick of two bombs on his first run and scored a near miss with a salvo of two bombs on his second. The others dropped their bombs and observed bursts, but could not pinpoint their location and headed home more in hope of success rather than expectation. Low cloud and rain had swept across the whole of England from the south coast to Yorkshire and provided treacherous conditions for returning crews to negotiate. Not all would make it, and among the casualties was the squadron's L7857 AA-C "Dopey", which was successfully abandoned by P/O Morton and crew as the last reserves of fuel dwindled away and crashed at 03.30 just north of Penrith on the edge of the Lake District.

During the course of the week, P/O Duncan McArthur was posted to 20 O.T.U. and P/O Eric Best to Leeming, where 7 Squadron was being reformed to introduce the first of the new generation of bombers, the Short Stirling, to operational service, although it would be the coming February before it first went to war. North-western Germany featured again on the night of the 21/22nd, when the shipyards at Hamburg became the main focus for the Feltwell effort. 75(NZ) Squadron briefed seven crews for this and another, freshman F/O Roy Pryce Elliot, for the Reisholz oil plant. They took off between 17.30 and 18.10, with S/L Boffee the senior pilot on duty and once more ran into challenging weather conditions on the route out and over the target. Some crews caught a glimpse of the ground through the cloud and haze, and all dropped their bombs in the general target area, but none was able to positively identify where the bomb bursts occurred. S/L Boffee and F/L Gilbert reported bombing the docks rather than the shipyards and the others described explosions and fires visible for some time, but no accurate assessment was forthcoming. Hit by flak, F/L Colin Gilbert's aircraft suffered an engine fire and lost a propeller on the way home, before crashing at 23.20 near Methwold after hitting trees while searching in the fog for somewhere to land. T2820 AA-B was wrecked, but the crew clambered out with an assortment of minor injuries and were taken off operations for a month to recuperate. Seventy minutes later, R3158 AA-J crash-landed in flames at Manston on return from Reisholz, after surviving a collision with a balloon cable at the coast. F/O Roy Elliott and crew emerged unscathed before attending debriefing to report their failure to locate the primary target and bombing Eindhoven aerodrome as a last resort target.

P/O Gordie Larney was posted to 7 Squadron on the 23rd, and that night just five of the squadron's crews were involved in operations to Berlin and Emden. Four were briefed to attack individual objectives in Berlin, S/L Boffee the Chancellory, P/O Gow Potsdam railway station, Sgt Noden area "T" and P/O Sanderson an undisclosed objective selected from the Charlottenburg and Klingenberg power stations or the Potlitzstrasse and Lehrte marshalling yards. The last mentioned was not in Berlin but is a town to the east of Hannover and 145 miles from Berlin, albeit on a direct route to the capital. F/O Kitchin was the odd man out, having been assigned to bomb the docks at Emden. They took off in a thirty-minute slot from 22.30 and flew into cloud, which would persist over enemy territory throughout the operations. S/L Boffee was separated from his aiming point by two layers of ten-tenths cloud and had no clue as to the fall of his bombs. Sgt Noden flew past the capital city and attacked a flarepath believed to be to the east, where his incendiaries were observed to fall three hundred yards short. P/O Gow bombed an aerodrome north-west of Berlin in the vicinity of Neuruppin and F/O Kitchen saw no results at Emden because of the intensity of the searchlights. P9292 AA-C is believed to have crashed into the sea off the Danish coast, taking with it to their deaths the crew of Aucklander P/O Rex Sanderson, which included the second pilot, P/O William John Finlayson RNZAF. Later, on the 24th, four crews were sent out in vain to search the North Sea for the Sanderson crew.

Nine of the squadron's crews were called to briefing on the 25th to learn that five of them, F/Os Elliott and Kitchin, P/O Hankins and Sgts Noden and Stubbs, were to attack an electrical power station in Hamburg, while P/O Wright went for the U-Boot yards at Bremen and P/Os Malcolm Hugh McFarlane and Clive King Saxelby and Sgt A.P. Jones an aerodrome at Evere near Brussels. The last-mentioned trio took off first at 19.00 and headed into poor weather conditions characterized by heavy cloud. P/O Saxelby failed to locate his primary objective and dropped his bombs on Haamstede aerodrome on the island of Schouwen in the Scheldt estuary on the way home. The other two delivered their bombs as briefed, before returning to report bursts and explosions in the general target area without being able to provide an accurate assessment. Four of the Hamburg quintet departed Feltwell between 20.00 and 20.12, but it was not until 23.10 that F/O Elliott got away and even later, 00.22, before P/O Wright took to the air bound for Bremen. The last-mentioned failed to locate his objective and returned his bombs to store, while those arriving early over Hamburg experienced difficulty in pinpointing their whereabouts. One bombed a large fire in the general target area, while the others released their loads based on estimated positions and returned to report bursts and burgeoning fires, which were confirmed by F/O Elliott and the local authorities.

The final operations of the month for 75(NZ) Squadron took place on the night of the 28/29th, when ten Wellingtons were made ready for attacks on Kiel and Wilhelmshaven docks, Wesseling oil refinery and Antwerp-Deurne and Evere aerodromes. P/O Hankins and Sgt Stubbs took off first for Kiel and F/O Elliott followed on an hour later. Cloud over the North Sea and Dutch coast cleared by the time that north-western Germany was reached and P/O Hankins was able to pick out the aiming point. He delivered his bombs in a single stick and observed them to overshoot the docks and fall into the ship-building yards on the south-eastern side of the harbour. Sgt Stubbs dropped a stick from 11,500 feet and watched two bombs and his incendiaries fall into the water, while another bomb hit the floating dock to which Gneisenau was moored. F/O Elliott was unable to observe the fall of his bombs because of searchlight glare and ground haze. P/O Morton took off at 17.35 for Wilhelmshaven and dropped his bombs in one stick, observing three explosions and small fires. He also lobbed a single bomb onto Wilhelmshaven aerodrome, possibly after it had hung up during the original run. P/O Saxelby and Sgt Jones departed for Wesseling at 17.40, but the former ended up bombing Eindhoven aerodrome, where an explosion and fire ensued, while the latter attacked Ostheim aerodrome to the east of Cologne and was prevented from assessing the outcome by cloud and gun flashes. P/Os Arthur George Lee Humphreys RAF/RNZAF and McFarlane were airborne by 18.15 bound for Antwerp-Deurne aerodrome, which the latter failed to locate and dropped his load into the middle of Antwerp docks instead. The former released three 250 pounders on a fire in the vicinity of the target but could provide no further details. Freshman Sgt Wilson and P/O Pownall took off at around the same time and the former reported the final bombs of the stick hitting the aerodrome, while the others started two fires to the south. The latter reported that heavy cloud and haze had obscured the primary target aiming point and he had attacked an alternative, the aerodrome at Ghent, where fires were started on the west side.

During the course of the month the squadron was sent against twenty-six targets and dispatched eighty-one sorties for the loss of four Wellingtons and one crew.

November 1940

By the onset of November, the Battle of Britain had run its course and the fear of invasion had been banished for the time being at least. Industrial Germany would now become the main focus of attention as the winter took hold, with oil related targets at the head of an impressive list drawn up by the Air Ministry in a new directive issued three weeks after the enthronement of C-in-C Sir Richard Peirse. However, this would not alter the pattern of small-scale and minimally effective operations and while November would be a month of reduced activity generally, 75(NZ) Squadron would still average almost one operation every three nights. 37 Squadron, which was still at Feltwell, had been notified of a posting to the Middle East and 75(NZ) Squadron inherited a dozen of its Wellington Mk 1Cs and a Mk 1A on the 6th.

Berlin was one of six German cities to be targeted on the night of 6/7th, when just two of the squadron's crews were involved. F/O Elliott and P/O Pownall took off just after midnight and headed into ten-tenths cloud with severe storms over the North Sea and icing conditions over Germany. Their target is believed to have been the Schlesinger railway station in central Berlin, but neither reached it, P/O Pownall turning back and jettisoning his bombs into the sea and F/O Elliott attacking what he believed to be an aerodrome at an undisclosed location.

Eight crews were called to briefings on the 8th, when five learned that they would be heading for southern Germany to attack the marshalling yards at Munich, while three others were assigned to the Hydrierwerke-Scholven synthetic oil refinery in the Buer district of Gelsenkirchen in the Ruhr. S/Ls Bain and Boffee were the senior pilots on duty as the Munich-bound quintet departed Feltwell between 17.12 and 17.35 and flew out in good weather conditions, which would persist for the long round-trip. Sgts Jones and Wilson took off at the same time for the Ruhr, where the conditions would prove to be less favourable, and they were able only to report fires and explosions in the general target area. P/O MacFarlane took off an hour later than the others and the poor visibility accounts for the bombing of Lastrup aerodrome, some ninety miles north of his intended target, where his bombs and incendiaries caused explosions on the airfield and two medium fires, which burned with red flames. Meanwhile, at Munich, S/L Bain carried out his attack from 3,000 feet, a brave and perhaps foolhardy venture in the face of very intense medium and light flak at one of the most heavily defended cities in Germany. He was rewarded with direct hits on tracks and sheds and was able to report explosions continuing as he left the target and fires visible for thirty minutes. P/O Pownall delivered his load in a single stick from west to east and observed bursts in the eastern side of the town and in the marshalling yards. P/O Morton bombed from 11,000 feet, and watched his incendiaries start fires and set off small explosions. S/L Boffee's attack from east to west resulted in a large row of fires within the yards and sixteen explosions of different colours, the effects from which were visible for sixty miles. P/O Hankins let his load go in a single stick and also observed the ensuing fires to be still burning as he flew away.

Gelsenkirchen was the destination for the squadron on the night of the 10/11th, when, according to the 3 Group ORB, the Hydrierwerke coal liquefaction plant at Scholven-Buer was the target for all twenty-five of its Wellingtons, eight of which represented 75(NZ) Squadron. The squadron ORB, however, specifies also the Gelsenkirchener Bergwerke (Nordstern) refinery at Horst as the assigned target for P/O Wright, leaving seven crews briefed for the former. There were no senior pilots on duty as they took off between 01.15 and 02.00 and headed into conditions of heavy cloud and icing. P/O Humphreys turned back at the Dutch coast with an unserviceable rear turret, leaving the others to press on to the target. P/O Pownall failed to locate the primary, concealed as it was beneath ten-tenths cloud, and made his way back to the area of the Scheldt, where he bombed Flushing aerodrome. P/O Saxelby experienced similar difficulties and dropped his bombs on the aerodrome at Eindhoven, without observing any results. P/O MacFarlane found what he believed to be marshalling yards at Münster, and deposited his load there, starting what he described as a long fire beside another that was already burning. P/O Wright claimed to have seen his bombs explode in the target area, presumably the Nordstern plant, while P/O Morton suffered a hang-up over the Scholven-Buer site and released only a 500 pounder and incendiaries. Even so, the incendiaries set off fifteen explosions over the ensuing twenty minutes as the Wellington retreated north-west towards Wesel, where another 500 pounder was dumped on the aerodrome. Sgt Stubbs was uncertain of his precise location as he carried out his attack from 13,000 feet and observed bomb flashes through the cloud. Sgt Jones reported his bombs detonating and causing a large fire and reported two further explosions as he turned away.

Two nights later, seven of the squadron's Wellingtons were made ready to join others from the group for an operation against the Nordstern refinery. S/L Bain was the senior pilot on duty as they departed Feltwell between 22.00 and 22.30 on another night of adverse weather conditions, which had not been forecast and would render the efforts ineffective. Within twenty miles of crossing the enemy coast, ten-tenths cloud had built up, producing severe icing conditions that would hold firm until the bombers reached the English coast homebound. S/L Bain and P/Os MacFarlane and Saxelby all failed to locate the primary target or suitable alternative and brought their bombs home, while Sgt Wilson dropped his load on an aerodrome at Arnhem. P/O Pownall was in the vicinity of the target but could not identify it and found a nearby railway line and canal as a last-resort recipient for his bombs. Sgt Stubbs turned back and dropped his 500 pounders onto the marshalling yards on the massive docks complex at Duisburg-Ruhrort, and only Sgt Jones reported bombing the refinery. He saw explosions and the glow of fires in the cloud, but no assessment was possible, and no reconnaissance was carried out.

P/O Frank Denton had finished his tour some time earlier and was posted to 15 O.T.U on the 13th, a departure followed on the 16th by that of F/L "Popeye" Lucas to 15 O.T.U at Harwell in Berkshire (now Oxfordshire). Nine crews gathered in the briefing room on the 14th and learned of diverse operations to be carried out over Germany and Holland that night. The main raid was to be against the Schlesinger railway station in Berlin, and the intention had been to target oil refineries also. However, after receiving intelligence that the Luftwaffe was planning to launch a major attack from Schiphol and Soesterberg aerodromes, the aircraft detailed for the oil targets were switched to them. This meant that four crews were briefed for Berlin, while two each were assigned to the aerodromes, and the newly-arrived F/L Garry Carlton Kain RAF/RNZAF was to be sent on a freshman sortie to an undisclosed French port.

The Schiphol duo took off first, P/O Humphreys at 17.20 and freshman P/O Brian Patrick McNamara at 18.00, followed by F/L Kain at 18.05, and they would be back home before another freshman, P/O Edgar Bernard Richard Lockwood RAF, and Sgt Wilson became airborne for Soesterberg either side of 22.30. In between, the departure of the Berlin quartet, consisting of S/L Boffee, P/O Pownall and Sgts Jones and Stubbs, took place during a twenty-five-minute slot from 19.15. Weather conditions over enemy territory were good and all crews arrived at their respective target areas to carry out their attacks. At Schiphol, both crews watched their bombs burst on the airfield setting off fires and explosions, which continued after they turned for home. F/O Humphreys landed first, at 20.20, ninety minutes before P/O McNamara, the former reporting fires visible from forty miles away. At Berlin, all four crews delivered their loads in a single stick from around 12,000 feet on different headings and observed explosions around the station and adjacent marshalling yards. P/O Lockwood attacked Soesterberg from 4,000 feet with 500 pounders and incendiaries and watched them fall among buildings on the south-eastern side of the airfield. As the Wellington retreated westwards, the crew watched two persistent fires burn until they eventually disappeared into the mist. Sgt Wilson and crew returned to report that their bombs had also found the mark and fires were burning as they left the scene. F/L Kain had little to report on his sortie, other than that his bombs had landed in the target area.

It was on this night, that more than five hundred Luftwaffe bombers attacked the industrial city of Coventry over a period of many hours and left the medieval central districts in ruins and unrecognisable and the cathedral gutted. The city, which was the centre of Britain's motor industry and also contained important aircraft, tank and machine tool factories, suffered the destruction of or damage to more than forty-one thousand houses along with seventy-one factories and 568 people lost their lives.

The night of the 15/16th brought a two-wave attack on Hamburg separated by eight hours, during which, a number of aiming points included the power station at Altona on the North Bank of the Elbe to the west of the city centre. Hamburg was also the destination for 130 aircraft on the night of the 16/17th, for which 3 Group detailed twenty-four Wellingtons, six of them belonging to 75(NZ) Squadron. The crews were briefed to attack a goods station and marshalling yards, while three others continued the assault on Schiphol and Soesterberg aerodromes. Those bound for north-western Germany took off between 18.00 and 18.15 on a night of adverse weather conditions, which would prevent more than half of the overall force from reaching Germany's second city. To their credit, all six 75(NZ) Squadron crews arrived in the target area, where they found nine to ten-tenths cloud obscuring the ground. P/O Hankins released his bombs in a single stick on a northerly heading and thought they fell a little to the west of the planned aiming point. Sgt Stubbs could not see his aiming point but carried out a run from the city centre and delivered his load from 13,500 feet, observing the bursts through the cloud. P/O Saxelby reported his load falling on the docks, Sgt Jones believed his exploded in the target area, F/O Elliott had no clue as to where his ended up, and P/O Pownall aimed at the docks through gaps in the cloud. Meanwhile, P/Os Humphreys and Lockwood had taken off for Schiphol at 17.30, but the former failed to locate it and brought his bombs back. The latter carried out his attack while being held in searchlights and delivered the bombs in a single stick but failed to observe the results because a flak shell exploded immediately beneath the aircraft, temporarily blinding the bomb-aimer. P/O Wright delivered his bombs at Soesterberg but was unable to comment on the outcome.

Berlin and Cologne provided the targets for ten of eleven 75(NZ) Squadron Wellingtons on the night of the 23/24th, while a single freshman crew was sent to bomb the docks at Boulogne. The Berlin element of seven took off either side of 17.45, two to attack Potsdam station, two others a power station, another two an unspecified target within the city and one area "T". F/L Kain, who was the senior pilot on duty, departed Feltwell for Cologne shortly after 18.00 accompanied in close order by P/Os Lockwood and Saxelby, all briefed to attack the inland docks. Sgt Drayton RAFVR was the last away at 18.15 on his freshman trip to the French coast, and he was also the first to return, having failed to locate his target beneath cloud and then responding to a recall signal. The skies over Cologne were relatively clear and all three crews reported fires and explosions in the target area on the eastern side of the Rhine. Conditions were equally helpful over Berlin, and Sgt Stubbs took advantage to deliver his load from 13,500 feet and observe them burst among buildings in area "T". P/O Saxelby and Sgt Jones identified Potsdam station and carried out their attacks, but observation of the results was hampered by searchlights and ground mist. P/O Hankins also bombed here after pinpointing on lakes east of Birkenwerder and then the Tiergarten, and his rear gunner watched bombs and incendiaries fall onto the station or adjacent yards. Sgt Wilson found low cloud and ground haze obscuring the results of his attack on the power station but was certain that his bombs had been close. P/O MacFarlane saw all his bombs and incendiaries burst at the same aiming point.

During the course of w.e.f. 24th, W/C Maurice Buckley was posted to the 214 Squadron Reserve Flight at Stradishall to be succeeded as commanding officer by the familiar and newly-promoted W/C Cyril "Cyrus" Kay, who arrived at the same time from Honington. Berlin and Cologne were again in the bomb sights on the night of the 26/27th, when ten crews were briefed at Feltwell. Unfortunately, the squadron ORB is confusing and adopts previously unseen target codes, upon which the 3 Group record sheds little light. What is clear is that weather conditions over Berlin were challenging, while those in the Cologne area were helpful. Take-off was accomplished safely between 17.35 and 19.15 and S/L Boffee, P/Os Hankins, MacFarlane and Saxelby and Sgt Stubbs, all of whom had been assigned to target M501(marshalling yards) in Berlin, arrived in the target area. P/O Saxelby alone claimed to have attacked it, while P/O MacFarlane bombed an alternative objective within the city and observed a reddish glow in the clouds that endured for fifteen minutes. S/L Boffee, P/O Hankins and Sgt Stubbs back-tracked to the Hannover area, where the first-mentioned pair bombed the aerodrome at Ncuruppin, while Sgt Stubbs found a recipient for his bombs within the city itself. Sgt Jones observed his bombs to explode in Berlin, as did F/O Elliott, but cloud prevented an assessment of results. P/O Humphreys was beaten by the conditions and found a flarepath at Stendal, some fifty miles west of Berlin, which he bombed on his way home without observing results. F/L Kain, in the meantime, had located his target, believed to be marshalling yards at Cologne, perhaps Gremberg or Kalk, and scored a near-miss to the east. P/O McNamara watched his bombs fall across the same target and his rear gunner reported three large explosions four minutes after they had turned for home.

All six of the squadron participants in operations on the 29th were briefed for marshalling yards in Cologne, and they took off between 17.50 and 19.00 with no senior pilots on duty. Despite fairly clear skies, it seems that few attacks were focussed on the primary targets and P/O McNamara was unable to release his bombs at all because of a fault in the release mechanism. P/O Wright saw his 500 pounders burst in the target area but was prevented by ground haze from assessing the result, and P/O Humphreys observed nothing after his load left the bomb bay. P/O Hankins dropped his bombs and incendiaries in a stick and witnessed three bursts and the splash of incendiaries across the docks on the western bank of the river, south of a railway and road bridge, where a fire was seen to be taking hold as they retreated. P/O Morton's load fell south of a Rhine bridge, while P/O Pownall was defeated by ground haze but found an aerodrome a mile-and-a-half east of the city.

This concluded another busy month for the Kiwis, who had operated without loss on nine nights and dispatched seventy sorties against nineteen targets.

December 1940

December was also to be a month of limited activity for the Command in general, and it was not until the night of the 6/7th that the squadron was called into action. Weather conditions over Germany precluded attacks on industrial targets and it was decided to launch nuisance raids against aerodromes in the vicinity of Paris instead, employing light calibre bombs. A new squadron record of thirteen Wellingtons was made ready, supported by two others from 214 Squadron at Stradishall, and the crews were allotted to three specific areas numbered 1, 2 and 3. The targets were at Velizy-Villacoublay, Villeneuve-Orly, Melun, Etampes, Chartres, Chateaudun, Orleans-Bricy and Tours, and the sorties were spread over a nine-hour period beginning with the departure of the freshman crews of P/O Herbert Douglas Newman, RAF/RNZAF and Sgt Rex Chuter RAF at 17.20. P/O Morton was the last to take off at 23.15 and the last to land six hours later. Weather conditions were not ideal and the plan was only lightly adhered to, providing a long list of targets actually attacked of Calais aerodrome and docks, St-Omer, Villacoublay, Glisy, Chateaudun, Boulogne docks, Orly, Tours, Chartres, Roye, Dunkerque, Abbeville, Nantes, Les Mureaux and Evreux. The results were not expected to be spectacular, and this was the case, but the attacks almost certainly restricted efforts by the Luftwaffe over England at a time when the Blitz on British cities was in full swing.

The night of the 9/10th was devoted to ports, Bremen in Germany and the others in Belgium and France. Eight 75(NZ) Squadron crews were briefed for Lorient and took off between 16.45 and 17.30 with S/L Boffee the senior pilot on duty. Weather conditions in the target area were favourable with clear skies, and most crews were able to observe their bombs bursting from a respectable height of around 12,000 feet. All returned safely to report many explosions among the dock installations and declare a successful night's work. Just five crews were called to briefing on the 11th, three to learn that they were to attack Mannheim, while two others were to head for Boulogne. Between 17.00 and 17.28, S/L Bain, P/O Lockwood and Sgt Wilson took off for southern Germany and P/O Arthur James Falconer RNZAF and Sgt White RAF for Boulogne, the former element adopting a more northerly route to cross the enemy coast over the Scheldt estuary. There, they met icing conditions, which persuaded P/O Lockwood to turn back and return his bombs to store and it seems that Sgt Wilson may have encountered similar difficulties as he chose to drop his bombs on Boulogne. It seems unlikely that S/L Bain pressed on to Mannheim, his time for the round-trip amounting to just five-and-a-half hours, which is considerably less than would be required to reach southern Germany and return. He described starting small fires along a railway, which resulted in two large explosions. P/O Falconer and crew were the only ones to carry out their brief, dropping their bombs in a salvo at Boulogne and observing two large fires on the north side of the docks area. Sgt White delivered his bombs across the docks at Dieppe but was prevented by cloud from assessing the results.

Friday the 13th turned out to be as bad as any superstitious planners at 3 Group HQ might have feared. The threat of adverse weather conditions over north-western Germany persuaded them to reduce the number of aircraft detailed for Bremen from thirty to twenty, and this meant the cancellation of three sorties by the squadron. Eight Wellingtons lined up for take-off between 16.40 and 17.05 with S/L Bain the senior pilot on duty, and they climbed away into heavy cloud, which persisted throughout the operation. In the target area the ground was obscured by ten-tenths cloud at around 6,000 feet, which prevented even the searchlights from breaking through. P/O Pownall could not identify his briefed aiming point and bombed on the flashes emanating from a flak position. S/L Bain experienced similar difficulties and unloaded his bombs on Schiphol aerodrome on the way home, observing them to straddle hangars and set off fires. The others simply bombed through the cloud and returned with nothing to offer in terms of an assessment.

The night of the 15/16th brought another reduction in the number of aircraft detailed for operations to Berlin and Frankfurt. 75(NZ) Squadron cancelled four sorties and made ready eight Wellingtons to be divided between the two. A late take-off saw the squadron participants airborne between 00.15 and 00.55 and adopt different routes to their respective targets. Conditions in southern Germany would prove to be more favourable for bombing than those at Berlin, where marshalling yards provided the objectives. The primary target was the Schlesinger goods station and adjacent yards, but P/Os Morton and Pownall failed to locate it and bombed those at Charlottenburg on the western side of the capital instead. P/O McNamara attacked an unspecified railway yard, while Sgt Wilson chose the docks at Bremen for his bombs, reporting a terrific explosion following a direct hit on a jetty with a 1,000 pounder. At Frankfurt ground detail could be identified, and P/O Falconer saw his bombs fall into the docks on the River Main. P/O Newman and Sgts Jones and Neate reported their bombs exploding in the target area but could not provide a detailed assessment.

The second visit of the month by the squadron to Mannheim was to participate in Operation Abigail Rachel, which was planned for the night of the 16/17th and was in retaliation for recent Luftwaffe attacks on English cities, particularly Coventry. The original intention had been to commit two hundred aircraft, but as the day drew on it became clear that the weather conditions over the bomber stations might cause problems and the force was cut to 134 aircraft, sixty-one of them provided by 3 Group. This was the largest force to date to be sent to a single target and it would be the first recorded "area" raid, in which the Command intentionally aimed for the city rather than military or economic objectives. 75(NZ) Squadron was represented by ten Wellingtons, which departed Feltwell between 22.25 and 00.30 with F/L Kain the senior pilot on duty. The Abigail part of the plan called for eight of the Command's most experienced Wellington crews to drop their all-incendiary bomb loads onto the city-centre aiming point to start fires and act as a beacon to the Rachel force following on behind. The weather conditions outbound persuaded perhaps a quarter of the force to turn back, but those reaching the target area found largely clear skies and a full moon, with only a modest defence in operation. In the event, the initial bombing was inaccurate and a scattered raid developed, which post-raid reconnaissance revealed had not produced the desired results, after the "path finder" element had missed the city centre. Even so, local reports provided a figure of 240 buildings either destroyed or seriously damaged, with more than a thousand people bombed out of their homes. Sgts Jones and Wilson failed to identify the primary target and the latter jettisoned his bombs onto waste ground near Aachen. The others carried out their attacks and returned safely to report that their bombs had set off explosions and fires.

S/L Boffee was posted to a training unit at Bassingbourn on the 18th to be succeeded as B Flight commander by the newly-promoted S/L Garry Kain. Garry Carlton Kain came from Ben Nevis, Central Otago in New Zealand, was educated at Christ's College, Christchurch, and had joined the RAF in 1936, serving in the Middle East. He was one of the pilots originally selected to fly Wellingtons back to New Zealand with the NZ Squadron, before war intervened. Although not related to Edgar "Cobber" Kain, the famous first fighter pilot "ace" of the war, his brother Dereck "Bill" Kain had been a great mate of Cobber's and flown with him at 73 Squadron, leading to some confusion around the relationship in the press at the time.

The Nordstern synthetic oil plant at Gelsenkirchen provided the next target for the squadron on the night of the 19/20th, for which eight Wellingtons were made ready. They took off between 23.06 and 03.05 with no senior pilots on duty and headed into ten-tenths cloud that would persist throughout the operation. Sgts Neate, White and Wilson and P/O Pownall all failed to locate the primary target, and while the last three-mentioned brought their bombs home, Sgt Neate dropped his over Homberg on the west bank of the Rhine opposite Duisburg, having glimpsed it through a gap in the overcast. Sgt Chuter was not certain of his exact position and dropped his bombs in a single stick from 11,000 feet in the general area. P/Os Faulkner, Lockwood and Newman effectively did the same thing in the face of the cloud cover, and some reflections of bomb bursts were observed.

The squadron hosted a group of VIP guests during the week, Sir Cyril Newall, the Governor General designate of New Zealand, Air Marshal Sir Richard Peirse, Commander-in-Chief, Bomber Command, and Air Vice-Marshal J. E. A. Baldwin, officer commanding 3 Group. Sir Cyril had asked to meet the officers and men before leaving for New Zealand and the party was challenged with a haka in the officers' billiards room, led by Sgt E. P. Williams DFM of Auckland. Sir Cyril was given two paintings to take with him for presentation to New Zealand and to be exhibited there. One was *"Return at Dawn"* by Charles Cundall, depicting a Wellington crew returning to their station at dawn after a night raid on Germany. The other was a portrait of Wing Commander M. W. Buckley by Oswald Birley. Both paintings still hang in the Officer's Mess at RNZAF Ohakea.

Mannheim was probably feeling somewhat persecuted by the time Wellingtons from 75(NZ) and 115 Squadron appeared overhead during the evening of the 22nd on the latest of an eventual seven attacks of varying sizes on the city during the month. Eleven from 75(NZ) Squadron had taken off from Feltwell between 16.45 and 17.25 led by S/L Kain and seven are known to have reached the target area to find low cloud and a spirited defence from what must have been by this time a bunch of trigger-happy flak crews. Three crews failed to locate the primary target, which, according to the target code in use, was the Rhine docks area. F/L Gilbert returned his bombs to store, P/O Morton bombed an aerodrome in the Reims area, while S/L Kain is recorded as having bombed railway installations at Koblenz. The return of T2474 AA-W was awaited in vain, and it was established later that it had come down a couple of miles from the French coast near Fecamp, north-east of Le Havre. Sgt Rex Chuter RAF and four of his crew survived to be taken into captivity but rear gunner, Sgt Alfred Henry Ritchie RNZAF, lost his life. The other crews returned home safely to report many explosions and fires and gave an impression of a successful raid, and the last crews to leave the target area reported the city to be ablaze on both sides of the river. While this operation was in progress, Sgt Drayton and crew carried out an attack on the aerodrome at Flushing and returned safely, unable to offer an assessment of damage.

The final operation of the year for 75(NZ) Squadron was a low-key affair involving three crews at Hamm marshalling yards on the night of the 29/30th. Sgt White took off at 17.20 and P/O McNamara at 20.15, but we are not given a time of departure for the recently-promoted F/L Newman. The target was covered by ten-tenths cloud with tops at around 12,000 feet and the loads of 500 pounders were delivered on estimated positions. F/L Newman RAF/RNZAF sent a message to confirm carrying out his attack, but R3211 AA-J did not arrive back at Feltwell. News eventually came through that all members of the crew had survived whatever befell them and had joined the growing list of Bomber Command personnel on extended leave in PoW camps.

The squadron had operated against fourteen targets during the month and dispatched seventy-five sorties for the loss of two aircraft and crews. It had been a curious year in some ways, which had started with the inactivity of the "Phoney War", before erupting into unimaginable fury in May. The struggle for survival during the summer had been followed by a less frenetic end to the year, when the best that could be achieved was the presentation of a defiant face to the as yet all-conquering enemy. Perhaps it was only at this point that the realisation came, that this was going to be a very long war indeed, and that much needed to be done before Bomber Command could become even remotely effective.

*Members of the New Zealand Squadron's 1st Mobile Flight, August 1939. Pilots seated at front (L-R): P/O Trevor Freeman, P/O WMC "Bill" Williams, F/O John Adams, F/O John Collins, F/O Arthur Greenaway, F/L Charles Hunter, S/L Maurice "Buck" Buckley, S/L Cyril "Cyrus" Kay, F/O Aubrey Breckon, P/O Neville Williams, P/O William "Bill" Coleman, F/O Fred "Popeye" Lucas. Wireless and aircraft technicians standing behind.
(Air Force Museum of New Zealand)*

*The Breckon crew that flew on the squadron's second wartime operation on the 13th of March 1940 (L-R): F/L Aubrey Breckon (captain), F/O Fred 'Popeye' Lucas (2nd pilot), Sgt Robert Hughes (navigator), AC Thomas Mumby (rear gunner), AC Eric Albert (front gunner), and LAC Edwin Williams (wireless operator). Taken during training at Feltwell.
(Popeye Lucas collection, courtesy of the Lucas family)*

*High Commissioner Mr Bill Jordan greeted on arrival at RAF Feltwell by ACM Sir Edgar Ludlow-Hewitt and AVM Baldwin (right). NZ Liaison Officer S/L Sidney Wallingford in the background. 20th of March 1940.
(AWMM, W J Jordan photo album)*

*High Commissioner Mr Jordan and ACM Sir Edgar Ludlow-Hewitt taking the salute of members of the New Zealand Squadron, Feltwell, 20th of March 1940.
(AWMM, W J Jordan photo album)*

Inspecting the assembled airmen with W/C Buckley, Mr Jordan shaking hands with wireless specialist LAC Joe White, with LAC Donald McGlashan next closest to the camera.
(AWMM, W J Jordan photo album)

Cpl Colin Beresford Graham Knight, DFM, recipient of the first RNZAF decoration of the war. (AWMM)

High Commissioner Bill Jordan presents the DFM to Cpl Colin Knight, Feltwell, 20th March 1940. (AWMM, W J Jordan photo album)

Mr Jordan meets members of the Collins crew, just prior to boarding the Wellington and observing operation of the gun turrets, Feltwell, 20th March 1940. (IWM)

W/C (later G/C) Maurice William "Buck" Buckley, MBE. (From "Return At Dawn")

S/L (later W/C) Cyril Eyton "Cyrus" Kay. (NZ Bomber Command Assn. archives)

75 (NZ) Squadron, RAF Feltwell, ca. November 1940. (Wayne Mellor)

F/L Breckon and crew flying Vickers Wellington Mark I, L4387 'LG-L', over parked Hawker Hurricanes at Wick, Caithness as they leave on a daylight reconnaissance of Narvik, Norway. (IWM)

A Wellington being bombed up, Feltwell, 1940. (From 'Early Operations with Bomber Command)

*Leaflet loading for a "Nickeling" raid, Feltwell, 1940.
(From "Return At Dawn")*

*The Breckon crew for the Narvik reconnaissance (L-R): LAC Edwin Williams, wireless operator; F/L Aubrey Breckon 1st Pilot; Lieutenant Commander Howie, R.N., observer; Sgt Robert Hughes, navigator; P/O Donald Harkness, 2nd Pilot, and AC Thomas Mumby, gunner observer.
(From "Early Operations with Bomber Command")*

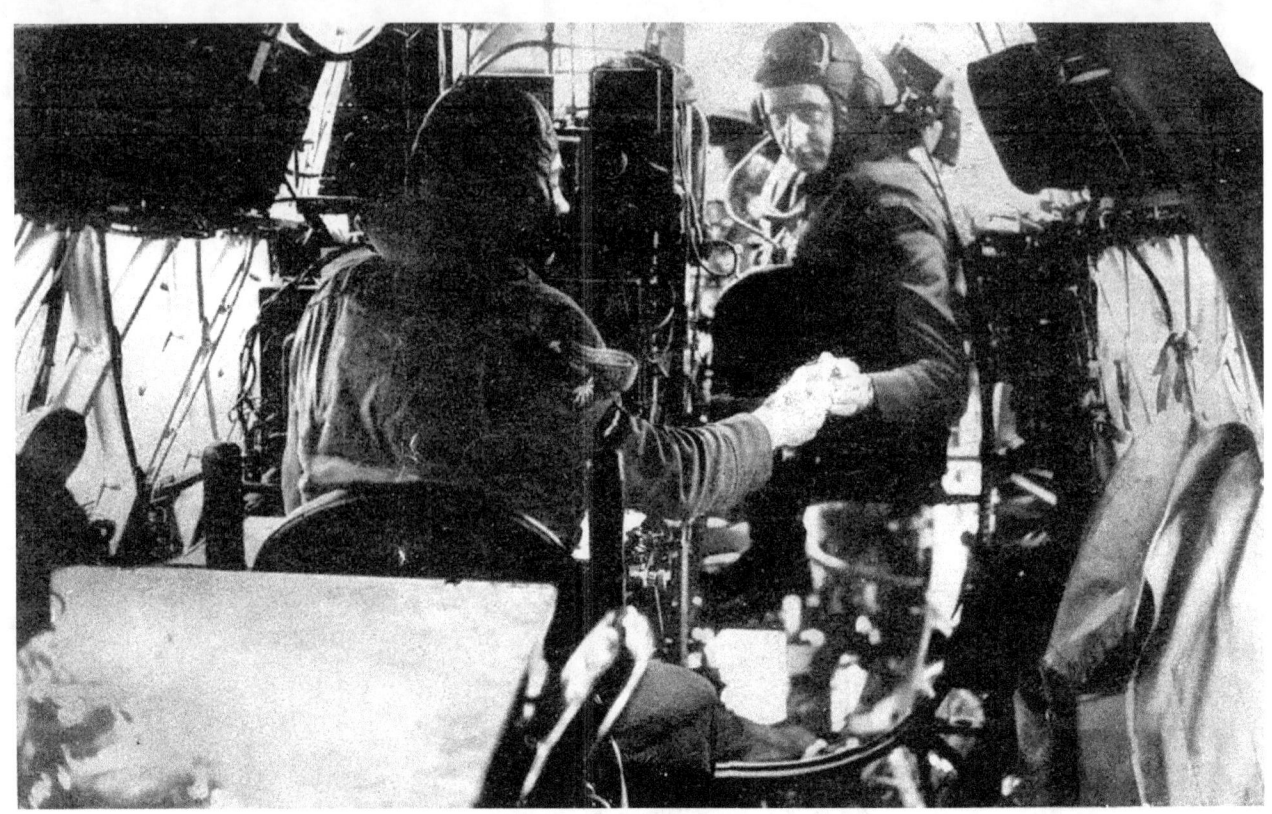

*P/O Donald Harkness receiving a message from wireless operator LAC Edwin Williams.
(From "Early Operations with Bomber Command")*

*F/L Aubrey Breckon was married to Dana (nee Waugh) on 23 July 1940. The wedding group pictured at RAF Feltwell, where the reception was held. F/L Breckon and bride flanked by S/L "Cyrus" Kay (right) and best man F/O Neville Williams. W/C Buckley to the left of Williams, S/L the Rev. Kayll, far right.
Squadron pilots make up almost all the back row.
(NZ Bomber Command Assn., Stan Brooks collection, via Anna Rhodes-Sayer)*

F/L Aubrey Breckon won a DFC for his role in the reconnaissance flights to Norway. (AWMM)

"Nickel" propaganda leaflet, "Die Freie Welt", October 1940. (Archives NZ)

Wireless operator LAC Edwin Williams at his set. (From "Early Operations with Bomber Command")

Wellington taxying. (From "Early Operations with Bomber Command")

RAF wireless operators, ACs "Smudge" Smith, "Stan" Brooks and Eric Albert.
(NZ Bomber Command Assn., Stan Brooks collection, via Anna Rhodes-Sayer)

S/L Wilfred Ira Collett (AWMM)

F/L John Noel Collins
(NZ Bomber Command Assn., Stan Brooks collection, via Anna Rhodes-Sayer)

*Crew boarding their Wellington.
(NZ Bomber Command Assn., Stan Brooks collection, via Anna Rhodes-Sayer)*

S/L "Cyrus" Kay and crew, May-July 1940, (L-R): Sgt Jim Carter (navigator), S/L Kay, P/O Alfred Charles (rear gunner), AC Eric Albert (wireless operator), P/O Eric Best (second pilot). (From "The Restless Sky")

"A squadron group" L-R: Sgt Jim Carter, Sgt Eric Albert, unknown, unknown, P/O WMC "Bill" Williams, F/O Alfred Charles, P/O Eric Best, S/L Cyril Kay; F/O John Adams, F/O Neville Williams, W/C Maurice Buckley, "Popeye" Lucas, unknown, F/L Aubrey Breckon. (From "Early Operations with Bomber Command")

75 (NZ) Squadron Wellingtons over East Anglia. The leading aircraft in the formation, P9206 'AA-A', was usually flown by the Squadron's Commanding Officer, S/L "Cyrus" Kay. (IWM)

The Neville Williams crew (L-R): Sgt Robert Noden, second pilot; F/O Donald Mackay DFM, navigator; F/O Neville Williams DFC, pilot; Sgt Alan White, DFM, rear gunner; Sgt Harold Smith, wireless operator. Note the "Bashful" nose art on the Wellington. (aircrewremembered.com, Michael Green)

F/O Samuel Miles Mackenzie Watson mid., (AWMM)

Flying Officer William Harcourt "Bill" Coleman, DFC (AWMM)

Wellington undergoing maintenance at Feltwell, 1940.
Several of the squadron's aircraft wore nose art inspired by Snow White & The Seven Dwarfs – this appears to be Sneezy.
(From "Early Operations with Bomber Command")

F/O Neville Williams, DFC, RNZAF.
(NZ Herald)

S/L Max Boffee
(www.214squadron.org)

Above: Fred "Popeye" Lucas in Wellington R3169, AA-P, the first of his aircraft to wear the famous 'Popeye' nose art.
(Popeye Lucas collection, courtesy of the Lucas family)

Incendiaries being loaded, Feltwell, 1940. (From "Early Operations with Bomber Command")

Sgt Ted Williams presented with his DFM by H.M. King George V. Williams was injured in the crash that killed S/L Collett, spending five weeks in hospital. (NZBCA archives)

The Sanderson crew ready for operations; P/O Rex Sanderson third from left, P/O William Finlayson far right. (From "Early Operations in Bomber Command")

"The Station church" - Feltwell's St George chapel covered in camouflage netting, and the squadron Padre, S/L the Rev. Arthur Kayll, a New Zealander from Waihi. (From "Return At Dawn")

A publicity photo taken in early November 1940, "Officers and men who have been decorated for gallantry" (L-R): Sgt John "Jack" Mylod, DFM, RAF, Sgt Jim Whitlaw Carter, DFM, RAF, F/O Duncan Harold McArthur DFC, RAF, F/O Neville Williams DFC, RNZAF; P/O Donald Mackay DFM, RAF, Sgt Ted Williams DFM, RNZAF and W/C M. W. Buckley, CO of 75 (NZ) Squadron. The nose art on the Wellington depicts "Eugene the Jeep", from the Popeye comic strip. (NZBCA archives)

Wellington and crew. (From "Return at Dawn")

Wellington T2820 AA-B crashed in fog 20th October 1940. (Colin Gilbert family collection, via Noel Baker)

Wellington T2820 AA-B crashed 20th October 1940. T2820 is believed to have carried "J Wellington Wimpey" nose art, one of several pieces on squadron aircraft said to have been created by D.W. Smith.
(Colin Gilbert family collection, via Noel Baker)

Wellington T2820 AA-B after it crashed into trees in fog near Methwold on 20th October 1940.
(Colin Gilbert family collection, via Noel Baker)

The Gilbert crew with Wellington T2835, AA-C. F/L Colin Gilbert 3rd from left, and his 2nd pilot P/O Norman Edwards 4th from left. December 1940.
(Colin Gilbert family collection, via Noel Baker)

*A Wellington being bombed up for a night operation.
(From "Early Operations with Bomber Command")*

Wellingtons of 75 (NZ) Squadron, 1940. (From "The Restless Sky")

Mark 1A Wellington L7784, AA-D, an early model that flew with the squadron between April and October 1940. (NZ Bomber Command Assn. archives)

*Feltwell maintenance ground crew (L-R): Thomas "Tutai" Read, "Chiefy" Healey, and P.W. "Spud" Murphy.
(Popeye Lucas collection, courtesy of the Lucas family)*

The Best crew, August-October 1940, in front of Wellington L7857, "Dopey". P/O Eric Best centre, wearing harness, then P/O Brian McNamara, second pilot. Unidentified are P/O Harry Albert Goodwin, navigator, Sgt Green, wireless operator, Sgt Emmett McMahon, rear gunner, and Sgt Lawler, front gunner.
(Brian McNamara collection, courtesy of Mary Ann Kane and Dave Homewood)

Early model Mk 1A Wellington showing small code letter and tail fin flash markings, 1940.
(Paul Nash collection, Tate Archive)

The Denton crew (L-R): Sgt Jimmy Farquhar (front gunner), Sgt "Chalky" White (second pilot), P/O Frank Denton (skipper), Sgt Andy Orrock (navigator), P/O Edward Jelley (rear gunner, killed on 29th September) and Sgt Len Hayter (wireless operator). (NZ Bomber Command Assn. archives)

75 NZ Squadron airmen enjoying a pint or three in The Ship, a pub near Feltwell, late 1940. Third from right is P/O Norman Edwards, 2nd pilot in F/L Colin Gilbert's crew. (Ian Carswell)

January 1941

January would be a fairly low-key month operationally and began with the Command's focus initially upon the city of Bremen, where the ship-building yards and the Focke-Wulf aircraft factory were the main attractions. Coastal targets in Germany and France would continue to dominate, with Wilhelmshaven taking prominence from the middle of the month, and there would be only occasional forays into the Ruhr region. 75(NZ) Squadron began its 1941 campaign by contributing seven Wellingtons to an attack on Bremen on New Year's Night, four crews briefed for the Focke-Wulf factory in the Hemelingen district to the south-east of the city centre and three for the Deschimag U-Boot yards. They took off between 17.00 and 18.00 with P/O Hankins, P/O McNamara and Sgt White the first away bound for the shipyards. P/O Hankins was about fifty miles out over the North Sea when starboard engine trouble forced him to jettison his bombs and turn back. The others pressed on to the target, which they found to be largely free of cloud and delivered their mixed loads onto the general area, P/O McNamara observing greenish flashes as his HE exploded. P/O Lockwood arrived later and made three runs across the target at 10,000 feet but failed to observe the burst of his bombs among the fires already burning. Sgt Wilson saw his explode four hundred yards to the west of the aiming point, while Sgt Drayton's fell to the south-east and P/O Falconer could not determine the fall of his.

Ten of the squadron's Wellingtons were made ready on the 4th for operations that night against Duisburg and Brest. S/L "Basher" Bain was the senior pilot on duty and he had a visitor, S/L James Foulsham RAF, on board acting as second pilot. The take-offs, as usual, were spread over an extended period between 18.45 and 20.25 with six crews bound for the Ruhr and four for Brest. P/O McNamara and crew had been briefed specifically to attack the main Rhine docks at Duisburg-Ruhrort, while the others sought out industrial targets generally within the city. The weather was most unhelpful and the entire operation was conducted over ten-tenths cloud, which coated the wings with ice as the Wellingtons climbed through it. S/L Bain was unable to locate the target and brought his bombs back, while the others bombed through the cloud and observed an occasional reflection or glow as they dodged the spirited flak defence. The Brest trio was equally hampered by the poor conditions, P/O Falconer failing to locate the target and dumping his bombs "safe" in the sea. The others bombed through cloud in the face of intense light and moderate heavy flak and returned safely with little to report.

There were no operations on the night of the 6th, but flying control reported that a German intruder had landed six bombs on the aerodrome, two of them on the tarmac and smashing windows in the watch office, fortunately without casualties. Wilhelmshaven was the destination for seven of the squadron's Wellingtons on the night of the 8/9th, when the docks and the battleship Tirpitz were the specific objectives. S/L Kain was the senior pilot on duty as they departed Feltwell between 21.50 and 23.25 and headed for the North Sea. Reports on the visibility in the target area were contradictory, some crews picking out ground detail, while others were thwarted by cloud. Generally, however, the attack was accurate and the town itself sustained quite heavy damage, while fires were reported in the docks area and some crews reported straddling the battleship Tirpitz with their bombs. S/L Kain failed to locate the target and attacked Leeuwarden aerodrome, the famed Wespennest (wasps' nest) in northern Holland on the way home.

P/O McNamara and crew took off at 11.30 on the 10th to carry out a night flying test (NFT) in T2550 AA-L, and afterwards proceed to Bassingbourn to drop off second pilot P/O Ryan and collect his replacement. The Wellington failed to arrive at its destination and was found later to have crashed near Stapleford, four miles south-east of Cambridge, killing P/Os Brian Patrick McNamara and Alexander James Ryan, both members of the RNZAF. Three other crew members also lost their lives, navigator Sgt Richard Booth Elliott RAF, wireless operator Sgt John Olive RAFVR, and front gunner Sgt Matthew Roy Ritchie RAF. The rear gunner P/O Ronald Edward Ashby-Peckham RNZAF was taken to hospital with very severe injuries.

Eight crews attended briefing on the 11th to learn of a return to Wilhelmshaven for five of them, while three others were to cross the Alps for the first time and attack the industrial city of Turin in northern Italy, which was home among other war supporting companies to Fiat's Lingotto and Mirafiori car plants, the Lancia motor works, the Arsenale army munitions factory, the Nebioli foundry and plants belonging to the American Westinghouse company. The Italy-bound trio of the crews of Sgt Neate, P/O Morton and P/O Saxelby took off at thirty-minute intervals from 20.00 and arrived in the target area to find low cloud, which restricted their vertical visibility. A number of fires and bright explosions were observed, but no detail could be ascertained and they were on their way home before the Wilhelmshaven contingent departed Feltwell between 01.20 and 02.15. S/L Kain was again the senior pilot on duty among these, and they, too, were impeded by thick cloud in the target area and were unable to observe the results of their efforts.

In a directive issued on the 15th, the Air Ministry had decided that an all-out assault against oil related targets would eventually take its toll on the German war effort and operations from now on would reflect this. A list of seventeen sites was drawn up, the top nine of which represented 80% of Germany's synthetic oil production, and of these, Scholven-Buer and Gelsenkirchen were in the Ruhr, Leuna, Zeitz, Böhlen and Lützkendorf were in the east near Leipzig, Magdeburg and Ruhland were north and east of Leipzig respectively and the other was at Politz close to the Baltic coast, but it would be February before Peirse was able to comply.

Wilhelmshaven continued to be the focus of attention on the night of the 15/16th, when a further seven crews were called to briefing to be told that they would be part of an overall force of ninety-six aircraft. They took off between 18.55 and 19.35 with S/L Kain the senior pilot on duty and climbed out into good weather conditions, which held firm for the entire operation. There were largely clear skies over northern Germany and vertical visibility was good as the bombers made their approach. Only Sgt Neate failed to arrive, after wireless failure forced him to turn back and jettison his bombs into the sea. Fires were already burning in the town, providing a beacon for those beginning their bombing runs and all from the squadron reported adding to the destruction with bombs and incendiaries. They returned safely to claim a successful operation, which was confirmed by local reports and mentioned the main post office and police station, army barracks, dockside offices and many commercial premises as suffering destruction or damage.

A week of inactivity preceded the next operation, which was a trip to Düsseldorf in the Ruhr on the night of the 22/23rd. The original plan called for 3 Group to lead the attack and start fires for the other groups, but poor weather conditions led to a reduction in the size of the force and ultimately, it became a 3 Group show of twenty-eight Wellingtons. Five of these were provided by 75(NZ) Squadron, which took off between 17.35 and 18.00 with no senior pilots on duty. They all reached the target area, where ten-tenths cloud completely blotted out the ground and bombs were delivered on estimated positions based on the flashes from flak batteries. It was a wasted effort, but at least all returned safely to offer the intelligence section what little information they could. S/L Bain was posted to 11 O.T.U at Bassingbourn on the 24th and P/O Arthur "Artie" Ashworth RAF came in the opposite direction for his first tour with the squadron.

Hannover was selected as the target for seven of the squadron's crews on the night of the 26/27th, and at briefing they were somewhat optimistically told to aim for the main post office and telephone exchange. This was, of course, code for an area attack on the city centre at a time when the fact of indiscriminate bombing was withheld from the public. The northern city of Hannover was a major centre of war production, the home among others to the Accumulatoren-Fabrik A G factory which manufactured lead acid batteries for U-Boots and torpedoes, the Continental tyre and rubber factory at Limmer, the Deurag-Nerag synthetic oil refinery at Misburg, the VLW (Volkswagen) metalworks, and the Maschinenfabrik Niedersachsen Hannover and Hanomag factories, which were producing guns and tracked vehicles. It was a very late take-off between 01.15 and 01.50 and the crews had to climb through low cloud to reach the North Sea, where S/L Kain was forced to turn back with engine problems. The others pushed on to find the cloud dispersing until clear skies greeted their arrival over the target area. Each Wellington was carrying a mixed load of a 1,000 pounder and 500 and 250 pounders, which were dropped in sticks across the city, setting off fires and explosions. All returned safely, confident in the quality of their work, but there was no post-raid reconnaissance or local report to confirm their success.

S/L Edward Ulric Guerin Solbe RAF was posted in from Bassingbourn on the 28th to succeed S/L Bain as A Flight commander, and P/Os Malcolm Hugh MacFarlane and John Morton were promoted to the acting rank of flight lieutenant (unpaid). The squadron operated against nine targets during the month and dispatched fifty-one sorties for the non-operational loss of one Wellington and crew.

February 1941

February began as January had ended, with ports occupying the bulk of the Command's attention, although the accent shifted to those in France and Belgium. The new month began in gentle fashion for 75(NZ) Squadron with the dispatch of two freshman crews to bomb the docks and shipping at Boulogne on the night of the 1/2nd. First-time captains Sgt Kilsby RAF and P/O Oliver Rayner Matheson RAFVR took off in fairly good weather conditions at 05.23 and 05.53 respectively and both reached the French coast, where the latter failed to locate the target because of cloud and the former reported bomb bursts in the general area. A similar operation took place on the evening of the 4th, when Le Havre was the destination for the freshman crews of P/Os Alec Herbert Burton RAF and Gilbert Theodore Kimberley RNZAF.

They took off shortly before 18.00 but failed to locate the port after encountering ten-tenths cloud in the target area, and jettisoned their bombs into the sea.

AM Sir Richard Peirse had decided upon a policy of one major operation each month and selected Hannover to host February's "Big Night" on the 10th, for which a record force for a single target of 222 aircraft was assembled, 103 of them 3 Group Wellingtons, eleven representing 75(NZ) Squadron. In addition to the main fare, a freshman raid on the oil storage tanks at Rotterdam involved forty-three aircraft including two 75(NZ) Squadron Wellingtons containing the crews of P/Os Leonard Rodney Hewitt RNZAF and George Ronald Simich RNZAF, who took off first at 18.40 and 18.50 respectively. In a demonstration of the burgeoning power of the Command, the contribution to the night's efforts by 3 Group of 119 aircraft would be the first time that any group had exceeded one hundred aircraft. Among them, as part of the Rotterdam force, were the first three sorties by the new four-engine Short Stirling in the hands of 7 Squadron. There was a delay in the departure of the main element due to enemy aircraft activity over Feltwell, but they eventually took to the air between 21.20 and 22.09 with S/L Kain the senior pilot on duty. They flew out over scattered cloud intending to enter Fortress Europe by way of the Dutch coast, but P/O Falconer's receiver broke down during the North Sea crossing and he bombed Rotterdam as an alternative target, observing his bombs to fall across the Y-shaped docks and leave three fires burning. The others pressed on in ideal weather conditions with clear skies and bright moonlight to assist navigation and map-reading, and most of the force pinpointed initially on the Steinhuder Lake to the west, and then the Maschsee to the south of the city centre. Over the target itself, around three-tenths cloud was reported at 7,000 feet, but it would have no influence on the course of the raid, which attracted what appeared to be only a limited and inaccurate flak defence. This emboldened crews to circle, if necessary, to establish their positions and decide upon a method of attack, and in some cases to descend to a fairly low level. A few crews adopted a glide approach, while most favoured a higher-level attack from between 10,000 and 14,000, the Feltwell crews aided by fires already burning. They returned to report many fires and explosions, which suggested a successful outcome, but no local report was forthcoming to confirm the extent of damage. L7848 AA-V "Cuthbert", Dick Curtis's old kite, was attacked four times by enemy aircraft, which scored hits with cannon and machine-gun shells, causing the hydraulics system to fail. F/L Morton decided to put the wounded Wellington down at Methwold, three miles north-east of Feltwell, and accomplished a crash-landing from which he and his crew were able to walk away. Thanks to F/L Morton's skill, the Wellington sustained little further damage and would be returned to flying condition.

75(NZ) Squadron was allowed the night off on the 11th, while a force of seventy-one Hampdens, Wellingtons and Whitleys was made ready for Bremen and eighteen Wellingtons and eleven Hampdens for a return to Hannover. It proved to be a good night to stay at home as fog over the bomber stations caused twenty-two returning aircraft to crash or be abandoned by their crews. A dozen 75(NZ) Squadron crews were called to briefing on the 14th, to learn that they were to join twenty-nine others from the group to attack the Nordstern synthetic oil plant at Gelsenkirchen. They took off between 18.30 and 19.25 with S/L Kain once more the senior pilot on duty and made their way out in good weather conditions. Searchlights were active from the Dutch coast to the target, which was reached by all crews and found to be under clear skies and protected by an accurate flak barrage. Extreme darkness and the usual industrial ground haze combined to prevent most crews from identifying the aiming point, and many sought out alternative targets in Essen and Duisburg. A German aircraft is said to have landed among the 57 Squadron returnees at Feltwell but took off again when the flare-path was extinguished. W/C "Cyrus" Kay had seen the aircraft taxy in, turn around and take off immediately, but thought nothing of it since Feltwell regularly received "strays". A phone call came through shortly afterwards from an unhappy A-O-C 3 Group, AVM Jack Baldwin, asking if he realised that an enemy aircraft had just taken off from Feltwell! As it happened, the lost pilot, low on petrol and realising how far he was from home, landed at another airfield and surrendered.

Wilhelmshaven found itself once more in favour on the night of the 21/22nd, after a planned attack on Berlin had first been scaled-down and then cancelled altogether. Seven of the squadron's Wellingtons were made ready to join forces with twenty-seven others for an all-3 Group operation, and they took off between 18.55 and 19.10 with no senior pilot on duty. P/O Kimberley and crew turned back with unserviceable front and rear turrets, leaving the others to press on over ten-tenths ice-bearing cloud. Four crews bombed in the general target area, two on estimated positions and the flashes from flak concentrations, and the others after a visual identification. Some bursts were observed across the docks and a number of fires were reported, but no local report exists to confirm the effectiveness of the raid. One crew attacked the port of Emden as an alternative and observed the 500 pounders explode in the docks. T2503 AA-P failed to return with the crew of P/O Falconer RNZAF, which contained the recently arrived A Flight commander, S/L Solbe, RAF. It was established later that the Wellington had crashed into the sea off the North German coast and that none had survived. P/O Falconer, P/O Anthony Vincent Muir and Sgt Andrew Moore Brodie were all members of the RNZAF. T2547 AA-F was another casualty on this night after colliding with the perimeter fence when landing at Feltwell at 00.30. The Wellington was written-off, but P/O Leonard Hewitt and crew walked away to fight another day.

Two nights later it was planned to put Wilhelmshaven under the spotlight again, until a forecast of adverse weather conditions led to a change of target to Boulogne, for which the squadron made ready eight Wellingtons. They were part of an overall force of thirty-five Wellingtons, almost all belonging to 3 Group, and took off between 18.50 and 19.10 with F/O John Kenneth Collins RAFVR the senior pilot on duty. They made their way to the French coast over cloud, which was at eight to ten-tenths by the time they arrived at the target. Three crews were unable to pinpoint its location, despite the intense searchlight and flak activity acting as a beacon, but the others carried out their attacks and returned to report bomb bursts across the docks resulting in small fires and explosions.

126 aircraft were made ready on the 26th for an operation that night against the Rhineland capital, Cologne. Ten 75(NZ) Squadron Wellingtons took off between 18.50 and 19.19 with S/L Kain the senior pilot on duty and P/O "Artie" Ashworth flying as second pilot to Sgt White. They flew out in good weather conditions and ran the gauntlet of searchlights all the way from the Dutch coast to the target area, where haze hampered identification of ground detail. Returning crews described explosions and large fires and all indications pointed to a successful raid, which, as often was the case, was not borne out by local reports. These recorded ten high explosive bombs and ninety incendiaries falling on the western fringes of the city out of a total of 353 and 15,000 respectively supposedly dropped.

Ten months after it had begun, an assessment of the efficacy of mining operations revealed that seventeen enemy vessels had been sunk in the Baltic's Great and Little Belts and eighteen damaged. It was believed that a further eighteen had probably been sunk and it was considered safe to estimate that for every known case of a sinking or damage, another would have occurred without news of it reaching England. Among the known sinkings was that of a troopship carrying three thousand men, of whom fewer than four hundred survived. This concluded the month's operations, of which there had been eight, generating fifty-four sorties for the loss of two Wellingtons and one crew.

March 1941

Ports would again feature prominently in March, although the first two operations of the new month would continue the assault on Cologne. Six Wellingtons were made ready on the 1st, and they were to join fifty-one others from the group in an overall mixed force of 131 aircraft. They took off between 20.50 and 22.00 with F/L MacFarlane the senior pilot on duty and crossed the North Sea via "corridor G" to make landfall over the Scheldt estuary in conditions of ten-tenths cloud, which dispersed over enemy territory to leave clear skies at the target. They delivered their loads of 1,000, 500 and 250 pounders in the face of an intense searchlight and heavy and light flak defence and observed bomb bursts in various parts of the city. P/O Simich and F/L MacFarlane specified theirs as falling a mile west of the Hohenzollern Bridge and near the cathedral respectively. All returned safely to report many fires, and local authorities confirmed significant damage, particularly in the docks areas on both sides of the Rhine.

Two nights later a reduced force of seventy-one aircraft returned to the city, among them thirty-two Wellingtons from 3 Group, of which eleven represented 75(NZ) Squadron. S/L Kain was the senior pilot on duty as they departed Feltwell between 19.25 and 19.55 and headed into fine weather conditions, which produced a little cloud over the Rhineland. One crew turned back with wireless problems and bombed Haamstede aerodrome on the way, while the remainder reached the target to deliver their bombs, before returning safely home. Just one crew reported the fall of their bombs on the eastern side of the Rhine, while the local authorities recorded no bombs in the main city area and just a few on the western fringes. S/L John MacKenzie Southwell RAFVR was posted to the squadron from 12 O.T.U at Benson on the 6th, and he would immediately assume command of A Flight following the loss of S/L Solbe.

Thereafter, the weather took a hand to keep most of the Command on the ground for the next week, and it was during this period on the 9th, that the Air Ministry responded to the urgent and burgeoning threat posed by U-Boots, which were claiming a massive tonnage of shipping crossing the Atlantic in convoys with vital war supplies. A new Directive was issued, which would unleash a concerted campaign against this menace and its partner in crime, the Focke-Wulf Kondor long-range maritime reconnaissance bomber. These two threats were to be attacked where-ever they could be found, at sea, in their bases in the occupied ports, and at their point of manufacture in the shipyards and in the assembly and component factories. A new target list was drawn up, which was headed by Kiel, Hamburg and Vegesack (Bremen), all of which were home to U-Boot construction yards, and Bremen itself, which also boasted a Focke-Wulf aircraft factory in its south-eastern Hemelingen district. Other related targets included the diesel engine plants at Mannheim and Augsburg, aircraft factories at Dessau, and, of course, the U-Boot bases at Brest, Lorient and St Nazaire. Until otherwise instructed, this was to be the focus of Peirse's efforts, and only occasionally would he be able prosecute the oil campaign.

The new directive was implemented first on the night of the 12/13th at the end of a day of hectic activity across the Command, as aircraft were made ready for three major raids to be conducted that night. Eighty-eight aircraft were to attack the Blohm & Voss shipyards at Hamburg, while eighty-six other crews were briefed for the Focke-Wulf factory and the city of Bremen, and finally, seventy-two aircraft were prepared for the long slog to Berlin to target two aiming points. The official records are confusing, with the 3 Group ORB recording 75(NZ) Squadron as contributing six Wellingtons to the Focke-Wulf factory in Bremen and four to Berlin, while the squadron ORB records nine aircraft to be involved in the night's activities but does not make clear how they were assigned. Landing times identify P/O Hewitt and Sgt Kilsby as targeting the capital, but as some crews attacked alternatives, the precise allocation of targets among the others is unclear. They took off between 19.45 and 20.06 with S/L Southwell the senior pilot on duty and headed for their respective targets in good weather conditions. One crew with wireless problems bombed Schiphol aerodrome as an alternative, and others reported their loads falling across the primary target, one specifying the docks area. P/O Leonard Hewitt was held for thirty minutes in searchlights over Berlin and was subjected to anti-aircraft fire for the entire period, which inflicted damage to W5621 AA-D and knocked out the hydraulics system. On return to Feltwell, a skilful crash-landing was carried out, which enabled the crew to walk away and the Wellington to be repaired and returned to service. Hewitt's second pilot, Sgt Ian Reid, a journalist before the war, wrote of the experience: "Over the airfield we found our undercarriage had been smashed. Reassuring voices from the ground as we turned in to crash land…. the fences, buildings, and flares rush past, there are tearing, splintering noises, crunching skid and a smell of fresh furrowed earth ripped up in our path. Silence and then a voice from outside inviting us to come out and have a smoke ...". Sgt Kilsby reported his bombs bursting in the vicinity of the Air Ministry building in Berlin, half a mile south-east of the Tiergarten (zoo), during what was a scattered and relatively ineffective operation that damaged sixty buildings. Post-raid reconnaissance at Bremen revealed that a dozen high explosive bombs had hit the Focke-Wulf aircraft factory.

On the following night, the entire force of 139 aircraft was sent to Hamburg to target the Blohm & Voss shipyards located on Kuhwerder Island on the bank of the Elbe to the west of the city centre. It was here that the mighty Bismarck had been built between 1936 and 1940. The 75(NZ) Squadron contingent of eight Wellingtons took off between 19.45 and 20.40, with S/Ls Kain and Southwell the senior pilots on duty and made their way across the North Sea in good weather conditions. Searchlights were very much in evidence over enemy territory, and the flak from Bremen to Hamburg was intense and accurate. P/O Kimberley's L7818 AA-R was badly beaten-up in the Bremen area and he dropped his bombs hurriedly in order to escape the unwanted attention. The others reported bombing within three miles of the aiming point and observing a number of fires that were visible for up to twenty minutes into the return journey. The general consensus among returning crews was of an effective raid, which local sources and post-raid reconnaissance confirmed had inflicted further damage to the main office block and two occupied U-Boot slipways at the Blohm & Voss shipyards. The raid also caused 119 fires in Hamburg generally, thirty-five of them classed as large.

Before the next operation took place, F/L Malcolm MacFarlane was posted to the Polish 18 O.T.U at Bramcote, near Nuneaton in Warwickshire, where he would join up again with F/L John Morton, who had departed the squadron a week earlier, also to take up instructional duties. Just five crews were called to briefing on the 15th, when they learned that they were to participate in a small-scale raid on a construction site on the Keroman Peninsula at Lorient. The first phase of the massive construction project had begun just weeks earlier, and would continue until January 1942, by which time K1, K2 and K3 would be completed and capable of sheltering thirty vessels and their crews under cover. The complex would boast a revolutionary lift system, which could raise U-Boots from the water and transport them across the facility to repair and servicing bays. The thickness of the concrete would render the structure impervious to the bombs available to Bomber Command at the time, and the purpose of the attacks was to destroy the town and its approaches to prevent access by road and rail, while extensive minelaying compromised access by sea. The 75(NZ) Squadron participants took off between 18.45 and 19.00 led by S/L Kain and reached the target to find clear skies but ground haze, which prevented all but one crew from assessing the outcome. Returning crews were met by fog over their stations in northern and eastern England and were diverted to the west country to land either at St Eval in Cornwall or at Boscombe Down in Wiltshire.

The squadron made ready eleven Wellingtons on the 18th, nine to attack the port of Kiel and two to carry freshman crews to bomb the oil storage tanks at Rotterdam. S/Ls Kain and Southwell were the senior pilots on duty as they departed Feltwell between 19.30 and 20.00, with the Rotterdam-bound freshman crews of P/O Frank Albert Andrews RNZAF and Sgt Phillip Ronald 'Pip' Coney RNZAF among the first to take off. Cloud over the Baltic coast forced some to bomb on e.t.a., but most seemed to identify the docks area and contributed to a very successful attack, which local reports claimed to be the most destructive thus far. Particular damage was inflicted upon the Deutsche Werke U-Boot yard, and the town centre also attracted many bombs. On return, T2736 AA-A ran short of fuel after F/O Collins had apparently become lost, and was abandoned over Yorkshire, ultimately crashing at Ryhill, some fifteen miles north of Sheffield. The parachute of wireless operator Sgt Daniel Gilmore RAFVR failed to deploy, and he was killed, while his crew colleagues came safely to earth.

S/L Reuben Pears Widdowson RAF was posted to the squadron from 11 O.T.U at Bassingbourn during the week ending Friday the 22nd, and he immediately took over command of B Flight as successor to S/L Kain, who was posted to 21 O.T.U at Moreton-in-Marsh. Kain was to serve later in the war as a flight commander with 487(NZ) Squadron of the 2nd Tactical Air Force (Mosquitos), where he teamed up with the other flight commander, "Popeye" Lucas. S/L "Ben" Widdowson was from Winnipeg in Canada, where he had learned to fly at Winnipeg Flying Club. He joined the RAF in 1934 and had served with No.2 (AC) Squadron on the North-West Frontier and later at No.1 OTU, RAF Silloth. Three crews were detailed for operations on the night of the 21/22nd, two to attack the Keroman U-Boot construction site at Lorient and one the docks at Ostend. Sgt Coney took off at 18.45 and freshman Sgt David Leo Nola RNZAF at 23.50, and we are not provided with information on the third crew involved or to which of the targets each was assigned. We are told that one crew bombed searchlights and a flak battery at Boulogne, another delivered its load onto the west bank of the river, and the third observed no results.

A force of sixty-three Wellingtons and Whitleys set out for Berlin on the evening of the 23rd, six of the former provided by 75(NZ) Squadron. No senior officers were on duty as they got away between 19.30 and 19.50 and headed towards a target shrouded in eight to ten-tenths cloud. Attacks were carried out and some explosions and fires were observed to be reflected in the clouds, but returning crews were unable to offer an assessment of the results.

Cologne and Düsseldorf were the destinations for small forces on the night of the 27/28th and 75(NZ) Squadron contributed eight to the raid on the former and a single freshman for Dunkerque. S/L Widdowson was the senior pilot on duty but flying on this occasion as "second dickey" to Sgt Kilsby. They took off between 19.45 and 19.55, and the fact that F/L Peter Gordon Frank Fletcher RAFVR departed last at 20.20, suggests that he and his crew may have been Dunkerque-bound. F/L Fletcher had arrived on the 16th from 115 Squadron at Marham, which he had joined on posting from Bramcote just three weeks previously and had flown a single operation as a second pilot. The main effort was hampered by cloud, haze and searchlight glare and most crews could only bomb in the general target area. No results were observed, and although some photographs were taken, they proved to be of Düsseldorf. The bombing at Dunkerque appeared to be on the mark and caused two fires. S/L Widdowson operated as crew captain with the squadron for the first time on the evening of the 30th, after being assigned as the sole representative of the squadron and the group for an attack on the docks and shipping at Calais. He took off at 20.00 and reached the target area to find good conditions with five to seven-tenths cloud and fairly heavy but inaccurate flak. He was back home a little over three hours after take-off, having dropped his 500 pounders and incendiaries in the target area.

On the 29th, the German cruisers Scharnhorst and Gneisenau were reported to be off Brest, and by the following morning had taken up residence. This was to be the start of a protracted and distracting ten-month saga, which would cost the Command dearly in crews and effort for precious little return. The first operation of the campaign against Brest and its lodgers, which would sometimes include Prinz Eugen, was carried out by over a hundred aircraft on the night of the 30/31st in the absence of 75(NZ) Squadron, and no hits were scored. The freshman crews of F/Os Cecil McKenzie Hill RAFVR and Graham Noel Parker RAF carried out the squadron's final sorties of the month on the evening of the 31st, when the oil storage tanks at Rotterdam were the target. They took off at 19.45 and reached their destination to find cloud, which prevented F/O Hill from identifying the aiming point. He jettisoned his bombs into the sea, while F/O Parker carried out an attack, but was unable to observe the results.

During the course of the month the squadron operated against fifteen targets and dispatched seventy-two sorties for the loss of one Wellington.

April 1941

The first week of the new month was reserved exclusively for operations on and around Brest with the intention of disabling its lodgers. Scharnhorst and Gneisenau were dubbed in the British press as Salmon & Gluckstein, in a comic reference to the country's largest tobacconist, established in 1873 by a German Jewish émigré and his English partner. The assault on Brest began with 5 Group launching a dozen Hampdens from St Eval in Cornwall for a daylight attack on the 1st, when all but one turned back in the absence of cloud.

Brest opened 75(NZ) Squadron's April account on the night of the 3/4th, when eight Wellingtons were dispatched as part of a force of ninety aircraft of assorted types. They took off between 18.30 and 19.15 with F/L Fletcher the senior pilot on duty and reached the target area to find nine to ten-tenths cloud, which prevented most crews from identifying the aiming point. Sgt Kilsby, P/O Matheson, F/O Hill and F/L Fletcher all delivered their bombs but saw no results, while P/O Andrews observed his to explode in the vicinity of the docks. P/O Simich reported jettisoning his bombs "live" in a salvo after a distributor froze up, and he watched them burst on the dockside close to the water. F/O Parker decided to bring his bombs home after failing to find a gap in the clouds, while F/O Dave Prichard and crew became involved in a fight for their lives. They had bombed successfully and were on their way home at 12,000 feet, when they spotted a Me110 flying 300 feet below and tracked it for five minutes before it came up to attack them. Rear gunner, F/O William Davenport Brown RNZAF shot it down in flames with three bursts, for which he would receive the immediate award of a DFC. Brown, from Wanganui, was the squadron gunnery leader and had already distinguished himself in February by fighting off a German intruder near Marham when flying with P/O Duncan McArthur. Coming back in over the English coast they next experienced heavy AA fire from the naval base at Portland Bill, from which they escaped, but that was not the end of their problems. Their Wellington, R1161 AA-W, was involved in a mid-air collision with a Blenheim travelling in the opposite direction and sustained severe damage, which culminated in a forced-landing at Boscombe Down. The crew walked away and the Wellington was eventually returned to flying condition and shipped off to 311 (Czech) Squadron. The only Blenheim failing to return from this operation was N3552, which was lost without trace with the crew of 101 Squadron's commanding officer, W/C Addenbrooke. While it can never be proved, it seems highly likely that this was the other aircraft involved in the collision.

On the 4th, Gneisenau entered a dry dock, which was to be drained on the following day for an inspection of the vessel. In the meantime, a force of fifty-four aircraft carried out an attack on the cruisers that night, some of the 5 Group Hampdens from low level, and one went in at 1,000 feet at 22.55 to score a direct hit on Scharnhorst, which was recognised in the flash as being in a dry dock precisely as depicted in the reconnaissance photos shown to the crews at briefing. The rear gunner confirmed the success, but it was impossible to determine which part of the vessel had been hit. Another of the low-level attackers was the 106 Squadron commanding officer, W/C Polglase, whose Hampden was seen to be shot down. The Continental Hotel in the town was also struck by bombs just as dinner was being served, and a number of naval officers were killed. When Gneisenau's dry dock was drained on the following day, the 5th, a single unexploded 500lb bomb was found nestling at the bottom, and the ship's captain, Kapitän-zur-See Otto Fein, decided to move his vessel out into the harbour while it was dealt with. The dock was refilled to allow Gneisenau to vacate it and she was spotted by a reconnaissance aircraft at some point, which led to the planning of an operation by Coastal Command to be carried out at first light on the 6th. The Coastal Command operation took place in poor weather conditions, which led to the six Beauforts becoming separated while outbound and F/O Kenneth Campbell and his crew alone pressed home an attack, which caused damage to Gneisenau that would require six months to repair. In the face of the most concentrated anti-aircraft fire, the Beaufort stood little chance of getting away with it and was shot down without survivors. F/O Campbell was posthumously awarded a Victoria Cross for his actions.

Ten of the squadron's Wellingtons were made ready for a return to Brest later that night as part of an overall force of seventy-one aircraft. They took off between 19.45 and 20.40 with S/Ls Southwell and Widdowson the senior pilots on duty and reached the target area to find ten-tenths cloud. Eight crews failed to locate the target and just two bombed on estimated position and the flashes from flak batteries.

In contrast, the weather conditions over north-western Germany on the night of the 7/8th were ideal for bombing operations, with clear skies and bright moonlight laying bare the port of Kiel. A force of 229 aircraft was made ready, 110 provided by 3 Group, which represented the largest effort yet sent against a single target. 75(NZ) Squadron briefed eleven crews, who departed Feltwell between 20.20 and 23.00 with S/L Widdowson the senior pilot on duty. The spread of take-off times reflected the fact that the bombing would be conducted over a five-hour period, which was common practice at this stage of the war for such a large-scale operation. They set course for Rømø Island on Denmark's western coast, where they would turn east to a position north of Flensburg to approach Kiel from the north. They encountered cloud at 6,000 feet for the first fifty miles of the North Sea crossing and benefitted from clear skies for the remainder of the outward flight, reaching the enemy coast at around 10,000 feet before traversing the Schleswig-Holstein peninsula and arriving in the target area to find the defences had already been stirred into action. The bright moonlight helped to tone down the glare from dozens of searchlights co-operating with medium calibre flak batteries that were hosing shells up to 12,000 feet, while heavy flak reached as high as 18,000 feet and the light stuff awaited any crew foolhardy enough to try to sneak in lower down. The Feltwell crews reached the target area and benefitted from the excellent conditions to deliver their bombs and incendiaries into the docks area and the town, and observed explosions and fires. Returning crews were confident in the effectiveness of the attack, and it was established later that much housing had been destroyed and particular damage had been inflicted upon the eastern docks area, where the Deutsche Werke and Krupp Germania Werft U-Boot yards lost a number of days' production.

A force of 160 aircraft was made ready during the following day to return to Kiel that night, and among them were sixty Wellingtons and a Stirling representing 3 Group but none from 75(NZ) Squadron. Returning crews reported a very large explosion that was followed by a column of black smoke and described the target area as a mass of flames as they retreated to the west. Local sources confirmed another damaging raid, which had fallen more into the town than the docks and seafront area and some eight thousand people had been bombed out of their homes.

Berlin was the target for a force of eighty aircraft on the night of the 9/10th, for which 3 Group detailed thirty-six Wellingtons and 3 Stirlings, nine of the former provided by 75(NZ) Squadron. They took off between 20.05 and 20.30 with F/L Fletcher the senior pilot on duty, and made their way into Germany via northern Holland, where intense searchlight and flak activity greeted the bombers at the frontier and a number were seen to be shot down. The weather conditions outbound and over the target were excellent, allowing crews to pick out other aircraft up to half a mile away. All from the squadron reached the target to carry out their attacks, P/O Simich observing his incendiaries to burn close to a railway line in the Charlottenburg district to the west. P/O Andrews bombed an aerodrome sixteen miles west of the city and F/O Prichard attacked a railway station in the north, but the others were unable to pinpoint the fall of their bombs. P/O Matheson brought back a photograph of Tempelhof aerodrome to the south of the city centre. He and his navigator, P/O Eric Fowler, were awarded an immediate DFC each for making a second run over the target to deliver their load, despite having sustained flak damage.

Brest had been targeted by elements of the Command on the nights of the 10/11th and 12/13th, and four bombs had struck Gneisenau on the former occasion, killing fifty men and injuring ninety. Ninety-four aircraft were made ready for another assault on the port on the night of the 14/15th, for which operation 3 Group provided thirty-six Wellingtons and three Stirlings, ten of the former belonging to 75(NZ) Squadron. They departed Feltwell between 21.35 and 22.30 with S/Ls Southwell and Widdowson the senior pilots on duty and headed for the French coast in fine weather conditions. Having found a thin layer of cloud hanging over the target, they all delivered their bombs into the general docks area, but few observed results in the face of intense searchlight and flak activity. A post-raid analysis would blame low cloud for an ineffective attack, but the experiences of some crews from other squadrons cast doubt on that assessment as they reported that the weather had cleared as the target drew near. Even though they could not identify the cruisers, they saw enough detail to enable them to dive through the flak to release their bombs.

The squadron was not included in a 3 Group contribution of thirty-nine aircraft detailed on the 15th for a return to Kiel as part of a force of ninety-six aircraft, which failed to produce an effective attack in the face of heavy cloud.

The Command returned to north-western Germany on the night of the 16/17th with a force of 107 aircraft bound for Bremen, almost half of them representing 3 Group. 75(NZ) Squadron made ready ten Wellingtons, which took off between 20.25 and 20.50 with F/L Fletcher and the newly-promoted F/L Gill the senior pilots on duty and Sgt Robert Ewen Ernest "Bob" Fotheringham RNZAF flying his first sortie as captain of his own crew. They reached the target area to find thin layers of cloud and haze obscuring the ground, which prevented both F/Ls Fletcher and Gill from identifying the target. The former brought his bombs home, while the latter dumped his on the centre of Hamburg without observing the outcome. The others carried out their attacks in the face of a spirited searchlight and flak defence and returned safely, mostly unable to offer an assessment of the results. 3 Group had been sending Photo Reconnaissance Unit (PRU) Wellingtons on recent raids and one failed to return from this one.

Berlin provided the objectives again on the night of the 17/18th, when a force of 118 aircraft was assembled, of which seven Wellingtons were provided by 75(NZ) Squadron. S/L Southwell was the senior pilot on duty as the Kiwi element departed Feltwell between 20.35 and 21.00 and made their way out over heavy cloud. Ground haze in the target area presented the usual difficulties and although all from the squadron found the target area, neither of the two aiming points, including the telephone exchange, could be identified. This was of no consequence as the purpose of the raid was to inflict as much damage as possible on the city centre and only S/L Southwell specified a location for his incendiaries on the outskirts of the city. On return, a damaged R1458 AA-E was landed at Ternhill by P/O Simich, who had P/O Ashworth beside him as second pilot. The Wellington overshot the runway because of an error in laying out only three hundred yards of flare-path (in the wrong direction) and ended up in a barbed-wire fence. The crew emerged unscathed and the Wellington, which sustained only slight damage, was soon returned to active duty. Twenty-four-year-old Auckland-born "Ron" Simich was later awarded a DFC, in part for his courage and skill during this operation.

P/O Graham Wellesley Hamlin and Sgt Ian Laurie Reid (both RNZAF) were dispatched at 20.35 and 20.45 respectively on freshman sorties to bomb oil storage tanks in Rotterdam on the evening of the 20th. The former reported three dull, red fires, suggesting that at least one bomb had found the mark, while the latter brought his bombs home. The squadron briefed twelve crews on the 24th, nine for an operation that night against Kiel, and three freshmen (the newest, P/O George William Curry, RAFVR) for Ostend. In the event, three crews failed to take off because of technical failures, and this left seven Wellingtons to depart for Kiel between 20.30 and 20.50 with S/L Widdowson the senior pilot on duty. These would be on their way home by the time that P/Os Hamlin and Curry left Feltwell at 00.20 and 01.00 respectively, bound for Ostend. S/L Widdowson returned a little over three hours after take-off, after his wireless operator had been found unconscious, and a number of other crews would also bring their bombs home. Those carrying out an attack returned to report bomb bursts and fires, but could offer no detailed assessment, while local reports described a scattered attack and little resultant damage. P/O Curry failed to locate Ostend, and although P/O Hamlin enjoyed greater success, he was unable to observe the fall of his bombs.

The squadron operated for the final time in the month on the night of the 29/30th, when Mannheim was the target for nine crews, while P/Os Curry, Hamlin and Alan Murray Hobbs RNZAF continued their freshman introduction programme at Rotterdam. The main element took off between 20.30 and 21.00 with F/Ls Fletcher and Gill the senior pilots on duty as part of an overall force of seventy-one aircraft, which experienced good weather conditions outbound but encountered ground haze at Mannheim. This, presumably, accounted for the poor bombing performance, which managed to deposit only fifteen bomb loads in the entire area of Mannheim and its neighbour Ludwigshafen on the other side of the Rhine, and destroy a total of four houses. F/L Fletcher brought his bombs back, while two other crews bombed flare-paths at Schiphol and Haamstede as alternatives. The freshman crews took off between 23.00 and 23.10 and carried out their attacks in the face of searchlights and flak, observing the burst of a number of incendiaries but no other results.

During the course of the month the squadron operated against twelve targets, dispatching eighty-eight sorties without loss.

May 1941

Germany's second city, Hamburg, would feature prominently during the first half of the new month and the Rhineland capital, Cologne, would also receive frequent visits mostly in the second half. The new month began with the posting of an operation to Hamburg on the 1st, but this was subsequently cancelled, only to be reinstated on the following day and a force of ninety-five aircraft assembled. Hamburg and Emden provided the destinations for thirteen 75(NZ) Squadron Wellingtons on this night, ten for the former and three for the latter. Those assigned to Emden, S/L Widdowson and P/Os Curry and Hobbs, took off first between 20.40 and 21.00, to be followed into the air over the ensuing thirty minutes by the main element, of which F/L Gill was the senior pilot on duty. The weather conditions were good for the outward flight and visibility in the target areas was conducive to accurate bombing, although S/L Widdowson reported Emden to be obscured, forcing him to seek an alternative recipient for his bombs. The Luftwaffe night-fighter aerodrome at Leeuwarden lay on his route home over northern Holland, and a large explosion followed the bursting upon it of his incendiaries. P/O Hobbs reported his bombs falling into the town of Emden and the incendiaries setting off a fire, while P/O Curry claimed that his load, all except for a hung-up 500 pounder, fell onto a railway bridge. The Hamburg contingent all bombed within the target area, where the searchlights were organised in stationary cones, and then returned safely to report a successful operation. Local reports described twenty-six fires, half of them large, but no serious incidents.

The squadron sat out the first attack of the month on Cologne on the night of the 3/4th, but thirteen crews attended briefing on the 4th for another assault on Brest that night. A force of ninety-seven aircraft was made ready, forty-four of them representing 3 Group, and the Feltwell departures were accomplished safely between 21.45 and 22.20 with S/L Widdowson the senior pilot on duty. Each was carrying a 2,000 pounder along with 500 and 250 pounders and all were delivered within the target area, some crews claiming to have hit the dry dock in which Gneisenau was under repair. Two crews reported straddling one of the ships and P/O Curry dared to believe that he may have scored a direct hit, as did returning crews from other squadrons, but no damage to the cruisers was confirmed.

The teleprinters on 1, 3, 4 and 5 Group stations began churning out the orders of the day on the 5th, to reveal that Mannheim was to be the destination that night for a force of 141 aircraft in the absence of 75(NZ) Squadron. The outward flight was attended by ten-tenths cloud, which persisted in the target area, and despite the claim by 121 crews that they had attacked the city, local sources reported some twenty-five bomb loads falling and causing only minor damage. It was back to Hamburg for a force of 115 aircraft on the 6th including ten Kiwi Wellingtons. They took off between 22.10 and 22.35 with S/L Widdowson the senior pilot on duty and reached the target to find complete cloud cover that persuaded many crews from other squadrons to seek alternative objectives. The 75(NZ) Squadron crews all delivered their bombs over Hamburg but had no idea what happened to them after they disappeared into the cloud, and local reports would confirm this raid as a wasted effort. It was always particularly tragic when death came to a crew after having completed its assigned task and returned to friendly airspace. R3169, Popeye's old Wimpey, since re-coded AA-O, collided with a balloon cable at the mouth of the Humber and dived into the water, and only the rear gunner, Sgt Craven RAF, survived from the crew of Sgt Nola RNZAF. Second pilot Sgt Alexander Coutts Mee RNZAF had baled out over Yorkshire only six weeks earlier when T2736 AA-A became lost on return from a raid on Kiel. Happily, and perhaps, remarkably, it would be a further two months before the Grim Reaper returned to the squadron.

On the 8th, S/L John Southwell was rewarded for his excellent service with a posting across the tarmac to 57 Squadron and promotion to wing commander rank to take command. In June 1942, he would occupy a similar position at 9 Squadron and see it through its posting to 5 Group and conversion from Wellingtons to Lancasters. Hamburg was earmarked to receive further attention that night and a force of 188 aircraft was made ready, 119 of them assigned to the Blohm & Voss shipyards and sixty-nine to target the city, while 133 Whitleys and Wellingtons attended to the A G Weser U-Boot construction yards in Bremen. Support and minor operations were also planned and raised the number of sorties to a new record in a single night of 364. A dozen of the Hamburg-bound Wellingtons were provided by 75(NZ) Squadron, and they took off between 22.00 and 22.55 with S/L Widdowson the senior pilot on duty. His sortie was curtailed by an unserviceable rear turret, however, and he brought his bombs home. F/L Fletcher attacked the docks at Den Helder in Holland as an alternative and observed the bombs burst, before returning to land shortly after 02.00. The others pressed on to find the target in good visibility under clear skies and carried out their attacks based on a visual identification of the aiming point. Many fires were observed, and all returned safely to Feltwell to report a successful operation. Local reports confirmed an effective raid, which caused eighty-three fires, thirty-eight of them classed as large, and resulted in 185 fatalities, the highest death toll to date from a Bomber Command attack.

Twenty-four hours later, attention shifted to southern Germany and the twin cities of Mannheim and Ludwigshafen, facing each other on the east and west banks respectively of the Rhine. The aiming point for the 5 Group element was the Badische Anilin & Soda-Fabrik (BASF) works in Ludwigshafen, which was part of the infamous I G Farben company, the largest manufacturer of chemicals and synthetic oil products in the world and major employer of slave workers. A dozen 75(NZ) Squadron Wellingtons departed Feltwell between 22.05 and 23.00 with S/L Widdowson the senior pilot on duty, and this time all reached the target area to encounter fine weather conditions and good visibility. This, and the modest searchlight and flak response enabled the crews to carry out their bombing runs with precision and all returned safely to report hitting the target and starting fires or adding to those already burning. The catalogue of damage included military, industrial, commercial and residential buildings on both sides of the river, and 3,500 people were bombed out of their homes. P/O Andrews and crew had a heart-stopping moment when both engines failed over the target, probably due to iced-up carburettor air intakes, but they were eventually able to re-start them after gliding down to 3,000 feet.

Hamburg was posted to face its fourth major operation of the month on the 10th, for which a force of 119 aircraft was assembled and the crews briefed to aim for shipyards, the Altona power station (Tiefstack) and the general city area. Returning crews were enthusiastic about the outcome, and local sources confirmed that 128 fires had broken out, forty-seven of them classed as large, with extensive damage resulting in the city centre. 75(NZ) Squadron was not involved but was called into action on the 11th, when Hamburg and Bremen were back in the bomb sights to face forces of ninety-two and eighty-one aircraft respectively. It was for the former that eleven 75(NZ) Squadron crews were briefed and S/L Widdowson was the senior pilot on duty as they took off between 22.20 and 23.20 to make their way out over the Norfolk coast in the continuing favourable weather conditions. As S/L Widdowson began the North Sea crossing, his Wellington, R1589, was fired upon by an unseen assailant at 4,000 feet and the rear gunner, Sgt Eric Francis "Pete" Gannaway RNZAF, was fatally wounded. The aircraft sustained severe damage but landed safely back at base after the bombs had been jettisoned in the sea. The others pushed on to the target, where the Kuhwerder-located Blohm & Voss shipyard was the assigned aiming point, and they were greeted by cones of searchlights and intense flak. Apart from ground haze, conditions for an attack were excellent and all delivered their mixed loads of HE and incendiaries before returning safely home to report a successful raid. This was confirmed by local reports, which mentioned eighty-eight fires, twenty-six of them large, although mostly in residential rather than industrial districts.

The squadron remained on the ground when operations were mounted against Mannheim, Ludwigshafen and Hannover and the month's other principal target, Cologne, on the nights of the 12/13th, 15/16th and 16/17th respectively, and not one of them was concluded successfully. Fourteen 75(NZ) Squadron crews attended briefings on the 17th, thirteen in preparation for another attack on Cologne as part of an overall force of ninety-five aircraft, while the single freshman crew of Sgt Jack Joll RNZAF was assigned to the docks at Boulogne. They departed Feltwell between 22.20 and 23.05 with S/L Widdowson continuing to lead from the front and made their way across the Channel to enter enemy territory via the Belgian coast, Sgt Joll having already peeled off to the south-west. F/O Hill was forced to turn back with a turret issue, and he returned his bombs to store. The others pressed on in fair weather conditions and found the city to be covered by ground haze and protected by intense searchlight and flak activity. In the absence of a moon to diffuse the searchlight glare, the crews found it difficult to pick out ground detail, but all bombed within the city, some observing bursts and others not. Local reports spoke of widely scattered bombing with a little concentration in southern districts, but no major incidents.

Before the next operation, F/O Hill was promoted to flight lieutenant rank and tour-expired P/O Ron Simich was posted to 18 O.T.U at Bramcote, where he would use his skill and experience to train Polish pilots. A year hence he would begin a second tour of operations flying Stirlings with 214 Squadron and would fail to return from Hamburg on the night of the 26/27th of July 1942. Happily, he and his crew all survived as PoWs, but sadly, Ron would lose his life in a flying accident with 75(NZ) Squadron back home in New Zealand in 1947.

After almost a week away from the operational scene, ten of the squadron's crews, including freshman, P/O William Jeffrey Rees RAF, were called to briefing on the 23rd to learn of the next assault on Cologne planned for that night. It should be noted that at this point of the war, "freshmen" had usually already flown ten operations as second pilot with an experienced captain. F/L Frank Gill was the senior pilot on duty as they took-off between 23.55 and 00.30 and headed for the Belgian coast as part of a 3 and 5 Group effort of fifty-one aircraft. A cone of twenty-two searchlights greeted their arrival over Dunkerque, where Sgt Reid chose to drop his bombs on docks 4, 5 and 6. The others reached Cologne to find some cloud and generally poor visibility, which led to scattered bombing and a disappointing outcome. The ORB states that no enemy aircraft were encountered, however, according to two logbooks, F/O "Darkie" Parker's crew in R1038 AA-H claimed a "probable" kill, after rear gunner, Sgt Alec Rowe RNZAF, fired at an attacking fighter, which was seen to go down in flames.

S/L F.J. "Popeye" Lucas returned to the squadron during the week, after spending seven months at the BAT Flight and 15 O.T.U at Hampstead Norris, a satellite of Harwell, and he succeeded S/L Southwell as A Flight commander. News came through on the morning of the 27th that the mighty battleship Bismarck had been sunk by elements of the Royal Navy in the North Atlantic following an epic chase. It had begun when she and the heavy cruiser, Prinz Eugen, had put to sea on operation "Rheinübung", which for Bismarck would be her first offensive action. They were being shadowed by Coastal Command aircraft as they slipped out of Bergen, heading for the Denmark Straits between Greenland and Iceland, where, on the 24th, the pride of the Royal Navy, HMS Hood, was blown out of the water with the loss of all but three of her crew. The Hipper class cruiser Prinz Eugen separated from Bismarck to create a diversion as Bismarck attempted to reach the safety of Brest, but her position was discovered and a torpedo delivered by a Fleet Air Arm Swordfish on the 26th jammed her rudder, rendering her unable to manoeuvre and restricted to a top speed of ten knots. At first light on the 27th, multiple units of the Royal Navy closed in on the helpless Bismarck and from 08.47, engaged her with guns and torpedoes until she slipped beneath the waves at 10.39.

Earlier, at 06.45, Sgt Reid and crew had taken off in the first of a dozen 75(NZ) Squadron Wellingtons, which were to join fifty-two other aircraft from the group to look for Prinz Eugen. S/L Widdowson was the senior pilot on duty in what turned out to be a fruitless search in unhelpful weather conditions, during which, crews spent up to two hours in the search area. All would return safely home, despite encountering many enemy aircraft sent out to protect the vessel. Two separate formations, one led by F/L Gill and the other by F/L Fletcher, were attacked by Arado seaplanes, as a result of which several Wellingtons sustained damage. The squadron ORB records the last aircraft, that of P/O Hamlin, landing at 19.20, after spending twelve hours and fifteen minutes in the air.

This was the final operation of the month, during which eleven targets had been attacked and 107 sorties dispatched for the loss of a single Wellington and all but one of its crew.

June 1941

June and July were to be significant months for the Command, as its performance began to be monitored in order to provide an assessment of its effectiveness for the War Cabinet. The project was initiated by Churchill's chief scientific advisor, Lord Cherwell, who handed the responsibility to David M Bensusan-Butt, a civil-servant assistant to Cherwell working in the War Cabinet Secretariat. During the month, Cologne would share top billing with Düsseldorf, and during the second half of the month no fewer than nine simultaneous raids would be directed at these important industrial cities.

The new month began operationally with the assembly of a force of 150 aircraft on the 2nd, the crews of which were briefed for Düsseldorf. Just three Wellingtons were detailed from 75(NZ) Squadron, those containing the crews of F/L Fletcher, first-time skipper P/O James Williamson Thomson RNZAF and Sgt Joll, and they departed Feltwell at 23.30 on a night of cloudy conditions. All three reached the target area, where they delivered their 500 and 250 pounders into the cloud on estimated positions and had no clue as to the results of their efforts, although a local report described a light raid with scattered, slight damage. There was no further operational activity for the squadron until the night of the 10/11th, when a force of 104 aircraft was made ready to attack Brest and its lodgers, which now included Prinz Eugen. Twelve 75(NZ) Squadron crews were invited to take part and they took off between midnight and 00.55 with S/L Widdowson the senior pilot on duty. The weather conditions outbound and over the target were fine, but ground haze combined with an effective smoke screen to obscure the aiming point, and although all delivered their bombs into the target area, no results were observed. It was established later that many bombs had fallen into the docks but had failed to score direct hits on the vessels.

The Ruhr cities of Düsseldorf and Duisburg provided the main targets for the night of the 11/12th, for which forces of ninety-two and eighty aircraft respectively were made ready. The squadron briefed three crews for the former and two freshmen for Boulogne and they took off together between 23.31 and 23.45 with S/L Lucas the senior pilot on duty and undertaking the first sortie of his second tour. The weather conditions were fine at both locations, which were only fifteen miles apart, but a layer of cloud obscured the ground and the bombing lacked precision. S/L Lucas had always favoured attacking a target from fairly low level, but tactics had moved on during his absence from the operational scene and low-level bombing was now considered to be too dangerous. Much to the discomfort of his crew on this night, he chose to carry out his attack at Düsseldorf from 8,000 feet and actually made three runs, the first resulting in an overshoot, the second to drop the bombs and the third to photograph his work. A chunk of flak passed through the cockpit, narrowly missing his head, and other pieces of shrapnel hit the port engine and shredded the fuselage, causing damage to the undercarriage and hydraulics system and holing a fuel tank. The wounded Wellington had sunk to 500 feet by the time the North Sea came into view, but somehow, made it over the water to reach the Feltwell circuit, now flying on fumes and the undercarriage having been hand-cranked down. They found Feltwell closed because of bomb damage, and Lucas had to coax R1177 AA-C the fifteen miles to Newmarket, only for his starboard engine to cut as he lined up on the runway. He was ordered to stand off and queue, while a damaged Stirling was brought in, but ignored the instruction and touched down to one side of the grass track. A maintenance team from Feltwell counted thirty-four holes and declared the Wellington a write-off, despite which, it would be returned to service. The other squadron participants in the night's operations returned safely to report explosions and fires, but otherwise an indeterminate outcome.

The following night brought a concerted effort against marshalling yards at Soest, Osnabrück and Hamm to the north of the Ruhr and Schwerte on its south-eastern rim, and it was to Hamm that the squadron dispatched ten Wellingtons. They departed Feltwell between 22.50 and 23.40 with S/L Widdowson the senior pilot on duty and made their way out to the Norfolk coast. It was shortly afterwards that one crew, believed to be that of P/O Parker, ran into three enemy fighters some fifty miles out from Southwold. The rear gunner claimed one as shot down, and although the remaining two gave chase, they were evaded and the journey to the target continued with landfall on the Dutch coast and a course skirting round the northern edge of the Ruhr to reach one of the most important railway hubs in Germany. P/O Curry reported large fires at the eastern and western ends of the yards, while the others could only report bombing in the general target area in the face of heavy and light flak and searchlights operating in cones. A local report described a few bombs in the town, but no serious damage.

The first of the simultaneous Cologne/Düsseldorf operations took place on the night of the 15/16th, but both were moderate efforts employing forces of forty-nine and thirty-one aircraft respectively. 75(NZ) Squadron's contribution amounted to two Wellingtons for Cologne, while two others were sent to bomb the docks and shipping at Dunkerque. They took off at 23.15 and climbed into ten-tenths cloud, which would remain in place all the way to the targets. P/O Thomson turned back with intercom failure before reaching Dunkerque, while first-time skipper, Sgt Francis Charles "Frankie" Fox RNZAF, arrived over the port to be thwarted by the cloud, and he also brought his bombs home. The aiming point for the Cologne force was the Gereon marshalling yards on the west bank of the Rhine, and although Sgts Breckon and Joll found the general target area and delivered their bombs, the latter did so on e.t.a. and the flashes from flak positions and had no idea where they fell. First-time captain, Sgt Ivan Oswald Breckon, RNZAF, was the younger brother of squadron founder-member, S/L Aubrey Breckon. The operation was a complete failure and would be one of many ineffective raids carried out over the summer months.

Cologne and Düsseldorf were "on" again twenty-four hours later, when the squadron dispatched a new record of fifteen Wellingtons, fourteen as part of the all-3 Group force of seventy-two aircraft assigned to the latter, and a freshman, Sgt Frederick Thomas Miniken RAFVR and crew, for the docks and shipping at Boulogne. They departed Feltwell between 23.05 and 23.50 with S/L Widdowson the senior pilot on duty, and all fourteen reached Düsseldorf to find poor visibility. Many were able to pinpoint on the River Rhine and make a timed run to the target, before returning home to report simply that their bombs had burst in the target area. The exceptions were Sgts Fotheringham and Joll, who specified a railway station on the west side of the target and marshalling yards in the same area. T2835 AA-C was attacked and badly shot-up by what was believed to be a Ju88 in the Antwerp area on the way home, but although some of F/O Thomson's crew picked up bullet holes in their clothing, none sustained injury and the assailant turned away sharply and disappeared after receiving return fire from the Wellington's rear turret. Returning crews reported scant flak activity, which one station commander found to be suspicious and questioned whether a dummy fire had attracted the bombs. Local reports, suggesting that only two heavy bombs had found their way into a southern suburb, would seem to support this view.

A new record was set by the squadron on the 18th, when dispatching seventeen Wellingtons to Brest for another tilt at the enemy warships. For the second operation running, Feltwell would launch thirty Wellingtons without a single take-off failure or early return. S/L Widdowson continued to lead from the front as they departed between 22.25 and 22.55 to rendezvous with the rest of the all-3 Group force of sixty-five aircraft. For P/O Clive Walter Scott, RNZAF, this was the first operation as captain of his own crew. All reached the target area to encounter a combination of ground haze and an effective smoke-screen, which prevented most crews from identifying the briefed aiming point of the Scharnhorst and led to the general bombing of the docks, which P/O Rees reported attacking in a dive. P/O Ashworth dropped flares to aid his search and made eight low-level runs across the target during a seventy-five-minute period, establishing in the process that Scharnhorst was not berthed where the raid planners had asserted. He ultimately delivered a stick of seven bombs through the smoke, aimed at a 10,000-ton vessel seen entering port, and believed the first one struck it as it passed between the east and south jetties. For his determination and perseverance on this night, "Artie" Ashworth, who had inherited the Southwell crew, would be awarded a well-deserved DFC. Sgt Miniken experienced a bomb-release system failure and brought his bombs home, while F/O Parker was forced to land at Boscombe Down after R1038 AA-H was hit by flak and lost the use of its starboard engine.

Fifteen Wellingtons were made ready on the 21st for operations that night against Cologne and Dunkerque, while elements of 4 and 5 Groups attended to Düsseldorf. Eleven crews were briefed for Cologne, with F/Ls Fletcher and Gill the senior pilots on duty, while P/Os Curry, Scott and Thomson and Sgt Breckon were assigned to the Belgian port, and all took off together between 23.10 and 00.16. The weather outbound was fine but cloud and ground haze over Cologne provided difficult conditions for bombing, and despite the claims of some crews to have identified ground features, most dropped their loads on estimated positions. Precisely where they fell is uncertain, but local reports recorded no bombs within the city boundaries and just a few in villages to the west. P/O Ashworth's Wellington was hit by flak, which caused damage to its geodetics and a fuel pump. The Dunkerque element seemed to fare better, although Sgt Breckon simply stated that he had bombed the target. P/O Thomson delivered a stick across the docks, P/O Scott claimed that a fire started in an oil tank two minutes after his bombs burst and P/O Curry confirmed the blazing oil tank after dropping his bombs onto the docks nearby.

Yet another new record was set by the squadron on the night of the 24/25th, when dispatching eighteen Wellingtons, ten to Kiel and eight to Düsseldorf. They were given a VIP send-off by the His Royal Highness the Duke of Kent, who visited the station that evening and met several of the crews. The Kiel element took off first between 22.10 and 22.30 led by S/L Widdowson and enjoyed the rare experience of a Spitfire escort half way to the target, while S/L Lucas led the Ruhr-bound section away between 23.15 and 23.40. Sgt Fotheringham experienced engine problems when sixty miles short of the north German coast and jettisoned his bombs before returning home. P/O Ashworth also jettisoned his bombs after being held in searchlights and subjected to heavy, accurate flak. This would be the only time during his long and distinguished wartime career, that "Artie" Ashworth would jettison his bombs. Despite fine weather conditions, most crews could only report bombing in the target area, but P/O Hobbs observed his bombs bursting along the docks in the U-Boot construction yards. His second pilot on this operation was Sgt James Ward, a young New Zealander, whose career and life in Bomber Command would be brief but illuminated by an act of extreme courage. It was a similar story over the Ruhr, where Düsseldorf was obscured by some cloud and lots of haze. F/L Fletcher was unsure as to where he had bombed, reporting only that it was either in the Düsseldorf or Cologne areas. The fact they are twenty-five miles from each other, demonstrates the difficulty of target location over the Ruhr. One crew claimed to have started a large fire, but in truth, both operations were too small to cause useful damage even had they been accurate, which they were not.

The squadron produced another sizeable effort on the 27th, when making ready sixteen Wellingtons for a raid on Bremen. An attempt to hit this target two nights earlier in the absence of a Kiwi element had been rendered ineffective by electrical storms outbound, which had prevented most aircraft from reaching the target. A force of seventy-three Wellingtons and thirty-five Whitleys prepared for a late take-off, the 75(NZ) Squadron participants departing Feltwell between 23.03 and 23.40 with S/L Lucas the senior pilot on duty. It would prove to be another night of adverse weather, which included storms and icing conditions, in addition to which, the crews would face, for perhaps the first time, a concerted effort by the Luftwaffe

Nachtjagd. Poor visibility in the target area led to many crews finding their way to Hamburg, some fifty miles north-east of Bremen, and seventy-six bombing incidents were recorded there. S/L Lucas reported bombing the city centre of Bremen and F/L Fletcher believed that he had identified and bombed the city's Focke-Wulf aircraft factory, while others saw a river as a reference point for their bombing runs. No report was available from Bremen, but it is unlikely that it sustained more than slight scattered damage in return for a new record loss of fourteen aircraft, eleven of which were Whitleys, 31% of those dispatched.

The squadron operated for the final time in the month on the night of the 30th, when Feltwell was the only 3 Group station operating and Cologne was the target for twenty-three Wellingtons, while elements from other groups sent small numbers to Duisburg and Düsseldorf. Eleven 75(NZ) Squadron Wellingtons took off between 23.10 and 23.30 with F/Ls Fletcher and Gill the senior pilots on duty and adopted the southerly route to Cologne via Belgium. The weather was fine as they made their way out and all reached the German frontier, where F/L Fletcher's R1237 AA-G, lost an engine when a cylinder head blew off, forcing him to jettison his bombs live over Aachen. As he retreated to the north-west, a large fire could be seen developing where his ordnance had fallen. F/O Prichard had just passed through a searchlight belt south-east of Antwerp and was some fifty miles short of Cologne, when X3194 AA-S was latched onto by a He111, which attacked from fifty yards astern and above, knocking out the rear turret and hydraulics system. The bomb doors flopped open, and the front turret became sluggish, but the attacker was shaken off through turning and diving evasive manoeuvres, which took the Wellington down to 2,000 feet. Despite the damage, the engines were good, and F/O Prichard continued on to bomb the target, the bomb doors remaining open for the return journey, which combined with a vibrating engine to make it difficult to maintain height. A landing was carried out without flaps and brakes and the undercarriage ultimately collapsed, but the crew was able to walk away. An inspection revealed the cause of the vibration to be a cannon shell hole about eighteen inches from the tip of one blade, despite which and the other damage, the Wellington would soon be returned to active duty. For his actions on this night, F/O David Leatham Prichard RAF was awarded a DSO, the first for the squadron. Prichard, from Dannevirke, New Zealand, had arrived in England on an RAF short service commission two days before war was declared and had served in France on Fairy Battles. Meanwhile, the others pressed on to the target through what was a very dark night, and found Cologne obscured by ground haze. All reported bombing in the target area, some after identifying ground detail such as the Rhine and its bridges, and bursts were seen but little else.

During the course of the month the squadron operated on eleven nights against sixteen targets and dispatched 126 sorties without loss.

July 1941

The hard-working Feltwell maintenance crews were acknowledged from the top when G/C Buckley received a letter of congratulations and praise from the A-O-C 3 Group, AVM Jack Baldwin, stating that 75(NZ) Squadron had topped the serviceability list of squadrons in the group for the month of June. The squadron opened its July account with an operation to Essen, for which sixteen Wellingtons were made ready on the 3rd. Making their debuts as captains on this night were P/O Hone Anderson Roberts, RAAF and Sgt James Reginald Fairfax Brookes RAF. At briefing, the crews were presented with the Krupp works as the aiming point, which failed absolutely to adequately convey an accurate impression of what Krupp in Essen represented.

The name Krupp conjures up a vision of a massive factory, but this is far from what actually existed. The Krupp organisation had been the largest manufacturer of weapons in Europe since before the Great War and had a hand in all aspects of German war production from tanks to artillery and ship and U-Boot construction and was given a controlling share in all major heavy engineering companies in Germany and the occupied countries. It also built manufacturing sites in other parts of Germany, many situated close to concentration camps and employed vast numbers of forced workers in all of its factories. Once known as "Die Waffenschmiede des Reichs", the weapons-forge of the realm, its manufacturing sites in Essen included among others the Friedrich Krupp steelworks, the Friedrich Krupp locomotive and general engineering works, six coal mines and ten coke-oven plants, the Altenberg zinc works, the Presswerk plastics factory and the Goldschmidt non-ferrous metals smelting plant, all situated either within or close to the four Borbeck districts in a segment radiating out from near the city centre to the Rhine-Herne Canal on the north-western boundary on the banks of the Emscher River. The steel and engineering works alone employed in the region of eighty thousand workers and the company's sites covered an area of more than two thousand acres, of which three hundred acres were occupied by factories and workshops. All of that required massive rail and canal access in the form of marshalling yards and its own harbour, and energy was provided by at least four nearby power stations.

The 75(NZ) Squadron element departed Feltwell between 23.00 and 23.45 with S/L Widdowson the senior pilot on duty and reached the target area to find clear skies but the usual impenetrable ground haze and a hostile and accurate defence from searchlights and flak. F/L Fletcher reported his bombs falling in the area of the Krupp works alongside three fires already burning, and F/O Prichard thought that his burst alongside what appeared to be coke ovens. The others all bombed in the general target area and observed bursts and fires, while P/O Hamlin reported terrific explosions in response to the dropping of his load. A local report described light damage to housing in Essen and scattered minor destruction in towns and cities across the Ruhr. W5621, which had been re-coded AA-E, failed to return with the others and was lost without trace with the crew of Sgt Reid RNZAF. Reid had been a journalist before the war and his accounts of bomber operations over Germany had been widely published in the press.

The first of a series of operations against Münster was mounted by elements of 3 and 4 Groups on the night of the 5/6th, for which the squadron made ready a dozen Wellingtons as part of a 3 Group effort of sixty-four. Situated in the agricultural flatlands immediately north of the Ruhr, Münster was a garrison town, home to infantry and armoured units and contained a large marshalling yard south of the town centre. It had been left in peace by the Command for five months by the time the squadron element departed Feltwell between 23.10 and 23.30, led by F/L Fletcher. They flew out in fine weather conditions and those arriving over the Münsterland region found it under clear skies. F/L Fletcher lost his port engine when almost at the target and let his bombs go on a section of the Dortmund-Ems Canal two miles north-east of the town before heading home. P/O Scott claimed to be the first on target and reported starting huge fires with his incendiaries, and he believed that three large explosions resulted from hitting a chemicals factory. P/O Ashworth bombed close to the marshalling yards near an existing fire and Sgt Joll dropped his load into the town centre, causing a large fire which was seen to increase in size. A number of other crews commented on the fires, which could be seen from sixty miles into the return journey, and someone from another squadron claimed smoke had risen to 9,000 feet by the time he left the target. P/O Scott was chased by a BF109, which closed to 150 yards but broke away after the rear gunner fired two bursts.

3 Group supported two of the three main operations taking place on the night of the 7/8th, at Cologne and Münster again, while 4 Group attended to Osnabrück. S/L Widdowson was the senior pilot among ten from the squadron assigned to the return to Münster as part of an all-Wellington force of forty-nine aircraft. They took off between 23.10 and 23.30 and headed out in fine weather conditions, which provided clear skies over the target area, despite which, Sgt Breckon was unable to pinpoint the target. However, the lack of a coherent defence from the ground allowed the others to run more-or-less unmolested across the aiming point to deliver their bombs, and most reported hitting the town centre, where large fires resulted. S/L Ben Widdowson and crew set off on the homeward journey in L7818 AA-R and were at 13,000 feet over the Ijsselmeer with the North Sea in sight, when a Me110 attacked from below. It scored hits with cannon shells and incendiary bullets, injuring the front gunner, damaging the hydraulics system and setting the starboard wing on fire inboard of the engine. The flames were being fed by fuel from a split pipe and the blaze threatened to spread along the entire length of the wing. The rear gunner, Sgt Allan "Shorty" Box, fired at the assailant and watched it fall away and, according to his testimony, dive into the sea. The action that followed has become legendary and involved second pilot Sgt James Allen Ward, a New Zealander born of English parents, who had arrived at Feltwell on the 13th of June and undertaken a number of operations with experienced crews, before being allowed to captain his own. The squadron Operations Record Book provided the following account.

"The crew forced a hole in the fuselage and made strenuous efforts to reduce the fire with extinguishers and even the coffee in their vacuum flasks, but without success. They were then warned to be ready to abandon the aircraft. As a last resort Sgt Ward volunteered to smother the fire with an engine cover (canvass), which happened to be in use as a cushion. At first, he proposed to discard his parachute to reduce wind resistance, but was finally persuaded to take it. A rope from the dinghy was tied to him, though this was of little help, and might have become a danger had he been blown off the aircraft. With the help of the navigator, he then climbed through the narrow astro-hatch, and put on his parachute. The bomber was flying at a reduced speed, but the wind pressure must have been sufficient to render the operation one of extreme difficulty. Breaking the fabric to make hand and footholds where necessary, and also taking advantage of existing holes in the fabric, Sgt Ward succeeded in descending three feet to the wing, and proceeding another three feet to a position behind the engine, despite the slipstream from the airscrew which nearly blew him off the wing. Lying in this precarious position, he smothered the fire in the wing fabric, and tried to push the cover into the hole in the wing, onto the leaking pipe from which the fire came. As soon as he removed his hand, however, the terrific wind blew the cover out, and when he tried again it was lost. Tired as he was, he was able, with the navigator's assistance, to make successfully the perilous journey back into the aircraft. There was now no danger of the fire spreading from the petrol pipe, as there was no fabric left nearby, and, in due course, it burned itself out. When the aircraft was nearly home, some petrol, which had collected in the wing, blazed up furiously, but died down quite suddenly. A safe landing was then made despite the damage sustained by the aircraft. The

flight home had been made possible by the gallant action of Sgt Ward in extinguishing the fire on the wing in circumstances of the greatest difficulty and at the risk of his life."

The Wellington was put down at Newmarket, where the grass runways of the racecourse were the longest in the country and the landing was accomplished without flaps and brakes, the bomber eventually coming to rest against the boundary hedge. For his courage, Sgt Ward RNZAF was awarded the Victoria Cross and would soon be deemed ready to begin operations as crew captain. S/L Widdowson RAF received the immediate award of the DFC, while rear-gunner, Sgt Allan Robert James Box RNZAF, earned a coveted DFM. Sgt Lawrence Alan "Joe" Lawton RNZAF would later receive the AFC, partly due to his role in this action.

Other returning crews reported a major fire in Münster, thought to be a gas works, and the aiming point was claimed to be completely demolished. Buildings were seen to disintegrate, and the marshalling yards were also left in a damaged state, a local report confirming that many bombs had, indeed, fallen within the town. Münster's ordeal was not yet over and seven 75(NZ) Squadron Wellingtons were made ready for a return twenty-four hours later. They were part of an all-3 Group force of fifty-one aircraft, which took off in the late evening in fine weather conditions that would hold firm all the way to the target. The Feltwell crews departed between 23.10 and 23.30 with no senior pilots on duty and reached the target area to find ground haze but no serious impediment to accurate bombing. All returned safely to report bombing in the target area and starting fires in the town and the marshalling yards that were described as more numerous and more concentrated than those on the previous night, some of which were still burning.

On the 9th, a new Air Ministry directive signalled the end of the maritime diversion, although Brest would still feature for the remainder of the year and beyond because of the continuing presence of the enemy cruisers as a "fleet in being". The War Cabinet had decided that the enemy's transportation system and the morale of its civilian population were its weak points and Peirse was directed to focus upon these. This meant that the moon period would now bring attacks on the major railway centres which ringed the Ruhr, to inhibit the movement in and out of raw materials and finished products. On moonless nights, when navigation would be more problematic, the Rhine cities of Cologne, Duisburg and Düsseldorf should be easy to locate, and when unfavourable weather conditions obtained, more distant targets in northern, eastern and southern Germany would come into the reckoning.

Cologne was the destination for ninety-eight Wellingtons and thirty-two Hampdens on the night of the 10/11th, and crews were briefed for two aiming points in the city centre and the Klöckner-Humboldt mechanical engineering works located on the eastern side of the Rhine in the Deutz district. 3 Group provided sixty-two Wellingtons, of which ten represented 75(NZ) Squadron, and they took off between 22.55 and 23.15, again with no senior pilots on duty. Sgt Anthony 'Tony' Saunders RAF was flying his first operation as skipper, having taken over P/O Curry's old crew. Adverse weather conditions seriously affected the operation and less than half of the force would report reaching and bombing the target. Those arriving over what they believed to be Cologne found the ground obscured by thick haze and had little idea of their true position. Sgt Miniken believed he was over the south of Cologne when he bombed, while P/O Thomson aimed his load at a fire already burning in the city of Bonn, some fifteen miles to the south. P/O Scott also reported starting a fire in a small town to the south, while the remainder dropped their loads more in hope than in expectation and the local authorities confirmed the raid as a complete failure.

The ports of Bremen, Vegesack (north-west Bremen) and Emden were the targets for forty-nine, twenty and two aircraft respectively on the night of the 13/14th, for which the squadron made ready eleven Wellingtons. Two were to contain first-time captains, Sgt Ralph Norman Allen RNZAF and Sgt John Anthony Matetich RAFVR. Their target was Bremen, for which they took off between 22.55 and 23.35 with F/L Fletcher the senior pilot on duty on a night of thick cloud and icing conditions. Sgt Miniken RAFVR and crew were climbing out over the East Anglian coast shortly after midnight, when the starboard engine cut without warning at 6,000 feet. Minikin turned back immediately, but rapidly lost altitude and had to put X9634 AA-F down in the sea about a hundred yards from the beach two miles north of Lowestoft. Miniken and navigator, Sgt Gilding RAF, were rescued from the water at 02.15, the former slightly injured, and the latter seriously so, but the other crew members lost their lives. The remaining squadron crews pressed on and those reaching the target area bombed on e.t.a. or astro-fix through the ten-tenths cloud and saw no results. P/O Scott began to lose height because of ice accretion and let his bombs go five miles short of the target in order to maintain height. Likewise, Sgt Saunders became another victim of the thunder and ice-laden clouds and jettisoned his load in the target area. F/L Fletcher bombed an aerodrome five miles north-east of Ijmuiden and left a fire in his wake, while Sgt Joll aimed his bombs at two ships seen five miles north of the Frisian island of Terschelling. They all returned safely but had nothing to show for their challenging night's work.

Only 3 Group ventured out on the night of the 15/16th, when sending thirty-eight Wellingtons from Feltwell and Marham to Duisburg. Nine 75(NZ) Squadron Wellingtons took off between 22.40 and 23.10 with F/L Fletcher the senior pilot on duty and Sgt Donald Frederick Streeter, RNZAF, on his first operation as skipper. They headed out in fine weather conditions but encountered a layer of low, thin cloud over the target, which presented the bomb-aimers with a difficult task of establishing their precise position. An intense and accurate searchlight and flak response, particularly between 9,000 and 16,000 feet, added to the difficulties and made it an uncomfortable place to be stooging around. One crew did positively identify and bomb a set of marshalling yards to the south of the planned aiming point, and F/L Fletcher obtained a fix on the Rhine and an autobahn, before delivering his bombs in a salvo onto a large fire within three miles of the target. Six other crews bombed on estimated positions, among them P/O Ashworth, who then demolished a building on an aerodrome six miles south of The Hague and left a fire burning.

P/O "Jeff" Rees RAF and crew were on their way home in W5663 AA-O and passing through a searchlight belt, when they were coned and engaged, first by flak and then by a night-fighter, which riddled the Wellington with bullets and cannon shells. One exploded in the cockpit, and another blew out the mid-under turret hatch, leaving a gaping hole in the floor. The second pilot, Sgt David Campbell Joyce RNZAF, died of his wounds almost immediately and the front gunner, Sgt David Henry Conibear RAFVR, was so seriously wounded that he would not survive. The rear gunner, Sgt Gwyn-Williams RAFVR, was temporarily blinded by a splinter, prompting the observer (navigator), P/O Robert Cyril Adair Hunter RCAF, to make his way aft to render assistance. He unwittingly fell through the missing hatch, but fortunately was wearing his parachute and landed safely to spend the rest of the war as a PoW. The wireless operator, Sgt Ian William Lewis RAFVR, was left shocked and deafened after the cannon shell exploded close to his head, but he recovered his composure and rendered assistance to the wounded men. He then repaired his radio and obtained a wireless fix, before collecting the navigator's charts and instruments and assisting the pilot to bring W5663 home to a safe landing. Sgt Conibear was taken to hospital, where he succumbed to his wounds, while his crew colleagues, P/O Rees and Sgt Lewis, were awarded the DFC and DFM respectively. R3171 AA-E failed to return after crashing into the sea off the Dutch coast, and a three-hour search by S/Ls Widdowson and Lucas based on their final radioed position was fruitless. Sadly, there were no survivors from the all-Commonwealth crew of Sgt "Bob" Fotheringham RNZAF, of which three others were members of the RNZAF and one each of the RAAF and RCAF.

The squadron prepared eleven Wellington on the 21st, ten for an operation that night against Mannheim and one for a freshman sortie by P/O P.F. Wilson to Cherbourg. S/L Widdowson was the senior pilot on duty as they departed Feltwell between 22.30 and 23.06 with P/O Wilson last away and headed out in fine weather conditions for their respective targets. This was S/L Widdowson's first sortie since the traumatic events of the night of the 8/9th, and as then, he had Sgt Ward beside him as second pilot. The main element reached southern Germany in good order and carried out their attacks in the face of scant resistance, before returning safely to report explosions and fires. Precisely where the bombs fell is unknown, but a local report claims that only four high explosive bombs landed in the city and one of those was a dud. P/O Wilson, meanwhile, attacked the docks at Cherbourg and reported hits on the north-western corner.

A major daylight raid on Brest and its lodgers had been planned for some time and was to involve 150 aircraft operating under Operation Sunrise, a complex plan, which included diversions. The intention was to send in three pressurized B17 Fortress Is of 2 Group's 90 Squadron at 30,000 feet to act as bait and draw up the enemy fighters, while 5 Group Hampdens performed a similar role at a more conventional altitude under an escort of fighters carrying long-range fuel tanks, much in the style of a 2 Group "Circus" operation. Meanwhile, 2 Group Blenheims would create a diversion at Cherbourg, and while all of this was on-going, a force of Halifaxes and Wellingtons was to take advantage of the distractions and descend upon Brest to attack the warships. However, a reconnaissance sortie on the 23rd revealed that Scharnhorst had slipped away to a berth at La Pallice, some two hundred miles to the south, and this development forced a last-minute change of plans. It was decided to send the Halifaxes to attend to Scharnhorst, while the original plan went ahead at Brest, employing seventy-nine Wellingtons from 1 and 3 Groups.

3 Group detailed thirty-six Wellingtons, of which six were provided by 75(NZ) Squadron, and they took off at 10.50 on the 24th with S/L Lucas the senior pilot on duty. Interestingly, the briefing was taken by W/C Trevor Freeman, now with 3 Group in a training role, and he would lead the formation. They made their way out over Cornwall in excellent weather conditions and approached the target in waves at around 15,000 feet. They were greeted by a far more intense flak and fighter response than had been anticipated, suggesting that the feints and diversions had failed in their purpose. Each Wellington was carrying twenty-four 250lb semi-armour-piercing (SAP) bombs, the fall of which Sgt Breckon did not track, while P/O Roberts watched his overshoot and score direct hits on sheds half a mile south-east of the aiming point.

Sgt Saunders reported one or two hits on the north end of the graving (dry) dock, but P/O Ashworth saw nothing of his and S/L Lucas could only confirm bombing in the target area. Ten Wellingtons were brought down, and among them was the squadron's N2854, AA-U, which was observed to be attacked by several BF109s and disappeared into the sea to be lost without trace with the crew of Sgt Streeter RNZAF. Meanwhile, P/O Saunders and crew in R1457 AA-P had also been involved in running battles with BF109s, both before and after bombing. The second attack was driven off by rear gunner, Sgt Edward Callander RAFVR, but not before the front gunner, Sgt Jack Thompson RAFVR, had been wounded. Coming back over Portsmouth they attracted some light flak from the Navy, but despite the starboard engine being down on power and without undercarriage or flaps, Saunders managed to bring the Wimpey safely back for a belly-landing at Boscombe Down.

While the six hits claimed on the Gneisenau by crews from other units were not confirmed, Scharnhorst was severely damaged in an epic fifteen-minute battle with the Halifax brigade, five of which were shot down, while all of the others sustained damage. Scharnhorst was forced to limp back to Brest, where superior repair facilities existed. As a result of the attack on Brest, F/O Charles Stokes RAF, rear gunner to S/L Lucas, was awarded a DFC, while Sgts Gwyn Martin and Edward J. Callander, navigator and rear gunner respectively to Sgt Saunders, and Sgt Herrold Raymond "Hank" Corrin RNZAF, rear gunner to Sgt Ivan Breckon, each received a DFM. Sgt Callander, a Scot known to his crewmates as "Jock", had already been awarded a Croix De Guerre during his service with the French Foreign Legion in Norway and France. His recommendation for the DFM read, "He is probably the finest Air Gunner to have passed through this squadron". He would go on to a second tour with 115 Squadron and would be shot down on the 6th of May 1942 to become a PoW, incredibly, meeting up with his old navigator and room-mate Gwyn Martin at Stalag Luft 3, Sagan. Callander escaped three times from PoW camps but was caught and shot by the Gestapo in April 1944, probably as a result of orders issued following what became known as the Great Escape.

That night, the squadron contributed five Wellingtons to a sixty-four-strong 3 and 5 Group joint effort against shipyards in Kiel, taking off in a fifteen-minute slot from 22.15 with S/L Widdowson the senior pilot on duty. Despite clear weather conditions in the target area, the raid was a failure and all but a few bombs missed the town.

Postings from the squadron to O.T.U.s at the end of the month included P/Os Curry, Evans, Johnson, Hamlin and Hobbs, F/O Prichard and F/L Gill. Hamlin would tragically die in a Hudson test flight at Whenuapai back in New Zealand, on 17 December 1942, the day before his wedding. F/O Prichard was awarded a DSO and S/L Widdowson a DFC, while Frank Gill would go on to earn a DSO and OBE, rising to Chief of the Air Staff in the RNZAF and later entering Parliament, serving as a cabinet minister and amongst other roles, Minister of Defence.

During the course of the month the Feltwell station commander, G/C Buckley, was posted to pastures new and was eventually succeeded by Group Captain John "Speedy" Powell, the gung-ho, high-spirited, uncompromising RAF officer who had relinquished command of 149 Squadron in May. His sometimes-abrasive personality would be in stark contrast to the almost fatherly approach to command of G/C Buckley and W/C Kay and would create a division between him and some of the New Zealanders, which would contribute to a dip in morale. He had been very prominent in the film documentary "Target for Tonight, which cast genuine crews in the appropriate roles and starred the legendary W/C Percy "Pick" Pickard as the pilot of F for Freddy, Powell as the squadron commander and G/C "Bull" Staton, the former 10 Squadron commanding officer, as the station commander.

At his first briefing to mostly freshman crews, Powell's comments implied criticism of the former highly popular and respected New Zealand leadership of the squadron. After informing his audience that he intended to cut down on petrol and increase bomb loads, a policy which, he may have omitted to explain, came from higher up the chain of command, he reputedly made a callous, and what for him was probably a "throw-away" remark intended for impact, the gist of which was, "what are six miserable lives when there's a job to be done". It is said that two crews got up and walked out. July had seen the squadron attack eleven targets, dispatching ninety-seven sorties for the loss of three Wellingtons, two complete crews and a number of individual airmen.

August 1941

The policy of dispatching small numbers of aircraft to various targets simultaneously had rarely produced effective results, but it would be persisted with throughout the remainder of the year, and in fact until a new Commander-in-Chief arrived in 1942 to provide a different direction. The squadron was the only 3 Group unit not to be called into action for the first major raid of August, which took place against Hamburg on the night of the 2/3rd. The following night was to bring Hannover into the bomb sights, for which operation the squadron made ready ten Wellingtons as part of an all-3 Group effort of thirty-four, while Whitleys attacked Frankfurt. The Kiwi element departed Feltwell between 22.25 and 22.50 with S/L Lucas the senior pilot on duty and those reaching the target area found ten-tenths cloud obscuring the ground. Sgt Matetich and crew were not among them, however, having been set upon over enemy territory by an enemy night-fighter. X9760 AA-P sustained damage to its hydraulics system and the rear gunner, Sgt Twisleton RAFVR, was wounded. The bombs were jettisoned, the assailant evaded, and a wheels-up landing carried out at Newmarket. While this drama was being enacted, the others bombed on DR, e.t.a. flashes from flak batteries and the glow of fires and returned home with nothing useful to report.

Mannheim was the destination for thirty-eight 3 Group Wellingtons on the night of the 6/7th, of which a dozen were provided by 75(NZ) Squadron, while another of its crews joined in on a freshman trip to Calais. The main element took off between 22.20 and 22.45 with S/L Lucas the senior pilot on duty, while first-time skipper, Sgt Anthony Henry Ryder Hawkins RNZAF, and crew set off for the French coast ten minutes before midnight. Two other first-time captains flew that night, Sgt Leopold Ian Adrian Millett RAFVR and P/O Timothy John Wilder Williams RNZAF. The weather conditions throughout were unhelpful with heavy cloud, thunder, electrical storms and icing and F/L Fletcher got caught up in an extensive thunder cloud at the east coast and used up too much time and fuel breaking free to be able to reach the primary target. He carried on as far as Ostend, where he deposited his bombs onto the outer harbour, while the others pushed on to Mannheim, where railway workshops were the specific target. While most crews were unable to determine ground detail through the ten-tenths cloud, S/L Lucas observed bomb bursts in the Rhine docks area and P/O Williams claimed direct hits on lock gates. P/O Wilson and crew were attacked three times by what they believed to be a

Ju88, which was eventually driven off by return fire from the rear turret of Sgt William Massey RAF.

Meanwhile, at Calais, Sgt Hawkins also encountered complete cloud cover and bombed a flak and searchlight concentration on e.t.a. R1648 AA-K failed to return from Mannheim with the crew of Sgt Millett after ditching in the North Sea. It was his first operation as captain, having served as second pilot in the Coney and Fox crews, and the occasion turned into a nightmare when a Me110 attacked them on their way home. The front gunner, Sgt Bottomley, fought off the attacker but the Wellington caught fire and was barely holding together. Navigator, Sgt Deryck Polley RAFVR, managed to put out the fire with an extinguisher, but the Wellington was gradually losing height as it crossed the Channel and the crew threw out everything they could lay their hands on to reduce weight. Tragically, they ran into a bank of fog and eventually flew into the sea, the impact of which killed Sgt Jack Wilson Bottomley RAFVR, while the rear gunner, Sgt William Neill Kennedy Mellon, RAFVR, was trapped in his turret and went down with the Wellington. Sgts Millet and Polley and two others survived six days in a dinghy and were rescued by the enemy to be taken into captivity.

The prospect of poor weather conditions over northern Germany caused a reduction in the numbers of aircraft detailed to attack railway and shipyard aiming points in Hamburg on the night of the 8/9th. 75(NZ) Squadron contributed eight of the 3 Group Wellingtons, whose crews were briefed to attack the Blohm & Voss shipyards, and they took off between 22.10 and 22.25 with F/L Fletcher the senior pilot on duty. Sgt Tony Saunders and crew in X9757 AA-S were set upon by two enemy night-fighters at the Dutch coast and jettisoned their bombs in the Westerhaven area of Rotterdam while taking evasive action. They managed a forced landing at Dishforth without brakes or flaps and reported a twelve-foot square hole in the starboard wing! Heavy cloud outbound and over the target provided difficult conditions for the others and all carried out their attacks on e.t.a. without ever catching a glimpse of the ground. P/O "Artie" Ashworth was posted to Harwell during w.e.f 13th, and before the month was out he would find himself on the island of Malta on the strength of 38 Squadron for service in the Middle-Eastern theatre.

Hannover and Berlin occupied forces of sixty-five and seventy aircraft respectively on the night of the 12/13th, when 75(NZ) Squadron made ready nine Wellingtons, eight for an all-3 Group attack on the former and one to join others from the group to bomb the docks at Le Havre. F/L Fletcher was the senior pilot on duty as they took off together between 21.00 and 21.20 and headed out in fine weather conditions, which would deteriorate somewhat over enemy territory. Thunderstorms over northern Germany had dissipated by the time the bombers reached the target area, leaving slight cloud and ground haze, which was sufficient to obscure ground detail and the main railway station aiming point could not be identified. Bombs were delivered across the built-up area without precision, after which, crews set off for home with little genuine impression of the outcome. X9764 AA-V was cruising westwards at 16,000 feet over the Ijsselmeer, when an enemy night-fighter latched on to it and fired a long burst. Rear gunner, Sgt Joseph Paul Andre Faguy RCAF, returned fire and the assailant was seen to dive away steeply and disappear. The Wellington sustained extensive damage to the hydraulics pressure pipes and the a.s.i. feed, which caused the bomb doors and undercarriage to flop down, the dinghy to be partially released and the aileron controls to the starboard side to be completely severed. The radio equipment was also put out of action and that prevented the transmission of an SOS signal. At one point, the controls jammed, sending the aircraft into a dive from which P/O "Hughie" Roberts managed to pull out at 2,000 feet. Having reached the English coast with the fuel remaining in the nacelle tanks, the crew hoped to reach Feltwell, but on requesting permission to land they were diverted to the longer runway at Newmarket. However, without warning, both engines cut and it would be established subsequently that these tanks had been holed and were empty. P/O Roberts ordered his crew to abandon the aircraft, which they did successfully, while he was left without time to follow and prepared for a forced-landing. With the aid of his landing light, he picked out a firebreak in a forestry plantation and put the Wellington down safely with little additional damage. Meanwhile, at Le Havre, P/O Rees dropped his bombs onto the east side of dock 6 and started a fire.

The night of the 14/15th was devoted largely to railway-related targets in northern and eastern Germany, Hannover again featuring along with Braunschweig (Brunswick), thirty-five miles to the east, and Magdeburg. 3 Group contributed sixty-seven Wellingtons to the force of 152 assigned to the first-mentioned, of which eight belonged to 75(NZ) Squadron and they took off between 21.15 and 21.30 led by S/L Widdowson. They flew out over heavy cloud, which dispersed to an extent in the target area to leave patches that combined with ground haze to partially obscure the railway station aiming points. All reported bombing within the city and starting fires, but an accurate assessment of the outcome proved to be impossible. Enemy aircraft were active over Feltwell when the squadron returned, and P/O Wilson in W5618 AA-F was attacked head-on by a Ju88 at 1,200 feet as he prepared to land, but the cannon and machine-gun shells missed.

Railway targets continued to occupy the Command's attention and marshalling yards and stations in Duisburg provided the targets for five of the squadron's Wellingtons on the night of the 17/18th. They were part of a force of forty-one aircraft, a number reduced late on because of deteriorating weather conditions, and they took off between midnight and 00.50 with no senior pilots on duty. Heavy cloud over the target precluded any chance of identifying ground detail and bombs were dropped more in hope than in expectation, their bursts followed by a number of fires. Sgt Hawkins dropped his bombs on an aerodrome near the target and straddled the flare-path.

A hammer blow to the morale of the Command was delivered on the 18th, when the "Butt Report" was released and sent shockwaves reverberating around the Halls of Power as it laid bare the inadequacies of the bombing campaigns to date. The conclusions were probably not a surprise in Bomber Command circles, where it had long been accepted that reaching, identifying and hitting a target over a blacked-out, cloud-covered, hostile country was beyond the ability of crews with the level of technology available to them. After analysing four thousand photographs taken during a hundred night operations in June and July, the report's author assessed that only a third of those claiming to have reached the target had actually done so. A tiny proportion of bombs had fallen within miles of the intended targets and the poorest performances were reserved for the industrial Ruhr region, which was particularly disappointing. Exaggerated claims of success born out of enthusiasm on the part of the crews had begun with the very first bombing of German territory in March 1940, but now incontrovertible proof was to hand, and it would not only unjustly blight the period of the incumbent C-in-C's tenure, but also lead to calls for the dissolution of Bomber Command and the redistribution of its resources to other theatres.

Just two freshman crews were sent out on the night of the 18/19th to bomb the docks and shipping at Dunkerque, Sgt Keith Vernon Dudley Roe RAFVR and P/O James Edward Johnson RAFVR departing Feltwell at 21.10 on a night of more favourable weather conditions than of late. Both reached and bombed the target, where, in the absence of cloud, searchlight glare presented the greatest obstacle to accuracy. They returned safely to report a poor blackout south of Dunkerque, and surprisingly over England also between Southwold and Feltwell. The return of adverse weather conditions allowed limited operational activity over the ensuing week, and 75(NZ) Squadron remained at home until the night of the 26/27th, when fourteen Wellingtons were made ready, ten for the main event at Cologne and four for Boulogne. The Cologne-bound element, including first-timer Sgt Robert Walter Bray RAFVR, took off either side of midnight as part of an overall force of ninety-nine aircraft and encountered cloud over the target with occasional gaps, through which some crews were able to identify ground detail. Bombs were dropped in the general target area, but other than bomb bursts, flashes and a number of fires, one described as large, there was little useful information to pass on to the intelligence section at debriefing.

The Boulogne element departed Feltwell either side of 01.30 and encountered ten-tenths cloud over the French coast. Sgt Neil Gordon Cresswell Ramsey RAFVR and crew failed to identify the target, despite searching beyond the endurance of their fuel supply, and jettisoned their bombs into the sea an hour after the petrol gauge showed empty. Sgt Talbot RAF bombed the docks, P/O Alfred Sydney Raphael RAF also, while Sgt Raymond Fullerton Curlewis RAAF was defeated by the cloud and returned his bombs to store.

W/C Kay was posted from the squadron during the w.e.f. 27.8.41 at the conclusion of his period in command and took up a new post at 8 Group *(a training group, not to be confused with the 8 Group designation given to the Path Finder Force on the 8th of January 1943.)* The main operation on the night of the 28/29th involved a force of 118 aircraft targeting railway installations in Duisburg. 3 Group supported it, but did not call upon the Feltwell brigade to take part, instead, sending three freshman crews from 75(NZ) Squadron and two from 57 Squadron to bomb the docks and shipping at Ostend. Sgts Ramsey and Cyril Taylor RAFVR and P/O Raphael took off either side of 21.30, and two of them for certain reached the target to deliver their bombs in the face of a hostile and accurate response from searchlights and flak. Sgt Taylor attacked Haamstede aerodrome, but it is not clear whether this was in addition to bombing the primary target or as an alternative.

Two major operations were planned over southern Germany for the night of the 29/30th, the larger, by 143 aircraft against Frankfurt and the other, by ninety-four Wellingtons at Mannheim, forty miles to the south. S/L Lucas was the senior pilot on duty as the nine 75(NZ) Squadron participants took off for the latter between 21.50 and 22.12 on another night of unfavourable weather conditions. The target was concealed beneath ten-tenths cloud and none was able to positively identify it. Sgt Roe brought his bombs back, while P/O Rees overshot the city and spent forty-five minutes searching, before heading home and dropping his bombs through cloud when engaged by a heavy concentration of searchlights and flak. P/O Roberts also bombed a flak concentration, which an astro-fix identified as in the vicinity of Frankfurt. A local report from Mannheim confirmed a scattered and largely ineffective raid, which caused little damage. During the course of the month the squadron operated on ten nights against twelve targets, dispatching eighty-one sorties without loss.

September 1941

Twenty-six-year-old W/C Reginald Sawrey-Cookson RAF was posted to the squadron from 21 O.T.U at Moreton-in-Marsh at the start of the month to succeed W/C Kay. He had most recently served as a flight commander with 149 Squadron and had been mentored, therefore, by G/C Powell. In his favour, he had been a member of the original 75 Squadron from 1937 until its absorption into the O.T.U system on the 4th of April 1940, and his posting to 149 Squadron had followed shortly afterwards. He had been awarded a DFC in December 1940 for a daring low-level attack on an unlighted aerodrome in the face of a hostile defence from the ground, and a DSO had been added in May 1941 in recognition of his outstanding operational career to date. For all that, his association and friendship with Powell would perhaps, unfairly colour opinions of him at a time of reduced morale resulting both from the strained relationship with the station commander and through losses, some of which were attributed to the "cutting down the petrol" policy. As the new commanding officer arrived, F/L Fletcher departed on posting to 20 O.T.U at Lossiemouth at the conclusion of his outstanding tour, P/O Rees went to 21 O.T.U at Moreton-in-Marsh and P/O Scott to 11 O.T.U at Bassingbourn.

September's operations began with the preparation on the 2nd of ten 75(NZ) Squadron Wellingtons and the briefing of their crews for a raid on Frankfurt, for which they were to join forces with 116 others. They took off from Feltwell between 20.15 and 20.35 with no senior pilots taking the lead, but soon lost the services of Sgt Curlewis and crew in X3205 AA-L, who were forced to turn back after the oxygen supply to the rear turret failed. Cloudless skies in the target area, for a change, provided conditions conducive to accurate bombing and P/O Roberts delivered a stick right across the marshalling yards. Sgt Hawkins let his load go from 16,000 feet and started a fire at the western end of the town north of the River Main, while the others also reported observing their bombs and incendiaries burst in the target area, setting off a number of fires. Sgt Allen made two additional runs across the aiming point to take photos, only to find that his camera had failed to work. Despite the confidence of the crews, a report from Frankfurt suggested that the raid had failed to make an impact.

Apart from three SOE sorties from Newmarket, Feltwell was the only 3 Group station to send aircraft to war on the night of the 6/7th, when the threat of deteriorating weather conditions led to a reduced effort. Eighty-six aircraft were detailed to attack a chemicals factory at Hüls, on the north-eastern edge of the Ruhr, for which thirteen 75(NZ) Squadron Wellingtons took off between 19.55 and 20.45 with S/L Lucas the senior pilot on duty. The I G Farben-controlled factory at Marl-Hüls was known locally as the "Buna" works because of the butadiene and natrium chemicals employed in the manufacturing process of synthetic rubber for tyres. The Chemische Werke-Hüls GmbH had been formed in 1938 after its acquisition by the I G Farben company in association with the Bergwerkgesellschaft Hibernia A G, and whether or not it was using slave workers at this time, the I G Farben company would become infamous for drawing its labour force from concentration camps and forcing tens of thousands to toil under the harshest conditions at its many manufacturing sites across Germany. All reached the target area, where they were greeted by clear skies and, because of its location, many searchlights operating in cones. Despite the favourable conditions, not all crews were able to identify the aiming point and among those failing to do so was Sgt Allen, who picked up an excellent reference point on a railway line, yet still saw nothing. P/O Wilson made two runs across the aiming point at 8,000 feet, believing that he scored direct hits on the first and was positive that he had scored with three 500 pounders on the second. Sgt Saunders blamed a change in the wind and searchlights for carrying him south and deeper into the Ruhr to find himself at 7,500 feet over Essen, which he bombed and started a large fire. A number of returning crews reported that they had observed an aircraft ensnared in a searchlight cone and brought down by flak about fifteen miles south-west of the target and another shot down over the Dutch/German frontier. X9767 AA-S did not return home with the others and it was established later that it had been dispatched by Oblt Emil Woltersdorf of III./NJG1 and had crashed about five miles inside Holland at Borculo with no survivors from the crew of P/O Johnson RAFVR.

Berlin was the principal target on the night of the 7/8th, for which a force of 197 aircraft was made ready. 3 Group supported the endeavour with a contribution from each of its stations except for Feltwell, and also sent aircraft to Kiel as part of a force of fifty-one aircraft. Feltwell dispatched just three crews on freshman sorties to Boulogne, that of Sgt William Bennett Megarry Smyth RAFVR the lone 75(NZ) Squadron representative. They took off at 20.20 and returned after three hours and twenty minutes to report attacking the target and starting fires.

Ten Wellingtons were prepared by the squadron during the 8th to participate in an operation that night by ninety-five aircraft against railway workshops and an armaments factory at Kassel, situated some eighty miles east of the Ruhr. They took off between 20.25 and 20.55 with no senior captains on duty, just three of pilot officer rank and seven sergeants. All reached the target area where the skies were clear and some ground detail could be identified. Sgt Allen pinpointed on a bend in the River Fulda, which guided him to the target, where he bombed from 8,500 feet, while Sgt Saunders made two runs at 12,000 feet and started large fires among buildings. The others reported bombing in the target area and either starting fires or adding to those already burning, and as a result of eliciting little response from the ground, not a single aircraft was lost. All from Feltwell returned safely home to report a successful operation, local sources confirming serious damage to a railway-wagon works and an optical instruments factory and strikes on other buildings including the main railway station.

Germany's Baltic coast was the destination for the majority of the aircraft operating on the night of the 11/12th, fifty-six of them assigned to the Heinkel works at Rostock, fifty-five to the shipyards in Kiel and thirty-two 4 Group Whitleys to the docks at Warnemünde. 75(NZ) Squadron briefed eleven crews for Kiel and the freshman crew of Sgt Isherwood for Le Havre, and it was the latter who departed first, at 19.40. The main element took off between 21.00 and 22.10 with W/C Sawrey-Cookson the senior pilot on duty and backed up by S/L Lucas. This was the first time that a commanding officer of the squadron had included himself on the order of battle, something that was standard practice elsewhere in the Command. It is likely that the advanced ages of W/Cs Buckley and Kay, who were well into their forties, was the reason behind their failure to operate. First-time captain Sgt S. J. G. Isherwood RAFVR and crew found Le Havre to be completely cloud-covered and brought their bombs back, as did W/C Sawrey-Cookson and Sgt Talbot, both of whom failed to locate the aiming point in Kiel through the ground haze, despite the otherwise clear conditions. S/L Lucas set off two fires in the target area and P/O Wilson observed his bombs to hit either the docks or warehouses to the north-east, where a large fire developed. Sgt Saunders was another who failed to locate the target and jettisoned his bombs to lighten the load after seven hours in the air. Sgt Keith Roe RAFVR and crew did not return home in R1038 AA-H, the Parker crew's old kite, and were lost without trace.

The German warships at Brest had been left in peace for some time when a force of 147 aircraft was dispatched on the night of the 13/14th to unsettle them again. The squadron prepared twelve Wellingtons, which took off between 21.40 and 22.15 with no senior officers on duty and Sgt Ward VC back in harness and operating for the first time as captain of his own crew. On this occasion, he was unable to locate the target and brought his bombs home. The others found the port, where an effective smoke-screen concealed the cruisers and returning crews could only report bombing on approximate positions and observing bursts in the general target area. Sgt Taylor and crew flew on a further seventy-five miles to bomb the U-Boot slipways at Lorient as an alternative, but were unable to comment on the outcome.

Two nights later, Hamburg was selected as the target for 169 aircraft, whose crews were briefed to aim for railway stations and shipyards. A dozen Wellingtons were made ready by 75(NZ) Squadron and took off between 19.40 and 20.15 again without any senior officers present. They found the skies over Hamburg to be clear, but this allowed searchlight glare to mask ground detail and cause the bombing to be scattered over many parts of the city. Sgt Bray reported his bombs landing in the docks area, Sgt Allen claimed that his burst in the marshalling yards and P/O Roberts started a fire after attacking from 12,000 feet, while the others could only confirm bombing in the general target area. Two crews were absent from debriefing, those of Sgt Ward VC, RNZAF and Sgt Hawkins RNZAF, and either of these could have been in the aircraft seen to be shot down over the target, where searchlights were co-operating with the flak batteries and night-fighters. X3205 AA-L was brought down by flak, killing Sgt Ward and three others, while two men survived to fall into enemy hands. There were two survivors also from X9759 AA-R, and they, too, became PoWs, but the pilot, Sgt Hawkins, was not among them.

Eight crews were called to briefing on the 17th, to learn that their destination that night was the city of Karlsruhe in southern Germany. It would be the second night running that a force of 3 Group Wellingtons visited the city and they departed Feltwell between 19.20 and 19.30 to make their way to the English Channel. Sgt Talbot was taken ill during the sea crossing and dropped his bombs on Calais before turning back and making two attempts to land at Feltwell, where X9918 AA-U came to a halt only after colliding with a gun post. The crew walked away and the Wellington would be repaired and returned to service. Meanwhile, P/O Raphael failed to identify the target in the hazy conditions and headed thirty-five miles to the north to bomb Mannheim instead. Sgt Curlewis hit a large military barracks, while the others could only report bombing in the general target area and observing bursts. X9834 AA-O crash-landed on fire at Holsthum, just a few miles from the border with Luxembourg, and Sgt Smyth RAFVR was killed along with two members of his crew. The second pilot and two others were taken into captivity and the wireless operator, Sgt Jeffrey Walter Reid RAFVR, would be shot and killed while trying to escape from Lamsdorf prison camp on the 29th of December. S/L Widdowson had now concluded his highly successful tour of operations as B Flight commander and was posted on the 20th to 20 O.T.U at Lossiemouth, to be succeeded by S/L Paul Burton Chamberlain RAF, who arrived from 23 O.T.U at Pershore. Before his posting to

Pershore in March 1941, twenty-five-year-old S/L Chamberlain had served since December 1936 exclusively in India and Iraq.

A force of seventy-four aircraft set out for Berlin on the evening of the 20th, while thirty-four others headed for Frankfurt-an-Oder, situated some fifty miles east-south-east of the capital on the border with Poland (not to be confused with Frankfurt-am-Main in southern Germany). 75(NZ) Squadron dispatched twelve Wellingtons, ten on the main operation and two containing the freshman crews of P/O John Frederick Fisher and Sgt Geoffrey Sidney Nunn (both RAFVR) to Ostend. They took off between 19.15 and 20.18, but Sgt Allen was soon back in the Feltwell circuit with engine problems, leaving the others to press on and reach Germany, only to be recalled because of deteriorating weather conditions over the home bases. Not all would pick up the message but of those who did, Sgt Curlewis bombed an aerodrome near the Dutch/German frontier and started large fires. Others targeted Osnabrück, Sgt Brookes bombing a flare-path to the south-east, while P/O Wilson bombed the town. W/C Sawrey-Cookson had S/L Chamberlain on board as second pilot and was an hour short of Berlin when he turned back, dropping his bombs on a town between Hannover and Osnabrück, possibly Bückeburg. Sgt Ramsey made it all the way to Frankfurt, where he started a fire that remained visible for seventy miles into the return journey and observed four explosions from fifty miles away. Sgt Matetich and P/Os Williams and Roberts bombed the centre of Berlin and the two freshman crews succeeded in attacking their target at Ostend, both leaving large fires burning in their wake. On return to home airspace, many found their stations shrouded in fog and a total of twelve aircraft crashed or were abandoned. P/O Raphael force-landed T2805 AA-D in a sixty-acre field nine miles north-east of Norwich at 04.00, after which, he and four others walked away from the wreckage. Sadly, one member of the crew, navigator Sgt Gerald Robert Craig RCAF, sustained severe injuries to which he succumbed in hospital on the following day. R1518 AA-X was abandoned by Sgt Matetich and his crew while trying to reach Horsham-St-Faith, and they floated safely down to mother earth, leaving the Wellington to crash at 04.30 near North Walsham in Norfolk.

Another recall was issued to 104 crews heading for Cologne, Emden, Mannheim and Genoa on the night of the 26/27th. Just three of these were from 75(NZ) Squadron, S/L Chamberlain, P/O Fisher and Sgt Nunn, who had departed Feltwell at 19.15 bound for Emden. They failed to respond to the recall and reached the target to find hazy conditions and intense light flak, which made it difficult for them to observe the results of their efforts. Nine Wellingtons were made ready by the squadron on the 28th, six to send to Genoa and three to Frankfurt-am-Main, the latter a joint operation by 3 and 5 Groups to target the main railway station and marshalling yards. The former was an all-3 Group raid on the Ansaldo engineering works, the Italian "Krupp", which was heavily involved in all aspects of engineering from shipbuilding to components and at this site manufactured rolling stock and railway control equipment. The Feltwell station commander, G/C J.A. "Speedy" Powell, put his name at the top of the order of battle and gathered together an experienced crew, which included F/L Kay in the rear turret and F/L Watkins from 3 Group HQ as navigator. *(It is believed that this was the future W/C W.D.G. Watkins, who would be appointed commanding officer of XV Squadron on 15.4.44., one of only a handful of navigators to attain command of a squadron. He would become a PoW on 16.11.44.)* S/L Lucas was the senior 75(NZ) Squadron pilot heading for Genoa on this night, while S/L Chamberlain took the lead for Frankfurt, and they became airborne for their respective targets between 18.50 and 19.20.

The cloud that had at first covered the route out cleared to leave clear skies over southern Germany, but intense darkness provided challenging conditions for the bomber crews. S/L Chamberlain failed to locate the primary target and dropped his bombs instead on a small town with a railway line running through it, missing the tracks by two hundred yards. He was also attacked by a Me110, which approached first from the port quarter, then from above and finally from dead astern, but no damage was sustained. P/O Fisher and Sgt Nunn both bombed at Frankfurt and observed bursts but could not assess the results. Sgt Isherwood bombed either a railway junction or an aerodrome on the southern edge of Frankfurt, probably as an alternative to pressing on across the Alps. G/C Powell reached Genoa and dropped his bombs in three sticks, the first on a factory near the aiming point, the second alongside, and the third on the north side of the docks, where a fire broke out. S/L Lucas observed flashes on the north side of the docks, while the others could not determine the precise fall of their hardware. Sgt Isherwood and crew successfully abandoned R1177, now re-coded AA-K, over Essex after becoming lost and running short of fuel, and the Wellington crashed three miles north-west of Halstead at 03.20.

The month ended with simultaneous operations against Stettin and Hamburg on consecutive nights, beginning on the 29/30th. Forces of 139 and 93 aircraft respectively carried out the attacks, which were claimed by returning crews as successful. 75(NZ) Squadron was not called into action on this night but made ready six Wellingtons on the 30th for a repeat performance, this time with reduced forces of eighty-two aircraft for Hamburg and forty for Stettin. The Kiwi element was divided between the two targets at a ratio of five to one in favour of Stettin, and they all departed Feltwell together between 19.00 and 19.20 with S/L Chamberlain the senior pilot on duty. The weather conditions outbound were reasonably good, but cloud and haze greeted Sgt Saunders at Hamburg and hampered his attempts to locate the aiming point. He delivered his bombs over the city, observing them to burst and contribute to the fourteen fires reported by the city authorities. The others arrived over the Baltic coast to find Stettin under clear skies but shrouded to an extent by ground haze. S/L Chamberlain dropped his bombs on fires already burning near the aiming point and took a photograph showing them to have fallen around 350 yards to the north-west. P/O Roberts bombed a large fire on the aiming point, while Sgt Curlewis saw his explode among oil storage tanks to the north-east. Sgt Allen attacked from 3,000 feet and observed bursts on the aiming point and Sgt Nunn simply reported bombing in the target area.

During the course of the month the squadron was assigned to sixteen targets and dispatched 111 sorties for the loss of eight Wellingtons and five crews.

October 1941

September had seen an increase in losses for the squadron, which would continue in October and two crews mentioned above, who had narrowly escaped misfortune, would have used up varying degrees of their ration of good fortune. There was little activity for the squadron's crews at the start of the month other than a small-scale attack on Dunkerque for three freshmen on the night of the 3/4th. P/O William Reginald Methven RAFVR and Sgts Ralph Holland Tye RNZAF and Richard Charlwood Barker RAFVR took off at 18.45 and bombed the target in the face of a spirited searchlight and flak defence, before returning safely after barely three hours aloft.

There were no operations between the 5th and the 10th as adverse weather conditions kept the entire Command on the ground, and when operations resumed on the night of the 10/11th, Essen and Cologne were the main objectives. Forces of seventy-eight and sixty-nine aircraft respectively were made ready, 75(NZ) Squadron providing eight Wellingtons for the latter, which departed Feltwell either side of midnight with S/L Chamberlain the senior pilot on duty. All reached Cologne to find low cloud with a number of gaps, but S/L Chamberlain was forced to jettison his bomb load west-south-west of the target after his hydraulics system failed, presumably after being hit by flak, and this left the Wellington unable to maintain height and the undercarriage partially deployed. The others carried out their attacks in the face of intense anti-aircraft fire between 4,000 and 12,000 feet and watched their bombs explode in the target area and start fires. Sgt Tye discovered a hung-up bomb after releasing his load from 9,700 feet, and it would fall out safely after landing. One aircraft was seen to crash and explode near the target and this may have been Z8969 AA-R, which failed to return with Sgt Curlewis RAAF and his crew. There were no survivors among the six occupants, which included two members of the RNZAF, second pilot, Sgt Colin Maurice Thompson, and rear gunner, Sgt Timothy Rowley Murphy.

Two nights later, a heavy night of operations brought a new record number of 373 sorties, of which 152 were detailed for Nuremberg, the city deep in southern Germany that had been the scene of massive Nazi Party rallies during Hitler's rise to power in the thirties. A force of ninety-nine aircraft was assigned to Bremen, while seventy-nine from 5 Group returned to the "Buna" works at Marl/Hüls. 75(NZ) Squadron made ready nine Wellingtons, but the ORB is most unhelpful in determining which crews were assigned to which target. They took off together between 19.00 and 19.59 but P/O Fisher, who was bound for Nuremberg, returned a little over two hours later with an overheating engine. It seems that not all crews located their primary target, the ORB recording that one aircraft bombed the docks at Ostend, while others released their loads within a fifty-mile radius of Nuremberg. The 3 Group ORB described the Nuremberg operation as very successful, reporting that the bombing took place from between 2,500 and 13,000 feet, and mentioned one crew feeling the shockwave from the explosion of their bombs at 6,000 feet. The whole centre of the town seemed to be ablaze with fires visible from ninety miles away, when in reality, very few bombs actually fell into the city, the majority hitting outlying communities to the south.

Bremen was cloud-covered and was reached and attacked by only two-thirds of the force, who were able to report fires but nothing specific. 5 Group fared no better at Marl/Hüls, rendering it a night of wasted effort and massive disappointment, which was compounded by the loss of thirteen aircraft. Among these was X9981 (probably AA-X), which crashed near Dinant in southern Belgium with fatal consequences for S/L Chamberlain RAF and his crew. Only two returning Wellingtons landed at Feltwell before conditions required the others to be diverted, three to Honington and one to Horsham St Faith. The other, AA-Q, was diverted to Stradishall, where Sgt Parker crash-landed as a result of damage caused by an encounter with a BF109, which wounded his second pilot, Sgt Ivor John McLachlan RNZAF, in the right thigh and killed the rear gunner, Sgt Maurice Ronald Day RAFVR. Curiously, the Barker crew is not listed in the ORB for this operation.

Bad weather attended a 3 Group operation to Düsseldorf on the night of the 13/14th, for which the squadron made ready six Wellingtons. They took off between 18.30 and 18.45 and encountered ten-tenths cloud and thick ground haze, through which no crew was able to locate the aiming point. Large cones of searchlights were co-operating with flak batteries to the north and west of the target and offered a formidable defence, through which the bombers carried out their attacks on estimated positions. No assessment could be made and the only interesting report on return was offered by Sgt Taylor and crew, who were followed for forty minutes by an enemy aircraft employing a headlamp.

According to the squadron ORB, Sgt Ramsey and crew were dispatched at 18.35 on the 14th to attack Düsseldorf. The 3 Group ORB makes no mention of 75(NZ) Squadron or indeed, Feltwell, operating on this night, when Nuremberg appears to be the only target. Heavy cloud was encountered during the flight out and in the target area, where intense heavy flak provided a further challenge. Sgt Ramsey was diverted to an alternative target and is reported to have dropped his 500 and 250 pounders on an aerodrome on the Dutch coast, before landing after six hours and twenty-five minutes in the air.

An all-3 Group attack on Cologne was mounted on the night of the 15/16th and involved twenty-seven Wellingtons and seven Stirlings. 75(NZ) Squadron dispatched nine Wellingtons to the main target, which took off between 18.15 and 18.30, leaving the single freshman crew of Sgt John Frederick Massey Parnham RAFVR to get away last at 18.55 and join a handful of others at Boulogne. He was back on the ground three hours later to report bombing the target and observing bursts but could offer no insight into the effectiveness of his efforts. There were no senior pilots among the Cologne element, which found the target to be covered by cloud and bombed on estimated positions on the west side of the city, employing concentrations of searchlights and flak as a reference. Local reports confirmed that very few bombs had fallen within the city and there were no casualties or any damage, but outlying communities to the east were hit, as was Duisburg, thirty miles away and a lucky strike on the Wesseling oil refinery seven miles south of Cologne caused eight thousand tons of fuel production to be lost. There were three empty dispersals at Feltwell on the following morning, two of them belonging to the 75(NZ) Squadron aircraft containing the crews of Sgt Barker and Sgt Matetich RAFVR. It was established later that W5663 had crashed near Düsseldorf, killing Sgt Barker RAFVR, his second pilot, P/O Trevor Bernard Robertson RNZAF and two others, while the two survivors had been taken into captivity. X9916 came down somewhere in the general target area with no survivors, and two of those who died, the second pilot, Sgt Frederick Lionel Roy Wood, and the navigator, F/Sgt Neville Henry Welsh, were members of the RNZAF. According to Feltwell Flying Control, the two aircraft lost were "X" and "S", but we can't be sure which was which.

The Squadron ORB recorded a single sortie on the following night undertaken by Sgt Ramsey and crew against Cologne between 18.25 and 23.25. However, the 3 Group ORB mentions Duisburg as the night's only target, with Marham and Wyton dispatching crews. One must conclude that the 75(NZ) Squadron scribe recorded the wrong target and his 3 Group counterpart was unaware of the Feltwell sortie. In the event, the operation was a complete failure, for which heavy cloud was mostly responsible. Bremen was selected to host a raid by 153 aircraft of 3 and 5 Groups on the night of the 20/21st, for which 3 Group contributed sixty-three aircraft, six of the Wellingtons belonging to 75(NZ) Squadron. They departed Feltwell between 18.20 and 18.40 on another night of adverse weather conditions and found the target to be concealed beneath ten-tenths low cloud, which forced them to bomb on estimated positions based on searchlight and flak activity. It turned into another night of frustration and failure, which added further to the pressure building upon AM Peirse to achieve some worthwhile results. Sgt Parnham crash-landed R1457, now re-coded AA-Y, at Marham on return, having experienced hydraulic issues with the undercarriage on take-off from Feltwell. The crew walked away, and the Wellington would soon be returned to service. Later, on the 21st, he and his crew were the only ones from the squadron to operate, when taking off at 18.45 to bomb the docks and shipping at Boulogne with a load of 500 and 250 pounders and containers of incendiaries. The weather conditions were as recently experienced with heavy cloud making identification of the aiming point impossible, and the incendiaries were dropped on estimated position over the primary target, while the bombs found their way onto an unspecified aerodrome, where a hangar was believed to be hit.

Mannheim was the objective for a force of 136 aircraft on the night of the 22/23rd, for which the squadron briefed six crews. S/L Lucas was the senior pilot on duty as they took off between 18.00 and 18.15 and headed into foul weather conditions, which included electrical, thunder and snowstorms and icing from the Belgian coast to the target. Fewer than half of the force reached the target area, where bombing took place on estimated positions and many others found alternative and last-resort recipients for their bombs. X9914 AA-M failed to return home and news eventually arrived to confirm that Sgt Cyril Taylor RAFVR and his crew had all lost their lives in the crash near Diksmuide, ten miles south of Ostend in Belgium. The second pilot, Sgt Frederick Alexander Spark, was a member of the RNZAF. Frankfurt was the principal target on the night of the 24/25th, but the operation did not involve aircraft from Feltwell, which dispatched two freshman crews each from the resident squadrons to attack the port and shipping at Emden. P/O John Frederick Kelly Sandys RCAF and Sgt John William Black RNZAF and their crews took off at 18.15 and proceeded towards northern Germany in weather conditions that prevented them from locating the target. They dropped their bombs on searchlight and flak concentrations believed to be in the target area and returned with nothing useful to report.

F/L Peter James Robert Kitchin RAF was posted in from 23 O.T.U at Pershore w.e.f. the 28th and would be promoted to succeed the missing S/L Chamberlain as B Flight commander. Kitchin was "family", having served with the original 75 Squadron between 1937 and 1939 and then with 75(NZ) Squadron between September and November 1940. A force of 115 aircraft set off for Hamburg on the night of the 26/27th, while a handful of freshmen tried their hand against the docks and shipping at Cherbourg. Five crews from 75(NZ) Squadron were briefed, four for the main activity and one, that of Sgt Black it is believed, for France. They took off between 18.10 and 18.30 and those bound for north-western Germany encountered heavy, low cloud, which began to break up a little towards the end of the raid. A large fire was started, which could be seen from thirty-five miles into the return journey, and this may have been the one reported to be burning north-east of the Aussen-Alster Lake near the city centre. It was estimated that 150 searchlights were operating in cones and seemed to be co-operating with night-fighters. A message was received from Sgt Isherwood, which stated, "Target abandoned", and Z1168 AA-H failed to arrive home. The news filtered through some time later that Sgt S.J.G. Isherwood RAFVR and all but one of his mixed RAF, RCAF and RNZAF crew had survived and were now in enemy hands. Their aircraft had been badly damaged by flak over Hamburg and all but one managed to bale out, while wireless operator Sgt Barney Walker Shelnutt RCAF went down with the Wellington.

During the course of the month the squadron operated on twelve nights against fourteen targets and dispatched fifty-seven sorties for the loss of five Wellingtons and crews.

November 1941

Following the damning disclosures of the Butt Report in August, matters would be brought to a head early in the new month and bring into question the very existence of a strategic bomber force. It all began very badly for the Command, with an attempt to raid the Deutsche Werke shipyard in the port of Kiel on the night of the 1/2nd. A force of 134 aircraft was assembled, of which eleven represented 75(NZ) Squadron and they took off between 17.35 and 17.56 with S/L Lucas the senior pilot on duty and the two freshmen crews of Sgt James Kenneth Climie RNZAF and Sgt Harry Machin RAFVR taking part. They climbed through ten-tenths cloud, which persisted all the way to the target area, where a little over 50% of the force arrived to carry out an attack. So dense was the low cloud that the searchlights were unable to penetrate it, and although heavy predicted flak reached 14,000 feet, it did not give away the location of the target and the bombers flew past. No bombs fell within the town and docks area, but local reports spoke of the sound of bombs over in the east.

The squadron made ready nine Wellingtons on the 4th for an attack that night on the Krupp complex in the Borbeck districts of Essen in company with nineteen others from 3 Group, but it seems that one failed to take-off. S/L Lucas was again the senior pilot on duty as they departed Feltwell between 17.45 and 18.10 and climbed into ten-tenths cloud, which would blot out the ground for the entire operation. Some crews bombed on estimated positions, while others sought out alternatives, but it was another wasted effort, which, happily, did not cost any crews.

On the 6th, the squadron briefed the five freshman crews of Sgt Shilleto RAF, Sgt Spence, RAFVR, Sgt K.M. Smith RAF, Sgt Machin and Sgt Sykes RAF for a raid that evening on the docks and shipping at Le Havre. They took off between 17.45 and 18.10 and reached the target area to find six-tenths cloud, which enabled them to make out some ground detail and deliver their bomb loads with a degree of accuracy. They returned after a round trip of about five hours to report that they had left extensive fires burning. *(The squadron ORB mentions Essen as a target for this night as well as Le Havre, but the reports speak of target area, not areas, as would be the case if more than one had been attacked.)*

AM Peirse, desperate to score a success after weeks of negative results caused partly by adverse weather conditions, made plans for a major and, indeed, record night of operations on the 7th. The original plan had Berlin as the main objective, for which over two hundred aircraft were initially detailed, but a late weather forecast predicted a large area of bad weather characterised by storms, thick ice-bearing cloud and hail over the North Sea, which the force would have to fly through to and from the target. The 5 Group A-O-C, AVM Slessor, was unhappy about the prospects for his seventy-five aircraft and was allowed to withdraw them and send them instead to Cologne. A third force of fifty-three Wellingtons and two Stirlings from 1 and 3 Groups was assigned to Mannheim, while minor operations involved more than ninety other aircraft. The total number of sorties, at 392, was a new record, but sadly this massive effort would not be rewarded with success. Despite the ominous weather warnings, the operations were allowed to go ahead, only now, the Berlin force had been reduced to 169 aircraft. 75(NZ) Squadron detailed fourteen Wellingtons, nine of them assigned to Berlin and five for freshman crews to employ against the docks and shipping at Ostend.

The Berlin-bound element took off first, between 17.30 and 17.45 with no senior pilots on duty, but was reduced during the outward leg by the early return of P/O Sandys with engine trouble and Sgt Parnham with an indisposed navigator. The others pressed on and may have been among the seventy-three crews claiming to have reached the target area, where ten-tenths cloud shrouded the capital from view, forcing crews to bomb indiscriminately on estimated positions. A barrage of heavy flak gave a clue as to the location of the target, but what happened beneath the clouds could not be determined. Meanwhile, the freshmen, including first-timer Sgt Allen Bruce Slater RAAF, had departed for Ostend an hour after the Berlin brigade with S/L Kitchin undertaking his first sortie since joining the squadron. They found the target and carried out attacks before returning safely home between 23.47 and 00.30 from what was probably the most successful raid of the night. Twenty-one aircraft failed to return from Berlin, 12.4% of those dispatched, and all they had to show for it was scattered damage in many parts of the city and fourteen houses totally destroyed. Among the missing were two Wellingtons from 75(NZ) Squadron, X9951 AA-L and X9976 AA-O containing the crews of P/O Methven and Sgt Black respectively. The former sent out an SOS signal at 22.28, before abandoning the aircraft to its fate over western Germany and parachuting into the arms of their captors. There were two members of the RNZAF on board, the sole fatality, second pilot, Sgt John Cuthbert McKechnie Gibson, and front gunner, Sgt Thomas Duffy. The latter Wellington was last heard from at 22.36 when sending a message, "Target not attacked." On the way home it was shot down by a night-fighter flown by the Luftwaffe Ace, Oblt Helmut Lent of 4./NJG1 and crashed at 01.21 at Aldeboarn, about ten miles south of the "Wespennest" night fighter aerodrome at Leeuwarden in northern Holland. There were no survivors from what, because of the colour-related surnames of four crew members, came to be known as "The Rainbow Crew" of Sgt Black RNZAF. The second pilot, Sgt Trevor Hedley Gray, wireless operator, Sgt Leslie Cyril Green and navigator, P/O Eric Lloyd, were also members of the RNZAF and the rear gunner was another Sgt Black RAF.

There were no losses from among the 5 Group contingent following their trip to Cologne, but it was established later that for all their efforts, they had managed to destroy only two houses in the city and who knows where the other bombs fell? To compound a thoroughly bad night for Peirse, the Mannheim force failed to land a single bomb within the city and lost seven Wellingtons in the process, while nine other aircraft went missing from the minor operations. The loss of thirty-seven aircraft in one night was more than twice the previous highest and it proved to be the final straw for the Air Ministry, which instructed the C-in-C on the 13th to restrict future operations while the future of an independent strategic bomber force was considered at the highest level. In the meantime, Peirse was summoned to an uncomfortable meeting with Churchill at Chequers on the 8th to offer his explanations for the debacle.

Twenty-four hours after Berlin, Essen was posted as the target for an operation by fifty-four aircraft drawn from all groups. 75(NZ) Squadron briefed eleven crews, who took off between

17.30 and 17.50 with S/L Kitchin the senior pilot on duty. They encountered patchy cloud on the way out and five to nine-tenths over the target, where they had to run the gauntlet of intense searchlights in cones and heavy flak. It was claimed that many large fires were started, bomb bursts and explosions were observed across a built-up area and a railway junction to the south was also attacked. Six aircraft failed to return, and all three missing Wellingtons belonged to 75(NZ) Squadron. Sgt John Stephen Wilson RNZAF sent a message "target abandoned" at 20.49 and was no more than three miles from the stretch of water known as the Haringvliet, which feeds into the North Sea in south-western Holland, when flak brought down Z8942, AA-J at 22.15, killing all but the rear gunner. Tragically, he, Sgt Lawrence Beresford Hamilton Hope RNZAF, would be killed on the 19th of April 1945 by Allied fighter-bombers, while being force-marched. The Wilson crew included Sgt Sir Charles Thomas Hewitt Mappin, RAFVR, a baronet and member of the House of Lords, who volunteered as a gunner in the RAF and is said to have refused a commission and a ground job. X9628, AA-A crashed near Krefeld in the Ruhr killing the rear gunner Sgt George McAra Thain, RAFVR, while Sgt K.M. Smith RAFVR and four others fell into enemy hands. Wireless operator, Sgt Raymond James Rugg RAFVR, sustained serious injuries, to which he would succumb a week later. X9977, AA-D fell victim to a night-fighter flown by Lt Werner Rowlin of III./NJG1 and crashed at Ijzevoorde in Holland, some ten miles from the border with Germany with no survivors from the crew of Sgt Nunn RAFVR.

Thereafter, the squadron remained at home as the Command almost withdrew into itself. A number of small-scale operations took place against ports and others were scheduled, particularly by 3 Group against the enemy warships at Brest but were cancelled before they got off the ground. During the lull in operations two Merlin-powered Mk II Wellingtons were taken on charge on the 19th, Z8441, AA-T and Z8495, AA-P. These aircraft would be employed, in particular, to carry 4,000lb "cookies" or "blockbusters", so called because of their high charge to weight ratio, although Mk 1C versions were now also able to lift one.

On the 23rd, seven Wellingtons were made ready for their freshman crews to take to Dunkerque, for which they took off between 17.10 and 17.30 to join thirty other aircraft from 3 Group. New captains included Sgt Robert Arthur Colville RNZAF, Sgt Evans RAF, Sgt Francis Charles Harrison-Smith RNZAF, Sgt Loch Lomond Bentley RNZAF, Sgt Eric Reginald Jones RNZAF and Sgt Ian James Shephard RNZAF. It became another ineffective operation in which just seven crews bombed in the target area, mostly after coming down below the ten-tenths cloud, while many others jettisoned their bombs in the sea or brought them home.

Almost as if to compensate for the lack of activity during the month, the squadron made ready seventeen Wellingtons on the 26th, fifteen for an attack on Emden and two for Ostend. They took off between 17.20 and 19.20, with S/Ls Kitchin and Lucas the senior pilots on duty, but it is not possible to determine which two crews were assigned to Ostend. They all encountered heavy cloud that prevented most from reaching their respective targets, but Sgt Evans returned early anyway with engine trouble. The winds were not as forecast, and this drove many crews north of their intended track, and a handful of them dropped their bombs on estimated positions, while most brought them home. Returning from Emden, first-time captain Sgt Giddens RAFVR and crew were flying on fumes with faltering engines and safely abandoned Z1144 at 23.15 over the Lincolnshire coast, eight miles north-east of Boston. The aircraft had arrived at the squadron only two days before. "Popeye" Lucas dropped one of the new "cookies" on Emden from Mk II Wellington, Z8495, AA-P and when he landed at 22.50, it brought to an end his second tour of operations. After a training course he would be posted across the tarmac in early January to command Feltwell's 1519 BAT Flight, but the death of his wife in December would prompt a return to New Zealand in March 1942. In November 1943 he would set sail again for England, and as previously mentioned, serve as a flight commander with 487(NZ) Squadron of the 2nd Tactical Air Force flying Mosquitos, completing his third tour of operations on the 11th of July 1944.

The final operations of the month were directed at north-western Germany on the night of the 30th, when the Blohm & Voss shipyards and three city-centre aiming points in Hamburg were the objectives for a force of 181 aircraft, while Emden was the target for fifty. 75(NZ) Squadron made ready eleven Wellington 1Cs and two Mk IIs to support both operations, sending ten aircraft to Germany's second city and three to Emden. G/C Powell was the senior pilot on duty, supported by S/L Kitchin, and they took off between 16.50 and 17.20 on a night of fine weather conditions, which provided clear skies over the target area with moonlight. The squadron ORB informs us that a few bombs were dropped in the target area, but many were brought home and the 3 Group ORB queries the lack of flak at such a hot spot. This latter point was contradicted by the squadron ORB, which mentioned heavy, medium and light flak and a large number of searchlights in operation. Only 122 of the returning crews claimed to have bombed the target, where some housing damage resulted, and six large fires were started along with sixteen smaller ones. Unaccountably, thirty-five crews attacked alternative targets, which, on a night of favourable bombing conditions, was strange.

The raid on Emden appeared to be more satisfactory and returning crews claimed good results. Fifteen aircraft failed to make it back from the two operations, thirteen of them from Hamburg, but it was from Emden that 75(NZ) Squadron's Z1099 AA-S went missing with the freshman crew of Sgt Harrison-Smith RNZAF. They had the misfortune to cross paths with Ofw Paul Gildner of 4./NJG1, a pilot who would go on to score forty-eight victories before his death in February 1943. He shot the Wellington down off the Dutch coast and it crashed into the Waddenzee without survivors.

During the course of the month the squadron operated against eleven targets, dispatching eighty-four sorties for the loss of seven Wellingtons and six crews.

December 1941

The continuing presence at Brest of the German cruisers Scharnhorst and Gneisenau prompted a renewed obsession with the port beginning on the 7th of December, which would continue until the affair was finally resolved in the infamous "Channel Dash" episode in the coming February. Numerous operations of varying proportions would be mounted against the port in general and the ships in particular, more at the insistence of the Admiralty than any desire on the part of the C-in-C to become involved with precision targets, which were difficult to hit and fiercely defended. There was no operational activity for 75(NZ) Squadron until the 11th, when four crews were dispatched at 16.40 to join thirty others in bombing the docks and shipping in the port of Le Havre. Only three of the freshman crews were listed in the ORB, and all returned safely with their bomb loads of 250 pounders between 21.35 and 23.30, after failing to locate the target in conditions of ten-tenths cloud.

The weather had improved by the following afternoon, when nine of the squadron's Wellingtons arrived over Brest to carry out a small-scale raid in conditions of two to four-tenths cloud. It was another freshman show, involving exclusively sergeant pilots, who had departed Feltwell between 14.45 and 16.36 each carrying a mixed load of a cookie and 1,000 and 500 pounders. They were met by searchlights operating in cones and an accurate barrage of heavy and light flak, as a result of which, no assessment of the raid was possible. The 3 Group ORB records that the squadron's X9825 AA-V suffered an undercarriage collapse on landing at Feltwell through enemy action, but no mention of this incident is made in the squadron records and the Wellington in question is not shown as operating on that night. Flying Control reported another drama that evening when a 57 Squadron Wellington returned with a full bomb load and dropped more than one hundred incendiaries in the middle of the flare path, some of which started to burn.

Five NCO crews were briefed on the 15th for a return to Brest by seventeen Wellingtons and seven Stirlings, by which time the weather conditions had taken a turn for the worse. They took off between 14.50 and 16.10 and reached the target area to encounter cloud and high winds, the latter having made navigation difficult. They were greeted by the same flak response but much reduced searchlight activity and all returned safely, unable to provide the intelligence section with an assessment of the outcome because of the cloud. Seven Wellingtons were made ready on the 17th, six for the same target as part of a force of 121 aircraft, and one for Le Havre, and this time the squadron participants were to be led to Brest by W/C Sawrey-Cookson with S/L Kitchin in support. They took off between 16.45 and 17.13 and arrived in the target area to find ten-tenths cloud but otherwise good visibility. Z1083 AA-K sustained flak damage over Le Havre and Sgt Climie landed at Exeter on return to allow P/O Stanley Holmes "Pete" Gunning RNZAF, the second pilot, to receive medical attention to a jaw wound inflicted by shrapnel. The Brest brigade returned safely with nothing concrete to show for their efforts.

The relentless assault on Brest continued on the 23rd, for which the squadron prepared seven Wellington Mk 1Cs and a Mk II as part of a force of thirty-eight Wellingtons and nine Stirlings. They departed Feltwell between 16.23 and 17.20 with W/C Sawrey-Cookson again the senior pilot on duty and flying in the Mk II, Z8441, AA-T. The weather over the target was good for a change and the reception hostile, as always, and crews bombed in the target area, where searchlight dazzle was largely responsible for obscuring the results. On return, Z8834 AA-P crashed at 23.45 near Elvedon in Suffolk, close to the boundary with Norfolk while awaiting landing instructions, and the pilot, F/Sgt Bentley RNZAF, was killed, while his crew sustained injuries.

The third wartime Christmas passed peacefully, and operations resumed on the 27th, when 5 Group's 50 Squadron supported the epic and successful Vaagso raid by Royal Marines off the Norwegian coast on the 27th. The final operations of the month were scheduled for the 27th, when Düsseldorf was to host a raid by 132 aircraft, including eight from 75(NZ) Squadron, while four others joined in another attack on Brest. As usual, the ORB is not explicit with regard to the assigning of crews to a particular target, but based on take-off times, three NCO crews departed Feltwell between 16.30 and 16.40, and although Sgt Machin's sortie is not mentioned, the location of his homecoming confirms that he was the fourth one bound for Brest. The remainder took off between 16.55 and 17.10 with W/C Sawrey-Cookson and S/L

Kitchin the senior pilots on duty. The Brest quartet joined up with other 3 Group Wellingtons and Stirlings on the way out and found the target concealed beneath cloud and the output from an effective smoke screen. A number of crews claimed to catch a glimpse of the docks, but the majority bombed on estimated positions before returning home. W/C Sawrey-Cookson, who was flying in Z1077 AA-N, filed a combat report for an attack by a Me110 night-fighter, which, perhaps, sustained damage. Z8971, AA-A suffered port-engine failure and was abandoned by Sgt Harry Machin RAFVR and crew over Devon. While they floated safely down to earth, the Wellington ended its career with a crash on Dartmoor. The skies were clear over Düsseldorf, and the bombers were greeted by the usual intense searchlight and flak response, in the face of which the attacks went ahead and many bomb bursts were reported in the town and the railway station.

During the course of the month the squadron operated against eight targets and dispatched forty-five sorties for the loss of two Wellingtons and one pilot. So ended a year of under-achievement and disappointment, which had left the Command languishing in the doldrums and with an uncertain future. There had been few advances on the performance of 1940 and the new bomber types, the Stirling, Halifax and Manchester, had all disappointed and fallen short of their design requirements, and each type had undergone periods of grounding while essential modifications were carried out. 1942 beckoned, a year which would bring changes and eventually the first signs of the emergence of an effective bomber force, but also the stark realisation that there was a very long and bloody struggle ahead, before any light would appear at the end of the tunnel. In actual fact, a bright light in the form of the Avro Lancaster was already undergoing proving trials in the hands of 5 Group's 44 Squadron and would enter the fray as the "shining sword" in the armoury of a new Commander-in-Chief in the spring.

Wellington R1162 AA-Y "Yorker" being serviced in the snow, Feltwell, early 1941.
(NZ Bomber Command Assn. archives, Mayhill collection)

Wellingtons in the snow.
(NZ Bomber Command Assn. archives, Mayhill collection)

P/O Brian Patrick McNamara RAF and four of his crew were the squadron's first losses for 1941, killed when Wellington T2550 AA-L crashed near Stapleford, on their way to Bassingbourn.
(AWMM)

The White crew, March 1941 (L-R): Sgt Kelly (wireless operator), Sgt Harrison (navigator), Sgt White (pilot), P/O Artie Ashworth (second pilot), Sgt East (front gunner), and Sgt Alan Campbell (rear gunner). Behind is Wellington R1458, AA-E, in which they flew two NFTs, 5 and 7 March 1941.
(Artie Ashworth collection, courtesy of Vince Ashworth)

The Matheson crew, March–April 1941 (L-R): P/O Oliver Matheson, pilot, Sgt Bob Fotheringham, second pilot, Sgt Crossley, front gunner, P/O Eric Fowler, navigator, Sgt Jack Wakefield, rear gunner, Sgt Robert Newton, wireless operator. (Jack Wakefield collection, The Wings Over New Zealand Show, via Dave Homewood)

The Fotheringham crew in front of R1162 AA-Y "Yorker", May 1941. Front, Sgt Bob Fotheringham (skipper), behind him, P/O Eric Fowler DFC, navigator, P/O George Curry, 2nd pilot, Sgt Crossley, front gunner, Sgt Robert Newton, wireless operator. Top is Sgt Jack Wakefield, rear gunner.
The famous nose art was created by the aircraft's previous Rear Gunner, P/O Ted Wilcox.
(IWM)

The nose art painted on the Matheson (and later Fotheringham) crew's regular Wimpey, R1162, AA-Y "Yorker" became famous after photographs appeared in the UK and NZ press – "RAF soda siphon spitting bombs". (IWM)

The "Berlin Boys" farewelled at the crew bus by W/C Cyrus Kay (left), S/L Ben Widdowson (second from left), and F/L W.D. Brown (squadron gunnery leader, right). Also P/O (later S/L) Eric Fowler (third from left), Sgt Jack Wakefield (fourth from left), and their skipper, Sgt Bob Fotheringham (seventh from left). Feltwell, 10 April 1941. (Jack Wakefield collection, The Wings Over New Zealand Show, via Dave Homewood)

Wellington R1409 AA-N "Nuts" is bombed up for a raid on Berlin, 10 April 1941. Below, take off. (NZBCA archives)

*Pilot and navigator in discussion: F/O Graham "Darkie" Parker (left) and P/O John Breckell.
(NZBCA archives, Stan Brooks collection, via Anna Rhodes-Sayer)*

*The Parker crew with their "kite", R1038, AA-H (L-R): unknown 2nd Pilot, Sgt Douglas Banks, F/O Graham "Darkie" Parker, P/O John Breckell, unknown front gunner, Sgt Alexander Rowe, unknown ground crew.
(Alexander Rowe collection, courtesy of Dion Rowe)*

Above: The Parker crew with R1038, AA-H (L-R): Sgt Douglas Banks, wireless operator; F/O Graham Parker, skipper; P/O John Breckell, navigator; Sgt Alexander Rowe, rear gunner.
(Alexander Rowe collection, courtesy of Dion Rowe)

Left: Sgt Alexander Rowe with his "office", the rear turret of R1038, AA-H.
(Alexander Rowe collection, courtesy of Dion Rowe)

One of the most famous 75 (NZ) Squadron photos, a PR photo supposedly taken before an operation to Hamburg, but in fact on 10 May 1941. S/L Ben Widdowson centre, with white overalls. Amongst the airmen shown, members of the Matheson, Fotheringham, Hill and Coney crews are identifiable.
(Alexander Rowe collection, courtesy of Dion Rowe)

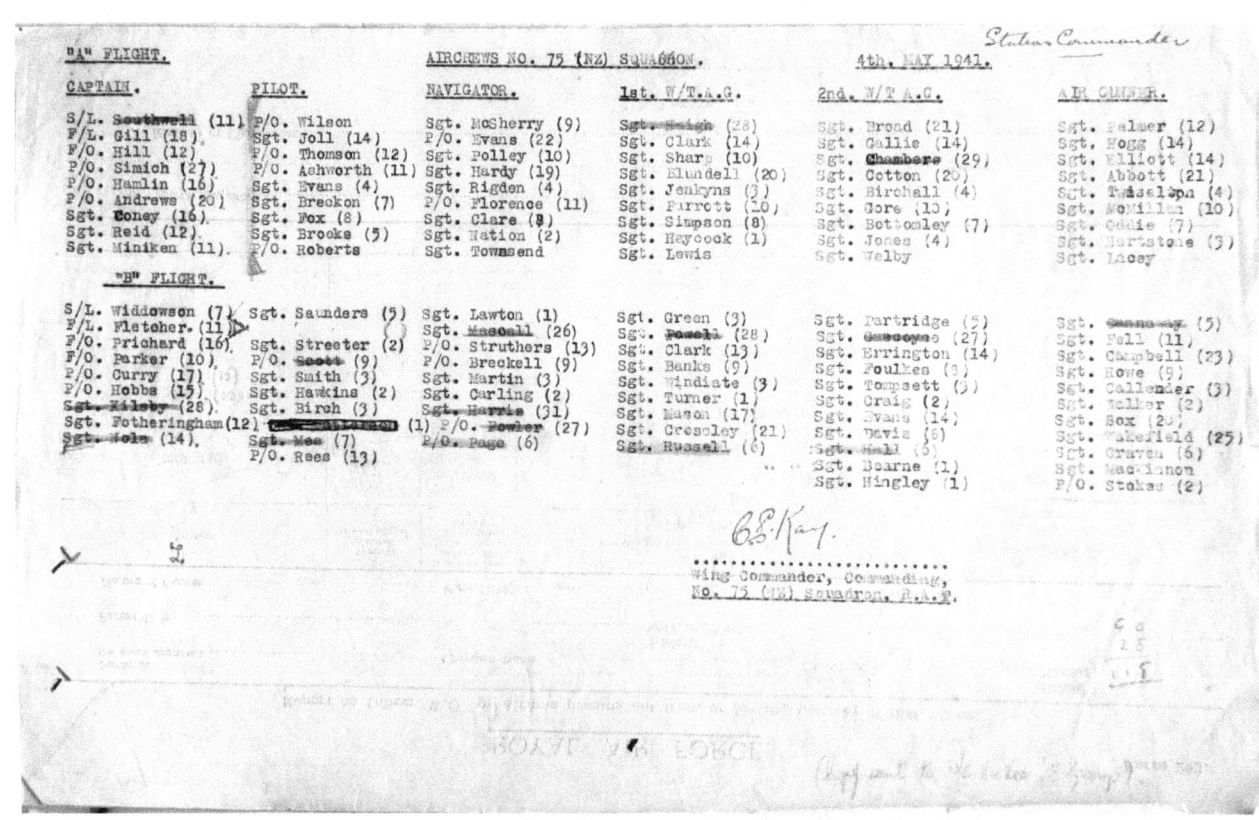

Aircrew lists, A and B Flights, 4th of May 1941. (Archives NZ, Maurice Buckley collection)

Sgt Eric Francis "Pete" Gannaway (feltwell.net)

F/O David Prichard, DSO. (NZ Herald)

Members of the Ashworth crew, May 1941 (L-R): Sgt Ted McSherry (navigator), P/O Artie Ashworth (pilot), P/O P.F. Wilson (second pilot), and Sgt Broad (front gunner). Artie inherited the crew from S/L Southwell; missing are Sgt Welby, wireless operator and Sgt Geoffrey Palmer, rear gunner. Ashworth and McSherry had rowed together back in Wellington, NZ.
(Artie Ashworth collection, courtesy of Vince Ashworth)

Popeye's shot-up Wellington. (Popeye Lucas collection, courtesy of the Lucas family)

Feltwell Op's Board for the night of 16 June 1941, listing crews detailed for operations from both 75 (NZ) and 57 Squadrons. Aircraft numbers and codes shown, those carrying a camera marked with an asterisk. (Popeye Lucas collection, courtesy of the Lucas family)

HRH the Duke of Kent and AVM Baldwin greeted on arrival by Feltwell station commander, G/C Buckley, 24th of June 1941. (Alexander Rowe collection, courtesy of Dion Rowe)

The Duke of Kent being introduced to Sgt Ted Williams DFM by W/C Kay, 24th of June 1941. Others identifiable in the line-up include pilots Maurice McGreal (next to Williams), Bob Fotheringham (next) and "Pip" Coney (next but one). (Alexander Rowe collection, courtesy of Dion Rowe)

P/O Clive Scott in the cockpit of his Wellington. (From "Return At Dawn")

*Armourers with bomb trolleys, Feltwell, 1941.
(NZBCA archives, Stan Brooks collection, via Anna Rhodes-Sayer)*

Sgt James Allen Ward, VC (IWM)

Wellington L7818, AA-R showing the holes Sgt James Ward made in the fabric, and damage from fire in the wing. Climbing out onto the wing via the astro-hatch (B) with a dinghy-rope tied around his waist, he made hand and foot-holds in the fuselage and wings (1, 2 and 3) and moved out across the wing from where he was eventually able to extinguish the burning wing-fabric. (IWM)

Damage to the fuselage and wing of L7818, AA-R after the night fighter attack and subsequent fire, 7/8th of July 1941. (Kerry Foster, via Simon Sommerville)

*Five of the Widdowson crew who were involved in Jimmy Ward's VC action (L-R): Sgt Allan Box, Sgt Jimmy Ward, S/L Reuben "Ben" Widdowson, Sgt W. Mason, and Sgt Joe Lawton.
(Air Force Museum of New Zealand)*

Widdowson crew members (L-R): Sgt Allan Box, S/L Ben Widdowson, Sgt Jimmy Ward, Sgt W. Mason, and Sgt Joe Lawton. Sgt T. Evans, the front gunner, was recuperating in hospital from the wounds to his foot sustained during the attack. (From "Vickers Wellington – The Backbone of Bomber Command")

*Sgt James Ward VC is congratulated by W/C Cyrus Kay. Third from left, Sgt Gwyn Martin (Saunders crew), fourth Sgt Ray Curlewis (Saunders crew), fifth Sgt Jimmy Ward, sixth Sgt Joe Lawton (Widdowson crew), seventh Sgt Charlie Black (Saunders crew), eighth W/C Cyrus Kay and twelfth P/O John Breckell (Parker crew).
(Gwyn Martin collection, courtesy of David Martin)*

*Sgt Lawrence Alan "Joe" Lawton, AFC, RNZAF, navigator in the Widdowson crew the night that Jimmy Ward won his VC.
(From "Early Operations with Bomber Command")*

Officers and airmen together celebrated the confirmation of Jimmy Ward's VC with a dinner and party in the Feltwell Officer's Mess on the 7th of August. (From "The Restless Sky")

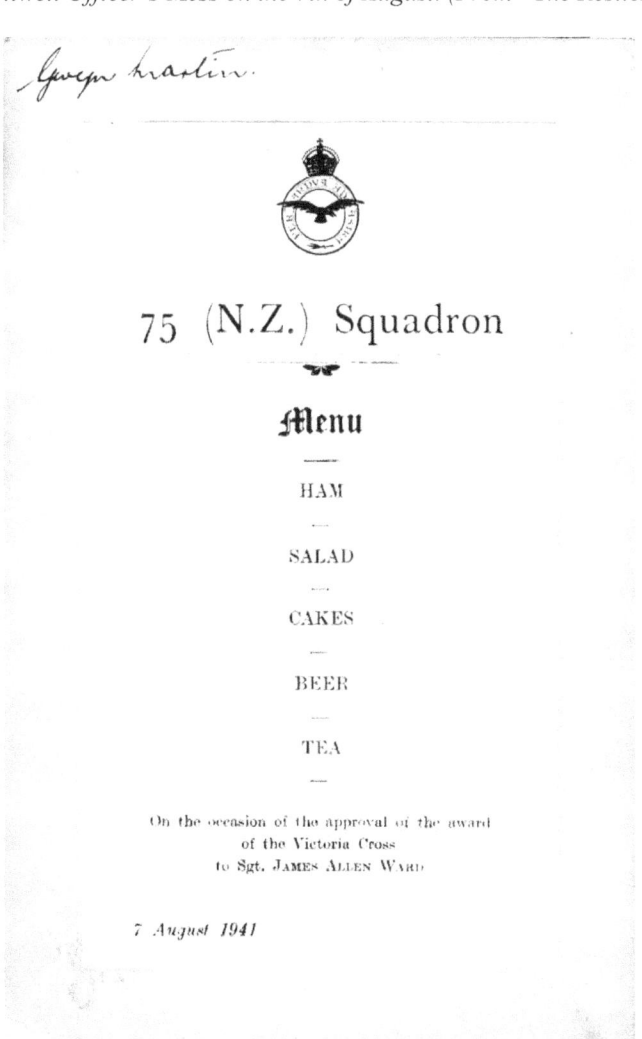

The menu for the celebration dinner on 7th of August "on the occasion of the approval of the award of the Victoria Cross to Sgt James Allen Ward". (Gwyn Martin collection, courtesy of David Martin)

Sgt James Allen Ward, VC. (NZ Bomber Command Assn. archives)

The Saunders crew (L-R): back - Raymond Curlewis (second pilot), Tony Saunders (pilot), Jack Thompson (front gunner), Gwyn Martin (navigator); front - Edward Callender (rear gunner) & Albert Windiate (wireless operator). (Gwyn Martin collection, courtesy of David Martin)

P/O William Jeffrey "Jeff" Rees DFC, RAF. (NZ Bomber Command Assn. archives)

Sgt Robert Ewen Ernest "Bob" Fotheringham, RNZAF, lost with all his crew on the night of the 15/16th of July. (AWMM)

Station Commander G/C J.A. "Speedy" Powell as he appeared in the movie "Target For Tonight".

Sgt Ian Millett, flying R1648, AA-K, ditched in the North Sea on 6/7th August 1941.
(Ian Millett collection, courtesy of Ursula Millett)

Wellington R1648, AA-K.
(feltwell.net)

"I had come down in the middle of a large plantation of young pine trees." Wellington X9764 AA-V in remarkably good shape after P/O Hughie Roberts crash-landed after running out of petrol on the 12/13th August 1941.
(NZ Bomber Command Assn. archives)

P/O Hughie Roberts with his aircraft, X9764 AA-V.
(feltwell.net)

Feltwell Operations Room, awaiting the return of crews from a night operation. Thought to be Station Commander G/C Speedy Powell seated at desk, centre, W/C Sawrey-Cookson standing behind him, S/L the Rev. Kayll at left. (From "Return at Dawn")

The Curry crew, April-June 1941, (L-R): back - Albert Windiate (wireless operator), Gwyn Martin (navigator), George Curry (pilot), Brian Smith (second pilot), Edward Callender (rear gunner), Stanley Tompsett (front gunner). Front – ground crew, names unknown. Tragically Tompsett was killed in a motorbike accident in June, in which Smith was also badly injured and hospitalised for a year. (Gwyn Martin collection, courtesy of David Martin)

Mr Peter Fraser, Prime Minister of New Zealand, visited the squadron in August 1941, meeting Sgt Ward VC., and spending time with NZ personnel. (NZ Bomber Command Assn. archives)

Bill Jordan, New Zealand High Commissioner, chatting with airmen, 1941. Sgt Alexander Rowe (rear gunner, Parker crew) third to the left of Mr Jordan. (Alexander Rowe collection, courtesy of Dion Rowe)

The crew de-briefing room, Feltwell.
(Jack Wakefield collection, The Wings Over New Zealand Show, via Dave Homewood)

Sgt. Sir Charles Thomas Hewitt Mappin.
(The Spectator)

P/O George Ronald "Ron" Simich, DFC, RNZAF.
(AWMM)

*Gunner checking his rear turret guns.
(From "Early Operations with Bomber Command")*

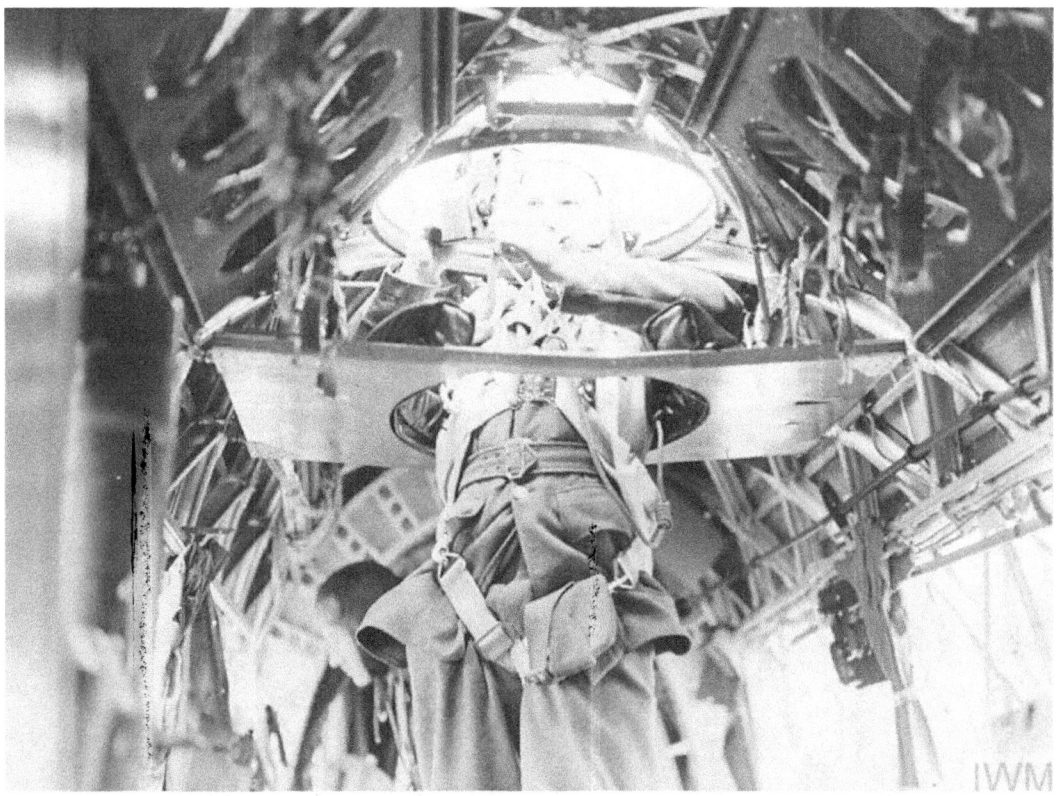

The observer (navigator) takes a bearing with his sextant from the astrodome. (IWM)

*Above "Shoot up"; below, "Night operations".
(NZBCA archives, Stan Brooks collection, via Anna Rhodes-Sayer)*

Another famous photo that appeared in the newspapers back home - armourers pose with a pair of 500-pounders and give the 'thumbs up' in front of the 'Wellington Devil', 10 May 1941. (IWM)

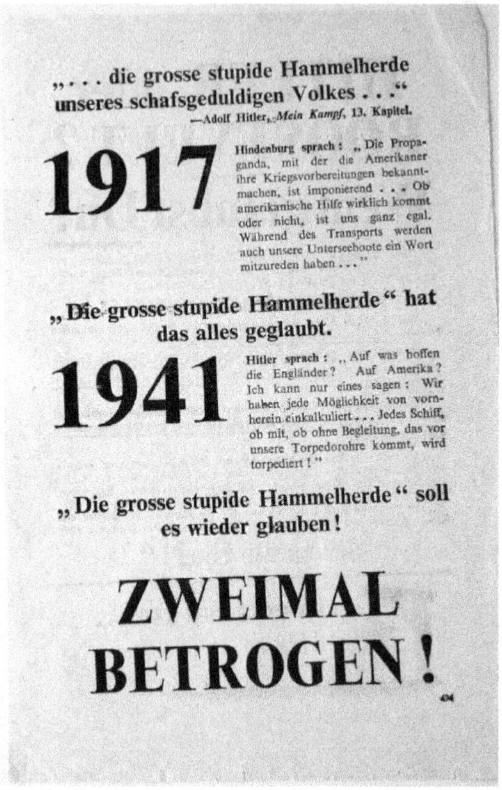

„. . . die grosse stupide Hammelherde unseres schafsgeduldigen Volkes . . .“

—Adolf Hitler, *Mein Kampf*, 13. Kapitel.

1917

Hindenburg sprach : „Die Propaganda, mit der die Amerikaner ihre Kriegsvorbereitungen bekanntmachen, ist imponierend . . . Ob amerikanische Hilfe wirklich kommt oder nicht, ist uns ganz egal. Während des Transports werden auch unsere Unterseeboote ein Wort mitzureden haben . . .“

„Die grosse stupide Hammelherde“ hat das alles geglaubt.

1941

Hitler sprach : „Auf was hoffen die Engländer? Auf Amerika? Ich kann nur eines sagen : Wir haben jede Möglichkeit von vornherein einkalkuliert . . . Jedes Schiff, ob mit, ob ohne Begleitung, das vor unsere Torpedorohre kommt, wird torpediert !“

„Die grosse stupide Hammelherde“ soll es wieder glauben!

ZWEIMAL BETROGEN!

Das verdankt Euch die Welt!

WARSCHAU im September 1939, nachdem Eure Bomber die Befehle Hitlers und Görings ausgeführt hatten. Das Bild stammt aus Goebbels' „Feuertaufe“, Eurem amtlichen Propagandafilm, den Ihr in allen neutralen Ländern aufführen liesst, um der Welt deutlich zu zeigen, was sie Deutschland verdankt.

ROTTERDAM — unter Hitlers „Schutz“. Der weisse Fleck — heute eine Wüste — war vor wenigen Monaten ein blühendes Stadtviertel. Dreissigtausend Menschen wurden hier innerhalb weniger Minuten durch deutsche Bomben getötet. Noch drei Wochen nach der Bombardierung wurden täglich dreihundert Leichen aus den Trümmern dieser unverteidigten Stadt geborgen.

Wollt Ihr das büssen?

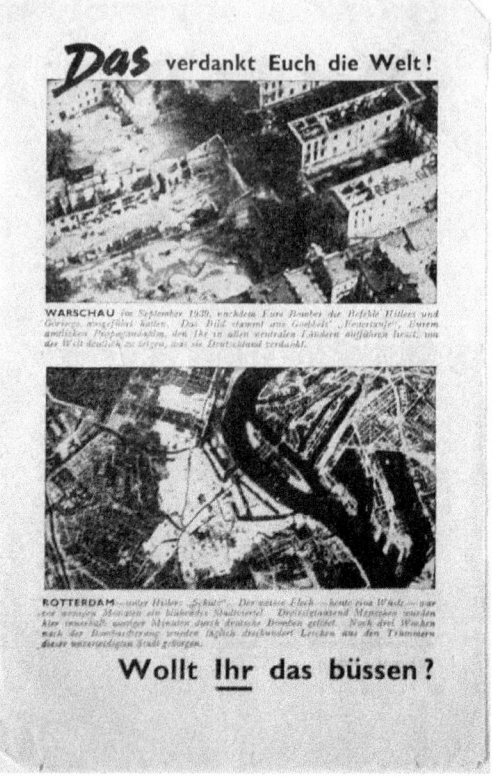

"Nickeling" – propaganda leaflets dropped over Germany, 1941.
(Archives NZ, Maurice Buckley collection)

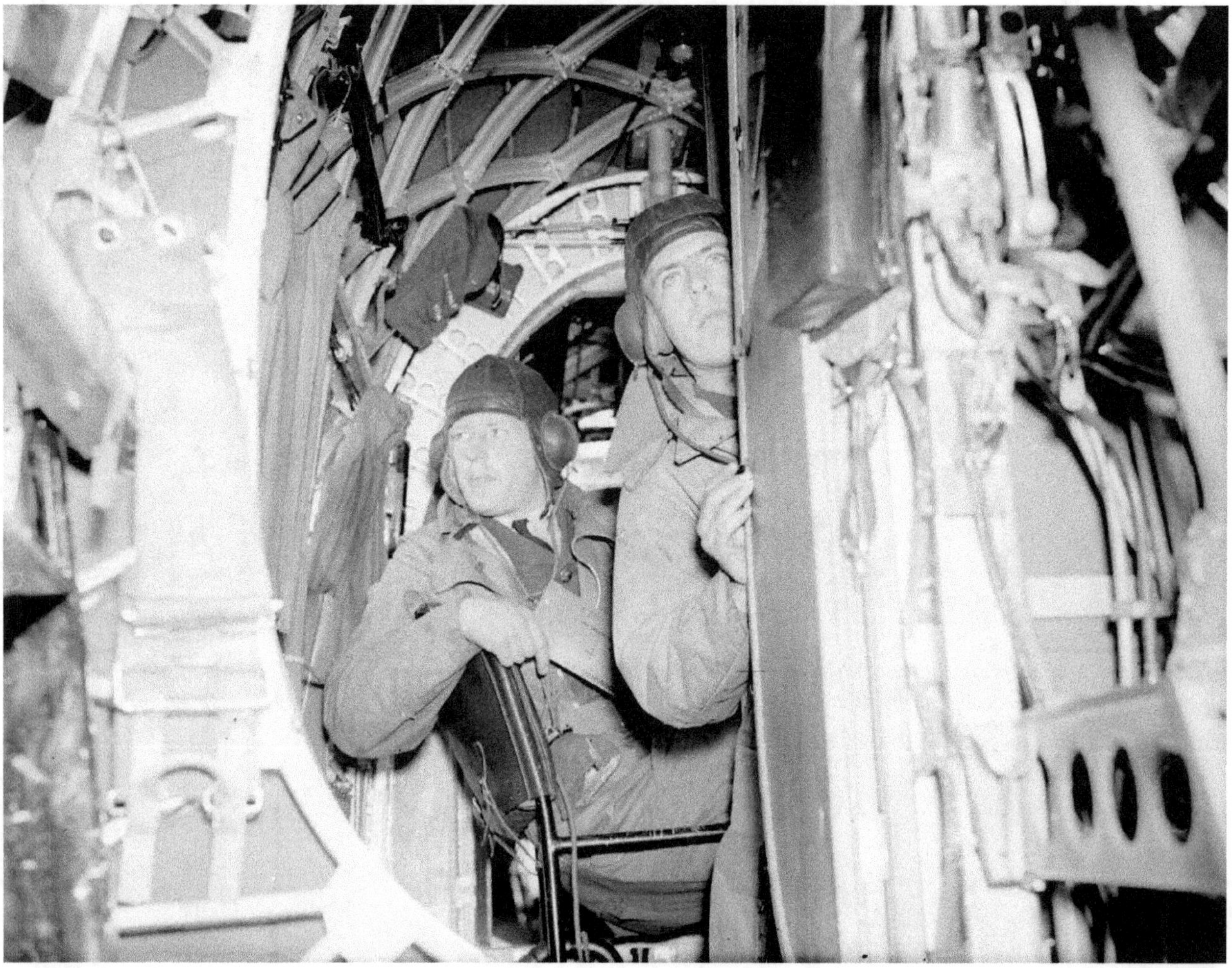

Navigator and Wireless Operator at their stations. (IWM)

RAF Feltwell from the air, home to both 75 (NZ) and 57 Squadrons in 1941. (IWM)

*Wellington T2747 AA-J was flown by the Ramsey and Nunn crews during September 1941.
(Popeye Lucas collection, courtesy of the Lucas family)*

S/L Frederick John "Popeye" Lucas DFC in Trafalgar Square. (Kerry Foster, via 75nzsquadron.com)

In an unusual mark of respect and collective grief, Joan Lucas, Popeye's wife, was given a military funeral at St Mary's Anglican Church, Feltwell, December 1941. She had passed away in her sleep on the 5th of December, leaving behind Popeye and their 2-year-old daughter Wendy. (Popeye Lucas collection, courtesy of the Lucas family)

January 1942

The first six weeks of the new year were dominated by the continuing campaign against the German raiders at Brest, and no fewer than eleven raids of varying sizes would be launched against the port and its guests during January alone. It would prove to be a low-key month for the Kiwis, with just two operations to keep them busy, beginning with the call to action of five freshman crews on the 2nd as part of a 3 Group force of thirty-one Wellingtons and Stirlings targeting Brest. P/O Fisher was the only commissioned pilot representing the squadron as they got away from Feltwell shortly after 18.00, each carrying six 500 pounders and two small bomb cases (SBCs) containing sixty 4lb incendiaries. These they hoped to use to good effect against the German warships, but in the event found the target to be protected by ten-tenths cloud and bombed on flares delivered by Stirlings, which they assessed as west and north of the aiming point. They all returned safely, Sgt Colville with his bombs still on board, some reporting bomb bursts, and all commenting on the fires caused by the incendiaries.

AM Sir Richard Peirse left his post as C-in-C Bomber Command on the 8th to be succeeded temporarily by AVM Baldwin, the A-O-C 3 Group. His period of tenure was blighted by the Butt Report, but in truth it was his misfortune to head Bomber Command at a time when navigation was an art rather than a science and the demands and expectations of his superiors were often unrealistic and unachievable with the technology available at the time. In February, Peirse would take up a new appointment as C-in-C Allied Air Forces in India and South-East Asia, but the sense that he had been "sacked" from Bomber Command would linger and perhaps unjustly tarnish his legacy.

Brest was posted as the target for a force of 151 aircraft that night, reconnaissance having revealed that Scharnhorst and Gneisenau had been joined by Prinz Eugen, and this operation was followed twenty-four hours later by another involving a force of eighty-two aircraft.

The squadron took part in no further operations until the evening of the 15th, by which time 124 aircraft had been sent against Wilhelmshaven on the night of the 10/11th and ninety-five against Hamburg on the 14/15th. The latter operation was to target the Blohm & Voss shipyard located on Kuhwerder Island opposite the Sanct Pauli district of Hamburg to the west of the city centre and the nearby Hamburger Flugzeugbau airframe factory on Finkenwerder Island. The former raid had been a dismal failure, while the latter resulted in seven large fires but no major incidents. Hamburg was the main target again on the night of the 15/16th, when a force of ninety-six aircraft was dispatched without a contribution from 75(NZ) Squadron. Representatives of the squadron were in action, however, and S/L Kitchin and P/O Sandys took off at 18.30 with the aerodrome at Schiphol as their destination. The former blew a cylinder in R1457 AA-Y while climbing out and was soon back on the ground, leaving the latter to press on alone with his load of a dozen 250 pounders. These were delivered onto Schiphol and a neighbouring aerodrome, where bursts were observed, and a safe return was completed at 21.55. The Hamburg force again failed to impress after a third of the aircraft either turned back or were unable to locate it and three large fires were all the others had to show for their efforts.

It was a similar story two nights later, when only eight of eighty-three crews reported bombing Bremen, while others found alternative targets, including Hamburg. As far as 75(NZ) Squadron was concerned, two operations and seven sorties summed up a month in which plenty of training filled the operational void and the Mk Ic Wellingtons began to be replaced by the Mk III variant. Acting F/L Newton arrived from 23 O.T.U during the last week of the month and was immediately elevated to acting squadron leader rank to succeed S/L Lucas as A Flight commander. S/L Raymond John "Ray" Newton, MiD, RNZAF came from Christchurch, New Zealand, having learned to fly with the Canterbury Aero Club and was commissioned as a pilot officer at Wigram in December 1940, before serving with 150 Squadron.

February 1942

There was also no operational employment at the start of February as heavy snow falls rendered Feltwell airfield unserviceable until the 7th. 3 Group contributed aircraft to a failed attempt to hit the enemy warships at Brest on the 6th, while snow-clearing and lectures kept the Feltwell crews busy during the period. W/C Sawrey-Cookson took off on the morning of the 7th to see if Lakenheath offered better prospects for operations, but nothing materialised, and fog then added to the difficulties on the 9th. The new Wellingtons were equipped with the Gee navigational device, and when conditions allowed, training focussed on becoming proficient in its use.

Among small-scale operations on the 11th was one against Brest by eighteen Wellingtons, the crews of which would have been unaware that they were the last to engage in this seemingly endless saga. As the sound of their engines receded into the eastern cloud-filled skies, Vice-Admiral Otto Cilliax, the Brest Group commander, whose flag was on Scharnhorst, put Operation Cerberus into action at 21.14, and Scharnhorst, Gneisenau and Prinz Eugen slipping anchor, before heading into the English Channel under an escort of destroyers and E-Boats. It was an audacious bid for freedom, covered by bad weather, widespread jamming and meticulously planned support by the Kriegsmarine and the Luftwaffe, all of which had been rehearsed extensively during January. The planning, and a little good fortune, allowed the fleet to make undetected progress until spotted off Le Touquet by two Spitfires piloted by G/C Victor Beamish, the commanding officer of Kenley, and W/C Finlay Boyd, both of whom maintained radio silence and did not report their find until landing at 10.42 on the morning of the 12th.

The British authorities had prepared a plan in advance for precisely this eventuality under the Codename, Operation Fuller, but so secret was it that few, it seemed, either knew of its full requirements or even of its existence. Once the enemy fleet was spotted in the late morning, frantic efforts were made to get Coastal and Bomber Command aircraft away, but only 5 Group was standing by at four hours readiness and it was after 13.00 hours before the first sorties were launched. The original 3 Group intention had been to catch the enemy at a position some thirty miles west of The Hague between 16.00 and 16.30 and attack from high level under the protection of a fighter escort. This idea was abandoned, however, and P/O Climie and crew took off at 15.10 as the first of three from 75(NZ) Squadron to try to locate the flotilla further north, twenty miles off Zandvoort on the Den Helder peninsula. They climbed out through low cloud and rain to find similar conditions in the target area, which made their task impossible, and although they caught sight of part of the fleet, they were unable to carry out an attack and were fired upon for their pains by light flak from two destroyers, at which the rear gunner popped off some rounds. They were also set upon by a pair of Me110s without sustaining damage. W/C Sawrey-Cookson departed Feltwell at 17.00, to be followed fifteen minutes later by S/L Newton, but the gathering darkness and weather conditions prevented them from making contact with the enemy and all bombs were returned to store. They had been part of the largest commitment of aircraft by daylight in the war to date, amounting to 242 sorties, most of which had been thwarted by the rainstorms and squally conditions that compounded the logistical difficulties of locating a fleet at sea. Fifteen aircraft failed to return, 5 Group alone posting missing nine Hampdens and crews all lost in the North Sea, six of them without trace. They could be added to all of those others sacrificed to this endeavour over the past eleven months.

Despite the heroic effort and sacrifice of the Bomber Command, Coastal Command and Fleet Air Arm crews, the enemy fleet made good its escape into open sea, although, its own trials and tribulations were not yet over. Scharnhorst struck a mine in the late afternoon and began to fall back, and at 19.55, a magnetic mine detonated close enough to Gneisenau, when off Teschelling, to open a small hole in the starboard side and temporarily slow her progress also. Later still, at 21.34, when passing through the same stretch of water, Scharnhorst hit another mine which stopped both engines and damaged steering and fire control. The vessel got under way again at 22.23 using its starboard engines and making twelve knots, while carrying an additional one thousand tons of seawater. The day's activities were not yet over for 5 Group, and the crews of fourteen Hampdens and nine Manchesters were briefed to lay mines in the Nectarine gardens off the Frisians through which the enemy fleet would have to pass to reach safety.

Gneisenau and Prinz Eugen reached the Elbe Estuary at 07.00 on the 13th, and tied up at Brunsbüttel North Locks at 09.30, while Scharnhorst arrived at Wilhelmshaven at 10.00 with three months-worth of damage to repair. The mines had been laid almost certainly by 5 Group Hampdens over the preceding nights and demonstrated the remarkable effectiveness of this war-long campaign. The entire episode was a major embarrassment to the government and the nation, but on a positive note, this annoying and distracting itch had been scratched for the last time and the Command could now concentrate its forces against the strategic targets for which it was best suited. Over at Feltwell, meanwhile, Sgt Miles Frederick Gordon Fraser RNZAF and crew cut a lonely furrow as the sole 75(NZ) Squadron representatives to be called to briefing on the 13th to learn that they were to join in on a small-scale raid on the docks and shipping at Le Havre. They took off at 18.25 and encountered nine-tenths cloud in the target area, which prevented them from delivering their load of 250 pounders.

A new Air Ministry directive issued on the 14th was to change the emphasis of bomber operations from that point until the end of the war. Lengthy consideration having been given to the Butt Report and the future of an independent bomber force, the new policy authorized the blatant area bombing of Germany's industrial towns and cities in a direct assault on the morale of the civilian population, particularly its workers. This had, of course, been going on since the summer of 1940, but no longer would there be the pretence of claiming to be attacking industrial and military targets. Waiting in the wings, in fact, at this very moment, four days into his voyage from the United States in the armed merchantman, Alcantara, was a new leader, a man well-known to 5 Group, who not only would pursue this policy with a will but also possessed the self-belief, arrogance and stubbornness to fight his corner against all-comers on behalf of his beleaguered Bomber Command. In the twenties and thirties AM Sir Arthur Harris had developed the theory and practice of bombing by both day and night and was a "Bomber Baron" through-and-through, who was determined to forge his Command into a war-winning weapon.

Air Chief Marshal Sir Arthur Harris took up his post as the new Commander-in-Chief of Bomber Command on the 22nd. He was a man well-known to 5 Group, having served as its A-O-C until November 1940, when he became second deputy to Sir Charles Portal, the Chief-of-the-Air-Staff. Harris arrived at the helm with firm ideas already in place on how to win the war by bombing alone, a pre-war theory, which no commander had yet had an opportunity to put into practice. It was obvious to him, that the small-scale raids on multiple targets favoured by his predecessor served only to dilute the effort, and that such pin-prick attacks could not hurt Germany's war effort. He recognized the need to overwhelm the defences and emergency services by pushing the maximum number of aircraft across the aiming point in the shortest possible time, and this would signal the birth of the bomber stream and an end to the former practice, whereby squadrons or even crews determined for themselves the details of their sorties. He knew also that urban areas are most efficiently destroyed by fire rather than blast, and it would not be long before the bomb loads carried in his aircraft reflected this thinking.

In the meantime, while he developed his ideas, he would continue with the fairly small-scale attacks on German ports favoured by his predecessor, and later on the evening of his appointment, he sent thirty-one Wellingtons and nineteen Hampdens to Wilhelmshaven to attack the floating dock likely to be employed during repairs to Scharnhorst. Three nights later, sixty-one aircraft were sent against Kiel to attack the floating dock at which Gneisenau was berthed, and a further operation by forty-nine aircraft was mounted on the 26th. The latter operation threw up one of the war's great ironies, after a high explosive bomb struck the bows of Gneisenau, now supposedly in a safe haven after enduring eleven months of constant bombardment at Brest, and not only did it kill 116 of her crew, it also ended her sea-going career for good. Her main armament was removed for use in coastal defence, and she was eventually towed to Gdynia, where she remained unrepaired for the remainder of the war. The British authorities were unaware of the success, however, and sent another raid of sixty-eight aircraft on the 27th.

75(NZ) Squadron took no part in operations during the second half of the month as its crews trained on TR1335, the Gee navigation device, and only experienced its first aircraft incident of the year on the afternoon of the 28th, when Sgt Colville, RNZAF took X3355, AA-Y on an air-test to check out an engine with three members of ground crew on board. They were over Suffolk when the starboard engine failed, to be followed shortly afterwards by its port counterpart, and the attempt to put the Wellington down safely resulted in a stall and crash near Brandon at 16.00. The wellington burst into flames and two of the ground crew lost their lives, while Sgt Colville and two others were pulled clear by local people and army personnel, alive but severely injured to the extent that Sgt Henry William Woodham RNZAF succumbed later in the day. Sgt Colville had been in the first class of New Zealand airmen to graduate as pilots under the Empire Air Training Plan. Despite almost losing both of his legs, he went on to fly again and would rise to the rank of wing commander in the RAF.

During the course of the month the squadron was involved in just two operations, launching four sorties for the non-operational loss of a single Wellington, one airman and two ground crew.

March 1942

Adverse weather conditions welcomed in the new month and kept the bomber force on the ground on the 1st. It was the same on the 2nd, and it was the 3rd before orders were received across the Command to prepare for an operation, which, in its bold conception was a clear indication of what was to come. Bomber Command's evolution to war-winning capability was to be long, arduous and gradual, but the first signs of a new hand on the tiller came early on in Harris's reign with this meticulously planned attack on the Renault lorry factory, which was located in a loop of the Seine in the district of Billancourt to the south-west of central Paris. The plant was capable of producing 18,000 lorries per year, which was a massive boon to the German war effort, and the attempt to destroy it came in response to an Air Ministry request. The operation would be conducted in three waves led by experienced crews and would involve extensive use of flares to provide illumination. An unprecedented average of 120 aircraft per hour would pass over the aiming point, a 50% increase over the previous highest concentration, and in the face of what was expected to be scant defence, crews were also encouraged to attack from as low a level as practicable, both for the sake of accuracy and in an attempt to avoid civilian casualties. In time, such operations would be led by Gee-equipped aircraft, but the 3 Group squadrons already employing the device were forbidden from taking part on this occasion, lest one be lost over enemy territory and its secrets revealed. This inevitably reduced 3 Group's presence and its maximum effort contribution would amount to thirty-nine Wellingtons and thirty-one Stirlings in a new record force for a single target of 235 aircraft. As a Gee-equipped unit, 75(NZ) Squadron was represented by just one crew, that of S/L Newton, who departed Feltwell at 18.40.

Those reaching the target area were greeted by bright moonlight that aided target location and most crews picked up the River Seine in good time to enable them to plan their bombing runs. 223 returning crews reported successful sorties, many describing the factory buildings as well alight as they turned away, and post-raid reconnaissance confirmed the operation to have been an outstanding success for the loss of just one aircraft. 40% of the factory's buildings had been destroyed and production was halted for four weeks, costing the Germans around 2,300 lorries, although sadly, not all of the bombs had fallen precisely where intended. Inevitably, adjacent residential districts were hit by stray bombs, killing 367 French civilians and severely injuring 341 others, some of whom would not survive, and a further nine thousand were rendered homeless. At the time, this was more than twice the heaviest death toll inflicted on a German target and the problem of avoiding collateral damage would remain unresolved for the remainder of the war. It was somewhat paradoxical, that, as a champion of area bombing, Harris should gain his first major victory against a precision target.

While the above was in progress, some 330 miles to the north, four Lancasters taxied to the runway under the approving eyes of the 5 Group A-O-C, AVM Slessor, each carrying four mines for delivery to the Yam and Rosemary gardens in the Schillig Roads and Heligoland Bight in what would be the type's maiden operation.

Despite the fact that Essen, as home to the Krupp organisation, was the beating heart of the Ruhr Valley's war production, it had not been paid particular attention thus far in the war. This was about to change as Harris fixed his gaze upon it and like a dog with a bone, would not abandon his quest to destroy it until that aim had been achieved. It was a fight he would win, but the first twelve months would be frustrating, unrewarding and expensive and began with the first of three raids on consecutive nights on the 8th. A force of 211 aircraft included a maximum effort by 3 Group of eighty-six aircraft, of which twenty Gee-equipped Wellingtons were assigned to the flare force to provide the illumination and would carry no bombs. They did, though, carry the great hope that Gee (TR1335) might solve the problem of blind target locating. The remaining 3 Group force numbered sixty-seven Wellingtons and Stirlings and each had an all-incendiary load winched into its bomb bay. Eleven 75(NZ) Squadron Wellingtons were made ready, three as part of the flare force, and it would be the first time since late December that the squadron had committed double figures to an operation. W/C Sawrey-Cookson was the senior pilot on duty, supported by S/Ls Kitchin and Newton, and it was after midnight before they got away from Feltwell with departures spread over several hours between 00.20 and 04.10. This was caused in part by the bogging down at its dispersal of X3597 AA-C, which required a ninety-minute effort by a tractor to free it. Perhaps there was some residual technical issue as Sgt Shepherd returned a little over two hours after taking off with the incendiaries still on board. The others arrived over the Ruhr to find clear skies and good visibility provided by a half moon, but also the ever-present industrial haze, which obscured ground detail, including the assigned aiming point "B", the Krupp complex. Few crews were able to make a positive identification after pinpointing on the Rhine and most bombed the general city area, some observing bursts and others not. Local sources reported a light raid with a little housing damage in southern districts and it was a disappointing outcome in view of the effort expended.

The following night brought a return to Essen for 187 aircraft, of which eleven represented 75(NZ) Squadron and were assigned to the flare force, while Sgt Bell and crew carried out a freshman sortie at Boulogne docks. The last-mentioned took off first at 19.31, and they were followed into the air between 20.00 and 20.45 by the others, of which S/Ls Kitchin and Newton were the senior pilots on duty. Some crews claimed to be able to see the flares over Essen even before reaching the Dutch coast, which confirmed that the horizontal visibility was reasonable, while vertical visibility at the target was again compromised by industrial haze. Major landmarks were identified through the five-tenths cloud with tops at around 8,000 feet, but not the Krupp districts in the western and north-western region of the city and the bombing was scattered over twenty-four other Ruhr towns and cities with Hamborn and Duisburg the chief beneficiaries. The Essen authorities reported the destruction of two buildings, with seventy-two others damaged, a fact not appreciated at 3 Group HQ, which described fires burning in the target area and the attack generally as a 100% improvement on the previous night's effort. There was also ground haze at Boulogne, but most crews were able to find something to bomb.

Essen was posted as the primary target again on the 10th, for which a force of 126 aircraft was made ready to attack two aiming points, the Krupp sector and the city centre, and it was for the former that thirty-two 3 Group crews were briefed in the absence of a 75(NZ) Squadron contribution. Cloud and industrial haze were responsible for another total failure, in which only half of the returning crews claimed to have attacked the primary target, while thirty-five others admitted to bombing alternatives.

The entire Command was rested on the 11th, and when crews sat down at briefing on the 12th, they learned that the Deutsche Werke U-Boot yard in the port of Kiel was to be their objective that night. The 75(NZ) Squadron ORB is contradictory and at variance with the 3 Group record, but it seems that eleven aircraft were made ready as part of an all-Wellington force of sixty-eight, and they took off between 19.30 and 20.25 with S/Ls Kitchin and Newton the senior pilots on duty. Sgt Maurice Perrott Bell RNZAF, meanwhile, headed for the port of Emden to join other freshmen, including fellow first-time captains Sgt Ivan George Edward McPhail RNZAF and F/Sgt Ivor John McLachlan RNZAF. The Bell crew found nine-tenths cloud, which persuaded them to bring their bombs home. The conditions on the eastern side of the Schleswig-Holstein peninsula were sufficiently clear to allow accurate bombing at Kiel, but this had to be carried out in the face of predicted light and heavy flak assisted by cones of searchlights. Both the Deutsche Werke and Krupp Germania Werft yards sustained damage, as did the naval dockyard and the town, and the success was gained at the fairly modest cost of five Wellingtons.

The squadron suffered badly, however, losing X3282 AA-F to the defences in the target area, with no survivors from the crew of Sgt John Parnham, RAF, while X3585 AA-V and X3588 AA-U were lost without trace, taking with them the crews of F/O Sandys RCAF and flight commander S/L Kitchin DFC, MiD, respectively. F/O Sandys was born on Jersey in the Channel Islands, and his highly experienced crew contained four members of the RNZAF, including F/L Thomas James Desmond Baber, only twenty-three years old, but already on his second tour with the squadron. Baber was one of the first RNZAF gunners to be commissioned, Mentioned in Dispatches and awarded the Czech medal for bravery. S/L Kitchin was another who had served with the original 75 Squadron pre-war and was now on his second tour with 75(NZ) Squadron. His second pilot and rear gunner were Kiwis, as were two members of Sgt Parnham's crew. F/L Cecil McKenzie Hill was immediately promoted to the acting rank of squadron leader to enable him to succeed S/L Kitchin as B Flight commander.

The main operation on the night of the 13/14th involved a force of 135 aircraft targeting Cologne, while 75(NZ) Squadron sent four freshman crews to bomb the docks and shipping at Dunkerque, including debutants Sgt Eric George Delancey Jarman RAAF and P/O Rufus Leggett RAFVR, both of whom were to make their mark in the squadron. They departed Feltwell between 19.55 and 20.50, but Sgt Leggett returned with engine trouble after just seventy-five minutes. The others reached the target area guided by Gee and found fine weather conditions but ground haze and only Sgt Bell released his load of 250 pounders, while the others brought theirs home.

There would be no further major operations for most of the Command for almost two weeks, during which period isolated mining and "moling" (daylight cloud-cover incursions) sorties occupied small numbers of aircraft. In preparation for Harris's next assault on Essen a new record force of 254 aircraft was assembled on the 25th and crews were assigned to three specific roles, to deliver flares to illuminate the target, incendiaries to start fires as a beacon and high explosives as part of the main strike force. 75(NZ) Squadron made ready a dozen Wellingtons, which took off between 18.55 and 21.15 with W/C Sawrey-Cookson bringing up the rear as the senior pilot on duty, and operating with the squadron for the first time as skipper was F/O Alfred William Doel RNZAF. The weather conditions outbound and over the target were good and vertical visibility was marred only by the expected industrial haze. 181 crews returned to report bombing as briefed, some claiming to have hit the Krupp districts, but photographic reconnaissance and local reports revealed this raid to have been another huge failure. A decoy fire-site eighteen miles away at Rheinberg had drawn off the main weight of bombs, and damage in Essen was slight in the extreme. Nine aircraft failed to return, and among them was X3652, AA-O, which crashed on German soil after P/O Slater RAAF and all but the second pilot had parachuted into the arms of their captors to spend the remainder of the war as guests of the Third Reich.

A much-reduced force of 104 Wellingtons and eleven Stirlings was made ready for a return to Essen on the following night, when, it is believed, that 75(NZ) Squadron provided seven aircraft for the main target and the freshman crew of P/O Peter John Wilson, RNZAF for Le Havre. They took off between 19.50 and 20.45 and arrived in the target area to find excellent weather conditions, with smoke and haze less troublesome than expected. The searchlight and flak defence, however, had increased substantially since the previous night and night-fighters were much in evidence throughout the operation. Once more the claims of a successful outcome were found to be exaggerated as only a few bomb loads found their way into the city, and the failure was paid for by the failure to return of eleven aircraft, more than 10% of those dispatched. The only casualty from Feltwell was a 57 Squadron Wellington, and this left both resident squadrons at full strength to answer the call to arms for a milestone operation in Bomber Command's development on the 28th.

Harris well understood the difficulties facing his crews in trying to identify a target over a blacked-out and often cloud-covered land in darkness, with only traditional methods of navigation at their disposal to take them to their destination hundreds of miles away. Gee could guide them to an approximate area, but was unable to pinpoint a precise location, and expertly-prepared decoy fire sites could easily be confused with the real thing. Despite this, Harris had faith in the ability of his crews to hit a target, if they were provided with the means to locate it, and coast lines seemed to offer the best prospects. The Hansastadt (ancient free-trade city) Lübeck lies on the River Trave some forty miles south-east of Kiel and was an ideal target for a number of reasons principal among which were its close proximity to an easily identifiable coastline, the paucity of its defences and the fact that it was an old city with narrow streets and half-timbered buildings, which would aid the spread of fire. The three-wave attack, involving 234 aircraft, was to be conducted along similar lines to those employed against the Renault factory early in the month, and the high proportion of incendiaries carried in the bomb bays reflected Harris's fire-raising intent. 75(NZ) Squadron prepared ten Wellingtons for the operation, and they would carry a variety of bomb loads, which included 4,000lb cookies, and 1,000, 500 and 250 pounders along with incendiaries.

The squadron participants took off between 19.30 and 22.05, with W/C Sawrey-Cookson last but one away, presumably, so that he could make an assessment at the end of the raid. The target lay beyond the range of Gee, but the device helped with preliminary navigation, enabling the first wave aircraft to reach the target area to be greeted by clear skies, bright moonlight and an absence of searchlights. The lack of defensive measures allowed crews to carry out their attacks from medium to low level, some descending to 2,000 feet, and this aided accuracy as four hundred tons of bombs, two-thirds of them incendiaries, fell within the city. Over the target, X3597, AA-C was hit by flak, igniting a flare inside the aircraft, upon which, P/O Rufus Leggett put the Wellington into a dive to keep flames away from the petrol tanks, shedding 5,000 feet in the process, until, after fifteen minutes, second pilot Sgt Arthur Osborne managed to extinguish the fire with his gloved hands and boots. Twelve aircraft failed to return home, and 75(NZ) Squadron was represented by X3462, AA-D, which crashed between Kiel and the target, killing P/O Maurice Bell RNZAF and his crew, which included two other members of the RNZAF. Photographic reconnaissance revealed that approximately 190 acres of the old town had been destroyed, mostly by fire, and this amounted to 30% of the city's built-up area. A total of 1,425 buildings had been destroyed, and almost two thousand others seriously damaged, and this was a triumph for Harris at a time when the very existence of an independent bomber force was still being questioned in high places. Lübeck was the first major success for the area bombing policy, but the principles put into operation on this night would form the basis of all similar operations in the future. There was an outcry following this unexpected attack on Lübeck, which was a vital port for the Red Cross, and an agreement was struck that largely ensured its future protection from bombing.

This was the final operation of a month which had seen the squadron operate against eleven targets, dispatching seventy sorties for the loss of five Wellingtons and crews.

April 1942

April began inauspiciously for the Command in general and for 3 Group in particular, when Operation Lineshoot, an attack on railway installations at Hanau and Lohr in southern Germany on the night of the 1/2nd, went disastrously wrong. 75(NZ) Squadron made ready eleven Wellingtons to be divided between the main operation and the docks and shipping at Le Havre, but the ORB does not provide details. Based on the take-off times and length of sorties it would seem that F/Sgt Thomas, P/O Leggett and Sgt McPhail were assigned to the latter and departed Feltwell at 20.05, 20.50 and 21.05 respectively, to be followed into the air by the others between 22.25 and 23.30. G/C "Speedy" Powell was the senior pilot on duty, and he had beside him W/C Peters-Smith, who had recently been appointed to command fellow Feltwell residents, 57 Squadron. S/Ls Hill and Newton were also on the order of battle for this operation, which was to be carried out at low level at the two locations east of Frankfurt. Sgt McPhail was back on the ground within twenty-five minutes after losing an engine, and F/O Doel would also fail to reach the target, bringing his bombs back after a flight of four hours and fifteen minutes. The others pressed on in unfavourable weather conditions, which made identification difficult, but returning crews claimed to have observed bomb bursts in the marshalling yards at Hanau and in the docks at Le Havre, without being able to comment on the results. Quite how the Kiwis escaped retribution is a mystery, after twelve Wellingtons, five from 57 Squadron and seven from 214 Squadron, were shot down, mostly it appears by night-fighters. There was no pattern to their fall, which occurred in Holland, Belgium, Rhineland Germany and the target area.

The Command set another new record on the night of the 5/6th, when dispatching 263 aircraft to Cologne. Nine 75(NZ) Squadron crews had attended briefing to learn that the aero-engine and military vehicle-producing Klöckner Humboldt A G mechanical engineering works in the

Deutz district to the east of the Rhine was to be the aiming point. W/C Sawrey-Cookson was the senior pilot on duty as they took off between 23.20 and 01.25 on a night of fine weather conditions, with five-tenths cloud and bright moonlight over the target, and F/O Edward Cecil Ball RNZAF was flying his first operation with the squadron. P/O Fisher returned early with engine trouble leaving the others to push on into Germany, where an intense searchlight and flak response awaited them. Returning crews reported bombing the target but not observing the results, and opinions as to the effectiveness of the raid were divided. Feltwell, Marham and Oakington expressed doubts, while Honington, Mildenhall, Stradishall and Wyton were confident that their bombs had landed in the city. A local report revealed scattered bombing across the city, with one industrial building hit and ninety houses destroyed. Two of the five missing aircraft belonged to 75(NZ) Squadron and the fate of their crews provided an example of the widely differing fortunes of war. X3489, AA-P crashed somewhere in the target area on the edge of the Ruhr, killing W/C Reginald Sawrey-Cookson DSO, DFC, RAF and his crew, which included second pilot P/O William Finlay Budge RNZAF and rear gunner F/O George Eric Mitchell DFM, RCAF. It was the commanding officer's ninth sortie since arriving at Feltwell, and he was the first of the squadron's commanders to be lost on operations. More fortunate on this night was the crew of F/Sgt Godfrey John Evan Thomas, who were at 10,500 feet when hit by flak and were forced to abandon X3661 AA-Q to its fate, while they escaped with their lives to become PoWs.

On the following day, W/C Edward George "Ted" Olson RNZAF arrived from Marham as the new commanding officer, having previously served as a New Zealand liaison officer at the Air Ministry. It is believed that he had been "lodging" with his friend and former 75(NZ) Squadron stalwart, W/C Trevor Freeman, over at 115 Squadron to bring himself up to operational status. He had flown with Freeman on the Lübeck raid, and also went to Poissy on the night of the Hanau debacle and the above-mentioned raid on Cologne. W/C Olson had been "Popeye" Lucas's initial flying instructor in New Zealand before the war, and like the unit's first two commanders, he was comparatively advanced in years and would use his maturity to lead a revival in morale.

Harris's campaign against Essen continued on the night of the 6/7th, for which a force of 157 aircraft was made ready, including seven Wellingtons representing 75(NZ) Squadron in a 3 Group contribution of fifty-seven. There was a late take-off on a night of unfavourable weather conditions, and six of the Feltwell contingent departed between 00.30 and 00.55 with S/L Hill the senior pilot on duty. They made their way to the Dutch coast in stormy conditions, having passed through ten-tenths ice-bearing cloud, and a large proportion of the force turned back at this time, landing times suggesting that S/L Hill, F/O Doel, P/O Leggett and Sgt McPhail were among those abandoning their sorties. According to the squadron ORB, those reaching the Ruhr found three to five-tenths cloud at 11,000 feet, although other sources report complete cloud cover. They were subjected to intense anti-aircraft fire, which actually drove off a single-engine night-fighter that had latched onto P/O Climie's X3636 AA-R. F/Sgt McLachlan in X3705 AA-F also reported an attack by a BF109, both front and rear gunners returning fire. The operation was another total failure at a cost of five aircraft, although none was missing from Feltwell.

Flying with Legget that night was wireless operator, Sgt Leonard "Len" Chambers, RNZAF. Len came from Karamea on the West Coast of New Zealand's South Island, and he was one of several "Coasters" on the squadron at that time. He had already completed a first tour with 460 Squadron RAAF and would add at least another thirty-one to his tally with 75(NZ) Squadron, becoming a radar specialist and eventually squadron signals leader. As a 'spare' wireless operator, he flew with G/C "Speedy" Powell, S/L Ray Newton, S/L Frank Denton, S/L Artie Ashworth and several other crews. From 75(NZ) Squadron he would go briefly to 26 O.T.U, then become a founder member of 617 Squadron as a member of F/L Mick Martin's crew, taking part in the famous Operation Chastise against the Ruhr dams in May 1943, for which he earned a DFC.

Briefings took place on all heavy bomber stations on the 8th, when crews were told that they were to be part of a new record force to attack Hamburg that night. 272 aircraft were made ready, nine of the Wellingtons provided by 75(NZ) Squadron, and they took off between 21.30 and 22.07 with S/L Newton the senior pilot on duty. Last off, flying his regular kite X3538, AA-N "Pruno", P/O Rufus Leggett was almost straight away on his R/T to say that the escape hatch over his head had blown off. In one of the moments that may have helped establish 75's reputation as a 'chop' squadron, Station Commander "Speedy" Powell ordered Leggett to continue on his way! The realities of communication and working in an open cockpit proved too much, however, and Leggett was back by 23.40. He was not alone, four other crews came home early, three with engine issues and one in response to a mysterious BBA (return to Base) signal. The others climbed through electrical storms and icing over the east coast, and those reaching the target area were confronted by ten-tenths cloud permeated by an intense flak barrage. On return, two-thirds of the crews reported bombing in the target area, but local authorities claimed that the equivalent of only fourteen bomb loads struck the city, causing three large fires. A load of incendiaries fell very accurately onto the Vulkan U-Boot construction yards at Bremen, some sixty miles to the south-west, but it was scant return for the failure of such a huge effort.

Rufus Leggett was another of the squadron's 'characters and was nicknamed "Pruno" for his resemblance to the cartoon RAF officer and for his cheeky grin. X3538 became his regular aircraft and "Pruno" nose art was duly applied. She carried Leggett and his crew safely through seventeen operations and then second pilot Arthur "Ossie" Osborne (by then skipper of his own crew) through another fourteen. Osborne kept the colourful nose art, and it survives to this day.

On the following afternoon the squadron dispatched three Wellingtons to join four others from 57 Squadron on a "moling" operation to Essen. The whole concept of sending inadequately armed bombers in daylight to the most heavily defended region of Germany, relying only on cloud for protection, was utter madness and one wonders who came up with the idea and who sanctioned it. Fortunately, it proved to be a passing phase, but brave and valuable crews would be lost until common sense prevailed. S/L Newton, F/O Ball and P/O Fisher took off at 12.30, 12.45 and 13.05 respectively, and the first two-mentioned turned back an hour out after the cloud began to break up. P/O Fisher, alone of the seven participants, continued on and dropped his bombs on the German border town of Geldern, north-west of Duisburg. What was achieved by putting these crews at extreme risk is difficult to fathom.

Essen was the target again on the 10th, only this time under cover of darkness. A force of 254 aircraft was assembled, of which eight were provided by 75(NZ) Squadron and they took off between 21.10 and 22.11 with S/Ls Hill and Newton the senior pilots on duty and P/O Allen Armistice Fraser, RNZAF operating for the first time as crew captain. The weather had improved considerably, and clear skies had been forecast at briefing, but on arrival at the target the crews encountered not only a layer of eight-tenths cloud across the central Ruhr at between 5,000 and 8,000 feet but also heavy predicted flak accompanied by fairly intense searchlight activity. Despite the delivery of the very first 8,000lb bomb by a 76 Squadron Halifax, the raid was scattered and ended as another failure, which destroyed a dozen houses and caused no industrial damage.

Harris would try once more in the current series and ordered the next attack on Essen to take place on the night of the 12/13th, for which a force of 251 aircraft was made ready. 75(NZ) Squadron briefed eight crews for the main event and two to join a raid on the docks and shipping at Le Havre. P/O Allen Fraser and his sergeant namesake, Myles Fraser, took off at 20.55 and 21.00 respectively to head for the Channel and the French coast, while the remaining crews departed Feltwell between 22.10 and 22.55 with S/Ls Hill and Newton the senior pilots on duty. Once over enemy territory, many night-fighter flares were in evidence along with red and green lights, and numerous searchlight cones were accompanied by fairly accurate medium and heavy flak. The weather conditions were good, with visibility estimated by some at a hundred miles, and this may have contributed to the slight improvement in performance. Five high explosive bombs and two hundred incendiaries hit the Krupp complex, causing a large fire, and there was also some destruction in residential districts, but bombing photographs captured many other Ruhr locations, and generally it was another disappointing performance that would provide further ammunition for the detractors. Eight major operations had been mounted against Essen since the night of the 8/9th of March involving 1,555 sorties, of which two-thirds had claimed to have bombed the city. This huge effort had resulted in very modest residential damage, only two incidents of industrial damage and had cost sixty-four aircraft and crews.

Mining and minor operations took care of the night of the 13/14th, when the Fraser pairing were the only 75(NZ) Squadron participants to take part in a freshman raid by four Wellingtons on the docks and shipping at Boulogne. They took off at 21.30, and one delivered his load of 250 pounders over the target, while the other brought his bombs home after failing to identify it.

Harris turned his attention upon another Ruhr giant for the next operation, which was directed at Dortmund on the night of the 14/15th. A force of 208 aircraft was made ready, of which six were provided by 75(NZ) Squadron, while F/Sgt Thomas Stanley Mahood RNZAF and crew undertook their maiden freshman sortie at Le Havre. The last-mentioned took off at 21.39 and returned a little under four hours later, presumably having fulfilled their brief. Those taking part in the main event departed Feltwell between 22.17 and 22.45 with S/L Newton the senior pilot on duty but P/O Fisher and F/Sgt McLachlan returned early, both with failed engines. The others found the weather in the target area to be fine with some ground haze, and there was surprisingly little response from the defences, despite which, Dortmund escaped with superficial damage after bombs were scattered across a forty-mile stretch of the Ruhr. S/L Ray Newton had been coned by searchlights over the target and a whole 5-inch shell had smashed his tailplane, half of the starboard elevator and the port aileron, requiring all of his flying skills to nurse the crippled aircraft home.

The same targets were on offer on the following night, with a reduced force of 152 aircraft assigned to Dortmund, seven of them representing 75(NZ) Squadron, while F/Sgt Mahood and crew returned to Le Havre, taking off first at 21.50 and returning safely at 01.30 to report clear weather conditions with a little ground haze. Those involved in the main event departed Feltwell between 23.30 and 00.05 with no senior officers present and had to contend with severe icing conditions on the southern approaches to the Ruhr, only then to run into intense searchlight and flak activity over the target, where two-tenths low cloud combined with the industrial haze to muddy the vertical visibility and create difficult bombing conditions. A little over half of the force reached the target area and some bomb bursts were observed, but it was another massive failure, which mercifully cost just four aircraft and crews.

The new Lancaster was announced to the Luftwaffe on the 17th during the audacious and epic daylight raid by elements of 44 (Rhodesia) and 97 (Straits Settlement) Squadrons on the M.A.N. diesel engine factory at Augsburg, deep inside southern Germany. Seven of the twelve participants were shot down, four by fighters while outbound over France and three at the target by flak, and 44 Squadron's S/L Nettleton was awarded the Victoria Cross. It would be almost two years before the Kiwis got their hands on this remarkable bomber.

Attention switched to Germany's second city, Hamburg, on the night of the 17/18th, for which a force of 173 aircraft was made ready, including seven Wellingtons of 75(NZ) Squadron. Sgt Turner RAF and his crew took off first, at 21.30, to carry out a freshman sortie to Le Havre, and they were on their way home when the participants in the main operation departed Feltwell between 23.40 and 23.59. Those arriving at the target found clear skies with ground haze and a fierce response from searchlights and flak, and when a searchlight beam latched onto Sgt Jarman's X3636 AA-R, the bomb load was jettisoned to aid its escape. 107 returning crews claimed to have bombed in the target area and local reports confirmed a more effective attack than had recently been the norm, detailing seventy-five fires of which thirty-three were classed as large.

Training filled the four-day void before the next operation on the night of the 22/23rd, which was an experimental raid on Cologne employing Gee as a blind bombing device. An all-Gee-equipped force of sixty-four Wellingtons and five Stirlings was made ready, and of these, eight were provided by 75(NZ) Squadron, while two freshman crews made the now familiar flight south to attack the docks and shipping at Le Havre. F/Sgt Mahood and Sgt Turner took off first at around 21.20 and only Sgt Turner and crew came home to land at 01.25. The body of F/Sgt Mahood's RAF rear gunner was recovered from the sea for burial in Le Havre, but the remaining five occupants of X3667 AA-D, all members of the RNZAF, were lost with the Wellington and are commemorated on the Runnymede Memorial.

Those bound for Cologne departed Feltwell between 22.00 and 22.30 and lost the services of the newly-promoted F/L Doel to an early return for an undisclosed reason. X3705, AA-F was attacked by a night-fighter on the way out and the second pilot, P/O Cedric Niel Fountain, was killed, while Sgt Desmond Stewart Tutty RNZAF in the rear turret sustained serious wounds. F/Sgt Ivor McLachlan brought the Wellington home to a crash-landing at 03.30 and there were no further casualties. X3487, AA-O was also attacked by an enemy night-fighter, a Ju88, while still over the North Sea outbound and was badly shot-up during the single pass. The rear gunner, Sgt Richard James Harris RNZAF, is believed to have been killed in the engagement, while the second pilot, P/O Trafford McRae Nicol, the only other member of the RNZAF on board, was mortally wounded and would lose his fight for life on the following day. Navigator Sgt William "Jock" Taylor and wireless operator Sgt John Fernie, both RAFVR, also sustained wounds and were grateful to P/O Eric "Riki" Jarman for bringing the damaged Wellington back to base, where a crash-landing was carried out and the wounded removed to hospital for medical attention. The others, meanwhile, arrived in the target area to find cloud and haze, which would render the bombing photography ineffective. At debriefing it became clear that less than half of the force had found the target and local authorities estimated that perhaps a dozen bomb loads had fallen within the city, while many others had landed up to ten miles away. The experiment demonstrated that Gee was useful in bringing an aircraft to a general area but was too imprecise to employ as a blind bombing device.

Following this series of unsuccessful operations, and perhaps recalling the success of the Lübeck raid a month earlier, Harris ordered a series of attacks on Rostock, situated some sixty miles further east along the Baltic coast on the southern bank of the Unterwarnow River some five miles south of the coastal town of Warnemünde. An additional attraction was the Heinkel Flugzeugwerke HQ and aircraft factory in the Marienehe district on the western bank of the Unterwarnow estuary. A force of 161 aircraft was assembled on the 23rd, 143 to attack the old town with predominantly incendiary bomb loads, while eighteen aircraft from 5 Group carried out a precision attack on the Heinkel works. 3 Group detailed sixty-seven aircraft, of which seven Wellingtons belonged to 75(NZ) Squadron and took off between 22.25 and 23.05 with S/L Newton the senior pilot on duty. All arrived at the target to find good visibility and bombing conditions and little in the way of defensive measures, which offered the opportunity to deal a telling blow against the town and the factory. Returning crews claimed to have done precisely that, describing explosions and many large fires, but as so often was the case, the crews misinterpreted what they were observing. Reconnaissance and local sources revealed that most of the bombing had fallen between two and six miles from the town centre, while the confident claims of the 5 Group crews belied the fact that the aircraft factory had escaped damage entirely.

Captain Peter Terry Wykes, Royal Artillery, S/L Newton's front gunner, was on attachment with 75(NZ) Squadron to observe German flak and searchlight techniques and was the only army officer to serve in the squadron. He flew ten operations with S/L Newton and as a result of this pioneering work he was Mentioned in Dispatches. Later he was to train as a pilot and serve as a forward observer with 658 (Air Observation Post) Squadron RAF, sadly to lose his life with his observer while flying an Auster over the front line near Rees in Germany on the 24th of March 1945.

On the following night, ninety-one aircraft were assigned to the town and thirty-four to the Heinkel factory in the absence of a contribution by 75(NZ) Squadron. This time the centre of the town sustained extensive damage, but the factory, despite claims to the contrary, was not hit. The squadron returned to the fray on the night of the 25/26th with six Wellingtons, while the freshman crew of P/O Wilson joined others from the group to attack the docks and shipping at Dunkerque. The main element took off between 22.15 and 22.35 with S/L Newton the senior pilot on duty, while P/O Wilson got away fifteen minutes later and carried out his attack in good visibility before returning safely at 01.10. Sgt Fraser was soon back in the circuit for an undisclosed reason, leaving the others to press on to the Baltic coast under clear skies, which persisted throughout the operation. There was a little ground haze at the target, where many bomb bursts were observed across the aiming point, and retreating crews watched numerous fires take hold. The Heinkel factory had been assigned to Manchesters of 106 Squadron led by its soon-to-be-famous commanding officer, W/C Guy Gibson, and they, at last, managed to land some bombs on it. The final operation in the series was mounted on the following night and involved 106 aircraft, although none from Feltwell. Another successful raid ensued, and by the conclusion of the campaign, 1,765 buildings in the town had been destroyed and a further five hundred seriously damaged, amounting to an estimated 130 acres or 60% of the town's built-up area. In his diaries, Propaganda Minister Göbbels used the phrase "Terrorangriff", terror raid, for the first time.

Cologne provided the main target on the night of the 27/28th, for which ninety-seven aircraft were made available, and it is believed that six of these were provided by 75(NZ) Squadron, while two other crews undertook the squadron's first gardening (mining) sorties in the Rosemary garden in the Heligoland Bight. They took off together between 21.50 and 22.20 with S/L Newton again taking the lead, but the ORB did not detail the allotting of crews to specific targets, which were roughly the same distance from Feltwell, thereby rendering landing times of little help in determining who went where. The weather in the Cologne area was favourable with good visibility and just a little ground haze, and the crews took advantage to deliver an unusually effective attack, which caused damage to nine industrial premises and more than fifteen hundred houses. P/O Leggett and crew were in X3538 AA-N and reported a brief skirmish with a Me110 just after bombing, at which rear gunner F/Sgt Newdick returned fire. The mining duo carried out their brief without interference and all aircraft returned safely to Feltwell after a successful night's work.

The final operation of the month to involve the squadron took place on the night of the 29/30th and was directed at the Gnome & Rhone aero engine factory at Gennevilliers, situated in the Port de Paris, in a loop of the Seine in north-western Paris. Eighty-eight aircraft were made ready, of which eight Wellingtons were provided by 75(NZ) Squadron and took off between 21.20 and 21.50, led for the first time by S/L Frank Henderson Denton RNZAF, who had been posted in from 218 Squadron on the 19th and promoted to succeed S/L Hill as B Flight commander. Denton was another familiar face, having already flown a tour and earned his DFC with the squadron in 1940. The good weather continued, and the force arrived in the target area to find perfect conditions and little defensive activity, which enabled them to deliver their attacks from an average of 7,000 feet. Returning crews described accurate bombing with hits on the factory and adjacent power station, and the 3 Group ORB described the operation as an undoubted success. Sadly, the crews were mistaken again, and the factory escaped damage, although other industrial buildings nearby were hit. Departures from the squadron at the end of the month included S/L Hill and F/L Doel, who relinquished their acting ranks on posting to 11 O.T.U. and 109 Squadron respectively.

During the course of the month the squadron attacked twenty-four targets, including the mining operation, and dispatched 122 sorties for the loss of five Wellingtons and three crews along with a number of individual crew members.

May 1942

The weather kept the Command on the ground on the night of the 1/2nd, but it had relented sufficiently on the following day for ninety-six aircraft from 3 and 5 Groups to be detailed for mining operations that night in German and French waters. Nine 75(NZ) Squadron crews attended briefing to learn that they had been assigned to the Beech garden off the Biscay port of St-Nazaire, for which they departed Feltwell between 20.45 and 21.05 with S/L Denton again the senior pilot on duty and last away. Weather conditions in the target area were unhelpful, with thick sea mist affording poor visibility but the 1,500lb parachute mines were apparently delivered according to brief and all aircraft returned safely.

Hamburg was the destination for eighty-one aircraft on the following night, of which only fifty-four reached it to deliver their bombs through ten-tenths cloud, which completely obscured the ground. Despite the challenging conditions, the results achieved were out of all proportion to the size of the force and local sources confirmed that fifty-seven large fires had broken out and many city-centre type buildings had been destroyed or damaged, along with others of a residential nature. 75(NZ) Squadron remained at home on this night but made ready eight Wellingtons on the 4th for the first of three attacks on the southern city of Stuttgart on consecutive nights. S/L Denton was the senior pilot on duty as they departed Feltwell between 22.25 and 22.40, each loaded with a cookie and SBCs of 4lb incendiaries. They were part of an overall force of 121 aircraft, a proportion of which had been briefed to aim for the Robert Bosch factory in the Feuerbach district to the north-west of the city centre, but it is not known whether any of the squadron's crews were among them. Located in a series of deep valleys, Stuttgart was difficult to find even in good conditions, and on this night eight to ten-tenths cloud concealed the ground, causing bombs to be scattered over a wide area, some drawn away by a decoy fire site at Lauffen, some fifteen miles to the north. It was defended by thirty-five searchlights and fifty flak guns in a clever ruse that would lure away many bomb loads during the course of the war, that might otherwise have caused damage in Stuttgart. Damage within the city was insignificant and the Bosch factory was not hit.

The squadron did not participate in the following night's operation, which was carried out by a smaller force and despite cloud-free skies, almost entirely missed the city. Ninety-seven aircraft were made ready on the 6th for the third raid, for which 75(NZ) Squadron put up eight Wellingtons. They departed Feltwell between 21.45 and 22.30 with S/L Denton the senior pilot on duty, but his trip was cut short when several BF109s were encountered near the Belgian coast and he and his crew found themselves in a desperate struggle to avoid being shot down. They escaped without combat damage to X3714 AA-W, "but one wing was torn owing to the very violent evasive action taken". As they headed home, the others pressed on to find thick haze concealing ground detail, and the operation was another massively ineffective affair, which again failed to land a single bomb in Stuttgart but did hit 150 buildings in Heilbronn, a large town situated five miles from the Lauffen decoy site and twenty miles from Stuttgart.

Another large mining effort occupied the night of the 7/8th, for which the squadron dispatched eight Wellingtons led again by S/L Denton. They took off between 22.10 and 22.45 bound for the Forget-me-not garden in the Kiel Bay region of the western Baltic, each carrying 1,500lb mines and 500lb bombs. They encountered clear conditions in the target area, where the vegetables were delivered according to brief, but most brought their bombs home after failing to find suitable coastal targets. The only incident of note involved P/O Wilson and crew, who were chased by an enemy fighter, which failed to press home its attack.

Having recently dealt a blow upon the town of Rostock and the local Heinkel aircraft factory, it was decided to return to the area on the night of the 8/9th to target the firm's other factory at Warnemünde, situated on the western bank of the Warnow estuary about six miles to the north. 75(NZ) Squadron was, perhaps, fortunate in not receiving an invitation to participate, as the operation became something of a disaster for little return. Nineteen aircraft failed to return from what was a largely low-level attack, and four of the casualties were 44 (Rhodesia) Squadron Lancasters, one of which contained the newly-appointed commanding officer and his crew.

The Kiwis were back in action on the following night, however, with eight Wellingtons returning to either the Forget-me-not or Wallflower gardens in Kiel Bay to plant a few more vegetables, and among the pilots was first-time captain, F/Sgt Summers RAF. S/L Newton was the senior pilot on duty as they departed Feltwell between 22.20 and 22.40 and reached the target area to find a continuation of the favourable weather conditions. Once again, the mines were delivered as briefed but most crews failed to find a suitable target for their 500 pounders and brought them home. The madness of "moling" saw four Wellingtons dispatched from Feltwell on the 13th to attack Essen by daylight. S/L Newton was the sole 75(NZ) Squadron representative, and he, like two of the 57 Squadron crews, delivered nine 500 pounders, not upon Essen but upon nearby Mülheim-an-der-Ruhr, before returning safely home.

Yet another gardening trip to Kiel Bay was ordered on the 15th, and the squadron contributed eight of the fifty aircraft involved. They took off between 22.45 and 23.30 with S/L Newton the senior pilot on duty and benefitted from fine weather conditions throughout the operation, which facilitated the planting of the vegetables in the briefed locations and the delivery of the 500 pounders on shipping, which responded with inaccurate anti-aircraft fire. X3482, AA-J failed to return home with the crew of F/Sgt Myles Fraser RNZAF, two others of which were also members of the RNZAF, and it was established eventually that the Wellington had come down in the sea off Sylt without survivors and was the squadron's first loss from a mining operation. A freshman operation to bomb the docks at Boulogne on the night of the 17/18th involved just a single crew from 75(NZ) Squadron, that of F/Sgt Summers, who took off at 22.50 but did not complete their sortie in the face of adverse weather conditions. On return to Feltwell in poor visibility at 01.40, X3420 AA-O came to grief, but no injuries were sustained, and crew and aircraft were returned to duty.

The first major operation for eleven days was mounted against Mannheim on the night of the 19/20th, for which 197 aircraft were made ready. A simultaneous operation by freshmen to St-Nazaire involved sixty-five crews, and 75(NZ) Squadron supported both efforts with a total of nine Wellingtons, including that of first-time skipper P/O Trevor Harry Smith RNZAF. They departed Feltwell between 22.50 and 23.20 with S/L Denton the senior pilot on duty, but as usual, the squadron ORB offers no clue as to the allotting of crews to specific targets. It seems likely that F/Sgt Summers was St-Nazaire-bound, but he returned with engine trouble and was sent to drop his load on Berners Heath bombing range. Those heading for southern Germany made landfall on the French coast and continued south until crossing into Germany south of Luxembourg, where they had to run the gauntlet of masses of searchlights before finding the target area under clear skies and in extreme darkness in the absence of a moon. Haze compounded the challenges and blotted out all ground features, compelling most crews to identify the general city area by means of a Gee-fix and the River Rhine but they were quite unable to pick out the main post office aiming point. The bombing was to be carried out from a higher level than normal, and aircraft were reported to have flown back and forth over the target searching for the aiming point, which delayed the opening of the attack. The Feltwell crews were airborne for up to six hours thirty minutes, and on return reported bomb bursts and explosions. In the event, local sources claimed that only about ten bomb loads fell within the city and bombing photographs showed mainly wooded areas and open country.

3 Group sent forty-eight Wellingtons and Stirlings on a mining expedition to the Cinnamon and Artichoke gardens off the Biscay ports of La Pallice and Lorient respectively on the night of the 21/22nd, for which 75(NZ) Squadron provided seven aircraft. They took off between 22.40 and 23.20 with S/L Newton taking the lead but encountered adverse weather conditions in the target area and most returned their mines and bombs to store. On the 22nd one of the inevitable training accidents cost the squadron P/O Andrew Donald MacKay RNZAF and four crewmen, two of them also members of the RNZAF, after Z1566, AA-K crashed into high ground near Leek in Staffordshire. Only the rear gunner, Sgt Chappell RNZAF, survived with injuries.

There now followed another lull in major operations as Harris prepared for his master stroke. At the time of his appointment as C-in-C, the figure of four thousand bombers had been bandied around as the number required to wrap up the war. Whilst there was not the slightest chance of procuring them, Harris, with a dark cloud still hanging over the existence of an independent bomber force, needed to ensure that those earmarked for him were not spirited away to what he considered to be less-deserving causes. The Command had not yet achieved sufficient success to silence the detractors, and the Admiralty was still calling for bomber aircraft to be diverted to the U-Boot campaign, while others demanded support for the North Africa campaign. Harris was in need of a major victory, and, perhaps, a dose of symbolism to make his point, and out of this was born the Thousand Plan, Operation Millennium, the launching of a thousand aircraft in one night against a major German city, for which Hamburg had been pencilled in. Harris did not have a thousand front-line aircraft and required the support of other Commands to make up the numbers. This was forthcoming from Coastal and Flying Training Commands, and in the case of the former, a letter to Harris on the 22nd promised 250 aircraft. However, following an intervention from the Admiralty, the offer was withdrawn and most of the Flying Training Command aircraft were found to be not up to the task, leaving the Millennium force well short of the magic figure. Undaunted, Harris, or more probably his able deputy, AM Sir Robert Saundby, scraped together every airframe capable of controlled flight or something resembling it, and pulled in the screened crews from their instructional duties. He also pressed into service aircraft and crews from within the Command's own training establishment, 91 Group. Come the night, not only would the thousand figure be achieved, but it would also be comfortably surpassed.

During the final week of the month, the arrival on bomber stations from Yorkshire to East Anglia of a motley collection of aircraft from training units gave rise to much speculation among crews and ground staff alike, but as usual, only the NAAFI staff and the local civilians knew what was really afoot. The most pressing remaining question was the weather, and as the days ticked by inexorably towards the end of May, this was showing no signs of complying. Harris was aware of the genuine danger that the giant force might draw attention to itself, and thereby compromise security, and the point was fast approaching when the operation would have to take place or be abandoned for the time being. Harris released some of the pressure by sanctioning operations on the night of the 29/30th, for which the Gnome & Rhone aero-engine and Goodrich tyre factories at Gennevilliers in Paris were the main targets. A force of seventy-seven aircraft took off and crews found it difficult to gain an accurate picture of the outcome, claiming a successful operation, when in fact, the only damage caused was to eighty-seven houses, in which thirty-four people were killed and 167 injured. Other small-scale operations on this night were directed against the docks and shipping at Cherbourg and Dieppe and mining in the Frisians and off Copenhagen. 75(NZ) Squadron briefed four freshman crews for Dieppe, including debutants F/Sgt John Charles Wilmshurst RNZAF, Sgt Robert Bertram RAFVR and F/Sgt Edward Leonard Haydon RNZAF), and they took off either side of 22.30, before reaching the target area to deliver their bomb loads. Cloud and poor visibility prevented them from assessing the results, but all returned safely home.

It was in an atmosphere of frustration and hopeful expectation, that "morning prayers" began at Harris's High Wycombe HQ on the 30th, with all eyes turned upon the civilian chief meteorological adviser, Magnus Spence. After careful deliberation, he was able to give a qualified assurance of clear skies over the Rhineland, while north-western Germany and Hamburg would be concealed under buckets of cloud. Thus, did the fickle fates decree that Cologne would bear the dubious honour of hosting the first one thousand bomber raid in history. At briefings, crews were told that the operation would adopt the now familiar three wave format and that the enormous force was to be pushed across the aiming point in just ninety minutes. This was unprecedented and gave rise to the question of collisions as hundreds of aircraft funnelled towards the aiming point. The answer, according to the experts, was to observe timings and flight levels, and they calculated also that just two aircraft would collide over the target. It is said that a wag in every briefing room asked, "do they know which two?"

3 Group assembled a force of 255 aircraft made up of eighty-eight Stirlings and 167 Wellingtons drawn from its front line and specialist squadrons and training units, and they were joined by ten other Wellingtons from non-operational units. They were assigned, along with 1 Group and any other units lodging on their stations, to attack aiming point A, the old city centre on the western bank of the Rhine, which included the cathedral to the north, and in its shadow, the main railway station. The northern quadrant of an outer ring adjoining the centre was designated aiming point X and was entrusted to 4 Group, while the southern quadrant, aiming point Y, belonged to 5 Group. A total of 1,047 aircraft lined up on dozens of stations in preparation for take-off for the Rhineland capital, forty-seven of the Wellingtons at Feltwell, a figure made up of a new record of twenty-three representing 75(NZ) Squadron, of which a number were aging hacks, twenty from 57 Squadron and four from Flying Training Command. Some of the older and more tired Mk 1As and 1Cs would climb almost reluctantly into the air, lifted more by the enthusiasm of their crews than by the power of their engines, and some of these, unable to achieve a respectable altitude, would fall easy prey to the defences or simply drop from the sky through mechanical failure. The Kiwi element became airborne between 23.05 and 23.55 with S/Ls Denton and Newton the senior pilots on duty, and three

first-time captains on duty, P/O Cecil William Phair Carter RNZAF, P/O Graham Edward Murdoch RNZAF, and P/O Stanley Holmes Gunning, RNZAF. Twenty-five aircraft departing from 3 Group stations returned early with technical difficulties, and among them for certain was the 75(NZ) Squadron crew of F/Sgt Haydon and, perhaps, one other. The bomber stream adopted a direct route that crossed the English coast between Southwold and Orfordness and made landfall on the enemy coast over the Scheldt estuary. Precisely as forecast, the clouds parted shortly after midnight to allow clear skies and bright moonlight, which 868 crews exploited to deliver 1,455 tons of bombs, two-thirds of them incendiaries.

Returning crews described a city on fire from end to end and never-before-witnessed scenes and claimed that the glow remained visible for a hundred miles into the return flight, which adopted a reciprocal route a little to the south of that employed outbound. The operation was, by any standards, an outstanding success, which left more than three thousand buildings in ruins and many times that number damaged to some degree. On the debit side, a new record number of forty-one aircraft failed to return, which, when measured against the size of the force and the scale of success in conditions favourable to attacker and defender alike, was acceptable, and at 3.9% of those dispatched, sustainable. Among the missing were thirteen representing 3 Group, one of them an elderly Wellington IA, N2894, which, with its pilot, P/O David Malcolm Johnson, was on attachment to the squadron from the Central Gunnery School at Sutton Bridge. Two crew members had been 'borrowed' from 75(NZ) Squadron for the trip, second pilot W/O Oldrich Jambor, RAF and navigator F/L Hector Austin Charles Batten, RAF. The Wellington fell victim to a night fighter over Holland, piloted by Oblt Emil Waltersdorf of III./NJG1, and only the rear gunner survived as a PoW. Five other 3 Group aircraft were involved in crashes in England. The heaviest casualties were sustained by the training units, which posted missing twenty-one aircraft and crews.

On the following night, just two 3 Group Wellingtons operated, while the rest of the Command remained at home to draw breath. One aircraft from each of the Feltwell squadrons returned to Cologne, S/L Newton captaining the 75(NZ) Squadron representative and taking off at 23.15. They found the city on this occasion to be concealed beneath cloud and were unable to observe the results of their efforts. During the course of the month the squadron undertook fourteen separate operations and dispatched ninety-five sorties for the loss of three Wellingtons and crews, one of them while training.

June 1942

While the Millennium force remained assembled, Harris wanted to exploit its potential again immediately, and was no doubt excited about the prospect of visiting upon the old enemy of Essen a similar ordeal to that just experienced by Cologne. A force of 956 aircraft was the best that could be achieved during the 1st, 3 Group managing to raise 229 of them after again raiding the training units, and eighty-four Stirlings and 145 Wellingtons would ultimately take to the air late in the evening. The leading twenty aircraft, all from 3 Group, were to act as the flare force, while a further sixty, all Gee-equipped, would bomb in the first wave, leaving the remainder to form part of the main force. Forty Wellingtons lined up at Feltwell, twenty from each squadron, with S/Ls Denton and Newton the senior 75(NZ) Squadron pilots on duty as the Kiwis took off between 22.50 and 00.10, the departure times reflecting their place in the grand scheme of things. Crews had been briefed to employ the sprawl of the Borbeck district-located Krupp sector as the aiming point and flew out under favourable weather conditions that promised the possibility of actually being able to identify ground detail. Eight 3 Group aircraft turned back early, while the 75(NZ) Squadron element all reached the target area, where they ran into five to ten-tenths cloud at 4,000 to 6,000 feet, which combined with industrial haze and smoke drifting over from Cologne to muddy the vertical visibility. A few crews claimed to have pinpointed on the River Ruhr and on the Krupp complex, but as usual at this target, bombing took place on estimated positions based on Gee, e.t.a., and dead-reckoning (DR), and as a result was spread over a wide area encompassing eleven population centres in and around the Ruhr. There were reports of scattered fires, some of them large and claims that they remained visible as a glow on the horizon from as far away as far as the Dutch coast. In fact, Essen had escaped lightly once more, and the operation was a huge disappointment at a cost of thirty-one aircraft. A dozen of these were from the training units, to add to those sacrificed to Operation Millennium, and the policy of employing instructors and students on major operations would continue to bleed the Command for much of the year.

A follow-up raid was planned for twenty-four hours later and a much-reduced force of 197 aircraft made ready, of which 3 Group provided fifty-seven Wellingtons and twenty-one Stirlings. The sixteen-strong 75(NZ) Squadron contingent took off either side of midnight with S/L Denton the senior pilot on duty and found clear skies over the Ruhr with the usual industrial haze impairing the vertical visibility. However, a low moon provided some illumination, and crews also benefitted from the deployment of flares, which highlighted the Rhine over to the west. Those equipped with Gee were able to confirm their positions over what they believed to be the Krupp complex aiming point and returned with confidence that they had attacked Essen. This was not borne out by local sources, who reported that just three high explosive bombs and three hundred incendiaries had fallen within the city and caused only minor damage. Such was the density of the Ruhr, with overlapping town and city boundaries, that it was difficult not to hit something urban, but concentration was the key to success and the scattering of bombs over a wide area was never going to achieve the knock-out blow that Harris was seeking. Stubborn to the end, he would keep trying, but it would be a further nine months before the means were to hand to make a genuine impact.

P/O "Willy" Carter and crew were in the target area at 10,500 feet when X3408, AA-Q was hit by flak. Carter had managed to keep the Wimpey in the air until one of the engines gave up, and it is unclear whether it was abandoned by the all-New Zealand crew or was crash-landed. What is known is that it broke in two on impact and its occupants, including ex-Leggett crew wireless operator Sgt Jack "Slim" Mayall, survived and set the wreckage alight before trying to evade capture. In the event, they were all in enemy hands by the end of the day and would spend the remainder of the war as PoWs, probably as the first all-Kiwi crew to be captured. On the way back over the Channel, the McLachlan crew in X3646, AA-M fought off a night-fighter, possibly the same one that attacked the Wilmshurst crew in X3720, AA-U shortly afterwards. The latter's wireless operator, Sgt Dick Sharp, spotted it first from the astro-hatch and rear gunner Sgt Raymond John Finlay "Browny" Hirst RNZAF took up the fight. After several passes, with skipper F/Sgt Wilmshurst RNZAF diving and weaving, the fighter was identified as a Ju88 and Hirst shot it down in flames to crash into the sea. It was the squadron's first "kill" of 1942.

The squadron sat out a raid on Bremen on the night of the 3/4th, when an initial force of 170 aircraft delivered an uncharacteristically effective attack, which caused damage to U-Boot construction yards, the harbour and residential districts. The freshman crews of Sgts Charles Croall and Arthur Gibson Osborne, both RNZAF, departed Feltwell at 23.20 on the 4th to bomb the docks and shipping at Dieppe with 250 pounders. Both returned safely, the former having done so early with a broken airspeed indicator and was sent to bomb Berners Heath range instead, while the latter claimed to have attacked the target without observing the results.

Essen was again the destination on the night of the 5/6th, this time for 180 aircraft, of which 75(NZ) Squadron provided thirteen Wellingtons, although only twelve were listed as taking off. S/L Denton was flying as second pilot to P/O Smith and may have been counted twice. They departed Feltwell between 23.10 and 23.35 and having flown out over Belgium under clear skies, some identified a bend in the River Ruhr to the south-east of the target, while others relied on a TR-fix, flares or evidence of searchlight and flak concentrations to establish their positions in conditions of poor vertical visibility caused by industrial haze. Bombs were dropped over a wide area of the Ruhr in the face of an intense searchlight and flak response, and returning crews were unable to offer any assessment of the outcome. It was another abject failure, which cost twelve aircraft and crews, and there was probably some relief when Emden was posted as the target for the following night. Among the 233 aircraft taking off for the naval port were a dozen Wellingtons representing 75(NZ) Squadron, which became airborne either side of 23.30 with F/L Ball the senior pilot on duty. They flew out in favourable weather conditions, which persisted in the target area, enabling many of them to observe a number of large buildings on fire. Searchlights were few, but flak quite intense as they delivered an effective attack, which left three hundred houses in ruins and many more damaged to some extent. One unspecified aircraft dived down to 200 feet to attack flak ships, but no results were observed.

The busy start to the month continued with another attempt to deal Essen a heavy blow on the night of the 8/9th, for which 170 aircraft were made ready, a dozen of the Wellingtons to represent 75(NZ) Squadron. They departed Feltwell between 23.25 and 23.45 with S/L Newton the senior pilot on duty and set course in favourable conditions that persisted all the way to the Ruhr. They were greeted by the expected blanket of ground haze, which, together with the glare from the intense searchlight activity, blinded them to ground features and rendered the attack something of a lottery. Bombing took place on TR and bomb bursts were observed, but those crews returning to base would have no detail to pass on at debriefing. Minor property damage was reported by local authorities and many other widely-spread Ruhr communities recorded bombs falling. This time the squadron did not escape retribution and two of its Wellingtons were among the nineteen aircraft failing to return. X3587, AA-S crashed near Düsseldorf, killing P/O Rupert John Smith RNZAF and his crew, the front gunner of which was also a member of the RNZAF. P/O Murdoch's Z1573, AA-T was brought down at the Dutch coast and crashed into the waters of the Krabbenkreek in the region of the Scheldt estuary, again with no survivors. One of the returning crews reported an encounter with two unidentified aircraft near the Dutch coast, which they managed to evade. Perhaps these were the ones responsible for the demise of the Murdoch crew, in which the pilot, navigator and front gunner were all members of the RNZAF. This would prove to be the last major operation for a week, during which period mining became the main activity.

There had been an intention to raid Essen again on the nights of the 13th and 15th, but unfavourable weather conditions caused a cancellation on each occasion. Not so on the 16th, however, for which a modest force of 106 aircraft had been made ready during the day, seven of them Wellingtons provided by 75(NZ) Squadron. All crews had been briefed to employ TR to locate the target and bomb blindly based on that, which, under the conditions of up to eight-tenths cloud on a moonless night with visibility down to three miles was the best that could be expected. The participating crews had to wait until late before getting away, those at Feltwell between 23.23 and 23.55 with F/L Ball the senior pilot on duty. He was forced to turn back early, presumably with technical difficulties, leaving the others to press on towards the target, the general area of which only sixteen aircraft attacked, while forty-five others, including the Kiwi element, dropped their bombs on the city of Bonn, south of Cologne. Essen escaped once more with light, superficial damage, and thus was concluded a five-raid series over sixteen nights, which had involved 1,607 sorties and the loss of eighty-four aircraft for no worthwhile return.

Only minor operations were mounted on the night of the 17/18th, for which the squadron briefed seven crews. Five were to plant vegetables in one of the Nectarine gardens around the Frisians, while two others joined in on a raid on the docks at St-Nazaire. They took off between 23.00 and 23.35 with F/L Ball the senior pilot on duty and those heading for the Biscay coast encountered low cloud and poor visibility, which contributed to just six aircraft out of twenty-seven bombing the French port. Many miles to the north, the gardeners found more favourable conditions and were able to plant their vegetables in the briefed locations. The Nectarine region encompassed the entire Frisian chain and was divided into three gardens, Nectarine I from Texel to the eastern tip of Ameland, Nectarine II, from east of Ameland to Memmert, and Nectarine III, Juist to Wangerooge.

The first of three attacks on Emden in four nights took place on the night of the 19/20th, for which 194 aircraft took off, including eleven Wellingtons belonging to 75(NZ) Squadron, among them one containing the crew of first-time captain, P/O Walter Jack Monk, RNZAF. They became airborne between 23.24 and 23.49 with F/L Ball the senior pilot on duty and set out for northern Germany in fair weather conditions. At briefings, Osnabrück, which lay eighty miles south of the primary target, had been offered as an alternative, and was found to be under clear skies as the bomber force passed by. Part of the flare force illuminated it, persuading a large element from the main force to deliver their bombs and returning crews reported observing bomb bursts in the marshalling yards and the town. The remaining two-thirds pressed on to reach Emden, where they carried out their attacks through eight-tenths cloud, although, what happened to the bombs is unclear, as according to local reports, only a handful of high explosives found their way into the town and port. P/O Fraser and crew, who were in X3760 AA-L "London", reported that they had been attacked by a BF109 just before bombing, but sustained no damage. P/O Smith was also attacked just after bombing, whereupon the rear gunner fired back, but Z1592 AA-O sustained extensive damage and bullets in an ammunition box began to explode. Unable to douse the incendiary rounds with a fire extinguisher, the wireless operator, Sgt McKenzie, pushed the whole box out through the escape hatch!

185 aircraft were made ready for the same target on the following night, of which a dozen Wellingtons represented 75(NZ) Squadron. F/L Ball was once more the senior pilot on duty as they departed Feltwell between 23.29 and 23.59, and, mentioned for the first time in the

squadron records, is the name Sgt R.S.D Kearns, who was flying as second pilot to F/Sgt Wilmshurst. Kearns, another West Coaster, from Reefton, would go on to complete a distinguished operational career, which would take him to 156 Squadron of the Path Finders, and then to 617 Squadron as a flight lieutenant in September 1943 to serve under W/C Len Cheshire. Known as "Terry" to his colleagues, he would eventually be selected to be one of 617 Squadron's Mosquito pilots, whose job was to mark precision targets from low level.

Also flying on this night was first-time captain John 'Jack' Leonard Wright, RNZAF and he and his crew were among those from 75(NZ) Squadron to reach their destination and find five-tenths cloud with thick ground haze. They noted also that the flak defences had been strengthened since the previous night, although searchlights were few. On the return flight near Terschelling, Sgt Jack Wright and crew were attacked by a Ju88, the fire from which damaged the Wellington's propellers, punctured the fuel tanks, blew away the astro-navigation hatch and tore large strips of the fuselage fabric away. Rear gunner, Sgt Bruce Neal, fired back and a very lucky wireless operator, Sgt Nick Carter, had the seat of his pants ripped by a piece of shrapnel, but no injuries were sustained, and X3646 AA-M made it safely back to Feltwell. Nine aircraft failed to return, and among them was the squadron's X3760, AA-L "London", which was shot down by a night-fighter and crashed into the sea west of the Frisian island of Ameland. There were no survivors from the all-RNZAF crew of F/O Allen Fraser, whose bodies, with the exception of the front gunner, were eventually recovered for burial. It was not possible to assess the outcome, but a local report stated that a hundred houses had been damaged. The above mentioned "Jack" Wright was a pilot who would go on to lead a famous crew and return to the squadron later in the war as a respected flight commander.

After a night's rest the next attack on Emden was mounted on the 22/23rd, for which the squadron made ready thirteen Wellingtons as part of an overall force of 227 aircraft. They took off between 23.10 and 23.59 led away by F/O Wilson, who found himself to be the senior pilot on duty. Sgts Colin Valentine McPherson RNZAF, Alexander George Sutherland RNZAF and Neville John Netscher Hockaday RAFVR were the three pilots undertaking their maiden operations as captain of their own crew. Weather conditions outbound were favourable, with five-tenths cloud at 15,000 feet, but this dispersed to leave clear skies to greet the arrival of the force over the German coast. A total of 196 returning crews claimed to have bombed in the target area, but a local report suggests that only part of the force had correctly identified Emden. Fifty houses were destroyed, a hundred others were damaged, and there was some unspecified damage in the harbour area, but decoy fire sites are believed to have drawn off many bomb loads and the operation, while the most effective of the three, still fell short of expectations.

On the following night, Feltwell waved off fifteen Wellingtons to mine the waters of the Beech garden off St-Nazaire and drop some bombs on the docks, and of these eight were provided by 75(NZ) Squadron, among them the one containing Sgt Arthur Grahame Johns RNZAF, who was flying for the first time as captain. F/L Ball was back for this one as the senior pilot on duty as they took off between 22.58 and 23.45 with Sgt Sutherland and crew the last away some thirty minutes adrift of the others. The last-mentioned returned two and a quarter hours later with an indisposed navigator and was diverted to Methwold, leaving the remainder to head for the French coast in fine weather conditions with a little ground haze. Vegetables were planted and some bombs dropped without any observation of results, and all returned safely from uneventful trips.

The final employment of the "Thousand Force" was planned for the night of the 25/26th, when the city of Bremen was selected as the target. Bomber Command was able to raise 960 aircraft in what was the most diverse force yet, which included 2 Group Bostons and Mosquitos, normally used only for daylight operations. Churchill ordered Coastal Command to take part, and this added 102 Wellingtons and Hudsons to the overall force, although their participation was classed as a separate effort not under the direct control of Bomber Command. The overall force of 1,067 aircraft exceeded that assembled for the highly successful Cologne raid, and certain elements were given specific targets to aim for. 5 Group's 142 aircraft, including twenty Manchesters on their final operation in Bomber Command service, were assigned to the Focke-Wulf aircraft factory, twenty 2 Group Blenheims were to attack the A G Weser shipyard, while the Coastal Command target was the rest of the Deschimag shipyard complex. All other aircraft were to deliver an area attack on the city, and it was planned to send the entire force across their respective aiming points in a sixty-five-minute slot, compared with the ninety minutes allowed at Cologne. They took off late in the evening, the 75(NZ) Squadron element of twenty Wellingtons departing Feltwell between 23.15 and 23.52 with S/L Newton the senior squadron pilot on duty. G/C Powell was also on the order of battle for this one and was the last to leave the ground. There were two debutants, Sgt George Edward Francis Bradey RNZAF and Sgt R.S.D. "Terry" Kearns RNZAF. Although not listed in the ORB, Sgt Wright and crew took off with the group but returned early with an unserviceable intercom.

It had been known that a band of cloud over northern Germany was pushing eastwards and it was hoped that clear skies would attend the attack, however, the wind dropped, and the city was completely concealed for the entire duration of the raid. Gee led the first-wave aircraft to the target area and those following behind were able to pick out the glow of fires beneath the cloud caused by their bombs, although the precision bombing of specific targets was out of the question. The attack was carried out in the face of an intense flak response, through which almost seven hundred returning crews claimed to have bombed in the target area. While not repeating the success at Cologne, the operation was substantially more effective than that at Essen and resulted in the destruction of 572 houses with damage to more than six thousand others. There was also some success at the Focke-Wulf factory and two shipyards, and a number of other important industrial firms were also hit. A new record casualty figure of forty-eight aircraft featured a disproportionately high number from the training units with a total of thirty-four from OTUs, conversion units and squadron conversion flights failing to return. Sgt Bertram's rear gunner fired off four bursts from Z1616 AA-D at an approaching BF109, possibly damaging it, before it disappeared below them. Otherwise, 75(NZ) Squadron came through unscathed and spent the following two nights at home, or more likely, in the watering holes of west Norfolk or even, perhaps, across the county line in Cambridgeshire. While they were, no doubt, enjoying themselves, 144 crews took part in the first of two follow-up raids on Bremen on the night of the 27/28th, and achieved a degree of success.

Following the brief respite, four freshman crews were called to briefing on the 28th to learn that they were to attack the docks and shipping at St-Nazaire. They took off at 23.00 and proceeded towards the south-west in fair but cloudy conditions and met intense flak at Vannes on France's north-western coast. Two 57 Squadron aircraft were approached by enemy fighters and the Kearns crew was shot at by E Boats on the way back, rear gunner Sgt Harold "Buck" Price copping a nasty wound in the backside, but the Kiwi quartet returned safely.

The second follow-up raid on Bremen was mounted on the night of the 29/30th, for which the squadron put up eighteen Wellingtons as part of an overall force of 253 aircraft, including that of first-timer F/Sgt William Ronald Parkes RNZAF. They took off between 23.25 and 23.59 with S/L Newton the senior pilot on duty, but tragedy struck almost immediately as Z1616, AA-D crashed at nearby Methwold at 23.28, killing P/O Robert Bertram RAFVR and his crew. Eyewitnesses reported the aircraft to be on fire and circling before diving into the ground. The wireless operator, Sgt Richard John Grenfell, and front gunner, Sgt Norman Mitchell, were both members of the RNZAF. The others set course across the North Sea, but it seems that the crews of F/L Ball, P/O Smith, P/O Gunning and Sgt Johns each returned early for unspecified reasons. Those reaching the target in the early stages of the raid found ten-tenths cloud, but this had diminished to five-tenths by the end of the attack and some crews were able to bomb visually. Unusually, it was industry that seemed to suffer most, with extensive damage inflicted upon five important war industry sites, including the Focke-Wulf factory and the A G Weser U-Boot construction yard. Eleven aircraft failed to return, and among them was the squadron's X3539, AA-T, which fell victim to a night-fighter and crashed into the Waddenzee between Ameland and the Dutch mainland. There were no survivors from the all-RNZAF crew of P/O Monk, and his was the only body not recovered for burial in the local churchyard at Holwerd. On the way out, Sgt Hockaday and crew in BJ837 AA-F "Freddie" spotted a Ju88 at 2,000 yards flying slightly below them and manoeuvred to place the enemy aircraft above them and in the moon. Rear gunner, Sgt Philip, fired off a thousand rounds in the ensuing dog fight, eventually sending the assailant down with smoke coming from its port engine and claiming it as possibly destroyed. Luckily, one of the other pilots saw the whole episode and was able to confirm the enemy aircraft as destroyed.

During the course of the month the squadron undertook sixteen operations and dispatched 174 sorties for the loss of six Wellingtons and crews.

July 1942

The new month began as the old one had ended, with a large-scale assault on Bremen on the night of the 2/3rd, for which a force of 325 aircraft was assembled, a dozen of the Wellingtons provided by 75(NZ) Squadron in a 3 Group contribution of eighty-four Wellingtons and thirty-four Stirlings. They Kiwis were all safely airborne by 23.30 with no senior pilots on duty but lost the services of Sgt Hockaday and crew when they returned early for an undisclosed reason. The others set course for the Dutch coast near Alkmaar and reached the target area to find favourable weather conditions, with excellent visibility, no low cloud, high cirrus at around 22,000 feet, a half moon and only a little haze to spoil the view below. Positions were established by TR-fix confirmed by a visual check, but searchlight glare created great difficulty for the bomb-aimers, particularly those assigned to specific aiming-points like the Focke-Wulf aircraft factory and shipyards, and most would settle for estimating the fall of their bombs. Returning crews reported many fires, but they were scattered over a wide area, particularly across southern districts, and most fell outside of the city boundaries. Even so, local reports specified a thousand houses damaged to some extent, and seven ships hit in the harbour, one of them sinking to create a navigation hazard.

The Feltwell crews all came home safely and enjoyed a few days away from the operational scene, before ten of them were called to the briefing room on the 7th to be informed that elements of 1 and 3 Groups would be carrying out an extensive mining programme in the Nectarine gardens around the Frisians that night involving over a hundred aircraft. By take-off time, shortly after midnight, one of the squadron's aircraft had been scrubbed, but the others got away safely, their bomb bays loaded with 1,500lb mines and 500lb bombs for coastal targets of opportunity. The weather in the target area was unhelpful with cloud and poor visibility, which persuaded some crews to bring their stores home, while others dropped them and hoped for the best. No opposition of any kind was encountered, and all returned without incident.

Northern Germany continued to provide the focus for operations, and the night of the 8/9th was devoted to the naval and shipbuilding port of Wilhelmshaven, for which a force of 285 aircraft was made ready. Twenty-four Wellingtons were bombed-up at Feltwell, thirteen of them provided by 75(NZ) Squadron as part of a 3 Group contingent of 113 Wellingtons and Stirlings. They took off either side of midnight with no senior pilots present and arrived at their destination to find around three-tenths thin cloud at 10,000 feet and haze below. This made it almost impossible for most to identify ground detail, including the docks and shipyard aiming-points, and positions were established on e.t.a. and by TR-fix, some backed up through a brief glimpse of the docks and waterways sparkling in the light of flares. The first bombs went down before the flare force had provided adequate illumination and appeared to fall to the west of the main town. Thereafter, the attack crept closer to the briefed aiming point, but post-raid reconnaissance would reveal that much of the effort had been wasted in open country. A local report admitted damage to housing and public buildings, along with isolated destruction of buildings in the harbour. The operation cost a modest five aircraft and among them was the squadron's X3557, AA-X, which had crashed into the Waddenzee off Rottumeroog Island at 01.30 while outbound. There were no survivors from the six-man crew of P/O Trevor Smith, who were all members of the RNZAF, and only the remains of the pilot and front gunner were ultimately recovered for burial.

Four crews were called to briefing on the morning of the 10th to be told that they were to be sent "moling" over the Ruhr that afternoon and would have to rely on cloud cover for protection. P/Os Jarman and McLachlan and Sgts Kearns and Wilmshurst and their crews took off during a forty-five-minute slot either side of 15.00 and headed for Düsseldorf loaded with 500 pounders. Three of them came back with their loads intact after flights lasting between one hour forty minutes and two hours fifty minutes, having been recalled due to a lack of cloud-cover. Carrying nine 500lb bombs, X3396 AA-S overshot the runway and ploughed through the perimeter barbed-wire fence and a sand-bagged gun emplacement, causing a few anxious moments for the Kearns crew. The return of X3720, AA-U and the crew of Sgt Wilmshurst was awaited in vain, and on the strength of a final wireless message, S/L Newton and P/O Jarman carried out a sea-search in the hope of finding a dinghy. The fate of the all-RNZAF crew remained a mystery until two bodies were eventually recovered from the sea for burial in Germany's Sage War Cemetery.

Having failed so spectacularly at Essen, Harris now moved on to its neighbour, Duisburg, not only hugely important for its war industry, but also as Germany's largest inland port and a vital component in the communications network. Over the next three-and-a-half-weeks, he would launch five operations against it, beginning on the night of the 13/14th, for which a force of 194 aircraft was made ready. 75(NZ) Squadron briefed nine crews as part of the 3 Group contribution of seventy-three Wellingtons and Stirlings, but one Kiwi sortie was cancelled, leaving eight Wellingtons to take off either side of 00.30 on the 14th with F/L Wilson the senior pilot on duty and F/O "Artie" Ashworth back in the fold for his second tour. They flew out through electrical storms and heavy cloud and reached the western edge of the Ruhr to find Duisburg concealed by ten-tenths cloud and could tell already that the bombing was widely scattered across the target area. The crews faced exactly the same problems as at Essen, in that even when the ground was visible, its detail was blotted out by thick industrial haze. A local report stated that eleven houses had been destroyed and some seventy others seriously damaged, but this was a poor return for the effort expended.

The squadron dispatched three sorties on the following night to plant mines in the waters of the Nectarine I garden off Terschelling in the Dutch Frisians. P/O Shepherd and Sgts Hockaday and Kearns were all safely airborne and on their way before 23.00, and were back on the ground within three hours, having completed a successful and uneventful operation. Training occupied the ensuing five days, and it was the 20th before the next operation was posted, which was to involve six crews in daylight "moling" sorties to Bremen during the afternoon. F/L Wilson and P/O Shepherd took off at 14.00, and the others between 17.05 and 17.30, but all returned with their bombs after failing to find sufficient cloud cover. Four enemy aircraft unsuccessfully attacked X3452, AA-A, which contained the crew of Sgt Charlie Croall, and that was the only incident of note.

A force of 291 aircraft was prepared on the 21st for the second attack of the series on Duisburg, for which 3 Group detailed 134 Wellingtons and Stirlings and 75(NZ) Squadron thirteen of the 170 participating Wellingtons. They departed Feltwell between 23.50 and 00.25 and lost the services of Sgt Croall and crew to a faulty rear turret in BJ599 AA-U. The others reached the target to find clear skies and the usual industrial haze, but sufficiently good vertical visibility aided by flares to confirm their TR-fixed positions visually. At least, there was no moon to aid the night-fighters, which had been taking an increasingly heavy toll of bombers in recent weeks. Returning crews would be enthusiastic about the success of the operation, but photographs taken during the raid showed that the flare force, relying on Gee, had illuminated an area on the western bank of the Rhine away from the main city, and a proportion of the bombing had fallen there. Despite this, the Duisburg authorities confirmed a moderately successful raid, during which ninety-four buildings had been destroyed and 256 seriously damaged. This represented something of a success at this elusive target, and it is believed that the Thyssen steelworks was among a number of important war industry factories to sustain some damage at a cost to the Command of twelve aircraft.

The squadron was able to offer fourteen Wellingtons two nights later for the next instalment of the Duisburg campaign, for which an overall force of 215 aircraft included a 3 Group contribution of 119 Wellingtons and Stirlings. There was another very late take-off for the Kiwis, who became safely airborne in a thirty-minute slot either side of 01.00 with F/L Wilson the senior pilot on duty and Sgt John Edward Gilbertson RNZAF captaining his own crew for the first time. They crossed the North Sea over ten-tenths cloud topping out at 5,000 feet and all reached the target area to find that nine-tenths of the white stuff remained beneath them at 8,000 to 12,000 feet, forcing them to establish their positions by Gee-fix. The bombs disappeared into the cloud in which their detonations and the burgeoning fires were reflected, and it was left to local sources to report housing damage and sixty-five fatalities but another unsatisfactory attempt to deliver a telling blow on this major centre of war production.

The fourth raid of the series was planned for the night of the 25/26th, for which the squadron prepared thirteen Wellingtons as part of a 3 Group contribution of 139 Wellingtons and Stirlings in an overall force of 313 aircraft. The 75(NZ) Squadron element departed Feltwell between 00.15 and 00.40 with F/O Ashworth the senior pilot on duty and reached the western Ruhr to encounter eight-tenths cloud with thick industrial haze below. Most crews established their positions by TR, before aiming their bombs at existing fires and could only assume that they were adding to the damage, which, according to local sources was on a smaller scale than that from the previous raids in the series. Returning crews commented on the intensity and accuracy of the flak and also the prevalence of night-fighters but had nothing to say about the effectiveness of the attack, which, it transpired, was not as damaging as the previous two. AA-Q is reported to have crash-landed at Mildenhall, the unidentified crew mistakenly believing that they were landing at Feltwell.

Looking back after the war, it was possible to see the pattern of operations each year during the last week of July. Hamburg always featured, and in this year of 1942, two large-scale operations were mounted, the first on the night of the 26/27th, for which a maximum effort was demanded and a force of 403 aircraft assembled. 3 Group contributed 137 aircraft, of which fifteen of the Wellingtons were provided by 75(NZ) Squadron. S/L Newton was the senior pilot on duty as they took off between 22.35 and 23.30 and set course for the North Sea to negotiate the frequently met conditions on this route of towering cloud, electrical storms and severe icing, and it was probably at this stage that most of the fifteen 3 Group early returns dropped out. The cloud diminished as the force made its way eastwards and those reaching the target area were drawn on for the last few miles by the sight of fires already burning in the docks area and the southern part of the old town. Apart from a little cloud at 15,000 feet, the skies were now clear and the city basking in bright moonlight as the Feltwell crews carried out their attacks. Soon, fires could be seen springing up all over the city, particularly in residential and semi-commercial districts, most noticeably in the old town north of the Elbe, but it was impossible to pick out individual bomb bursts among the many detonations and the hostility of the searchlight and flak defences dissuaded crews from loitering to make an assessment. The flak defence was described as accurate, but the effectiveness of the searchlights was nullified by the bright moonlight. "Terry" Kearns and crew reported destroying seven searchlights, while damaging others and silencing a machine-gun post. Flying at roof-top level, front gunner Jack Moller and rear gunner "Buck" Price fought a running battle with searchlights and machine gun posts, while Kearns tried to avoid trees and high-tension wires. Smoke was drifting across the city as the bombers retreated into the clutches of the waiting night-fighters, which played their part in bringing down a massive twenty-nine bombers, or 7.2% of those dispatched, many of them falling in the coastal regions and over the North Sea. Returning crews were unanimous in their assertion that the operation had been an unqualified success, almost on a par with Cologne, and this was borne out by local reports, which catalogued eight hundred fires, 523 of them classed as large and detailed 823 houses as destroyed with five thousand others damaged to some extent. The squadron's X3714, AA-W disappeared without trace with the six-man all-RNZAF crew of F/Sgt Colin McPherson, while Z1596, AA-K went down somewhere over northern Germany and only the rear gunner survived as a PoW from the crew of P/O Ian Shepherd. The four who died were all members of the RNZAF.

Feltwell and Wyton were ordered to send eight "moling" Wellingtons between them to northern Germany on the afternoon of the 27th to attack Bremen, Hamburg or Emden. F/L Wilson and Sgt Johns represented 75(NZ) Squadron and took off at 14.00 and 15.25 respectively for the former, where thick cloud concealed the ground. F/L Wilson delivered his load of 500 pounders blind and observed bombs bursting in what was believed to be the built-up area, while Sgt Johns brought his hardware home. 57 Squadron's commanding officer, W/C Peters-Smith, failed to return through enemy action and died with his crew, and a 156 Squadron aircraft was lost through engine failure, with all but one of the crew surviving in enemy hands. This represented a 25% loss rate, which on this occasion, was not entirely attributable to the folly of a daylight "moling" operation.

Worse was to come, however, when Hamburg was revisited on the night of the 28/29th by what remained of a much-depleted force after adverse weather over 1, 4 and 5 Group stations caused their participation to be scrubbed. Ultimately, it became a 3 Group operation involving ninety-four Wellingtons and seventy-four Stirlings, along with ninety-one aircraft drawn from O.T.Us, among which were twenty-four Whitleys, a type no longer in front-line service. 75(NZ) Squadron made ready seventeen Wellingtons, which departed Feltwell between 22.35 and 23.01 with S/L Newton the senior pilot on duty, although he was back on the ground within thirty minutes, presumably with a technical malfunction. Three pilots, P/O William Guy Horne RNZAF, Sgt George Alister Hutt RNZAF and Sgt John Jackson, RAFVR, were captaining a crew for the first time. Deteriorating weather conditions during the outward flight caused the O.T.U element to be recalled, and thirty-one 3 Group crews also turned back early. The remainder pressed on, and sixty-eight crews would later claim to have bombed after finding clear skies over the target city. The attack was scattered, but left fifty-six fires burning, fifteen of them classed as large, in return for which, the defenders hacked down twenty-five 3 Group aircraft, 15.2% of those dispatched, and four O.T.U Wellingtons, along with a Whitley that crashed in the sea. "Artie" Ashworth was the first to land back at Feltwell at 04.25, and over the ensuing sixty-three minutes another ten landed, leaving six empty dispersals to contemplate in dawn's early light.

Sgt Charles Croall's X3452, AA-A had been coned by searchlights over the target and hit by light flak as he lost height in an effort to break clear. He was forced to carry out a ditching, from which he and three others of the all-RNZAF crew survived to be taken prisoner. The body of the rear gunner, Sgt Thomas Eric Crarer RNZAF, eventually came ashore further north on the Schleswig-Holstein peninsula and was buried at Tönning. X3452 had only returned to the squadron the day before after being patched up following a previous skirmish. X3558 AA-Z crashed somewhere on the southern bank of the Elbe estuary, killing F/Sgt Sutherland RNZAF and his crew of four, three of whom were also members of the RNZAF. X3664 AA-Y came down near Stade on the western bank of the Elbe some eighteen miles west of the centre of Hamburg, and there were no survivors from the six-man all-RNZAF crew of F/L Peter Wilson. The shattered remains of BJ599 AA-U were also found in this area, at Steinbeck, some eight miles south of Stade, and the bodies of the all-RNZAF crew of F/Sgt Hutt were found inside. It was Hutt's third operation and his first as captain. Another casualty was the Ball crew's old kite Z1570, AA-B, which, it is believed, crashed much further south and again there were no survivors from the five-man crew of Sgt Arthur Johns RNZAF, three others of whom were members of the RNZAF. BJ661, AA-X was shot down into the Ijsselmeer by a night-fighter at 03.05 while homebound, and F/Sgt John Gilbertson RNZAF perished along with two of his crew, including the Kiwi navigator. The wireless operator and front gunner, both members of the RNZAF, survived to be taken into captivity.

In the thick of the hellish cauldron of fire over Hamburg, "Artie" Ashworth and his crew in BJ584 AA-C not only dropped their bombs but made three passes over the city, capturing three good target photographs. Their diligence was rewarded a day later when a telegram arrived on W/C "Ted" Olson's desk: "THE AOC CONGRATULATES F/O ASHWORTH C/75 SQDN ON HIS PHOTOGRAPHS OF HAMBURG NIGHT 28/29 JULY".

Losses were a fact of life in Bomber Command and could not be allowed to interfere with the process of war. A team from the Committee of Adjustment would descend upon the billets of the missing men and remove all trace of them to prepare the way for the next occupants. Such was the size of a bomber squadron and the constant turnover of arrivals and departures, particularly in 1943 and beyond, that close friendships beyond one's own crew were discouraged. Perhaps it was different among officers, who were fewer, and were more frequently in each other's company in the officers' mess, but generally, the faces of the missing soon faded from memory and those returning within a matter of months after evading capture were often shocked to discover how few of their former colleagues remained.

The mood at Feltwell was dark on the following day, the squadron members left stunned by the loss of thirty of their mates and angry that other squadrons had been withdrawn while they felt they had been "sent in like sitting ducks". The station community also was shaken that so many familiar faces had been torn from their midst, in all probability as far as they were concerned, never to be seen again. This was the squadron's heaviest loss to date in what would be a horrendously expensive month, which was not yet at an end. With no time to lick its wounds, the squadron called ten crews to briefing on the 29th for an operation that night against the capital of the coal-producing Saarland, Saarbrücken, situated on the frontier with north-eastern France to the south of Luxembourg. A force of 291 aircraft included a 3 Group contribution of eighty-three Wellingtons and Stirlings for what would be the largest raid by far on this major industrial target. It was expected that the local defences would be weak, and crews were encouraged to deliver their bombs from as low a level as practicable. The Feltwell element took off between 23.45 and midnight with the newly-promoted acting S/L Ashworth the senior pilot on duty for the first time since succeeding S/L Newton as A Flight commander on the 27th. There was one debutant, in the person of Sgt Thomas Smith Barclay RNZAF. They joined up with the rest of the 290-strong force as they made their way south to the French coast, from where they would hug the Belgian and Luxembourg frontiers before crossing into Germany. Initially, cloudy conditions gave way to clear skies in the target area, and three-quarters of the crews heeded the briefing and bombed from below 10,000 feet. On return, all were unanimous that the operation had been highly successful and this was confirmed by local reports, which listed almost four hundred buildings as destroyed, predominantly in central and north-western districts, and two war industry factories as damaged. "Terry" Kearns and crew were attacked by a Ju88, which they successfully evaded.

The final operation of the month was a huge affair involving 630 aircraft from the front-line and training units, which had Düsseldorf as their target for what was the largest non-1,000 raid to date. As a sign of the burgeoning power at Harris's disposal, more than a hundred Lancasters were to operate together for the first time. 75(NZ) Squadron made ready eleven Wellingtons in a 3 Group force of 133 aircraft, and they departed Feltwell between 00.20 and 00.50 with S/L "Artie" Ashworth again the senior pilot on duty. Those reaching the southern Ruhr in the first wave found bright moonlight, clear skies and good visibility that enabled them to confirm their TR-fixed positions visually by an S-bend in the River Rhine. They left developing fires for the second wave crews, whose identification of the aiming-point was impeded by the resulting smoke. The 75(NZ) Squadron crews carried out their attacks in the face of an intense and accurate searchlight and flak defence and reported many explosions and fires and a column of black smoke rising through 10,000 feet as they turned away. At debriefing, they expressed confidence in the quality of their work, having contributed to the delivery of more than nine hundred tons of bombs. Some was wasted in open country, but the remainder had been scattered across all parts of the city and neighbouring Neuss on the opposite bank of the Rhine. Local sources confirmed the destruction of 453 buildings, with varying degrees of damage to fifteen thousand more, and sixty-seven large fires among 954 conflagrations had to be dealt with. Had it not been for the high casualty rate of twenty-nine aircraft, the operation could have been declared an unqualified success. The Kiwis came through unscathed, apart, that is from F/Sgt Alan Lewis, the rear gunner in Sgt Bradey's X3646 AA-M, who was hit and injured by a 4lb incendiary dropped from above.

This operation brought to an end what had been an expensive month, during which the squadron had operated on fifteen occasions, and dispatched 147 sorties for the loss of ten Wellingtons and crews. W/C Olson completed his tour as commanding officer towards the end of the month and would be appointed station commander at Oakington on the 3rd of September, by which time it had become a Path Finder station and the continuing home of 7 Squadron and its Stirlings. The reins of command at 75(NZ) Squadron were passed to W/C Victor Mitchell, RAF, a Scot who, it is believed, was posted in directly from his flight commander role at 149 Squadron during w.e.f the 4th of August.

August 1942

Unfavourable weather conditions on the nights of the 1/2nd and 2/3rd led to the cancellation of operations against Düsseldorf and Flensburg respectively, and Flensburg was substituted for Essen on the night of the 4/5th, for which a force of thirty-eight aircraft was dispatched. Feltwell was the only 3 Group station in action and called five 75(NZ) Squadron crews to briefing along with four from 57 Squadron. They took off between 22.30 and 22.55 with S/L Ashworth the senior pilot on duty and those reaching the central Ruhr had battled their way through towering storm clouds that extended to 20,000 feet, which persuaded six Feltwell crews and fourteen others to turn back. The squadron ORB spoke of fairly good weather over the target with cloud in places, which the searchlights lit up as they co-ordinated with flak batteries to produce an intense barrage. The loads of 500 pounders were dropped in the target area, but no assessment was possible and only eighteen returning crews claimed to have bombed in the target area.

The last of five attacks on Duisburg in the current series was planned for the night of the 6/7th, for which 216 aircraft were made ready, ninety of them provided by 3 Group and eight of the

Wellingtons by 75(NZ) Squadron. S/L Ashworth was the senior pilot on duty as they lined up for a late take-off between 01.00 and 01.50, and once airborne, headed out over ten-tenths cloud in generally good weather conditions. It was common for the assessment of cloud conditions to vary markedly, and on this occasion, it was reported at between zero and ten-tenths with tops at 10,000 feet and barrage balloons tethered as high as 12,000 feet. Positions had to be established by TR-fix confirmed by visual reference on evidence of fires, flak and flares, and the bombs were delivered blindly. The flak was heavy, but thick ground haze at least nullified the searchlights, despite which, most of the bombs fell into open country to the west. X3636 was hit by flak, which wrecked the hydraulics system and Sgt Jackson had to carry out a crash-landing on return. He and his crew walked away unscathed, and the Wellington was eventually returned to service. Local reports from Duisburg listed eighteen buildings as destroyed and more than sixty damaged, but this was yet another poor return from a large effort. Over the course of the three-week campaign, 1,229 sorties had been dispatched on five operations and forty-three aircraft had been lost in return for the destruction of 212 houses, the serious damage of 741 others and significant industrial damage resulting from just one raid.

The squadron made ready seven Wellingtons on the 9th for an operation that night against Osnabrück as part of an overall force of 192 aircraft, of which ninety-nine were provided by 3 Group. Departure from Feltwell was accomplished safely by thirty minutes after midnight with S/L Ashworth once more leading from the front and F/O Laurence St George Dobbin RNZAF captaining his crew for the first time. The squadron participants carried flares in addition to a bomb load of 500 pounders and incendiaries as they flew out over the Norfolk coast on their way to the Den Helder peninsula on a direct course to the target, situated between Bremen to the north and the Ruhr to the south. There were clear skies over the flatlands of the Münster region as they closed on the target, but haze contributed to the poor visibility that awaited the approaching bombers. The crews found that they were unable to establish their positions by TR after it was jammed by the enemy on crossing the Dutch coast. On final approach to the target, flares were dropped by the lead aircraft to thinly illuminate the ground and some crews picked out railway lines, a canal and the River Hase, but it was mainly the fires, searchlights and flak that pointed the way to the aiming-point. The target area was ringed by searchlight concentrations, but only a small amount of light flak came up from the ground and a proportion of the bombing found the mark. Returning crews reported many fires both inside and outside the target area, and a number also spoke of a large explosion and fire with a pall of smoke visible from the Dutch coast. According to local reports, more than two hundred houses were destroyed and four thousand others damaged to some extent, mostly superficially.

A force of 154 aircraft was assembled on the 11th to undertake the long trip to Mainz in southern Germany on the 11th, and among the 3 Group contingent of sixty-seven aircraft were nine Wellingtons representing 75(NZ) Squadron. They departed Feltwell shortly before 23.00 with no senior pilots on duty and turned towards the south-east on course for what was the first major raid on this city, perched on the west bank of the Rhine, south-west of Frankfurt. BJ837 AA-F "Freddie" was five minutes from the English coast when the fabric covering the Wellington's nose was torn off, forcing Sgt Neville Hockaday to jettison the bomb load and return to base. The others crossed the North Sea to make landfall on the French coast near Dunkerque and continued on the well-worn route to southern Germany in largely favourable weather conditions to be greeted in the target area by up to eight-tenths cloud with tops at

11,500 feet and a base at around 5,000 feet. F/O Gunning and crew were in BJ725 AA-H and briefly exchanged fire with a Ju88, but no damage resulted. The bomb loads consisted mostly of a cookie with 1,000 and 500 pounders, and these were employed to good effect in central districts, where many historic and cultural buildings were destroyed or seriously damaged.

Sixteen aircraft failed to return on a bad night for Feltwell, which had five empty dispersal pans to contemplate on the following morning. Three of them should have been occupied by 75(NZ) Squadron Wellingtons, the fate of which would take time to filter through. According to the testimony of the rear gunner, the sole survivor, X3646, AA-M was hit by flak, it is believed at the Dutch coast, and P/O George Bradey RNZAF sustained what was probably a fatal wound to the abdomen. The aircraft crashed into the sea after Sgt J.E. London had taken to his parachute to become a PoW, and only one body was ultimately recovered for burial. Lost with the Bradey crew that night was S/L Ronald Ernest Kimber RAF, who was filling in as navigator and was probably the squadron's navigation leader. BJ767 AA-V went down over south-eastern Holland close to the border with Germany and may well have been caught by the extensive flak belt protecting the western fringe of the Ruhr. F/L Dobbin RNZAF and his Kiwi front gunner lost their lives, while the other three crew members, including the Kiwi wireless operator, joined the growing list of 75(NZ) Squadron members on extended leave in the Reich. It was Dobbin's third operation and second as captain. Based on the location of the cemetery containing the four RNZAF crew members from BJ625, AA-T, it seems likely that this Wellington also crashed to the south or west of the Ruhr. The rear gunner in F/Sgt Barclay's crew, Sgt John Atkin RNZAF, was the only survivor, and he, too, ended up in enemy hands.

A force of 138 aircraft was put together for a return to Mainz on the following night, when among sixty 3 Group aircraft were five Wellingtons representing 75(NZ) Squadron. P/O Hornes was the senior pilot on duty, and he, F/Sgts Parkes and Wright and Sgts Hockaday and Kearns and their crews had all been on the previous night's operation. They took off either side of 22.30 and arrived at the target some three hours later to find cloudy conditions, despite which they contributed to another effective attack. There was some stray bombing, but much further destruction was inflicted on the city's central districts and also in industrial areas and the main railway station was severely damaged. All from the squadron returned safely, P/O Horne bringing back photographs of the target area.

On the 15th the squadron moved to Mildenhall, where 115 Squadron had been stationed since April, but it would prove to be a relatively short residency. The equipment was ferried out by motor transport, while W/C Mitchell led the air party consisting of all serviceable Wellingtons on the ten-mile hop due south. Shortly afterwards, G/C Powell arrived from Feltwell to command the station.

It was on this day also that the Path Finder Force came into existence and all four founder heavy squadrons arrived on their stations in Huntingdonshire and Cambridgeshire. 83 Squadron moved into Wyton, the Path Finder HQ, as the 5 Group representative operating Lancasters, while 35 (Madras Presidency) Squadron flew its Halifaxes into Graveley and would draw its new crews from 4 Group. Although having served thus far in 3 Group, 156 Squadron would now represent 1 Group and retained its Wellingtons for the time-being at Warboys, leaving the Stirling-equipped 7 Squadron to remain at Oakington as 3 Group's contribution to the new force. In addition to the above, 109 Squadron was posted in to Wyton, where it would spend the next six months developing the Oboe blind-bombing device and marrying it to the Mosquito under the command of W/C Hal Bufton. The new force would occupy 3 Group stations, falling nominally under 3 Group administrative control and receiving its orders through that group, which was commanded by AVM Baldwin, whose tenure, which had lasted since just before the outbreak of war, was shortly to come to an end.

A "Path Finder Force" was the brainchild of the former 10 Squadron commanding officer, G/C Sid Bufton, Hal's brother, and now Director of Bomber Operations at the Air Ministry. He had used his best crews at 10 Squadron to find targets by the light of flares and attract other crews by firing off a coloured Verey light, and it could be said that the concept of target-finding and marking had been born at 10 Squadron in late 1940 and early 1941. Once at the Air Ministry, Bufton promoted his ideas with vigour and gained support among the other staff officers, culminating with the idea being put to Harris soon after his enthronement as Bomber Command C-in-C. Harris rejected the principle of establishing an elite target-finding and marking force, a view shared by the other group commanders with the exception of 4 Group's AVM Roddy Carr, a Kiwi. However, once overruled by higher authority, Harris gave it his unstinting support and his choice of the former 10 Squadron commanding officer and still somewhat junior, G/C Don Bennett, as its commander was both controversial and inspired and ruffled more than a few feathers among more senior officers. Australian, Bennett, was among the most experienced aviators in the RAF, a pilot and a Master Navigator of unparalleled experience with many thousands of hours to his credit. He was blessed with a brilliant mind, which made him prone to set standards that few others could achieve, and this created a demanding, exacting, but fair leader. He had been entrusted with setting up the Atlantic Ferry Service earlier in the war to transport much needed aircraft over from America, and he could also bring to his role his recent and relevant experience as a bomber pilot through his commands of 77 and 10 Squadrons. He had demonstrated his strong character and resourcefulness when evading capture and returning from Norway after being shot down while attacking the Tirpitz in April. Despite his reserve, total lack of humour and his impatience with those whose brains operated on a lower plane than his, he would inspire in his men great affection and loyalty, along with an enormous pride in being a Path Finder. He would forge the new force into a highly effective weapon, although this would not immediately be apparent.

It had been intended to "blood" the Path Finders at Osnabrück on the night of the 17/18th, but they were still settling in at their new homes and learning about their new roles and would not be ready in time. The operation went ahead without them and involved 139 aircraft, fifty-five of them provided by 3 Group, of which just three represented 75(NZ) Squadron. Sgts Hockaday and Kearns and F/Sgt Parkes were well-rested after four nights at home and took off at 22.30 to head for the Dutch coast. They were hounded by searchlights and flak all the way across enemy territory, and reached the target to find a thin layer of cloud. They were carrying a 4,000 pounder each with practice flash bombs and incendiaries, and these were deposited mainly in northern and north-western districts, where seventy-seven houses and four military buildings were destroyed and 125 other buildings seriously damaged.

The Path Finders took to the air in anger for the first time on the 18th, when contributing thirty-one aircraft as part of a 3 Group contingent of sixty-nine in an overall force of 118 bound for the naval and shipbuilding port of Flensburg. It had been selected as the Path Finders' first target because of its easy-to-find location on the eastern coast of the Schleswig-Holstein peninsula close to the border with Denmark, where the U-Boot pens were the briefed aiming-point. Over time, Path Finder equipment and tactics would evolve to highly sophisticated levels, but at this early stage, its role was simply to lead the main force crews to a target and establish its position with incendiaries and illumination. They crossed the Schleswig-Holstein peninsula unaware that the wind forecast guiding their navigation was incorrect and that the entire force was being pushed to the north of the intended track and over southern Denmark. The fact that the ground was largely concealed by haze and extreme darkness added to the difficulties, and what appeared to be Flensburg Fjord was identified and illuminated. In fact, they had strayed over a similar-shaped coastal inlet across the Danish frontier, and this led to a scattering of bombs across territory up to twenty-five miles north of the frontier and into the towns of Abenra and Sønderborg. Flensburg remained untouched by this inauspicious operational debut of a force, which, in time, would become a highly efficient, successful and vital component in Bomber Command's armoury.

75(NZ) Squadron had not been involved in the Flensburg operation and next took to the air on the evening of the 20th, when five crews were among twenty-nine from 3 Group and twenty-eight from other groups for wide-ranging mining operations from Biscay to the eastern Baltic. All were first-time captains, Sgt Kenneth Howard Blincoe RNZAF, P/O Leo George Trott RNZAF, Sgt Alan Gray Tolley RNZAF, Sgt John McCullough, RNZAF and F/Sgt Eliner Knud Alfred Andersen RAFVR. The Kiwis were St-Nazaire-bound as they took off either side of 21.00 and reached the target area, the Jellyfish garden to find bright moonlight, which aided their search for coastal pinpoints from which to make their timed runs, but also exposed them to the highly active flak batteries. BJ774, AA-X failed to return to Mildenhall and was lost without trace with the crew of F/Sgt Andersen DFM, who were on their maiden operation together and consisted of two Englishmen and three Canadians.

The second Path Finder-led operation was mounted on the night of the 24/25th against Frankfurt and involved 226 aircraft, including a 3 Group contribution of ninety-seven aircraft, of which thirty-seven were Path Finders and eight of the Wellingtons were put up by 75(NZ) Squadron. Two other Kiwi crews, those of Sgt Tolley and first-time captain, Sgt Frank Burrill RCAF, were assigned to mining duties in one of the Nectarine gardens off the Frisians. The main element departed Mildenhall first between 21.20 and 21.45 with F/O Gunning the senior pilot on duty and headed out across the North Sea on course for the Belgian coast to enter Germany over the Eifel region. They encountered five to ten-tenths cloud at between 7,000 and 9,000 feet and with ground haze compounding the difficulties of locating the aiming-point, it was the flak that guided some Path Finders to the approximate location of the target to deliver their 1,000 pounders and incendiaries. Most of the bombs missed the target and fell into open country to the north and west, although the few loads that found the mark started seventeen large fires and more than fifty smaller ones. Sixteen aircraft failed to make it home, five of them Path Finders, and "Terry" Kearns and crew might have joined them after X3396 AA-S was attacked by a FW190, which his gunners drove off before any damage was sustained. This was the only incident of note in an otherwise uneventful operation for the squadron. Meanwhile, the gardeners had taken off at 21.55 and headed out across the Norfolk coast, where X3936 AA-T was almost shot down by a British convoy, and it may have been as a result of the evasive action that the compass malfunctioned, forcing Sgt Tolley to return early.

Sgt Burrill found favourable weather conditions in the target area and delivered his 1,500lb mines as briefed before returning safely home.

Kassel was posted as the target for the night of the 27/28th, for which a force of 306 aircraft was made ready, 113 provided by 3 Group in the form of thirty-three Path Finders and eighty as part of the main force. 75(NZ) Squadron bombed and fuelled up a dozen Wellingtons, which departed Mildenhall either side of 21.00 with W/C Mitchell undertaking his first operation since assuming command, and two newcomers in the persons of F/L Andrew Francis Atterbury Osborn RAF and Sgt Francis Lawrence Curr RAAF. They set out for the Dutch coast in fine conditions, each carrying a cookie, 500 pounders and incendiaries, unaware that a major night-fighter response awaited them. Sgt Frank Burrill RCAF and crew were some thirty miles from the target when they were attacked by a Ju88, which injured the navigator, Sgt Albert Edward Rey RCAF, knocked out the port engine and caused other damage. Rear gunner, Sgt Ralph Ernest Gorman RCAF, replied in kind and watched their assailant fall in flames to the ground. The bomb load was jettisoned, and Sgt Burrill turned for home, unable to maintain height and was down to 700 feet at the Dutch coast. This made BJ584 AA-C an irresistible target for the light flak batteries, which followed it out to sea with their fire without scoring any hits. Still losing height, the Wellington reached the Suffolk coast and belly-landed on the 2 Group airfield at Wattisham without injury to the crew. The Kearns crew in X3396 AA-S were also attacked on the way to Kassel, front gunner Sgt Jack Moller firing back at what they identified as a Me110. Meanwhile, the Path Finders had managed to locate the target and illuminate it for the main force, which took advantage to deliver an effective attack. The main weight of bombs fell mainly in the south-western districts and destroyed 144 buildings, while seriously damaging more than three hundred others. It was not a one-sided affair, however, and thirty-one bombers, 10% of the force, failed to return home, a third of them belonging to 3 Group squadrons. 75(NZ) Squadron was represented among the missing by BJ708, which crashed a dozen or so miles south of Kassel, killing F/L Osborn DFC and his crew, three of whom were members of the RNZAF. Osborn, twenty-five years old and starting his second tour, had only arrived on the squadron four days earlier.

Two operations were posted on the 28th, one against Saarbrücken in an experiment to ascertain the ability of the main force crews to find and bomb a lightly defended target in favourable weather conditions, which, on this night, included a four-fifths moon. The force consisted of seventy-one Wellingtons with predominantly freshman crews, seventeen Hampdens, a type with fewer than three weeks front-line service ahead of it, and twenty-four Halifaxes, a type with a cloud hanging over it because of a spate of unexplained crashes caused by a rudder design flaw. 3 Group's contribution amounted to eight Wellingtons and a single Stirling from Feltwell, Marham and Stradishall. The main event on this night was directed at Nuremberg, for which a force of 159 aircraft was made ready and involved eighty-one aircraft representing 3 Group, including thirty-one Path Finders. Ten 75(NZ) Squadron Wellingtons departed Mildenhall between 20.40 and 21.05 with P/Os Horne and Trott the senior pilots on duty, and Sgt Eric Perks RNZAF and Sgt Sydney Bernard Thomas Davis RAFVR the debutants. Losses were now so heavy that new pilots were generally flying only one "second dickey" operation before captaining their own crew, and sometimes none at all.

The weather conditions were excellent and ideal for bombing but exposed the crews to the waiting night-fighter response. The Path Finders were to employ rudimentary markers for the first time rather than just provide illumination, and they were delivered in adapted 250lb bomb casings with great accuracy onto the aiming point. The main force crews had been briefed to attack the target from as low as practicable and the clear conditions with moonlight enabled them to see the ground clearly, despite which, many bomb loads were scattered outside of the confines of the city. There were numerous concentrations of searchlights, with heavy but inaccurate anti-aircraft fire, and night-fighters were very much in evidence. Sgt Hockaday reported four bombers and a fighter falling in flames and also commented on the sight of a city ablaze with fires visible up to seventy miles into the return journey. He landed BJ837 "Freddie" at Tangmere on the Sussex coast short of fuel and burst a tyre on touch-down. X3936 AA-T was attacked by a Me110, which was hit by return fire from the rear turret, but the engagement ended inconclusively and P/O Trott RNZAF brought the Wellington and crew safely home. The operation was only modestly successful, and the Command sustained another bloody nose with the failure to return of twenty-three aircraft, fourteen of them Wellingtons, a figure which represented a massive 34% of those dispatched. 75(NZ) Squadron lost two aircraft, firstly DF673, which crashed outbound at 23.15 at Moerbeke in northern Belgium with no survivors from the crew of F/Sgt Sydney Davis RAF, three of whom were members of the RCAF. X3389 came down in southern Germany with no survivors from the crew of F/Sgt Eric Perks RNZAF.

S/L Ashworth was posted to HQ Bomber Command at the end of the month, and would be attached immediately to Wyton, the site of Bennett's Path Finder HQ. It would be a month before his successor as A Flight commander arrived, but the long-vacant post of B Flight commander was finally filled by S/L Edgar Bernard Richard Lockwood, RAF, who arrived during w.e.f the 22nd. Lockwood had already completed a tour with the squadron between August 1940 and February 1941, and just the month before had rescued a crew member from a Wellington that had crashed into a building and caught fire, earning for himself an OBE.

During the course of the month the squadron undertook eleven operations, including mining, and dispatched seventy-four sorties for the loss of seven Wellingtons and crews.

September 1942

Multiple losses were now a fact of life for all squadrons, and this trend was to continue during the course of September, a busy month for the Command and one which was to require of 75(NZ) Squadron its highest number of operations to date. The first half of the new month would distinguish itself through an unprecedented series of effective operations, although it would begin ignominiously for the Path Finder Force on the night of the 1/2nd, when it marked the wrong target. The city of Saarbrücken, which, as described above, had been attacked ineffectively four nights earlier, had been briefed out as the objective to 231 crews, of which twenty-six were Path Finders in a 3 Group contribution of around seventy-six aircraft. The 75(NZ) Squadron element of eleven Wellingtons departed Mildenhall between 23.35 and 23.55, with S/L Lockwood the senior pilot on duty for the first time and two debutant crews, those of Sgt Eric Richmond Hunting RAFVR and Sgt Roy William Raharuhi RNZAF, the squadron's first Maori pilot. They turned towards the south and encountered ten-tenths cloud over the North Sea, which began to disperse at the Belgian coast and had cleared completely by the time that the target drew near. The good visibility enabled the Path Finders to confirm their TR-established positions visually using the River Saar as a reference, and the leading main force wave followed hard on their heels, finding little in the way of defensive measures.

The developing fires were visible to the Mildenhall crews when still twenty minutes short of the target and some would later report the entire area of the North Bank of the Saar to be on fire. A very large explosion occurred in the midst of the conflagration and there was no question in the minds of the crews as they retreated to the west that this had been an outstandingly accurate attack, which left a glow in the sky visible from up to 140 miles into the return flight. It was only later that the truth emerged, that the Path Finders had not marked Saarbrücken, but the non-industrial town of Saarlouis, situated thirteen miles to the north-west on a bend in the river similar to that at the intended target. Much to the chagrin of its inhabitants, and those in surrounding communities, the main force bombing had been particularly accurate and concentrated and heavy damage had been inflicted. This could have been an ill-omen for the month's efforts, but in fact, the Command now embarked on the unprecedented run of effective operations mentioned above.

This was the Kearns crew's final operation with 75(NZ) Squadron after logging forty-nine flights, both operational and non-operational, in Wellington X3396 AA-S over a period of two months. This aircraft would be shot down over Emden only two days later with the loss of all on board. The Kearns crew had completed twenty-seven operations, and after three more would have earned a six-month break from operations. However, they had volunteered for the new Path Finder Force and were immediately posted to 156 Squadron at Warboys, where they would go on to complete their tour after fifty-seven operations. Others would soon follow, members of the Frankie Curr, Neville Hockaday (F-Freddie) and Jack Wright (D-Duck) crews volunteering for Path Finder duty, along with veteran 75(NZ) Squadron gunner Ken Crankshaw. From this group of battle-hardened airmen, 156 Squadron's famous "Thomas Fredrick Duck" crew would emerge.

The accent remained on southern Germany on the following night when two hundred aircraft were made ready for an operation against the city of Karlsruhe, for which 3 Group provided a combined Path Finder and main force contribution of around sixty. The city was home to a factory belonging to the Deutsche Waffen und Munitionsfabriken A G, better known as DWM, which manufactured all types of firearms from pistols to automatic weapons for infantry and aircraft. The six-strong 75(NZ) Squadron element departed Mildenhall between 22.50 and 23.10 with F/L Geoffrey Harland Womersley RAF the senior pilot on duty and undertaking his first operation since arriving in August. He would remain only briefly with the squadron before moving to 156 Squadron of the Path Finders towards the end of the month, where his reputation would flourish. They set course for the Belgian coast, before tracking along the Franco-Belgian frontier to the target, which they found under clear skies, bathed in moonlight and naked to the eyes of the bomb-aimers high above. The Autobahn and the Rhine, with its distinctive finger-shaped docks, stood out clearly as a guide to the aiming-point and the Path Finders exploited the conditions to provide accurate marking of the city for the main force element. Returning crews reported as many as two hundred fires, the glow from which remained visible for a hundred miles into the homeward journey and post-raid reconnaissance confirmed much residential and some industrial damage, local reports mentioning seventy-three fatalities. The crews of Sgt Blincoe and Sgt Parkes in BJ790 AA-J and X3867 AA-P respectively reported attacks by Ju88s, which were defended by bursts from both front gunners, but neither made claims and no damage was done.

On the night of the 3/4th, 3 Group dispatched nine freshman crews to the port of Emden, six of them 75(NZ) Squadron Wellingtons from Mildenhall, and the other three, 149 Squadron Stirlings from Lakenheath. The Kiwi element included first-time captains Sgt Eric Lees RAFVR, F/O Leo Vernon Harcourt RAFVR, P/O Gerald Howard Jacobson RNZAF, Sgt James Law RAFVR and Sgt Kenneth John Bettles RAFVR, who were safely airborne by 23.30 before heading into heavy cloud that would persist throughout the operation. F/O Harcourt and P/O Jacobson returned early for unspecified reasons, possibly as a result of icing conditions, while the remainder located the general target area without ever seeing the ground and bombed on estimated positions through thick cloud. Two of them failed to return, Gerry Kearns' old kite, X3396 AA-S, crashing in northern Germany with no survivors from the crew of Sgt Law RAF, who was the only non-RNZAF member on board. X3794 is presumed to have gone down over the sea with the crew of F/Sgt Eric Hunting RAF, on just their second operation together, and only the body of the rear gunner eventually came ashore for burial in southern Holland.

The hectic start to the month continued on the night of the 4/5th with a major operation against Bremen. The Path Finder Force had been developing its tactics, and on this night unveiled what would become its basic standard operating procedure for the remainder of the war. The three-phase marking system would begin as always with illuminators to light up the target area with white flares and they would be followed by the marker element, to identify the briefed aiming point visually and drop coloured markers onto it, while backers-up maintained the aiming point for the duration of the raid with all-incendiary bomb loads. In time the system would become more sophisticated with the introduction of electronic aids and improved marking devices, but the basic principles would remain.

A force of 251 aircraft was assembled to put the new development to the test, for which 3 Group detailed eighty-eight, twenty-five of them Path Finders. A dozen 75(NZ) Wellingtons lined up for take-off at Mildenhall at midnight, one of them piloted by W/C Trevor Freeman RNZAF, who was a squadron original and had relinquished command of 115 Squadron in June. He was currently occupying a 3 Group post overseeing training, a job which required him to visit the operational stations. His association with 75(NZ) Squadron allowed him a free pass, and this was almost certainly an unofficial sortie, for which he accompanied the inexperienced crew of Sgt Raharuhi. The senior squadron pilot on duty was S/L Lockwood, and F/L Womersley was also on hand to lend his experience to the raid, while Sgt George William Sharman RNZAF was flying for the first time as captain. They flew out in good weather conditions, which would persist all the way into north-western Germany, by which time the crews of Sgts Bettles, Lees and Sharman had turned back with technical malfunctions. A thin layer of cloud lay over Bremen at 5,000 feet, but a hint of moonlight glinting on the surface of the River Weser and the distinctive shape of the docks and nearby woods enabled the leading crews to establish their position. The Focke-Wulf aircraft factory in the Hemelingen district was the aiming-point assigned to a 5 Group element, while the bulk of the main force targeted the general city area including the docks. The first Path Finder flares and incendiaries went down at around 01.50 and having run the gauntlet of searchlights and intense heavy and light flak, the main force element arrived to deliver an accurate and effective attack, which fell across the city and the docks area. Returning crews described large fires with smoke rising to 8,000 feet, and there was no doubt in their minds, that they had delivered a telling blow. It would be established later that 460 houses, six large industrial premises and fifteen smaller ones had been destroyed, and that severe damage had been inflicted upon a further 1,360 houses and thirty-five industrial concerns, including a shipyard and an aircraft factory.

A month after the last attempt to bomb Duisburg effectively, a force of 207 aircraft was assembled on the 6th for another crack at it. 3 Group contributed twenty Path Finders and fifty-four Wellingtons and Stirlings for the main force, fifteen of the former representing 75(NZ) Squadron, which departed Mildenhall between 01.05 and 01.35 with W/C Mitchell the senior pilot on duty and the last away. Captaining their crews for the first time were Sgts Thomas Otto Metcalfe and Eric William Peter Johnson, both RNZAF. They found the target to be partially concealed by cloud with the usual industrial haze rendering ground detail indistinct. The Path Finders established their positions by TR and confirmed them as far as possible by visual reference, but the searchlight and flak defences provided a firm indication as to the general whereabouts of the target, the flak shells bursting well above the bombing level. The reflection of the Path Finder flares on the haze combined with the smoke to obliterate ground detail as the main force arrived and most crews bombed on e.t.a. after failing to make a positive identification. Returning crews described large fires growing in intensity as the raid developed, and F/L Womersley reported being attacked from the rear by an enemy fighter, which the gunner drove off with a well-aimed burst. The Duisburg authorities reported the most destructive attack yet on their city, with 114 buildings destroyed and more than three hundred seriously damaged. The loss of eight aircraft was relatively modest, but two of the missing Wellingtons belonged to 75(NZ) Squadron and involved the fairly inexperienced all-RNZAF crews of F/Sgt William Parkes and Sgt George Sharman. X3867 AA-P contained the former and was shot down by the night-fighter of Hptm Walter Ehle of Stab II./NJG2 over Holland, to crash a couple of miles south-west of Tilburg close to the Belgian frontier. Sgt Sharman and crew rest in Reichswald CWG Cemetery, which suggests that BJ765 AA-L came down somewhere in the Ruhr area.

Minor operations took place on the night of the 7/8th, one of them a 3 Group raid by sixteen aircraft on the Heinkel aircraft works at Warnemünde on the Baltic coast. F/L Womersley was the sole 75(NZ) Squadron representative and took off at 20.15, only to be recalled with the rest of the force when ninety minutes out. Three other crews from the squadron were sent on gardening duties in one of the Nectarine gardens off the Frisians, and they were all airborne by 21.00 to fulfil their briefs despite cloud and sea haze in the target area.

There had been no pattern to the choice of targets thus far in the month, southern and north-western Germany and the Ruhr all featuring during the busy first week, and Frankfurt in south-central Germany was posted as the latest target on the 8th, for which a force of 249 aircraft was assembled. 3 Group put up twenty-nine Path Finders and fifty-six Wellingtons and Stirlings for the main force, of which nine Wellingtons were provided by 75(NZ) Squadron, including that of first-time skipper F/Sgt Kenneth John Dunmall RAFVR. They took off between 20.40 and 21.10 with S/L Lockwood the senior pilot on duty and set course for the Belgian coast with the intention of following the frontier with France as far as southern Luxembourg, before turning east and crossing into Germany. Those reaching the target area offered the usual mixed opinions concerning the conditions, some describing clear skies and good visibility, while others reported up to eight-tenths cloud at between 2,000 and 13,500 feet, with poor to moderate visibility made worse by searchlight glare. The intensity of the searchlight and flak activity should, perhaps, have helped to guide the Path Finders to the aiming-point, but surprisingly, they failed to locate the city and most delivered their flares and incendiaries on DR, TR and e.t.a. more on Rüsselsheim, some fifteen miles to the south-west. Returning crews spoke of large fires, numerous searchlights and moderate flak, but the impression was of a scattered and ineffective raid. The squadron's BJ596 was hit by flak and caught fire, forcing the all-RNZAF crew of Sgt Eric Johnson, who were on only their second operation together, to take to their parachutes and float down into the arms of their captors. Local sources in Rüsselsheim confirmed that the Opel tank works and Michelin tyre factory had sustained damage, which compensated in small measure for the failure to hit the primary target.

The Path Finder Force was constantly evolving in tactics and equipment and had a new weapon in its armoury for the next operation, which was to be against the Ruhr city of Düsseldorf on the 10th. "The Pink Pansy", which weighed in at 2,800lbs, was the latest attempt to produce a genuine target indicator and employed converted 4,000lb cookie casings. A force of 479 aircraft included a contribution from the training units of 91, 92 and 93 Groups, while 3 Group provided thirty-nine Path Finders and sixty-six Wellingtons and Stirlings for the main force. The thirteen 75(NZ) Squadron Wellingtons departed Mildenhall between 21.09 and 21.25 with F/L Womersley the senior pilot on duty and Sgt Henry Edwin Rousseau, RAFVR undertaking his first sortie as crew captain. The crews of P/O Jacobson and Sgt Rousseau returned early with aircraft malfunctions, leaving the remainder to press on in favourable weather conditions via the Scheldt estuary to the cauldron of the Ruhr. Those in the vanguard of the Path Finder element found clear skies but also the usual industrial haze to impair the vertical visibility and established their positions on Gee-fix aided by illuminator flares, which highlighted the Rhine and other ground features. The marker incendiaries were released either side of 20.30 and other elements of the Path Finders dropped red and green flares to maintain the marking for the main force crews, by the time of whose arrival, fires had taken hold and smoke was becoming a problem. Sgt Curr and crew, who were in BJ721 AA-A "Achtung ANZAC", reported a brief skirmish with a Me110 just after bombing, during which they probably sustained a hit in the port wing and fuselage, although it was difficult to determine because of other, considerable flak damage to the aircraft.

It was clear at main force debriefings that the crews were fairly confident about the outcome of the raid, some reporting the glow of the fires to be visible from the Scheldt homebound, and post-raid reconnaissance and local reports confirmed this operation to have been probably the most successful since Operation Millennium at the end of May. Other than the northern districts, all parts of the city and its neighbour across the Rhine, Neuss, had been hit, and 911 houses had been destroyed with a further fifteen hundred seriously damaged. In addition to the destruction also of eight public buildings, fifty-two industrial firms in the two cities sustained damage sufficient to cause a total shut down of production for varying periods. It had been an expensive victory for the Command, however, with thirty-three failures to return, 7.1% of the force, and this was a bitter pill to swallow particularly for the training units, to which thirteen of the missing belonged. 75(NZ) Squadron posted missing three crews, and it would be established later that none of the fifteen crew members had survived. BJ828 and BJ968 AA-W were both lost without trace with the crews of Sgt Eric Lees and F/Sgt Frank Burrill respectively, each with a RNZAF navigator, while the rest of the former crew was all-RAF and the latter all-RCAF. Sgt Thomas Metcalfe's BJ974 went down somewhere in the western Ruhr area and all but the rear gunner were members of the RNZAF.

The crews were, no doubt, glad to spend the next three nights at home, before being called to briefing on the 13th to learn that they would be returning to Bremen that night as part of a force of 446 aircraft, again bolstered by aircraft and crews from the training groups. Thirty-one Path Finder crews attended briefings on 3 Group stations along with seventy-two others assigned to the main force, among them eight belonging to 75(NZ) Squadron. The ORB listed only five crews, which departed Mildenhall shortly after 00.30 with F/L Womersley the senior pilot on duty and each Wellington loaded with a cookie and incendiaries. They headed for the Norfolk coast to begin the North Sea crossing and were greeted over the Dutch/German frontier region by eight-tenths cloud, which gave way to clear skies by the time the target drew near. However, thick haze concealed ground features other than the River Weser and the docks, forcing some of the early Path Finders to release their incendiaries on e.t.a. Fires and searchlight concentrations drew on the remaining Path Finder and main force crews, who bombed through haze and smoke. The 5 Group ORB described the Path Finder performance as unhelpful, but the success of the operation suggested otherwise and by far exceeded the destruction resulting from June's Thousand Bomber raid. A total of 848 houses was destroyed, and much damage was inflicted on the city's industry, including to the Lloyd Dynamo works, where two weeks production was lost, and parts of the Focke-Wulf factory were put out of action for between two and eight days. Of the twenty-one aircraft lost, fifteen belonged to the training units and conversion flights, two to 156 Squadron of the Path Finders and one to 3 Group's 214 Squadron.

The end of the Hampden era arrived on the following night, when the naval and shipbuilding port of Wilhelmshaven was posted as the target for 202 aircraft, 3 Group providing twenty-six Path Finders and forty-seven main force Wellingtons and Stirlings. Six 75(NZ) Squadron Wellingtons departed Mildenhall between 19.45 and 20.00 with F/L Womersley the senior pilot on duty and flew out over considerable amounts of cloud, which dispersed in the target area to leave something between clear skies and seven-tenths cloud at 5,000 feet. The Path Finders located the target by Gee and confirmed it visually by the shape of the coastline in Jade Bay, but extreme darkness and ground haze impaired vertical visibility, leaving the waterline and the docks to provide an adequate pinpoint for them to aim at. The main force crews also employed the shape of the coastline and Gee to establish their positions before bombing from between 14,000 and 17,000 feet. It was difficult to assess the outcome, but local reports confirmed this as the most destructive raid yet on this significant port, during which housing and public buildings bore the brunt, particularly in central districts.

The following night brought mining operations in the Nectarine gardens around the Frisians by forty aircraft of 1 and 3 Groups, to which 75(NZ) Squadron contributed four Wellingtons. P/O Trott was the senior pilot on duty as they took off at 19.45 and headed into electrical storms over the North Sea, in spite of which, the crews located their pinpoints and delivered their mines in the briefed locations before returning safely home.

With so much success attending recent operations, it is not surprising that Harris decided to have another crack at the old enemy, Essen, for which a force of 369 aircraft was assembled on the 16th, again bolstered by elements from the training units. 3 Group contributed twenty Path Finders and sixty-eight main force Wellingtons and Stirlings, 75(NZ) Squadron responsible for eight of the former, which got away from Mildenhall between 20.28 and 20.38, all captained by NCO pilots. A rather unhealthy and alarming twenty-four 3 Group aircraft turned back early, while those reaching the central Ruhr encountered between three and eight-tenths cloud but generally good visibility despite the industrial haze, which could be penetrated sufficiently for some ground detail to be identified visually by the light of Path Finder flares. Even so, the overlapping boundaries of the Ruhr towns and cities made it difficult to establish positions with absolute certainty, and some of the crews dropping their bombs on e.t.a. would find from the evidence of their bombing photos, that they had been over Bochum, Oberhausen or some other built-up expanse. Some of the Path Finder flares were estimated to be falling up to twenty miles east of Essen, which would have put them over Dortmund and Hagen. Returning crews reported the glow of fires to be visible for a hundred miles into the return journey, and local sources would confirm this to be Essen's worst night of the war to date. In addition to much housing damage and more than a hundred medium and large fires, fifteen high-explosive bombs had found their way onto the Krupp complex, as did a crashing bomber loaded with incendiaries. A post-raid analysis revealed that bombs had been scattered across a large part of the Ruhr, with Bochum, Wuppertal and Herne among the hardest hit, and until the advent of Oboe in the coming spring, such inaccuracies remained a fact of life.

It was far from a one-sided affair, however, and cost the Command a massive thirty-nine aircraft, 10.6% of those dispatched, nineteen of them from the training units. BJ790, AA-J was two minutes from bomb-release when a flak shell punched a large hole between the starboard engine and the fuselage. Damage to the controls made it impossible to turn to port, but Sgt Kenneth Blincoe RNZAF coaxed the wounded Wellington towards the Dutch coast, where it was attacked from below by an unseen enemy fighter and sustained several hits, one of which wounded the wireless operator, P/O Harold Lowe RAFVR, in the back. By the time Mildenhall hove into sight, the hydraulics system had drained completely, and Sgt Blincoe was compelled to carry out a belly-landing, which he accomplished successfully without further injury to the occupants. On the way home, F/Sgt Wright's BJ772 AA-D "Donald" was attacked by a Ju88, which was engaged by the front gunner, F/Sgt Reynolds, who with other members of the crew watched their assailant explode in the air. This achievement finally restored equal bragging rights with their mates in the F for "Freddie" (Hockaday) crew, who had managed a 'kill' on only their second operation, and the episode became one of the early chapters in the "Thomas Fredrick Duck" legend. As already mentioned, members of both crews, along with gunner Ken Crankshaw from the Curr crew, would later combine to form a crew under Jack Wright at 156 Squadron of the Path Finders, applying a copy of the "Donald Duck" nose art from BJ772 to their Lancaster, GT-T for Tommy. So, in a nice piece of compromise, Donald became Thomas Fredrick Duck, and the story of the crew's exploits was made famous in Alan Mitchell's 1946 book, "New Zealanders in the Air War". Sadly, BJ772 would be destroyed on the ground only ten days after the Wright crew's Ju88 success, when a stray Boston bomber crash-landed at Mildenhall and smashed into "Duck", which was sitting at its dispersal. A fire ensued, which detonated the Boston's load of two 500lb bombs and killed its navigator.

If any period in the Command's gradual evolution to war-winning capability could be seen as a turning point, then perhaps, the first half of September 1942 qualified. It can be no coincidence that the Path Finder Force was emerging from its hesitant start as the crews got to grips with the complexities of their demanding role, and new tactics and aids were being brought to bear against the enemy. It would be no overnight transformation and failures would still outnumber victories for some time to come, but the encouraging signs were there that all of the elements of technical and tactical advance were coming together, and with other technological wizardry in the pipeline, it boded ill for Germany's industrial towns and cities.

Much of the remainder of the month would find the squadron engaged in mining duties in French waters and around the Frisians, and the night of the 18/19th brought extensive activity involving 115 aircraft operating from the Biscay coast in the south-west to the Baltic waters off Danzig in the north-east. It was for the Beech garden off St-Nazaire that five all-NCO 75(NZ) Squadron crews were bound on the 18th, having taken off from Mildenhall at 19.00. They found clear skies and good visibility in the target area and a little light flak coming from the town with isolated searchlights as they sought out their pinpoints. Each delivered their 1,500lb mines at the briefed location before returning safely home from what had been an uneventful operation.

The Path Finders were required to mark two targets on the night of the 19/20th, Saarbrücken for a force of 118 and Munich for eighty-nine Lancasters and Wellingtons. 3 Group sent nine Path Finders and nineteen main force Stirlings to the Bavarian capital and fifteen Path Finders and thirty Wellingtons and Stirlings to the Saarland capital, 75(NZ) Squadron contributing eight Wellingtons to the latter, which took off between 20.16 and 20.35 with W/C Mitchell the senior pilot on duty. They were carrying a cookie and incendiaries each and enjoyed good weather conditions during the outbound flight across France via the familiar route running parallel to the Belgian and Luxembourg frontiers. The two forces followed a common route as far as Saarbrücken, leaving the Munich element with a further 220 miles to travel to reach the birthplace of Nazism, a city of cultural and industrial significance. The Saarbrücken contingent reached the target to find good visibility hampered only by ground haze, which caused problems for the Path Finder element. The moonlight on haze produced a kind of glare that added to the difficulties and some Path Finder crews spent forty minutes seeking out the aiming point before admitting defeat, and a study of one crew's bombing photo would reveal that they had attacked the French city of Nancy, some fifty miles south-west of the intended target. Crews were left with an impression of a scattered raid, about which they had little of use to pass on at debriefing. Local sources reported damage to be superficial and confirmed that the raid had largely missed the city to the west.

3 Group sent seventeen aircraft mining in the Baltic on the night of the 21/22nd, and three failed to return. Three 75(NZ) Squadron crews were sent on a sea-search during the afternoon of the 22nd to look for dinghies from ditched aircraft but found nothing. Five crews set off at 19.30 on the 24th for gardening duties in the Nectarine I garden off the Frisian island of Texel, and encountered no enemy response of any kind, only difficult weather conditions in the form of heavy thunderstorms and low cloud. All fulfilled their briefs by delivering their mines on visually-established pinpoints and returned safely home from another uneventful outing.

S/L Robert Stanway Crawford RAFVR was posted in from 91 Group on the 25th to assume the post of A Flight commander that had been left vacant since the departure a month earlier of S/L "Artie" Ashworth. F/L Womersley left the squadron at the same time to join 156 Squadron and would be given command of 139 Squadron of 8 Group's Light Night Striking Force in 1944.

Operations on the night of the 26/27th involved a force of Halifaxes at Flensburg, while seventy-one Wellingtons and Stirlings carried out mining duties in the Baltic and around the Frisians. Eleven 75(NZ) Squadron Wellingtons were made ready, seven for the Baltic, probably in one of the Silverthorn gardens in the Kattegat and four for one of the Nectarine gardens, and the latter took off first between 19.15 and 19.30 with F/L Parish the senior pilot on duty. Sgt Alexander Scott RNZAF, Sgt John Mathers Bailey RNZAF, F/L Charles Woodbine Parish, RAF and Sgt Benjamin Allan Franklin RNZAF were all flying their first operations as crew captains. The remainder departed Mildenhall from 21.00, led by P/Os Horne and Trott, and were well on their way to the target area when a recall signal was sent out to all aircraft, probably because of deteriorating visibility at home stations. The Frisian element had already returned home by this time and was not affected by the recall. F/Sgt Dunmall and Sgt Curr failed to pick up the signal and continued on in cloudy conditions to carry out their orders to deliver mines into the required locations and drop 500lb bombs on coastal targets of opportunity. The visibility had, indeed, become poor by the time Sgt Dunmall approached Mildenhall in BK207 to land at 05.15, and the sortie ended with a crash from which no injuries were reported and the Wellington was eventually returned to flying condition.

Three crews were briefed on the 28th for a "moling" operation that afternoon to Lingen, a town just a few miles from the frontier with Holland in north-western Germany. The signs were good as they took off shortly after 14.00 with F/L Parish the senior pilot on duty and headed out in thick cloud across the North Sea. However, once they reached the enemy coast, the cloud broke up and they decided to turn back. The crews of Sgts Curr and McCullough reported a brief encounter with BF109s, which ended inconclusively, and all were safely back on the ground by 17.15.

The final operation of a very busy month involved four freshman crews mining in the Nectarine I garden off the Frisian Island of Terschelling on the evening of the 30th. They were all debutants in the persons of Sgt Howard James Hugill RNZAF, Sgt George William Rhodes RAFVR, Sgt James Allison McConnell RNZAF and Sgt Peter John Oswald Buck RNZAF. They took off at 19.30 and reached the target area to find fine weather conditions with patches of thick sea haze, through which they delivered their mines as briefed and strafed an enemy convoy, before returning home either side of 23.00.

During the course of the month the squadron carried out twenty operations, including recalls, and dispatched 138 sorties for the loss of eight Wellingtons and crews.

October 1942

October was to bring a change in equipment for the squadron as it bade farewell to the trusty and reliable old Wellington in favour of the manoeuvrable but flawed Stirling. What would never change for 75(NZ) Squadron, however, was the attrition rate in aircraft and crews, which would find it at war's end the squadron with the second highest overall losses. The new month began for 3 Group with an operation against Lübeck by twenty-five Stirlings in defiance of the arrangement with the Red Cross to leave the city in peace. Briefings across the Command on the 2nd identified Krefeld as the target for a force of 188 aircraft, of which 3 Group provided twenty-seven Path Finders and thirty-nine for the main force. Located at the western edge of the Ruhr, a few miles to the south-west of Duisburg, Krefeld's industry had been based on silk and velvet textiles, but the presence of a Thyssen-Krupp steelworks was sufficient to attract the attention of Bomber Command. At Mildenhall, 75(NZ) Squadron made ready thirteen Wellingtons, which took off between 18.45 and 19.40 with W/C Mitchell the senior pilot on duty and accompanied by Jack Wright's crew, which he was shepherding through the final sortie of their first tour. They headed for the Dutch coast loaded with a cookie each and incendiaries and ran the gauntlet of a flak before arriving in the target area to find it enveloped in dense industrial haze, which thwarted the Path Finders' best efforts to provide a reference for those following behind. Bombing took place predominantly from between 12,000 and 15,000 feet on e.t.a., Gee and whatever target indicators were visible, and returning crews reported some scattered fires, while local sources confirmed that three streets in the northern part of the city had sustained damage but nothing commensurate with the size of the force and the effort expended.

All heavy groups were alerted on the 5th to prepare for an operation that night against Germany's most westerly city, Aachen, which sits close to the frontiers of both Holland and Belgium. A force of 257 aircraft was prepared, 3 Group providing twenty-one Path Finder and forty-four main force aircraft, among the latter fifteen Wellingtons representing 75(NZ) Squadron. They took off in a creditable fifteen minutes from 19.15 carrying all-incendiary bomb loads and with S/L Crawford the senior pilot on duty for the first time, before climbing away into challenging weather conditions that caused problems particularly in the 3 Group region. They were forced to negotiate an electrical storm as they headed for the Essex coast to begin the North Sea crossing to Belgium and despite the squadron ORB describing the weather conditions in the target area as good, the consensus was that they were unfavourable with eight-tenths cloud at between 8,000 and 14,000 feet. This led to the failure by the Path Finders to locate the planned aiming point and returning crews expressed doubt that Aachen had been the built-up area beneath them through which large fires had spread. Local authorities confirmed that perhaps ten bomb loads, including a cookie, had found their way into the southern district of Burtscheid, and had caused a surprising amount of damage to both residential and industrial buildings. It would become clear later that the marking had fallen mostly around the Dutch town of Lutterade, situated some seventeen miles from Aachen, and this would have unforeseen, if minor consequences for the development programme of the Oboe blind-bombing device, which was currently undergoing trials in the Mosquitos of the Path Finders' 109 Squadron.

Osnabrück was posted as the target on the 6th for an operation that would involve a force of 237 aircraft, of which twenty-three Path Finders and forty-five main force were provided by 3 Group, fourteen of the latter 75(NZ) Squadron Wellingtons. S/L Crawford was the senior pilot on duty as they departed Mildenhall between 19.00 and 19.20, each carrying a cookie and incendiaries. The Path Finders dropped flares over Makkum in Holland and the Dümmer See to the north-east of the target as route markers, and these proved to be very effective in guiding the main force in, although inevitably, some bomb loads were released early during the twenty-mile leg between the Dümmer See and the city. Four to eight-tenths cloud lay over the target area at 8,000 feet and provided challenging conditions for accurate bombing, although opinions varied as to the quality of the visibility. Returning crew described many fires and a glow visible by some from the Dutch coast homebound, and most had confidence in the effectiveness of the raid. According to local reports, 149 houses and six industrial buildings were destroyed, 530 houses seriously damaged and more than 2,700 others slightly damaged, mostly in central and southern districts. Six aircraft failed to return and among them was 75(NZ) Squadron's DF639, which crashed near Hardenberg, close to the German border in east-central Holland at 23.30, killing Sgt George Rhodes RAFVR and his crew.

The squadron now embarked on a period of gardening operations, beginning on the night of the 8/9th, when five freshman crews were briefed, two of them to plant their vegetables in the Artichoke garden off the Ile de Groix, to catch enemy naval shipping, including U-Boots, entering and leaving the port of Lorient via the Blavet Estuary. Sgts Franklin and McConnell and their crews took off at 18.50, but the latter were forced to return early with an electrical malfunction, leaving the former to fulfil their brief during an uneventful trip in good weather conditions. Newcomers Sgts Charles Raglan Davey RNZAF, Charles John Shalfoon RNZAF and Ventry Watters RNZAF departed Mildenhall at 21.45 for gardening duties in the Turbot garden off the port of Ostend, which two of them completed, while the third returned early in the belief that a recall signal had been received. The Right Honourable Mr W J Jordan, the High Commissioner for New Zealand, visited the squadron on the 9th and was photographed with crews.

That night, seven of the squadron's Wellingtons were dispatched with NCO-crews to mine the waters of the Nectarine I garden off the southern Frisians, departing at 18.00 on an evening of poor weather conditions and ten-tenths cloud. All reached the target area to carry out their briefs and returned safely to report another uneventful outing. The gardens for the night of the 11/12th were in the western Baltic, Carrot or Endive in the Little Belt and Silverthorn in the Kattegat, for which nine crews were briefed. They took off shortly after 18.00 with F/L Parish the senior pilot on duty and all reached the target area to find clear skies and good visibility. As usual, they were carrying 500 pounders in addition to the 1,500lb parachute mines, and F/Sgt Curr and crew aimed theirs at a bridge at Middelfart, which linked the Danish Island of Fyn with the Schleswig-Holstein peninsula. The first bomb fell short, but the others were very close and may have hit the bridge. BK341 failed to return with the others after crashing into the sea at 23.29 between the island of Langli and the Skallingen peninsula to the north of the port of Esbjerg and there were no survivors from the crew of Sgt Shalfoon RNZAF, who was the only Kiwi on board.

A return to bombing operations on the night of the 13/14th brought thirteen of the squadron's crews to the briefing room, to learn that the port of Kiel was to be their target and that they were to be part of an overall force of 288 aircraft. The plan called for the Path Finder target-locaters and illuminators to fly out over the Baltic, before turning back onto a westerly heading to drop special markers over the Selenter Lake, the second largest body of water in Schleswig-Holstein, situated some eight miles east of Kiel. The locaters were to lay sticks of flares across the target area at the opening of the attack at 21.09, or if the aiming-point had definitely been identified, to bolster the efforts of the illuminator crews and drop their flares onto it during the time-on-target slot between 21.10 and 21.18, leaving the way clear and the aiming-point primed for the main force element to do their job. 3 Group raised thirty-two Path Finders and fifty-one Wellingtons and Stirlings for the main force, the 75(NZ) Squadron element departing Mildenhall between 18.20 and 18.50 with F/L Parish the senior pilot on duty.

They reached the target area to find almost clear skies and good visibility and the target illuminated and marked by the Path Finders, to which the defenders responded with an effective smoke screen and intense searchlight activity. The consensus among returning crews was of an effective raid, but a post-raid analysis and local sources revealed that a decoy fire site had been successful in drawing off half of the attack, and damage in Kiel, although substantial, particularly in the eastern district of Elmschenhagen, was less than might otherwise have been. Eight aircraft failed to return and among them was the squadron's X3954, which crashed in the target area, killing Sgt Watters RNZAF and his crew, two of whom were also members of the RNZAF. BJ837 "Freddie" arrived back short of fuel and was crash-landed at Lakenheath by Sgt Davey RNZAF, who, along with his crew, sustained injury as a result. Front gunner, Sgt John Brewick Redhead RAF, was the most seriously injured and finally lost his fight for life on the 19th.

On the 15th, the crews of B Flight were ferried by road to Oakington under the command of F/L Parish to begin conversion training on Stirlings under S/L Crompton. Oakington's station commander just happened to be 75's old commanding officer, G/C "Ted" Olson. The first of the type to be taken on charge was N3704 on the 16th, while R9243 and R9247 would follow on the 21st and BF396 and BF397 two days later. A Flight, meanwhile, remained at Mildenhall, where seven of its crews were called to briefing on the 15th to learn of an operation against Cologne, which had been left unmolested for a considerable time. A force of 289 aircraft was made ready, which included thirty-two Path Finders and fifty other 3 Group aircraft to support the main force. The 75(NZ) Squadron element departed Mildenhall in a five-minute slot from 19.15 led by S/L Crawford and headed out over Southwold on course for Goeree island in the Scheldt estuary. The force encountered stronger-than-forecast winds, which would create difficulties for the Path Finders as they attempted to establish their position, those at the point of the spear finding the Rhineland capital to be concealed beneath a layer of five to ten-tenths cloud with visibility so poor that few crews were able to establish a firm position in relation to it. Apart from throwing the operation behind schedule, this ruined the marking sequencing, with the result that there were insufficient markers to attract the main force crews, although the Path Finder flares did illuminate the Rhine to provide something of a reference point. However, the presence of a large decoy fire site was a more powerful lure, and most crews were persuaded by that to waste their effort in open country. Most of the bombs, including the all-incendiary loads dropped by the Kiwis, were wasted and damage in Cologne was light and superficial. This proved to be S/L Edgar Lockwood's final sortie with the squadron after completing his tour, and he was posted to 81 O.T.U on the 20th.

Following a week of operational inactivity, five crews were briefed on the 22nd for daylight "moling" forays over Germany, two to attack the town of Lingen in the north-west and three, including debutant Sgt Raymond Herbert John Broady RNZAF, to present themselves over Essen in the heart of the Ruhr. The Lingen-bound duo took off at 12.30, to be followed twenty minutes later by the Essen element, which included S/L Crompton flying as second pilot to Sgt Buck. Sgt Jackson and F/Sgt Curr made their way across northern Holland in low cloud with a base at 700 feet and carried out their attacks with 500 and 250 pounders and 30lb incendiaries from low level, causing damage to the railway station. The Essen trio ran out of cloud before reaching their objective, and it is assumed that they brought their bombs home. On the following day the 3 Group A-O-C, AVM Cochrane, visited Mildenhall to interview and congratulate the crews on their daylight endeavours.

Other than an audacious 5 Group attack by daylight against the Schneider armaments works in France on the 17th, the following week brought largely minor operational activity. The lull came to an end on the 22nd, when a new campaign began against Italian cities in support of land operations in North Africa under Operation Torch. The target for the opening round was the city-port of Genoa and the naval dockyard, where part of the Italian fleet was sheltering and the Ansaldo shipyards were supporting the Italian war effort. It was the eve of the opening of the Battle of El Alamein, which, after twelve days' fighting, would see Montgomery push Rommel's forces all the way back to Tunisia and out of the war. Ten 5 Group squadrons mustered between them 101 Lancasters, while 83 Squadron of the Path Finders contributed eleven more to take care of target marking. Some returning crews described the raid as a "miniature-Cologne", and local sources confirmed heavy damage in central and eastern districts, which, because of the need for fuel over bombs, had been achieved with just 180 tons of high-explosives and incendiaries, and, remarkably, without loss.

Plans were put in place to immediately follow-up the 5 Group raid on Genoa, for which thirteen Path Finders would mark the target for a main force of forty-eight and sixty-one aircraft respectively drawn from 3 and 4 Groups. Eight 75(NZ) Squadron Wellingtons were bombed and fuelled up for the trip across the Alps and they departed Mildenhall at 18.15 led by G/C "Speedy" Powell, who had commandeered Sgt Broady and most of his crew, with navigation officer, S/L Watkins, riding as front gunner. They set course for Dungeness on the Kent coast and Berck-sur-Mer on the other side of the Channel and initially enjoyed good weather conditions as they pressed on across France. It was only as the target drew near that the force ran into a considerable amount of cloud with tops at 4,000 feet and a base at 3,000, which obscured most ground detail. The bombing took place from between 12,000 and 16,000 feet, although some crews opted to come below to deliver their loads of 1,000, 500 and 250 pounders and incendiaries. Bursts and fires were observed, but there was an inkling that the attack had actually been directed at Savona, a town situated some twenty miles along the coast to the west, and this proved to be the case.

5 Group attacked Milan at dusk on the 24th, and elements of 1 and 3 Groups were scheduled to followed up after dark with the support of seventeen Path Finders. The 3 Group main force element consisted of just six Mildenhall Wellingtons, five provided by 75(NZ) Squadron and one by 115 Squadron, and eight Stirlings in an overall force of seventy-one aircraft. The Kiwis took off either side of 19.00 led by W/C Mitchell and flew out over ten-tenths cloud that persisted all the way across France, where storms dispersed the stream and sent some straying over Swiss territory, from where warning shots were fired. Only thirty-nine returning crews claimed to have bombed the target, and the operation failed to create more than superficial damage. Four Wellingtons and two Stirlings were missing, two of the former belonging to 75(NZ) Squadron and both came down in France, Z1652 AA-D at Ville-sur-Retourne in the north-east and BJ725 AA-H near Valenciennes, further north still and closer to the Belgian frontier. There were no survivors from the crew of Sgt James McConnell RNZAF in the latter, two others of whom were also members of the RNZAF. The former had turned back with engine issues, unable to make it over the Alps, then crash-landed after being attacked by a Me110, only for the fuel to cause an explosion, which killed Sgt Howard Hugill RNZAF and his observer, Sgt Edmund John Pete, RAFVR. The Kiwi wireless operator, Sgt Edwin Worsdale, and the RAF rear gunner, Sgt L. Newbold, managed to evade capture, while the

RNZAF front gunner, Sgt James George Barnes, was taken into captivity. These would prove to be the last Wellingtons to be lost in service with 75(NZ) Squadron.

Operations on Wellingtons continued in the hands of A Flight, however, and two crews were sent to lay mines in one of the Nectarine gardens off the Frisians in the early hours of the 26th, while two others, under first-time skippers Sgt Martin Lord RNZAF and Sgt Herbert James Dalzell RNZAF, headed for the Jellyfish garden in the approaches to Brest to fulfil a similar task. They began taking-off at 03.00, but Sgt Buck, who had S/L Crawford alongside him as second pilot, was forced to turn back after about half an hour through the failure of his radio equipment. F/Sgt Jackson was successful in planting his mines in the briefed locations despite cloudy conditions over the Frisians, and clear skies at the French coast helped Sgts Lord and Dalzell also to complete their tasks.

This was the final Wellington operation for the squadron, and on the 29th, A Flight travelled by road to Oakington under the command of S/L Crawford to begin its conversion to Stirlings. During the course of the month the squadron carried out fifteen operations and dispatched 105 sorties for the loss of six Wellingtons and five crews.

November 1942

On the 1st of November the squadron changed address once more with a move to Newmarket, although the squadron HQ was actually at the satellite airfield at Rowley Mile on the northern side of the racecourse. S/L George Eric Fowler RAF was posted in during w.e.f the 2nd, and despite being a bomb-aimer rather than a pilot, he would succeed S/L Lockwood as B Flight commander. He had served with the squadron previously as an observer, completing a tour of operations between November 1940 and August 1941 as a member of the Matheson, Lockwood and Fotheringham crews, and was renowned for his piano-playing in the Feltwell officers' mess. Over at Oakington the process of working up to operational status with the Stirling would occupy the first eight days of B Flight's month, by which time twenty Stirlings had been taken on charge. B Flight moved to Rowley Mile between the 8th and the 10th, where the seven converted crews would continue the working up process to operational status under the watchful eye of W/C Mitchell. Training was intensive, and surprisingly accomplished without a single accident, remarkably, not even one involving the type's notoriously weak and unstable undercarriage.

The campaigns against Italy and Germany would have to run side-by-side for the time being, and Genoa was posted as the target on the 7th for a force of 175 aircraft, which included twenty Path Finders and seventeen other 3 Group aircraft as part of the main force. In a break from Italy, Hamburg was named as the target on the 9th, when no mention was made by the "met boys" during briefing of strong winds and ice-bearing cloud of the type that often lay in wait across the bombers' path to Germany's second city. The four heavy groups put together a main force of 183 aircraft, a modest nine representing 3 Group, to which was added a contribution from the Path Finders of thirty aircraft. Nine Path Finder Stirlings from 7 Squadron accompanied a 5 Group force in a return to Genoa on the 13th, while the rest of 3 Group spent the night at home. The third raid on Genoa was mounted on the 15th for which the Path Finders put up thirteen aircraft in an overall force of seventy-eight, before attention switched back to Turin on the 18th. Twenty Path Finders and twenty-four other 3 Group aircraft took off, but adverse weather conditions led to just seven of the main force 3 Group element reaching the target.

The 75(NZ) Squadron crews were not declared to be operationally ready until the 20th, when four of them attended briefing to learn of that night's operation to Turin. They would be part of an overall force of 232 aircraft, which would prove to be the largest sent to Italy during the current campaign. 3 Group detailed twenty-four Path Finder aircraft and thirty-five others to support the main force and the 75(NZ) quartet consisting of the crews of F/L Parish, P/O Trott, F/Sgt Bailey and Sgt Franklin departed Rowley Mile between 18.20 and 18.33 with an almost four-hour outward flight ahead of them. They headed for the Channel, where Sgt Franklin turned back with a technical problem and jettisoned his bombs in the Wash. The others flew out over France in good conditions, but F/L Parish also turned back for an undisclosed reason before crossing the Alps and jettisoned his bombs over southern France. This left P/O Trott and F/Sgt Bailey to negotiate the remaining seven hundred miles to the target without incident and arrive to find a considerable amount of haze, which had presented the Path Finder crews with some difficulty in identifying the aiming-point. Even so, their efforts enabled those in the vanguard of the main force to establish their position and follow the illuminated autostrada into the heart of the city to deliver their all-incendiary loads in the face of scant resistance. The attack left massive fires raging in the city centre with smoke rising through 6,000 feet and drifting across the area to prevent an accurate assessment of the outcome. The crews turned for home in confident mood, and although no details of damage emerged, a death toll of 117 people was an indication of the severity of the attack.

In another break from Italy, Stuttgart was named as the target on the 22nd for a force of 222 aircraft, of which twenty-four Path Finder and thirty-one main force aircraft were provided by 3 Group with a contribution from 75(NZ) Squadron of two Stirlings. F/L Parish and Sgt Scott departed Rowley Mile shortly before 18.30, but the former was out of luck again and had to turn back after an hour with an unserviceable rear turret. The head of the bomber stream reached the target area after an outward flight of some three-and-a-half hours, and unusually, found that it was the vertical rather than horizontal visibility that proved to be favourable. Located in a series of valleys, Stuttgart was generally a difficult city to identify, but on this night crews were able to carry out timed runs from Lake Constance and pick out the River Neckar and its tributaries to establish their positions through six-tenths cloud between 6,000 and 8,000 feet. By the time that the first of the main force crews arrived, the Path Finders had presented them with a well illuminated city, which invited them to take advantage and carry out their attacks predominantly from between 12,000 and 15,000 feet. They returned with reports of many fires, the glow from which lingered on the horizon for a considerable distance into the homeward flight, but post-raid analysis and local sources suggested that the majority of the eighty-eight houses destroyed and 330 seriously damaged had been in suburbs to the south and south-west. However, two bombers had attacked the main railway station from low level and had caused damage.

The inevitable first Stirling accident to befall the squadron occurred on the evening of the 24th during an air-firing exercise, when R9246 AA-S had to be force-landed wheels-up at 17.20 by Sgt Buck at Holme, ten miles north-north-west of Huntingdon. The crew was able to walk away from the wreckage with only a slight injury to one of the gunners, and the cause of the incident was given as bad weather. Four days later, on the 28th, a second training accident involved an A Flight crew at the Conversion Unit at Oakington and had a more serious outcome. BF399 AA-O stalled as Sgt Raymond Broady RNZAF tried to avoid a head-on collision with another Stirling in the circuit and crashed close to the airfield at 22.29, killing five of the six occupants and seriously injuring the rear gunner, who would lose his fight for life on the 30th. Two of the regular Broady crew were not taking part in that particular night flying test, their places taken by O.T.U personnel, and navigator, Sgt John Charles Kennedy Fabian RNZAF, and wireless operator, Sgt Edward Henry Gray RNZAF, were consequently 'orphaned'. Sgt Fabian teamed up with the Bettles crew and would later earn a DFC for his deeds with the squadron. Sgt "Ted" Gray eventually joined the Bennett and then Way crews, but, sadly, was to lose a second skipper, W/O James Oscar Way RCAF, in April 1943 and would complete his tour with S/L Jack Joll.

The target for an initial force of 228 aircraft on the 28th was Turin, for which the squadron made ready four Stirlings as part of a 3 Group contingent of twenty-nine Path Finder and thirty-five main force aircraft. W/C Mitchell, P/O Trott and Sgt Blincoe took off either side of 18.15, while F/L Parish is recorded as taking off an hour later. They made their way to the Alps in cloudy conditions, at which point one of the Kiwi aircraft lost an engine and could not maintain height, let alone traverse the mountains. Based on the duration of the flights as recorded in the ORB, it seems likely that F/L Parish's luck continued to thwart his attempts to complete a Stirling operation, and he jettisoned the bombs in the foothills of the Alps before turning back. The others reached the target area, where the Path Finder crews had been greeted by wispy cloud and a half moon and identified the River Stura-di-Lanzo leading south towards its confluence with the Po in the city centre. It was reported that a number of main force crews bombed before the Path Finders officially opened proceedings, but it did not compromise the attack and the city would endure another torrid experience. The flares, markers and main force bombs went down with a degree of concentration mostly from between 10,000 and 15,000 feet and the high explosives were observed to burst on or near the aiming-point. Among the detonations were the first two 8,000 pounders to fall on Italy, dropped by the 106 Squadron crews of W/C Guy Gibson and F/L Whamond. At debriefings, crews reported hits on the Fiat works and one counted forty-seven fires when fifteen minutes into the homeward journey. Others confirmed that the city was a mass of flames and commented on a particularly large blaze in the centre, while some mentioned hits on the Lancia and Fiat works and other conflagrations around the Royal Arsenal. BK608 AA-T arrived over East Anglia short of fuel with engines faltering and was down to 900 feet when Sgt Blincoe gave his crew the option of remaining on board or bailing out. The navigator and rear gunner chose the latter course and survived their descent from 600 feet, while Sgt Blincoe crash-landed safely at Stradishall at 03.15. It was also on this night that 149 Squadron pilot, F/Sgt "Ron" Middleton, earned a posthumous Victoria Cross, one of only two to be awarded to a Stirling crewman.

On the following night, 3 Group detailed fifteen Path Finder Stirlings and Lancasters and a dozen main force Stirlings to return to Turin, where the Fiat works was the designated aiming point. 75(NZ) Squadron made ready two Stirlings, loading them with 1,000 and 500 pounders and dispatching them either side of midnight with the crews of Sgt Scott and F/Sgt McCullough on board. They flew into very poor weather conditions, and neither would reach their destination. Sgt Scott and crew were back within three hours having jettisoned their bombs into the Wash, while F/Sgt McCullough was about to cross the Alps when the bomb-aimer found the bomb release gear to be faulty. Their load was jettisoned sixty-six miles west of

Turin, and despite the foreshortened flight distance, petrol consumption gave cause for concern on the way home over France. It was a great relief when the Essex coast slid by below and a landing was carried out at Bradwell Bay at 07.05 after seven hours aloft. BK609 AA-R ran off the end of the runway and was written off, but the McCullough crew walked away with only a slight injury to the bomb-aimer. The operation was a failure, for which the weather conditions were blamed, and only half of the force, mostly the Path Finder element, reached the target area.

This was the final operation of the month, during which the squadron had taken part in four operations, dispatching twelve sorties for the loss of four Stirlings in crashes at home and one crew.

December 1942

So far, none of the squadron's Stirlings had failed to return from an operation, but this state of affairs could not continue and the first missing crew was registered on the night of the 2/3rd. Earlier in the day, Frankfurt had been posted as the night's target and a force of 112 aircraft made ready, of which thirty-four Path Finder and twenty-three main force aircraft represented 3 Group. Five of the squadron's Stirlings had been detailed and loaded with 4lb incendiaries, and they were at start-up when one had to be withdrawn because of exactor trouble. A second aircraft swung so badly on take-off, that after two failed attempts to become airborne, its participation was also scrubbed, leaving the crews of F/O Trott, Sgt Scott and Sgt Franklin to get away safely at 02.00, 02.02 and 02.12 respectively. The last mentioned returned ninety minutes later with a dead port-outer engine, BK615 having struck a Drem airfield lighting pole on take-off. The two remaining 75(NZ) Squadron representatives headed south to fall in line behind the Path Finders and fly out over Dungeness on the Kent coast on course for the French coastal town of Cayeux-sur-Mer, and traversed France to arrive in the target area some three hours after take-off and encounter cloud and patches of thick haze, which severely impaired the vertical visibility. Three or four searchlight cones of fifteen beams each combined with the haze to create an impenetrable glare, which would render aiming-point identification impossible for most crews. Those in the vanguard of the Path Finder element established a pinpoint on a bend in the Rhine at Oppenheim to the south-west of the target and dropped white flares over the city, some of which were observed to be illuminating open country to the north-west and south-east. Already, this condemned the raid to be scattered and ineffective and most of the bombing fell into open country south-west of the city. P/O Trott and crew returned safely to report that they had found clear skies and good visibility and had dropped their incendiaries from 10,000 feet, but the fires that they observed to be taking hold may have been at a decoy site. BK618 AA-Q was shot down by a night-fighter to crash at Idar-Oberstein, some thirty miles from the Luxembourg frontier, and Sgt Alexander Scott RNZAF and rear gunner, Sgt Alexander Watson Mcmorrine RAF, were killed. The six others on board were taken into captivity, and mid-upper gunner, Sgt Robert Edward Preston RAF, would lose his life in April 1945, almost certainly as the result of an Allied strafing attack.

Four crews were briefed for an unspecified target on the 4th, but the operation was cancelled late on and was replaced by a hastily-arranged mining foray in one of the nectarine gardens around the Frisians. This put a great strain on the armourers, who had to swap the bomb load of 1,000 pounders for 1,500lb parachute mines. One Stirling developed engine problems at start-up and was scrubbed, leaving Sgt McCullough to get away at 21.50, F/L Parish at 23.00 and F/O Trott at 23.15. The operation took place under clear skies with good visibility and without any response from the enemy, and all mines were delivered to the briefed locations, which, in view of the short duration of each sortie, was almost certainly in the Nectarine 1 garden. A message of congratulations to the armourers was received from the A-O-C on the following day.

The eight crews of A Flight finally completed their conversion and joined B Flight at Newmarket on the 6th. They arrived with their seven Stirlings but with much further training to carry out, as one crew had not yet undertaken a daylight solo and three were still awaiting their first night solo. It had taken longer than expected to complete the initial course because of adverse weather and serviceability problems, but the squadron was once more a single unit and looked forward to playing its part in the coming offensives.

Mannheim had been posted as that night's target, and three 75(NZ) Squadron Stirlings were made ready to join an overall force of 272 aircraft, of which thirty-one Path Finder and forty-four main force aircraft were provided by 3 Group. F/Sgt Rousseau led the trio away at 17.35, followed closely by F/Sgt Bailey and P/O Bettles, but the first and last-mentioned were forced to turn back when less than two hours out, one with a dead starboard-inner engine and the other through an inability to climb. F/Sgt Bailey and crew completed the outward flight across France and reached the target to encounter eight to ten-tenths cloud at between 4,000 and 12,000 feet, which rendered ineffective the Path Finders' efforts to illuminate the city with flares and mark the aiming point. Some released parts of their load on estimated positions or on evidence of flak, but not in sufficient quantity or concentration to assist the main force crews. The main force bombing was based on Gee and e.t.a. with little genuine clue as to their proximity to the target, and a decoy site operating some twenty miles to the south inevitably attracted a proportion of the bombing. The response from the ground was intense and accurate and BF398 AA-F would require a new tailfin before it could fly again. Returning crews reported the glow of fires penetrating the cloud, but local reports confirmed that only an estimated five hundred incendiaries had hit the city and the operation was a failure.

Two Stirlings were made ready for a gardening trip to the Frisians on the following night, but one became unserviceable with an engine problem, leaving F/Sgt Dunmall and crew to take off alone at 17.29. They found the target area despite poor weather conditions and watched the mines drift down under their parachutes into the required locations, before returning safely from an uneventful sortie that lasted less than four hours, suggesting that the Nectarine I garden had been the destination. Two Stirlings were prepared for a similar operation in the Baltic twenty-four hours later, probably in one of the Silverthorn gardens in the Kattegat again, but one was unable to take-off and F/L Parish and crew set off alone at 17.00. A change in the wind strength and direction caused them to make landfall over Denmark, well to the south of the intended track, but once corrected, the sortie proceeded according to plan, and the mines were delivered into the correct location. There was no response from the enemy and R9247 AA-W arrived safely home after a round trip of seven hours. The main operation on this night had been the first of a series of three raids in four nights on Turin, which would bring the current campaign to a conclusion. It was a 5 Group and Path Finder show involving 133 aircraft and was highly successful in causing extensive damage in both residential and industrial districts.

S/L Crawford was posted to Mildenhall on the 9th, and it would be the New Year before his successor as A flight commander arrived. That night, a force of 227 aircraft was assembled for a return to Turin to capitalize on the success of the previous night's effort and included fifty-four 3 Group aircraft with equal numbers representing the Path Finders and main force. 75(NZ) Squadron briefed five crews, and they departed Newmarket between 17.10 and 17.35 with debutant F/L Frank Albert Sandeman RAFVR the senior pilot on duty. They were each carrying a load of 4lb incendiaries and enjoyed an apparently uneventful outward flight, guided the final few miles to the target by the fires still burning from the previous night. This would prove to be a double-edged sword, as the smoke hanging over the city created challenging conditions for the Path Finders in their quest to illuminate the aiming-point. Time on target for the first illuminators was 21.15, but they were behind schedule, and it was 21.26 before the first crew delivered forty-eight illuminator flares and a single red one with green stars. The raid was spread out over more than thirty minutes, during which bombing took place predominantly from between 11,000 and 16,500 feet. Many new fires broke out to produce even larger volumes of smoke that obscured much of the ground from those arriving at the tail end of proceedings, and while returning crews reported explosions and fires and a huge column of smoke, the consensus at Bomber Command HQ was of a moderately successful raid that had failed to match the previous night's performance. The ORB recorded this as the squadron's most successful Stirling operation to date, but sadly, the events of a week hence would wipe away any smiles and sense of satisfaction.

It was intended to target Turin again on the following night, but the operation was scrubbed to the relief of all. The crews were becoming tired of the slog across the Alps and the opinion was that Turin had had its moment in the spotlight and it was time to move on. Higher authority disagreed, and another operation was called for the night of the 11/12th. This was to be a small-scale attack, involving eighty-two aircraft from the Path Finders and 1, 4 and 5 Groups, which crossed the Channel to make landfall near Abbeville and everything proceeded according to plan until they ran into ten-tenths ice-bearing cloud between the French coast and Paris. The adverse conditions persuaded around half of the force to turn back, while those pressing on reported some improvement east of the Alps, but it was still almost impossible to establish their position and local reports confirmed that hardly any ordnance fell into the city.

Nine 75(NZ) Squadron crews were briefed on the 16th for a mining operation that night in the Deodar garden in the Gironde estuary on the approaches to the important port of Bordeaux, and they lined up for take-off shortly before 21.45 with F/L Sandeman the senior pilot on duty. There was a strong crosswind as the first three took off, causing each to swing violently before becoming airborne, and it was at this point that the wind backed further to leave the flare-path at right angles to the wind direction, just as Sgt Franklin was about to start rolling. R9245 AA-N swung as violently as the others but seemed to straighten and left the ground later than it should have, causing the starboard undercarriage leg to strike Devil's Dyke, a seven-mile-long embankment and natural hazard at the end of the runway. The impact, just four feet from the top of the dyke, is believed to have torn out the oil tank to the starboard-inner engine, causing it to seize at a critical moment as the Stirling was straining for flying speed. It span into the ground a mile beyond the airfield, setting off two mines and killing all on board. The remaining five sorties were scrubbed, leaving the three airborne crews to complete their sorties successfully under variable weather conditions, which included heavy rain and hailstorms, but also some clear skies.

The following night turned into one of unmitigated disaster for the Command in general and for 3 and 5 Groups in particular. Small-scale operations rarely produced worthwhile results, but always offered a risk of losses, although not to the level experienced on this night. 5 Group sent twenty-seven Lancasters to attack eight small towns in Germany, while sixteen Stirlings and six Wellingtons of 3 Group attacked what was reported to be the Opel motor works at Fallersleben, a town situated some thirty-five miles east of Hannover, which would be renamed Wolfsburg after the war. In fact, a giant Volkswagen factory complex had been built there during the mid to late thirties, where the VW "Beetle" had been born and was currently in production along with military vehicles. Five 75(NZ) Squadron crews were briefed and told to fly at low level, before climbing to 5,000 feet to deliver their loads of 1,000 pounders. They departed Newmarket either side of 18.00 led by W/C Mitchell, who was flying with a freshman crew as good commanders often did, in this case, that of W/O Trevor Horace Bagnall RNZAF. P/O McCullough and crew returned fifteen minutes after midnight to report flying out under clear skies but encountering rain and poor visibility in the target area, which prevented them from identifying the factory. They found an aerodrome to attack on the way home and observed bomb bursts across the flare path and hangars. Anti-aircraft fire was fairly heavy, and Stirling R9250 AA-C was attacked twice by night-fighters, which were driven off on each occasion, but four holes discovered on return were attributed to one of them. The arrival home of the others was awaited in vain, and the realisation dawned that the squadron had sustained 80% losses. BF396 AA-X disappeared without trace with W/C Victor Mitchell RAF, the squadron commander, while R9247 AA-W crashed on or near the aerodrome at Vechta, thirty miles south-west of Bremen with no survivors from the crew of F/Sgt Henry Rousseau RAFVR, three of whom were members of the RNZAF. BF400 AA-G came down at Ankum, only some twenty miles further south-west, killing F/O Gerald Jacobson RNZAF and his crew, which included four other members of the RNZAF. BK620 AA-A was shot down by a combination of flak and night-fighters over Holland, and crashed into the Westeinderplassen Lake, south-west of Amsterdam. F/Sgt Dunmall and his crew all escaped with their lives to fall into enemy hands, and P/O Eric Williams, the captain and bomb-aimer, would be one of those escaping from Stalag Luft III PoW camp in Sagan in a cleverly executed plan made famous in his book "The Wooden Horse". On his return after liberation, he would be decorated with a Military Cross. In all, 3 Group posted missing six Stirlings and two Wellingtons, while five Group lost a third of its Lancasters, all for little or no gain.

The weather on the following day was unsuitable for flying, and the ORB described the mood. *"The squadron tried to get its breath back after the tragedy of last night, but it must be recorded that morale was completely unbelievable. Nearly all young men, many merely boys, yet they faced the recent disaster with incredible calm. No finer example of sincere and earnest determination could possibly have been shown. During the afternoon a soccer game was arranged, and the exercise did much to relieve mind and body alike."* S/L Fowler took temporary charge of the squadron while F/L Parish stepped into his shoes as B Flight commander.

Apart from isolated "moling" daylight operations, the Ruhr had been left in peace since Krefeld at the start of October while attention had been focused on Italy. Now, on the 20th, Duisburg was posted as the target, and this would mask another operation of great significance for the Command that was taking place at the same time over Holland. Although, in the event, not all would proceed according to plan, it would be a mere blip in the development of the Oboe blind-bombing device. A force of 232 aircraft was assembled for the main event and included forty Path Finder and thirty-two main force aircraft provided by 3 Group. Two 75(NZ) Squadron crews were briefed to take part, but one aircraft could not be made ready in time, and this left F/O Trott and crew to take-off alone at 18.05 carrying a load of 4lb incendiaries. They crossed the North Sea in favourable weather conditions and bright moonlight, which prevailed all the way to the western Ruhr, where good visibility enabled crews to peer through the unusually slight ground haze and identify the River Rhine and the distinctive fingers of the Ruhrort docks complex to establish a firm visual reference. The Trott crew bombed in the face of heavy and accurate flak and returned safely from what they believed was a successful operation.

Meanwhile, six 109 Squadron Oboe-equipped Mosquitos had targeted a power station at Lutterade in Holland, in a test to gauge the device's margin of error, believing the target to be free of bomb craters so as not to impair the data. Unfortunately, three of the Mosquitos suffered Oboe failure, and went on to bomb Duisburg instead, leaving W/C Hal Bufton and two other crews to deliver the bombs. What they hadn't bargained for was a whole carpet of bomb craters left over from the attack on Aachen, seventeen miles away, in October, and it proved impossible to identify those aimed by Oboe. The calibration tests would continue, however, and come the spring, Oboe would be ready to unleash with devastating results against the Ruhr.

Christmas was celebrated in traditional fashion during a period of adverse weather as far as flying was concerned, and a shortage of serviceable aircraft also meant that the remainder of the month was spent largely on the ground with lectures, film shows and snow clearing to occupy idle hands. During the course of the month the squadron undertook nine operations and dispatched twenty-six sorties for the loss of six Stirlings and crews. This had been a sad end to 1942 for the squadron, and it did not portend well for what lay ahead in 1943, when major campaigns would be launched into the enemy heartland and the quality of the aircraft and resolve of the crews would be tested to the limit. While most airmen were preparing to celebrate the countdown to 1943, eight Lancasters and two Mosquitos were continuing the Oboe trials programme at Düsseldorf, all but one of the former returning home in time to share in the festivities.

Vickers Wellington Mark III, X3597, AA-C, received 25th January 1942. Despatched 28th October 1942 to 15 Squadron. (NZ Bomber Command Assn. archives, Osborne collection)

S/L Raymond John "Ray" Newton, mid, RNZAF. (NZBCA archives, Crankshaw collection)

*The Parnham crew (L-R): back - Sgt John Brown (2nd pilot), Sgt Campbell Aitcheson (front gunner), Sgt. Murray McDonald (wireless operator), Sgt Joseph Godfrey (rear gunner). Front - Sgt. Robert McGibbon (observer), Sgt John Parnham (pilot). They were all lost on the night of 12/13th March 1942.
(Stuart Godfrey, via 75nzsquadron.com)*

*W/C Edward George "Ted" Olson.
(NZ Herald)*

Three of the Leggett crew and their damaged Wimpy, X3597, AA-C showing the damage from flak and a flare fire over Lübeck, 28/29th March 1942 (L-R): Sgt Arthur Osborne (second pilot), P/O Rufus Leggett (skipper) and Sgt Jack Mayall (wireless operator). (NZ Bomber Command Assn. archives, Osborne collection)

F/L Frank Denton DFC (left) welcomes the new commanding officer, W/C "Ted" Olson, and visitors S/L John Gamble, NZ Air Liaison Officer to the Air Ministry, and W/C Trevor Freeman, DSO, DFC, a founding member of 75 (NZ) Squadron. Feltwell, April 1942. (NZ Herald)

One of a set of group photos taken shortly after W/C Ted Olson arrived, April 1942. Members of the Ball, Doel, AA Fraser, Fisher, Hill, Jarman, Leggett, McLachlan, McPhail and Newton crews can be identified. W/C Ted Olson standing centre with arms folded, next to S/L John Gamble and S/L Ray Newton (hands in pockets). (National Library of New Zealand.)

Sgt Len Chambers.
Len was promoted to squadron Signals Officer and later went on to become a
foundation member of 617 Squadron, flying on the famous Dam Busters raid.
(NZBCA archives, Len Chambers collection, courtesy of the Chambers family)

The McPhail crew, around April 1942. Sgt Leslie Fraser, (wireless operator/front gunner) at left,
F/Sgt Ivan McPhail (skipper), third from left. (Kerry Foster)

*S/L Ray Newton (A Flight Commander), W/C "Ted" Olson (Commanding Officer) and F/L Frank Denton (B Flight Commander), April 1942.
(NZ Bomber Command Assn. archives, Crankshaw collection)*

Captain Peter Terry Wykes, mid, RA. A rare combination, Royal Artillery uniform and Air Gunners wings. (Brian and Margaret Wykes)

Feltwell, April 1942 (L-R): F/L Walter Fenton (rear gunner with S/L Newton), F/L Ces Ball, F/L Bill Bridget (navigator, Ball crew), S/L Newton (Flight Commander), F/Lt Alfred Doel, S/L Frank Denton (Flight Commander), F/O Frank Green (navigator with S/L Lucas), P/O Reg Clarke (rear gunner, Ball crew), P/O Cyril Ingelby (front gunner, Ball crew). (NZ Bomber Command Assn. archives, Bridget collection)

P/O Rufus "Pruno" Leggett in the cockpit. (NZBCA archives, Osborne collection)

The Leggett crew, April 1942 (L-R): rear - P/O Rufus Leggett, Sgt Jack "Slim" Mayall, Sgt Kerrison Morris, Sgt Arthur "Ossie" Osborne. Front - F/S Gordon Newdick, Sgt James Robinson. (NZBCA archives, Osborne collection)

"Our new Wimpy". Ground and aircrew inspecting the new artwork on Wellington X3538, AA-N "Pruno". Dated 4th of April 1942. (NZBCA archives, Osborne collection)

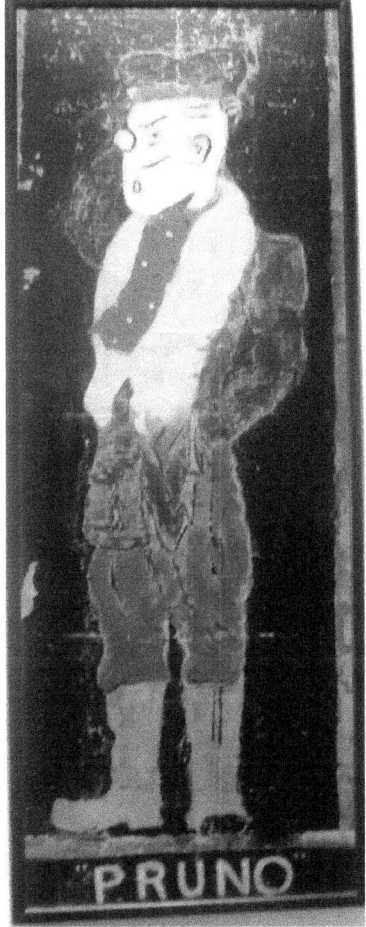

Left: The "Pruno" nose art from Leggett and Osborne's Wellington X3538, AA-N survives to this day. (NZBCA archives, Osborne collection)

F/Sgt Thomas Stanley Mahood RNZAF. (AWMM)

*The AA Fraser crew pose for a photo beside Wellington X3586 AA-A, April 1942.
L-R: P/O "Pete" Gunning (2nd pilot), P/O JJ Manson (navigator), unknown, F/O Allen Fraser (skipper), unknown, unknown. (Kerry Foster)*

F/O Allen Armistice Fraser RNZAF and his crew were shot down by a German night-fighter with no survivors on 20/21 June 1942, crashing into the sea west of Ameland, near the Frisians. (Feltwell.net)

P/O Allen Fraser (second from right) and crew, whose regular Wellington was X3760, AA-L "London". Next to him, with navigator's map bag, is P/O J.J. Manson. (Air Force Museum of NZ)

The Jarman crew, in front of X3636 AA-R (L-R): Back - Sgt John Fernie, wireless operator, P/O Trafford Nicol, 2nd pilot, P/O Eric Jarman, skipper, Sgt Stanley Hall, navigator. Front - Sgt Jim Harris, rear gunner, Sgt Ron Davey, front gunner / bomb aimer.
Sgt Harris was killed and P/O Nicol was mortally wounded in an attack by a night fighter on the night of the 22/23rd April 1942. Taylor and Fernie were also wounded. Nicol died the following day.
(NZ Bomber Command Assn, Stan Brooks collection, via Anna Rhodes-Sayer)

The funeral procession for P/O Trafford Nicol, P/O Cedric Fountain and Sgt Jim Harris leaves Feltwell for St. Nicholas Churchyard, 27 April 1942. (Barbara Ogilvie)

F/Sgt Miles Frederick Gordon Fraser RNZAF. He and his crew failed to return on the night of 15/16th May 1942, the squadron's first loss from a mining operation. (AWMM)

P/O Andrew Donald MacKay RNZAF, lost with four of his crew on 22nd May 1942 in a training accident. (AWMM)

Sgt Richard Stansfield Derek "Terry" Kearns, RNZAF. (NZ Bomber Command Assn. archives)

F/Sgt Colin Valentine McPherson RNZAF, lost with all his crew on 26/27th of July 1942. (AWMM)

The CWP Carter crew, said to have been taken at Feltwell on the 2nd of June 1942, the day before they were shot down (L-R): Sgt Larry Coy (front gunner), Sgt Bert Ives (navigator), P/O Willy Carter (skipper), Sgt Jack "Slim" Mayall (wireless operator), F/Sgt "Spike" Howard (rear gunner). Bert Ives had already survived a crash near Feltwell on 23rd December 1941 which killed his skipper, F/Sgt Loch Lomond Bentley RNZAF. All survived a controlled crash landing at 0310hrs in a forest near the village of Aalst in the Netherlands but were captured shortly afterwards. (Jack Mayall collection, courtesy of Adrian van Zantvoort, via Raimondo Bogaars)

"Len, with unknown West Coasters" (L-R): Sgt Len Chambers and (thought to be) Sgt Ken Crankshaw, Sgt Norman Mitchell, P/O Nathaniel Hodson and S/L Frank Denton, who all hailed from the West Coast of the South Island of New Zealand. Chambers, Hodson and Crankshaw all flew in S/L Denton's crew on 2nd/3rd and 5/6th of June 1942. (NZBCA archives, Len Chambers collection, courtesy of the Chambers family)

The Ball crew (L-R): P/O Cyril Ingelby (front gunner), P/O Reg Clarke (rear gunner), F/Lt Ces Ball (skipper), F/Sgt Douglas Semmence (wireless operator), F/Lt Bill Bridget (navigator).
(NZ Bomber Command Assn. archives, Bridget collection)

Reg Clarke (left) and Cyril Ingelby cleaning the rear turret guns on Z1570, AA-B.
(NZ Bomber Command Assn. archives, Bridget collection)

*The NZ High Commissioner Mr Bill Jordan visited the squadron at Feltwell to meet the aircrews and see them take off for Essen that evening, 5th of June 1942. After air tests and lunch, the men talked with Jordan for an hour outside the crew rooms, and then had a briefing from W/C Ted Olson. Sitting front and centre, G/C Speedy Powell (station commander, wearing sunglasses), Bill Jordan, W/C Ted Olson, and W/C Trevor Freeman (3 Group training, and foundation member of 75(NZ) Squadron). S/L Ray Newton (A Flight commander) 3rd from left, back.
(NZ Bomber Command Assn. archives, Croall collection)*

*Vickers Wellington Z1570, AA-B.
(NZ Bomber Command Assn. archives, Bridget collection)*

"A group of 'sprogs'". Unknown (left) with the Wright crew (L-R): Sgt Jack Wright (skipper, behind unknown), Sgt Victor Westerman (2nd pilot), Sgt Charles Kelly (navigator), Sgt Bruce Neal (rear gunner), Sgt Raymond "Podge" Reynolds (front gunner), Sgt Maurice "Nick" Carter (wireless operator). Westerman only flew one operation with the crew, on the 21st of July 1942. (NZ Bomber Command Assn. archives, Carter collection)

Sgt Charles Kelly, Jack Wright's navigator, inspects the damage to X3646, M-Mother from a night fighter attack on 20/21 June 1942.
(NZ Bomber Command Assn. archives, Kelly collection)

*"D-Donald's aircrew, Feltwell, June 1942". Photo taken by Cpl Jack Way, an Airframe Fitter in A Flight.
(Air Force Museum of NZ, Jack Way collection)*

*A pencil drawing by Jack Wright's wireless operator Nick Carter,
said to be the origin of the D-Donald nose art applied to Wellington BJ772,
and the later inspiration for 156 Squadron's famous Thomas Fredrick Duck.
(NZ Bomber Command Assn. archives, Carter collection)*

The Hockaday crew with BJ837 AA-F for "Freddie" (L-R): Sgt M.H. Hughes (wireless operator), F/Sgt Alf Drew (navigator), Sgt Neville Hockaday (skipper), Sgt Bill Gordon (front gunner), Sgt Bruce Philip (rear gunner). "Freddie", the crew's mascot, was a green and yellow creature that survives in original drawings, a soft toy and in a poem written by navigator Alf Drew. (NZ Bomber Command Assn. archives, Hockaday collection)

The Jarman crew in May-July 1942 after the loss of Nicol and Harris, with Wellington X3751, AA-P (L-R): P/O Francis Chunn (rear gunner), Sgt. John Fernie (wireless operator), P/O Rick Jarman (skipper), P/O William Taylor (navigator), Sgt. Ron Davey (front gunner).
(NZ Bomber Command Assn. archives, Stan Brooks collection, via Anna Rhodes-Sayer)

X3751, AA-P, the Jarman crew's regular Wellington.
(NZ Bomber Command Assn. archives, Stan Brooks collection, via Anna Rhodes-Sayer)

The Osborne crew with X3538, AA-N "Pruno", July 1942. Skipper Arthur "Ossie" Osborne centre.
(NZ Bomber Command Assn. archives, Osborne collection)

F/L Peter John Wilson RNZAF, lost with all his crew, 28/29th of July 1942. (AWMM)

Sgt Arthur Grahame Johns RNZAF lost with all his crew 28/29 July 1942. (AWMM)

F/Sgt John Edward Gilbertson RNZAF, lost with two of his crew, on the night of 28/29th of July 1942. (AWMM)

P/O George Edward Francis Bradey, RNZAF, lost with all but one of his crew on the night of the 11/12th of August 1942. (AWMM)

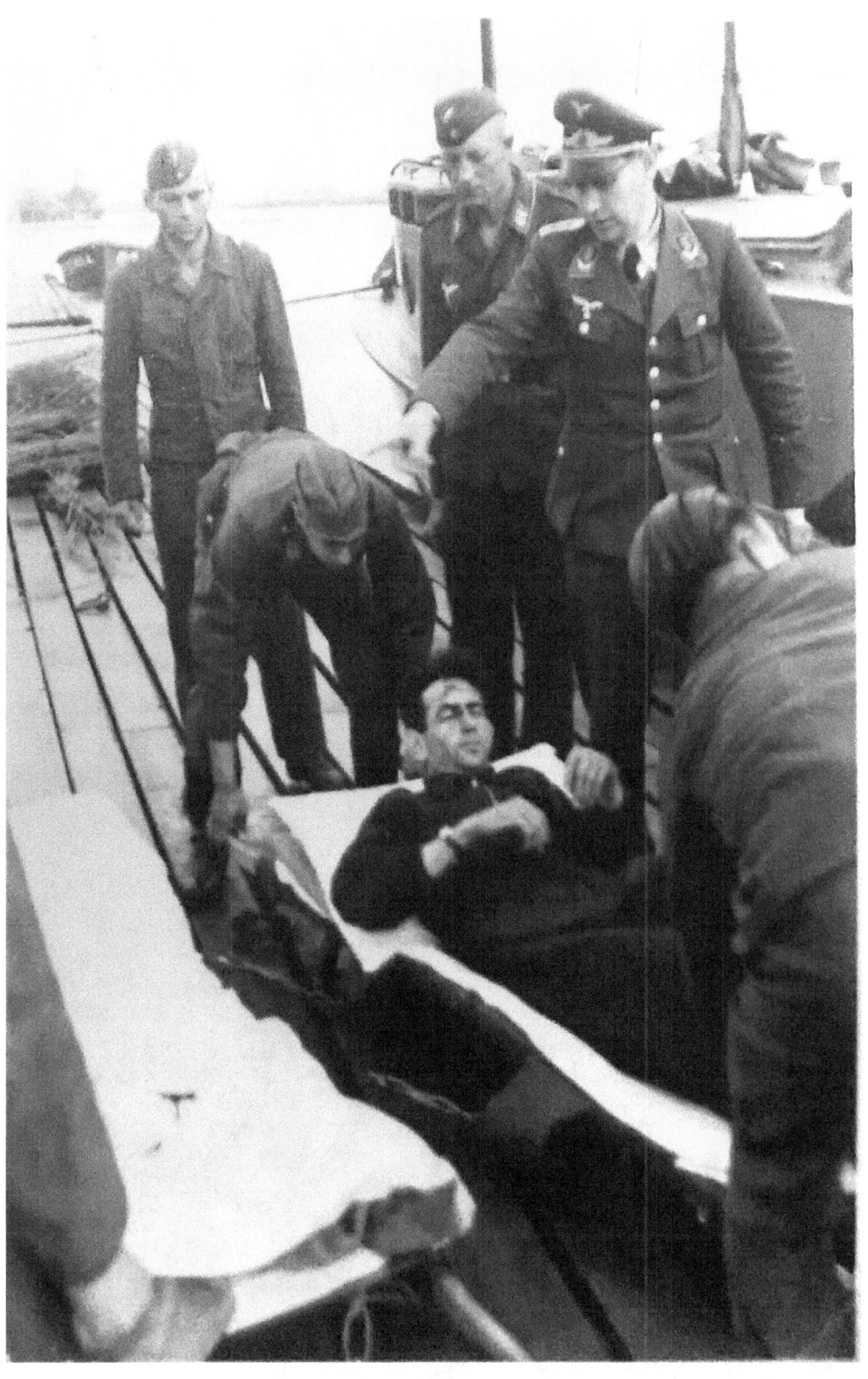

A Luftwaffe officer directs the recovery of Sgt Alan Rutherford, one of the two survivors from the Gilbertson crew, shot down into the Ijsselmeer 28/29th of July 1942. (Kerry Foster)

Only hours after the Gilbertson crew were shot down, a German salvage crane was used to raise the wreckage of BJ661 from the Ijsselmeer, with the bodies of F/Sgts Gilbertson and Byrne still in their seats. The German authorities were apparently aware that the Wellington was fitted with the new Gee system. 29th of July 1942. (Both photos thanks to Kerry Foster)

3 copies

OC 75 28

R.A.F. 30 JUL 1942 SIGNAL OFFICE

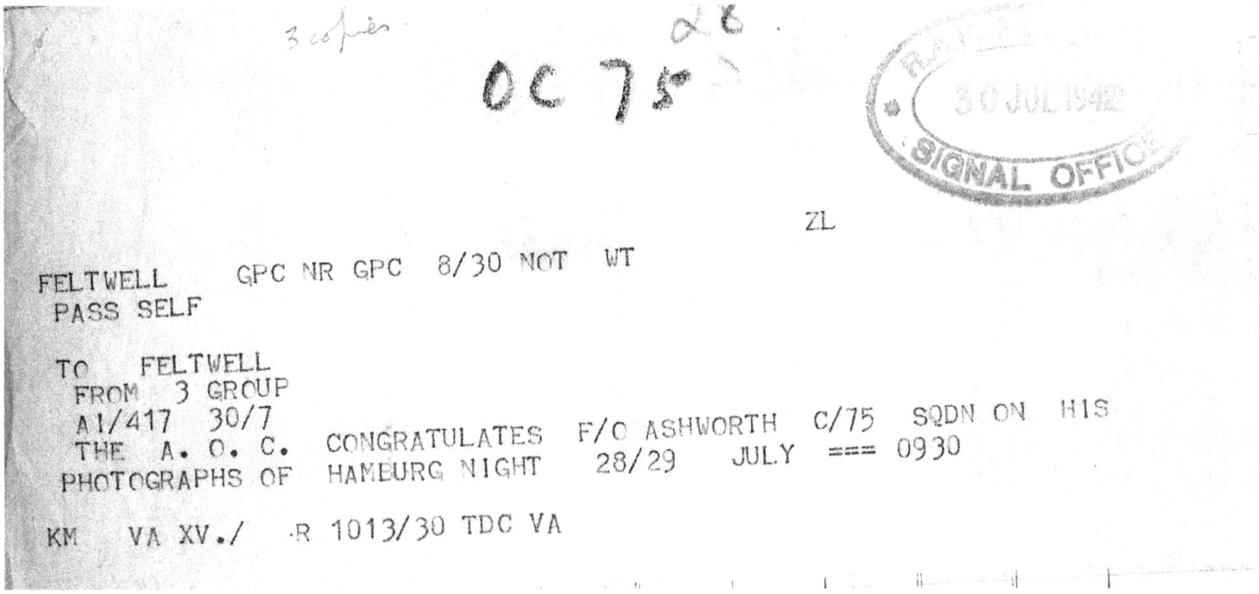

ZL

FELTWELL GPC NR GPC 8/30 NOT WT
PASS SELF

TO FELTWELL
FROM 3 GROUP
A1/417 30/7
THE A. O. C. CONGRATULATES F/O ASHWORTH C/75 SQDN ON HIS
PHOTOGRAPHS OF HAMBURG NIGHT 28/29 JULY === 0930

KM VA XV./ R 1013/30 TDC VA

AOC 3 Group AVM Jack Baldwin's telegram congratulating F/O Artie Ashworth on his target photos from Hamburg 28/29th July 1942.
(Artie Ashworth collection, courtesy of Vince Ashworth)

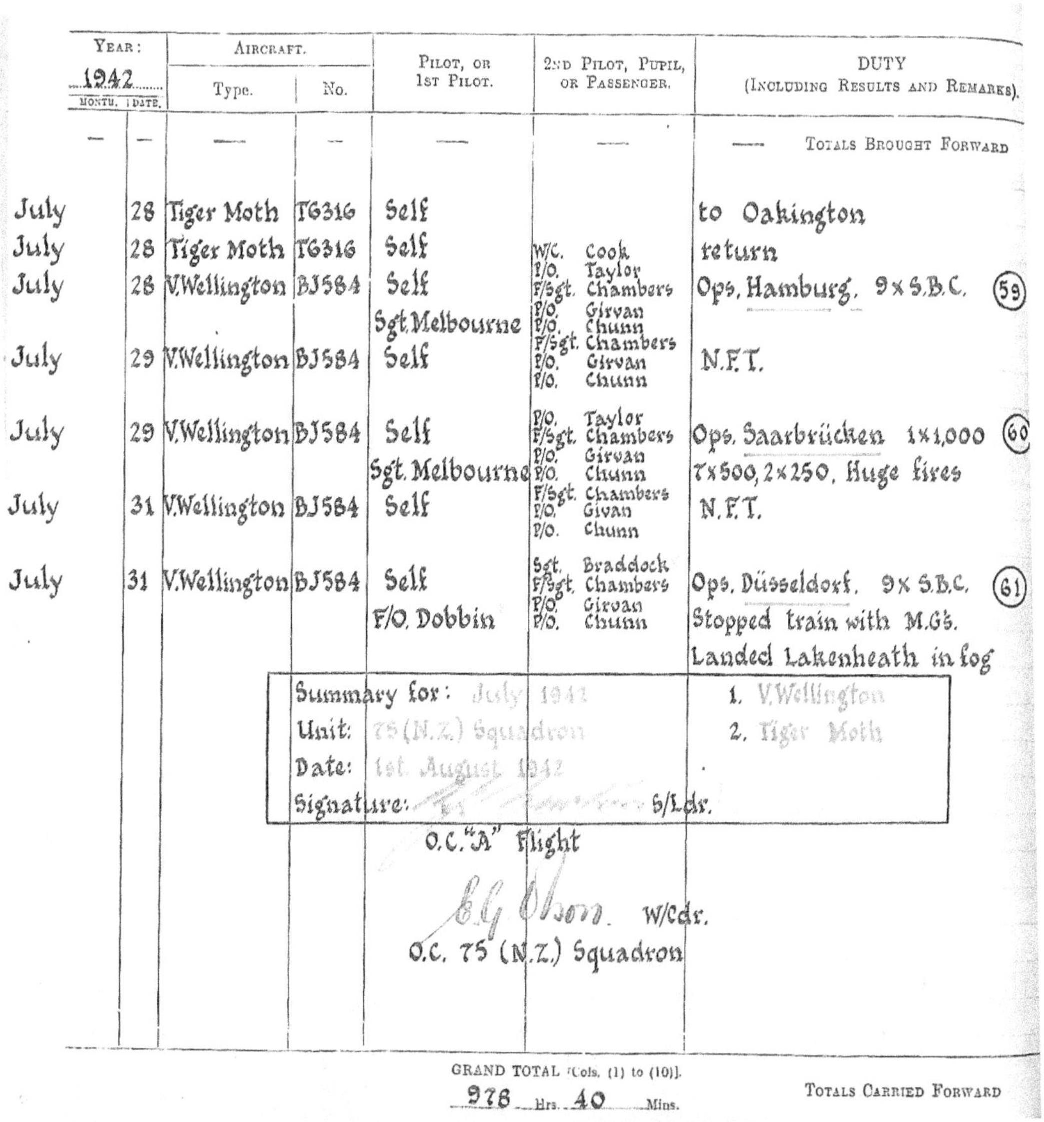

Year: 1942 Month	Date	Aircraft Type	Aircraft No.	Pilot, or 1st Pilot	2nd Pilot, Pupil, or Passenger	Duty (Including Results and Remarks)
—	—	—	—	—	—	— Totals Brought Forward
July	28	Tiger Moth	T6316	Self		to Oakington
July	28	Tiger Moth	T6316	Self		return
July	28	V.Wellington	BJ584	Self Sgt. Melbourne	W/C. Cook F/O. Taylor F/Sgt. Chambers P/O. Girvan P/O. Chunn	Ops. Hamburg. 9 × S.B.C. (59)
July	29	V.Wellington	BJ584	Self	F/Sgt. Chambers P/O. Girvan P/O. Chunn	N.F.T.
July	29	V.Wellington	BJ584	Self Sgt. Melbourne	P/O. Taylor F/Sgt. Chambers P/O. Girvan P/O. Chunn	Ops. Saarbrücken 1×1,000 7×500, 2×250. Huge fires (60)
July	31	V.Wellington	BJ584	Self	F/Sgt. Chambers P/O. Givan P/O. Chunn	N.F.T.
July	31	V.Wellington	BJ584	Self F/O. Dobbin	Sgt. Braddock F/Sgt. Chambers P/O. Girvan P/O. Chunn	Ops. Düsseldorf. 9× S.B.C. (61) Stopped train with M.G's. Landed Lakenheath in fog

Summary for: July 1942 — 1. V.Wellington 2. Tiger Moth
Unit: 75 (N.Z.) Squadron
Date: 1st August 1942
Signature: [signature] S/Ldr.
O.C. "A" Flight

[signature] W/Cdr.
O.C. 75 (N.Z.) Squadron

GRAND TOTAL (Cols. (1) to (10)). 978 Hrs. 40 Mins. — Totals Carried Forward

A page from Artie Ashworth's immaculately kept logbook, July 1942.
(Artie Ashworth collection, courtesy of Vince Ashworth)

The crew of F-Freddie at debriefing after an operation, circa August 1942 (L-R): Sgt Bruce "Foo" Philip (rear gunner), Sgt M.H. Hughes (wireless operator), Sgt Neville "Hock" Hockaday (skipper), F/Lt John Duncan (intelligence officer), Sgt Alf Drew (navigator) and Sgt William "Flash" Gordon (front gunner).
(NZ Bomber Command Assn. archives, Hockaday collection)

F/Sgt Cyril Vincent Green, RNZAF, P/O Bradey's front gunner on 11/12th August, had been a regular member of S/L Frank Denton's crew. (AWMM)

P/O Ventry Watters, RNZAF, lost with all his crew on the night of 13/14 October 1942. (AWMM)

F/L Laurence St. George Dobbin, RNZAF and his front gunner lost their lives on the night of the 11/12th of August 1942. (AWMM)

Sgt James Allison McConnell, RNZAF, lost with all his crew near Valenciennes on the night of 24/25 October 1942. (AWMM)

The wreckage of Wellington BJ767, AA-V after the Dobbin crew was shot down on the night of the 11/12th of August. (aircrewremembered.com, Anneliese Autenrieth)

75 (NZ) Squadron veterans reunited in March 1943 for their investitures at Buckingham Palace (L-R): Alf Drew (navigator, Hockaday crew), Neville Hockaday, Mrs Hockaday, Terry Kearns, and Hone Barclay (navigator, Kearns crew). (NZ Bomber Command Assn. archives, Hockaday collection)

The Curr crew with X3597 AA-C "Achtung ANZAC", (L-R): Sgt Leslie Kennedy (front gunner), F/Sgt Ken Crankshaw (rear gunner), Sgt Frankie Curr (skipper), P/O Ronald Hull (wireless operator) and Sgt Ivan "Sully" Sullivan (navigator). (NZ Bomber Command Assn archives, Crankshaw collection)

*The Trott crew circa September 1942 (L-R): Sgt Harold Hamerton (rear gunner), P/O Dugald Poppelwell (front gunner), Sgt Mikaere Manawaiti (wireless operator), P/O Leo Trott (pilot) and P/O Bill Scollay (navigator). Poppelwell and Scollay would go on to serve as squadron Bombing and Navigational Leaders respectively.
(NZ Bomber Command Assn archives, Hamerton collection)*

*Below: A 75 (NZ) Squadron Wellington returns to Feltwell. The move to Mildenhall foreshadowed the end of the Wellington era.
(From "Return At Dawn")*

*A squadron group at Mildenhall, 9 October 1942. CO W/C Victor Mitchell gives 'three cheers' for High Commissioner "Bill" Jordan front centre in suit, with Station Commander G/C J.A. "Speedy" Powell behind him. To the right of Powell, at front, Trott crew members Harold Hamerton and Dugald Poppelwell.
(NZ Bomber Command Assn. archives, Hamerton collection)*

*Another group photo taken the same day. High Commissioner Jordan front centre, between CO W/C Victor Mitchell (left) and Station Commander G/C "Speedy" Powell (right). Mildenhall, 9 October 1942.
(NZ Bomber Command Assn. archives, Hamerton collection)*

Members of the Trott crew with one of the new Stirlings (L-R): Sgt Joseph Sansoucy (flight engineer), Sgt Harold Hamerton (rear gunner), and Sgt Mikaere Manawaiti (wireless operator).
(NZ Bomber Command Assn. archives, Hamerton collection)

Photo from "The Weekly News", probably taken at Mildenhall, "A Maori team at a British air station" (L-R): Sgt Roy Raharuhi (pilot), Sgt Marama Parata (wireless operator, Raharuhi crew), Sgt "Mana" Manawaiti (wireless operator, Trott crew), and Sgt "Ted" Gray (wireless operator, Broady crew). Courtesy of the Raharuhi family.
(Air Force Museum of New Zealand)

The mighty Stirling. AA-C "Charlie" in flight. (NZ Bomber Command Assn. archives)

New Zealand armourer Cpl Charlie Shepherd bombing up a Stirling, late 1942. (NZ Bomber Command Assn. archives, Shepherd collection)

Sgt Raymond Herbert John Broady RNZAF, killed with three of his regular crew during Stirling conversion at RAF Oakington, 28th of November 1942. (AWMM)

Sgt Benjamin Allan Franklin RNZAF, killed with all crew when they hit the Devil's Dyke and crashed on take-off from Newmarket, 9th of December 1942. (AWMM)

AM Sir Arthur Harris, Commander-in-Chief of RAF Bomber Command. (NZ Bomber Command Assn. archives, Jack Moller collection, via Tony Moller)

January 1943

The new year was to be one of campaigns, which would bring significant successes, punctuated by gallant and expensive failures, but the first official act of the New Year was the formation of 6 Group, a fully-fledged Royal Canadian Air Force bomber group financed by the Canadian government but operating under Harris. The group was stationed on former 4 Group airfields in northern Yorkshire and County Durham and would ultimately operate a mixture of Halifaxes and Lancasters, although most squadrons began with Wellingtons. Eventually, all Canadian squadrons would find a home in 6 Group, but it began life with eight founder members.

The Oboe trials programme would dominate the first two weeks of the year as seven small-scale attacks on Essen and one on Duisburg were mounted, although these would involve only Lancasters of 1 and 5 Groups and the Mosquitos of 109 Squadron. For the first time, the cloud cover and ever-present blanket of industrial haze should have no bearing on the outcome of the raid as reliance on e.t.a., DR and Gee was cast aside in favour of Oboe, at least that is, at targets within the device's range. Until the advent of mobile transmitter stations late in the war, Oboe would be restricted by the curvature of the earth and the altitude at which Mosquitos could fly to pick up the pulse, but this meant that the entire Ruhr lay within range of Harris's bombers. That said, the success of a raid would still rely on the ability of the Path Finders to back up the initial Oboe markers and maintain a supply of target indicators (TIs) on the aiming-point. In the midst of this on the 8th, the Path Finder Force was granted group status as 8 Group, and duly took ownership of the 3 Group stations upon which it had lodged since its formation in August. For the purpose of this book the terms Path Finder and 8 Group are interchangeable.

W/C Gerald Arthur Lane RAF was officially posted to 75(NZ) Squadron w.e.f the 1st of January as the new commanding officer but was detached immediately to 1657 Conversion Unit to learn the ways of the Stirling. Born in Somerset in 1916, Gerald Lane joined the RAF in 1936 and at the outbreak of war was serving with 4 Group's 51 Squadron flying Whitleys. After completing a tour and earning a DFC, he was posted to 35 Squadron, which had been reformed late in 1940 to introduce the new four-engine Halifax to operations. He took part in the first Halifax operation over Germany against Hamburg in March 1941 and completed a second tour before being posted as a squadron leader to Wellesbourne in Warwickshire to establish a bomber training unit, which became 22 O.T.U. While there he took part in the first Thousand Bomber raid on Cologne and was appointed chief flying instructor, before being rewarded for his outstanding service with promotion to wing commander rank and a posting to 75(NZ) Squadron.

New Year's Day found the 75(NZ) Squadron crews attending lectures as snowstorms swept the country. The weather improved on the 2nd, however, and flying training took place on most days thereafter, leading to the first operational activity on the 8th. Three crews were called to briefing to learn that they would be heading for the western coast of Denmark for mining duties in one of the Hawthorn gardens. F/Sgt Jackson was first to leave the ground at 17.20, closely followed by F/Sgt Bailey and P/O McCullough, but F/Sgt Bailey lost his port-inner engine over the North Sea and had to turn back. Unable to maintain height, the Stirling sank into ice-bearing cloud and it became necessary to jettison the mines. The other two crews carried out their sorties successfully in favourable conditions and returned safely after a five-hour round-trip.

Three crews, including that of first-time captain Sgt Roy Arthur Williams RAFVR, were briefed on the following day for another mining operation in the waters north of the Frisian Island of Terschelling in the Nectarine I garden, but one Stirling suffered engine trouble and had to be withdrawn. The crews of Sgts Lord and Williams took off at 17.25 and 17.50 respectively and completed their assigned tasks during uneventful three-hour sorties. The maritime theme continued on the night of the 12/13th, when four Stirlings were made ready for a longer trip to the Deodar garden in the Gironde Estuary on the south-western coast of France. This time there were no serviceability issues and all got away safely either side of midnight, P/Os Bettles and McCullough and Sgts Davey and Williams completing their sorties as briefed in around six and a half hours.

On the 14th, a new Air Ministry directive was issued, which forced Harris to focus his resources against the French ports offering shelter and support facilities to U-Boots, which were continuing to cause havoc among Allied convoys in the North Atlantic. Lorient, St Nazaire, Brest and La Pallice were to be subjected to a campaign of heavy bombing, which would distract the bomber force from its primary role of attacking the industrial towns and cities of Germany. There was no delay in implementing the directive and a force of 122 aircraft made ready to attack Lorient that night included seventeen Stirlings and two Wellingtons representing 3 Group. The truth was, that the concrete structures built on the Keroman peninsula to house the U-Boots were still just as impregnable with the bombs available now as they had been when the first maritime campaign had been launched in the spring of 1941. As then, the only effective course of action was to destroy the town and communications to make it inaccessible from land, while mining compromised access from the sea. Three Stirlings of 75(NZ) Squadron were loaded with 1,000 pounders and 4lb incendiaries and departed Newmarket either side of 22.30 with the crews of F/L Parish and Sgts Buck and Lord on board. They reached the target area to find large gaps in the cloud cover, and watched their bombs fall into the town from 10,000 feet to add to the burgeoning fires. All returned safely to report a successful operation, which post-raid reconnaissance did not entirely confirm, and a local report mentioned that just 120 houses had been destroyed.

This was just the first of nine operations against the port over the ensuing five weeks, however, and the second one was mounted twenty-four hours later. A force of 157 aircraft was assembled, which included twenty-six aircraft representing 3 Group, and when the time came, 75(NZ) Squadron could only muster three Stirlings. The day had begun badly with four crews travelling by road to Stradishall and Bourn at the crack of dawn to collect new Stirlings, but when the ground crews started work to prepare them for the raid, they discovered that they were not new at all and required far more servicing than could be accomplished in the hours remaining. The trio took off between 17.45 and 18.30 loaded with 1,000 pounders and 4lb incendiaries, but Sgt Buck turned back with engine problems and was back on the ground within ninety minutes. P/Os Bettles and McCullough pressed on to the target and bombed through cloud in the face of a spirited flak defence, observing the glow of fires as the town began to burn fiercely. This was a much more successful operation, which left eight hundred houses in ruins, and as most of the residents had evacuated themselves the day before, there were modest casualties among French civilians.

3 Group was not involved in operations on the 16th and 17th against Berlin, which were predominantly Lancaster affairs and failed to produce the hoped-for outcomes. The crews of Sgts Dalzell and Raymond Frederick Bennett RNZAF took off at 17.15 on the 18th for mining duties in one of the Nectarine gardens off the Frisians, but the serviceability curse struck again, forcing the former to turn back after losing their intercom over the North Sea. Sgt Bennett and crew in BK624 AA-A pressed on in bright moonlight on what was their maiden sortie and were set upon three times by enemy fighters. The crew performed magnificently and shook off their assailants with good defensive flying, before returning home to examine the bullet holes in their aircraft and report fulfilling their brief.

S/L Gilbert Meston Allcock RAF was posted to the squadron during w.e.f the 18th, and he would step into the A Flight commander's post left vacant since the departure of S/L Crawford almost six weeks earlier. A force of seventy-nine Lancasters and three Mosquitos resumed the Oboe trials programme at Essen on the 21st, while seventy others took part in a major mining effort around the Frisians. The third attack of the series on Lorient was posted on the 23rd, for which 121 aircraft were made ready, including twenty-eight Stirlings of 3 Group, nine contributed by 75(NZ) Squadron, which would represent their best effort to date on the type. They departed Newmarket either side of 17.30 with the newly-promoted F/L Trott the senior pilot on duty, and all made it to the target area, where ahead of them, the Path Finder illuminator and marker crews had arrived to find some thin cloud at 3,000 feet but generally clear conditions and good visibility, which enabled them to carry out timed runs from Groix Island to the aiming-points A, B and Y. The main force crews followed the line of the Blavet and Scorff estuaries to reach the built-up area, those from Newmarket delivering their loads of 1,000 and 500 pounders and 4lb incendiaries in good visibility. Returning crews reported many fires with smoke beginning to obscure ground detail and the glow from the burning port lingered on the horizon for seventy miles into the homeward flight. Bombing photos confirmed the accuracy of the raid at a cost of a single Stirling belonging to 75(NZ) Squadron. R9248 AA-H was hit by flak on the way home and crashed about six miles south-east of Morlaix in France with the English Channel in sight. The pilot, Sgt Robert Miln Kidd RNZAF, who was on his first operation with the squadron, was the only survivor and he managed to evade capture. The others all returned safely on a rare night of 100% serviceability.

The squadron was not required for the fourth Lorient raid on the night of the 26/27th, for which a force of 157 aircraft took off, among them a dozen Wellingtons from 115 Squadron as the 3 Group representatives. Sgts Andrew James Newel Scott and Desmond Lewis Thompson (both RNZAF) were briefed to carry out the final sorties of the month on the night after, a gardening effort in the Nectarine I garden off Terschelling, for which they set off at 17.40 to find cloudy and hazy conditions offering poor visibility. Despite the challenges, both crews delivered their mines into the assigned locations and returned safely.

Other squadrons from other groups completed the month's operations at Düsseldorf on the 27/28th, Lorient on the 29/30th and Hamburg on the 30/31st. At the first-mentioned, Mosquito-laid Oboe ground markers were used for the first time to provide a reference for the Path Finder heavy brigade and were designed to burst and cascade just above the ground. The presence of a thin layer of cloud over the target, which pre-Oboe, would have turned the attack into a lottery, had no detrimental effect and the bombing was concentrated in southern districts, where a significant amount of damage resulted. Hamburg lay beyond the range of Oboe, and the ground-mapping H2S radar was employed for the first time in Path Finder Halifaxes and Stirlings. In time, H2S, particularly in updated form, would become a useful tool, but it would take time for the operators to learn how to interpret the jumble of images on their cathode-ray tube and bombing was scattered on this night.

Operationally, it had been a less-than-satisfactory month for the squadron, through no fault of its own, and operated just eight times, dispatching twenty-eight sorties for the loss of a single Stirling and crew.

February 1943

The new month was a time of honing and refining for Bomber Command in preparation for the launching of a major campaign a month hence. February opened with the posting of the Rhineland capital Cologne as the target for an experimental raid on the 2nd, during which two marking methods were to be employed to further explore target marking techniques at a target situated just to the south of the Ruhr and well within range of Oboe. The plan called for the initial marking to be carried out by Oboe Mosquitos of 109 Squadron, followed by H2S-equipped Stirlings and Halifaxes from 7 and 35 (Madras Presidency) Squadrons, all with red TIs, and for the Path Finder Lancaster element to back up with green TIs. A force of 159 heavy aircraft included a Path Finder contribution of twenty-six Lancasters, Halifaxes and Stirlings with two 109 Squadron Mosquitos but no contribution from 3 Group. It is interesting to note that the 3 Group ORB was still recording Path Finder numbers as if it were still part of the group. In the event, the experiment was not successful, and bombing was scattered across the city, causing no significant damage.

A force of 263 aircraft was assembled on the 3rd to send against Hamburg, this number including a contribution from 3 Group of twenty-seven Stirlings and three Wellingtons, nine of the former representing 75(NZ) Squadron. W/C Lane had completed his conversion course and would oversee this, his first operation as commanding officer, from the ground. His arrival also allowed S/L Fowler to resume command of B Flight, which had been looked after by F/L Parish. They departed Newmarket between 18.15 and 18.55 with S/L Allcock the senior pilot on duty and each Stirling loaded with 4lb incendiaries, before setting course for the North Sea on a night of heavy cloud with icing conditions, having been told at briefing to turn back if the conditions proved to be too challenging. Twenty-two 3 Group crews took advantage of the get-out-of-jail-free card, among them five Kiwis in the face of the towering storm-laded cumulonimbus cloud that often formed a barrier over the North Sea, and on this night extended beyond 22,000 feet. The recently-commissioned P/O Kenneth Blincoe DFC, RNZAF and crew, who had survived a crash-landing in November, were outbound over Holland, when they ran into a night-fighter, which shot down R9250 AA-C to crash near Tiel, thirty miles east of Rotterdam at 02.00, killing all eight occupants. The second pilot and two others on board were also members of the RNZAF. Thirteen minutes later, BK604 AA-S also crashed in Holland some fifty miles further to the north-east near Almelo, following an encounter with another night-fighter, this one flown by Hptm Wolfgang Thimmig of III./NJG1. P/O John McCullough DFC, RNZAF, who likewise, had survived a crash on the night after Blincoe's, found his luck had run out on this operation too, and he died with three of his crew, while the four survivors were taken into captivity. These were two of the squadron's most experienced crews, and their loss would be keenly felt. A total of nine members of the RNZAF were lost to the squadron on this night, and two freshman crews were left at Newmarket without a pilot.

The others pressed on and once in German airspace, followed the briefed track, which approached the target from the south, passing to the east of the designated alternative target of Bremen. The plan called for the Path Finder heavy brigade to open the attack with red skymarker flares with green stars at 21.00, but the conditions intervened, and the operation did not proceed as intended. North-western Germany was found to be covered by ten-tenths cloud with tops at 10,000 to 12,000 feet and positions over Hamburg had to be established by the Path Finder crews blindly on H2S. In the event, they were unable to provide more than a few scattered skymarkers for the main force crews, among which were those of F/L Trott and Sgt Buck, and the bombing reflected this. On return, most could only report the reflection of fires in the cloud.

Turin was posted as the main target on the following day and a force of 188 aircraft assembled, of which thirty-three Stirlings and three Wellingtons were provided by 3 Group. While this operation was in progress, 128 other aircraft, mostly Wellingtons, were to continue the assault on Lorient. The seven-strong 75(NZ) Squadron element departed Newmarket between 18.00 and 18.50 with S/L Allcock the senior pilot on duty, ably supported by F/Ls Sandeman and Trott. F/L Sandeman's sortie lasted an hour and was curtailed because of a defective turret and intercom, while S/L Allcock's R9243 was unable to climb sufficiently to cross the Alps and he bombed an alternative target in occupied France. The five remaining crews flew the length of eastern France over heavy cloud and were able to make the necessary height to clear the Alps, guided by route markers dropped over Lake Bourget in the foothills on the French side. On the Italian side they found clear skies and excellent visibility and the 75(NZ) Squadron crews had red marker flares in their bomb sights as they delivered their loads of 1,000 and 500 pounders and 4lb incendiaries. They observed large fires develop, including a particularly extensive one in the city centre as they retreated and their reports were corroborated by returning Path Finder crews, who had identified ground features like the marshalling yards and sports stadium and had witnessed many bomb detonations in the city centre.

Four of the squadron's crews were among nineteen from the group to be sent mining in one of the Nectarine gardens off the Frisians on the evening of the 5th. They took off either side of 18.00, with F/L Sandeman the senior pilot on duty and flew out in ten-tenths cloud from the English coast to the garden area. At 19.43 a message was received from BK617 AA-D to say that the crew had something to communicate to base, but nothing further was heard, and a report came through that a Stirling had been seen to crash in flames two miles off the Norfolk coast at Cromer. It was established later that the aircraft had caught fire in the air when outbound at 1,500 feet and had dived into the North Sea, taking with it the first-time crew of Sgt Randolph Ernest Redding RNZAF, which contained two other members of the RNZAF, two of the RCAF and two of the RAF. A search was made, but no trace of the Stirling and its crew was ever found. The other three crews delivered their mines into the briefed locations and returned safely after uneventful sorties.

The squadron made ready nine Stirlings on the 7th as part of a 3 Group contingent of fifty-five of the type for the seventh raid on Lorient scheduled for that night. It was to be a large-scale operation in two phases involving 323 aircraft, for which F/Ls Sandeman and Trott took off at

18.05 as part of the early shift, leaving the remainder to depart Newmarket between 19.10 and 19.50 with S/L Allcock the last away. P/O Bennett returned early after the intercom failed, but the others exploited the clear conditions and concentrated Path Finder marking to deliver an outstandingly destructive attack. The town was seen to be well ablaze with smoke rising to 8,000 feet as the bombers retreated, and all from Newmarket returned safely. The squadron spent the following week at home, training when conditions allowed, and a number of crews sat through a briefing for a mining sortie to the Elderberry and Furze gardens located on the Biscay coast close to the Franco-Spanish frontier, only for it to be cancelled.

The experienced F/L Geoff Rothwell arrived at this time with his new crew, which included three members of the RNZAF, and was returning to familiar ground. Born in Greater Manchester in 1920, Rothwell had joined the RAF in the summer of 1939 on a short service commission, and after training was posted to Newmarket in May 1940 to join 99 Squadron. In November he completed a tour of thirty-seven operations, for which he was awarded a DFC in January 1941. After a frustrating period as an instructor, he joined an RAF delegation to Washington DC, where he engaged in public speaking and guest appearances, touring many airfields in the process. On his return to the UK, he was posted to 1657 Conversion Unit to learn to fly the Stirling, before being posted to 75(NZ) Squadron. On the 11th, Sgt Kenneth Atherton Crankshaw RNZAF was posted out to 156 Squadron of the Path Finder Force. A notable "character", he had originally operated as a 'spare part" gunner flying with a variety of crews, including those of S/Ls Denton, Newton, and Ashworth. He had previously completed a tour of thirty operations flying as a gunner in Defiants, and his tally now stood at sixty-six. Without a break, he continued at 156 Squadron, earning a commission and a DFC along the way, flying two operations with Frankie Curr, his old skipper from 75(NZ) Squadron, ten with another ex-75er, Terry Kearns, (along with his old crew members Jack Moller, Morrie Egerton, Hone Barclay and Buck Price), and then another fifteen with ex-75 pilot Jack Wright and the "Thomas Fredrick Duck" boys. This brought his operations to a grand total of 93!

During this lull for 75(NZ) Squadron, other elements of the Command carried out a raid on Wilhelmshaven on the night of the 11/12th, which was conducted through complete cloud cover, employing H2S-guided skymarking, the least accurate of all marking methods. An enormous explosion lit up the clouds with a glow that lingered for ten minutes, and it was discovered later that it came from the naval ammunition dump at Mariensiel in the south of the town. The eruption devastated an area of 120 acres and caused major destruction in the town and dockyard.

It was not until the 13th that the next operation was posted on the board at Newmarket, and that was for a return to Lorient that night for what would prove to be the penultimate and heaviest raid of the war on this target. A force of 466 aircraft was made ready, which included sixty-four 3 Group Stirlings, eleven of them belonging to 75(NZ) Squadron. They again took off in two shifts between 17.40 and 19.00, with S/L Allcock the senior pilot on duty and P/O Douglas Charles Lowe, RAFVR and crew on their first operation together. One crew returned early with unserviceable turrets, leaving the others to push on to the target, which they found under clear skies with good visibility. The plan called for a number of Path Finder aircraft to station themselves over the Ile-de-Groix, an island situated some five miles off the mouth of the estuary leading to the port and illuminate it continuously as a navigation point. They arrived at 20.30 and, under perfect conditions of clear skies and bright moonlight, delivered three white and one red flare from 14,000 feet, and, ten minutes later, ten white flares and four green TIs, which fell to the north-west of the aiming-point. The other Path Finder crews followed up over Lorient itself with flares, green TIs and 1,000 pounders in a number of passes from 11,000 to 14,000 feet between 20.35 and 20.56, paving the way for the main force element to carry out their attacks. This was the first non-1,000 operation to drop a thousand tons of bombs on a single target, and returning crews reported massive fires right across the town and the port area. F/L Trott's W7469 AA-O was hit by flak over the target, holing the No 2 petrol tank on the port side and damaging a trimming tab, and the aerial was also shot away. The Stirling held together for the flight back to England, where a safe landing was carried out at Middle Wallop. R9316 AA-K was another victim of flak over the target and was partially abandoned before crashing a dozen miles north-north-east of Lorient. The pilot, Sgt Roy Williams RAFVR, and his RNZAF rear gunner died in the wreckage, while four members of the crew were captured and the Canadian mid-upper gunner, Sgt Leonard Willis RCAF, ultimately evaded a similar fate.

Two operations were mounted on the following night, the larger, by 243 Halifaxes, Wellingtons and Stirlings against Cologne, while 142 Lancasters of 1, 5 and 8 Groups targeted Milan. 3 Group offered fifty-three Stirlings, eight of them made ready by 75(NZ) Squadron and loaded with 1,000 pounders and 4lb incendiaries, which took off between 18.20 and 18.50 with S/L Allcock the senior pilot on duty. He returned after two hours because of engine problems, leaving the others to fly out in broken cloud, which built up from the Scheldt estuary and was at ten-tenths with tops at around 7,000 feet by the time that the Path Finders arrived in the target area to establish their positions by H2S and the evidence of the accurate flak penetrating the cloud tops. They opened the attack bang on scheduled at 20.15 with red flares with green stars and 1,000 pounders, which the main force bomb-aimers had in the sights as they let their high explosives and incendiaries go. The cloud prevented an assessment of the results, and the intensity of the flak dissuaded crews from hanging around, but they observed some evidence of burgeoning fires that gave some hope of a successful raid. Local sources confirmed only limited success in western districts, the failure to achieve better results, perhaps in part, caused by a bunch of red flares with green stars observed to fall ten miles to the north.

Preparations were put in hand on the 16th for the final attack on Lorient, to be delivered that night by an initial force of 377 aircraft, of which 3 Group contributed forty-one Stirlings and six Wellingtons, the latter belonging to 115 Squadron, the groups only operator of the type until its impending conversion to Mk II Lancasters. Seven 75(NZ) Squadron crews attended briefing, while their aircraft were loaded with 2,000lb and 500lb bombs and 4lb incendiaries. It was not often that a crew member, other than a pilot commanded a bomber, but S/L Eric Fowler, B Flight commander, made his debut as captain on this operation, flying as bomb-aimer with the crew of F/Sgt Charles Arnold Rothschild RCAF. (In RAF Squadrons the pilot was always captain, irrespective of rank.) F/L Sandeman led the first section away at 18.40, and they were followed between 19.00 and 19.20 by the second section in which S/L Allcock was the senior pilot on duty. The plan called for two Halifaxes and four Lancasters of 8 Group to drop sticks of flares across the town, before the remaining Path Finders delivered red TIs onto the aiming-point and maintained the illumination as required. They arrived in the target area to find widely-dispersed low cloud and excellent conditions and the initial illuminator crews opened the attack with thirty-two white flares from 14,000 feet a minute ahead of schedule at 20.44. The main force crews were able to identify the river and its bridges and braved an intense searchlight and flak response in the early stages until it became overwhelmed. One of the squadron's Stirlings was coned for eight minutes, during which the pilot took violent evasive action and only escaped the situation with extreme difficulty. A massive explosion was witnessed at 21.20, which sent a huge column of smoke into the air. As few buildings remained standing in Lorient, this final attack had been predominantly an incendiary affair, and the glow from the resultant fires remained visible for fifty miles into the return flight. During the course of the series, 1,967 sorties had been sent against the port, which was now a deserted ruin with little other than the impervious K1, K2 and K3 U-Boot structures still standing. While this operation was in progress, F/L Trott and P/O Lowe delivered mines into the Deodar garden in the Gironde estuary leading to Bordeaux, and returned safely from uneventful sorties.

The crews slept late into the morning of the 17th, and as no operations were posted, a rugger match was arranged for the afternoon against the O.T.U at Wescott. The opponents cancelled at lunchtime, and one wonders if the fearful reputation of the "All-Blacks" had perhaps caused a change of heart. The game was eventually contested between A and B Flights, whose Kiwi element, no doubt, kicked chunks out of their RAF colleagues. On the 18th the squadron received a visit from A/C Neville, A-O-C RNZAF Overseas, and G/C Manson, RNZAF HQ, to present an advance copy of the book "Return at Dawn", the first official history of the squadron covering the period from June 1939 to July 1942, edited by Hilary A St. George Saunders. A copy signed by the personnel mentioned therein was to be presented to Mr Jordan, the High Commissioner.

The main operation on the night of the 18/19th was the first of a series of three against Wilhelmshaven and did not involve 75(NZ) Squadron, which instead, briefed seven of its crews for a mining operation in the Deodar garden in the Gironde Estuary and two for the Furze garden off St-Jean-de-Luz close to the Spanish frontier. The Gironde estuary feeds into the Rivers Garonne and Dordogne, which diverge north of the port of Bordeaux, the latter winding its way inland, while the former serves the port. Not only was the waterway the gateway to the Atlantic for Bordeaux's U-Boot fleet but was also the site of oil plants at locations on an island and along its banks at Pauillac, Bec-d'Ambes and Blaye, which would become significant targets for Bomber Command in 1944. In the event, only eight took off, becoming airborne in a ten-minute slot from 18.40 with S/L Allcock the senior pilot on duty. One of the Spain-bound duo experienced low revs on take-off because of an exactor problem, and after two failed attempts to gain enough speed, was withdrawn. The other one, containing the crew of Sgt Lord, turned back early with a similar port-inner engine exactor problem, which was traced on inspection to an unserviceable rev-counter. Six of the others reached their target area to deliver the 1,500lb mines as briefed, and all returned safely from round-trips of between five-and-a-half and seven hours.

Eight of the squadron's crews were briefed on the 19th for the second attack on Wilhelmshaven, for which an overall force of 338 aircraft was assembled, forty-one Stirlings and four Wellingtons provided by 3 Group. The Stirlings were loaded with 1,000 pounders and 4lb incendiaries, and all but one of the 75(NZ) Squadron representatives took off between 17.45 and 18.26 with S/L Allcock the senior pilot on duty and last away. F/L Trott turned back after seventy-five minutes with a defective compass, leaving the others to press on to find the target, where the Path Finders were to drop preliminary green warning flares by H2S, before skymarking the release point and ground marking the aiming-point with red TIs. The port was covered by a thin layer of ten-tenths low cloud and was further protected by a smoke screen, which prevented any from determining what was happening on the ground, although the TIs were visible. The previous night's raid had failed dismally after most of the bombs found their way into open country to the west of the town, and this night's effort would prove to be equally ineffective. Some returning crews reported the glow of fires spreading quickly through the town, while Sgt Lord described being held in a searchlight cone for three minutes. In fact, the Path Finder marking had led to the bombing of an area of open country north of the town, and this would be put down later to the use of out-of-date maps.

Bad weather kept the squadron on the ground over the ensuing days, and the time was filled with lectures, rugger and soccer matches and a demonstration of dinghy drill by F/L Trott and crew in the static water pool. The last of the three raids on Wilhelmshaven was mounted on the night of the 24/25th in the absence of 3 Group in what was another inconclusive operation, after which, the port would be left in peace until October 1944.

Seven 75(NZ) crews were called to briefing on the 25th to learn that their destination was to be Nuremberg in southern Germany, for which a force of 337 aircraft was drawn from 1, 3, 4, 5 and 8 Groups, 3 Group represented by forty-four Stirlings. The plan called for all Path Finder aircraft to drop a yellow TI as a route marker, and for the H2S-equipped Halifaxes and Stirlings to release a white TI each fifteen miles from the target. These were then to deliver a red TI onto the aiming-point, which the remaining Path Finder Halifaxes and Lancasters would back up with greens. The Stirlings' petrol tanks were filled to the top and their bomb bays loaded with 1,000lb and 500lb bombs and 30lb and 4lb incendiaries, those from Newmarket taking off either side of 20.00 with W/C Lane the senior pilot on duty for the first time and flying with the crew of P/O Lowe. After battling their way through a bank of towering ice-bearing cloud over south-eastern England, they crossed the Channel and or North Sea to make landfall over north-eastern France and maintained a course parallel with the Franco-Belgian frontier to enter Germany south of Luxembourg. F/L Sandeman and P/O Bailey returned early, at 22.30 and 23.30 respectively, one in an aircraft failing to maintain height and the other with an indisposed navigator, while F/L Trott's BK602 AA-R was hit by flak near Mannheim, around a hundred miles west of the target. He was forced to jettison the bombs but decided to carry on to the target and act as an observer. The route markers were dropped over Speyer on the West Bank of the Rhine south of Mainz, by which time the Path Finder element had already fallen behind schedule by some margin on what was a dark night with clear skies and no moon. Thick haze in the target area blotted out ground detail, but the leading Path Finder crews established their positions by H2S and dropped red TIs and 1,000 pounders at 23.16, sixteen minutes after the attack had been due to begin. The TIs fell around eight hundred yards from aiming-point C and were backed up by greens from other aircraft. The late arrival of the Path Finders forced the main force crews to orbit, and many bombed on the first markers, with the result that the main weight of the attack fell into northern and western districts. The consensus was of a moderately effective raid, which was confirmed by local reports of damage to three hundred buildings and these sources also revealed that bombs had fallen onto other communities and open country up to seven miles to the north of the city.

Following the long round-trip, the crews were given little to do during the day on the 26th, but F/Sgt Rothschild height and load-tested one of the new Mk III Stirlings and managed to wring

20,000 feet out of it. Cologne was selected for its third raid of the month that night and a force of 427 aircraft was assembled from all heavy groups, 3 Group detailing forty Stirlings and three Wellingtons, seven of the former belonging to 75(NZ) Squadron. They departed Newmarket either side of 19.00 with F/L Sandeman the senior pilot on duty, but Sgts Davey and Thompson failed to complete their sorties because of engine issues. The bomber stream made its way to the target via the Scheldt estuary, the crews of the heavy brigade unaware that three of the four Mosquitos had dropped out with technical problems leaving just one to mark the target with a red TI. The skies over Cologne were clear, but haze and smoke impaired the vertical visibility and most main force crews were drawn to the target area by red and green TIs and the burst of incendiaries. Many explosions and fires were observed, the glow from which remained visible to some for a hundred miles into the return flight. A post-raid analysis revealed fires in the city centre and decoys to the west of the city, and bombing photos showed fire tracks and smoke that suggested an effective raid. Some Path Finder bombing photos depicted open countryside between eight thousand and six thousand yards west of the aiming-point and an assessment confirmed that a large proportion of the effort had fallen to the south-west of the city, with perhaps, only a quarter landing in the built-up area, where it inflicted much damage upon housing, minor industry and public buildings. However, with Oboe about to be unleashed on all targets within its range, the picture would soon change and the ratio of successful to unsuccessful operations would swing decisively in the Command's favour. A combat report filed by P/O Lowe and crew in BK646 AA-N described being attacked by two enemy aircraft over Holland on the way home, but that return fire and evasive tactics had been successful in evading them.

While the main raid went ahead at Cologne, other aircraft were sent mining in the Nectarine gardens off the Frisians, and the squadron contributed four Stirlings with F/L Rothwell the senior pilot on duty and undertaking his first sortie since joining the squadron. The senior officer on duty was, in fact, S/L Fowler, flying as bomb-aimer with the crew of F/Sgt Rothschild. The other two new captains were W/O John Arthur Ernest Walsh RNZAF and F/Sgt Kevin Frederick Debenham, RNZAF. The quartet took off at 18.25 and found favourable weather conditions in the target area, which enabled all to carry out their briefs, before returning home safely.

The night of the 27/28th was devoted to mining operations from the Frisians to the south-west of France, and 75(NZ) Squadron contributed seven crews, two assigned to the Furze garden off Saint-Jean-de-Luz, close to the Franco/Spanish border, one to the Deodar garden in the Gironde Estuary and four to the Nectarines. They set off together either side of 18.30 with Sgt Davey and P/O Bennett having the furthest to travel, but the former turned back with engine trouble when ninety minutes out and jettisoned his mines "safe". The latter reached the target area to find six-tenths cloud and poor visibility in the form of sea mist and returned after eight hours aloft having planted his vegetables in the briefed location. Sgt Dalzell completed his sortie to the Gironde without incident, and F/L Rothwell led the Frisian-bound contingent also to a successful conclusion in good conditions, although they had to run the gauntlet of heavy and accurate predicted flak in the target area.

Having effectively wiped the town of Lorient from the map, the Command now turned its attention upon St-Nazaire in accordance with the January directive and assembled a force of 437 aircraft on the 28th. 3 Group detailed fifty-three Stirlings and four Wellingtons, six of the former from 75(NZ) Squadron, which departed Newmarket between 18.15 and 18.43 with S/L Fowler the senior officer present, flying as bomb-aimer with F/Sgt Rothschild, and F/L Sandeman the senior pilot on duty. Crews had learned at briefing that three Oboe Mosquitos would be operating to mark singly with green TIs at ten-minute intervals, which the Path Finder Halifaxes and Lancasters would back up with greens also. The main force arrived in the target area in clear skies but only fair visibility because of haze, those in the rear-guard drawn on for the final forty miles by the fires already burning fiercely. They delivered their 1,000 pounders and mixed incendiaries into the target area, adding to the extensive damage inflicted upon the town and port area, and a local report suggested that 60% of the town had been destroyed in this one raid.

It had been a busy month for the squadron, characterized to some extent by serviceability problems, particularly with engines and eighteen operations had produced 103 sorties for the loss of four Stirlings and crews.

March 1943

Harris was about to embark on the first major campaign of the year, and the first for which the Command was adequately equipped and truly prepared. Since joining the Path Finder Force in the previous August, 109 Squadron had been carrying out magnificent work under W/C Hal Bufton, preparing the Oboe blind-bombing device for operational use and marrying it to the Mosquito. The endeavours were about to bear fruit and would finally negate the Ruhr's protective cloak of industrial haze, first, however, the crews had two major operations to negotiate, beginning with Berlin on the night of the 1/2nd. A force of 302 aircraft was assembled made up of 156 Lancasters, eighty-six Halifaxes and sixty Stirlings, with 3 Group responsible for thirty-eight of the Stirlings and 75(NZ) Squadron eight of them including two of the new Mk III variant in the hands of F/L Rothwell and P/O Bennett. The crews learned at briefing that six Path Finder Halifaxes and ten Stirlings equipped with H2S were to drop a "landmark" yellow TI each at Butzow, situated some eighty miles north of Berlin, which were to be backed up by seven Halifaxes and sixteen Lancasters. The "special" (H2S-equipped) aircraft were then to release red warning flares twelve miles short of the target followed by red TIs on the aiming-point at the time-on-target of 22.00, which the seven Halifaxes and sixteen Lancasters would back-up with green TIs. As always, the plan was based on a forecast of favourable conditions, in the absence of which, skymarkers would substitute for TIs.

The 75(NZ) Squadron element departed Newmarket between 18.30 and 19.00 with F/Ls Rothwell and Sandeman the senior pilots on duty and S/L Fowler accompanying the Rothschild crew. Each was carrying 1,000lb and 500lb bombs and 30lb and 4lb incendiaries, not all of which was destined to reach the target as the crews of F/L Sandeman and Sgt Davey turned back early, one with intercom problems and the other with an unserviceable turret. The remaining six crews pressed on to cross the Schleswig-Holstein peninsula and approach Berlin from the Baltic and find on arrival a small amount of cloud but good visibility, which enabled them to identify ground detail and drop their bombs on the Path Finder red and green skymarkers. This operation would highlight the flaws in the early version of the H2S device when seeking an aiming-point over a massive urban sprawl like Berlin. It would take experience and great skill on the part of the H2S navigators to interpret the jumble of indistinct images on their screens, and on this night, the marking fell predominantly over the south-western districts, well short of the city centre. It was clear that the marking had been scattered over a wide area, with a particular concentration over the southern half of the city, despite which, some returning crews claimed exultantly that the concentrated bombing had eclipsed even the thousand bomber raid on Cologne, with the glow of fires visible from Bremen, some two hundred miles away. A post-raid analysis based on bombing photos revealed the attack to have been spread over an area of a hundred square miles, but because of the increasing bomb tonnages now being carried, more damage was inflicted on the city than on any previous raid. 875 buildings, mostly houses, were destroyed and twenty factories seriously damaged, along with railway workshops in the Tempelhof district. Seventeen aircraft failed to return, four of them Stirlings, and it is interesting to analyse the percentage loss rate of each type on this night, as it would be an accurate indicator of their future fortunes. The statistics revealed the loss rate of Lancasters to be 4.5%, and those of the Halifaxes and Stirlings to be 7%. P/O Bailey and crew, who were in BF443 AA-V, reported a brief skirmish with a Me110, at which rear gunner, Sgt Thompson, opened fire at 200 yards with a one second burst but made no claim.

It had been a challenging night for Geoff Rothwell and crew in BF456 AA-J, who were intercepted over Fehmarn Island in the Baltic by a twin-engine enemy fighter. They were able to shake it off and make their way to Berlin, where they delivered their bombs on a north-south heading before turning to the west and adopting a direct course for home south of Hannover to the Dutch coast. They had reached the outskirts of Osnabrück at 13,500 feet when both gunners spotted another fighter manoeuvring to attack from 400 yards astern. Each turret fired a two-second burst, and the enemy was seen to dive away. Almost immediately, the Stirling was bracketed by flak and hit by shrapnel, which shattered the windscreen and severely holed the fuselage but missed the crew and anything else vital to the aircraft's ability to remain airborne. Twenty-eight minutes later, when north of Münster, a Ju88 was seen on the port bow and slightly above, which the front and mid-upper gunners engaged with a two-second burst at maximum range. The night fighter was seen to dive away steeply, and a few seconds later a red glow appeared beneath the cloud, before slowly disappearing from sight. They diverted to Stradishall, where a safe landing was carried out at 03.00, and they were eventually able to claim the Ju88 as a "probable".

Hamburg was posted as the target for the night of the 3/4th and a force of 417 aircraft assembled, which included forty-two Stirlings and four Wellingtons of 3 Group. Nine 75(NZ) Squadron Stirlings were loaded with a selection of 2,000lb and 500lb bombs and 30lb and 4lb incendiaries, while three others, including those to be occupied by the debutant crews of Sgt Richard Otway French RNZAF and Sgt Raymond Cyril Going RNZAF, had mines winched into their bomb bays for delivery into the Nectarine I garden off the Frisian Island of Terschelling. After one Hamburg-bound aircraft dropped out with a burst tail-wheel tyre, the remaining eight took off between 18.20 and 19.00 with S/L Allcock the senior pilot on duty. The ORB mentions one aircraft returning early with a malfunctioning rear turret, but the flight duration of each is consistent with the operation being completed. They headed out above ten-tenths cloud, but otherwise, excellent weather conditions, which would hold firm for the entire operation and provide clear skies over both Hamburg and the garden area off Terschelling. Visibility in the target area was fairly good with some haze and the wide River Elbe provided strong H2S returns, despite which, some Path Finder navigators misinterpreted what they saw on their screens and a batch of red and green TIs was released well to the west of the planned aiming-point and onto the town of Wedel, situated on the northern bank of the Elbe thirteen miles downstream of Hamburg city centre. To the crews high above, everything appeared normal, with cones of searchlights and intense light and heavy flak, and many bombed on the Path Finder markers assuming them to be accurate. Meanwhile, other Path Finders had identified and marked the intended aiming point, and main force crews had bombed the central area encompassing the Hamburg-America landing stage, the Blohm & Voss shipyards, the Binnen-Alster Lake and the main railway station, and on return reported an apparently successful raid, which left a pall of rising black smoke and a hundred fires to be dealt with before the city's Feurwehr could go to the aid of their neighbour.

While this operation was in progress, the gardeners had arrived off the Frisians, having departed Newmarket either side of 20.00 and had delivered their mines into the assigned locations in excellent weather conditions. BF398 AA-F came through a brief encounter with a Ju88 on the way home in which shots were exchanged but no damage sustained, and Sgt French and crew landed safely. Veteran Stirling N6123 AA-Q "Queenie" did not return with the crew of Sgt Going RNZAF, which contained two other members of the RNZAF, and no trace of them or the Stirling was ever found. Sgt Going came from Maromaku in the north of New Zealand, and three of his younger siblings were to become famous for their rugby exploits, in particular Sid, the legendary All Black halfback.

The decks were now cleared for the opening of the Ruhr offensive, which, over the ensuing months, would change the face of bombing and provide for the enemy an indication of the evolving power of the Command. This was a momentous occasion, a culmination of all that had gone before during three and a half years of Bomber Command operations. The backs-to-the-wall desperation of 1940, the tentative almost token offensives of 1941, the treading water and gradual metamorphosis under Harris in 1942, when failures still far outnumbered successes, had all been leading to this night, from which point would begin the calculated and systematic dismantling of Germany's industrial and population centres. The only shining light during these dark years had been the quality and spirit of the aircrews, and this had never faltered.

To the residents of bomber stations from County Durham to Cambridgeshire, the 5th of March probably felt no different from any other day on which a major operation was posted. By its end, however, Germany's industrial heartland had lost its invulnerability to Bomber Command attacks, and notice had been served, that the Ruhr Valley was to be taken apart piece-by-piece. The campaign was to begin at Harris's nemesis, Essen, and a force of 442 aircraft included a contribution from 3 Group of fifty-four Stirlings and four 115 Squadron Lancasters, nine of the former provided by 75(NZ) Squadron. The main force element was to bomb in three waves, Halifaxes first, followed by Wellingtons and Stirlings with Lancasters bringing up the rear. Six Path Finder Halifax and fifteen Lancaster crews had been briefed to drop a warning yellow TI each when fifteen miles from the target, before backing up the Mosquitos' red TIs on the aiming-point with greens, and the force was to adopt the southern route to the central Ruhr, making landfall over the Scheldt estuary.

The 75(NZ) Squadron element departed Newmarket between 19.10 and 19.30 with S/L Allcock the senior pilot on duty and S/L Fowler flying as usual with the Rothschild crew, but matters instantly went awry for P/O Bennett after BK647's port-inner engine seized as it took to the air, and the Stirling, AA-M, had to be crash-landed. Fortunately, the bomb load did not detonate, and the crew was able to walk away from the wreckage. Sgt Dalzell and crew turned back with engine trouble before reaching the coast, and they were just one of eleven 3 Group early returns in an unusually high number of fifty-six "boomerangs" representing 13% of the force. Critically, among them were three of the eight 109 Squadron Mosquitos, whose markers would provide the initial reference for their colleagues in the heavy marker aircraft. The spearhead of the bomber stream arrived in the target area to be greeted by a thin layer of stratocumulus between 16,000 and 18,000 feet, which blotted out ground detail but allowed the red TIs on the aiming point to be visible. This was the game-changer, the fact that a "blind" attack was reliant entirely upon electronics and made irrelevant the need to identify ground detail. The 75(NZ) Squadron Stirlings were carrying 2,000lb and 1,000lb bombs with 30lb and 4lb incendiaries, which were used to good effect and contributed to a highly successful outcome. The overwhelming impression was of a concentrated attack, which left many fires burning and a glow in the sky reported by some to be visible from the North Sea homebound. Some reported a terrific explosion at 21.18, which lit up the sky, and a pall of smoke hanging above the dull, red centre of the resulting conflagration. Twenty-four crews reported attacking alternative targets, and together with the early returns, this reduced the numbers attacking the primary target to 362 aircraft. Post-raid reconnaissance revealed the destruction of 3,018 houses in 160 acres of devastation, and fifty-three buildings had been hit within the giant Krupp complex. This stunning victory was gained at a cost of fourteen aircraft, and a message of congratulations from the C-in-C was received on participating stations on the following day.

A week would elapse before the next operation to a Ruhr target, and, in the meantime, Harris switched his focus to three important industrial cities in southern Germany, beginning with Nuremberg on the night of the 8/9th. Such operations were beyond the range of Oboe, and thus, success would rely upon the skill of the H2S operators to accurately interpret what they were seeing on their cathode-ray tubes. Crews learned at briefing that zero hour was to be 23.15, and that three Path Finder Stirlings and two Halifaxes were to drop illumination flares across the target in two sticks by H2S, to be followed by six Stirlings and three Halifaxes dropping green TIs on the aiming-point, also by H2S, and employing additional flares if necessary. The remaining Path Finder markers were to back up with green TIs, unless cloud negated the illuminator flares, in which case, red TIs were to be dropped by the H2S-equipped aircraft and backed up by the others with greens. All Path Finder aircraft were to deliver yellow route markers on the way in and out. A force of 335 aircraft included fifty-four 3 Group Stirlings, nine representing 75(NZ) Squadron, which departed Newmarket between 19.35 and 20.00, with F/L Rothwell first away and S/L Allcock the senior pilot on duty. They were carrying a load of 2,000, 1,000 and 500 pounders with incendiaries, which F/L Rothwell jettisoned as starboard-inner engine failure forced him to turn back when deep into France.

The Path Finders reached the target to find clear skies but also ground haze and extreme darkness, which seemed to impede their ability to locate the city centre blind using H2S, although equipment failure also played its part in the widely scattered nature of the illumination and marking. The backers-up went in at 18,000 to 20,000 feet between 23.27 and 23.38, each to deliver a 2,000 pounder and 504 x 4lb incendiaries and thirty-six of the 30lb variety. They were followed by the main force crews, who experienced the same difficulty in identifying ground detail, and allowed themselves to be guided to the aiming-point by a few red and green TIs, which appeared to lack concentration and soon burned out. The marking and bombing spread along a ten-mile-long corridor, which resulted in half of the bomb loads falling outside of the city, but returning crews described many fires and one large explosion emanating from the centre of the target seen from a hundred miles into the return journey. On return, 83 Squadron's S/L Cooke reported a cookie and yellow TIs being jettisoned east of Heilbronn, some forty miles short of the target, and being accurately backed-up by other Path Finders. Inevitably, this would have drawn off other bomb loads, and local sources confirmed the marking and bombing of Nuremberg to have been spread along a ten-mile stretch, half of it falling short of the city boundaries, while the rest destroyed six hundred buildings and damaged fourteen hundred others, including a number of important war-industry factories.

A modest eight aircraft failed to return, half of them Stirlings and absent from its dispersal at Newmarket on the following morning was BF437 AA-L, which was brought down a dozen miles north-north-east of Karlsruhe with no survivors from the crew of Sgt Charles Davey RNZAF, who was the only Kiwi on board. BK646 AA-N was attacked by an enemy night-fighter near Saarbrücken on the way home, and some cannon shells found their way into the cockpit. One of them exploded near the second pilot's leg, wounding him and inflicting some facial cuts on P/O Lowe RAF, the pilot, but the damaged Stirling returned safely after a trip of seven-and-a-half hours. Many years later P/O Lowe would become ACM Sir Douglas Lowe, GCB, DFC, AFC, RAF.

On the following day, preparations were put in hand to return to southern Germany to attack the city of Munich, situated deep in the Bavarian mountains of south-eastern Germany, a round-trip of more than 1,200 miles. A force of 264 aircraft was assembled, which included thirty-one 3 Group Stirlings, five of them provided by 75(NZ) Squadron. Three others from the squadron, including first-timer P/O Kelvin Havelock Green Groves RNZAF, were assigned to mining duties in the Deodar garden in the Gironde Estuary, and they departed Newmarket first either side of 19.30. F/Sgt Debenham and crew returned after two hours with engine problems, leaving the others to continue on to south-western France, where they found the target area beneath ten-tenths cloud and in poor visibility. They delivered their mines as briefed in an area that was well-defended by flak batteries, which were protecting the previously mentioned oil-storage facilities at Pauillac, Blaye, Bec-D'Ambes and in Bordeaux itself. Sgt French's BF398 AA-F sustained damage from a battery at Blaye, but he and P/O Groves and crew returned safely home.

Those participating in the main event were informed at briefing of the plan of attack, which called for white TIs to be dropped by the Path Finders as route markers to aid the main force crews, and white and green flares over the northern tip of the Ammersee, a large lake situated some twenty miles to the west-south-west of the city centre, which the 5 Group crews in particular would use as the starting point for their time-and-distance runs. Nine Stirlings and four Halifaxes were to ground mark by H2S with red TIs at the same time as releasing white flares, and four Lancasters were to drop flares also, if required, and then join with eleven Lancasters and four Halifaxes to back up with green TIs. The 75(NZ) Squadron element took off either side of 20.30 led by the two flight commanders, but one crew, believed to be that of Sgt Buck, lost its way and after futile attempts to get back on track, abandoned the sortie. The leading Path Finders were greeted by clear skies and good visibility but watched a layer of stratus cloud approach at 19,000 feet and begin to drift across the city at 00.15, which prevented them from establishing a visual reference to confirm the H2S data. However, the remaining four Kiwi crews arrived at the target to find excellent visibility, which enabled them to identify ground detail and deliver their all-incendiary loads accurately, guided by the red and green skymarkers. A massive explosion was witnessed in the vicinity of the marshalling yards to the west of the city centre at 00.17, followed by another at 00.25, which lit up the sky for twenty seconds, illuminating an area of ground with a ten-mile radius that was described by some as the largest they had experienced. Yet another particularly large detonation occurred at 00.43 and the burgeoning fires produced a large pall of smoke that rose above the city to 10,000 feet as the bomber force withdrew to the west, and all but a relatively modest eight would make it back.

A post-raid analysis concluded that a strong wind had pushed the attack into the western half of the city, where 291 buildings had been destroyed and 660 severely damaged. The aero-engine assembly shop at the B.M.W factory was put out of action for six weeks, and many other industrial concerns also lost vital production. Many other industrial premises were also hit, as were military, retail, public and cultural buildings, and this was achieved for the loss of eight aircraft. F/L Rothwell and crew had a close call when both outer-engines cut as they were on final approach to land, and they had to carry out a forced-landing on Newmarket Heath.

The trio of operations to destinations in southern Germany concluded with the highly industrial city of Stuttgart, for which a force of 314 aircraft assembled on the 11th included forty-three Stirlings belonging to 3 Group. The briefing of eight 75(NZ) Squadron crews at Newmarket revealed that the Path Finders were to deliver flares and red TIs by H2S across the aiming point, to be backed up with green TIs visually. The Kiwi Stirlings were loaded with 30lb and 4lb incendiaries and took off either side of 20.00 with S/L Allcock the senior pilot on duty. They adopted the familiar route across France, before entering Germany near Strasbourg with Stuttgart fifty miles straight ahead. The visibility in the target area was found to be excellent as the lead Path Finders arrived, already behind schedule because of wrongly forecast winds. The arrival of the main force coincided with the expiration of many of the Path Finder TIs on the ground, which left the way clear for dummy TIs to lure the bombing away from the city centre. In this endeavour the enemy was largely successful, although, to the bomb-aimers high above, the green TIs appeared to be legitimate and were bombed by the remaining main force crews. The 75(NZ) Squadron element reached the target area intact and deposited their incendiaries in the centre of the city, where large fires became concentrated. One unidentified aircraft from the squadron was held in a searchlight cone for two minutes, but managed to escape without being hit, and all returned safely, confident in the success of the raid. It emerged later that most of the effort had been wasted in open country, but the south-western suburbs of Vaihingen and Kaltental were hit and 118 buildings, mostly houses, destroyed in what was a disappointing outcome, which cost eleven aircraft.

A week after the spectacular success of the opening round of the Ruhr offensive at Essen, the same city was selected to host round two. A force of 457 aircraft was made ready on the 12th, of which forty Stirlings and four Lancasters were provided by 3 Group, 75(NZ) Squadron responsible for seven of the former. Briefings revealed that the force was to adopt the northern route to the Ruhr, and sixteen Path Finders were to ground mark the town of Dorsten with white TIs as a track guide. With a time-on-target for the Path Finders of 21.15, they would then back up the Mosquito-borne Oboe red TIs with greens to provide the main force crews with a solid aiming point. The Kiwis departed Newmarket between 19.40 and 19.55 with P/Os Bailey, Bennett and Thompson the senior captains, but P/O Bailey and crew were forced to return early in BF443 AA-V with an unserviceable rear turret. The others all reached the target under clear skies but found the visibility to be compromised to an extent by haze and smoke, and intense searchlight and flak activity made it an uncomfortable place to spend time. As was the case a week earlier, and for all future attacks on Ruhr targets, visibility was no longer a consideration, as Oboe allowed the Path Finders to mark an area within the Krupp complex. Large fires lit up the entire area, and a number of explosions were reported to have emanated from the munitions plant. Post-raid reconnaissance showed that the bombing had centred on the Krupp-dominated area of the city, where even more damage was inflicted than a week earlier and a further five hundred houses were also destroyed. The loss of twenty-three aircraft reminded the crews that success at the Ruhr would not be gained cheaply, but for the third operation running to a German target, the squadron kept a clean sheet, and indeed, there would be no further losses during the month.

The ensuing nine days had seen operations posted for Berlin, Augsburg and St-Nazaire, but all had been cancelled, while persistent fog had restricted training. It was the 22nd before a briefing took place for an operation that actually went ahead, while out on the dispersals on 3 Group stations, fifty-nine Stirlings and seven Lancasters were being made ready. Nine 75(NZ) Squadron Stirlings were loaded with 30lb and 4lb incendiaries to deliver on the town of St-Nazaire in compliance with the January directive. As happened so frequently before every operation, aircraft would become unserviceable at the last moment, and just eight Stirlings departed Newmarket either side of 19.00 with S/L Fowler the senior captain on duty, flying as always with F/Sgt Rothschild's crew. They must have been very close to the target when a recall signal was sent out to 3 Group aircraft at 21.00, to which all but a handful of crews responded. Concern had been growing over the landing conditions at 3 Group stations and it had been decided to get them back on the ground rather than risk accidents.

On the following evening P/O Tolley and crew were sent mining in the Nectarine I garden off the Frisian Island of Texel, departing at 19.32 and returning at 23.11 to report a successful and uneventful sortie. Operations were posted to Kiel, Cologne and Duisburg over the next three days, the first two falling by the wayside, while the last-mentioned, the third raid of the Ruhr campaign, went ahead after the Stirling element had been withdrawn. Despite the commitment of 455 aircraft and the use of Oboe, it was not a successful operation, largely because five of the nine Oboe Mosquitos turned back with equipment malfunctions and a sixth was forced to ditch in the North Sea.

Orders were received on stations across the Command on the 27th to prepare for a trip to the "Big City" that night, for which a force of 396 aircraft, including a 3 Group contribution of sixty-six Stirlings and six Lancasters, was assembled. At briefings, the Path Finder crews were told of their part in the plan, which required eleven Stirlings and eight Halifaxes to drop green route marker flares and yellow warning flares by H2S, before marking the aiming-point with red TIs for two Stirlings, five Halifaxes and twenty-one Lancasters to back up with green TIs. In the event of cloud blotting out the ground, skymarking would be employed. 75(NZ) Squadron's eleven Stirlings took off between 19.35 and 19.50 with S/L Allcock the senior pilot on duty. The route took them into enemy territory between the Frisian Islands of Texel and Vlieland, and then on a course a little north of Hannover to a point to the south-west of the capital for the run-in to the intended city-centre aiming-point. W/O Walsh turned back when ninety minutes out because of an inability to maintain altitude, and his was one of eleven 3

Group early returns, while the others pressed on to approach the capital from the south-west. The Path Finders were reliant upon H2S and established two areas of marking, both well short, and the main force had little choice but to aim for them. There was the usual discrepancy in the reported cloud state of zero to nine-tenths as the main force crews carried out their attacks predominantly from between 16,500 and 19,000 feet either side of 23.00, before returning to report moderate flak, extensive searchlight activity and many fires within the city. The truth was, that the nearest bombs to the city centre were plotted five miles short, and the creep-back resulted in most falling between seven and seventeen miles along the line of approach. According to local sources, 25% of the bombs were "duds", and if true, this was another reason behind the lack of serious damage, but at least the losses were modest at nine aircraft. At debriefing, F/L Rothwell reported delivering his load onto red and green target indicators (TIs) from a very low 8,500 feet in the face of a spirited flak defence and landed safely after a round-trip of seven hours and forty-four minutes to hand back his flak-holed BF451 AA-Z to the tender care of its ground crew.

On the following night, two freshman crews took off either side of 19.30 to join with twenty-eight others from 3 Group in an overall force of 321 aircraft for the latest raid on the port of St-Nazaire. First-time captain Sgt Donald Gordon McCaskill RNZAF and P/O Tolley successfully delivered their all-incendiary loads into the target area and returned safely from what had been uneventful sorties.

The month's final operation was posted on the 29th, when the red tape on the briefing-room wall maps ended again at Berlin. A force of 329 aircraft was made ready, of which sixty Stirlings and eight Lancasters were detailed by 3 Group, while a main force of 149 Wellingtons continued the Ruhr campaign at Bochum. The plan for the main event required all Path Finder aircraft to drop yellow route markers at predetermined points, and the marker crews to illuminate the Müggelsee, to the south-east of Berlin, with sticks of white flares and bundles of green flares with red stars by H2S. They were then to carrying out a DR run to the aiming-point to deliver red TIs, and the backers-up were to follow a similar procedure. Ten 75(NZ) Squadron crews were briefed, but when the time came to take-off between 21.05 and 21.30, only eight Stirlings were serviceable, and five other 3 Group aircraft also dropped out.

The route to Berlin on this night took the bomber stream further north than two nights earlier, to cross Denmark's Jutland peninsula, but bad weather in the form of heavy ice-bearing cloud and static electricity extending from the North Sea to the Baltic forced many crews to turn for home, among them a massive seventeen from 3 Group and an alarming twenty-four from 4 Group. F/L Rothwell had been the senior pilot on duty, but he and his crew and those of F/Sgt Debenham and P/O Bennett were among the "boomerangs". P/O French and crew were in BK602 AA-R and were attacked by a Me110, at which both gunners returned fire before they managed to escape. Damage to the aircraft was recorded as eight strikes by machine gun bullets on the port main plane and a cannon shell through the tail plane and rudder. The others pressed on through the front and reached the "Big City" to find good visibility that enabled them to identify the Müggelsee to the south-east as a reference point from which to run in on the aiming-point. Inaccurately forecast winds may have contributed to the Path Finders marking an area some six miles to the south of the planned aiming point, and the main force arrived late, by which time some of the markers had burned themselves out. The main force crews bombed in the face of a heavy searchlight and flak defence and set off home in the belief that the fires they had left behind, the glow from which was still visible from 150 miles away, indicated that an effective attack had been delivered. In fact, most of the bombing had been wasted in open country to the south-east of the city, and an accurate figure for damage was not forthcoming, although 148 houses were believed to have been destroyed in the suburbs.

While the bombers had been outbound to Berlin, debutant Sgt Walter Donald Whitehead RNZAF and crew carried out a freshman mining sortie in one of the nectarine gardens off the Frisians. They returned after five hours to report a successful sortie and were tucked up in bed by the time their colleagues began to return shortly after 05.00. While operations beyond the range of Oboe were still something of a lottery, the device had demonstrated great promise for the Ruhr campaign.

During the course of the month the squadron carried out fifteen operations, dispatching ninety-one sorties for the loss of three Stirlings and two crews.

April 1943

April saw the establishment of a C Flight, which, with the increase to twenty-four aircraft IE (immediate equipment) plus 3 IR (in reserve), the improved serviceability of the Stirling and the efficiency of the ground crews, would enable the squadron to achieve a consistently high sortie rate. The new flight was declared "operationally fit" by the 1st of April, but a temporary flight commander was needed while F/L Richard Broadbent RNZAF, who had arrived on the 23rd of March, was away undergoing Stirling Conversion. P/O Lowe was promoted to acting flight lieutenant rank to lead the flight until Broadbent returned.

In his 2005 memoir "The Man with Nine Lives", F/L Rothwell remembers that he himself was nominated as C Flight commander. However, late in March, possibly on the 31st, he was apparently informed by A/C Andrew "Square" McKee, that it was the policy of the New Zealand government to fill senior posts with New Zealanders, and that consequently, he was to be posted from the squadron with immediate effect. Rothwell was dismayed and stunned at the news but was offered the consolation of keeping his crew. It seems unlikely that such a policy existed, as the incumbent flight commanders, S/Ls Fowler and Allcock, one of the next flight commanders to be appointed, S/L Appleton, and the current commanding officer, W/C Lane, were all Englishmen. Either way, 75(NZ) Squadron's undoubted loss was 218 Squadron's gain, as S/L Rothwell was soon appointed A Flight commander under his old friend, the straight-talking Australian, W/C Don Saville, and was back on operations, his forty-seventh, on the night of the 4/5th. Geoff Rothwell would be posted to a training role in July, for a frustrating and unhappy spell, before returning to operations in May 1944 as a flight commander with 138 Squadron, one of two top-secret SOE units operating out of Tempsford in Bedfordshire. In September, when about to be handed command of the squadron on the posting of W/C Wilf Burnett, his Stirling collided with the cable of a drifting balloon off Vlieland and crash-landed on the Island, where he and the surviving crew members were taken into captivity.

S/L Broadbent would arrive back at Newmarket on the 17th and received his promotion to squadron leader rank on the 25th to fill the C Flight commander's post. He had spent nineteen months at an O.T.U., during which time he undertook three sorties to add to the full tour of operations he had completed with 40 Squadron.

April would prove to be the least rewarding month of the spring/summer offensive, largely because of the number of operations mounted to targets beyond the range of Oboe. It began with a flourish, however, and in the absence of the Stirling brigade, with the third successful tilt at Essen, which took place on the night of the 3/4th. Ten 75(NZ) Squadron crews were called to briefing on the 4th to learn of that night's operation to Kiel and they would probably have been excited to hear that it was to be conducted by 577 aircraft, the largest non-1,000 force of front-line aircraft thus far in the war, although sadly, it would be an inauspicious start to the month's operations for the Kiwis. They were part of a 3 Group force of seventy-six Stirlings and eleven Lancasters, whose crews learned at briefing that the plan of attack called for a time-on-target of 23.00 and for yellow TIs to be dropped by the Path Finders as route markers, before the H2S marker crews in ten Stirlings and six Halifaxes illuminated the aiming-point with flares and marked it with red TIs. Two Stirlings, five Halifaxes and fifteen Lancasters were to back up with green TIs, leaving two of each type to bomb with the main force. The Newmarket brigade took off between 20.30 and 20.45, each carrying all-incendiary bomb loads, S/L Allcock the senior pilot on duty and Sgt John Webb RAFVR and crew operating together for the first time. The ORB is confusing, stating that one aircraft failed to take-off and four others returned early with engine trouble, when in fact, all ten have a recorded take-off time and six a landing time consistent with completing the operation. Sgt Webb landed at 22.50, followed by P/O Tolley ten minutes later, P/O Thompson at 23.45 and Sgt Dalzell at ten minutes after midnight, leaving six to continue on via the Schleswig-Holstein peninsula to the western Baltic. The bomber stream encountered ten-tenths cloud from the midpoint of the North Sea at 3 degrees east, which would persist for the remainder of the operation, topping out over the target at 8,000 feet. The marker element arrived on time, but the failure of H2S equipment reduced the numbers and the red and green TIs could be seen only dimly through the clouds. It seems likely that strong winds caused the skymarkers to drift, and this along with decoy fire sites conspired to draw the main weight of the attack away from the town. In BF412 AA-Y, S/L Fowler and crew were shadowed by a Ju88, at which all three gunners fired without reply, and this left them to speculate that it was a decoy, although no other enemy aircraft were seen. Returning crews were unable to offer an assessment of the raid, other than to report the glow of fires beneath the cloud. Local reports confirm that damage was light and restricted to the destruction of eleven houses, which was a massive disappointment in view of the effort expended, and the only consolation for the Command was that losses amounted to a little over 2% of the force.

The sea lanes around the Biscay ports were targeted by forty-seven miners on the night of the 6/7th, with two freshman crews provided by 75(NZ) Squadron assigned to the Deodar garden in the Gironde Estuary. Sgts Keith Halliburton RNZAF and Whitehead departed Newmarket at 21.00 and planted their vegetables successfully and unopposed in the briefed locations in excellent weather conditions, before returning safely home.

The Ruhr offensive continued at Duisburg on the night of the 8/9th, for which a force of 392 aircraft was made ready, forty-four of them representing 3 Group. Crews learned at briefing that ten Oboe Mosquitos would provide the initial marking, backed up by the Path Finder heavy brigade consisting of four Stirlings, twenty Lancasters and eight Halifaxes. 75(NZ) Squadron loaded nine Stirlings with 1,000 pounders and incendiaries and sent them on their way between 21.20 and 21.55 with no senior pilots on duty. Time-on-target was set for 23.15, before which, the ten Oboe Mosquitos were to drop red warning flares and then greens with red stars and green TIs over the aiming-point. If the weather conditions permitted, one Stirling, seven Halifaxes and fourteen Lancasters would back up with red TIs, while the remaining 8 Group aircraft supported the main force. The bomber stream had to climb through ten-tenths ice-bearing cloud and electrical storms over the North Sea and reach 12,000 feet before breaking into clear air, which proved impossible for fifteen of the 3 Group Stirlings. Five of the Newmarket brigade recorded landing times between 23.15 and 00.35, and BK770 AA-L was homebound over Norfolk when a message was received from W/O John Walsh RNZAF and crew at 01.10. Nothing more was heard, until news came through that a Stirling had crashed shortly after that time at Brassingham, three miles west-north-west of Diss, exploding on impact and killing all on board. This was the first loss by the squadron of a Mk III Stirling. The cloud over Duisburg extended to 20,500 feet, and for whatever reason, Oboe failed to provide the main force crews with anything more than the hint of red and green TIs on which to bomb, before returning with nothing of use to pass on at debriefing. Local sources confirmed a widely scattered raid, which hit at least fifteen other Ruhr locations and destroyed just forty buildings in Duisburg at a cost to the Command of nineteen aircraft.

While this operation was in progress, Sgt McCaskill and crew successfully carried out a mining sortie in the Deodar garden in the Gironde Estuary.

A 5 Group main force returned to Duisburg on the following night to find similar weather conditions and Oboe again failed to facilitate a successful assault, resulting in a disappointing raid that managed to destroy just fifty houses in return for the loss of nineteen aircraft or 7.7%. The city would continue to enjoy a relatively charmed life for another five weeks.

Frankfurt was posted as the destination on the 10th for a force of 502 aircraft, of which the 144 Wellingtons would represent the most populous type, demonstrating that this trusty old warhorse still had an important part to play in Bomber Command operations. The plan was standard for a target beyond the range of Oboe and required eleven Stirlings and six Halifaxes to drop yellow TIs as route markers by H2S, followed by preliminary warning flares, all of which were to be backed up by two Stirlings, ten Halifaxes and seventeen Lancasters. Cloud conditions permitting, the aiming-point was then to be marked by red TIs on H2S, and if not, by green flares with red stars and a white flare, with appropriate backing up with green TIs or coloured flares. 3 Group contributed ninety aircraft, a dozen of the Stirlings provided by 75(NZ) Squadron, which were led off from Newmarket by F/Sgt Rothschild and crew at 23.55, and all were safely in the air by 00.20 on a night when F/L Lowe was the senior pilot on duty. The ORB stated that three of the nine 3 Group early returns had been unable to maintain height, and the crews of Sgts Dalzell and Whitehead were certainly among them.

The bomber stream adopted the usual course to this region of Germany, following the line of the Franco/Belgian frontier to cross into Germany on an east-north-easterly heading north of Saarbrücken. The H2S marker crews arrived in the target area to be confronted by ten-tenths cloud with tops at between 8,000 and 12,000 feet but found that their red TIs were visible and opted not to sky mark. This was fine in the early stages, until it became impossible to distinguish the genuine TIs from decoys among the incendiaries and searchlights, and the backers up experienced great difficulty in establishing an aiming-point. Largely ineffective heavy and light flak was operating in concert with searchlights, and BF455 AA-Y was unlucky enough to be hit and damaged over the target, before being chased at some point on the way home by enemy night-fighters. Evasive action caused excessive fuel consumption, which was becoming critical as F/Sgt Rothschild and crew began the Channel crossing, but textbook radio procedure had alerted the rescue services and two Spitfires were waiting at the French coast to escort the Stirling, while a Walrus air-sea-rescue flying boat was standing by to pick the crew up. They were just three miles off Shoreham when the fuel gave out, but F/Sgt Rothschild carried out a perfect ditching at 07.15, and the crew transferred safely to the dinghy. The only hitch was a collision between the Walrus and the dinghy, which pitched the crew into the sea, but all eight men were hauled on board and returned to terra-firma, and the Stirling remained afloat for twenty-five minutes.

S/L Fowler was not flying with the crew on this night, but among the regular members were the Canadian Tod twins, who were wireless operator and front gunner. Sadly, both would lose their lives later in the year. Sgt Robert Ernest Tod, RCAF, the wireless operator, was awarded the DFM for his role in this episode. Sgt McCaskill in BF465 JN-K reported a fighter attack in his logbook, but after returning fire with an initial short burst, the rear gunner was unable to continue because of an issue with the servo-feed. The return of BF456 AA-J was awaited in vain, and it was established later that it had crashed at Steeg, south of the Ruhr, with no survivors from the crew of Sgt John Webb RAF. While this operation was in progress, the freshman crews of Sgt Alfred Edward Lewis RAAF and P/O Douglas Vincent Hamer RAFVR successfully carried out mining sorties off the Frisians, despite the presence of ten-tenths cloud and only moderate visibility.

F/L Leo Trott RNZAF had by now concluded his tour and was awarded a DFC on his posting to 12 O.T.U on the 11th. The busy round of non-Ruhr operations would continue at Stuttgart, for which a force of 462 aircraft was made ready on the 14th, and as for the Frankfurt operation, Wellingtons were again the most populous type with 146 on duty. 3 Group was represented by seventy-five aircraft, seven of the Stirlings made ready at Newmarket by 75(NZ) Squadron. At briefings, the crews took in the details of the plan, which involved Path Finder aircraft dropping yellow TIs as route markers at two locations, while at the target, nine Stirlings and eight Halifaxes would ground mark the aiming-point with red TIs on H2S, at the same time as releasing a short stick of flares. One Stirling and four Lancasters were then to identify the aiming-point visually, and mark it with green TIs, for three Stirlings, six Halifaxes and eleven Lancasters to back up also with greens. This would leave three Stirlings, three Halifaxes and five Lancasters to bolster the efforts of the main force.

The 75(NZ) Squadron element took off between 21.35 and 22.00 with all-incendiary bomb loads and no senior pilots on duty. P/O Tolley turned back after an hour because of faulty controls, leaving the others to push on in favourable weather conditions, attracting attention from the flak belts at the French coast and the Franco/German frontier. The bomber stream entered Germany under high cirrus cloud and bright moonlight to approach Stuttgart from the north-east and found it clearly visible with just a little haze to impair the vertical visibility. The Path Finder ground marker crews established their positions by H2S confirmed by visual reference, but as evidence of the shortcomings of H2S in its early form, they were actually short of the city centre when they delivered bundles of white flares, red TIs and 1,000 pounders between 00.47 and 00.56. The backers-up were carrying four green TIs, one of them of the long-burning variety, four 1,000 pounders and a single 500 pounder each, which they dropped between 00.50 and 01.14, also to the north-east of the planned aiming-point. The main force crews were greeted by plentiful red and green TIs concentrated in a built-up area, and some would claim later to have picked out ground detail such as the River Neckar, marshalling yards, the railway station and the Bosch factory, which reinforced their belief that they were over the briefed aiming-point. Smoke rising through 8,000 feet and a concentration of fires was all that crews could report as they turned for home, and debriefings gleaned little in the way of a useful assessment either of the fall of the bombs or of the raid in general.

Bombing photos and post-raid reconnaissance confirmed that the Path Finders had not marked the centre of the city, and that a "creep-back" had developed, which had spread along the line of approach. Creep-back was a feature of many large raids and was caused by crews bombing the first fires they came upon, rather than pushing through to the planned aiming-point. It could work for or against the effectiveness of an attack, and on this night, worked in the Command's favour by falling across the industrial district of Bad-Canstatt, situated to the north-east of the city centre on the East Bank of the River Neckar. The bombing continued to spread further back along the line of approach onto the residential suburbs of Münster and Mühlhausen, and it was here that the majority of the 393 buildings were destroyed and more than nine hundred others severely damaged. A number of bombs did find their way into the city centre, and one killed four hundred French and Russian PoWs in an air-raid shelter. Twenty-three aircraft failed to return, among them eight 3 and 8 Group Stirlings, almost 10% of those dispatched. P/O Groves' rear gunner in BF455 AA-Y fired briefly at a Me110 before his skipper's evasive actions shook the would-be attacker off, and P/O Bennett in BF465 AA-K had a similar experience with an unidentified single-engine enemy aircraft. BF513 (JN-E according to P/O McCaskill's logbook) was shot down on the way home by a night-fighter flown by Lt Fritz Graef of 1./NJG4 and crashed at 02.25 at Regniessart in Belgium, close to the border with France some twenty-five miles south of Charleroi. There were no survivors from the crew of P/O Donald McCaskill RNZAF, whose navigator and rear gunner were also members of the RNZAF.

On the following night, Sgt Alan Joseph Lyall Sedunary RAAF and crew were sent on a freshman mining sortie to the Deodar garden in the Gironde Estuary, departing at 21.03 and returning at 03.52 to report a successful and uneventful trip.

Preparations were put in hand on the 16th for a major night of operations, which would see 327 Lancasters and Halifaxes head for the Skoda armaments works at Pilsen in Czechoslovakia, while a predominantly Wellington and Stirling force of 271 aircraft carried out a diversionary raid on Mannheim. 3 Group put up eighty-five Stirlings for Mannheim and eight Lancasters for Pilsen, 75(NZ) Squadron represented by eleven Stirlings, although the ORB specified the target as Ludwigshafen, which faces Mannheim from the west bank of the Rhine. It became common practice to attack both cities simultaneously with an approach from the west and an aiming point in the eastern side of Mannheim to allow a natural creep-back to spill into Ludwigshafen. The plan of attack for Pilsen called for the Path Finders to drop route markers at the final turning point seven miles from the target, which the crews were to then locate visually in the bright moonlight and bomb from as low a level as practicable. It was asking for trouble, and many crews became confused and bombed the route markers, which happened to be over an asylum at Dobrany, situated some seven miles short of the factory, which escaped damage. Not only was the operation an abject failure, but it also cost thirty-six aircraft, divided equally between the two types.

The Kiwi element departed Newmarket for Mannheim either side of 22.00 with S/L Allcock the senior pilot on duty, but Sgt Halliburton and P/O Hamer were forced to turn back with engine problems. The others pressed on in good weather conditions and those reaching the target found considerable haze blotting out ground detail. In compensation the Path Finder marking was accurate and the subsequent bombing by the main force concentrated within the city. Heavy and light flak batteries were co-operating to good effect with searchlights, and F/L Lowe's BK664 AA-M was one of two from the squadron to be hit, one unspecified navigator sustaining a leg wound. On landing, F/L Lowe discovered that his throttle controls were jammed open, and the Stirling careered across the airfield to collide with a partially-built hangar. The Stirling was wrecked, but the crew survived, albeit with an assortment of injuries. Eighteen aircraft were missing from this operation, and among them were two of the 75(NZ) Squadron participants. W7469 AA-O crashed at Katzenbach, some forty miles north-west of Mannheim, and only Sgt D. Wainwright RAFVR, the flight engineer from the crew of F/Sgt Kevin Debenham RNZAF, survived to be taken into captivity. BF451 AA-Z fell victim to a night-fighter and crashed six miles south of Reims, killing all eight occupants. P/O Kelvin Groves and his mid-upper gunner were both members of the RNZAF, and second pilot, W/O James Oscar Way RCAF, was about to be granted crew captain status after completing his quota of second pilot sorties. Post-raid reconnaissance and local reports established that 130 buildings had been destroyed with more than three thousand others damaged to some extent, and many war industry factories had lost production. The combined losses for the night of fifty-four aircraft represented a new record.

The main operation on the night of the 20/21st was against Stettin, the large port situated some thirty miles south of Swinemünde at the centre of Germany's Baltic coast. A force of 339 aircraft included eleven 115 Squadron Lancasters, while eighty-four 3 Group Stirlings and two from 7 Squadron of 8 Group were made ready for a simultaneous attack on the Heinkel aircraft works at Rostock further west along the coast. 75(NZ) Squadron prepared nine aircraft, filling their bomb bays with 1,000 pounders and an assortment of incendiaries, and sent them on their way from Newmarket between 21.47 and 22.15 with W/C Lane the senior pilot on duty. All reached the target area, having flown out in excellent weather conditions with good visibility, but found an effective smoke-screen in operation, which led to scattered bombing and an unsatisfactory outcome. Sgt Dalzell and crew reported colliding with a Lancaster on the way home, which must have been part of the Stettin force, and although BK624 AA-A sustained only minor damage, the rudder was jammed, and Dalzell's subsequent four-hundred-mile trip home and perfect landing was considered worthy of an immediate DFM. At debriefing, 25% of crews reported attacking the factory and the remainder the town. Eight Stirlings failed to return, which represented around 9% of those dispatched, and among them was the squadron's BF506 AA-P. A message was received from P/O Alan Tolley's crew at 03.00 stating that the starboard-inner engine was on fire, it is believed as the result of an engagement with a night-fighter, and the Stirling came down at 03.26 at Bøgballe in Denmark's mid-Jutland region with no survivors. P/O Tolley, his bomb-aimer, wireless operator and rear gunner were all members of the RNZAF.

The night of the 22/23rd was one of little activity and provided an opportunity for 3 Group to send out a force of thirty-two gardeners to the Biscay sea lanes. Eight 75(NZ) Squadron Stirlings were loaded with 1,500lb parachute mines and dispatched either side of 21.00 to the Deodar garden in the Gironde Estuary, which all reached to find eight-tenths cloud and two flak ships, which were co-operating with searchlights but were not overly troublesome. Patchy cloud provided cover when necessary, and all returned safely, mostly to report having observed the mines' parachutes deploying. F/L Sandeman was posted to 20 O.T.U on the 23rd after completing his tour.

Night flying tests (NFTs) were carried out during the afternoon of the 26th in preparation for that night's operation to Duisburg, for which a force of 561 aircraft was assembled, the numbers bolstered by the inclusion of 135 Wellingtons, while 215 Lancasters represented the largest contribution by type. 8 Group was boosted by the operational debut of 97 (Straits Settlement) Squadron and 405 (Vancouver) Squadron RCAF, which had recently been transferred from 5 and 6 Groups respectively. The plan that called for eight Oboe Mosquitos to drop yellow route markers and red TIs on the aiming-point and for the yellows to be backed up by others of the same colour delivered by a dozen Lancasters, while three Stirlings, five 35 (Madras Presidency) Squadron Halifaxes and seven Lancasters backed up at the aiming-point with green TIs. 3 Group detailed eighty-three aircraft, eight of the Stirlings provided by 75(NZ) Squadron for what was the largest raid yet on this particular target. Take-offs from Newmarket took place between 23.55 and 01.07 in the absence of one unspecified crew, who failed to get away because of an indisposed pilot. There were no senior pilots on duty, but F/L Ronald Laud RAF had returned to the squadron on the 16th for a second tour as A Flight commander elect and was flying as second pilot to P/O Thompson. F/L Edward Robert Appleton RAF had also been posted in on the 16th as B Flight commander elect, and he was flying on this night as second pilot to P/O Buck. To make it a full set, freshly-promoted S/L Richard Broadbent RNZAF, the new C Flight Commander, was flying his first operation and captaining his own Stirling. After climbing out, they set course for the Dutch coast near The Hague for the northern approach to the Ruhr, joining the bomber stream as they crossed the North Sea. P/O Thompson returned early for an unspecified reason and P/O Buck in BF517 AA-O was some thirty miles north of the target when attacked by an unseen night-fighter. The rear gunner, Sgt Brian Arthur Rogers RAFVR, was mortally wounded and the Stirling sustained damage to the tail and rudder. In a second attack, the starboard outer engine was hit, the flaps damaged, the M.W. aerial shot away and incendiaries in the bomb bay ignited. The enemy aircraft was evaded and all removable items jettisoned to save weight, leaving P/O Buck to carry out a textbook crash-landing at base, from which all but the rear gunner walked away with minor injuries. For his airmanship in covering the three-hundred-mile return trip in a badly damaged aircraft and landing it safely, P/O Peter Buck RNZAF would be awarded the DFC. The wireless operator, P/O John Henry Symons RCAF, would be similarly decorated for his dedication to duty despite sustaining a wounded hand during the engagement. The others reached the target area after approaching from the north-east, finding largely clear skies and good visibility and green TIs backing up the reds delivered by the Oboe Mosquitos. By the end of the raid, many fires were evident, although opinions were divided as to the degree of concentration achieved. A large orange explosion was witnessed to the east of the aiming-point at 02.34, and although fires had not fully gained a hold as the last of the bombers turned away, black smoke was rising through 7,000 feet. The operation was only partially successful, daylight reconnaissance revealing that many bombs had fallen to the north-east of the city, probably as a result of some main force crews bombing too early rather than pressing-on to the aiming point at what was a recognised flak hotspot. Even so, three hundred buildings had been destroyed, and for a change, only two Stirlings were among the seventeen failures to return.

Two massive mining operations were mounted on the nights of the 27/28th and 28/29th, the former employing 160 aircraft, of which five of the Stirlings represented 75(NZ) Squadron. S/L Broadbent and F/L Appleton were the senior pilots on duty as they took off either side of 01.00 and set course for the Frisians. The other three were debutants, Sgt Leslie Charles Wright RAFVR, Sgt Alfred John Thomas RAFVR and Sgt Hilton Clifford 'Speed' Williams RNZAF. Sgt Thomas must have been almost at the target area when he turned back with engine problems, leaving the others to locate their pinpoints through heavy cloud and rainstorms, but in reasonable visibility. All carried out their tasks in accordance with instructions and returned safely from an uneventful trip.

207 aircraft were made ready for the following night's gardening expeditions, of which eight Stirlings were provided by 75(NZ) Squadron and took off for the Radish garden in the Baltic's Fehmarn Belt at 20.30 with no senior pilots on duty. One crew is recorded as returning early with a defective compass and this may have been P/O French, whose landing time was the earliest. The force encountered heavy cloud over the Danish and German coasts, which persuaded many crews to descend to low level to establish a pinpoint for the timed runs to their drop sites. This put them within range of flak ships and coastal batteries, which sprayed lethal light flak into their paths and brought down twenty-two of them. Seven of thirty-two Stirlings were shot down and four of them belonged to 75(NZ) Squadron. Sgt Keith Halliburton RNZAF and his crew were lost without trace in W7513 AA-G, while R9290 AA-Y, containing the crew of F/Sgt Alfred Lewis RAAF, went into the sea off Denmark's Lolland Island on the northern side of the Fehmarn Belt. BF467 AA-W was a victim of a naval flak battery and crashed at 00.08 off Naksov at the western end of Lolland, taking with it P/O Desmond Thompson RNZAF and his crew, and BK807 AA-M was brought down in the same manner and crashed into the Baltic close by at 00.23 with the crew of P/O Douglas Hamer RAFVR. There was not a single survivor among the twenty-eight crewmen, eleven of whom were members of the RNZAF. This was the highest casualty figure of the war from a mining operation, in exchange for the planting of a record 593 mines.

Stirlings were excluded from the month's final operation, which was by 305 aircraft against Essen on the night of the 30th, for which 3 Group contributed eleven 115 Squadron Lancasters, five of which returned early. The operation was based on Oboe skymarking over a cloud-covered target and destroyed 189 buildings, while inflicting further damage on the Krupp complex. During the course of the month, 75(NZ) Squadron undertook fourteen operations and dispatched ninety-six sorties for the loss of twelve Stirlings and ten crews. On top of the losses, the number of sorties not completed was at an all-time high and morale an all-time low.

May 1943

May would bring a return to winning ways and some spectacular successes, and the new month began for 75(NZ) Squadron with the briefing of five crews for a mining operation in the Deodar garden in the Gironde Estuary on the 1st. In the event, poor weather resulted in just two Stirlings departing Newmarket shortly after 21.30, with the experienced S/L Broadbent and F/L

Appleton at the controls. They reached the target area to find seven-tenths cloud and good visibility and delivered their mines into the allocated locations before returning safely. Ten Stirlings were at the point of take-off for Duisburg on the following evening, when a cancellation order was received. On the 3rd, S/L Michael Wyatt RAF was posted in from his flight commander post at XV Squadron at Bourn, to which he had recently returned after crash-landing his Stirling in Spain during an operation to Turin. Wyatt had been tasked with improving operational efficiency, and in his own words, "to get them out of the rut". He was promoted and appointed to succeed W/C Lane as commanding officer, while W/C Lane took up a new post at Harwell. One of Wyatt's early assessments was that Newmarket, one of England's premier horse racing courses, was not an ideal location as it continued to put on race meetings and was too close to the social life of the easily accessed town.

An operation to Duisburg planned for that night was cancelled during the afternoon, and it was on the following evening that the month's first major operation was mounted. During the afternoon of the 4th ten Stirlings were loaded with 2,000 and 1,000 pounders along with incendiaries, while their crews were being briefed for the first attack on Dortmund during the current Ruhr campaign. They learned that they were to be part of a new record non-1,000 force of 596 aircraft, of which seventy-five Stirlings and a dozen Lancasters were being made ready on 3 Group stations. The plan of attack called for Oboe Mosquitos to drop yellow track markers, before eight of them ground-marked the aiming-point with green TIs, leaving two in reserve to bomb with the main force if not required for marking duties. Twenty-two Lancasters and two Halifaxes were to back up with red TIs, and all remaining Path Finder aircraft were to bomb with the main force. One Kiwi sortie was scrubbed because of an engine issue, leaving the remaining nine to get away either side of 23.00 with F/L Appleton the senior captain on duty and F/L Laud flying as second pilot to Sgt Dalzell. Sgts Thomas and Williams returned early with engine issues, while the rest of the bomber stream crossed Holland to enter Germany to the north of the Ruhr and make its way to the eastern end, where crews found clear skies, good visibility and only industrial and smoke haze to spoil the vertical view. The Oboe markers were due to go down at 01.00, but the first greens were two minutes early, after which the initial Path Finder marking was accurately placed around the city centre. Some of the backing-up fell short and inevitably attracted some bomb loads and a decoy site was also successful in luring away others, but most crews were guided by the yellow approach markers and red and green TIs on the ground. Returning crews reported many sizeable explosions, including a particularly large one at 01.12, which may have been the one reported by a 50 Squadron crew that threw flame to a height of 2,000 feet and burned for ten seconds. They also described developing fires, the glow from which could be seen, according to some, from 150 miles into the return flight. Post-raid reconnaissance revealed that approximately half of the force had bombed within three miles of the aiming-point, destroying 1,218 buildings and seriously damaging more than two thousand others, while a number of important steelworks were hit, as were many facilities in the inland docks area. Local reports confirmed a death toll of 693 people, which was a record from a Bomber Command attack. It was not a one-sided affair, however, and the loss of thirty-one aircraft was a foretaste of what was in store for the bomber crews operating over "Happy Valley". At debriefing, Sgt Sedunary crew reported a short combat with a Ju88 on the run in to the target, the rear gunner claiming it as "probably destroyed".

3 Group sent twenty-one Stirlings to lay mines in one of the Nectarine gardens off the Frisians on the following night, and five of them were provided by 75(NZ) Squadron, the number including newcomers Sgt Cyril Philip Bailie RAFVR and Sgt Reginald Francis Westwood RAAF. They were all airborne by 22.00 with F/Ls Andrews and Laud the senior pilots on duty and found broken cloud and good visibility in the target area. Some light flak was encountered, but it was described as ineffective, and four crews returned home to report planting their vegetables in the briefed locations and observing the parachutes to open. EF340 AA-Q failed to arrive back with the others after being shot down by a flak battery at 01.15 and crashing into the Waddenzee south-east of Vlieland. There were no survivors from the crew of P/O Westwood RAAF, which included three members of the RNZAF, and no bodies were recovered.

The garden for the night of the 9/10th was Cinnamon, off the Ile-de-Re, through which waters naval vessels entering and leaving the Biscay ports of La Rochelle and La Pallice would have to pass. Six 75(NZ) Squadron Stirlings took off either side of 22.00 with F/L Laud the senior pilot on duty and Sgt Robert Frederick Harvey RNZAF and Sgt John Lefevre Mitchell RAFVR operating as crew captains for the first time. The weather conditions were good, and all completed their sorties in accordance with briefing before returning safely from an uneventful trip. The weather on the 10th prevented any flying, and W/C Wyatt took the opportunity to deliver a lecture to the crews. S/L Fowler was sent on leave pending his posting on the 18th to take up a training role at 1665 Conversion Unit, and he was succeeded as B Flight commander by the freshly-promoted S/L Appleton. S/L Allcock was posted to 12 O.T.U on the 11th and was succeeded as A Flight commander by the similarly newly-promoted S/L Ron Laud, who was a New Zealander from Campbell's Bay and had joined the RAF in 1939.

An operation to Bochum planned for the evening of the 11th was cancelled, and the following day Duisburg was posted as the night's target. A force of 572 aircraft was made ready, of which eighty-five were provided by 3 Group, among them nine Stirlings representing 75(NZ) Squadron. The plan allowed for nine Mosquitos to drop yellow TIs on track as a preliminary warning and red TIs on the aiming-point, which would be backed up with green TIs by five Stirlings, five Halifaxes and twenty Lancasters. A late take-off slot meant that it was thirty minutes after midnight before the 75(NZ) Squadron element began to roll and 00.37 when BK721 AA-Z's starboard-inner engine failed, robbing the heavily-laden Stirling of the necessary flying speed to clear Devil's Dyke on the airfield boundary. It crashed almost immediately, killing six of the eight occupants, three of whom were members of the RNZAF, while S/L Appleton and his Kiwi wireless operator, F/Sgt Stanley Gordon Cocks, RNZAF, sustained serious injury. The two remaining aircraft had their take-off cancelled, leaving seven to head for the North Sea to rendezvous with the bomber stream and make landfall on the Dutch coast in the area of Castricum-aan-Zee. F/Sgt Rothschild was taken ill during the outward flight and was forced to return early, while the others pressed on to reach the target area guided by the yellow tracking flares. They found ideal bombing conditions with no cloud and good visibility, which helped the Oboe and H2S crews to mark with great accuracy and focus. The main force crews were able to identify ground features and exploit the opportunity to produce a display of unusually concentrated bombing on red and green TIs, predominantly from between 17,000 and 20,000 feet. Perhaps, for the first time at this target, the attack proceeded according to plan, and Duisburg finally succumbed to a devastating assault. Returning crews described a large explosion at 02.30, streets outlined by fire and a highly successful outcome, the best yet witnessed by some, and their impressions were confirmed by photo-reconnaissance, which revealed extensive damage in the city centre and the Ruhrort Rhine docks, Germany's largest inland port, where thirty-four barges and other vessels were sunk, and a further sixty damaged to some extent. 1,596 buildings were totally destroyed and the Thyssen steelworks was hit, but the success was paid for by a new record loss for the campaign of thirty-four aircraft. The loss rates by type again made interesting reading and confirmed the established food chain, the Lancasters sustaining a 4.2% loss, compared with 8.9% for Wellingtons, 7.1% for Stirlings and 6.3% for Halifaxes. Such was the level of destruction that Duisburg would now be left in peace for a year.

S/L Frank Albert Andrews was installed as the new B Flight commander on the 13th in place of S/L Appleton, who would recover from his injuries only to lose his life in a USAAF B17 on the 31st of August. S/L Andrews was another who had returned for a second operational tour, having spent his first stint at 75(NZ) Squadron between December 1940 and June 1941.

On the following day, 124 Lancasters of 5 Group were detailed to join forces with thirty-two other Lancasters and twelve Halifaxes of 8 Group for an attempt to rectify the recent failure at the Skoda armaments works at Pilsen. A simultaneous raid on Bochum, a city built on coal mining and situated some ten miles west of Dortmund would involve a force of 442 aircraft, of which 3 Group contributed ninety, a dozen of the Stirlings made ready by 75(NZ) Squadron. They departed Newmarket between 00.07 and 00.42 with S/L Broadbent the senior pilot on duty and lost the services of the crews of Sgts Bailie and Thomas and P/O Bennett to engine trouble, leaving the others to press on in favourable conditions and follow Oboe-laid yellow track markers to the target area. They had to run the gauntlet of heavy predicted flak co-operating with searchlights and were greeted over the central Ruhr by clear skies but the usual industrial haze to obscure ground detail.

The first Oboe Mosquitos dropped red TIs onto the aiming point, before a gap developed in the marking, and although the backers-up kept the aiming point marked with green TIs throughout, the bombing lacked a degree of concentration, possibly as a result of the appearance of decoy markers some fifteen minutes into the attack. Enemy aircraft were also in evidence, and a Me110 latched onto BF561 AA-O, before opening fire from four hundred yards and slightly below. Sgt Mitchell's mid-upper gunner fired a medium burst, and the enemy was seen to be on fire as it passed beneath. The rear gunner then fired a long burst at three hundred yards range, after which the night-fighter rolled onto its back, dived into the ground and exploded. Mitchell's mid-upper gunner was kept busy with two further combats, one a Ju88 just after bombing, and another, unidentified, about half an hour later on the way home. Sgt Thomas and crew in BK614 JN-H were also attacked, in their case by a FW190, the rear gunner, Sgt A.E. Parker RAFVR, sustaining wounds but continuing to fire back. The mid-upper unleashed a long burst, causing the fighter to turn on its back and dive straight down in flames to be claimed as "probably destroyed". Returning crews reported that the target was rocked by many explosions and appeared to be a mass of flames by the end of the raid. Photo-reconnaissance revealed the operation to have been moderately effective and local sources admitted to the destruction of 394 buildings, with more than seven hundred others seriously damaged.

While the above was in progress, debutant Sgt Arthur William Burley RAFVR and crew took off at 01.20 bound for one of the Nectarine gardens off the Frisians, and completed their sortie according to brief in favourable conditions and without incident.

It was on the night of the 16/17th, during a nine-night lull in main force operations, that 617 Squadron wrote its page in history by attacking the Ruhr dams under Operation Chastise, and contrary to popular belief, the nineteen special Lancasters were not the only Bomber Command aircraft flying that night. Shortly after 01.00, while the flood waters from the Möhne Dam were engulfing communities to the west of the reservoir, four Stirlings departed Newmarket with the freshman crews of Sgt Norman Bradford Bluck RNZAF, Sgt Burley, Sgt Williams and P/O William Rosser 'Ross' Perrott RNZAF. They were bound for the Frisians, where they successfully delivered their mines into the briefed locations. Preceding them into the air for a training flight had been BF398, now re-coded AA-P, with the crew of Sgt Leslie Wright on board, plus a second pilot and a member of the ground crew, AC1 Bailey. When over Staffordshire, both outer engines failed and the pilot gave the order to abandon the aircraft, which seven of eight accomplished safely. Realising that he was over a built-up area, Sgt Wright remained at the controls to attempt a forced-landing but crashed at 01.00 on farmland four miles north-west of Stoke-on-Trent and was killed. The mayor of Stoke-on-Trent contacted the squadron to express the admiration of the townsfolk for Sgt Wright's selfless act. The body of rear gunner, Sgt Alan John Francis RAFVR, remained missing for four days before eventually being located.

On the following night, the squadron sent two crews to the Cinnamon garden off the Ile-de-Re in the approaches to the Biscay ports of La Rochelle and La Pallice. Sgts Thomas and Bailie took off either side of 22.45 and exploited the excellent weather conditions to complete their sorties in accordance with instructions, before returning safely after more than six hours aloft. The squadron was ordered to provide eleven Stirlings to be part of a force of 104 aircraft for mining duties on the night of the 21/22nd, five crews for the Deodar garden in the Gironde Estuary and six for one of the Nectarine gardens off the Frisians. Among the crews assigned to the former was that captained by F/O Jack 'Jacky' Joll RNZAF, who had come back for a second tour with the squadron. The Frisians contingent were all debutants, Sgt Thomas William Darton RNZAF, Sgt Stephen Muir Tietjens RNZAF, Sgt John Milward Mee RNZAF, Sgt Benjamin Brinley Wood RAFVR, Sgt Sidney Russell Thornley RNZAF and Sgt Ernest Stanley Wilkinson RNZAF. Those heading east took off first either side of 22.00, to be followed immediately into the air by the south-bound quintet and all completed their sorties in favourable weather conditions before returning to report uneventful trips.

By the time that the next major operation was posted on the 23rd, the main force squadrons had undergone an expansion with the addition to many units of a third or C Flight, which in most cases, would eventually be hived off to form the nucleus of a brand-new squadron. The giant force of 826 aircraft was the largest non-1,000 effort to date and surpassed the previous record set three weeks earlier by a clear 230 aircraft. The number of available Lancasters had leapt by eighty-eight, Halifaxes by forty-eight, Stirlings by forty and Wellingtons by forty-one, and their destination for the second time in the month was Dortmund. The Command had been restored to full health and vigour, and activity on all participating stations was hectic as preparations were put in hand to resume the Ruhr offensive. The ground crews and armourers worked tirelessly, while the aircrews attended briefings to learn of their part in the grand plan.

Eleven Oboe Mosquitos were to drop yellow preliminary warning TIs on track, before marking the aiming-point with red TIs, which eight Stirlings, eleven Halifaxes and fourteen Lancasters were to back up with greens. 3 Group detailed a record 118 aircraft, and 75(NZ) Squadron achieved its best effort yet by making ready fifteen Stirlings, which took off between 23.01 and 23.49 with S/Ls Broadbent and Laud the senior pilots on duty. They set course under cloudless skies for the Castricum region of the Dutch coast on the northern approach to the eastern Ruhr and lost Sgt Burley and crew to an early return caused by engine trouble.

The others all reached the target area to find clear skies but smoke already drifting across the city and combining with industrial haze to obscure ground detail, a situation, which, before the advent of Oboe, would have rendered the attack a lottery. The 109 Squadron Mosquitos marked the centre of the city accurately, after which the backers-up fulfilled their briefs to ensure that the aiming-point was maintained throughout the raid. Main force crews reported that they could observe the TIs from twenty miles away on approach, and after bombing witnessed many explosions and fires, which merged into a large area of conflagration that sent thick columns of black smoke rising up through 18,000 feet as they turned away. Returning crews reported fierce night-fighter activity over the target and on the way home, and this was reflected in the high casualty rate of thirty-eight aircraft, the largest loss of the campaign to date, of which almost half were Halifaxes. Among six missing 3 Group Stirlings was the squadron's BK783 AA-Q, which was shot down by a night-fighter over Holland and crashed at Beesd, twenty miles east of Rotterdam. Sgt Tietjens RNZAF and five of his crew, including two other members of the RNZAF, were killed, but the rear gunner, Sgt Leslie R. Vale RAFVR, survived to be taken into captivity. At debriefing, Sgt Whitehead and crew reported that their aircraft, BF461 JN-B, had returned with its port-outer propeller shot off by flak, and two other crews reported short and inconclusive engagements with night-fighters. Post-raid reconnaissance and local reports confirmed massive damage in central, northern and eastern districts, where almost two thousand buildings had been destroyed and many important industrial premises had suffered a loss of production.

Just like Duisburg, Dortmund would be allowed an entire year to lick its deep wounds before next hosting a visit from the heavy brigade, and in the meantime, the Bomber Command juggernaut moved on to its neighbour, Düsseldorf, for which a force of 759 aircraft was made ready on the 25th. The plan called for the standard procedure of Mosquito-laid yellow preliminary warning TIs on track, and red TIs delivered by Oboe onto the aiming-point. Eight Stirlings, twelve Halifaxes and twenty-three Lancasters were to back these up with green TIs, leaving five Stirlings, fourteen Halifaxes and twenty-five Lancasters to bomb with the main force. 3 Group detailed 113 aircraft, of which sixteen Stirlings were loaded with 1,000 pounders and 4lb and 30lb incendiaries at Newmarket to break the squadron's own record set just forty-eight hours earlier. They took off either side of midnight with F/Ls French and Lowe the senior pilots on duty, but Sgt Wilkinson was back in the circuit before 01.00, to be joined on the ground by F/Sgt Rothschild, F/L Lowe and F/Sgt Whitehead within an hour, all with engine issues. This was the second time in two weeks that the squadron had put up double figures only to experience a 25% rate of early returns.

The bomber stream set course for the Scheldt estuary for the southern approach to the Ruhr, the crews expecting to find the forecast favourable conditions over the target, for which a ground-marking plan had been prepared. When the Oboe Mosquitos arrived, however, they were greeted by two layers of cloud with tops at 18,500 feet, and although they delivered their TIs with great accuracy, they could not be seen by the backers-up and the marking became scattered. Some main force crews arriving at the Dutch coast towards the rear of the bomber stream were able to observe feverish activity at the target, still some one hundred miles and thirty minutes flying time away. The 75(NZ) Squadron participants delivered their attacks onto red and green TIs from around 16,000 feet and all returned safely to pass on their impressions to the intelligence section. Some reported a huge explosion at 01.49 as they were lining up for the bombing run and gained an impression of large fires developing beneath the clouds, despite which, many thought the raid to have been scattered.

Post-raid reconnaissance and local reports confirmed that the raid had failed to achieve concentration, possibly as the result of the deployment by the enemy of decoy markers and dummy fire sites, and it had developed into an "old-style" scattering of bombs across a wide area. Düsseldorf suffered the destruction of fewer than a hundred buildings, in return for which, twenty-seven aircraft failed to return, among them the squadron's BK602 AA-R, which was shot down by a night-fighter off the Belgian coast while on its thirtieth operation. There were no survivors from the crew of F/Sgt Darton RNZAF, which contained two other members of the RNZAF. The sea eventually gave up four bodies for burial in Ostend, Dunkerque and Bergen-op-Zoom. On the way home, Sgt Sedunary's BF564 JN-W was attacked by a FW190, at which both rear and mid-upper gunners returned fire. This and the pilot's continual corkscrewing allowed them to escape without damage or injury.

Essen was posted as the target for the night of the 27/28th, for which the squadron began to prepare fourteen Stirlings. However, shortly after briefing, the Stirling element was cancelled and the operation went ahead without them, employing a force of 518 aircraft. This also developed into a scattered attack based on skymarking in the face of cloud cover, but even so, almost five hundred buildings were destroyed. While this operation was in progress, 75(NZ) Squadron dispatched five freshman crews between 22.49 and 23.05 to one of the Nectarine gardens off the Frisians, including first-time captains Sgt George Vincent Helm RNZAF, F/O Richard Berry Vernazoni RNZAF and Sgt John Henry Roy Carey RNZAF. All returned safely having planted their vegetables in the briefed locations, assisted by favourable weather conditions and a lack of response from the enemy.

Ten miles to the east of Düsseldorf on the southern fringe of the Ruhr, the twin towns of Elberfeld and Barmen nestle in the Wupper Valley, which gave them their joint name of Wuppertal. They had become wealthy by exploiting the rich coal deposits beneath their feet and now boasted much industry helping the German war effort. A force of 719 aircraft was assembled on Saturday the 29th to pitch against this new Ruhr target, the aiming-point for which was to be the Barmen half at the eastern end of the conurbation. On this occasion, the route markers were to be dropped by two 8 Group Stirlings and two Halifaxes, while ahead, the Oboe Mosquitos took care of ground marking with red TIs. These would be backed up by four Stirlings, eleven Halifaxes and twenty-three Lancasters with greens, at the same time as thirteen Stirlings, twenty Halifaxes and twenty-one Lancasters acted as fire raisers by dropping incendiaries. This would leave two Stirlings, five Halifaxes and seven Lancasters to bomb with the main force. 3 Group detailed ninety-nine Stirlings and sixteen Lancasters and the ground crews and armourers at Newmarket pulled out all the stops to prepare a magnificent twenty Stirlings, a new squadron record.

All but one presented themselves for take-off between 23.02 and 23.41 with S/L Andrews the senior pilot on duty but lost the services of the crews of F/Sgts Bluck and Rothschild to undisclosed technical issues. Sgt Burley and crew were in in BF434 AA-Y and encountered a Ju88 on the outward journey, which the mid-upper gunner fired at to end any contact between the two aircraft. The bomber stream negotiated the southern approach to the Ruhr, running the gauntlet of searchlights and flak in the Cologne and Düsseldorf corridor to be greeted by clear skies in the target area, with the usual industrial haze extending up to 10,000 feet. The yellow tracking flares clearly identified the final turning-point and the backers-up went in at 16,000 to 18,000 feet between 01.03 and 01.51 to reinforce the red TIs with greens. Meanwhile, the thirteen fire-raisers had attacked with a 2,000 pounder and 1,164 x 4lb incendiaries each, leaving the way clear for the main force to exploit the opportunity to deliver a massive blow. The operation proceeded precisely according to plan, with accurate Path Finder marking preceding concentrated main force bombing, which caused damage on an unimaginable scale. High above, the crews watched the narrow streets of the old town become engulfed in flame, which almost certainly developed into a minor firestorm. The defences of flak and searchlights were described by returning crews as ineffective, and a few enemy night-fighters were seen, but the impression was of a one-sided affair.

In fact, thirty-three bombers failed to return home, and in many cases, they were the ones that experienced an up-close-and-personal encounter with the night-fighter that shot them down. 75(NZ) Squadron posted missing four crews, 25% of those pressing on to the target, and they were all likely victims of the Luftwaffe Nachtjagd. EF398 AA-A was definitely shot down by Oblt Manfred Meurer of 1./NJG1 and crashed in the Roerdalen region of south-eastern Holland, killing F/O Richard Vernazoni RNZAF and his crew, which included three other members of the RNZAF. BF561 AA-O crashed at Gladbeck-Rentfort on the northern edge of the Ruhr, and there were no survivors either from the crew of F/Sgt Sidney Thornley RNZAF, which contained two other members of the RNZAF. P/O Raymond Bennett RNZAF had four Kiwis among his eight-man crew, three of whom managed to save themselves before BK776 AA-R crashed at Odenspiel, killing the remaining five occupants. The crash site, some thirty miles to the south-east of the target, suggests that the Stirling may have been chased off course by a night-fighter before succumbing. EH881 AA-Z crashed just to the east of Aachen, killing F/Sgt John Carey RNZAF and both gunners, one of whom was a member of the RNZAF, but four men survived to be taken prisoner, and three of these were also RNZAF.

Wuppertal had been the victim of the outstanding raid of the entire Ruhr campaign, in which a thousand acres of built-up area had been reduced to ruins by fire. Four thousand houses had been destroyed, along with five of the six largest factories and more than two hundred other industrial premises. A further eighteen hundred houses and seventy industrial building had sustained serious damage, and the death toll was put at 3,400, many times greater than any previous figure arising from an attack on an urban target.

During the course of the month the squadron operated fifteen times, dispatching 114 sorties for the loss of nine Stirlings, seven complete crews and seven individual airmen from two other crews.

June 1943

The new month began for 8 Group with the arrival of two Mosquito squadrons from 2 Group, which had left Bomber Command on the previous day to become part of a new organisation called the 2nd Tactical Air Force. 105 and 139 Squadrons had illustrious careers behind them, having been part of the AASF during the battle for France, and had served 2 Group with distinction, thereafter, flying Blenheims until the advent of the Mosquito. Unlike the Mosquitos of 109 Squadron, which operated at maximum altitude for the purpose of Oboe reception, 2 Group Mosquitos had been employed mostly in a low-level strike role against shipping and precision land targets, where speed was their greatest asset. 105 Squadron was to be the second Oboe unit, while 139 Squadron's initial role would be to drop cookies in nuisance raids on German cities as a forerunner of the Light Night Striking Force (LNSF), which would form in 8 Group with the addition of further Mosquito units in 1944. For the time being, both squadrons remained at Marham in Norfolk, which was transferred to 8 Group control, and 109 Squadron would move there from Wyton in the following month.

The main force stayed on the ground for the first week and a half of June, providing a welcome respite for the crews. The Command was rarely totally inactive, however, and 3 Group contributed ten Stirlings to mining operations off the Frisians on the night of the 1/2nd. The freshmen crews of F/O Charles Eddy RNZAF and Sgt Wood were the 75(NZ) Squadron representatives, and they took off at 00.40, before heading eastwards under clear skies. The target area was located without difficulty in good visibility and the mines delivered into the briefed locations. One of the Stirlings flew over two flak ships and picked up a number of holes in the fuselage, but nothing vital was hit and both aircraft returned safely.

It was left to 3 Group to send a dozen gardeners back to the Nectarine I garden in the southern Frisians on the night of the 5/6th, the force consisting of eleven Stirlings and a solitary 115 Squadron Hercules-powered Mk II Lancaster. Five of the Stirlings belonged to 75(NZ) Squadron, including those of newcomers Sgt John Herbert Russell RAFVR, Sgt Andrew Rankin RAFVR, Sgt Gerald Scott Phillips RNZAF and F/Sgt Kenneth Alfred Burbidge RNZAF. They took off shortly before 23.00 with F/O Eddy the senior pilot on duty and encountered favourable conditions in the target area apart from haze, and all completed their sorties without incident, before returning safely after barely three hours in the air.

8 Group HQ moved out of Wyton on the 10th to Castle Hill House in Huntingdon, where it would remain for the rest of the war. Despite the fact that bomber crews had one of the most dangerous jobs in military service, they became bored and listless during extended periods of operational inactivity, and most preferred the dangers to the alternatives, like lectures and PT. Many cricket matches were played while the crews kicked their heels on the ground, and there was, no doubt, relief, when the operations against Düsseldorf and Münster planned for the 11th actually resulted in briefings taking place. The bomber stations from north to south became a hive of industry as ground crews and armourers got to work preparing 783 aircraft for the night's main event over the southern Ruhr and for an 8 Group show 180 miles to the north, which, in effect, was a mass H2S trial involving seventy-two aircraft. 8 Group's H2S-equipped Stirlings and Halifaxes had thus far been referred to as "special aircraft" in operational plans, but now that 83 Squadron had begun to take on H2S-equipped Lancasters, they would be referred to as "Y" aircraft. The plan for Düsseldorf would follow the standard pattern, in which

Mosquito yellow preliminary warning flares would be backed up by the other 8 Group aircraft, and the Oboe-laid red TIs on the aiming-point backed up with greens. However, uncertainty concerning the weather conditions resulted in the Mosquitos also carrying target-marking red flares with green stars.

3 Group detailed 112 aircraft for Düsseldorf and sixteen 75(NZ) Squadron Stirlings had their bomb bays filled with 2,000 and 1,000 pounders and mixed incendiaries and took off from Newmarket between 23.24 and 23.48 with W/C Wyatt the senior pilot on duty. He had adopted F/O Eddy and crew for the night, and S/Ls Broadbent and Laud were also on the order of battle as the Ruhr offensive was reignited. They adopted the southern approach to the region via the Scheldt estuary and Belgium and had to contend with static and lightning conditions in towering ten-tenths cloud as they made their way across the North Sea, some reporting the tops to be at 23,500 feet. It was probably at this stage that Sgts Burley and Thomas returned early with engine issues, and later when the squadron's BK817 AA-B was shot down by Oblt Wilhelm Telge of Stab II./NJG.1 and crashed at 01.35 six miles north of Verviers and within sight of the German frontier. S/L Laud and six others lost their lives, and only the rear gunner from this all-RAF crew survived to fall into enemy hands. The cloud had largely dissipated by the time that the others reached the southern Ruhr to find just small amounts at 2,000, 5,000 and 10,000 feet, dependent upon the time of arrival on final approach. Those in the vanguard of the main force were drawn on by yellow tracking flares from 01.05 and red skymarkers with green stars at 01.16, while those a little further back in the bomber stream were guided on by red and green skymarkers. The Paramatta marking (ground-marking TIs) did not seem to appear until these crews were turning away, but they were clearly visible to the crews in the rear-guard, who delivered their payloads from between 16,000 and 21,300 feet and described a sea of flames covering a massive area with columns of smoke rising through 21,000 feet. The searchlight and flak defences were at their formidable best, and S/L Broadbent's BK778 JN-U was coned and only escaped with great difficulty after violent evasive action, which caused the wireless operator to burst an eardrum. Others reported seeing night-fighters and a number were involved in brief and inconclusive engagements.

When all aircraft had been accounted for, thirty-eight were found to be missing, a figure that equalled the heaviest loss of the offensive to date. Returning crews described many large fires and huge explosions, and it was clear, that the target city had undergone an ordeal of extreme proportions. Post-raid reconnaissance revealed an area of 130 acres to have been destroyed, and local reports detailed an area of fire of eight by five kilometres covering the city centre. Almost nine thousand separate fire incidents were recorded, and massive damage was inflicted upon housing and industry, leading to the complete stoppage of production at forty-two war industry factories. The death toll in Düsseldorf amounted to almost thirteen hundred people, while 140,000 others were bombed out of their homes. This level of destruction was achieved despite the fact that an Oboe Mosquito had inadvertently dumped a bunch of TIs fourteen miles from the aiming point, which caused a proportion of the bombing to be wasted in open country.

F/O Jack Joll had been posted back to the squadron on the 24th of April and had since been promoted to acting flight lieutenant rank. As happened so often during the war, the substantive ranks of aircrew officers rarely caught up with their acting ranks, and while still officially a flying officer, Joll would be promoted again to squadron leader rank to fill the vacancy for A Flight commander created by the failure to return of S/L Laud. Lancasters and Halifaxes made up the main force for a heavy raid on Bochum on the following night, when, despite complete cloud cover, Oboe skymarking allowed massive damage to be inflicted upon the city centre. The Stirling brigade spent this night at home and 75(NZ) Squadron had the next night off as well, while a number of other Stirling units contributed to a mining effort off the Biscay ports.

The main operation on the night of the 14/15th was an all-Lancaster affair at Oberhausen, the heavily industrialized Ruhr city nestling in the eastern shadows of Duisburg. Oboe Mosquitos again provided the reference, and the heavies caused major damage to the Altstadt through complete cloud cover. 75(NZ) Squadron was back in action on this night, sending six Stirlings with freshman crews, including debutant F/O John Lloyd Edwards RAFVR, to lay mines in the Deodar garden in the Gironde Estuary. They took off in a half-hour slot from 22.29 with F/O Edwards the senior pilot on duty, but Sgts Rankin and Thomas returned early, one with an engine issue and the other with a failed intercom. BK646 AA-N was hit by flak at the French coast and was finished off by a night-fighter to crash near Bretteville-sur-Laize, south of Caen. F/O Edwards remained at the controls to enable the crew to abandon the aircraft, and sacrificed his life, while four, including both members of the RNZAF, fell into enemy hands and two others ultimately evaded a similar fate.

More than two hundred aircraft from 1, 5 and 8 Groups undertook a raid on Cologne on the night of the 16/17th, for which the marking was carried out, not by Oboe, but by sixteen Path Finder aircraft employing H2S. The experiment was not entirely successful after the late and sparse skymarking led to scattered bombing. Even so, four hundred houses were destroyed in a foretaste of what was in store for the Rhineland capital in the near future.

In the previous October 5 Group had mounted an audacious daylight attack by more than ninety Lancasters on the Schneider armaments works at Le Creusot and its power source, the nearby Henri Paul power station at Montchanin, situated in east-central France. Labelled the French "Krupp", the company was founded by the famous family, whose name will forever be associated with the Schneider Trophy, for which Britain, France, Italy and the USA competed bi-annually in float plane speed trials between 1913 and 1931. The competition ended when Britain won the trophy outright after three straight victories, the last of which was achieved by the Supermarine S6B powered by the forerunner of the Rolls Royce Merlin engine. The attack, code-named Operation Robinson, which was believed initially to have been successful, was later shown to have caused little damage, and a new attempt to halt production of artillery pieces for use by the Germans was planned for the night of the 19/20th.

290 aircraft were made ready on 3, 4, 6 and 8 Group stations, of which eighty-seven Stirlings were provided by 3 Group, eight of them belonging to the newly-formed 620 Squadron, which was making its operational debut. Just two Lancasters were to take part, both representing 7 Squadron, which was in the process of converting from Stirlings. 75(NZ) Squadron prepared fourteen Stirlings and among the participating crews was F/L Thomas Fraser Mccrorie RAFVR, who was undertaking his first sortie since arriving at Newmarket. The plan called for fourteen Stirlings and ten Halifaxes to drop green flares and yellow TIs as route markers by H2S, and for four Stirlings and two Lancasters to illuminate the aiming-point blindly with long sticks of flares. These and the remaining illuminators would keep the aiming-point highlighted, while the main force went about its business, before flying on to Montchanin to repeat the process. The 75(NZ) Squadron contingent took off either side of 22.00 with S/Ls Andrews,

Broadbent and Joll the senior pilots on duty, but F/L French was back after two hours for an unspecified reason.

Time-on-target for the leading Path Finder crews was scheduled for 01.45, and there were no further early returns among the Newmarket element during the 450-mile outward flight. On arrival in the target area, the weather conditions were found to be excellent, enabling the crews to identify lakes and other landmarks with ease. There was no opposition, which was fortunate, as Path Finder crews would have to make up to five passes over the aiming-points, not counting dummy runs, depending upon their respective roles. The 75(NZ) Squadron crews established their positions by Gee, confirmed visually, and delivered their 1,000 and 500 pounders from between 4,500 and 10,000 feet. A flak shell hit S/L Joll's EH880 AA-D and exploded in the port mainplane, causing a large volume of oil to flood into the fuselage, while also severing the electrical feed to the fuel pumps. Unable to ascertain the source of the leak, Canadian flight engineer, Sgt Falloon, used an axe to hack a two-foot-square hole in the fuselage to enable him to crawl into the wing to effect repairs, doing so while still in the target area and with complete disregard for his own safety. Once inside, he was able to operate the fuel pumps by hand and stem the leak from a punctured hydraulic line to one of the turrets. He also took advantage of the situation to examine the port main tyre for shrapnel cuts. The Stirling would return safely and Sgt George Hugh Falloon RCAF would be rewarded for his actions with a well-deserved DFM. BF564 JN-W also returned safely after losing its starboard-outer propeller just before bombing but having continued on to carry out its attack in the hands of P/O Sedunary and crew.

Returning crews reported explosions, fires and blue electrical flashes and the consensus was of a successful operation. However, while bombing photos revealed the attack to have fallen within three miles of the aiming-point, only about 20% of the bombs had hit the target and it was established later that drifting smoke had hampered target identification and that the Breuil steelworks had attracted most of the bombs in error, while the transformer station had escaped damage altogether. The problem was partly that main force crews had been trained to aim at TIs from medium to high level and were unused to identifying targets visually from medium to low level.

The 3 Group A-O-C, AVM Harrison, visited the squadron on the 20th, and at a ceremonial parade at 15.00, presented the squadron crest to W/C Wyatt. Afterwards it was given a prominent place in the officers' mess. A hectic round of four major operations to the Ruhr in the space of five nights began at Krefeld on the 21/22nd, for which a force of 705 aircraft was made ready, which included 113 provided by 3 Group. Situated on the West Bank of the Rhine south-west of Duisburg and north-west of Düsseldorf, this was the most westerly Ruhr town to be targeted during the campaign. At briefings, the 8 Group crews were told that ten Mosquitos would ground mark the aiming-point with red TIs, and if they proved not to be visible, nine Stirlings, thirteen Halifaxes and eight Lancasters were to ground mark with yellow TIs by H2S, backed up with reds and greens by twenty-five Lancasters, six Stirlings and six Halifaxes. 75(NZ) Squadron loaded fifteen Stirlings with 30lb and 4lb incendiaries and launched them from Newmarket either side of midnight with S/Ls Andrews and Joll the senior pilots on duty. Sgt Wood returned early with engine trouble, but the remainder flew on to the target, which lay under cloudless, moonlit skies with just drifting smoke from fires to impair the vertical visibility. Path Finders produced a near-perfect display of target marking for the main-force crews to exploit and three-quarters of them delivered their bombs within three miles of the aiming point. The 75(NZ) Squadron element carried out their attacks on red and green TIs and watched a concentrated area of fire develop, which would remain visible for a hundred miles into the return journey. At debriefings across the Command, crews described a sea of red fire giving off masses of smoke, with one particular jet-black column rising through 18,000 feet as they turned away. All were convinced of the success of the operation, and one crew likened it to the Wuppertal-Barmen raid. The searchlight and flak defences were described by most as moderate, and it was the night-fighters that were responsible for the majority of the forty-four missing bombers, a new record for the campaign. Seventeen Halifaxes were lost, six of them from 35 (Madras Presidency) Squadron of the Path Finders, and this represented an 8.1% loss rate for the type, which was marginally more than the 7.7% registered by the Stirlings, but appreciably in excess of the 3.4% for the Lancaster brigade. In return for this huge loss, Krefeld had suffered the destruction of 5,517 houses in an area of devastation in the centre representing 47% of the built-up area, leaving 72,000 people homeless and a death toll of 1,056.

Crews were back in their briefing rooms on the following afternoon to learn about that night's operation against Mülheim-an-der-Ruhr, a medium-size town situated south-east of Duisburg and south-west of Essen. A force of 557 aircraft was prepared, along with a plan that called for eight Oboe Mosquitos plus two in reserve to drop yellow preliminary warning TIs on track, before marking the aiming-point with red TIs for twenty-nine Path Finder Lancasters to back up with greens. 3 Group detailed 105 aircraft, of which fifteen Stirlings were loaded with 4lb and 30lb incendiaries by 75(NZ) Squadron and departed Newmarket between 23.34 and 23.56 with S/L Joll the senior pilot on duty and a dozen crews captained by NCO pilots and one debutant, P/O Francis Max McKenzie, RNZAF. After climbing out, they set course for the North Sea to join up with the rest of the bomber stream and, for once, there would be no early returns, but EH889 AA-Z had just crossed the Dutch coast when it was intercepted by the night-fighter of Oblt Lothar Linke of IV./NJG.1 and shot down into the Ijsselmeer. There were no survivors from the crew of F/L Thomas McCrorie RAFVR, which contained the previously-mentioned Canadian Tod twins and one member of the RNZAF.

The others reached the target to find a thin layer of three-tenths stratus cloud at 10,000 feet, through which it could be seen that the Path Finders had produced another example of near-perfect marking. The main force crews bombed on red and green TIs and observed the development of many fires, while witnessing a large red explosion at 01.34. The defenders fought back again to claim thirty-five bombers, with the Halifaxes and Stirlings representing two-thirds of them and suffering a respective loss rate of 7.7% and 11.8%. F/Sgt Burbidge RNZAF sent a message at 02.25 indicating that EF399 AA-O had been severely damaged by flak, and soon afterwards, it ran into the night-fighter of Hptm Egmont Prinz zur Lippe Weissenfeld of III./NJG.1, who shot it down at 02.47 to crash near Markelo in eastern Holland. There were no survivors from the crew, which included three other members of the RNZAF. BK810 AA-G was another victim of a flak/night-fighter combination and its loss was credited to Hptm Wilhelm Herget of I./NJG.1. It crashed at 02.10 near Venray in south-eastern Holland, killing P/O Francis McKenzie RNZAF and his RNZAF bomb-aimer. Three of the five survivors, who fell into enemy hands, were also members of the RNZAF. EF408 AA-P contained the crew of F/Sgt Wood RAFVR and succumbed to flak over the target, somehow making its way eastwards towards Gelsenkirchen before crashing and killing the crew, which included two members of the RNZAF.

While this operation was in progress, RNZAF debutants P/O Allan Mason Forbes Alexander and F/Sgt Osric Hartnell White took advantage of the distraction to deliver mines into the waters off the Frisians. Post-raid reconnaissance at Mülheim revealed an accurate and concentrated attack, which destroyed eleven hundred buildings, mostly in central and northern districts and damaged to some extent twelve thousand more. A post-war survey would suggest that 64% of the built-up area had been destroyed on this one night, when bombing also spilled into the eastern districts of Oberhausen to the north, inflicting further extensive damage.

The Command rested on the 23rd, the day on which F/L French and crew were posted to 7 Squadron of the Path Finders. Having destroyed the Barmen half of Wuppertal at the end of May in one of the most devastating attacks to date, it was time to visit the same catastrophe on the western half, Elberfeld, for which a force of 630 aircraft was made ready on the 24th. On this occasion, six Lancasters, three Stirlings and three Halifaxes of 8 Group were to deliver the yellow route markers on H2S, while seven Oboe Mosquitos marked the aiming-point with red TIs and eighteen Lancasters, seven Halifaxes and three Stirlings backed them up with greens. 3 Group supported the operation with 105 aircraft, of which thirteen of the Stirlings were provided by 75(NZ) Squadron and loaded with incendiaries. They took off either side of 23.30 with S/Ls Andrews and Joll the senior pilots on duty and only F/Sgt Mee returned early with an unserviceable rear turret. The others made landfall over the Scheldt and ran the usual gauntlet of searchlights and flak from the Cologne and Düsseldorf defence zones, which were aided by the formation of condensation trails at between 18,000 and 21,000 feet to advertise the presence of the bomber stream. It seemed to some that fewer guns were firing at them over the target, where small amounts of cloud with tops at 17,000 feet were insufficient to obscure the ground.

The Path Finder marking was accurate and concentrated, and the main force went in at between 14,000 and 19,000 feet to deliver their bombs onto the TIs before a creep-back developed that hit urban areas to the west. Those arriving at the tail end of the attack described thick columns of smoke already passing through 19,000 feet and the glow of fires visible from the Dutch coast. Post-raid reconnaissance and local sources revealed another massively concentrated and accurate attack, which had reduced to rubble an estimated 90% of Elberfeld's built-up area, including three thousand houses and 171 industrial premises. It had also severely damaged 2,500 houses and dozens of important factory buildings, and the fact that more buildings were destroyed than damaged provided a telling commentary on the conditions on the ground. The number of fatalities stood at around eighteen hundred, and some of the survivors might have been cheered to know that thirty-four bombers, containing 240 of their tormentors, would not be returning to England that night. Among them was EH902 AA-K, which crashed into the sea off the island of Beveland in the Scheldt Estuary and took with it the lives of P/O Norman Bluck RNZAF and his crew, two of whom were members of the RNZAF.

Instructions were received across the Command on the 25th to prepare for the first major attack on the Ruhr city of Gelsenkirchen since 1941, when it had been a regular destination under the Oil Directive. A force of 473 aircraft was assembled and the crews briefed to focus on the Nordstern synthetic oil plant (Gelsenberg A G), which was a Bergius-process manufacturer of high-grade petroleum products, particularly aviation fuel. 8 Group was to provide seven Oboe Mosquitos plus two in reserve to drop route markers and skymark the aiming-point, and two to bomb after the main force, but none of its heavy aircraft was to be involved. The 3 Group contribution amounted to seventy-three Stirlings and a dozen Lancasters, eleven of the former loaded with 30lb and 4lb incendiaries and sent on their way between 23.28 and 23.41 for what would prove to be the final time from Newmarket. S/L Broadbent was the senior pilot on duty as they took off, by which time the freshman crew of P/O George Morrison Duncan RAFVR were well on their way to the Deodar garden in the Gironde Estuary, having taken-off at 22.45 loaded with 1,500lb parachute mines.

The route out for those involved in the main event was the standard one for a target located on the northern side of the Ruhr, with landfall over the Den Helder peninsula, before passing to the north of Amsterdam and heading south-east across the Münsterland to the final turning point towards the south. There were no early returns among the Kiwi element and they arrived over the east-central Ruhr to be greeted by ten-tenths stratus with tops at 10,000 to 15,000 feet, which would not have been a problem had five of the Oboe Mosquitos not suffered equipment failures. This caused tracking flares to be late and to drop in the wrong sequence in a somewhat scattered manner at a time when the crews were contending with an intense flak barrage. Searchlights illuminated the cloud as the main force crews bombed on red flares with green stars from up to 20,000 feet, and on return they would report a large explosion at 01.43 and the glow from the target to be visible from the Dutch coast. The retreating bombers had been chased to the sea by a large deployment of enemy night-fighters, which, together with flak, would bring down thirty of them.

The crew of BF434 AA-Y reported being attacked by a night-fighter, which appeared astern and was evaded when Sgt Burley threw the Stirling into a violent corkscrew. The mid-upper and rear gunners managed to fire off a burst and the enemy aircraft was seen to dive towards the ground, where a flash and fire seemed to confirm its fate. The crew claimed it as destroyed. P/O Alexander spotted a Ju88 on his starboard bow and turned towards it in BF443 AA-V, allowing his mid-upper gunner to get a short burst in before the night-fighter disappeared. S/L Broadbent and crew were aboard BK778 JN-U and were approached by an unidentified single-engine aircraft, which the mid-upper and rear gunners fired at with a couple of medium bursts. This caused a large, bright flash from the fighter, which immediately went into a steep dive and disappeared from sight to be claimed as destroyed. BK768 AA-L failed to return after crashing into the Ijsselmeer, and there were no survivors from the crew of P/O "Ross" Perrott RNZAF, two others of whom were members of the RNZAF. The Duncan crew returned from the south-western coast of France at 05.57 and brought an end to the squadron's operational association with Newmarket.

There was no flying on the 26th as preparations were put in hand for the move to Mepal in Cambridgeshire, which took place between the 27th and 29th. F/L Lowe was posted at this time to 26 O.T.U at the conclusion of his tour. Construction of the new airfield at Mepal, situated six miles west of Ely, had begun in July 1942 and 75(NZ) Squadron would be its first and only resident unit, remaining there until after war's end. Operationally it was a big improvement over Newmarket's grass field and converted racecourse facilities, with brand new runways, taxiways, dispersal areas and maintenance hangars, although construction was still going on when they moved in and would continue well into 1944. Mepal's identification letters were "M.P." and its radio call-sign was "Mawkish". The new station would be commanded by G/C Kenneth Michael Macleod Wasse DFC, who had been station commander at Newmarket. As a consequence of the change of address, the squadron missed the opening round of a devastating three-raid series of attacks on Cologne on the night of the 28/29th, which 3 group supported with sixty-eight Stirlings and fourteen Lancasters. A massive 6,400 buildings were destroyed, a further fifteen thousand were damaged to some extent and the death toll on the ground exceeded 4,700 people, a new record for a Bomber Command attack.

During the course of the month the squadron was involved in eleven operations, dispatching one hundred sorties for the loss of eight Stirlings and crews.

July 1943

The first two days of the new month were beset by poor weather conditions, which kept all but a few gardeners and Mosquitos on the ground and caused 3 Group gardening operations planned for the 1st and 2nd to be cancelled. The second attack of the current campaign against Cologne was scheduled for the night of the 3/4th, and crews were called to briefings on all operational stations during the late afternoon as a force of 653 aircraft was assembled. The Path Finder crews listened with interest as they were told that ten Mosquitos would drop green flares four-and-a-half miles from the target as a preliminary warning, and red, green and white flares and red TIs on the aiming-point. On this night, the aiming-point was on the East Bank of the Rhine in the industrial Deutz district, where the Klöckner-Humboldt-Deutz works manufactured aero-engines and heavy and tracked vehicles for the Wehrmacht, served by the nearby Kalk and Gremberg marshalling yards. Nine Halifaxes and twenty-four Lancasters were to back up the red TIs with greens, but, in the event that cloud concealed the TIs, they were to bomb on H2S with the main force along with the remaining nine Halifaxes and seventeen Lancasters. 3 Group made ready eighty Stirlings and fourteen Lancasters, 75(NZ) Squadron loading thirteen of the former with incendiaries for its maiden operation from Mepal.

They took off between 23.00 and 23.30 with W/C Wyatt the senior pilot on duty and among them were an additional four Stirlings bearing aloft the freshman crews of Sgt Philip Albin Miles Moseley RAFVR, Sgt Trevor Fear RAFVR, Sgt Phillip Hartstein RAFVR and Sgt James Arthur Couper RNZAF, who were bound for mining duties off the Frisians. F/Sgt Mee was forced to return from Cologne early because of engine trouble, leaving the others to continue on in the expectation of finding nine-tenths cloud from the English coast all the way to the target, as forecast by the meteorological experts. What the leading Path Finder heavy crews actually encountered, however, was a clear sky and red Oboe-laid TIs in the bomb sights, which they backed up with greens. There was a certain amount of haze, but this did not interfere with the accuracy of the attack, which developed in concentrated form in the face, initially, of an intense flak defence. By the time the raid reached its crescendo, it was nine-tenths smoke rather than cloud that hung over the city, through which the 75(NZ) Squadron participants delivered their incendiary loads from an average 16,000 feet. Returning crews described a highly successful raid, which left the city a mass of flames with smoke rising to 10,000 feet and blotting out ground detail. Some noticed a tendency to creep-back, but the overall impression was of another operation more successful than the Thousand raid against this city at the end of May 1942. Post-raid reconnaissance and local reports confirmed another stunningly accurate and concentrated attack, in which twenty industrial premises and 2,200 houses had been destroyed, 588 people had been killed and 72,000 bombed out of their homes at a cost to the Command of thirty aircraft.

The gardeners all completed their tasks as briefed, and there were no empty dispersals to contemplate at Mepal on the following morning.

Some crews commented on the presence over Cologne of day fighters, and this was clear evidence of the introduction of a new tactic by the Luftwaffe. The newly formed JG300 was operating for the first time, employing the Wilde Sau (Wild Boar) tactics, which was the brainchild of former bomber pilot, Major Hans-Joachim (Hajo) Herrmann. The unit had been formed in June with borrowed standard BF109 and FW190 single-engine day fighters to operate directly over a target, seeking out bombers silhouetted against the fires and TIs. On this night, the unit would claim twelve victories, but would have to share them with the flak batteries, which claimed them also. Unaccustomed to being pursued by fighters over a target, it would take time for the bomber crews to work out what was happening, and until they did, friendly fire would often be blamed for damage incurred by unseen causes.

On the following night four crews were sent mining in the Cinnamon garden off the Ile-de-Re and the ports of La Rochelle and La Pallice, taking off either side of 22.00 and completing their tasks as briefed under clear skies and in excellent visibility. The crews of P/O Clifford Charles Pownall Logan RAAF, F/O Geoffrey Turner RCAF, Sgt Michael Henry Charles Ashdown RAFVR and Sgt Henry Nichol RAF were all debutants. It was similar fare on the night of the 5/6th for four crews, who took off at 23.40 for the Frisians, and again encountered favourable weather conditions and good visibility. EF436 AA-A went missing without trace with the debutant crew of F/Sgt Raymond Thomas RNZAF and the circumstances are clarified by Bill Chorley in Bomber Command Losses for 1943. According to a reliable source in the Netherlands, the Stirling was shot down by Oblt Hermann Greiner of IV./NJG1 at 02.31, when some twelve miles north-west of Terschelling.

The last of the three attacks on Cologne was carried out by an all-Lancaster heavy force on the night of the 8/9th, again with great accuracy, and once the dust had settled the city authorities were able to confirm that the three-raid series had caused the destruction of eleven thousand buildings, killed 5,500 people and rendered homeless of a further 350,000. This massive success for the Command was gained at a cost of sixty-two heavy bombers. 75(NZ) Squadron was also active on this night, sending six gardeners to the Deodar garden in the Gironde estuary between 22.15 and 05.45. All delivered their mines as briefed in good visibility, despite the presence of patchy cloud and sea mist, and one unspecified aircraft returned with minor damage to the rear turret, sustained in a brief encounter with an enemy night-fighter.

There were no operations for the Stirling units on the next four nights, and poor weather conditions during the day curtailed some training activity for the squadron, particularly the very useful fighter affiliation exercises. Operations were mounted by other elements of the Command during that period to Gelsenkirchen on the night of the 9/10th and Turin on the 12/13th, the former unsuccessfully after equipment failure afflicted many of the Oboe Mosquitos, and the latter with great success, but at the cost of the life of W/C Nettleton VC of 44 (Rhodesia) Squadron, who had earned his award for his part in the epic daylight raid on the Augsburg-based M.A.N factory in April 1942.

Although two more operations to the Ruhr region would be launched late in the month, the campaign was winding down and Harris was already planning his next attempt to shorten the war by bombing alone, buoyed by the success of the spring offensive. He could look back on the past four and a half months with genuine satisfaction at the performance of his squadrons, and, as a champion of technological innovation, take particular pride in the success of Oboe, which had been the decisive factor. Although losses had been grievously high and the Ruhr's reputation as "Happy Valley" well earned, its most important towns and cities had suffered catastrophic destruction. In Britain, the aircraft factories had more than kept pace with the rate of attrition, while the training units both at home and overseas were pouring eager new crews into the fray to fill the gaps. With confidence high in the ability of his Command to destroy almost any target at will, Harris prepared for his next major campaign, the erasure from the map of a prominent German city in a short, sharp series of maximum effort raids to be launched during the final week of the month.

In the meantime, a force of 374 aircraft from all but 5 Group was assembled on the 13th for an operation that night against the Spa city of Aachen, the most westerly German city and an important railway hub and industrial centre situated right on the frontiers with Belgium and Holland. The plan called for ten Halifaxes to drop yellow TIs as route markers and six Oboe Mosquitos to ground mark the aiming-point with red TIs, backed up with green TIs by nineteen Halifaxes. The main force element consisted of Halifaxes, Wellingtons and Stirlings, with just eighteen Lancasters among the 8 Group contribution. 3 Group weighed in with fifty-Stirlings and eighteen Lancasters, including nine of the former belonging to 75(NZ) Squadron, each loaded with incendiaries. They were launched from Mepal either side of midnight with no senior pilots on duty, and after crossing Holland and Belgium, found seven to nine-tenths cloud lying predominantly over the eastern half of the city with tops at around 9,000 feet. A strong tail wind had driven the first wave to the target ahead of schedule and an unusually large number of aircraft bombed as soon as the Path Finder markers went down, giving rise to a sudden proliferation of fires. On the run in to the target, Sgt Nicol's BF518 AA-E was attacked by a Ju88, which the rear gunner had sighted shortly after receiving a "Boozer" radar warning signal. As the enemy opened fire and made a subsequent pass, both the rear and mid-upper gunners returned fire, driving it off and claiming it as damaged.

Returning crews reported that large areas of the town seemed to burst into flames at once, and also commented on the effectiveness of the searchlights and flak and the prevalence of night-fighters. P/O Logan's EE878 AA-P sustained flak damage to the starboard-outer engine, the fin and elevator, and he landed safely at the emergency landing-strip at Ford on the Sussex coast. BK646 AA-N was attacked by a Ju88, during which engagement the wireless operator, F/Sgt Thorstenson, was wounded. P/O Rankin's rear gunner returned fire, forcing the enemy to break away and then return for another attack from astern. The rear gunner fired a long burst, observing a flash from the night-fighter, which performed a half-turn and fell away into cloud, after which, an explosion on the ground seemed to confirm its destruction. P/O Alexander and crew sighted a Me210 a hundred yards away on the port beam and slightly below, and as it passed underneath the Stirling, the front gunner engaged it with a short burst, observing it then to dive into the clouds, upon which he claimed it as possibly destroyed. It was the Alexander crew's first outing in F/L French's "kite", BK777 AA-U, and they would quickly label it as their own with colourful nose art proclaiming "Alexander's Ragtime Crew". EE886 AA-L arrived in home airspace with a burst tyre, and during the emergency landing at Oakington, the undercarriage collapsed, causing the Stirling to overturn and catch fire before coming to rest. F/O Eddy was seriously wounded in the incident but remained on board to assist his bomb-aimer's escape. Having then vacated the burning wreckage, he heard that the mid-upper gunner was trapped and ventured back inside to assist a medical officer in a vain attempt to rescue him. Only when the heat, smoke and fumes became too much did he give up and collapsed immediately on exiting the aircraft. It is believed that the mid-upper gunner had been killed on impact. In May 1944, F/O Charles Eddy RNZAF would be made an additional member of the Military Division of the Most Excellent Order of the British Empire in recognition of his outstanding courage and gallantry.

The Aachen authorities confirmed the destruction of 2,927 buildings containing more than 16,800 dwelling units, and eight large war industry factories were also hit along with many public and cultural buildings.

Hamburg had been a regular target for the Command throughout the war to date, and had been attacked, amongst other occasions, during the final week of July in 1940, 1941 and 1942. It had been spared by the weather from hosting the first "One Thousand" bomber raid at the end of May 1942, but Harris now identified it as the ideal candidate for destruction under Operation Gomorrah, the intention of which was to cause the maximum impact to the enemy's morale in a short, sharp campaign, employing ten thousand tons of bombs. Hamburg's political status was second only to Berlin's, and its value to the war effort in terms of ship and U-Boot construction and other war production was undeniable, but it suited Harris's criteria also in other respects. Its location close to a coastline aided navigation and made it accessible from the North Sea without the need to spend time over hostile territory, and its relatively short distance from the bomber stations enabled a force to approach and retreat during the few hours of darkness afforded by mid-summer. Finally, lying beyond the range of Oboe, which had proved so decisive at the Ruhr, Hamburg had the wide River Elbe and the distinctive Binnen and Aussen-Alster Lakes to provide a solid H2S signature for the navigators high above.

The first operation in the campaign was actually posted on the 22nd, for which 75(NZ) Squadron was required to provide twenty-two Stirlings, until it was cancelled during the afternoon. The same thing happened on the 23rd, by which time there had been no operations for most squadrons for nine days, despite a number being posted, and by the time that 791 crews trooped into their respective briefing rooms on the 24th, they probably expected the day to end with yet another scrub. Instead, they were read a special message from the commander-in-chief to announce the beginning of the Battle of Hamburg. They listened intently to the revelation that they would be aided by the first operational use of "window", aluminium-backed strips of paper of precise length, which, when released in bundles into the airstream at a predetermined point, would drift down slowly in vast clouds to swamp the enemy night-fighter, searchlight and gun-laying radar systems with false returns and render them blind. The device had actually been available for a year, but its use had been vetoed in case the enemy copied it for use against Britain. It was not realized that Germany had, in fact, already developed its own version called Düppel, which it had withheld for the same reason.

The plan of attack called for eleven Lancasters and nine Halifaxes to drop yellow TIs as route markers, before continuing on to mark the aiming-point with yellow TIs, and if conditions permitted, illuminator flares. The route markers were to be backed up by six Stirlings, thirteen

Lancasters and nine Halifaxes, and six Lancasters and two Halifaxes were to use the yellow TIs as a guide, and with the aid of flares, mark the aiming-point with red TIs, which would be backed up with green TIs by the remaining marker crews. 3 Group detailed 115 Stirlings and seventeen Lancasters, 75(NZ) Squadron contributing a record twenty-three of the former, the bomb bays of which were loaded with 2,000lb and 1,000lb bombs and incendiaries. They departed Mepal between 21.45 and 22.38 with all three flight commanders on the order of battle and lost the services of Sgt Thomas and P/O Rankin to intercom and engine failure. The remainder continued on across the North Sea and at a predetermined point, the designated crew member, in most cases the wireless operator, began to dispense "window" through the flare chute, beginning shortly after 00.30. The effects appeared to be immediate as few night-fighters rose to meet the approaching bombers and although a number of aircraft were shot down over the sea during the outward flight, two of them 103 Squadron Lancasters, they were off course and outside of the protection of the bomber stream and may well have been among those returning early with technical difficulties.

The efficacy of "window" was made more apparent in the target area, where the crews noticed an absence of the usually efficient co-ordination between the searchlights and flak batteries and defence appeared random and sporadic. This offered the Path Finders the opportunity to mark the target by visual reference and H2S virtually unmolested, and although the red and green TIs were a little misplaced and scattered, they landed in sufficient numbers close to the city centre to provide the main force crews with ample opportunity to deliver a massive blow. It rarely happened that aircraft arrived in strict bands according to their task, and some main force crews were already over the target from the opening of the raid at 01.00. The 75(NZ) Squadron crews carried out their attacks from up to around 16,000 feet and returning crews reported a successful operation that had left part of the city ablaze with a column of smoke rising through 20,000 feet.

Post-raid reconnaissance revealed that a six-mile-long creep-back had developed, which cut a swathe of destruction from the city centre along the line of approach, out across the north-western districts and into open country, where a proportion of the bombing had been wasted. In fact, less than half of the force had bombed within three miles of the city centre during the fifty-minute-long raid, in which 2,284 tons of bombs had been delivered, despite which, the city had suffered a telling blow and fifteen hundreds of its inhabitants lay dead. For the Command it was an encouraging start to the campaign, particularly in the light of just twelve missing aircraft, for which "window" was largely responsible. Three Stirlings failed to return, among them 75(NZ) Squadron's EE890 AA-L, which was shot down by a night-fighter flown by Feldwebel Meissner of II./NJG.3 and crashed at Neumünster in the centre of the Schleswig-Holstein peninsula on the way to the target. W/O Henry Nicol RAF and three of his crew were killed, while three others, including both RNZAF members, were taken into captivity. EH935 JN-K was one of a few aircraft to be caught in a searchlight cone, and while taking evasive action, collided with a Ju88 as it approached head-on. The Stirling lost four feet of its starboard wing, while the fighter was seen to crash. F/O Geoffrey Turner RCAF struggled to keep the wounded Stirling on an even keel during the three-hour return flight, but assisted by the bomb-aimer, managed to regain Mepal and land safely. Returning crews spoke of large areas of fire and black smoke rising to 14,500 feet as they withdrew.

On the following night, and in the expectation that Hamburg would be covered by smoke, Harris switched his force to Essen, where he could take advantage of the body blow dealt to the enemy defensive system by "window". A force of 705 aircraft was made ready and a plan prepared, which called for Halifaxes and Lancasters of 35 (Madras Presidency) and 156 Squadrons to drop preliminary yellow warning TIs on track by H2S, which would be backed up by elements of 7 and 156 Squadron. Ahead, fourteen Oboe Mosquitos would mark the aiming-point with red TIs, which nineteen Lancasters, nine Halifaxes and five Stirlings were to back up with greens. 3 Group detailed ninety-nine Stirlings and sixteen Lancasters, nineteen of the former provided by 75(NZ) Squadron, which had two debutant captains operating in the persons of W/O Gordon Kenneth Williams RNZAF and F/Sgt Jack Neville Darney RNZAF. The Kiwi element departed Mepal between 22.10 and 22.35 with no senior pilots on duty and lost the services of the crews of F/Sgt Whitehead and F/O Duncan to engine and intercom issues. The others flew out in good, if hazy, conditions over the North Sea and visibility was good from the Dutch coast eastwards as far as the central Ruhr, where four to five-tenths cloud hung out to the west, leaving clear skies over the aiming-point and just the usual ground haze to spoil the vertical visibility. The Path Finder marking was accurate and concentrated more towards the eastern side of the city, and crews watched on as a highly concentrated attack developed, which left the ground enveloped in smoke from the many fires and explosions. Returning crews reported concentrated fires around the aiming-point in a one-and-a-half-square-mile area of the city, two large, red explosions at 00.36 and 00.39 and a column of smoke rising through 20,000 feet as they withdrew to the west, the glow remaining visible as far away as the Dutch coast. Twenty-six aircraft failed to return, and among them was EE892 AA-F, containing the crew of Sgt Michael Ashdown RAFVR. The Stirling was observed to crash in flames into the sea off Southwold on the Suffolk coast on the way home, and there were no survivors. The Aldeburgh lifeboat recovered four bodies for burial, and the remaining three are commemorated on the Runnymede Memorial. There were no members of the RNZAF on board.

At debriefing it emerged that EH936 JN-W had been held in a searchlight cone for three minutes before diving and twisting its way clear. F/Sgt "Speed" Williams's rear and mid-upper gunners alerted him to an enemy aircraft at four hundred yards approaching from astern, upon which, he threw the Stirling into a corkscrew manoeuvre. The gunners fired a long burst, and the enemy was seen to explode and fall to the ground. One Stirling sustained slight flak damage but returned safely for the crew to describe the target area as a mass of flames with many huge explosions in their midst. Post-raid reconnaissance and local sources confirmed the raid to be another outstanding success against this important war materials producing city, in which the complex of Krupp manufacturing sites suffered its heaviest damage of the war to date. Of 134 other industrial premises hit, fifty-one suffered complete destruction, along with more than 2,800 houses. It is believed that Dr Gustav Krupp suffered a stroke on the following day, from which he never recovered.

A night off preceded the second round of Operation Gomorrah on the night of the 27/28th, for which a force of 787 aircraft was made ready. 3 Group contributed 108 Stirlings and seventeen Lancasters and at Mepal, twenty-two Stirlings were loaded with 2,000lb and 1,000lb bombs and a selection of incendiaries. The crews attended briefing to learn that yellow route markers would be dropped by H2S on the enemy coast and backed up, and that "Y" aircraft (H2S blind markers) were to deliver red TIs and a stick of flares over the aiming-point, for visual markers to confirm and back up with green TIs. The 75(NZ) Squadron element took off either side of 22.00 with S/Ls Andrews and Joll the senior pilots on duty and one first-time captain in the form of F/Sgt Eric John Roberts RNZAF. Two returned early with engine trouble, while the remainder pushed on towards Hansastadt (Ancient Free Trade City) Hamburg, crossing the coast over the Schleswig-Holstein peninsula to the north, none of them having any concept of the events that were to follow their arrival.

A previously unknown and terrible phenomenon was about to present itself to the world and introduce a new word "firestorm" into the English language. A number of factors would conspire on this night to seal the fate of this great city and its hapless inhabitants in an orgy of destruction that was quite unprecedented in air warfare. An uncharacteristically hot and dry spell of weather had left the city a tinderbox, and the spark to ignite it came with the Path Finders' H2S-laid yellow and green TIs, which fell with almost total concentration some two miles to the east of the intended city-centre aiming-point and into the densely populated working-class residential districts of Hamm, Hammerbrook and Borgfeld. To compound this, the main force, which had been drawn on to the target by yellow release-point flares, bombed with rare precision and almost no creep-back, and deposited much of its 2,300 tons of bombs into this relatively compact area. The Mepal crews found three-tenths cloud in the target area and smoke already beginning to drift across the city to obscure ground detail. They observed many explosions and a sea of flames developing below as they carried out their attacks and a ship was observed to be on fire in a dock south of the main attack. Those bombing towards the later stages of the raid observed a pall of smoke rising through 20,000 feet, and the glow of fires was reported to remain visible for up to two hundred miles into the return journey.

On the ground, individual fires began to join together to form one giant conflagration, which sucked in oxygen from surrounding areas at hurricane speeds to feed its voracious appetite. Trees were uprooted and flung bodily into the inferno, along with debris and people, and temperatures at the seat of the flames exceeded one thousand degrees Celcius. The defences were overwhelmed and the fire service unable to pass through the rubble-strewn streets to gain access to the worst-affected areas. Even had they done so, they could not have entered the firestorm area, and only after all of the combustible material had been consumed did the flames subside. By this time, there was no-one alive to rescue, and an estimated forty thousand people died on this one night alone. A mass exodus from the city, which would ultimately exceed one million people, began on the following morning and this undoubtedly saved many from the ravages of the next raid, which would come two nights later. Seventeen aircraft failed to return, reflecting the enemy's developing response to the advantage gained by the Command through "window". No gain was ever permanent, and the balance of power would continue to shift from one side to the other for the next year. For a change, it was the Lancaster brigade that sustained the highest numerical casualties on this night, accounting for eleven of the failures to return. Three of the squadron's Stirlings picked up minor flak damage, while F/Sgt Roberts and crew in EE897 AA-G described coming under attack twice from the port beam and once from starboard by a Ju88. Both the front and mid upper turrets were put out of action, a bomb door was shot off and a petrol pipe severed, before the assailant was driven off by return fire and claimed as damaged. F/Sgt White was also attacked by a Ju88, but evasive action and a short burst from the mid-upper gunner was enough to discourage him, and EF435 JN-J and her crew escaped unscathed.

Bomber Command's heavy brigade stayed at home on the following night, while four Mosquitos carried out a nuisance raid on Hamburg to ensure that the residents' sleep was disturbed. A force of 777 aircraft was put together to continue Hamburg's torment on the 29th, while the crews attended briefings to learn of their part in the proceedings. They were told that red TIs and flares were to be employed as route markers, before seventeen Lancasters and eight Halifaxes marked the aiming-point with yellow TIs by H2S to be backed up by thirty-four Lancasters, six Stirlings and nine Halifaxes. 3 Group provided 110 Stirlings and fifteen Lancasters, seventeen of the former loaded with 30lb and 4lb incendiaries at Mepal, and they took off between 21.55 and 21.25 with S/L Broadbent the senior pilot on duty. Sgt Mitchell and P/O Alexander returned early, leaving the remainder to push on in good weather conditions, which persisted all the way to the target, where smoke-haze was the only impediment to vertical visibility. The plan was to approach from due north to hit the northern and north-eastern districts, which thus far had escaped serious damage, but the Path Finders strayed two miles to the east of the intended track and dropped their markers just to the south of the already devastated firestorm area. Many bombs fell into the still smouldering ruins, before a four-mile creep-back rescued the situation by spreading along the line of approach into the residential districts of Wandsbek and Barmbek, and parts of Uhlenhorst and Winterhude. The 75(NZ) Squadron crews carried out their bombing runs at around 15,000 feet and released their loads on yellow and green TIs, before returning to report smoke rising through 17,000 feet and fires visible for two hundred miles into the homeward journey. The defences were very active on this night, suggesting that the flak and searchlight systems had recovered somewhat from the "window" setback, and two crews described being held in a searchlight cone, one for ten minutes and another for eight, which would have seemed like a lifetime. They ultimately escaped with extreme difficulty, but sustained shrapnel damage. Four other crews, those of Sgt Hartstein, F/O Duncan, F/Sgt Wilkinson and F/Sgt Darney, reported encounters with night-fighters, none of which resulted in damage to either side. P/O Sedunary lost an engine shortly after bombing but made it home to a perfect landing.

Before the final Hamburg raid took place, the Ruhr campaign was brought to a conclusion on the 30th with an attack on the town of Remscheid, situated about six miles south of Wuppertal, where the main industries were mechanical engineering and tool-making. Up until this point, only twenty-six people had lost their lives in this town as a result of stray bombs, but it was now to face a modest force of 273 aircraft consisting of roughly equal numbers of Lancasters, Halifaxes and Stirlings with six Oboe Mosquitos to mark out the aiming-point with red TIs. Thirteen of the eighty-seven 3 Group Stirlings were provided by 75(NZ) Squadron carrying all-incendiary loads, and they took off between 22.23 and 22.45 with S/L Joll the senior pilot on duty. One aircraft returned early with an unserviceable rear turret, but the others reached the target to find clear skies and good visibility, along with pinpoint marking by Oboe Mosquitos backed up by the Path Finder heavy brigade. The main force bombed with great accuracy at this virtually virgin target and returning crews reported many fires and explosions. On the way in, and shortly after witnessing a combat just above and to starboard, F/Sgt "Speed" Williams and crew, who were once more in EH936 JN-W, had been approached by an unidentified twin-engine aircraft. The front gunner fired three bursts before the attacker rolled to starboard and fell to the ground on fire. The captain and gunner both saw it explode when it hit the ground, and it was claimed as destroyed. F/Sgt White's EF435 JN-J was attacked three times by an unidentified enemy aircraft, which was damaged by return fire and eventually broke away.

Post-raid reconnaissance confirmed a devastatingly effective raid, which destroyed more than 3,100 houses and 107 industrial buildings and killed 1,120 people. It was a stunning example of what the Command could achieve with a force of moderate size if all went according to plan. Fifteen aircraft failed to return, eight of them Stirlings, and two of those missing belonged to 75(NZ) Squadron. BF458 JN-P came down at Krefeld-Uerdingen, twenty-five miles north-west of the target, probably while outbound, and only two survived from the crew of P/O Thomas to be taken into captivity. Among the fatalities was the RNZAF bomb-aimer. EE915 AA-X was lost without trace with the crew of F/Sgt Darney RNZAF, which included two other members of the RNZAF. Also lost with this crew was the squadron's flight engineer leader, F/L Leonard Charles Dive-Robinson RAF. While this operation was in progress, the freshman crew of Sgt Allan Johnson Mayfield RNZAF successfully carried out a mining sortie off the Frisians.

During the course of the month the squadron received twenty-eight new Mk III Stirlings from Austin's at Marston Green and Short's at Swindon, although four of them were passed on immediately to the recently-formed 620 Squadron. The squadron took part in eleven operations and dispatched 131 sorties for the loss of six Stirlings and five crews and S/Ls Andrews and Broadbent were awarded the DFC at this time in recognition of their operational careers to date. W/C Wyatt received a message of appreciation from 3 Group A-O-C, AVM Harrison, passing on the thanks of Bomber Command chief ACM Harris for the efforts made by the personnel of all units in the group for the month, adding, "May I add my personal congratulations to the 75th (New Zealand) Squadron for producing by far the largest effort of any squadron in the group."

August 1943

Preparations for the last of the four rounds of Operation Gomorrah kept ground crews and armourers busy after NFTs had been completed on the afternoon of the 2nd. A force of 740 aircraft was assembled, which included 102 Stirlings and fourteen Lancasters belonging to 3 Group. At Mepal, seventeen Stirlings were loaded with incendiaries, while their crews attended briefing to learn that the Path Finders were to mark the aiming-point with red TIs by H2S, which the visual markers would confirm with yellow TIs, backed-up by greens for the duration of the bombing. The 75(NZ) Squadron element took off between 23.14 and 23.40 with S/L Andrews the senior pilot on duty and headed for the rendezvous point over the North Sea. The weather conditions, initially, were favourable, until the bomber stream came into contact with a towering bank of ice-bearing cumulonimbus cloud at 7 degrees east, a not unusual feature of this regular route into north-western Germany, but on this occasion, a particularly imposing one, which could not be circumnavigated and stretched upwards to 20,000 feet and beyond. Upon entering it, aircraft were thrown around by violent electrical storms characterised by enormous flashes of lightning, thunder, electrical discharges and instruments going haywire. According to F/O Alexander, it was "the most terrifying experience I had ever had, on the ground or in the air", and he was not alone in that opinion as a massive forty-four 3 Group crews turned back early. Six of the squadron's crews were persuaded to abandon their sorties, either through the conditions or as a result of engine trouble, leaving the others to press on to the target, which they found under ten-tenths cloud.

Some of those battling through the conditions to reach the target area caught a glimpse of the Elbe and isolated yellow and green Path Finder flares, which might have been jettisoned rather than placed, and the majority bombed on e.t.a. Bombs were spread over a hundred miles of the Schleswig-Holstein peninsula, the town of Elmshorn, some fifteen miles to the north-west of Hamburg seeming to attract the most attention and 254 houses were destroyed. Few crews had any idea of their precise location and bombed on the glow of fires beneath the cloud and the smoke rising through it. On return, they expressed themselves to be shaken by their experience and were unanimous in their conviction that the operation had been a total failure. The outcome was of little consequence in view of what had gone before, but the Command suffered the relatively heavy loss of thirty aircraft, some of them having fallen victim to the weather conditions. There were two absentees from among the ranks of 75(NZ) Squadron, one of them, EH928 AA-A having been shot down by Hptm Hans-Joachim Jabs of IV./NJG1 off Terschelling with no survivors from the eight-man crew of P/O Cyril Bailie RAFVR. His was the only body to be recovered, after it drifted in the current to eventually wash ashore on the Danish coast. The navigator was the single member of the RNZAF on board. BF577 JN-M collided in the air with a Do217 flown by Feldwebel Krauter of II./NJG3 and crashed at Kaiser-Wilhelm-Koog on the northern bank of the Elbe Estuary, again with no survivors. F/Sgt James Couper and his bomb-aimer and wireless operator were all members of the RNZAF. During the course of the four raids of Operation Gomorrah, the squadron despatched seventy-nine sorties, sixty-six of which bombed as briefed and lost three Stirlings and crews. (The Battle of Hamburg. Martin Middlebrook).

On the 5th the squadron was visited by a Mrs Arnott Robertson, a novelist, and F/O Colville of RNZAF HQ, London, to meet and discuss the making of a film. The project was intended to showcase the efforts of the RNZAF in Europe but was apparently scaled back and eventually appeared in 1945 as "New Zealand Was There", an eleven-minute short film made up mostly of old news clips. Colville, a pilot, who almost lost both legs in an air test crash with 75(NZ) Squadron in 1942, appears briefly in the film with the NZ High Commissioner, Bill Jordan.

Adverse weather over the ensuing days caused a number of mining operations to be cancelled, until the 6th, when five Stirlings were loaded with 1,500lb parachute mines, while their crews were briefed for the Deodar garden in the Gironde Estuary. Three were debutants, F/Sgt Keith Alexander McGregor RNZAF, F/Sgt Warwick Harold Batger RNZAF and F/Sgt John Russell Mayo RNZAF. They began taking off at 21.30, but F/Sgt McGregor was soon back in the circuit with intercom failure. Cloud in the target area was at 1,000 feet, above which, visibility was fair to good and three returning crews reported observing the parachutes to deploy. A little flak was encountered, and several enemy aircraft were spotted, one making an ineffective attack on BF461 JN-B containing the crew of F/Sgt Roberts. On the way home over France, F/Sgt Mayfield's gunners in EH901 JN-O shot up a train, and watched the locomotive blow up with a brilliant flash. BK614 JN-N failed to return home with the crew of F/Sgt John Mayo RNZAF, and no trace of the Stirling or its occupants was ever found.

Italy was now teetering on the brink of capitulation and Bomber Command was invited to help nudge it over the edge with a short offensive against its major cities. It began with the preparation of an all-Lancaster force drawn from 1, 5 and 8 Groups for an attack on Genoa, Milan and Turin on the 7th, and with preparations already in hand for, perhaps, the most important operation of the war to date to be launched in ten days' time, the Turin raid was to be used to test the merits of employing a raid controller, or Master of Ceremonies, in the manner of W/C Gibson during Operation Chastise. The man selected for the job was Group Captain John Searby, currently serving as commanding officer of 83 Squadron, and before that, Gibson's successor as commanding officer of 106 Squadron. His brief was to remain in sight of the target for the entire attack, assessing the marking and bombing and directing and encouraging the crews. It is believed that all 197 aircraft reached their respective targets after flying out in excellent weather conditions, and although the Master Bomber experiment at Turin was not entirely successful, experience was gained which would prove useful for the forthcoming Operation Hydra.

The main operation on the night of the 9/10th was a Lancaster and Halifax raid on Mannheim, which set off fifteen hundred individual fires and destroyed more than thirteen hundred buildings. While this operation was in progress, F/Sgts Victor Trevor Parkin RNZAF and Neville Bruce Whitta RNZAF and F/O Wilson and their crews carried out a further mining operation, this time in the Nectarine I garden off the southern Frisians and completed their sorties according to instructions under clear skies and in bright moonlight between 22.00 and 01.40.

The following night brought a return to southern Germany, this time to Nuremberg, for which a force of 653 aircraft was made ready. As far as the Halifax crews of 4 and 6 Groups were concerned, the return of Stirlings for this raid was likely to provide respite for them, as in a Lancaster/Halifax force, they invariably came off second best. 3 Group's contribution of 116 Stirlings and fourteen Lancasters included eighteen of the former belonging to 75(NZ) Squadron, which were loaded with 4lb and 30lb incendiaries and took off between 21.55 and 22.20 with S/Ls Andrews and Joll the senior pilots on duty. After climbing-out, they set course for Beachy Head to follow a route similar to that of the previous night and there were no early returns to blunt the squadron's effort. The Path Finders had been told to expect clear skies, and had prepared a ground-marking plan, but conditions in the target area also reflected those of twenty-four hours earlier with eight to ten-tenths cloud at 12,000 feet, despite which, the Path Finders proceeded with the ground-marking plan. Consequently, there were no release-point flares to draw the main force on, but the green TIs were visible to most as bombing took place predominantly from between 15,000 and 18,500 feet over central and southern districts, where a useful attack developed that inflicted heavy residential and industrial damage. At debriefing crews reported a good concentration of fires, the glow from which remained visible for 150 miles into the return journey. P/O Logan's navigational tools broke down on the way home, and this allowed their Stirling to wander off track and eventually use up its reserves of fuel. The crew members were preparing to abandon ship when they came across Marston Moor airfield in north Yorkshire, and landed safely at 07.10, after nine hours and ten minutes aloft.

Briefings took place on the 12th for an attack that night on Turin by 152 aircraft of 3 and 8 Groups, while a much larger Lancaster and Halifax force attended to Milan, home to many war factories, including the Isotta Fraschini luxury car works, which had been converted to military vehicle and aero engine manufacture, the Pirelli rubber works, Alfa Romeo, the Caproni aircraft plant, the Breda locomotive, armaments and aircraft works and the Innocenti machinery and vehicle factory. 75(NZ) Squadron loaded eighteen Stirlings with 1,000lb and 500lb bombs and mixed incendiaries, and launched them skyward between 21.15 and 21.35 with AVM Harrison, A-O-C of 3 Group watching on, and S/Ls Joll and Broadbent the senior pilots on duty. BF443 AA-V took off with W/O Moseley at the controls for the final operational sortie with the squadron of a Mk I Stirling. There were no early returns, but disaster almost struck BF434 AA-Y as it passed between Chartres and Paris on the outward leg. An enemy night-fighter attacked from astern, severely damaging the port-outer engine, which had to be shut down. Return fire and corkscrewing shook the fighter off, and despite having 380 miles still to cover and the Alps to cross, P/O Burley decided to press on. He and his crew reached their destination along with the others from the squadron and bombed the target under clear skies and in bright moonlight. The attack took place almost unopposed from the ground and colossal fires and heavy explosions were observed. P/O Burley and crew set off on the 718-mile return journey and landed safely at base after an eight-hour round trip. For his perseverance and airmanship P/O Arthur Burley RAFVR was awarded an immediate DFC. It was during this raid that pilot, F/Sgt Aaron of 218 Squadron, won the posthumous award of a Victoria Cross, the second and final Stirling crewman to be so honoured.

An all-Lancaster force continued the assault on Milan on the night of the 15/16th, while four 75(NZ) Squadron Stirlings carried out mining sorties in the Deodar garden in the Gironde estuary, among them first-time captain, F/Sgt Frank Douglas Higham RNZAF. They took off shortly before 21.00 and three returned to report finding the target area under clear skies and in good visibility, which enabled them to identify their drop zones without difficulty, although F/O Wilson's BF465 JN-K was damaged by fire from flak ships. On the way home over France at 200 feet, F/Sgt Parkin's gunners shot up four trains and watched one of the locomotives explode. The return of EE891 AA-Q was awaited in vain and it was established later that it had crashed into the sea off the Biscay coast. The bodies of F/Sgt Neville Whitta RNZAF and four of his crew eventually washed ashore for burial, but his RNZAF navigator and one other were never recovered.

The Italian campaign was brought to an end with a raid on Turin by elements of 3 and 8 Groups on the night of the 16/17th. 75(NZ) Squadron loaded a dozen Stirlings with 1,000 pounders and incendiaries and dispatched them between 20.15 and 20.45 with W/C Wyatt leading the squadron for the final time. They all reached the target area to find good weather conditions with ground haze, but P/O Williams's aircraft suffered an electrical fault when they were a tantalizing ten miles north-west of Turin, and the bomb load had to be jettisoned. Returning crews reported huge explosions and very large fires spreading through the city and there were claims of damage to the Fiat works. Conditions over 3 Group stations were unsuitable for landing, and this included Mepal where mist was the problem, and the entire force was diverted to airfields in the south of England. It would take time to recover them on the 17th, and many would not be made ready in time to participate in one of the war's most important operations, which was to take place that night.

Since the very beginning of the war, intelligence had suggested that Germany was researching into and developing rocket technology, and although scant regard was given to the reports, photographic reconnaissance had confirmed the existence of an establishment at Peenemünde at the northern tip of the island of Usedom on the Baltic coast. The activities there were monitored through Ultra intercepts and surreptitious reconnaissance flights, and the V-1, known to the photographic interpreters at Medmenham because of its wingspan as the "Peenemünde 20", was captured on a photograph. The brilliant scientist, Dr R V Jones, had been able to gain vital information concerning the V-1's range, which would ultimately be used to feed disinformation to the enemy, largely through the double agent "Zigzag", otherwise known as Eddie Chapman. Unfortunately, Churchill's chief scientific adviser, Professor Lindemann, or Lord Cherwell as he became, steadfastly refused to give credence to the existence and feasibility of rocket weapons and held stubbornly to his viewpoint even when presented with a photograph of a V-2 on a trailer, taken by a PRU Mosquito as recently as June. It required the combined urgings of Duncan Sandys and Dr Jones to persuade Churchill of the urgency to act, and Operation Hydra was planned for the first available opportunity, which occurred on the night of the 17/18th.

Earlier in the day, the USAAF 8th Air Force had carried out its first deep-penetration raids into Germany to attack ball-bearing production at Schweinfurt and the Messerschmitt aircraft plant near Regensburg, and to the shock of its leaders, had learned the harsh lesson that unescorted daylight raids in 1943 were not viable. The folks at home would not be told that sixty B17s had failed to return.

It was vital that the Peenemünde installation be destroyed, ideally at the first attempt, and a force of 596 aircraft was assembled made up of 324 Lancasters, 218 Halifaxes and fifty-four Stirlings, sixty Stirlings short of what should have been the available number. The operation had been meticulously planned to account for the three vital components of Peenemünde, the housing estate, where the scientific and technical staff lived, the factory buildings in which the weapons were assembled and the experimental site, where testing took place. Each was assigned to a specific wave of aircraft, which would attack from medium level, with the Path Finders bearing the huge responsibility of re-directing the point of aim accordingly, for which each one of its squadrons was to provide one crew as a "shifter". That apart, once route markers had been dropped on Rügen island, the Path Finder markers and backers-up were to follow the standard routine of red, yellow and green TIs. After last minute alterations, 3 and 4 Groups were given the first-mentioned aiming point, 1 Group the second, and 5 and 6 Groups the third. The whole operation was to be overseen by a Master of Ceremonies (referred to hereafter as Master Bomber), and the officer selected for this hazardous and demanding role was G/C John Searby of 83 Squadron, who, as already mentioned, had stepped into Gibson's shoes at 106 Squadron after Gibson was posted out to form 617 Squadron. Searby's role was to direct the marking and bombing by VHF and to encourage the crews to press on to the aiming-point, a task requiring him to remain in the target area and within range of the defences throughout the attack. In an attempt to protect the bombers from the attentions of enemy night-fighters for as long as possible, eight Mosquitos of 139 Squadron were to carry out a spoof raid on Berlin beginning at 23.00, seventy-five minutes before the opening of the main event, and would be led by the highly experienced and former 49 Squadron commander, G/C Len Slee. In the expectation of encountering drifting smoke as the last wave on target, the 5 Group crews were instructed to employ their oft-used time-and-distance approach to the aiming-point and had practiced this over a stretch of coast near the Wainfleet bombing range at the mouth of the Wash in Lincolnshire, progressively cutting the margin of error from one thousand to three hundred yards.

Twelve 75(NZ) Squadron Stirlings were loaded with 2,000lb, 1,000lb and 500lb bombs and incendiaries, and took off between 20.50 and 21.05 with S/L Joll the senior pilot on duty. The various groups made their way individually to a rendezvous point some ninety minutes flying time or three hundred miles from the English coast and sixty miles from Denmark's western coast, where they formed into a stream. The overall early-return rate was lower than normal, suggesting that crews had taken to heart the importance of the operation and only W/O Hartstein and crew returned to Mepal after two hours because of an unserviceable rear turret. Darkness had fallen as they crossed the North Sea, and twenty miles short of landfall over the southern tip of Fanø island, south of Esbjerg, "windowing" began, in order to simulate a standard raid on a northern or north-eastern city. Southern Denmark was traversed by the Lancaster brigade at 18,000 feet, twice the altitude required for the attack, but, worryingly, in a band of cloudless sky under a bright moon, which the enemy night-fighter force failed to exploit. They adopted an east-south-easterly course and began to shed altitude gradually during the 240-mile run to the target a little over an hour away, and, at the rear of the stream, the 5 Group crews focused on the island of Rügen, the ideal starting point for their timed run to Peenemünde, which lay some fifteen miles beyond to the south-east.

The skies over the target area were clear and the visibility good despite the deployment of a smoke screen, but even so, the initial marking of the housing estate went awry, and some target indicators fell onto the forced workers camp at Trassenheide, more than a mile south of the intended aiming-point. Inevitably, many of the 3 and 4 Group bombs fell here, inflicting grievous casualties on friendly foreign nationals trapped inside their wooden barracks. Once rectified, however, the attack proceeded according to plan and a number of important members of the technical staff were killed. The Mepal crews had green TIs in their bomb sights as they attacked from 5,000 to 8,500 feet between 00.15 and 00.35 in accordance with the instructions from the Master Bomber, and all were satisfied that they had straddled the aiming point. The 1 Group second-wave crews encountered strong crosswinds over the narrow section of the island where the construction sheds were located, but this phase of the operation largely achieved its aims, and they were on their way home before the night-fighters arrived from Berlin, having been attracted by the glow of fires well to the north. On arrival at Rügen, the 5 Group crews began their timed run and reached the experimental site to encounter the expected smoke, before bombing on green TIs between 00.36 and 00.52. They and the 6 Group Halifaxes and Lancasters then ran into the night-fighters, which proceeded to take a heavy toll, both in the skies over the target, and on the route home towards Denmark. Twenty-nine of the forty missing aircraft came from this third wave, seventeen of them belonging to 5 Group and twelve to 6 Group, which represented a loss rate for the Canadians of 19.7%. Some had fallen victim to the new Schräge Musik (slanting or jazz music) upward-firing cannons, which were being employed by the Luftwaffe Nachtjagd for the first time. The Mepal brigade all returned safely and reported fires visible from 150 miles away. There was sad news concerning the former 75(NZ) Squadron pilot, P/O Alfred Sydney Raphael DFC, who failed to return from this operation after crashing into the Baltic while outbound. He was serving as a squadron leader and flight commander with 467 Squadron RAAF. On the main force stations there was praise for the work of the Path Finders and the Master Bomber, and post-raid reconnaissance revealed the raid to have been sufficiently effective to delay the V-2 development programme by a number of weeks and ultimately to force the manufacture of secret weapons underground at Nordhausen. The flight testing of the V-2 was eventually withdrawn eastwards into Poland, beyond the range of Harris's bombers, and thus Peenemünde had been nullified as a threat.

On the 19th, W/C Wyatt left the squadron on posting to 3 Group HQ, but would return to operations in May 1944 as the commanding officer of 514 Squadron at Waterbeach. He was succeeded at 75(NZ) Squadron by W/C Roy Douglas Max DFC, a battle-hardened veteran, who arrived from 1657 Conversion Unit on promotion. He had flown Fairey Battles with 103 Squadron as part of the Advanced Air Striking Force in France between September 1939 and June 1940 when a flying officer and returned to the squadron briefly as a flight lieutenant in July 1941 after serving for a time as a ferry pilot.

The main operation on the night of the 22/23rd was against the Ruhr city of Leverkusen, situated on the Rhine just a stone's throw north of Cologne, where it was home to a factory belonging to the infamous I G Farben chemicals company. It was engaged in the development and production of synthetic oil and rubber and employed slave labour at all of its factories, including 30,000 from the Auschwitz concentration camp, where it had built a plant. One of the company's subsidiaries manufactured the Zyklon B gas used during the Holocaust to murder millions of Jews. A force of 462 aircraft carried out the raid in the absence of a 3 Group presence and failed to produce the hoped-for outcome after a partial failure of the Oboe signal. While this operation was in progress, three Kiwi crews took off either side of 20.30 for mining duties in one of the Nectarine gardens off the Frisians, the number including debutant F/Sgt Francis Patrick Lundon RNZAF. They were to rely entirely on Gee to find their release points, but two of them failed to complete their sorties after the Gee signal faded and they brought their mines home, while the third crew completed its sortie according to instructions.

Harris had long believed that the key to ultimate victory lay in the destruction of Berlin, the seat of the Nazi government and the symbol of its power. On the 23rd, orders were received on stations across the Command to prepare for a maximum effort that night against Germany's capital city, which had not been visited by the heavy brigade since the end of March. The crews, of course, could not know that this was to be the first of an eventual nineteen raids on the "Big City", in an offensive which, with an autumn break, would drag on until the following spring. It was a campaign that would test the resolve of the crews to the absolute limit, whilst also sealing the fate of the Stirlings and the Mk II and V Halifaxes as front-line bombers. There are varying opinions concerning the true start date of what became known as the Berlin offensive or the Battle of Berlin, some commentators believing these first three operations in August and September to be the start, while others point to the sixteen raids from mid-November. However, there was little doubt in Bomber Command circles that this was it, a fact demonstrated by the comments in numerous squadron ORBs, which spoke of the "long-awaited Berlin campaign" and similar sentiments.

There would be a Master Bomber on hand for this operation, and the officer chosen was Canadian W/C "Johnny" Fauquier, the tough, grizzled and one-time bush pilot and frequent brawler, who was enjoying his second spell as the commanding officer of 405 (Vancouver) Squadron, once of 4 Group, but since April, proud to be the only Canadian Path Finder unit. The route had been planned to take the bomber stream to a rendezvous point over the North Sea, before crossing the Dutch coast near Haarlem and entering Germany between Meppen to the north and Osnabrück to the south. It would then follow a path between Bremen and Hannover to bypass the southern rim of Berlin, before turning back sharply on a north-westerly course to fly across the city centre. After bombing, they were exit Germany via the Baltic coast and head for landfall on the Schleswig-Holstein peninsula. Seventeen Mosquitos were to precede the Path Finder and main force elements to drop route markers at key points in an attempt to keep the bomber stream on track.

A force of 727 aircraft included 124 Stirlings and thirteen Lancasters representing 3 Group, and an additional ten 139 Squadron Mosquitos were to provide a "window" screen in advance of the bomber stream. The Oboe Mosquitos were to mark the route with red and green TIs, backed up by H2S Lancasters, but as Berlin was beyond the range of Oboe, the aiming-point was to be marked with red TIs by H2S, backed up by greens. The 75(NZ) Squadron element of twenty-three departed Mepal between 20.25 and 20.50 with S/Ls Andrews and Joll the senior pilots on duty and carrying a mixed load each of high explosives and incendiaries. F/Sgt Higham was the first of five early returns to arrive back in the circuit, landing at 22.30, to be followed over the ensuing fifty-five minutes by P/O Burley, W/O Mitchell and F/Sgts Roberts and Mee. P/O Burley and crew in EH877 JN-C had been subjected to a brief attack by an unidentified enemy aircraft on the way back, but no damage had been sustained. After flying out over scattered cloud, those reaching the target area found clear skies and moonlight, but the Path Finders were unable to identify the aiming-point in the centre of the city, a result of the inherent difficulties of interpreting the H2S images over such a massive urban sprawl and marked the southern outskirts instead. It would be established later, that many main force crews had cut the corner to approach the city from the south-west rather than south-east, and this had resulted in the wastage of many bomb loads in open country and on outlying communities. The Mepal crews aimed their bombs at the centre of green TIs from around 14,000 feet, reporting on return large explosions and many fires and a pall of smoke rising to meet them as they turned towards the north-west. The glow from the burning city remained visible for at least 140 miles into the homeward flight, and, curiously, only a few crews commented on hearing the Master Bomber and finding his instructions helpful.

It was during debriefing that individual stories emerged and F/Sgt White and two of his crew had quite an epic tale to relate to the intelligence officer sitting with them. They had been on final approach to bomb when EF435 JN-J became ensnared in a searchlight cone and was hit repeatedly by heavy flak. Severe damage was inflicted upon the port mainplane, despite which, F/Sgt White continued on to the target, even though still held fast in the beams. This enabled a Ju88 to latch on to the Stirling from astern and shatter the rear turret with cannon fire, killing the occupant, Sgt Poole. The aircraft was forced into an uncontrollable dive, during which the captain warned the crew to prepare to abandon ship. It was in mid-message that the intercom failed, leaving the crew unable to communicate and uncertain as to whether the Stirling's descent was terminal. The wireless operator, navigator and bomb-aimer decided for themselves, quite understandably, that it was time to go and took to their parachutes. The bomb load was jettisoned right over the target, and F/Sgt White finally regained control at 6,000 feet, before beginning the long and hazardous return trip with a reduced crew complement of a flight engineer and mid-upper gunner. Against the odds, and thanks to the superb airmanship of F/Sgt White and his depleted crew, the Stirling made it back to base, where a text-book belly-landing was carried out in the absence of lights, flaps and undercarriage. F/Sgt White RNZAF would be commissioned soon afterwards and receive a coveted Conspicuous Gallantry Medal, while the two crewmen who had remained on board with him would each be rewarded for their devotion to duty with a DFM.

Meanwhile, a Ju88 passed above F/Sgt Wilkinson's EH901 JN-O, presenting the mid-upper and rear gunners with a tempting target, and strikes were seen on the enemy's belly before it was lost from sight. F/Sgt Whitehead and crew in EF465 AA-H were also over the target when they spotted an enemy aircraft three hundred yards away on the starboard quarter. The rear gunner fired a five-second burst, and the enemy was seen to fall to earth in flames to be claimed as a "probable". Another unidentified enemy aircraft then appeared in the same relative position, into which the rear gunner poured a five-second burst, causing it to explode and disintegrate. F/O Alexander and crew in BK777 AA-U were, likewise, over the target when a Me110 approached from the starboard quarter above with its guns blazing. The mid-upper and rear gunners replied with long bursts, and the enemy aircraft was seen to be in flames. A fire on the ground suggested that it had crashed, and it was claimed as probably destroyed. Returning crews reported concentrated areas of fire, huge columns of smoke and heavy explosions, and there was little doubt in their minds that a decisive blow had been struck.

A new record of fifty-six aircraft failed to return, and this was made up of twenty-three Halifaxes, seventeen Lancasters and sixteen Stirlings, representing a percentage loss rate respectively of 9.1, 5.1 and 12.9, which perfectly reflected the food chain when all three types operated together. The Stirling losses were disproportionately high, and this continued to sound alarm bells at Bomber Command HQ, where the type was already unpopular with Harris because of its low operating ceiling and inability to carry anything larger than a 2,000 pounder in its split bomb bay. 75(NZ) Squadron posted missing three crews, the fate of which eventually filtered through to Mepal. BF465 JN-K crashed about fifteen miles north-north-east of Berlin on the way out of the target area, and only the mid-upper gunner survived from the crew of P/O Andrew Rankin RAFVR, among which were two members of the RNZAF. BF564 JN-W went down about the same distance south-east of Berlin while approaching to bomb, and the experienced P/O Alan Sedunary DFC, RAAF perished with the other seven occupants, of which two were members of the RNZAF. One of the crew members, flight engineer Frank Kitchener Alcock, MiD, RAF, had served as ground crew with the squadron at Feltwell, and wanting to do his bit in the air, had subsequently re-trained as aircrew. W/O Trevor Fear RAFVR and crew were also preparing to start their bombing-run when EE938 AA-X was shot down some seven miles east-south-east of the capital, and there were no survivors.

Despite the difficulty in marking, this was the most successful raid to date on Berlin and resulted in the destruction of or serious damage to 2,611 buildings in mostly residential districts. A few bombs did fall in the centre, into the government quarter, and the industrial districts of Marienfelde and Mariendorf were also hit. The death toll on the ground stood at 854, and an unusually high number of these were civilians, who had declined the opportunity to enter their allocated air-raid shelters.

On the following night, debutant F/Sgt Douglas Charles Henley RNZAF and crew took off at 20.45 to carry out a freshman mining sortie off the Frisians, where they found ideal weather conditions and good visibility. The mines were delivered in accordance with instructions, and they returned safely from an uneventful trip. Two nights later the same crew was sent to the Gironde Estuary, where they enjoyed similarly good weather conditions, and again planted their vegetables as briefed.

Orders were received on the 27th to prepare for an operation that night against Nuremberg and a force of 674 aircraft was duly assembled, which included a contribution from 3 Group of 112 Stirlings and ten Lancasters, nineteen of the former made ready at Mepal, where their bomb bays were filled with all-incendiary loads. They took off between 21.15 and 21.40 with no senior pilots on duty and the crew of F/Sgt Henley undertaking their third operation in four nights. The bomber stream flew out in cloud, which dispersed to leave clear skies and good horizontal visibility in the target area but extreme darkness that obscured ground detail. The Path Finders had been briefed to check their H2S equipment by dropping a 1,000 pounder on Heilbronn, and some crews complied, while others, it seems, experienced technical difficulties. Despite accurate initial marking, a creep-back developed, which the backers-up and the Master Bomber could not correct. The Mepal crews observed red, yellow and green TIs and most had the greens in their bomb sights as they let their loads go from around 15,000 feet. Many concentrated fires were reported and the consensus of returning crews was of an effective raid, which would not be entirely supported by an analysis and local sources that revealed that many bomb loads had fallen into open country, while others had hit south-eastern and eastern districts. Thirty-three aircraft failed to return, eleven of each type, which again confirmed the vulnerability of the Stirlings and Halifaxes when operating alongside Lancasters. The loss rate on this night was 3.1% for the Lancaster, 5% for the Halifax and a disproportionately high 10.6% for the Stirlings. 75(NZ) Squadron was represented by EE955 AA-D, which crashed on the northern bank of the River Main some ten miles east of Würzburg, killing F/Sgt Frank Higham RNZAF and his crew, whose wireless operator was also a member of the RNZAF. F/Sgt Phillips and crew in EH948 AA-Q reported a brief and inconclusive skirmish with a Ju88.

The main event on the night of the 30/31st was a two-phase attack on the twin towns of Mönchengladbach and Rheydt, the first time that either would experience a major Bomber Command assault. Situated some ten miles west of the centre of Düsseldorf in the south-western Ruhr, they would face an initial force of 660 aircraft of four types, in what for the crews, was a short-penetration trip across the Dutch frontier and a welcome change from the recent long slogs to eastern and southern Germany. The plan called for the first wave to hit Mönchengladbach, before a two-minute pause in the bombing allowed the Path Finders to head south to mark Rheydt. 3 Group put up 107 Stirlings and eleven Lancasters, eighteen of the former provided by 75(NZ) Squadron, their crews having been briefed to bomb in the first wave. They took off between midnight and 00.35 with S/L Broadbent the senior pilot on duty and W/C Max flying as his second pilot and each crew sitting on an all-incendiary bomb load. There were no early returns, and the seven to nine-tenths cloud attending the outward flight across Holland persisted at the target, where it lay at 8,000 feet without impairing the good visibility. The operation proceeded according to plan with scarcely any creep-back and approximately half of the built-up area of each town was reduced to rubble. This amounted to more than a thousand buildings in Mönchengladbach and almost thirteen hundred in Rheydt, at a cost to the Command of twenty-five aircraft.

At Mepal, returning crews reported very large, concentrated and spreading fires, and were confident that they had contributed to a highly successful raid. F/Sgt Batger's front gunner in EF491 AA-O fired a long and a short burst at an enemy aircraft six hundred yards ahead and claimed it as possibly destroyed, while F/Sgt McGregor's rear gunner had a similar encounter with a Me110, which returned fire. The mid-upper gunner then managed to fire off a long burst as the Stirling was flung into a corkscrew, after which, the enemy was seen to dive away with smoke issuing from its engines and was claimed as possibly destroyed. F/Sgt Victor Parkin RNZAF and his crew were not present at debriefing, and it was established later that EH938 AA-F had crashed at Lommel in Belgium, close to the frontier with Holland, and only the bomb-aimer had managed to save himself, ultimately to evade capture. The navigator, F/Sgt

Terrence Watters, was a member of the RNZAF. While this operation was in progress, the squadron sent the freshman crews of F/O James Samuel Battersby RNZAF and F/Sgt William Stuart Masters RNZAF to mine the waters off the Frisians, and both completed their sorties as briefed in conditions of four-tenths cloud.

The month ended with preparations for the second of the Berlin operations on the night of the 31st, for which 622 aircraft were made ready, more than half of them Lancasters. 3 Group detailed 101 Stirlings and five Lancasters, sixteen of the former belonging to 75(NZ) Squadron, which were loaded with a mixture of high explosives and incendiaries before departing Mepal between 20.20 and 20.40 with F/L Turner the senior pilot on duty. The route on this night took the bomber stream on an east-south-easterly heading across Texel to a position between Hannover and Leipzig, before turning to pass to the south-east of Berlin and approach the city-centre aiming-point on a north-westerly track. The return leg would involve a south-westerly course to a position south of Cologne for an exit over the French coast, but despite the attempts to outwit the enemy night-fighter controller, he would be able to predict to some extent where to concentrate his night-fighters. This would be the first occasion on which the Command registered the German use of "fighter flares" to mark out the path of the bombers to and from the target. The 3 Group effort was depleted by the early return of a massive twenty-five aircraft for a variety of reasons. The Path Finders encountered five to six-tenths cloud in the target area, which combined with H2S equipment failure and a spirited night-fighter response to cause the markers to be dropped well to the south of the planned aiming-point. The main force crews reported between four and nine-tenths thin cloud and bombed on green TIs from 14,000 to 18,000 feet, observing many fires over a wide area. It was noted by some that two groups of green TIs were ten miles apart, and both attracted bomb loads, which possibly contributed to an extensive creep-back stretching some thirty miles into open country and outlying communities. The outcome was a major disappointment, brought about by woefully short marking, and resulted in the destruction of just eighty-five houses, a figure in no way commensurate with the effort expended and the loss of forty-seven heavy bombers.

The lower-flying Stirlings were particularly vulnerable to both night-fighters and flak, and this was demonstrated by a 16% loss rate and five empty dispersals at Mepal on the following morning. The latter figure could so easily have been higher had it not been for the determination and resourcefulness of the 75(NZ) Squadron crews. Having spotted a Ju88 five hundred yards astern, F/Sgt Wilkinson's rear gunner fired a long burst, to which the enemy replied, causing damage to the rear fuselage, fin and rudder of EE898, AA-N. The mid-upper gunner joined in and the enemy aircraft was observed to stall and fall away, encouraging the crew to claim it as probably destroyed. Two BF109s latched onto P/O Alexander's EH880 (by now re-coded as AA-J), and one opened fire from the starboard quarter, to which the rear gunner replied with a short burst. This assailant also seemed to stall, and the mid-upper gunner took the opportunity to fire a short burst, which sent the fighter diving to the ground, where it exploded. The second BF109 then opened fire from the port bow to the port quarter, before being hit by a return burst from the Stirling's rear turret, which sent it diving away to be claimed as possibly destroyed. A window near the navigator's station was blown out, along with all of his charts and papers, and this made for a tricky trip home. W/O Moseley's gunners in EE958 AA-V combined to pour fire into a Me110 on the port quarter, causing it to turn over and fall away with smoke issuing from its starboard side. P/O Logan's gunners claimed a BF109 as damaged, after it closed to sixty yards astern and was seen to be hit by tracer from the rear turret of EE881 JN-G. The Stirling was flung into a corkscrew manoeuvre, and the assailant was lost from view to be claimed as damaged. Just after bombing, W/O Hartstein's EF454 AA-A was attacked by a Ju88, which was hit by both mid-upper and rear gunners and claimed as damaged. "AA-A" was also damaged and crash-landed at West Malling.

One of the absent Mepal Stirlings was accounted for when news came through from Coltishall in Norfolk that EF491 AA-O had crash-landed there after being hit by fire in the port-outer engine, possibly from another Stirling, and fending off a night-fighter attack over the North Sea. Happily, F/Sgt Batger and crew were able to walk away from the wreckage. P/O Douglas Henley RNZAF died with the two other Kiwis on board EE878 AA-P, after it was shot down on the way home by a night-fighter near Ahrweiler, some thirty miles from the Belgian frontier. The four RAF survivors were taken into captivity. EE918 AA-D was attacked on the way home and the rear gunner killed, before it exploded a few minutes later and ejected the Australian mid-upper gunner, who survived as a PoW. The wreckage was found near Höxter, a town between Hamelin to the north and Kassel to the south, and inside were the remains of F/Sgt Eric Roberts RNZAF and the rest of his crew, two of whom were members of the RNZAF. EF501 AA-K was shot down by a night-fighter at Potsdam, close to which the bombers passed both outbound and inbound, and two men survived, while F/Sgt Keith McGregor RNZAF and the others, including three more members of the RNZAF, perished. One of them was navigator F/O James Benjamin Lovelock from Christchurch, who was the younger brother of 1936 Berlin 1,500m Olympic gold medallist and world record-holder, Jack Lovelock. EH905 AA-R was hit by bombs from above, which was an ever-present danger for Stirlings, and struggled on before crashing some ten miles south-east of Potsdam. The bodies of P/O George Vincent Helm RNZAF and four of his crew were found in the wreckage, and these included two other members of the RNZAF. Both gunners survived, and they were taken into captivity.

During the course of the month the squadron operated on sixteen occasions and dispatched 175 sorties for the loss of fourteen Stirlings and thirteen-and-a-half crews.

September 1943

September began for the Command with extensive mining operations on the night of the 2/3rd, for which 3 Group detailed twenty-five Stirlings and a single Lancaster. Ten of the Stirlings were assigned to the Cinnamon garden off the Ile-de-Re in the approaches to La Pallice and La Rochelle, while the remaining fifteen and the Lancaster were to ply their trade off the Frisians. 75(NZ) Squadron briefed five freshman crews for the Nectarine garden and two for Cinnamon, which departed Mepal between 20.10 and 20.55. Five were debutants, F/O Laurence John Kirkpatrick RNZAF, F/O Ian Robert Menzies RNZAF, F/Sgt Alan Robert Speirs RNZAF, F/O John David Grubb RNZAF and F/Sgt Richard Charles Whitmore RNZAF. P/O Grubb and crew in EF130 JN-M returned early with their mines because of navigational problems and experienced two brief and inconclusive combats on the way back. The others all completed their sorties in conditions of fog and patchy cloud over the Frisians and seven-tenths cloud off the French coast.

It was similar fare on the following night for five crews dispatched between 19.35 and 19.50 to the Deodar garden in the Gironde estuary. They found clear skies and a few ineffective searchlights and flak guns and all returned safely after fulfilling their briefs. The first bombing operation of the month was mounted on this night and was the third and last in the current series against Berlin. Probably as a result of the heavy losses incurred by the Halifaxes and Stirlings in the two previous raids, it involved an all-Lancaster heavy force of 316 aircraft Much of the effort fell short, but local sources confirmed severe damage, principally in the largely residential districts of Tiergarten, Wedding, Moabit and Charlottenburg, but also in the industrial Siemensstadt, which resulted in a significant loss of war production. Twenty-two Lancasters failed to return, 7% of those dispatched, demonstrating that in the absence of Halifaxes and Stirlings, they were equally vulnerable to night-fighters.

Whether by design or as a result of the losses sustained, Berlin was now shelved for the next ten weeks, while Harris sought other suitable targets, of which there were many. He would shortly begin a four-raid series against Hannover stretching over a four-week period, but first he focused on southern Germany, beginning on the 5th with the twin cities of Mannheim and Ludwigshafen, facing each other from the eastern and western banks respectively of the Rhine. The plan was to exploit the creep-back phenomenon that attended most large operations, by approaching the target from the west and marking the eastern half of Mannheim, with the expectation that the bombing would spread back along the line of approach across western Mannheim and into Ludwigshafen. A force of 605 aircraft was assembled, which included 111 Stirlings, the crews of which learned at briefing that the blind markers were to identify the target area with red TIs and flares, by means of which the visual markers would confirm the aiming-point with yellow and green TIs.

The nineteen-strong 75(NZ) Squadron element departed Mepal between 19.45 and 20.17 with S/Ls Andrews and Joll the senior pilots on duty and each Stirling carrying an all-incendiary bomb load, which F/Sgt Phillips was forced to jettison four miles north of Cambridge after EH948 AA-Q developed technical difficulties shortly after becoming airborne. The bomber stream tracked across France to a point five miles south of Luxembourg, where route markers established the final turning point for a direct run on the target. The Path Finders were routed in over Kaiserslautern some thirty miles due west of Mannheim, from where they were to carry out a timed run to the aiming-point. They benefitted from almost clear skies and excellent visibility, which enabled them to carry out their tasks according to brief and prepare the way for the approaching main force. The invitation to exploit the opportunity was accepted and the main force crews delivered their attacks from between 11,500 and 19,000 feet, those arriving towards the later stages of the raid drawn on by the burgeoning fires fifty miles ahead. A number of large, red explosions were observed at 23.12, 23.23 and 23.27, the last of which was followed by a purplish-red mushroom of fire. Searchlights were numerous, but the flak negligible, and it was the abundance of night-fighters that posed the greatest risk to life and limb. Black smoke was rising through 15,000 feet as the bombers withdrew to the west, and the glow from the burning cities was visible for 150 miles into the return journey, which thirty-four aircraft would fail to complete.

Thirteen Lancasters, an equal number of Halifaxes and eight Stirlings were missing, and the percentage loss rates continued to tell the same story, a 7.2% loss rate for the Stirling, compared with 6.6% for the Halifaxes and 4.3% for the Lancasters. F/O Menzies and crew were in BK777 AA-U and reported a brief, inconclusive combat with an unidentified enemy aircraft. EF435 (re-coded "Y" according to the combat report) was extensively damaged by fire from a fighter attack from the port quarter, and the flight engineer, Sgt Dalkins, sustained serious wounds.

F/Sgt Batger threw the Stirling into a corkscrew, and the gunners opened fire, sending their assailant diving to the ground in flames. F/Sgt Whitmore's EH877 JN-C was stalked by a night-fighter, which was spotted when only a hundred yards astern and immediately attracted fire from the rear and mid-upper turrets. The enemy aircraft was seen to turn over and spin into the ground, before another night-fighter approached soon afterwards, flying from starboard to port astern, but this broke away when engaged by the Stirling's gunners. A minute later the same crew spotted an unidentified aircraft attacking a Lancaster, which was on fire. Both gunners again opened fire, and the enemy aircraft disappeared, while the Lancaster was seen to break up. One unidentified 75(NZ) Squadron Stirling lost two engines to flak at the French coast homebound, but made it to Hunsdon airfield in Hertfordshire, where a belly-landing was carried out safely. EE893 JN-N failed to return with the crew of P/O Ernest Wilkinson RNZAF after crashing near Bensheim, a dozen miles north of Mannheim. The pilot and three others lost their lives, while the three survivors, two of whom were members of the RNZAF, were taken into captivity.

Local reports confirmed that both Mannheim and Ludwigshafen had suffered catastrophic destruction, with almost two thousand fires in the latter alone, 986 of them classed as large. Mannheim's reporting system broke down completely, and little detail emerged of this raid, although it would recover in time for the next assault in fewer than three weeks' time. What is known, is that the main railway station in Mannheim and three suburban stations were destroyed, and the tank and military tractor factories belonging to Heinrich Lanz and Josef Vogele respectively sustained serious damage, as did the Rashig & Sulzer chemicals plant.

Four hundred Lancasters and Halifaxes targeted Munich on the night of the 6/7th and scattered bombs over the southern districts in the face of extensive cloud cover. In the absence of Stirlings, thirteen Halifaxes were lost, a percentage loss rate of 8.8, compared with 1.2 for the Lancasters.

Operation Starkey was an attempt to mislead the enemy into believing that an invasion was imminent and had begun in mid-August with highly visible troop movements and the assembly of landing craft and gliders. It involved British, Canadian and American forces, and intimated that the area around Boulogne was to be the landing ground. Harris was not amused at being ordered to participate in what he considered to be play-acting, but in the event, bad weather prevented the planned Bomber Command involvement during the final week of August. It was not until the night of the 8/9th of September that the opportunity arose for him to carry out his orders to bomb heavy gun emplacements at either end of the small resort town of Le Portel near Boulogne. Perhaps in a gesture of his attitude towards the whole Starkey affair, and he was not the only senior commander in opposition to it, he committed only his two Oboe Mosquito squadrons and two heavy Path Finder units, along with the Stirlings of 3 Group and Wellingtons from the Polish 300 Squadron and the training units. Phase I was aimed at the northern site, code-named Religion, and phase II at the southern site, code-named Andante.

75(NZ) Squadron made ready seventeen Stirlings, each of which was to carry its maximum bomb load, which on this occasion consisted of 1,000 and 500 pounders. Two crews were debutants, those of F/Sgt Walter Willoughby Morgan RNZAF and F/Sgt Henry Leonard Burton RNZAF. The Mepal element began to take off at 20.45 with no senior pilots on duty, and it was 21.30 when BK809 JN-T's brakes were released by F/O Ian Menzies RNZAF as the twelfth to depart. The Stirling swung violently as it gathered speed, struck a petrol bowser and careered across the airfield to collide with two houses standing on the boundary beyond the perimeter track. A fire broke out immediately and some of the bombs went off, causing the deaths of the pilot and bomb-aimer, along with a WAAF officer, S/O Joan Marjorie Easton WAAF/RAF and a RNZAF airman, F/Sgt Peter Gerald Dobson MiD RNZAF, all of whom were rendering assistance. Two civilians also lost their lives and the flight engineer succumbed to his injuries soon afterwards. F/Sgt Dobson was navigator in the Whitehead crew, and while on leave, had been helping with the harvesting on a local farm when the accident occurred. The remaining take-offs were completed by 21.45, and the ORB records two aircraft aborting their sorties, although the landing times do not identify them. Returning crews reported numerous large explosions, but few fires, and it seemed to them to have been a successful operation. In fact, neither battery had been hit, but the town of Le Portel had suffered extensive damage and many casualties. (For a detailed analysis of this operation, see the excellent book, The Starkey Sacrifice, by Michael Cumming, published by Sutton).

Generally adverse weather and fog ensured that the crews remained on the ground over the ensuing few days, and they were kept busy at Mepal with lectures and an escape and evasion exercise. It was no doubt a relief when the weather improved and they were called to briefing on the 15th, with 3 Group commander AVM Harrison again in attendance, and learned of that night's operation to hit a Dunlop plant at Montluçon in the Vichy region of central France. It was to be carried out by 369 aircraft of 3, 4, 6 and 8 Groups, with Halifaxes and Stirlings making up the main force element. 3 Group contributed 120 Stirlings and at Mepal, seventeen of them had 1,000 pounders and incendiaries loaded into their bomb bays, before sixteen took off between 20.15 and 20.45 with S/L Joll the senior pilot on duty. They all reached the target, where eight to nine-tenths cloud at 4,000 feet failed to prevent a view of the factory and the red, green and yellow TIs marking it out. A Master Bomber in the person of W/C "Dixie" Deane of 35 (Madras Presidency) Squadron was on hand to direct the attack and the 75(NZ) Squadron crews bombed in bright moonlight from between 4,700 and 10,000 feet. It wasn't long before black smoke was seen to rise through 12,000 feet from the developing fires, and it was clear to all that the factory complex had been severely damaged. Opposition was negligible, and just two Halifaxes and a single Stirling failed to return. Post-raid reconnaissance confirmed that every building in the factory area had been hit, for which some of the credit must go to the Master Bomber.

The American confidence in the ability of its eighth Air Force to deliver daylight attacks on military and war production targets in Germany had been shaken by the high loss rates, which were not sustainable. They had been toying with the idea of operating at night and this operation brought the maiden participation by five B17s launched under the control of 3 Group.

On the following day, the same groups were alerted to an operation that night against the important and extensive railway yards at Modane, situated on the main line between France and Italy in the foothills of the Alps in south-eastern France. A force of 340 aircraft was assembled, which included 127 Stirlings and five B17s, nineteen of the former made ready at Mepal, which took off between 19.50 and 20.30 with W/C Roy Max the senior pilot on duty, and he was ably supported by S/Ls Andrews and Broadbent. The marking was to be dependent upon a visual reference, but in case the conditions in the target area proved to be unfavourable, red spotfires were to be dropped on Grenoble. A careful timed run from there would culminate in the delivery of red TIs on e.t.a., followed by backing-up throughout the raid with green TIs. F/Sgt Burton returned to the circuit after three hours in the air, while the rest of the force crossed the Normandy coast with more than 230 miles still to negotiate, and it was at around this time that S/L Broadbent's BK778 JN-U was suddenly fired upon by a Stirling in front, which then dived away to port! Fortunately, no damage was done, and the offending aircraft disappeared into the night. The others reached the target area to find between zero and two-tenths cloud at 10,000 feet with good visibility and moonlight. Zero hour was set for 00.01, but a patch of cloud right over the aiming-point delayed the start for a brief period. The target was situated in a steep valley, which presented the Path Finders with difficulties that they were unable to overcome, and the subsequent bombing lacked accuracy. Most of the main force crews arriving early believed that they had identified it visually, assisted by the red TIs backed up by greens that formed a good concentration. Bombing was carried out from between 14,000 and 17,000 feet and crews turned for home to report an apparently highly successful attack attended by heavy explosions and large fires, which appeared to be spreading.

Ground defences were not particularly troublesome, but one Stirling returned to Mepal on three engines after the port-inner had been set on fire by flak and had to be shut down. P/O Williams and crew flying in BF461 JN-B reported an encounter with a Ju88, which they claimed as destroyed, and four minutes later a second Ju88 was claimed as damaged. Trigger fingers were apparently twitchy that night, as on the way home, P/O Mitchell and crew in EF135 AA-T also had a Stirling drift in front of them and open fire while corkscrewing. Mitchell immediately took evasive action, but not before their aircraft had been hit several times in both wings, the fin and rudder. Sadly, the confidence in the success of the operation was not borne out by post-raid reconnaissance, which revealed that the marking had missed the mark and the yards had escaped damage.

S/L Broadbent had now concluded his tour and would soon be posted to the RAF Staff College. It was only on the 25th of July that his substantive rank had been confirmed as flight lieutenant, which meant that for three months, he had been C Flight commander in the substantive rank of flying officer. This was not unusual under war conditions, when casualties and tour expirations frequently catapulted relatively junior officers up the ladder of promotion, but they often had to relinquish their exalted status when posted to non-operational roles afterwards.

Three crews were dispatched at 19.40 on the 18th to carry out gardening duties in the Deodar garden in the Gironde estuary, and among them was that of first-time captain F/O Eric Francis Witting RNZAF. Their efforts were blessed with good weather conditions, bright moonlight and excellent visibility, which allowed the crews to witness the opening of the parachutes attached to the mines, and all returned safely from an uneventful operation. Two debutant crews took off at 19.30 on the 21st to plant their vegetables in the sea lanes in one of the Nectarine gardens off the Frisians, and F/Sgt Noel Norman Parker RAAF and Sgt Ralph Egerton Martin RNZAF carried out their briefs in good conditions with three-tenths cloud, and absolutely no opposition. However, the weather had deteriorated back at base and all three were diverted to Tangmere.

When the tannoys called the faithful to prayer on the 22nd after a five-night break, crews learned that they were to be part of a force of 711 aircraft, including 137 Stirlings and seven Lancasters of 3 Group plus five B17s, to attack the ancient city of Hannover, situated in northern Germany midway between the Dutch frontier and Berlin. They were told that it was home to much war industry, and that the plan of attack called for the Path Finder blind marker crews to use their H2S to mark the general target area with red TIs and illuminator flares, and that the visual markers would confirm the exact aiming-point with yellow TIs, which the backers-up were to maintain throughout the attack with green TIs. What was not known at the time among the Allies was that the region was also the location of seven Nazi concentration camps.

According to Martin Middlebrook and Chris Everitt in Bomber Command War Diaries, the first two operations produced concentrated bombing, but mostly outside of the target, while only the third one succeeded in causing extensive damage, which, if the figures are to be believed, seem to be massively out of proportion. The author contends that the reports of the crews after the first two operations suggest strongly that the damage to Hannover was accumulative over the first three raids and did not result from just one, as will be explained in the following narrative. The telling feature is, perhaps, that no reports came out of Hannover to corroborate the testimony of the crews on the first two raids, although post-raid reconnaissance by the RAF after the second one did show that some of the bombing had fallen into open country and the Path Finders did admit to at least one poor performance.

The twenty-strong 75(NZ) Squadron element departed Mepal either side of 19.00 with S/L Joll the senior pilot on duty and each Stirling loaded with 1,000 pounders and incendiaries. They climbed out and headed for the coast and the North Sea, where they would rendezvous with the rest of the bomber stream. Not all would complete the 430-mile outward leg, and the crews of F/Sgt Morgan and P/Os White and Williams were among fourteen 3 Group early returns, in their cases for unspecified reasons. The others encountered clear skies and good visibility but stronger-than-forecast winds that would play their part in pushing the marking and bombing towards the south-east. The attack was scheduled to begin at 21.30 and the first red TIs were observed three minutes later, before another was seen to cascade over the city after overshooting it by an estimated four miles. This was followed by other red TIs overshooting by one to four miles with many greens falling among them. However, the yellows seemed to be undershooting the reds by two miles and were closer to the city centre aiming-point. The main force crews carried out their bombing runs in the face of intense searchlight activity and heavy flak bursting at their level, those from 75(NZ) Squadron bombing on cascading green TIs. Some main force crews reported a line of fires developing from west to east, with smoke rising through 14,000 feet, while others claimed that fires ran from the aiming-point in a north-north-westerly direction across the city. One 101 Squadron crew described it as, "Excellent attack – should be the end of Hannover". All, it seems, were unanimous, that the raid had been highly successful, and confirmed that the glow of fires remained visible from the Dutch coast two hundred miles away. Twenty-six aircraft failed to return, five of them Stirlings, but the Halifaxes again sustained the highest numerical losses, this time, at 5.3%, even exceeding the Stirlings' loss rate. EH949 JN-P was almost another casualty after it was hit by fire from an unseen night-fighter, which caused damage to the tail, port mainplane and port petrol tanks and knocked out an engine. Despite this and a small fire in the fuselage, which was extinguished by the crew, the aircraft made it back to base, where F/L Turner carried out a crash-landing from which all on board walked away. Sadly, it seems that the Turner crew had exhausted its reservoir of good fortune in this incident.

Let us now consider the claim that the main weight of bombs fell two to five miles south-southeast from the city centre, and that the operation largely failed as a result. Firstly, two to five miles in any large city means that the bombing fell within the boundaries, and, therefore, within the built-up area. Secondly, the majority of crews, if not all, reported a highly successful raid with fires right across the city, smoke rising to 14,000 feet as they left the scene and the glow visible from the Dutch coast. It is true that crews were very frequently mistaken in their belief that an attack had been successful, but the evidence on this occasion would seem to confirm their testimony. Decoy fire-sites did not produce a glow visible from a distance of two hundred miles, or sufficient volumes of smoke to reach bombing height during the short duration of a raid in a density visible at night. In fact, fifty-six factories had sustained damaged, railway installations had been severely disrupted, the line to Hildesheim cut and a four-track railway bridge brought down as the result of a direct hit.

On the 23rd, and for the second time in the month, Mannheim was posted as the target, for which a force of 628 aircraft was assembled, 3 Group providing 116 Stirlings, six Lancasters and five USAAF B17s. At the Mepal briefing, while eighteen aircraft were being loaded with 4lb and 30lb incendiaries, the crews learned that Mosquitos were to drop red and green route markers, before the Path Finder blind marker crews delivered flares and red TIs over the target by H2S to guide the visual markers to the precise aiming-point. That was located in the less-severely afflicted northern districts, which they would mark with yellow TIs, followed by the backers-up with greens. The 75(NZ) Squadron element took off between 19.20 and 19.40, and there were no early returns to blunt the squadron's impact. The bomber stream adopted the familiar route across France and entered Germany south of Luxembourg, where they encountered largely clear skies and good visibility. Zero hour had been set for 21.45, and following a competent performance by the Path Finders, the main force crews bombed on green TIs from between 12,000 and 18,000 feet from around 22.00 onwards.

At debriefing, crews reported a successful operation with heavy explosions and large, concentrated fires spreading towards the west from which smoke had reached around 6,000 feet as they turned away. They also claimed that the glow of fires remained visible for 150 miles into the return journey and commented on the abundance of night-fighters, which were involved in a number of skirmishes with 75(NZ) Squadron crews. EE958 AA-V sustained damage during a combat with a Ju88, which inflicted slight injury upon the pilot, W/O Moseley, and his mid-upper gunner, but their assailant was claimed as probably destroyed. P/O Burley and crew in EF137 JN-Y survived three engagements with enemy fighters, claiming one as destroyed and the other two as damaged. EF152 JN-T captained by P/O Mitchell had two combats over the target, one with an unidentified single-engine fighter, and three minutes later by a FW190, which was claimed as damaged.

Thirty-two aircraft failed to return and this time, eighteen of them were Lancasters, compared with seven Halifaxes and seven Stirlings. This provided a somewhat topsy-turvy and unusual loss-rate of 5.7%, 3.6% and 6% respectively. 75(NZ) Squadron's EH936 JN-W was approaching the target when crashing five miles north-west of Frankenthal and about a dozen miles north-west of Mannheim, and there were no survivors from the crew of F/L Geoffrey Turner DFC, RCAF, which included a second pilot in the person of F/O Kenneth Albiston RAFVR. The bomb-aimer, F/O Arthur Douglas Howlett, was the only member of the RNZAF on board. BF459 JN-G came down about seven miles north of Mannheim, killing F/O Clifford

Logan RAAF and four of his crew and delivering both gunners into enemy hands, the mid-upper gunner, Sgt Frederick Edward William Crowther RAFVR, so critically injured that he died on the 3rd of October, leaving rear gunner, F/Sgt Albert John Knox RNZAF, as the sole survivor. The navigator, F/Sgt Geoffrey Phillips Sowerby, was also a member of the RNZAF. EH935 JN-K crashed at Edesheim, well to the south-west of the target, presumably after bombing, and took the lives of F/O Laurence Kirkpatrick RNZAF and four of his crew, including the RNZAF navigator, F/O Hugh Powell Sands. The bomb-aimer, F/O William Richard Allan Mason, who was a member of the RNZAF, and the mid-upper gunner Sgt J. Elliot, RAFVR, survived to be taken into captivity.

Post-raid reconnaissance and local reports revealed that the marking had been accurate and concentrated, although later bombing had spilled over into the northern fringe of Ludwigshafen and out into the nearby towns of Oppau and Frankenthal, where much damage resulted. A total of 927 houses and twenty industrial premises had been destroyed in Mannheim, and the I G Farben factory in Ludwigshafen had been brought to a standstill.

Two freshman crews were sent mining off the Frisians on the following night, Sgt George John Stewart Kerr RAFVR and F/Sgt Desmond George Geddes Horgan RNZAF and their crews taking off at 19.15 and encountering eight-tenths cloud in the target area along with intermittent rain. The conditions did not affect their ability to carry out their orders, however, and they returned safely after uneventful sorties.

The second Hannover operation was posted on the 27th, for which a force of 678 aircraft was assembled, 111 Stirlings provided by 3 Group with five USAAF B17s. Sixteen crews attended briefing at Mepal to learn of their part in the overall plan, while out on the dispersals, the armourers spent the late afternoon loading incendiaries into the Stirlings' bomb bays. The Steinhude Lake to the north-west of the city was to be employed again by the Path Finder blind marker crews as the starting point for a timed run to the aiming point, which would be marked with yellow TIs on H2S and identified visually by the backers-up and marked with reds and greens. The 75(NZ) Squadron element took off between 19.40 and 20.05 with S/L Andrews the senior pilot on duty accompanied by F/L Lawrence flying as second pilot. One unspecified aircraft is recorded as returning early with an unserviceable rear turret, but the landing times all reflect a completed operation.

They climbed out through ice-bearing cloud before setting course towards poor weather conditions over the North Sea, the bomber stream pressing on behind the Path Finder spearhead, who were unaware that the weather forecasts on which their performance would be based were incorrect. The result of that would be to push the marking some five miles from the city centre towards the north of the city, but at least the weather improved markedly over northern Germany to present the crews with clear skies at the target. The main force crews carried out their attacks on green TIs and observed widespread fires and black smoke rising through 12,000 feet, before returning to again report a city on fire with the glow visible from the Dutch coast. Confidence in the success of the operation was unanimous across the Command, giving lie to the claim that little damage resulted. Post-raid photos did reveal many bomb craters in open country, but also that the main force crews had performed with distinction to hit fifteen square miles within the built-up area and achieve 130 tons of bombs per square mile. Again, the fire and smoke evidence did not support decoy fire-sites, but no local report was forthcoming to shed further light.

The ground defences were described as ineffective, but night-fighters were very much in evidence and a number of the squadron's crews were involved in combats. F/Sgt Masters' rear gunner in BF461 JN-B fired at a Me110, while S/L Andrews in EF507 AA-P sustained some damage in an exchange with a twin-engine assailant, F/Sgt Horgan and crew in EF148 AA-R reported shooting down a Ju88, and F/Sgt Burton's rear gunner in EF465 AA-H claimed another one. The weather for the return flight was not particularly good, and EF135 AA-T arrived on final approach in poor visibility and at too high a speed. The Stirling bounced back into the air on initial touch-down, and P/O Mitchell cut the throttles, causing it to stall onto the runway at 01.35, writing it off, fortunately, without injury to the occupants. The loss of thirty-eight aircraft was probably something of a shock, but common sense had returned to the statistics to re-establish the status-quo after the topsy-turvy outcome of the Mannheim raid. Seventeen Halifaxes, ten Lancasters, ten Stirlings and one Wellington failed to return, giving loss-rates for the four-engine types of 9% for the Stirling, 7.3% for the Halifax and 3.2% for the Lancaster. The squadron posted missing two crews, those of Sgt Ralph Martin RNZAF in EF515 AA-F and P/O Richard Whitmore RNZAF in EH877 JN-C, both of which crashed in Germany. The former came down near Havebeck, about twenty-five miles south-west of Hannover, and all but the mid-upper gunner survived to be taken into captivity. The latter crashed at Sarstedt, about a dozen miles south-east of the target, and only the wireless operator survived to join his squadron colleagues in German hands. The navigator and rear gunner were both members of the RNZAF.

While this operation was in progress, the freshman crews of Sgt Harvey Johnson Middleton RAFVR and F/Sgt Alfred George Humphreys RAAF carried out mining sorties off the Frisians, encountering ten-tenths cloud and rain but delivering their stores into the briefed locations. The Stirling brigade remained at home on the night of the 29/30th, while 343 Lancasters and Halifaxes set off for Bochum in the Ruhr, and, once there, heaped further misery upon it, particularly in the Altstadt and in residential districts.

During the month the squadron donated some crews to 513 Squadron, which was being formed at Mepal, and some Stirlings would also be posted over in October. However, a decision was taken to re-equip 3 Group with Lancasters, and this would lead to the disbandment of the new unit before it attained operational status. The squadron operated on twelve occasions and dispatched 138 sorties for the loss of eight Stirlings and six and a half crews.

October 1943

The first week of the new month would place a heavy burden on the Lancaster squadrons, which would be called upon to operate five times in the first seven nights. It began at Hagen in the Ruhr on the night of the 1/2nd and moved on to Munich twenty-four hours later. While the latter was in progress, extensive mining operations involved 117 aircraft plying their trade between the Biscay coast and the Baltic. 3 Group assigned thirty-nine Stirlings to two Baltic regions, the Kraut garden in Lim Fjord between Hals and Aalborg off Jutland's north-eastern coast and one of the Silverthorn gardens in the Kattegat, and a further eighteen Stirlings and a Lancaster to the Nectarine region off the Frisians. It was to the Baltic that five 75(NZ)

Squadron Stirlings headed after taking off between 17.45 and 18.00, and they were followed into the air an hour later by three debutants, P/O Sidney Alfred Clark RNZAF, F/L Kenneth Aubyn Hassell Lawrence RAFVR and F/Sgt Alan Roy Single RAAF, who were all bound for the Frisians. One Stirling had been withdrawn, after its pilot, F/O Battersby, while waiting at dispersal, had fallen from the leading edge of the wing, breaking his wrist. For a fall of around fifteen feet onto concrete, it's surprising that he wasn't injured more seriously. They delivered their stores as briefed, and apart from the Baltic brigade having to fly through an electrical storm on the way home, the night was uneventful.

The Halifaxes and Stirlings were included on the order of battle for the next operation, which was against the highly industrialised city of Kassel on the 3rd, for which a force of 547 aircraft was assembled, consisting of 223 Halifaxes, 204 Lancasters, 113 Stirlings and seven Mosquitos. 75(NZ) Squadron provided fifteen of the Stirlings, which were loaded with incendiaries and took off either side of 19.00 with W/C Max the senior pilot on duty. The plan of attack called for the Mosquitos to provide route markers and for the Path Finder H2S crews to mark the target blind with yellow TIs and flares. The visual markers were then to identify the aiming-point and mark it with red TIs for the backers-up to maintain with greens. For Kassel, the industrial city located some eighty miles to the east of the Ruhr, this night's visit would be the first of two during the month, which, forever after would leave their mark upon it. As home among other war industry concerns to the Henschel and Fieseler aircraft factories and the Henschel tank works where the much-feared Tiger Tank was in production, it was a priority target that needed to be dealt with.

F/O Alexander turned back early after his navigator became ill and bombed searchlight and flak batteries at Texel so as not to waste their load. The others traversed Holland and the Münsterland in favourable weather conditions to reach the target area, where they were met by largely clear skies but thick ground haze, which should not have, but did cause the Path Finder blind markers to overshoot the planned aiming-point. The light from the flares reflected off the haze to prevent the visual markers from determining the location of the aiming-point, and as a consequence, they withheld their red TIs. The Germans were operating decoy markers, which, together with the absence of the red TIs, conspired to lead a quarter of the main force crews astray and waste their bombs outside of the built-up area. The main force crews carried out their part in the operation from between 14,000 and 20,000 feet and turned away from what appeared to be a good concentration of fires from which a pall of smoke was rising through 10,000 feet. In fact, the main weight of the attack had fallen onto the western suburbs, where the Henschel aircraft and tank factories and the Fieseler aircraft plant were hit, but also onto woodland beyond. However, a stray bomb load had fallen onto one of the largest ammunition dumps in Germany, situated three miles north-east of the aiming point at Ihringshausen, close to the suburb of Wolfsanger, and the resulting explosion at 22.06 devastated the area and attracted more bomb loads. A second explosion ten minutes after the first added to the destruction and left eighty-four buildings on the site flattened and the ground pockmarked by craters, one of which was three hundred feet in diameter.

Twenty-four aircraft failed to return, fourteen Halifaxes, six Stirlings and four Lancasters, which gave a loss-rate of 6.3%, 3.2% and 2.9% respectively. The 75(NZ) Squadron crews played their part, and all made it back to England, confident that they had participated in a successful operation. F/Sgt Parker and crew were, perhaps, lucky to be among them after

LK378 JN-G was hit by flak over the target and sustained damage to the starboard elevator, starboard tailplane and the rear turret. Part of the turret had been shot away and its occupant, Sgt Stanley Winston Riddler RNZAF, did not accompany the rest of the crew home. On landing at Wing, it was discovered that the turret hatch was open, and it was hoped that Sgt Riddler had baled out rather than fallen.

The busy schedule of operations continued with the posting of Frankfurt as the target for 406 aircraft on the 4th, for which 3 Group detailed sixty-nine Stirlings and three USAAF B17s in what was the final night operation for the Americans. Crews learned at briefing that they would be following a somewhat circuitous route, which departed England over the Sussex coast and tracked across France as if heading for southern Germany, before swinging to the north-east and passing to the west of Frankfurt for the final run-in of around eighty miles. This added significantly to the mileage but avoided the flak hotspots from the Dutch coast and the Ruhr's southern defence zone. Thirteen 75(NZ) Squadron Stirlings took off between 18.45 and 19.00 with S/L Joll the senior pilot on duty and set course for the Channel, each carrying an all-incendiary bomb load. Sgt Kerr, P/O Mee and F/L Lawrence returned early, two with technical issues, and one with an indisposed mid-upper gunner, while the others reached the target after a four-hour outward flight, up to an hour of which was accounted for in climbing-out and gaining height before setting course. Frankfurt was found to be clear of cloud, and the Path Finder crews excelled to deliver the H2S-laid markers and illuminator flares all within three miles of the aiming-point and the visual markers within a mile-and-a-half, leaving the city at the mercy of the main force.

Bombing was carried out on red and green TIs predominantly from 14,000 to 19,000 feet in the face of searchlights co-operating with night-fighters, which were very much in evidence. A large red explosion was observed at 21.37, which threw flames up to 3,000 feet, and smoke was rising through 8,000 feet as the bombers turned away, some crews reporting the glow from the burning city to be visible for up to 150 miles into the homeward leg. S/L Joll and crew were in EH880 AA-J and reported an engagement with a BF109, which the gunners claimed as possibly damaged. A modest ten aircraft failed to return, just two of them Stirlings, and one of these belonged to 75(NZ) Squadron. EF130 JN-M crashed at Rüsselsheim, ten miles south-west of the target, and there were no survivors from the crew of Sgt Harvey Middleton RAFVR. Post-raid reconnaissance revealed massive damage in the eastern half of the city and in the inland docks area, both of which were described locally as a "sea of flames". This was the first major success at this target.

While this operation was in progress, the freshman crews of Sgt Single and F/O Clark carried out successful mining sorties in the Deodar garden in the Gironde estuary, the former in EJ901 JN-O landing at Herne on the south coast after sustaining minor flak damage. Debutant captain F/O Spencer Francis Fauvel RNZAF and crew were the only ones from the squadron to be detailed for operations on the evening of the 7th, and they delivered mines into the waters of one of the Nectarine gardens off the Frisians during an uneventful sortie conducted over five-tenths cloud.

The main operation on this night, at the end of a busy first week of the month, was directed at Stuttgart, for which a force of 343 Lancasters was drawn from 1, 3, 5, 6 and 8 Groups. A new weapon in the Command's armoury was introduced for the first time in numbers on this night with the participation of a night-fighter-communications-jamming device called "Jostle" fitted in 101 Squadron Lancasters. It required a specialist operator in addition to the standard crew of seven, who, though not necessarily a German speaker, could recognise the language and on hearing it, jam the signals on up to three frequencies by broadcasting engine noise over them. At 101 Squadron the device was referred to as ABC or Airborne Cigar, and once proved to be effective, ABC Lancasters would be spread throughout the bomber stream for all major operations, whether or not 1 Group was otherwise involved. The Lancaster would also carry a full bomb load reduced by 1,000lbs to compensate for the weight of the equipment and its operator. The operation was inconclusive in the face of ten-tenths cloud but cost a remarkably modest four aircraft. Whether or not the presence of the radio-countermeasures Lancasters was responsible could not be proved, but it was a promising start and would lead ultimately to the formation of the dedicated 100 RCM Group in November.

The following night brought the third raid in the series against Hannover, for which a force of 504 aircraft was made ready, thirteen of the Lancasters representing 3 Group in the absence of the Stirling brigade. Twenty-six Wellingtons from 300 and 432 Squadrons were included, for what would be the type's bombing swansong. 3 Group had been asked to provide ninety-five Stirlings and twelve Mk II Lancasters as the main force for a diversionary raid on Bremen, some seventy miles north-west of the main target, and the dozen 75(NZ) Squadron participants departed Mepal either side of 23.00 with no senior pilots on duty and their bomb bays containing 1,000 and 500 pounders along with incendiaries. There were no early returns, and they reached north-western Germany to find eight to nine-tenths thin cloud at 6,000 feet, through which the Path Finder markers were clearly visible. The accuracy of the bombing was not of overriding importance on a spoof raid, the primary purpose of which was to confuse the night-fighter controller and split the defences. Some fires were reported, and three Stirlings were lost, although all from Mepal returned safely, F/Sgt Humphreys landing EF462 AA-M at Coltishall after a brief skirmish with a Ju88 on the way home. At debriefing, F/Sgt Spiers and crew in EF512 AA-A claimed a BF109 as probably destroyed, and a Me110 as damaged, while P/O White and crew in EH949 JN-P claimed another BF109 as damaged. Meanwhile, F/L Lawrence and F/Sgt Morgan and their crews carried out mining sorties in clear conditions in the Deodar garden in the Gironde estuary and returned safely to report an uneventful trip.

Hannover had been found to be clear of cloud and a highly successful operation ensued, in which all parts of the city, except for the western districts, sustained massive damage. Local reports claimed that 3,932 buildings had been destroyed and thirty thousand others damaged to some extent, figures which seem excessive for a single operation in which fewer than five hundred aircraft had bombed. This lends weight to the author's contention that the earlier raids, which had been dismissed largely as failures, had in fact caused much destruction and the above figures were accumulative over the three raids. Despite the Bremen diversion, night-fighters appeared on the scene while the raid was in progress and twenty-seven aircraft failed to return.

The Path Finder and main force squadrons would effectively stand down now for a period of ten days, while Mosquitos of 8 Group took the war to Germany. For a time at least, Stirlings would be precluded from deep penetration forays into the Reich and 75(NZ) Squadron would spend the rest of the month engaged in mining operations. Poor weather conditions hampered training and operations, and it was the evening of the 17th before three crews managed to get away, debutants Sgt Thomas Gregson Buckley RAFVR and F/Sgt John Cecil Turner RNZAF departing at 18.10 for the Frisians, and F/O Fauvel at the same time for the Gironde estuary. All completed their sorties in favourable weather conditions and returned safely.

The final events in the mini-campaign against Hannover were played out on the night of the 18/19th, when a force of 360 Lancasters produced scattered bombing, much of which fell into open country at a cost of eighteen aircraft. The series against Hannover had involved 2,253 sorties from which 110 aircraft had been lost, in return for which, much of the city had been reduced to ruins. F/O James Kenneth Climie RNZAF was posted in from 12 O.T.U on the 19th, and, according to the squadron ORB, was granted the acting rank of squadron leader as C Flight commander elect to succeed S/L Broadbent. This would be Ken Climie's second tour with the squadron, having completed thirty-three operations between September 1941 and April 1942, twenty-three as crew captain, for which he was awarded a DFC. He was allowed no time to settle in at Mepal before being packed off to 1651CU to learn the ways of the Stirling. There is an entry in the January 1944 record confirming that his acting rank was bestowed upon him on the 10th of November, the day on which he arrived back at the squadron following his conversion training. Whether or not this date, rather than the 19th of October is correct, is difficult to establish, but it would not be unreasonable as his absence from the squadron would render his elevated status ineffective.

The main operation on the night of the 20/21st was against Leipzig in eastern Germany, the first time that it had been targeted in numbers. Unfortunately, the raid was hampered by appalling weather conditions, and the bombing was scattered and probably ineffective. While this was in progress, first-timer F/Sgt Francis Alexander Jack Scott RNZAF and crew went alone to the Frisians and deposited their mines in the allocated locations.

Sgt William Morton Allen RAFVR and F/Sgts Colin Archibald Gunn McKenzie RNZAF and Ritchie Millar RNZAF ploughed the same furrows two nights later, and P/O McKenzie's rear gunner in EF513 JN-E fired at an unidentified aircraft, which disappeared without firing back. The main event on this night was the second raid of the month on Kassel, for which a force of 560 Lancasters and Halifaxes was assembled. No one could have predicted the scale of destruction that took place within the city on this night, but a tragedy of extreme proportions was played out on the ground, out of sight of the bomber crewmen, for whom this was just another operation against an industrial city and one more towards the end of their tour. 4,349 blocks of flats containing 26,782 apartments were destroyed and a further 6,743 blocks with 26,463 apartments were damaged, rendering 63% of the city's living accommodation unusable. Vast numbers of industrial, public, administrative and military buildings were also destroyed or damaged, the transport systems were put out of action, and 5,600 people lost their lives. The city's three Henschel factories, engaged at the time in the construction of the Tiger tank, locomotives and aircraft under licence, and the Fieseler works, where the V-1 flying bomb was in development, were also severely damaged, and this would impact the introduction of the new weapon and the numbers initially available to unleash on London. It was, perhaps, fortuitous for the Stirlings that they were not included in the operation, which claimed twenty-five Halifaxes and eighteen Lancasters. One can only imagine the carnage amongst Stirlings, had they been available for the night-fighters to target.

It was the turn of F/Sgts James Robert Randle and Bernard Forfar Wallis, both members of the RNZAF, to service the same Nectarine garden off the Frisians on the evening of the 24th, but the latter had to return early because of defective navigational equipment. F/Sgt Randle and crew completed their sortie and were on final approach to land, when EF142 AA-C crashed a mile and a half south-west of the airfield and immediately burst into flames. The mid-upper gunner was able to scramble clear uninjured, while the flight engineer and rear gunner would require hospital treatment, but F/Sgt Randle, his navigator and bomb-aimer, both also members of the RNZAF, and the wireless operator, all lost their lives. The squadron operated for the final time during the month on the night of the 25/26th, when contributing three crews to a 3 Group mining effort involving twenty-three Stirlings in one of the Silverthorn gardens in the Kattegat region of the western Baltic. F/Sgt Spiers, P/O White and F/O Grubb completed uneventful sorties, before being diverted on return because of adverse weather conditions at Mepal.

During the course of the month, S/L Joll was awarded a DFC to add to his DFM and the squadron operated fourteen times, dispatching sixty-five sorties for the loss of two Stirlings and the better part of two crews.

November 1943

The next four months would bring the bloodiest, hardest-fought air battles between Bomber Command and the Luftwaffe's Nachtjagd and test the hard-pressed crews to the limit of their endurance. In a minute to Churchill on the 3rd, Harris stated, that with the participation of the American 8th Air Force, he could "wreck Berlin from end to end". He estimated that the campaign would cost the two forces between four and five hundred aircraft, but that it would cost Germany the war. This would remove the need for the kind of bloody, expensive and protracted land campaign, which he had personally witnessed during the Great War and had prompted him to "get into the air" at the earliest opportunity. It should be remembered that this was the first time in the history of air warfare, that the means had existed to prove the theory, that an enemy could be defeated by bombing alone. It is only in the light of more recent experiences, that we have learned of the need, in a conventional conflict at least, to occupy the enemy's territory to secure submission. The Americans, however, were committed to victory on land, where film cameras could capture the glory, and would not accompany Harris to Berlin.

S/L Joll was posted to the newly-forming 513 Squadron on the 1st, and the vacancy for an A Flight commander would remain unfilled for some time. The unfavourable weather that had kept the squadron at home during the final days of October continued into November, relenting sufficiently on the 3rd to allow F/Sgts Turner RNZAF and Wallis and F/O Fauvell and their crews to go mining off the Frisians. The main event on this night involved a force of 577 Lancasters and Halifaxes at Düsseldorf, and while the raid was in progress, thirty-eight Mk II Lancasters of 3 and 6 Groups were to conduct the first large-scale test of the G-H bombing system against the city's Mannesmann Rohrenwerke (tubular steel works) on the northern outskirts. In the event, five returned early, sixteen suffered G-H equipment failure, two were lost and only fifteen bombed the factory, destroying in the process a number of assembly halls. Development of G-H would take a considerable time and it would be a further twelve months before it was unleashed to great effect on the enemy in the hands of 3 Group. Central and southern districts of the Ruhr giant bore the brunt of the main attack, and all the indications were that it was a successful operation at a cost of eighteen aircraft. A destructive diversionary raid was also mounted by 8 Group against Cologne.

The squadron briefed four crews for mining duties in the Kattegat on the following night, and they took off at around 16.00, before flying into ten-tenths cloud, generally poor weather conditions and enemy night-fighters operating over Denmark. F/O Witting landed EJ108 AA-O at Mepal at 23.20 with a damaged port wing, starboard flap and rear turret, many large holes in the fuselage and a fatally wounded rear gunner in the person of F/Sgt Walter Hurdle RNZAF. The crew reported an engagement with a night-fighter in the target area and had jettisoned the mines while taking evasive action. The return of the other three aircraft was awaited in vain, and news of their fate would eventually find its way to Mepal via the Red Cross. BF461 JN-B fell victim to a night-fighter and crashed at Kallerup, on the western side of North-Jutland, and the wireless operator failed to survive. P/O Gordon Williams RNZAF and four of his crew, one of them another member of the RNZAF, became PoWs, while the RNZAF navigator managed to evade a similar fate. P/O William Masters RNZAF and his crew were less fortunate when BK778 JN-U met a similar end in the same area, and they were all killed. There were a further three members of the RNZAF in this aircraft. EE897 AA-G was lost without trace, probably in identical circumstances, and took with it the crew of F/O Norman Wilson RNZAF, of which three others were Kiwis.

On the night of the 7/8th thirty-five aircraft were sent mining off France's Biscay coast from north to south, the quartet of freshman crews from 75(NZ) Squadron targeting the familiar waters of the Gironde estuary. They took off at 23.30, and all reached the drop zones to deliver their mines through nine-tenths cloud, before returning safely to report uneventful sorties. There was a much earlier start for F/Sgts Ronald Hunt RAFVR and McKenzie bound for the same region on the evening of the 10th. They took off shortly after 17.00 and flew out in eight-tenths cloud, which had largely dispersed by the time the target was reached. A number of enemy aircraft were seen and EF152 JN-T was attacked by a Ju88, which F/Sgt Hunt's gunners engaged and claimed as damaged. F/Sgt McKenzie and crew in EF514 AA-D were also involved in a short combat with a Ju88, but both Mepal aircraft returned safely after depositing their mines in the allocated locations and landed at Tangmere either side of 00.30. Twenty-four hours later it was the turn of newcomer F/O Derek Warren RAFVR and F/Sgt Wallis to keep the Gironde estuary well-stocked with mines, and they enjoyed incident-free sorties between 17.00 and 01.05.

S/L Andrews relinquished his role as B Flight commander on the 14th, and with it went his acting squadron leader rank. He was posted in the rank of flight lieutenant to 11 O.T.U. and was succeeded as B Flight commander on the 15th by S/L David Stewart Gibb DFC RNZAF, who had arrived from 1657 Conversion Unit on the 6th.

Undaunted by the American response to his invitation to join the Berlin party, Harris would return alone, and the rocky road to the Capital was re-joined by an all-Lancaster heavy force on the night of the 18/19th, while a predominantly Halifax and Stirling contingent of 395 aircraft acted as a diversion by raiding Mannheim and Ludwigshafen three hundred miles to the south-west. An innovation for the Berlin operation was a shortening of the bomber stream to reduce the time over the target to sixteen minutes. When the first Thousand Bomber raid had taken place in May 1942, with an unprecedented twelve aircraft per minute crossing the aiming-point, there was considered to be a high risk of collisions. The number had since been increased to sixteen per minute, with large raids lasting up to forty-five minutes, but on this night, twenty-seven aircraft per minute were to pass over the aiming-point.

The diversionary force consisted of 248 Halifaxes, 114 Stirlings and thirty-three Lancasters drawn from 3, 4, 6 and 8 Groups, 75(NZ) Squadron making ready nineteen Stirlings loaded with 2,000 pounders and incendiaries. They departed Mepal between 17.20 and 18.00 with S/L Gibb the senior pilot on duty and lost the services of the crews of F/Sgts Humphreys and McKenzie for unspecified reasons, while the rest of the bomber stream was driven by stronger-than-forecast winds to arrive at the target a little ahead of time, which upset the planned schedule to a degree and may have led to what became a scattered attack. They were greeted by clear skies, ground haze, and a fairly active ground defence backed up by numerous night-fighters. On the way in, F/Sgt Spiers' rear gunner fired at an approaching BF109, claiming it as damaged, and over the target, while bombing and coned by searchlights, Sgt Allen's gunners exchanged ineffective fire with an unidentified single-engine fighter. Some crews made a visual identification of the aiming-point after following yellow route markers, and confirmed their positions by H2S, while others relied on the red and green TIs and bombed from between 14,000 and 19,000 feet, observing fires and black smoke. The Path Finders had relied on H2S to position their ground markers, and the main weight of the attack fell into the northern districts, where 330 buildings were destroyed and a similar number seriously damaged. The Daimler-Benz car factory suffered a 90% loss of production for an unknown period. Returning crews described large, concentrated fires and huge explosions, and a number reported inconclusive encounters with night-fighters. The squadron's participants all returned safely, but nine other Stirlings failed to do so, a loss rate of 7.9%, and unknown to the squadrons operating the type, its career as a front-line bomber was about to become severely restricted.

Crews returning from Berlin had nothing useful to pass on to the intelligence section at debriefing, and most considered the bombing to have been scattered and probably ineffective. Local sources confirmed that there had been no concentration and catalogued the destruction of 169 houses and a number of industrial units, with many more damaged to some extent. The loss of a relatively modest nine Lancasters was credited partly to the diversion at Mannheim, but the night's overall losses were still high.

Acting S/L Climie, who was still shown in the movements record as a flying officer, arrived back at the squadron on the 10th following his conversion at 1651 Conversion Unit and officially succeeded S/L Broadbent as C Flight commander. On the 19th, 3, 4, 6 and 8 Groups combined to put together a force of 266 aircraft, 170 Halifaxes, eighty-six Stirlings and ten Mosquitos to attack the city of Leverkusen, situated on the eastern bank of the Rhine on the south-western fringe of the Ruhr a few miles north of Cologne. The Mepal element of sixteen took off between 16.55 and 17.41 with no senior pilots on duty, and after Sgt Buckley and crew had returned early to land at Chedburgh, the others joined the bomber stream and adopted the southern route to the Ruhr, passing north of Antwerp. They found ten-tenths cloud in the target area with tops at 10,000 to 12,000 feet but no TIs to guide them to the aiming point, a situation caused by mass Oboe equipment failure among the Mosquito element and the decision by the backers-up not to confuse the issue by releasing their markers. Sparce and scattered marking caused bombs to be sprayed over a wide area to the north, where twenty-seven towns reported bombs falling. Fortunately, the failure was not compounded by high losses, which amounted to four Halifaxes and a single Stirling, which happened to be the squadron's LJ442 JN-F. This was shot down by Lt Otto Fries of 5./NJG1 and crashed at Horrues in the Hainaut region of Belgium, from where F/Sgt Parker RAAF and his navigator evaded capture, while the Kiwi bomb-aimer was picked up and sent to a PoW camp and the other members of the crew, including the RNZAF wireless operator, lost their lives. Two combats were also reported by F/Sgt Horgan in LJ462 AA-O, the first one involving a FW190 that attacked head-on, forcing Horgan to drop one wing to avoid a collision, and the second one three minutes later by a Ju88, which was claimed as damaged. On return, fog at Mepal required the other fourteen aircraft to be diverted to Bramwell Bay.

Harris called for a maximum effort on Berlin on the 22nd, and 764 aircraft were made available, of which fifty Stirlings and eighteen Lancasters were provided by 3 Group, four of the former belonging to 75(NZ) Squadron. They were loaded with 1,000 pounders and incendiaries as they began taking off at 17.00 with no senior pilots on duty and after climbing out, adopted an outward route similar to that employed by the all-Lancaster force four nights earlier. This took the bomber stream from Texel to a point north-west of Hannover, where a slight dogleg to port put them on a due-easterly heading directly to the target. Unlike the previous raid, however, rather than the circuitous return south of Cologne and out over the French coast, they would come home via a reciprocal route. This was based on a forecast of low cloud and fog over Germany, which would inhibit the night-fighter effort, while broken, medium-level cloud over Berlin would facilitate ground marking. An additional bonus was the availability to the Path Finders of five new H2S Mk III sets, while a new record of thirty-four aircraft per minute passing over the aiming-point would be achieved by abandoning the long-standing practice of allocating aircraft types to specific waves. On this night, aircraft of all types would be spread through the bomber stream, and this was bad news for the Stirlings, which, by the very nature of their design, would be below the Lancaster and Halifax elements and in danger of being hit by friendly bombs.

F/O Clark and crew returned after three and a half hours with oxygen failure, while the others pressed on over ten-tenths cloud which persisted all the way to the target and topped out at around 12,000 feet, in defiance of the meteorological forecast that had been offered at briefing. The blind markers employed H2S to establish their positions before releasing both red TIs and skymarkers, but the TIs disappeared as soon as they hit the cloud and were largely ineffective. This meant that the least reliable Wanganui (skymarking) method was all that was available to the main force crews as they began their bombing runs in the face of intense predicted flak and a mass of searchlights. The Path Finder backers-up maintained the aiming point with red flares with green stars and also released green TIs, which the main force crews bombed from between 14,000 and 20,000 feet, observing the glow of fires beneath the clouds and a very large explosion that lit up the sky at 20.10. They flew home with a notion that they had taken part in a successful operation, but a meaningful assessment had been impossible, and they would have to wait for post-raid reconnaissance to reveal the truth. This and local reports would confirm that Berlin had suffered its most destructive raid of the war to date, which had left a swathe of destruction from the city centre through the western residential districts of Tiergarten and Charlottenburg as far as the suburb town of Spandau. A number of firestorm areas were reported, and the catalogue of destruction included three thousand houses and twenty-three industrial premises. Many thousands more sustained varying degrees of damage, costing

175,000 people their homes and an estimated two thousand their lives, and by daylight on the 23rd, the smoke had risen to almost 19,000 feet.

Twenty-six aircraft failed to return, eleven Lancasters, ten Halifaxes, and five Stirlings, which amounted to a loss-rate among the types respectively of 2.3%, 4.2% and 10.0%. F/O Fauvel landed at 00.10 to report bombing the target, and it soon became evident that the two outstanding aircraft had been lost. Information was received eventually, that EF148 AA-R had crashed north-north-east of Osnabrück, killing F/Sgt John Turner RNZAF and his crew, which contained an RNZAF navigator and wireless operator. LJ453 AA-K crashed some forty miles further south near Ahlen, north-east of the Ruhr, and F/Sgt Single RAAF died with his crew, which included three members of the RNZAF.

As far as Harris was concerned, the Stirling losses proved to be the final straw for a type, which, because of its short wing design, was restricted to a low service ceiling and by the configuration of its bomb bay to small calibre bombs. Unlike the Lancaster and Halifax, it lacked development potential and was immediately withdrawn from future operations over Germany. It would still have an important role to play on secondary duties, however, bombing over occupied territory, mining, and, in 1944, it would replace the Halifax to become the aircraft of choice for the two SOE squadrons, 138 and 161, at Tempsford. Many of those released from Bomber Command service would find their way to 38 Group, where they would give valuable service as transports and glider-tugs for airborne landings.

Having heard preliminary reports of the previous night's success, Harris ordered another immediate attack on Berlin, a decision that would stretch the nerves of the aircrew, who were still in recovery mode. A heavy force of 365 Lancasters and ten Halifaxes was made ready with some difficulty on the 23rd, because such back-to-back long-range operations also put a strain on those charged with the responsibility of getting the aircraft off the ground. At Ludford Magna, for example, the armourers would be unable to load all nineteen 101 Squadron Lancasters with the intended weight of bombs, and would have to send them off 2,000lb short. In further manifestations of the effects of back-to-back long-range operations, forty-six aircraft returned early, and others intending to continue on to the target dumped part of their loads over the North Sea to gain more height. It involved largely those from 1 Group, who were shedding their cookies in protest at their A-O-C's policy of loading each Lancaster to its maximum all-up weight at the expense of altitude. The slogan "H-E-I-G-H-T spells safety" could be found on the walls of most bomber station briefing rooms at the time.

Berlin was found to be covered by ten-tenths cloud with tops at between 10,000 and 15,000 feet, and, guided by the glow of fires still burning beneath the clouds from the night before, the Path Finders located the town of Rathenow on H2S and carried out a thirty-five-mile timed run to the city centre. Skymarkers were released and red and green TIs formed a triangle into which the bulk of the bombing fell and returning crews described a column of smoke reaching 20,000 feet and the glow of fires visible again from the Hannover area some 150 miles from the target. Fake broadcasts from England, which had begun a few nights earlier, caused annoyance to the night-fighter force by ordering them to land because of fog over their bases. There were arguments between the fake and real controllers as each claimed to be the legitimate voice, but despite the confusion, night-fighters still played a major hand in the bringing-down of twenty Lancasters. Post-raid reconnaissance and local reports confirmed that this operation had destroyed a further two thousand buildings and killed around fifteen hundred people.

The removal of Stirlings from operations over Germany was not immediately communicated to 3 Group Squadrons and 75(NZ) Squadron was ordered to make ready four for Frankfurt, which was posted as the target for the night of the 25/26th. These were cancelled and the operation, which was only moderately effective, went ahead with a main force of 236 Halifaxes from 4 and 6 Groups. 75(NZ) Squadron did operate also on this night, when sending five aircraft among thirty-two Stirlings to mine the sea lanes from the Biscay coast in the south to the Frisians in the north. The Kiwi target areas were either Cinnamon or Deodar off the Biscay coast, Greengage in the approaches to the port of Cherbourg and Nectarine off the Frisians. The first-time captains were F/Sgt Colin Roy Baker RNZAF, F/Sgt Alexander Hugh Baird RAAF, F/Sgt Edgar Lawrence Burke RNZAF, F/Sgt Arthur Russell Young RNZAF and F/Sgt Cyril William McCardle RNZAF, who took off between 17.20 and 17.40 and encountered between five and ten-tenths cloud in their respective target areas. All but one crew, who had to jettison their load in the mining area, fulfilled their briefs and returned safely from uneventful sorties.

The squadron sent a further four aircraft including those of debutants Sgt W Kay RAFVR and F/O Harold Wright Bruce Heney RNZAF, to the Frisians on the evening of the 26th, the night on which the next assault took place on Berlin. The marking was misplaced around six miles north-west of the city centre, but most of the bombing fell within the city boundaries, and caused much further damage to residential property, while destroying thirty-eight factories in the Siemensstadt district.

The month's operations concluded for 75(NZ) Squadron on the evening of the 30th, when four crews were sent to lay mines in the Baltic, led for the first time by S/L Climie. This is not mentioned in the 3 Group ORB, which specifies the northern and western coasts of France as the target areas. During the course of the month the squadron operated thirteen times and dispatched sixty-nine sorties for the loss of six Stirlings and their crews.

December 1943

The new month began for the squadron with participation in a 3 Group mining operation off Denmark on the evening of the 1st, for which the three participating Stirlings from Mepal were assigned to the Kraut garden in Lim Fjord, the inland sea area of north-eastern Jutland. F/Sgt Kerr and P/Os Moseley and White were airborne by 15.30 and reached the target area to find ten-tenths cloud, two unidentified crews releasing their mines at the allocated location but were unable because of the cloud to confirm that the parachutes had opened. On return, they were diverted to Acklington in Northumberland, but EH880 AA-J undershot the runway and crashed into a farmhouse at Togston, killing F/Sgt George John Stewart Kerr RAFVR and five of his crew, and severely injuring the mid-upper gunner, F/Sgt Kenneth Gordon Hook, RAFVR. Tragically, five children in the farmhouse also lost their lives, while their parents were badly injured and taken to hospital.

The Berlin campaign continued on the night of the 2/3rd, when a predominantly Lancaster main force delivered a scattered attack across mainly southern districts and open country, although a number of war industry factories in the east and west also sustained damage. It was an expensive operation for the Command, which lost forty aircraft, or 8.7%. Amends were made on the following night, when Leipzig was targeted by a force of more than five hundred aircraft and much destruction occurred in both residential and industrial districts at a more modest cost of twenty-four aircraft.

Poor weather settled over the bomber counties thereafter, and it was left to the Mosquitos of 8 Group to harass the residents of the Ruhr cities. S/L Raymond Johnson Watson DFC RNZAF finally succeeded the long-departed S/L Joll as A flight commander on the 4th, following his posting to the squadron as a flight lieutenant from 1651 Conversion Unit on that very day. Major operations resumed on the night of the 16/17th, when an all-Lancaster heavy force returned to Berlin. The Stirling force was also called into action, twenty-six for a special operation against flying bomb sites and twenty-seven for gardening duties. 75(NZ) Squadron prepared eight Stirlings for the special operation, four for mining off the Frisians and three more for the Bay of Biscay. The two mining sections took off between 16.50 and 17.15, with newcomers F/O Thomas Leo Whigham Teasdale RCAF and F/Sgts Roy Alexander Evans RNZAF, Colin John Kinross RNZAF and Robert Albert Potts RAAF bound for the Frisians, and P/O White and F/Os Fauvel and Warren heading south-west for the French coast.

The special operation was one of two to be carried out by small forces in the Abbeville area of France, one by nine Lancasters of 617 Squadron at Flixecourt and the other by twenty-six 3 Group Stirlings at Tilley-le-Haut and were the first attacks on V-1 sites under Operation Crossbow. The targets were very small and hidden in wooded areas, and the marking was to be carried out by Oboe Mosquitos, which offered the best chance of accuracy. Six of the 75(NZ) Squadron element took off safely between 17.50 and 18.15 with S/L Climie and S/L Watson the senior pilots on duty, while two others failed to become airborne and apparently crashed on take-off, incidents for which no details are provided in the ORB. We are told that one aircraft returned early, but the landing times offer no clue as to which. They flew out in good weather conditions, which persisted to provide clear skies in the target area with just a little ground haze. The Mosquitos marked at both sites as planned, but the TIs fell 450 yards from the aiming point at Tilley, and 350 yards at Flixecourt, which at an urban target, would have represented pinpoint accuracy. At a precision target, however, it was not good enough, and although the bombing fell close to the markers, the targets escaped destruction. This would happen on a number of subsequent occasions, and the frustration caused at 617 Squadron would lead to a breakthrough in marking techniques, which would ultimately allow 5 Group to become effectively independent.

This night will forever be remembered for the very low cloud that blanketed the airfields as the bombers returned from Berlin and the other operations, and it was the 1, 3, 6 and 8 Group airfields that were most severely affected. The tired crews stumbled around in the murk seeking somewhere to land, most without the reserves of fuel to reach other regions of the country. Twenty-nine Lancasters either crashed or were abandoned by their crews, and around 150 airmen lost their lives in tragic circumstances when so close to home and safety. EF163 JN-L also fell foul of the conditions on return from the Frisians, and crashed at Biddington Farm, Sutton in Cambridgeshire, four miles west of Peterborough. P/O Kinross RNZAF and five of his crew died, including the RNZAF navigator, and only the mid-upper gunner survived with injuries. There is a possibility that a hung-up mine may have altered the aircraft's centre of gravity and contributed to the accident.

Five NCO crews took off at 17.15 on the 20th for mining duties off the Frisians, and all returned safely from uneventful sorties. They included three newcomers, F/Sgt Desmond Marriott Dawe RNZAF, Sgt J Pryse RAFVR and Sgt Frederick Gregory RAFVR. Frankfurt was the target for a force of 650 aircraft on the following night, while the Mepal crews remained at home. Unexpected cloud caused difficulties for the Path Finders and the raid was only moderately successful. Sgt Gregory and F/Sgt Potts took off at 17.00 on the 22nd and delivered mines into the allocated positions in the Anemone garden off Le Havre in excellent weather conditions, and as they were making their way home across the Channel, six other Stirlings departed Mepal between 21.00 and 21.35 to join in on another attack on the flying bomb sites. F/Os Warren and Witting were the senior pilots on duty as they made their way towards the Channel and the northern coast of France, each carrying 500 pounders. They delivered their loads onto the Oboe markers in favourable conditions and a little patchy cloud, before returning safely to report concentrated bombing and large explosions.

The next round in the Berlin offensive, the seventh since the resumption, was posted on the 23rd and involved a predominantly Lancaster heavy force of 371 aircraft, which sprayed bombs across the south-eastern suburbs. Cloud and unserviceable H2S sets resulted in only modest damage at a cost of sixteen Lancasters.

The Christmas period was spent at home, either on the ground or in training in the air, and it was the 29th before the Kiwis were called once more to briefing. This was the night when more than seven hundred aircraft took off for Berlin, for what would be the first of three raids on the capital over five nights spanning the turn of the year. It was another moderately effective attack, which produced disappointing results in view of the size of the force deployed, and it cost twenty aircraft. Meanwhile, nine Stirlings had been loaded with 1,500lb parachute mines, five to deliver to the Cinnamon garden in the approaches to La Pallice and La Rochelle and two each for Deodar and Nectarine respectively in the Gironde estuary and off the Frisians. They departed Mepal between 17.00 and 17.25, and all reached their respective target areas to encounter cloud of between eight and ten-tenths. F/Sgts Buckley and Evans attracted heavy flak on their way to the Gironde estuary and one Stirling sustained slight damage. Three of the Cinnamon contingent brought their mines back, one with technical issues and two owing to navigational problems relating to the poor visibility. The others delivered their mines into the allocated locations, but the cloud prevented them from confirming the deployment of the parachutes.

F/O Teasdale and Sgt Pryse took off at 02.16 and 02.35 respectively on the 30th for a further mining effort in the Gironde estuary, and they returned after six hours for a hearty breakfast and to report successful and uneventful sorties. At 17.14 F/Sgt Young and crew took off to carry out the squadron's final sortie of the year, to lay mines in the waters between the Anemone and Greengage gardens off Le Havre and Cherbourg. They also enjoyed an uneventful trip and returned after three hours to report fulfilling their brief. Later, on the 30th the station hosted a group of VIP visitors including High Commissioner Mr Jordan, RNZAF Liaison Officer G/C Manson, and war correspondent Alan Mitchell.

During the course of the month the squadron took part in twelve operations and dispatched forty-three sorties for the loss of the two Stirlings and twelve crewmen at home. The squadron would not have wanted to be removed from the front line, but the Stirling was no longer suited to the demands of operating over Germany, and for 3 Group's main force squadrons the future lay with the Lancaster. 514 Squadron had been formed in September and since November had been operating Mk II Lancasters alongside 115 Squadron and the first examples of Mk I/III had arrived at Mildenhall during December for the conversion of 15 Squadron. For the next two months, the 75(NZ) Squadron crews could only look on with envy as they waited for Lancasters to reach Mepal.

W/C Gerald Arthur Lane, RAF.
(The Herald, Scotland)

P/O Kenneth Howard Blincoe DFC, RNZAF, lost with all his crew on the night of the 3rd/4th February 1943, shot down on the way to Hamburg. (AWMM)

S/L Gilbert Meston Allcock, RAF.
(214squadron.org.uk)

Sgt Randolph Ernst Redding RNZAF and his crew came down in the sea two miles off the Norfolk coast near Cromer on the 5th February 1943, all lost without trace. (AWMM)

The grand view from on top of a Stirling. (NZ Bomber Command Assn. archives, Alexander collection)

"Return At Dawn", by Hilary A. St. George Saunders. The Official story of the New Zealand Bomber Squadron of the RAF, from June 1939 to July 1942.

Above: Stirling at dispersal. (NZ Bomber Command Assn. archives, Alexander collection)

P/O Donald Gordon McCaskill RNZAF and his crew were shot down at Regniessart in Belgium on 14/15th of April, 1943, with no survivors. (AWMM)

F/L Geoffrey Maurice Rothwell RAF. (AWMM.)

Sgt Charles Raglan Davey RNZAF, lost with all his crew, shot down near Karlsruhe, 8/9 March 1943. (AWMM)

Sgt Kenneth Atherton Crankshaw RNZAF. (NZ Bomber Command Assn. archives, Crankshaw collection)

W/O John Arthur Ernest Walsh RNZAF, lost with all his crew returning from Duisburg 8/9 April, 1943. (AWMM)

The crash site where BK604 AA-S and the McCullough crew came down near Almelo on the night of 2nd/3rd of February. P/O John McCullough and three of his crew were killed, the other four became PoWs. (Diederick ten Brinke (taken by his grandfather), via Russell Murphy)

The four McCullough crew graves, L-R: P/O John McCullough RNZAF, Sgt Francis Frederick Allen RAFVR, Sgt Paul Rodney Trevayne RAFVR, Sgt Terence Austin "Terry" Murphy RNZAF. (Russell Murphy)

*Sgt Raymond Cyril Going RNZAF,
lost with all his crew on their first operation, 3rd/4th March 1943.
(AWMM)*

Four members of the Going crew with Stirling N6123 AA-Q "Queenie" (L-R): Sgt Francis Barkhouse (Frank) Stewart (mid-upper gunner), Sgt Clarence Sydney (Syd) Burton (rear gunner), Sgt Kenneth Cedric Eyre (wireless operator) and possibly Sgt Emrys Herbert Weaver (flight engineer). The crew was lost on their first operation, mining off the Frisians, 3rd/4th March 1943. (Martin Stewart)

P/O (later Sir) Douglas Charles Lowe DFC (far right) and crew. (Telegraph)

Stirling BF465 AA-K was involved in a combat with the McCaskill crew on the night of 10/11th April. (NZ Bomber Command Assn. archives)

P/O Norman Bradford Bluck RNZAF was lost on 24/25th June 1943, with all his crew. (AWMM)

P/O William Rosser Perrott RNZAF, failed to return 25/26 June 1943. (AWMM)

The Halliburton crew with their regular Stirling W7513 AA-G, the one they were flying when lost the night of 28/29th of April. L-R: Sgt David Church (wireless operator), Sgt Patrick Hunter (navigator), Sgt Devinder Singh Sidhu (flight engineer), Sgt Keith Halliburton (pilot). Others unidentified but probably Sgt Alexander Howell (rear gunner), Sgt Thomas Scarfe (air bomber) and Sgt Charles Boxall (mid-upper gunner).
(David Church/75 Squadron Association UK, via 75nzsquadron.com)

The Alfred Lewis crew, lost the night of 28/29th April 1943. Third from left Sgt Victor Howes (rear gunner), 5th from left Sgt Henry Corin (navigator), 7th from left Sgt Frederick Moulton (wireless operator). Others unidentified but probably include F/Sgt Alfred Lewis (pilot), P/O Charles Bickham (air bomber), Sgt John Whitehart (mid-upper gunner) and Sgt Andrew Graham (flight engineer). (AWMM)

"M 'Mother', Newmarket", April 1943. Stirling BK807 AA-M appears to have been lost on its first operation, the night of 28/29th April 1943, along with the Hamer crew. 2nd from left AC Harold Goadby (ground crew, FMA), 3rd from left F/Sgt Ross Buckley (air bomber), then LAC Tom McGibbon (ground crew, FME). 6th from left Sgt Malcolm Shogren (rear gunner), 8th from left Sgt Desmond Ross (navigator), right F/Sgt William Brian (wireless operator). (Air Force Museum of New Zealand, Jack Way collection)

The D.L. Thompson crew with their regular Stirling, BF467 AA-W, all lost the night of 28/29th April 1943. 2nd from left, Sgt Ernest Jenkins (wireless operator), and third from left, P/O Des Thompson, skipper. (NZ Bomber Command Assn. archives)

*W/C Michael Wyatt RAF.
(From "Forever Strong")*

*W/C Roy Douglas Max DFC RAF, RNZAF.
(AWMM)*

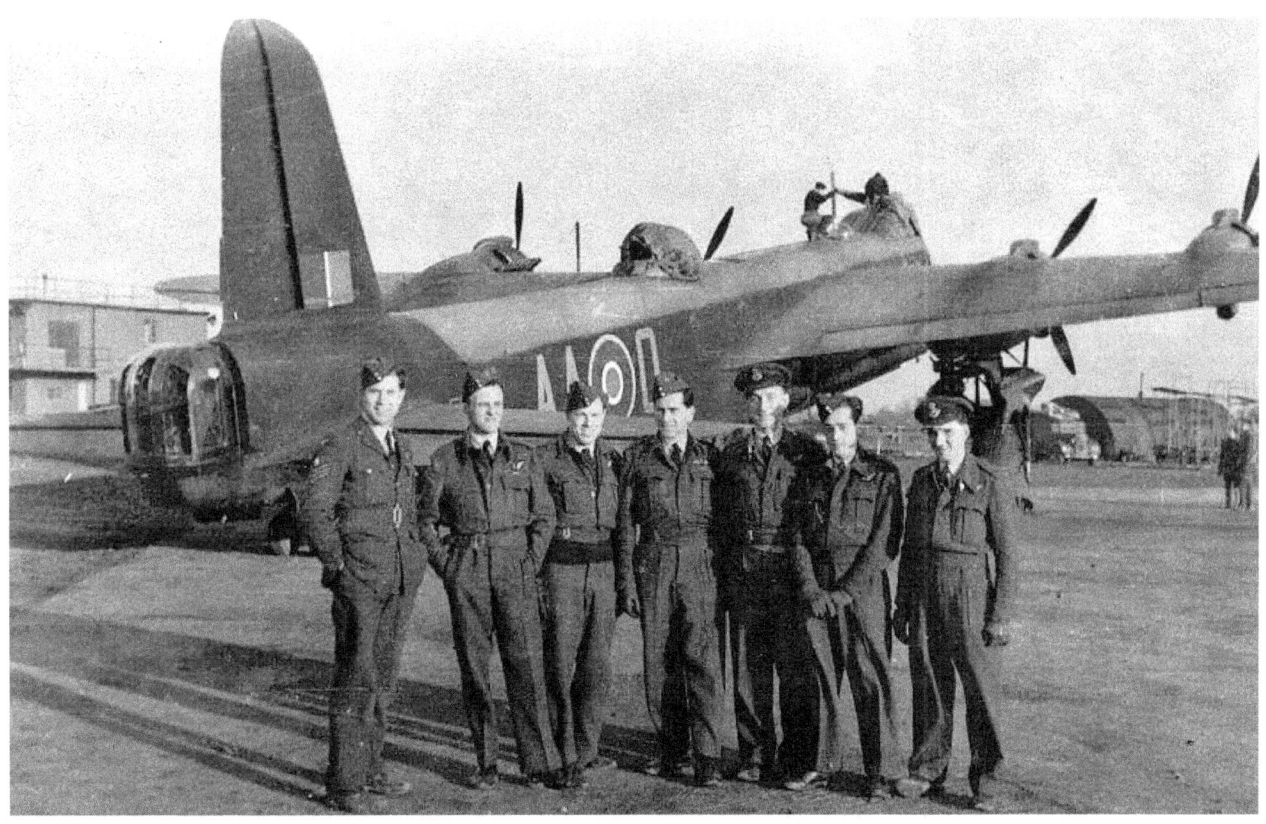
*W/C Roy Max (centre) and crew flew EJ108, AA-O to Modane on 16/17th September 1943.
(NZ Bomber Command Assn. archives)*

A Stirling group, (L-R): back - F/Sgt Vincent Jamieson, F/O Maurice Parker DFC, F/Lt (later S/L) Dick Broadbent DFC, mid (C Flight Commander), F/Lt (later S/L) Ronald Laud (A Flight Commander), F/Lt Guy Heywood DFC. Front - F/Sgt Charlie Parker, P/O Desmond Thompson, F/O John Fabian DFC, F/Sgt (later F/O) Don Whitehead DFM, P/O Raymond Bennett, F/O John Johnston, F/Sgt Pat Middleton. Dated between 16 and 28 April 1943. (NZ Bomber Command Assn. archives, Whitehead collection)

"Airmen overseas", April 1943. Members of the Appleton, Bailey, Bennett, Broadbent, Lewis, Rothschild, Thompson, and Whitehead crews, and the squadron cat, in front of Stirling W7513 AA-G. Centre with arms folded is F/L (later S/L) Ronald Laud. (NZ Bomber Command Assn. archives, Broadbent collection)

S/L Dick Broadbent (left) and visiting NZ fighter ace W/C Bill "Hawkeye" Wells inspecting the damage to the tail of P/O Peter Buck's Stirling BF517 AA-O, in which Sgt Brian Rogers was mortally wounded on the night of 26/27th April. (NZ Bomber Command Assn. archives, Broadbent collection)

The Bailey crew flew 15 op's with BF443, AA-V, this their second-to-last on 28 April 1943 to Kiel Bay, pictured with ground crew. L-R: Sgt Roe, LAC Lobley, F/O Charles "Slim" Ormerod, Sgt Bruce Hosie, Sgt Jack Wall, P/O Jack Bailey, Sgt Tom Lillystone, Sgt Freddie Ottaway, Sgt Wally Thompson, LAC Murdoch and Cpl Gibson. Bailey would return to the squadron in 1944 as Flight Commander, Wall as his bomb aimer, and Ormerod as squadron Navigation Leader. (NZ Bomber Command Assn. archives, Hosie collection)

*Armourers hoist two 1500lb sea mines into a Stirling's bomb bay.
(NZ Bomber Command Assn. archives)*

The Whitehead crew (L-R): Rex Jamieson (rear gunner), Morris Parker (air bomber), Charlie Parker (wireless operator), George Stokes (mid-upper gunner), Hugh McLellan (flight engineer), Don Whitehead (pilot), and Peter Dobson Navigator. Dated 24 April 1943. (NZ Bomber Command Assn. archives, Whitehead collection)

F/O Allan Alexander (left) with unknown in front of BK777 AA-U 'Alexanders Ragtime Crew'.
(NZ Bomber Command Assn. archives, Alexander collection)

Below: RAF Mepal from 16,000 feet, taken by S/L Dick Broadbent's air bomber on 20th of October 1943. It was Broadbent's last flight in his regular Stirling BK778 JN-U "Uncle".
(NZ Bomber Command Assn, archives, Broadbent collection)

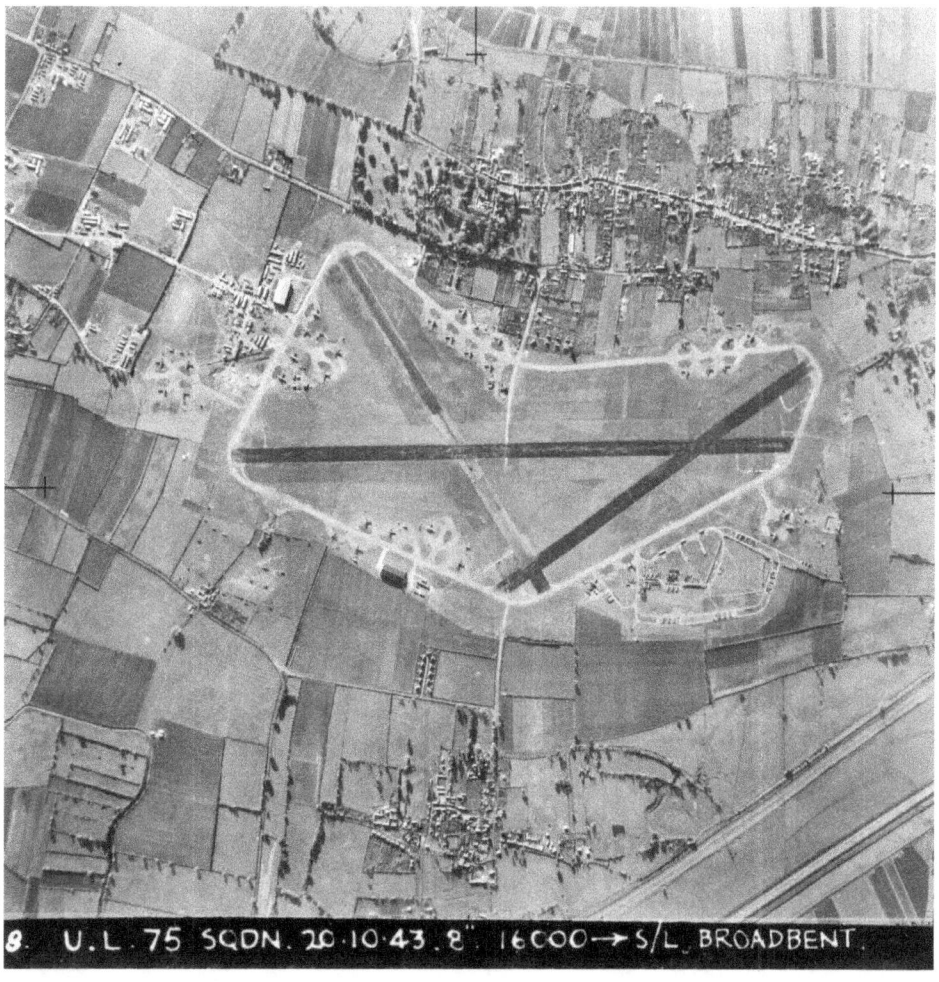

The Alexander crew (L-R): Sgt William McDonald (rear gunner), F/Sgt Desmond Andersen (navigator), Sgt Frank Howard (flight engineer), Sgt Armstrong Lyon (mid-upper gunner), F/O Allan Alexander (skipper), Sgt Thomas Mayhew (wireless operator) and Sgt Philip Pullyn (air bomber).
(NZ Bomber Command Assn. archives, Alexander collection)

The Williams crew, Mepal, September 1943 (L-R): Hilton 'Speed' Williams (skipper), Ivon Kaye (rear gunner), Adrian 'Shorty' Carson (air bomber), 'Taffy' Williams (wireless operator), Trevor Dill (navigator), 'Dicky' Dickinson (flight engineer) and William 'Billy' Hemsley (mid-upper gunner).
(NZ Bomber Command Assn. archives, Dill collection)

The Joll crew in front of Stirling EH880, by now re-coded AA-J "Johnny", ca. August 1943. Second from left, standing, F/Sgt Edward 'Ted' Gray (wireless operator), 4th from left, S/L 'Jacky' Joll (skipper), far right, LAC Tom McGibbon (ground crew, FME). (Tom McGibbon collection, via nordicul, Wings Over NZ forum)

P/O Douglas Charles Henley RNZAF died with two of his crew on the night of 31st August/1st September 1943, shot down by a night fighter near Ahrweiler on the way home from Berlin. (AWMM)

F/Sgt Eric John Roberts RNZAF was lost with all but one of his crew on the night of 31st August/1st September 1943. Four crews failed to return that night. (AWMM)

F/Sgt Keith Alexander McGregor RNZAF was lost on the night of 31st August/1st September 1943. Two of his crew survived. (AWMM)

F/O James Benjamin Lovelock RNZAF, brother of Olympic champion Jack Lovelock and navigator in the McGregor crew, was lost on the night of 31st August/1st September 1943. (AWMM)

F/O Laurence John Kirkpatrick RNZAF lost 23rd September 1943 during a raid on Mannheim. (AWMM)

P/O George Vincent Helm RNZAF died with four of his crew on the night of 31st August/1st September 1943. (AWMM)

P/O Ernest Stanley "Tom" Wilkinson RNZAF and three of his crew were killed when their Stirling crashed near Bensheim, 5/6th of September 1943. (AWMM)

F/Sgt Peter Dobson (fourth from left) with members of his crew (L-R): F/Sgt Charlie Parker, F/Sgt Morris Parker, F/Sgt Don Whitehead, F/Sgt Rex Jamieson. Dobson died assisting at the scene of the crash of Stirling BK809 at Mepal on the 8th of September 1943. (NZ Bomber Command Assn. archives, Whitehead collection)

F/Sgt Armstrong "Doc" Lyon, American mid-upper gunner in Allan Alexander's crew.
(NZ Bomber Command Assn. archives, Alexander collection)

Armourer with 4000lb 'Cookie'.
(NZ Bomber Command Assn. archives, Tomlin collection)

*Refuelling a Stirling.
(NZ Bomber Command Assn. archives, Alexander collection)*

The Witting crew with Stirling EJ108 AA-O (L-R): Sgt R.E. Morfett (mid-upper gunner), Sgt Reg Gunn (flight engineer), P/O Jack Thomas (air bomber), F/O Eric Witting (skipper), F/O Ted Anderson (navigator) Sgt Glen Marshall (wireless operator), Sgt Walter Hurdle (rear gunner). (NZ Bomber Command Assn. archives)

*Witting crew navigator F/O Ted Anderson in the doorway of Stirling EJ108 AA-O.
(NZ Bomber Command Assn. archives)*

*AVM Harrison, 3 Group A-O-C, visited the squadron on the 20th of June 1943 and presented the squadron crest to W/C Wyatt. The design features a tiki, representing New Zealand personnel, in front of two crossed mining hammers (in saltire), taken from the New Zealand coat of arms.
(Simon Sommerville)*

F/Sgt Walter Hurdle RNZAF cleaning his guns. Walter was killed when a night fighter attacked the Witting crew's Stirling EJ108 AA-O on the 4th of November 1943. (NZ Bomber Command Assn. archives, Hurdle collection)

F/Sgt Walter Hurdle's funeral, November 1943. (NZ Bomber Command Assn. archives, Hurdle collection)

F/Sgt Walter Hurdle's grave, Cambridge City Cemetery. Next to him is F/Sgt Patton Mason East RNZAF, killed in a crash at Mepal on the 24th of October. (NZ Bomber Command Assn. archives, Hurdle collection)

Sgt John Henry Roy Carey RNZAF, lost with two of his crew on only their second operation together, 29/30th May 1943.

Carey and five others in the crew had survived baling out of a cross country flight only two weeks earlier when their Stirling suffered double engine failure, as a result of which the pilot and one other died.
(AWMM)

P/O Gordon Kenneth Williams RNZAF was shot down on the 4th of November and became a PoW. (AWMM)

F/O Norman Clarence Bruce Wilson RNZAF and his crew were lost without trace, 4th of November 1943. (AWMM)

P/O William Stuart Masters RNZAF, lost with all his crew on the 4th of November 1943. (AWMM)

P/O Colin John Kinross RNZAF and all but one of his crew were killed when they crashed in low cloud at Biddington Farm, Sutton, returning from mining in the Frisians, 16/17th of December, 1943. (AWMM)

*The F.H. Turner crew, (L-R): back - F/Sgt Eric McNamara (wireless operator), F/O Murray Fearon (navigator), F/Sgt Francis Turner (skipper), Sgt W.J. Todd (flight engineer). Front - Sgt S. Bellis (rear gunner), F/Sgt Roy Young (air bomber), Sgt Robert More (mid-upper gunner). Sgt Robert McLeod More, RAFVR was tragically killed on 22.11.43, flying as replacement M/U/Gnr with the J.C. Turner crew. Their regular mid-upper gunner, Sgt Frederick Hulbert RAF, took Sgt More's place in this crew.
(NZ Bomber Command Assn. archives, Fearon collection)*

Stirlings at Mepal. (NZ Bomber Command Assn. archives, Tomlin collection)

Sgt S. Belliss (right), rear gunner with the F.H. Turner crew, and two unknown "erks".
(NZ Bomber Command Assn. archives, Fearon collection)

Larking around at dispersals.
(NZ Bomber Command Assn. archives)

75 (NZ) Squadron RAF, Mepal, December 1943 - full squadron photo. Centre front is W/C Roy Max, and to the right of him, station commander G/C Michael Wasse with Mambo, the squadron mascot. (NZ Bomber Command Assn. archives)

75 (NZ) Squadron and RAF Mepal command, December 1943 (L-R): S/L Raymond Watson DFC (A Flight commander), W/C Roy Max DSO, DFC (squadron commander), G/C Michael Wasse (station commander), S/L David Gibb DFC (B Flight commander), S/L Ken Climie DFC (C Flight commander), F/Lt Charles Bewsher (adjutant). (NZ Bomber Command Assn. archives)

*75 (NZ) Squadron B Flight, December 1943, S/L David Gibb DFC (B Flight commander) centre front.
(NZ Bomber Command Assn. archives)*

*75 (NZ) Squadron C Flight, December 1943, S/L Ken Climie DFC (C Flight commander) centre front (wearing gloves).
(NZ Bomber Command Assn. archives)*

*Unidentified Stirling ("R" or "P"?) "pranged" at Mepal.
(NZ Bomber Command Assn. archives, Tomlin collection)*

The Burke crew, late 1943 (L-R): Sgt Alf Newnham (rear gunner), Sgt Walter Pickering (flight engineer), Sgt John Cooper (mid-upper gunner), F/Sgt Edgar Burke (pilot), F/O John Downing (navigator), Sgt Frank Page (air bomber) and Sgt Alan Bromley (wireless operator). (Kevin King)

January 1944

One can assume with some degree of certainty, that the beleaguered residents of Berlin and the hard-pressed crews of Bomber Command shared a common hope for the coming year, that Germany's capital city would cease to be the focus of Harris's attention. Proud to be Berliners first and Germans second, the residents were a hardy breed, and just like their counterparts in London during the blitz of 1940, they bore their trials with fortitude and humour. During this, their "winter of discontent," they paraded banners in the streets, which proclaimed, "You may break our walls, but not our hearts", and the melodic song, Nach jedem Dezember kommt immer ein Mai, After every December there's always a May, was played endlessly over the air waves, hinting at a change of fortunes with the onset of spring. Both camps would have to endure for some time yet, however, and before New Year's Day was over, a force of 421 Lancasters would be winging its way towards the "Big City", most of them to arrive overhead in the very early hours of the 2nd. The operation was a failure, which was repeated twenty-four hours later at a combined cost to the Command of fifty-five Lancasters.

This first season of the New Year must have seemed strange to the Stirling crews of 3 Group, when, all around them the Command was fighting its way to Berlin and to other distant targets as the winter campaign ground on. News was, no doubt, filtering through from other stations of the grievous losses incurred in the process, and the strain of back-to-back long-range operations was beginning to drain morale, a situation reflected in the increasing number of early returns. For the time being, the Stirling units would continue to be restricted to mining duties, with occasional "special" bombing operations in northern France. There is no question that mining was a vital part of Bomber Command's work, but 3 Group had been at the forefront of operations from the very start, and it was a matter of pride that they resume their rightful place as soon as possible. As mentioned, 3 Group was being represented over Germany by the two MK II-equipped Lancaster squadrons, 115 and 514, but it must almost have felt as though they were gate-crashing a 1, 5 and 8 Group party. However, XV and 622 Squadrons were in the final stages of their conversion to Mk I/III Lancasters and would soon be available for operations. It was while the second Berlin operation of the year was in progress on the night of the 2/3rd, that three 75(NZ) Squadron Stirlings set off to mine the waters around the Frisians. Sgts John Carey RAFVR, Anthony Cook RAFVR and John Wainwright RAFVR and their crews took off at 22.15 and reached the target area to deliver their stores into the briefed locations through seven-tenths cloud.

The night of the 4/5th was busy for 75(NZ) Squadron, which had made ready twenty Stirlings for operations during the afternoon. Ten were loaded with 500 pounders for use against a flying bomb site, while ten others were to carry mines, six to the Elderberry garden in the waters north of Biarritz off south-western France and four for the Deodar garden in the Gironde estuary a hundred miles to the north. The weather conditions at base were marginal as the gardeners took off first, the ones with the greater distance to travel departing Mepal between 22.10 and 22.45, more than an hour ahead of those bound for the Bordeaux region. Finally, between 02.05 and 02.25, the bombers set off with S/L Watson the senior pilot on duty, and they, like the others before them, headed south in improving weather conditions, with some cloud in the target areas but excellent visibility. There were no early returns and all ten gardeners planted their vegetables into their respective allocated locations, before returning home from what most described as uneventful sorties. It was certainly uneventful for W/O Horgan and crew until they attempted to land at Mepal, where they overshot the approach, and it is believed, wiped off LJ473 AA-R's undercarriage against a steep bank, before belly-landing at 07.10. The crew walked away without a scratch, but the Stirling was declared a write-off.

There was three-tenths cloud over the flying-bomb site, which was one of two under attack, one at Bristillerie near Cherbourg and the other near Abbeville in the Pas-de-Calais, code-named Crossbow Robin and Crossbow Blackcap. 3 Group was present at both, but it is uncertain to which one the Kiwi element was assigned. There was a small amount of light flak at Robin and heavy flak at Blackcap, but it was not troublesome, and the bombing went ahead with precision and concentration. A few seconds after their bombs had gone, F/Sgt Burke's mid-upper and rear gunners in BK695 AA-N fired at a FW190, but it disappeared, possibly carrying damage. There were no losses from among the eighty aircraft involved and post-raid reconnaissance suggested that both operations had been effective.

This was the night on which Bomber Command made its first written reference to the "special operations" being undertaken from Tempsford on behalf of resistance organisations, despite the fact that they had been on-going for two years. In addition to the eighteen Halifaxes and a Hudson of 3 Group's 138 and 161 "moon" Squadrons detailed for operations this night, were six Stirlings of 214 Squadron, and from this point on, for as long as the group had Stirlings on strength, they would supplement the increasing call on Tempsford's resources. As already stated, later in the year, the Stirling would replace the Halifax as the main heavy equipment for clandestine operations.

Adverse weather conditions kept the squadron on the ground on the night of the 5/6th, while a predominantly Lancaster force went to distant Stettin and destroyed 504 houses and twenty industrial buildings in central and western districts, seriously damaged a further 1,148 houses and twenty-nine industrial buildings and sank eight ships in the harbour. The following night was devoted to minor operations and mining, for which the squadron made ready eight Stirlings and dispatched them to the Gironde estuary either side of 16.30 with S/L Climie the senior pilot on duty. They flew out in good weather conditions, which persisted to leave clear skies in the target area and all succeeded in fulfilling their briefs. A number of enemy aircraft were seen, and one brief engagement resulted in Sgt Carey and crew in EF454, now re-coded AA-C, claiming a Ju88 as damaged. The dangers inherent in the Stirling's lofty dimensions were again highlighted on the 8th when EF466 suffered an undercarriage collapse, presumably while sitting on its dispersal pan. An LAC working inside the aircraft injured his ankle and knee in the fall. An investigation found that a corporal should not have been working on the undercarriage emergency mechanism with the weight of the aircraft on its wheels. Apart from the shock, the culprit was no doubt lucky to survive the incident in one piece.

The following week brought little activity with no bombing operations by the heavy brigade, and it was the 14th before the Lancaster crews were next called to arms for a raid by 496 of them on Braunschweig (Brunswick), the historic and culturally rich city to the east of Hannover. It would be the first major operation to this target, and it would also be the maiden Lancaster operation for XV and 622 Squadrons. Tragically, during the day 75(NZ) Squadron lost one of its pilots in the strangest of circumstances, when F/Sgt William Allen RAFVR "borrowed" a visiting Hurricane KX581 of the Air Fighting Development Unit, while its pilot,

F/Lt Miller, was having lunch in the mess. Neither F/Sgt Allen nor the Hurricane were ever seen again, presumably having gone down into the North Sea when the fuel ran out.

Fifteen 75(NZ) Squadron crews were called to briefing on this day, to learn of their participation in another attack in the Crossbow series. A force of 82 aircraft, fifty-nine of them Stirlings, was made ready and the crews assigned to one of three sites at Ailly, Bonneton and Bristillerie, the last-mentioned the target for the Kiwi element. They took off between 18.00 and 18.25 with S/L Gibb the senior pilot on duty, and two are recorded as returning early, one with navigation equipment failure and the other through an inability to maintain height. The landing times do not positively identify which aircraft they were. The others pressed on to find clear skies and excellent visibility and delivered their 500 pounders onto the Oboe markers, which were described as scattered, and returning crews were uncertain as to the effectiveness of their efforts. While this operation was in progress, debutants F/Sgt Cecil Ernest "Snow" Armstrong RNZAF and F/Sgt William Jarvis Willis RNZAF and their crews went mining off the Frisians, one returning early after experiencing navigational problems and the other completing their sortie as briefed in favourable weather conditions.

Braunschweig had been a sobering occasion for the Lancaster squadrons, after thirty-eight failed to return home from what had been a highly disappointing raid, which all but missed the city on its southern extremity. The Path Finders, in particular, had suffered a torrid time since the turn of the year, and 156 Squadron alone had lost fourteen aircraft and crews from the two Berlin and the Braunschweig operations. A force of 769 aircraft was made ready on the 20th for the next round of the Berlin offensive, while 75(NZ) Squadron loaded six Stirlings with mines and sent them off to the Frisians between 16.45 and 17.15 with S/L Watson the senior pilot on duty and the crew of F/Sgt Harold Henry Bruhns RNZAF operating for the first time. There were no early returns, the weather was favourable with good visibility and they met no opposition of any kind. Meanwhile, the Lancasters and Halifaxes were fighting their way through night-fighters both to and from Berlin and lost thirty-five of their number in the process. It was established later that the main weight of the attack had fallen in an eight-mile swathe across the eastern districts from Weissesee in the north to Neukölln in the south, where substantial but not excessive damage had resulted.

On the following day, twenty Stirlings were made ready at Mepal and loaded with 500 pounders for an attack on one of three flying bomb sites. The 3 Group ORB specifies eighty-nine Stirlings divided equally between targets at Abbeville, Hazebrouck and Cherbourg, and the 75(NZ) Squadron element became airborne between 18.05 and 18.40 with F/Ls Fauvel, Grubb, Warren and Witting the senior pilots on duty and two first-time captains in the persons of F/O Robert Weir Herron RNZAF and F/Sgt Geoffrey Warren Rowberry RNZAF. There was five-tenths cloud at Abbeville, which affected the accuracy of the bombing, but the impression at the other sites, where the skies had been clear, was that the bombing had been concentrated and effective. The main operation on this night was the first major attack of the war on the eastern city of Magdeburg, for which a force of 648 aircraft took off in mid-evening. The operation was a failure in return for a new record loss of fifty-seven aircraft, the Halifaxes suffering a 15.6% casualty rate and poor weather resulted in seven returning 6 Group Lancasters diverting to Mepal.

The same three Crossbow sites were targeted again on the night of the 25/26th, when 75(NZ) Squadron detailed twenty Stirlings, all but one of which took off either side of midnight with S/L Gibb the senior pilot on duty. Reading between the lines of the 3 Group ORB, it seems that the squadron effort was directed at the Abbeville site, which was covered by six to seven-tenths cloud with tops at 8,000 feet. The Path Finder element was very late in arriving and also experienced equipment failure, which led to sparse and scattered marking. A high wind added to the difficulties, making it a challenge for aircraft to remain on station as they waited for the markers, and four crews decided to bring their bombs home. The others dropped theirs, but the expectation of success was low.

On occasions during the Battle of Berlin, a large force of mine-layers would be sent up ahead of the main force to mislead the enemy fighter controller. If he could be persuaded that they represented the main threat, the night-fighters might be on the ground refuelling and re-arming as the bomber stream passed through. This ruse was partially successful on the night of the 27/28th, when a total of 140 aircraft took part in extensive diversionary and support operations ahead of a five hundred-strong all-Lancaster heavy force making its way to the capital. 3 Group sent seventy-four Stirlings to mine the waters of the Rosemary and Silverthorn gardens, situated respectively in the Heligoland Bight and off Denmark's Baltic coast, and 75(NZ) Squadron supported both efforts with thirteen for the former and four for the latter. With further to travel to the Baltic, the latter took off first at 16.40, led by S/L Watson, and they were followed into the air from 17.00 by the others, among which F/Ls Heney and Warren were the senior pilots. The weather conditions were excellent, apart from a little sea haze, and the operations proceeded according to plan with almost no opposition off Heligoland, although several of the squadron's crews strayed a little too close to the island and almost drew the attention of a few patrolling enemy aircraft. While the gardeners were attracting the attention of the night-fighter controller, the Berlin-bound Lancasters slipped across the northern coast of Holland and headed south-east as if threatening an attack on Hannover, Brunswick, Magdeburg or Liepzig. At a point south of Hannover, they turned abruptly to the north-east to make for Berlin, while Mosquitos maintained the fake course dropping flares. The diversionary measures were successful in delaying the arrival of the night-fighters, but they still scored heavily over Berlin and on the way home, claiming the bulk of the thirty-three Lancasters that failed to return.

A force of 673 Lancasters and Halifaxes was made ready on the 28th for a return to Berlin, for the second of three attacks on the city in the space of an unprecedented four nights. 75(NZ) Squadron loaded nineteen Stirlings with 1,500lb mines for delivery to the Forget-me-not garden in the Kiel Bay area as part of the diversionary measures, and they departed Mepal either side of 19.00 with S/Ls Climie and Gibb the senior pilots on duty. F/L Fauvel, P/O Burton and W/O Humphreys returned early with technical problems and two of the remaining crews dropped their mines in alternative locations, but the others carried out their briefs in the face of variable weather conditions of five to ten-tenths cloud and ineffective anti-aircraft fire. There was also some night-fighter activity, and on the way home icing conditions, and it was while homebound that EF512 AA-A was raked from the tailplane to the navigator's compartment by machine-gun and cannon fire from a Me110 and sustained considerable damage. The mid-upper gunner, Sgt H R Renwick RAFVR, was slightly wounded in the left foot and right lower leg, and the flight engineer, Sgt W. P. Watson RAFVR, seriously so in the stomach, but P/O Baker RNZAF brought the Stirling back to a crash-landing at Coltishall without further injury to the occupants. It had been another expensive night for the Command, which lost forty-six aircraft on the Berlin raid.

After a night's rest, 534 aircraft set out once more for Berlin, while six 75(NZ) Squadron Stirlings made their way south-west to the familiar waters of the Gironde estuary. They had taken off either side of 17.00 all captained by flight sergeants and had encountered adverse weather conditions of ten-tenths cloud and poor visibility in the target area, which persuaded five crews to bring their mines home. Just one crew completed its sortie as briefed but was unable to confirm the deployment of the parachutes through the cloud. A further thirty-three aircraft failed to return from Berlin after this final concerted effort to bring the capital to its knees, and just two further operations would be mounted against it before the winter campaign drew to a close at the end of March. This was the final outing of the month for 75(NZ) Squadron, which had taken part in fourteen operations and dispatched 135 sorties for the loss of a single Stirling at home.

February 1944

Although major operations were planned early in February, none took place for the first two weeks, and the only event of significance was an attack by 617 Squadron on the Gnome & Rhone aero-engine factory at Limoges on the night of the 8/9th, which tested and proved the efficacy of the low-level marking technique and led, ultimately, to the independence of 5 Group. 75(NZ) Squadron would spend the month exclusively engaged in mining duties, which began on the night of the 3/4th with six Stirlings taking off between 03.25 and 03.55, two each for drop zones in the Upas Tree garden off Morlaix in St-Malo Bay and Greengage off Cherbourg. The squally weather conditions were not ideal, and at Morlaix only one crew found a pinpoint from which to make a timed run, while the others returned their mines to store. One of the Cherbourg duo, EF465, which had been re-coded "K" and was skippered by P/O McCardle, had its starboard-inner engine catch fire ten minutes from the target, but it was feathered and the sortie completed without further incident. On the following evening the squadron dispatched six Stirlings at 19.10 to lay mines in the Deodar garden in the mouth of the River Gironde. F/L Clark was the senior pilot on duty for what was expected to be a challenging operation in adverse weather conditions of rain and icing conditions, but in the event they were tested only by low cloud in the target area and all fulfilled their briefs before returning safely.

Four crews were assigned to gardening duties in the Cinnamon garden off La Rochelle on the evening of the 10th, and they got away at 18.45 with F/Ls Clark and Grubb the senior pilots in action. As one of several ports of residence for the German navy, it was a well-defended area and threw up heavy and light flak, none of which troubled the Stirlings, but F/O Herron in EE958 AA-A had an inconclusive encounter with a Ju88 night-fighter. One of the photographs taken by F/L Grubb showed a sunken merchant vessel. Fifteen crews attended briefing on the following afternoon to learn that they were to be divided among four gardens. Debutant F/O Henry James Murray RNZAF and crew were the first to take off at 18.05, bound for the Hyacinth garden in St Malo Bay, and they were followed into the air minutes later by F/Sgt Evans and Sgt Scott, who had been assigned to Upas Tree off Morlaix. Next to depart Mepal were F/L Warren, P/O Turner and F/Sgt Burke, whose target area was an inland stretch of the River Adour, which had no codename.

The nine remaining crews took off last, either side of 18.30, after being briefed for the Elderberry garden at a location off the mouth of the River Adour, which passes through the town of Bayonne deep in south-western France on its way to the sea north of Biarritz. S/Ls Climie and Watson were the senior pilots on duty as they headed for the Channel's south-western approaches and out across north-western France for the three-and-a half-hour outward flight. They had to pass through severe icing conditions to reach their destination, and one crew was forced to jettison its mines in order to maintain height. The others of this element all completed their sorties according to instructions, before returning safely home. Meanwhile, P/O Turner and F/Sgt Burke had been defeated by cloud in the River Adour area and had brought their mines back. F/L Warren believed that he had delivered his stores accurately, but when his photos were examined, it was determined that he had, in fact, mined the River Boucau, which is not shown on a map. On modern-day maps, Boucau is a district close to the north-eastern bank of the Adour.

The penultimate major raid on Berlin, and the first large-scale activity of the month, turned all of the bomber stations into hives of activity on the 15th. A force of 891 aircraft was made ready for the main event, and this represented not only the largest force ever sent against Berlin, but also the largest non-1,000 force to date. 75(NZ) Squadron was to play its part by contributing fifteen Stirlings to mining operations in the Forget-me-not garden in Kiel Bay as part of the support and diversionary measures put in place to confuse the enemy, while also sending six other mine-layers back to the mouth of the River Adour. The main element took off either side of 17.30 with S/L Watson the senior pilot on duty and only F/Sgt Kay returned early with starboard-outer engine failure. The others reached the target area, where they delivered forty-two mines in ten minutes in what was a highly successful operation. As they were landing, their six fellow crews were taking off at 23.30 for south-western France, with F/Ls Clark and Warren the senior pilots on duty. Three of them returned with aiming point photos and the others with pictures of a nearby factory, and it may have been the movement of produce from the factory that prompted the mining of an otherwise strategically unimportant river. The diversions and the wide sweep over Denmark of the Berlin-bound bomber stream succeeded in keeping the night-fighters at bay until the capital was reached, from which point on they scored steadily, and forty-three aircraft were lost in return for a very destructive attack on central and south-western districts.

Leipzig was posted as the target for a force of 823 aircraft on the 19th, and among the diversions was another mining effort in Kiel Bay, for which thirteen 75(NZ) Squadron Stirlings took off between 23.15 and 23.50 with S/L Gibb the senior pilot on duty. They all reached the target area, where unusually, Path Finder markers pinpointed the drop site and each delivered their 1,500lb mines from high level without incident. In contrast, the Leipzig operation was a disaster, which cost the Command a staggering seventy-eight aircraft and a 13.3% loss rate amongst the Halifaxes. The less efficient Merlin-powered Mk II and V variants were immediately withdrawn from further operations over Germany, thus substantially reducing 4 Group's contribution to the main offensive.

Despite the losses, a force of 598 aircraft was put together on the following night for a raid on Stuttgart, while ten 75(NZ) Squadron Stirlings continued with their mining role off France and the Frisians. F/L Warren and P/O Baker were assigned to the Morlaix region, while F/Sgts

Armstrong and Wainwright had St Malo Bay as their target area. F/L Witting and F/Sgt Pryse were to mine the waters of the Greengage garden off Cherbourg and newcomer F/L Euan Wilfred Sachtler RNZAF was the senior pilot of the quartet briefed to plant their vegetables in the Nectarine II garden off the Frisian island of Borkum. They took off for their respective gardens between 18.20 and 19.05, and all returned safely after completing their briefed tasks without incident. The Stuttgart raid achieved some very useful industrial damage, and in contrast to the previous night, resulted in the loss of a more modest nine aircraft.

For the third night running, the squadron was required to operate and provided three Stirlings for mining duties in the Nectarine II garden to the north of Borkum. They took off at 18.05 and made their way through moderately turbulent weather to the drop site, where they delivered six mines each into the allocated locations. Twenty-four hours later Kiel Bay was the intended destination for fifteen 75(NZ) Squadron Stirlings, which departed Mepal between 16.25 and 17.05 with S/L Climie the last to leave the ground. After being airborne for an hour, they were recalled because of doubts about the weather conditions over the bases at the scheduled time of their return.

A major operation against the ball-bearing production town of Schweinfurt was posted on the 24th and a force of 734 aircraft made ready. At briefings, crews were told of a new tactic to be employed in an attempt to reduce the recent heavy losses to night-fighters. The force was to be divided into two waves with a two-hour interval between them, in the hope of catching the night-fighters on the ground re-arming and refuelling as the second wave passed through. 75(NZ) Squadron's part in the night's activities involved fifteen of its Stirlings returning to Kiel Bay to add to the ever-increasing density of mines threatening enemy shipping. They took off between 17.00 and 17.20 with S/L Climie the senior pilot on duty and last off the ground, and fourteen returned some five to six hours later to report a successful operation. F/Sgt Harold Bruhns RNZAF and his crew were not among them, and EH948 AA-Q "Queenie" is presumed to have crashed into the sea in the target area. One body was recovered for burial at Abenra on Denmark's Baltic coast in the Little Belt region, while the others, including F/Sgt Laurie Licence Butler, the RNZAF bomb-aimer, are commemorated on the Runnymede Memorial. The main operation was not successful, but the second phase lost 50% fewer aircraft than the first in an overall casualty figure of thirty-three, and this suggested some merit in the ploy.

The following night was devoted to an attack on Augsburg, the beautiful, culturally significant and historic city in southern Germany, which had been the scene in April 1942 of the audacious daylight raid by 44 and 97 Squadron Lancasters on the M.A.N diesel engine factory. A force of 594 aircraft was assembled and the crews briefed for another two-phase operation, while 75(NZ) Squadron prepared fifteen Stirlings for mining duties in the Daffodil garden at the southern end of Oresund (The Sound) off the eastern seaboard of Zealand, the large Danish island upon which Copenhagen is situated. The Mepal brigade took off between 19.35 and 20.00 with F/Ls Grubb, Sachtler and Witting the senior pilots on duty, but P/O McCardle and F/Sgt Millar were forced back early with engine failures. The others pressed on in excellent weather conditions to find the target area under clear skies, and all delivered their stores into the allocated locations before returning safely. The safe return of F/Sgt Willis and crew in EH949 JN-P was accomplished despite encountering six Ju88s, four of which fired short bursts without causing any damage and elicited an equally ineffective response from the Stirling's gunners. The Augsburg raid was devastatingly concentrated and accurate and destroyed forever centuries of cultural history and priceless treasures, while also hitting some of the city's important war-industry factories in northern districts.

During the course of the month the squadron conducted nineteen mining operations and dispatched 109 sorties, not including the fifteen recalled, and posted missing a single Stirling and crew.

March 1944

By the beginning of March only four Stirling units remained in 3 Group, 75(NZ), 90, 149 and 218 Squadrons and a new task was about to be handed to them to supplement their mining responsibilities. The new month began for the Command with another large-scale attack on the recently-raided city of Stuttgart on the night of the 1/2nd by an initial force of 557 aircraft, and those reaching the target produced destructive bombing through cloud, which hit central, western and northern districts and claimed some important industrial scalps. Six 75(NZ) Squadron crews had been briefed for a special operation, which was subsequently cancelled, only to be reinstated on the 2nd and increased to ten Stirlings, while four gardeners were divided between the Greengage and Anemone gardens respectively off Cherbourg and Le Havre. P/Os Burton and McKenzie took off for Le Havre at 18.50, to be followed into the air minutes later by F/Sgt Willis and Sgt Scott bound for Cherbourg. Sgt Scott and crew returned early after their navigational equipment let them down, but the others all completed their sorties as briefed.

Tempsford was arguably the RAF's most secret airfield during the Second World War and was located on the site of Gibraltar Farm in Bedfordshire, close to the Cambridgeshire border, with the main LNER railway line running along its western boundary. Since 1942 it had been home to Bomber Command's two "Moon" Squadrons, 138 and 161, which operated in 3 Group, but on behalf of the Special Intelligence Service and the Special Operations Executive, the latter a shadowy, anonymous organisation run out of offices in Baker Street. The two squadrons were responsible for the delivery of agents and supplies into the occupied countries, mostly by parachute, although 161 Squadron employed Lysanders and occasionally other small aircraft to enable them to land in fields to disgorge agents and pick up others to bring home. The main role, particularly for 138 Squadron, was to deliver agents, arms and equipment by parachute to the resistance organizations fighting the Nazis, and they operated in all weather conditions over France, Belgium, Holland, Scandinavia, Poland and even Germany and Austria, sometimes remaining airborne for up to fourteen hours. They operated predominantly for two weeks each month during the moon period, and such was the demand upon their services by this stage of the war, that other squadrons were called upon to contribute aircraft and crews to supplement their efforts. *(A full account of 138 Squadron's wartime history can be found in RAF Bomber Command Profiles, Vol 6. 138 Squadron, by Chris Ward and Piotr Hodyra, published by Mention the War Publications in 2017.)*

And so it was that 75(NZ) Squadron embarked upon a new phase in its illustrious wartime career on the night of the 2/3rd of March 1944, when dispatching ten Stirlings to the Garonne region of south-western France to deliver containers under Operations WHEELWRIGHT 67, 68, 69, 70, 71, 72, 79 and 80 and TRAINER 115B and 175. SOE operations could be massively frustrating and often failed because of adverse weather conditions or the absence of a reception committee, and on this night, all reached their respective reception areas, where low cloud prevented seven of them from locating a precise pinpoint, and the stores were returned to base. W/C Max departed Mepal at 21.03 on WHEELWRIGHT 72 and reached the target area at 00.36 to find no low cloud for a ten-mile radius, which allowed him to see the reception lights clearly. He delivered fifteen containers, before setting course for home at 00.45 and dropping eight bundles of leaflets near Marmande, south-east of Bordeaux, on the way. He landed safely at 04.09 after a round-trip of seven hours and was able to greet the return seventeen minutes later of P/O Young and crew, who had taken off at 20.45 on TRAINER 115B. They had reached their pinpoint, the junction of a river, a canal and a railway line, at 00.26 in good visibility and dropped fifteen containers onto the flashing reception light from 450 feet at 00.35. They also delivered leaflets on the way home over Agen. P/O Turner and crew had been the first of the successful participants to land, at 03.40, having taken off at 20.55 on WHEELWRIGHT 67, and found their pinpoint, a bend in the river and a railway bridge at Tonneins at 00.08. Having established the presence of a reception committee, fifteen containers were released from 450 feet at 00.23 and leaflets were dropped over Angouleme during the course of an uneventful return flight.

Mining operations on the night of the 3/4th involved eight 75(NZ) Squadron crews in pairs, which took off between 19.00 and 19.45 for St Malo, Morlaix, Le Havre and Cherbourg. Seven completed their sorties as briefed and one lost track of its position and dropped to the west of the allocated location. All sorties were unopposed and uneventful. On the following night fifteen of the squadron's Stirlings were made ready for SOE operations deep inside France, and their crews were assigned to operations TRAINER 121 (two aircraft), 124 (four aircraft), 129 (three aircraft), 174 (three aircraft) and 178 (three aircraft). They began taking off at around 20.45, with an outward flight of three hours or more ahead of them, but W/O Hunt experienced engine trouble and was forced to jettison his sixteen containers from 4,000 feet at 23.25, when about ten miles short of what would be the Normandy invasion beaches three months hence. Nine others became victims of the conditions and failed to deliver their containers, citing variously snow, ice-bearing cloud, low cloud, dense haze and lack of a reception committee as the reasons, but all delivered leaflets at assigned locations on the way home.

Of the four successful sorties, F/Sgt Young was the first to take off, at 20.45, on TRAINER 129 and reached the target area at 23.52, where the visibility was good apart from a little haze. The drop site was pinpointed at 23.52 by a north-south road running through a wood, and a reception committee made itself known by flashing the correct letter in white. The sixteen containers were dropped from 600 feet between 00.14 and 00.17, before a course was set for home via Brive to deliver leaflets, and they arrived safely back at base at 04.10. The Young crew were flying their usual Stirling LK384 JN-X, "Excuse please Mr, I go, I come back". P/O Humphreys and crew took off on TRAINER 174 at 20.50 and reached their drop zone at 23.34 after pinpointing on a lake at Chancelade, some fifty miles east of Bordeaux. The weather was good, with gaps in a layer of thin cloud reaching to 7,000 feet, and good visibility in the space below where the crew was searching for a light flashing the correct identification letter. This was picked up and sixteen containers dropped from 480 feet, before a course was set at 23.59 for Aubusson to deliver leaflets and then home for a landing at 03.25.

P/O Turner and crew were recorded as taking off at the same time on TRAINER 178, the drop point for which they reached at 00.20 after encountering low cloud with a variable base of between 500 and zero feet and snow showers. They identified the drop site by a road running north to south and were greeted by a light flashing the correct identification letter. The sixteen containers were dropped from 600 feet at 00.38, and a course was set for home seven minutes later. They were unable to deliver the leaflets because of a frozen hatch but made it back without further incident and landed at 04.10. F/Sgt Armstrong and crew had been assigned to TRAINER 129 and they reached their target area at 00.02 after an outward flight of almost three hours. Visibility was good over south-central France and the drop site was identified by a road and rail junction at Mauriac, where three white lights greeted them, rather than the expected red. Sixteen containers were dropped from 400 feet at 00.12 and a safe return made via Tulle to the west, where leaflets were delivered. S/L Ray Watson DFC, RNZAF and crew had taken off at 20.51 on TRAINER 124 and did not return. It was established later that EF215 AA-M had crashed at Rochefort-Montagne, west-south-west of Clermont-Ferrand and to the north-west of the target area, killing all but the mid-upper gunner, Sgt Colin Armstrong, RAFVR, who fell into enemy hands. Three others of those on board were members of the RNZAF.

Twelve Stirlings were made ready for nine separate SOE operations on the night of the 5/6th, when an absence of reception committees would render six of them unsuccessful. This was a matter of great frustration after flying for up to four hours to reach a tiny pinpoint on a map, only to have to return the containers to base. There could, of course, be many reasons for a no-show, ranging from enemy activity to weather conditions, and the crews of 138 and 161 squadrons soon became accustomed to the lottery aspect of the job. Those that failed on this night were two of the TRAINER 149 sorties, FOOTMAN 9, PETER 24, PETER 47A and AUTHOR 11A. P/O Buckley and crew were first away, at 20.20, on AUTHOR 18, which they reached under clear skies and in good visibility three and a half hours later. Sixteen containers were dropped from 400 feet at 23.59 and a package of leaflets released over Brive on the way home to a landing at 03.00. F/L Clark and crew departed Mepal at 20.30 bound for southern France on PETER 8, the drop site for which was reached under clear skies after a four-hour outward flight. The reception lights were dim, but the correct letter was flashed, and sixteen containers fell away from 450 feet at 00.40. They also delivered leaflets over the Brive area on the way home and touched down safely at Mepal after seven and a half hours in the air.

F/L Grubb and crew took off at 20.45 on FOOTMAN 10, reached the target at 23.33 and dropped fifteen containers from clear skies, before returning over Limoges to deliver leaflets. The crews of P/O McCardle and F/O Herron were assigned to TRAINER 153 and took off at 20.41 and 20.53 respectively, to arrive in the target area within four minutes of each other and service the two reception sites. They dropped thirty containers between them from 400 to 500 feet either side of 23.50, and then added to the volume of paper floating down over Brive on their way home to safe landings shortly before 03.30. The newly-commissioned P/O Young and crew took off on TRAINER 149 at 21.04 and reached the target area two hours fifty minutes later, where the reception lights were obscured by a wood and were only visible from directly above. Nevertheless, the correct signal letter was confirmed, and fifteen containers were dropped from 500 feet at 00.22, before a course was set for Limoges to deliver leaflets on the way home.

Ten crews were briefed for SOE operations on the night of the 6/7th, but adverse weather conditions led to nine cancellations, leaving only P/O Turner and crew to take off at 19.57 on Operation DIRECTOR 60. It took almost four hours to reach the target area, where the drop site was identified by a field and two woods and a reception committee of at least seven men. Three red lights provided the signal to drop fourteen containers from 400 feet at 00.18 and as they set course for home via Brive, a twin-engine aircraft approached but withdrew without incident. An uneventful return journey brought them to a safe landing after eight hours thirty-eight minutes aloft.

It was on this night that the opening salvoes were fired in the Transportation Plan, the pre-invasion campaign to dismantle by bombing thirty-seven railway centres in France, Belgium and western Germany to prevent their use by the enemy to bring forces to bear to counter the Allied landings. While the Lancaster and Mk III Halifaxes were fully engaged in the continuing winter offensive, it was left initially to the demoted types, the Stirling and MK II and V Halifaxes, to carry the torch. It was the Halifaxes of 4 and 6 Group that undertook the maiden operation against the marshalling yards at Trappes, situated some ten miles west-south-west of Paris, and their excellent work there was repeated on the following night at Le Mans, with a little help from the Mk II Lancasters of 3 Group's 115 and 514 Squadrons.

On the 7th, ten 75(NZ) Squadron crews were briefed for SOE operations AUTHOR 11A (two aircraft), AUTHOR 17 (two aircraft), WHEELWRIGHT 70, WHEELWRIGHT 71 (one aircraft each) and TRAINER 121 (four aircraft). Seven would remain uncompleted, mostly as a result of ten-tenths low cloud and the consequent inability to establish a reception. P/O Burton and crew took off at 20.28 on AUTHOR 17 and reached the target area at 23.40, where a single light appeared in a gap in a wooded valley. It was only after they circled for some time below the 4,000-foot cloud base that three lights appeared and the correct letter was flashed, whereupon the fifteen containers were dropped. They set off on the return flight at 00.22 and delivered four packages of leaflets to the residents of Poitiers as they passed overhead. F/Sgt Millar and crew took off at 20.29 to undertake WHEELWRIGHT 70 and reached the drop site, identified by a wood and a road, at 23.57. On receipt of the correct signal the fifteen containers were disgorged into the night from 400 feet at 00.01, before a course was set for base via St Foy and La Force, east of Bordeaux, where leaflets were dispensed. F/Sgt Rowberry and crew departed Mepal at 20.31 and headed for their WHEELWRIGHT 71 drop zone, which was reached three hours later and found under a 2,000-foot cloud base. Fifteen containers were dropped from 400 feet at 23.50, before a course was set for base via Mussidan, also east of Bordeaux, where four packages of leaflets were released into the slipstream.

Nineteen Stirlings were made ready for operations on the 10th, and, this time, in contrast to recent experiences, the majority would be concluded successfully. Operation TRAINER 121 was responsible for three of the night's five failures and began badly, when F/Sgt Armstrong's aircraft lost an engine on take-off and was landed safely after all stores, other than a special package, had been jettisoned. S/L Climie and P/O Humphreys reached the target area, only to fail to raise a reception committee at both the primary and secondary locations. F/Sgt Potts and crew reached their destination for MONGREL 11 but failed to locate a reception committee despite excellent visibility, and it was a similar story for F/O Fauvel and crew, who observed cars patrolling the roads around both the primary and secondary sites but no light signal. MONGREL 18 involved the crews of P/O Buckley, P/O McKenzie, P/O Burton and F/O

Herron, who took off for south-eastern France between 20.01 and 20.38 and reached the target area to find excellent weather conditions. P/O Buckley arrived at 00.01 and pinpointed on steep cliffs in the form of an oval. A flashing white light was clearly seen, towards which a dozen containers were dropped from 3,000 feet and leaflets were then dispensed over Roanne during an uneventful return journey. P/O McKenzie turned up at 00.20 and observed a man standing in a hollow flashing a torch. The reception consisted of three bonfires, onto which twelve containers were dropped from 500 feet, before a course was set for home via Aix-les-Bains and St-Genix. P/O Burton found no reception committee at the primary target and flew on to the alternative, which was reached at 23.40. Here he was greeted by reception lights, which invited him to drop twelve containers from 1,500 feet at 00.05, before returning home via the Vichy region, where leaflets were delivered. F/O Herron and crew were unable to identify their primary drop site but found a reception between Bourgoin and Grenoble and dropped a dozen containers there from 1,200 feet at 23.50.

MONGREL 20 also involved four crews, those of F/Ls Clark and Warren, P/O Young and F/Sgt Wainwright, who departed Mepal between 20.00 and 20.40, before setting course for the foothills of the Alps deep in south-eastern France. They arrived in the target area in fine weather conditions to find a layer of cloud with a base at 2,000 feet and haze in the valleys but otherwise good visibility. The drop sites were pinpointed by a deep ravine with steep cliff walls and a wood, which stood out against the snow, and reception lights were strong and easily picked up. Forty-eight containers were delivered from 600 to 1,000 feet between 23.46 and 00.20 and leaflets delivered to Chambery on the way home, where they all arrived safely between 03.30 and 04.15. P/O Turner, W/O Horgan and F/Sgt Rowberry were the three successful crews assigned to MONGREL 11, having taken off between 19.58 and 20.30 for the same general area of south-eastern France. They encountered similar conditions and terrain and also found the receptions to be clear and unambiguous, which enabled them to deliver a total of thirty-six containers from 600 to 1,000 feet between 23.34 and 00.16. They dispensed their leaflets over Lyons, Roanne and Culoz, and arrived home after round-trips of between seven and eight hours. F/L Grubb took off at 20.20 on NEWSAGENT 5 and reached the drop site, recognised by a river and a rising hill, three hours and ten minutes later. After circling to confirm the reception lights, fifteen containers were dropped at 23.45 and leaflets were dispensed over Saint-Chamond on the way to a safe landing at 03.00. P/O Baker reached MONGREL 6 at 00.17 and established his position and the presence of a reception committee, before releasing his twelve containers from a perilously low 300 feet and dispensing his leaflets over the Chambery area on the way home. W/O Hunt and crew enjoyed an uneventful trip out and dropped a dozen containers from 600 feet at 23.35 to the reception at MONGREL 17. During an equally uneventful return flight, they delivered leaflets for the benefit of the residents of Montelimar.

Seven crews were briefed for SOE operations on the night of the 11/12th and involved the crews of F/L Sachtler on WHEELWRIGHT 63, W/C Max on WHEELWRIGHT 66, F/O Fauvel on WHEELWRIGHT 67, W/O Hunt on WHEELWRIGHT 78, Sgt Scott on WHEELWRIGHT 84, W/O Horgan on PAUL 57 and P/O Burton on TRAINER 110. They headed for southern France, to regions further to the west than on the previous night, and encountered ten-tenths cloud with moderate icing, which prevented six crews from completing their sorties and they brought their stores home after delivering leaflets to Auch, Aiguillon and Nicole, south-east of Bordeaux and Poitiers further to the north. P/O Fauvel and crew took off at 20.30 and arrived in the target area at 23.24 to find a cloud base at 3,000 feet and visibility at one mile. The drop site was identified by a river and a road, and the reception lights were clearly visible, allowing fourteen containers to be dropped from 400 feet at 23.37. Tonneins was the location for the leaflet drop, and a successful sortie was completed with a touchdown at Mepal at 03.00.

It had been known for some time that Lancasters were coming to Mepal, and the first example, probably ND747, arrived on the 13th to be followed by eighteen more by the end of the month. B Flight appears to have been the first to be equipped, a process noted as completed on the 18th, and the first crews earmarked for conversion training, F/L Witting, F/O Fauvel and P/O Burton, were packed off to 3 Lancaster Finishing School (3LFS) at Feltwell on the following day. During the afternoon, sixteen crews were briefed for mining duties off the French ports providing shelter for the German navy, and four crews each were assigned to Beech (St-Nazaire), Artichoke (Lorient), Cinnamon (La Rochelle) and Jellyfish (Brest) with S/L Climie the senior pilot on duty. They departed Mepal in that order between 21.45 and 23.00, but an aileron control rod broke in EF236 AA-J as it headed over Wiltshire towards Brest, and this necessitated an emergency landing. P/O Baker put the aircraft down on the short runway at Castle Combe airfield, but quickly exhausted its length and the Stirling came to a halt in the overshoot area with a collapsed undercarriage. The crew walked away, but three of the five mines eventually exploded to leave the Stirling a burnt-out wreck. LJ462 AA-O failed to return home from St-Nazaire, and while thought to have been hit by a flak ship on the run in to the drop zone, no trace of it or the crew of F/Sgt Geoffrey Rowberry RNZAF was ever found. The navigator was the only other member of the RNZAF on board, and sadly, the rear gunner, Sgt Alfred Newnham RAFVR, was "on loan" from W/C Max's crew. The remaining crews returned home safely to report fulfilling their briefs without incident.

Fifteen crews were called to briefing on the 15th for the next round of SOE operations, for which W/C Max put his name at the top of the order of battle. The main action on this night was a massive raid by an initial force of 863 aircraft on Stuttgart, the third attack on the city in three weeks. This was not a successful operation, and cost thirty-seven aircraft, most of them falling victim to night-fighters during the final leg to the target. The drop sites for the 75(NZ) Squadron crews were in more central regions of France than of late, but weather conditions would prove to be challenging and reception committees elusive, and only three sorties would be concluded successfully. The operational details were as follows; F/L Sachtler and crew were assigned to ARCHDEACON 4, but a lack of oil pressure in the port engines resulted in an early return. F/Sgt Potts and crew were assigned to BOB 154, which failed through the lack of a reception committee. W/O Horgan's attempt to complete BOB 151 failed through the inability to confirm an ambiguous reception signal and F/O Murray and crew were similarly thwarted on BOB 157. P/O Humphreys' MUSICIAN 3 failed because of cloud and lack of reception, as did F/L Grubb's TOM 43. F/Sgt Wainwright's BOB 136 failed through poor visibility and lack of reception, P/O Buckley's BOB 156 through lack of reception, F/L Warren's BOB 155 through lack of reception, F/Sgt Armstrong's MUSICIAN 5 through lack of reception and W/C Max's ARCHDEACON 10 through excessive cloud and lack of reception. P/O Young's TOM 46 failed also through lack of reception and suspicious activity around the drop site. On the way home from these operations, leaflets were dropped over Dijon, Corbigny, Bohain, St-Quentin, Montmirail, Dampierre-sur-Saonne, Guise and Mons.

Sgt Scott and crew took off at 23.42 for BOB 78, but on arrival, found no reception and decided to press on to an alternative drop site, which was identified by a wood and a field with two men standing in it. Fifteen containers were dropped from 300 feet at 03.17 and leaflets delivered over Chatillon on the way home to a safe landing at 06.05. F/O Herron and crew were assigned to BOB 118, which they reached at 02.43 after a three-hour outward flight. The drop site was identified by a wood and a reception signal was received, upon which, fifteen containers were dropped, and leaflets dispensed over Perreuil in east-central France on the way home and at Cabourg on the coast. S/L Climie took off at 23.45 for BOB 54, and also had to switch to an alternative drop site, BOB 149, which was reached at 02.30 and was identified by a field surrounded by woods and a large white farmhouse. Fifteen containers fell away, before a course was set for home via Chatillon, where leaflets were delivered.

The Transportation Plan continued on the night of the 16/17th with an attack on the marshalling yards at Amiens, for which a heavy force of eighty-one Halifaxes and forty-one Stirlings was made ready. This would be the first time that Stirlings had been invited to take part in the campaign, Mepal providing eleven of them, which took off between 20,00 and 20.35 with F/L Clark the senior pilot on duty. They all reached the target area, but one unspecified aircraft then developed engine problems and had to jettison the bomb load in order to maintain height. The others carried out their part in the raid and returned safely home to report a successful outcome.

The three crews sent to 3LFS for Lancaster conversion returned to the squadron on the 18th, and that night, Frankfurt became the target for more than eight hundred Lancasters and Halifaxes. They delivered a devastating attack, which left around six thousand buildings of all types destroyed or seriously damaged in eastern, central and western districts. It was back to mining for seven 75(NZ) Squadron crews on this night, who had been briefed to sow their vegetables in the waters of the Rosemary garden in the Heligoland Bight. Six Stirlings got away either side of 19.00 with S/L Climie the senior pilot on duty and they were followed into the air at 19.20 by F/O Murray and crew, whose late departure would see them arrive too late to benefit from the flares and consequently, unable to deliver their mines, which were brought home. The others managed to complete their sorties despite poor visibility caused by haze, and all returned safely.

Six crews were briefed for mining duties on the 19th, four for the River Adour and two for the nearby Furze garden off St-Jean-de-Luz, both close to the Franco-Spanish frontier. They took off together in a five-minute slot from 19.00 and all reached their respective target areas, where one of the Adour quartet had an engine catch fire and jettisoned its load. The other five crews planted their vegetables as briefed and returned home without incident after round-trips of between eight and nine hours duration. Acting S/L Lindsay Johnson Drummond RNZAF was among a number of crews posted to the squadron from 31 Base on the 19th, and he would fill the vacancy for A Flight commander left by the missing S/L Watson. S/L "Lin" Drummond had completed thirty operations with 149 Squadron, where he was awarded an immediate DFC for safely returning a damaged Stirling and it's wounded crew from a mining operation.

The squadron dispatched seven crews to French coastal waters on the 21st, four to St-Malo, two to Cherbourg and one to Le Havre. The St-Malo quartet took off either side of 19.00 with S/L Climie the senior pilot on duty and completed their sorties without incident. F/O Murray departed Mepal at 19.30 bound for Le Havre and was barely airborne before a broken propeller forced him to jettison his mines and land twenty minutes later. Debutants F/Sgt Alexander George Gray RNZAF and Sgt John Carter Bateman RAAF had set course for Cherbourg by this time, but one of them would be hampered by the failure of navigation equipment and only one would complete the sortie as briefed.

Frankfurt wilted under its second massive blow in five nights on the 22/23rd, and this time, half of the city was left without gas, electricity and water for an extended period. Thirty-six hours later, 162 B17s of the American 8th Air Force would bomb Frankfurt as a secondary target and add to the destruction, after which, according to local commentators, the city that had grown up since the Middle Ages ceased to exist. 75(NZ) Squadron sent four Stirlings to the Forget-me-not garden in Kiel Bay on the 22nd, departing Mepal between 18.00 and 18.20 and completing their sorties without incident. 143 aircraft from 3, 4, 6 and 8 Groups were made ready to continue the interdiction raids on railways on the 23rd and six crews were briefed at Mepal for the marshalling yards at Laon in north-eastern France. As they were about to take-off shortly after 19.30, one mid-upper gunner sustained an injury, and this caused the cancellation of the sortie. This left just five Stirlings to take off with S/L Climie the senior pilot on duty and they found clear skies in the target area, despite which, for some reason, the bombing began to fall into adjacent residential areas and the Master Bomber called a halt to proceedings after only half of the force had carried out an attack. The Kiwis were among those delivering their bombs and all returned safely. Post-raid reconnaissance revealed that some housing had been hit up to a mile away from the yards, and that the yards had sustained damage in the form of severed tracks, but they were repaired later that day, probably by pressganged civilians.

Nine crews returned from 3LFS on the 24th eager to go to war in a Lancaster, but they would have to wait a further two and a half weeks before any had their wish fulfilled. That night, while the Kiwis stayed at home, Bomber Command sent a force of heavy bombers to Berlin for the final time during the war. 811 Lancasters, Halifaxes and Mosquitos took off in the early evening and encountered for the first time what would become known as "Jetstream" winds. These were previously unknown currents of air at higher altitudes moving at speeds in excess of one hundred mph, which, if not detected, would drive the bomber stream wildly off course, break its cohesion and ruin the operation. Each squadron had designated "windfinder" crews, whose job was to ascertain wind speed and direction during the course of the operation and transmit their findings back to HQ, where the readings would be collated and broadcast back to the bombers. Such was the strength of the wind on this night, however, that windfinder crews felt unable to trust their readings and modified them before sending them to group. At group the amended figures were disbelieved and were further modified, so that navigators were working with false information, and many were unaware of the degree to which they were being driven south of their intended track. The result was that only in Berlin's south-western districts was there significant damage, largely to housing, while much of the effort was wasted on 126 outlying communities. The wind continued to push the homeward-bound bombers towards the south and many strayed inadvertently over the heavily-defended Ruhr region, where the flak batteries claimed two-thirds of the massive total of seventy-two failures to return.

On the following day, while the main force licked its wounds, preparations were put in hand to attack the marshalling yards at Aulnoye in north-eastern France. A mixed force of 192 aircraft was made ready, which included thirty-seven Stirlings, seven of them provided by 75(NZ) Squadron. This number was reduced just before take-off, when one Stirling developed engine problems and another put a wheel off the peri-track and became bogged down. The remaining five took to the air at 19.15, three of them containing the debutant crews of F/Sgt Lester Lascelles Bonisch RNZAF, W/O Frank Ernest Stott RNZAF and F/Sgt Colin Arthur Megson RNZAF, while F/O Murray was the senior pilot on duty. When they returned five hours later, they reported a well-concentrated attack, and while this may have been the case, it had been concentrated outside of the target, for which inaccurate Path Finder marking was held responsible.

A force of 702 aircraft was made ready for Essen on the 26th, while 3, 4, 6 and 8 Groups put together seventy Halifaxes, thirty-two Stirlings and seven Mosquitos for an attack on the railway yards at Courtrai (Kortrijk) in north-western Belgium. The assault on Essen took place through complete cloud cover, the effects of which were negated by Oboe, and more than seventeen hundred houses were destroyed and forty-eight industrial buildings seriously damaged, thus continuing the remarkable run of successes against this once elusive target since the introduction of Oboe a year earlier. Meanwhile, seven 75(NZ) Squadron Stirlings departed Mepal at 19.45, led for the first time by S/L Drummond, and including three other first-time skippers, Sgt Frederick William Hubbard RAFVR, Sgt Christopher Nigel Charles Crawford RAFVR and F/Sgt Mauson Lammas RNZAF. All reached the target area, where a not-entirely-accurate attack took place that hit and damaged to some extent the marshalling yards, but 313 buildings in the town were destroyed and 252 civilians killed. The Germans drafted in 1,650 local workers to repair the damage, and the yards were operating again three days later. One unnamed 75(NZ) Squadron crew had the frustration of being unable to release the bomb load because of a fault in the electrical circuitry.

The final operation of the long, bitterly-fought and costly winter campaign was directed at Nuremberg on the night of the 30/31st. This was to be a standard deep-penetration operation for which 795 aircraft were made ready. Under normal circumstances the operation would be planned by 8 Group and would incorporate feints, diversions and a circuitous route to the target to keep the enemy controllers guessing. This plan, however, offered 5 Group-inspired direct route, which would involve a 250-mile straight leg across Germany to a point fifty miles north of Nuremberg, from where the final run-in would commence, and was based on the belief that a layer of high cloud would protect the bomber stream from the moonlight, but that the target area would be clear. The A-O-Cs of the Lancaster-equipped groups were happy with the plan, but Roddy Carr of 4 Group was less enamoured about the prospects for his Halifaxes, even though they were the new Hercules-powered Mk III version, and AVM Bennett, the 8 Group A-O-C, was apparently incandescent with rage when he was told, and it is said, predicted a disaster.

A report from a Meteorological Flight Mosquito cast doubt on the weather forecast, particularly the amount and altitude of the cloud, and many expected the operation to be scrubbed. It was not, and what had been planned as a sixty-eight-mile-long bomber stream, which would pass across the aiming point in seventeen minutes, made its way in late-evening towards the fulfilment of Bennett's prediction. It was not long before the crews began to notice some unusual, unsettling and, perhaps, even freak features about the conditions, which included uncharacteristically bright moonlight. This created crystal clear visibility, which enabled the crews to see other aircraft around them, something to which they were not accustomed. Often, they would feel totally alone all the way to the target and only as they funnelled towards the aiming point would they become aware of the presence of other aircraft. They also noted the fact that the forecast high cloud was absent, and instead, a layer of white cloud below them acted as a backdrop to silhouette them like flies on a tablecloth. The two final insults were the formation of condensation trails to further advertise their presence in the hostile skies, and the close proximity of the route to two night-fighter beacons. All of these circumstances served to hand the bomber stream on a plate to the waiting night-fighters, and the route to the target could be traced by the burning wreckage on the ground of Lancasters and Halifaxes.

The carnage began at Charleroi in Belgium and continued all the way to the target, and at least eighty aircraft were lost during the outward leg. The same "Jetstream" winds that had so adversely affected the Berlin raid in the previous week, were also present, only this time from the south, and those crews who either failed to notice or refused to believe the evidence, were driven up to fifty miles north of the planned route. Again, the windfinders and groups did not believe the findings, as the result of which, many crews turned towards Nuremberg from a false position and when they came across Schweinfurt and observed some Path Finder markers, they believed it to be the target. These and the losses reduced dramatically the numbers bombing at Nuremberg, and the city escaped serious damage. When all returning aircraft had been accounted for, ninety-five were missing, and many others had been written off in crashes at home or with battle damage too severe to repair.

While this tragedy was on-going, four 75(NZ) Squadron Stirlings took off between 02.10 and 02.25 for mining duties, two each for Nectarine I off Texel and Anemone off Le Havre and completed their sorties without incident in clear weather conditions. During the course of the month the squadron carried out eighty-nine SOE sorties over eight nights, fifty-two mining sorties on seven nights and twenty-eight bombing sorties on four raids, all for the loss of three Stirlings and two crews.

April 1944

The winter campaign had brought the Command to its low point of the war and was the only time when the morale of the crews was in question. What now lay before the hard-pressed men of Bomber Command was in marked contrast to that which had been endured over the seemingly interminable winter months. In place of the long slog to Germany on dark, often dirty nights, shorter range hops to France and Belgium in improving weather conditions became the order of the day. However, these operations would be equally demanding in their way, and would require of the crews a greater commitment to accuracy, to avoid casualties among friendly civilians. Despite this, a decree from on high insisted that such operations were worthy of counting as just one third of a sortie towards the completion of a tour, and for a time afterwards, the hint of a mutinous air would pervade the crew rooms. In fact, the number of sorties to complete a tour would fluctuate between thirty and thirty-eight from this point until the end of hostilities. Despite the horrendous losses of the winter campaign, the Command was in remarkably fine fettle to face its new challenge, with 3 Group gradually changing to

Lancasters and the much-improved Hercules powered Halifaxes equipping 4 Group and half of 6 Group. Harris was now in the enviable position of being able to achieve what had eluded his predecessor, namely, to attack multiple targets simultaneously with enough strength to be effective. Such was the hitting-power now at his disposal, he could assign targets to individual groups, to groups in tandem, or to the Command as a whole, as dictated by operational requirements. Although invasion considerations would now take priority over all others, Harris would never entirely shelve his favoured policy of city-busting and would sneak one in whenever an opportunity arose.

The first eight nights of the new month required little of the heavy brigade, and operations involving them were restricted to gardening forays by the Stirlings and older Halifaxes, while the Mosquitos of 8 Group roamed far and wide over Germany. The railway yards at Trappes, Le Mans, Amiens, Laon, Aulnoye and Courtrai had all now received attention, and would continue to do so along with many others for as long as the campaign endured. S/Ls Climie and Gibbs and F/Ls Clarke and Warren and their crews were among those returning to Mepal from 3LFS on the 1st and were immediately put to work to hone their Lancaster skills with circuits and landings, fighter affiliation exercises and height and load tests. S/L Gibb was posted to 90 Squadron on the 4th and would be succeeded as B Flight commander by the newly-promoted S/L Sachtler, who was currently under conversion training at 3LFS. The first operational activity of the month came on the 5th, when S/L Drummond led a section of five Stirlings into the air at 19.00 to mine the waters of the Cinnamon garden off La Rochelle. There was one debutant crew, that of F/Sgt Lawrence Michael O'Connor RNZAF, and all completed their tasks as briefed, before returning safely to Colerne by 02.30, having been diverted because of poor weather conditions at base.

During the course of the 9th, two forces were made ready as the interdiction campaign moved into top gear. 239 crews of 3, 4, 6 and 8 Groups were briefed for an attack on the Lille-Delivrance goods station and among them were four from 75(NZ) Squadron, who would be flying Stirlings. Meanwhile, 225 others, drawn from all of the groups, learned that their target was the important marshalling yards at Villeneuve-St-Georges on the southern outskirts of Paris. Among the participants for this operation were eleven 75(NZ) Squadron crews, who would be going to war for the first time in Lancasters. These took off first, between 21.25 and 21.45 with S/L Climie the senior pilot on duty and P/O Buckley and crew in ND747 AA-T having the honour to be in the first Kiwi Lancaster to take off operationally.

It was a further hour before the Lille element got away led by F/L Grubb, but debutant F/Sgt Desmond Charles Brown RNZAF and crew had to jettison their load after an engine failed, and they landed safely at Wing shortly after midnight. The Lille group included one other newcomer in the person of F/Sgt Donald George Gibson RNZAF. The weather conditions were good as the two forces flew out to cross the French coast at 14,000 feet and returning crews would confirm clear skies over both targets and concentrated marking. The attack at Villeneuve was carried out from between 13,000 and 14,000 feet, a relatively modest height to aid accuracy, and was based on red and green TIs that had been accurately placed by the Path Finder Oboe Mosquitos. Many bomb bursts were observed along with orange explosions, and to those high above, the raid appeared to be highly successful. However, many bomb loads fell into adjacent residential areas damaging four hundred houses, and it would be established in time that ninety-three people on the ground had been killed. On the run in to the target, F/L

Witting's rear gunner had spotted a FW190 approaching their Lancaster, ND752 AA-O "Oboe". Evasive action was taken, and although fire was delayed due to the proximity of other Lancasters astern, both mid-upper and rear gunners managed short bursts before the attacker disappeared.

At Lille, crews were greeted by up to seven-tenths patchy cloud at 8,000 feet, but good visibility and favourable bombing conditions and confirmed their positions by H2S before bombing from between 12,000 and 13,000 feet on red and green TIs dropped by six Oboe Mosquitos and backed up by the Path Finder heavy brigade. Forty-nine bombs fell into the target area, destroying 2,124 items of rolling stock, more than two-thirds of what was present in the yards, and also damaging buildings and tracks. Many crews witnessed two particularly noteworthy explosions at 00.52 and 00.53, the former accompanied by an uprush of orange flame that reached several thousand feet and lasted for a few seconds before fading to leave a pall of black smoke. Crews arriving towards the end of the attack reported another violent explosion at 01.04, by which time the smoke was passing through 10,000 feet. Unfortunately, much of the effort strayed into the nearby built-up area, particularly the residential district of Lomme, where five thousand houses were damaged and 456 people killed. The problem of collateral damage would never be solved, but the French people stoically accepted such casualties as a price that had to be paid to gain liberation from a hated enemy. Only one Lancaster was lost during the two raids, although one from 75(NZ) Squadron, ME702 AA-Q flown by P/O Wainwright and crew, was hit by a bomb jettisoned from above on the way home and landed at Ford on the south coast with Category 'AC' damage.

On the following night, F/L Grubb was the senior pilot on duty as four Stirlings, including one captained by first-timer F/Sgt Henry John Burtt RNZAF, took off shortly before 21.00 to mine the waters of the Cinnamon garden off La Rochelle. They found clear skies and good visibility in which to carry out their runs and were on their way home by the time that eight of their Lancaster-equipped fellow crews began to depart Mepal as part of a 3, 6 and 8 Group heavy force of 148 aircraft with 8 Group Mosquito support assigned to attack five marshalling yards at Tours, Tergnier, Laon and Aulnoye in France and Ghent in Belgium. F/L Fauvel was the senior pilot on duty as they departed Mepal shortly before 01.30 and headed south for the Channel crossing to Laon. They carried out their attacks from between 9,000 and 11,500 feet in good visibility and returning crews described a concentrated and accurate attack, which was not confirmed after the post-raid photographs revealed that only a corner of the yards had been hit.

The city of Aachen, nestling on the frontiers with Holland and Belgium, contained two major marshalling yards, Aachen West and Rothe Erde to the east, which provided the main link to France. Any attack upon such objectives within a German city would be viewed by the Command, inevitably, as an opportunity for an area attack, and this was reflected in the 341-strong Lancaster force drawn from 1, 3, 5 and 8 Groups on the 11th. Among them were three representing 75(NZ) Squadron, which took off at 21.00 with F/L Witting the senior pilot on duty. They had actually been preceded into the air thirty-five minutes earlier by the Stirling of F/Sgt Brown, which was bound for the sea lanes off La Rochelle. Sadly, excessive cloud prevented him from pinpointing the drop zone, and he brought his mines back.

Meanwhile, the Aachen force climbed to between 18,000 and 20,000 feet by the time it reached the Belgian coast at 3 degrees east and maintained that altitude all the way to the target, where six to ten-tenths thin cloud was encountered at 7,000 to 8,000 feet. Red and green TIs identified the aiming point and the main force crews attacked it from 17,000 to 20,000 feet either side of 22.45, setting off many bomb bursts and fires, which suggested that the attack was accurate. The crews maintained height on the way home until fifty miles from the coast, at which position they began a gentle descent to exit enemy territory at 15,000 feet or above. Post-raid reconnaissance and local sources revealed that Aachen had experienced its most punishing attack of the war, in which central and southern districts bore the brunt as fires took hold, and severe damage was inflicted also upon communications and utilities, while fifteen hundred people lost their lives. There was a scare at Mepal later that day when Flying Fortress PU-J of the 360th Bomb Squadron based at RAF Molesworth crashed on the short runway, but fortunately, none of the crew was injured. The Station Log also reported that H2S was used operationally by the squadron this week for the first time.

On the 14th, Bomber Command became officially subject to the Supreme Headquarters of the Allied Expeditionary Force (SHAEF), under General Dwight D Eisenhower, in preparation for D-Day and would remain thus shackled until the Allied armies were sweeping towards the German frontier at the end of the summer. It was during the lull in main force operations that 83 and 97 (Straits Settlement) Squadrons were posted on what amounted to a permanent loan from 8 Group to 5 Group, from whence they had come in August 1942 and April 1943 respectively. They were to act as 5 Group's heavy marker force and were joined by the Mosquitos of 627 Squadron, which were to take over the low-level marking role from 617 Squadron. All three squadrons retained their Path Finder status, of which the crews were fiercely and justifiably proud, but they now had new masters. The already fractious relationship between AVMs Cochrane of 5 Group and Bennett of 8 Group plunged to new depths and from this point on, 5 Group was referred to in 8 Group circles as "The Lincolnshire Poachers" or "The Independent Air Force".

The 18th was to be extremely busy on stations across the Command as 1,125 aircraft were made ready for the night's operations against four marshalling yards in France, which would involve more than eight hundred of them, while a further 168 were to be sent mining in the Baltic. 75(NZ) Squadron would support both endeavours with nine Lancaster and six Stirlings, the former for an attack on the marshalling yards at Rouen in northern France and the latter for an extensive mining operation in Kiel Bay. The gardeners took off at 20.40 with S/L Drummond the senior pilot on duty, and it was approaching 23.00 before the first of the bombers took to the air with F/L Fauvel the senior captain. While they were away from Mepal, an enemy intruder dropped bombs on the runway, and this would necessitate a diversion for all but three of the returning crews. The bombing brigade, including newcomer Sgt Andrew David MacKenzie RAFVR and crew, found clear skies over the target area, although haze impaired vertical visibility to a degree, despite which, the operation appeared to progress according to plan, and Bomber Command claimed a successful raid. The conditions over Germany's Baltic coast were also ideal for the gardening element, and five of the squadron's participants returned home to report delivering their vegetables as briefed. EH955 AA-K (previously coded JN-K) failed to return, having been shot down by a night-fighter and crashing at Jenning in southern Denmark. F/O Henry Murray RNZAF was killed with three of his crew, but the other two members of the RNZAF were among three survivors to be taken into captivity. Navigator Sgt

'Paddy' McFarland RAFVR later reported that his desk had shattered without warning as the cannon shells hit, and he believed they had been attacked from below by upward-firing cannons.

Cologne provided the next objective for the squadron's Lancasters on the night of the 20/21st, when eight of them joined forces with 349 others from 1, 3, 6 and 8 Groups. Four Stirlings preceded them into the air at 21.00, each with an NCO crew on board, all bound for mining duties in the Jellyfish garden, specifically in the estuary leading to Brest. Debutant F/Sgt Hugh Edward Gilmour RAAF and crew jettisoned their mines because of technical difficulties, but the others successfully delivered theirs into the allocated locations and returned safely.

The bombers departed Mepal between 00.15 and 00.40 with F/L Witting the senior pilot on duty, but P/O Willis was forced to turn back with an ailing wireless operator. The others crossed the enemy coast in the Scheldt region at 20,000 feet, before climbing further to allow a gentle dive and increase in speed as they passed through the defended zone. According to 3 Group, the Path Finders were between six and twelve minutes late in arriving over the target, which was hidden beneath ten-tenths cloud, and some crews bombed on e.t.a. before the markers went down. Beneath the cloud and out of sight of the crews, Cologne was experiencing a torrid time, particularly in its northern and western districts, which were partly industrial in nature. Massive damage was inflicted upon industrial, public and residential buildings and more than eighteen hundred houses or apartments were destroyed, while twenty thousand others sustained damage to some extent. At 02.00, not long after the Lancasters had left, another enemy intruder attacked Mepal, strafing the aerodrome at low level with cannon and machine gun fire, damaging one dispersed bomber (thought to be ND801, originally coded JN-A), but not affecting operations.

On the 22nd a force of 596 aircraft, including eighty-seven 3 Group Lancasters, was made ready to attack Düsseldorf as Harris continued to pursue his own city-busting agenda on what was to be another very busy night for the Command. At the same time, a 5 Group force of 238 Lancasters and seventeen Mosquitos crews was to test the low-level Mosquito-based marking system for the first time at a heavily-defended German city, for which Braunschweig had been selected. Finally, 181 crews from 3, 4, 6 and 8 Groups were briefed to attack the marshalling yards at Laon in north-eastern France in a two-phase operation. At Mepal, S/L Drummond and crew led a quintet of Stirlings off the ground shortly after 22.00 as part of the second wave bound for Laon, and they all reached the target area to contribute to a highly effective raid, which caused considerable damage to the yards. The Ruhr-bound contingent of eight Lancasters remained on the ground for another hour before taking to the skies with F/L Fauvel the senior pilot on duty. They all reached the target and contributed to the 2,150 tons of bombs that rained down predominantly onto the northern districts of the city, where two thousand houses were either destroyed or severely damaged, fifty-six large factories were hit, of which seven were reduced to rubble, and more than a thousand people lost their lives. Night-fighters penetrated the bomber stream, and the failure to return of twenty-nine aircraft was a reminder that the Ruhr was still a dangerous place to visit. At debriefing two Mepal crews reported firing at enemy aircraft.

On the following night, the squadron dispatched Stirlings for the final time, when five took off at 20.40 to join in an extensive mining effort involving 114 aircraft in five areas of the Baltic.

The 75(NZ) Squadron element was assigned to the Forget-me-not garden in Kiel Bay, which F/Sgt Gibson and crew failed to reach after engine failure forced them to turn around and head for home. Three of the others returned after 03.00 to report successful sorties, but EF137, now re-coded AA-E, did not make it back to Mepal and news eventually filtered through that it had caught fire following an attack by a night-fighter and had crashed at 23.15 near Vemmenaes, on the eastern side of Tåsinge Island in southern Denmark. There were no survivors from the crew of P/O Mauson Lammas RNZAF, which included a RNZAF navigator, F/Sgt Douglas William Vaughan, and bomb-aimer, F/Sgt Robert Bailey, and their names were the last to be added to the squadron Roll of Honour for the Stirling era.

Thus ended an association which had begun in October 1942, during which an unusually high number of enemy night-fighters had been claimed as destroyed or damaged. This suggests that the Luftwaffe either targeted the lower-flying Stirlings specifically as "easy meat" or simply came upon them first as they climbed through them to reach operational altitude. Now a new allegiance was being forged with the Lancaster, and it was probable that a misplaced feeling of confidence had accompanied the arrival of the type, the losses of which, in a mixed force, were generally considerably lower than those of the poorer performing Merlin-powered Halifaxes and the Stirlings. When operating alone, however, Lancasters were equally at the mercy of the defences, as the ensuing months would graphically demonstrate. B and C Flights were now fully equipped with Lancasters, and the re-equipping of A Flight was underway.

Karlsruhe was posted as the target on the 24th, and the 1, 3, 4, 6 and 8 Group stations responded by preparing 637 Lancasters, Halifaxes and Mosquitos, eighty-six of the Lancasters provided by 3 Group. Meanwhile at 5 Group, 234 Lancasters and sixteen Mosquitos were made ready for another test of its low-level marking technique at a heavily defended Munich 150 miles to the south-east, to which destination they would be accompanied by ten 101 Squadron Lancasters from 1 Group to perform a Radio Countermeasures (RCM) role. 75(NZ) Squadron loaded fifteen Lancasters with bombs and sufficient fuel for the round-trip to southern Germany and sent them off from Mepal between 22.10 and 22.35 with F/Ls Clark, Fauvel, Warren and Witting the senior pilots on duty. There were no early returns and they flew out to the target over ten-tenths cloud, which would persist all the way and obscure all sight of the ground. About two hours into the trip, F/Sgt Bateman in LL865 AA-V came under attack from a BF109, but his rear and mid-upper gunners drove it off before it could open fire. An electrical storm between Liege and Strasbourg lasted for an hour and affected some H2S sets, and sixty to seventy searchlights were operating as the Karlsruhe-bound bomber stream passed close to Mannheim. At the target, crews were greeted by moderate flak coming up through the nine to ten-tenths thin cloud that reached up to 18,000 feet and were guided to the aiming point by release point flares and TIs. The Path Finders relied on H2S and skymarking, and the stronger-than-forecast wind pushed the whole attack further north than intended. The bombing became scattered and fell mostly in the northern districts, where nine hundred houses were either destroyed or seriously damaged. Bombs also fell in Mannheim, thirty miles to the north, and in Ludwigshafen, Darmstadt and Heidelberg, which suggests that much of the effort was wasted in open country in between. Nineteen aircraft failed to return, but there were no empty dispersal pans to contemplate at Mepal.

Another busy night on the 26th would involve more than a thousand aircraft, 493 of them made ready for Essen, while 5 Group went to Schweinfurt and a Halifax main force attended to the marshalling yards at Villeneuve-St-Georges. 75(NZ) Squadron briefed fifteen crews for the Ruhr, but two of these would have their sorties cancelled before take-off. The remaining thirteen got away safely between 23.05 and 23.35 and set course in favourable weather conditions, with F/Ls Clark, Fauvel and Warren the senior pilots on duty. Accurate and concentrated Path Finder ground-marking led to a destructive attack, and returning crews were unanimous in their assessment of a job well done. F/Sgt Gray and crew in veteran Lancaster, R5692 JN-P, reported an encounter with a Me210, which they claimed as damaged, and P/O Armstrong in ND768 AA-F reported two inconclusive encounters, one with a Ju88 and the other with a Me210. These were the only incidents of note in an otherwise uneventful operation.

The final operation of the month for 75(NZ) Squadron took place on the night of the 27/28th and involved a 1, 3, 6 and 8 Group force of 322 aircraft including eighty-two Lancasters representing 3 Group. The destination was the highly-industrialized town of Friedrichshafen, situated deep in southern Germany on the shores of Lake Constance, close to the border with Switzerland, where the principal target was a factory manufacturing engines and gearboxes for German tanks. Such was the compact nature of the built-up area, that the operation had to be conducted in moonlight to ensure accuracy, and feints and diversions were incorporated into the plan in an attempt to avoid a repeat of the Nuremberg disaster, which had taken place four weeks earlier in similar meteorological conditions. The sixteen 75(NZ) Squadron participants departed Mepal either side of 22.00 with W/C Max the senior pilot on duty and flew out over France in clear weather conditions, which persisted all the way to the target. The night-fighters had been unable to infiltrate the bomber stream before the target was reached, but then took a heavy toll during the attack and for a time on the route home. P/O Wainwright's rear gunner in R5692 JN-P spotted a FW190 and opened fire, without effect or response, and P/O Hunt in ND747 AA-T had a similar experience with a BF109. F/L Witting's mid-upper gunner saw a single-engine fighter following a bomber that was falling in flames, before it turned its attention upon ME691 AA-R and attacked it, the rear gunner opening fire without appearing to cause any damage. This Lancaster carried the name "Organ Grinder's Swing", no doubt applied by her original 'owners', W/O Des Horgan and his crew. Then, over the target, P/O Burke in ND802 JN-D "The Flying Scotsmen", was attacked by an unidentified fighter and his rear gunner fired off 500 rounds without apparent effect.

Returning crews described an accurate and concentrated operation, which was confirmed in a post-raid assessment that estimated ninety-nine acres or 67% of the town's built-up area to have been devastated, with a number of war-industry factories damaged and the tank engine factory destroyed. German sources would admit post-war, that this was the most damaging raid of the war on tank production. Among the eighteen missing Lancasters was the squadron's ND796 AA-J, which was shot down by a night-fighter to crash near Langenhart, some twenty-five miles north-west of the target, and there were no survivors from the crew of F/O Robert Weir Herron RNZAF, which contained three other members of the RNZAF. This was the first 75(NZ) Squadron Lancaster and crew to be lost.

The last two Stirlings left Mepal on the 28th, by which time twenty-six Lancasters were on squadron charge. S/L Drummond and the remaining Stirling crews returned from their conversion training at 3LFS on the 30th. Installation of the "Fishpond" defensive radar across the Lancaster fleet was now complete, and crews were quickly learning to use the equipment to provide extra warning of imminent attacks by night-fighters. During the course of the month the squadron operated seventeen times, dispatching thirty-four Stirling and ninety-one Lancaster sorties for the loss of two Stirlings and one Lancaster and their crews.

May 1944

The French and Belgian railway systems would remain the overriding priority during May, but, with the invasion looming ever nearer, airfields, ammunition and fuel storage dumps and coastal defences would begin to feature more prominently as the weeks passed. Most important of all was the need to reinforce in the minds of the enemy the belief that the invasion force would come ashore in the Pas-de-Calais region, and to that end, the main focus of attacks on coastal defences would be in that area rather than Normandy. Briefings took place for fourteen separate targets on the 1st, which would involve eight hundred sorties, 3 Group providing eighty-one Lancasters and sixteen Stirlings for a joint effort with 8 Group against a railway stores and repair depot at Chambly, located some twenty miles north of the centre of Paris. Sixteen 75(NZ) Squadron Lancasters took off between 22.44 and 23.00 led by S/L Sachtler and reached the target area to find clear conditions and accurate Path Finder marking in progress. The Stirling element bombed from 14,000 feet and the Lancasters from 7,000 to 10,000 feet, and the operation was concluded with a high degree of success. The enemy night-fighters got amongst the returning bombers over France, and F/Sgt "Lucky" Megson's rear gunner, F/Sgt Rowe in ND908 JN-M, shot inconclusively at a Do217. ME689 AA-Y became one of five failures to return and S/L Sachtler RNZAF and his crew, which included a RNZAF mid-upper gunner, were posted missing. In time, the squadron was notified that they had crashed south-west of Amiens and that there had been no survivors. S/L Sachtler had graduated in the same Wigram "wings" class as the last flight commander lost by the squadron, S/L Watson.

S/L Roy John Alexander Leslie AFC, RAF arrived on the 3rd from 311 Flying Training Unit as the new commanding officer elect, but he was sent immediately on detachment to 3LFS, as was F/O Richard Bruce Berney DFM, RNZAF, who would fill the vacant B Flight commander vacancy before the month was out. "Jack" Leslie was a New Zealander from Inglewood, who had served in the RAF on Fairey Battles earlier in the war, and then for two years had commanded a unit for reinforcing the Middle East forces with crews and aircraft. He was a driven individual who could be a hard taskmaster, admired, but not universally popular with his men. F/O Berney had picked up the 'headless' Turner crew at 1657 Heavy Conversion Unit at Stradishall, F/O Frank Turner having been hospitalised with a bad case of pneumonia. He returned to the squadron on the 6th but was not included on the order of battle for an attack on Chateau Bougon aerodrome near Nantes on the 7th, which involved ten of the squadron's crews as part of a 3 and 8 Group heavy force of ninety-three Lancasters with Mosquito support. They departed Mepal either side of 00.30 with F/Ls Clark and Fauvel the senior pilots on duty and all reached the target to find good visibility. The initial marking was a little scattered, but the Master Bomber took control as the bombing was carried out accurately from between 9,000 and 10,000 feet, and returning crews reported the explosion of bombs on the airfield.

S/L Leslie returned to the squadron from 3LFS on the 8th, but he was not among fifteen crews briefed for an attack on a heavy coastal battery at Cap-Gris-Nez scheduled to take place in the early morning of the 9th. More than four hundred aircraft were to be involved in attacks on seven such sites on the Pas-de-Calais coast, as the attempt continued to deceive the enemy over the invasion. S/L Climie was the senior pilot on duty as they took off either side of 03.00 and made their way south in clear weather conditions. Bombing was carried out from between 7,000 and 9,000 feet and returning crews reported an accurate and effective attack.

The ground crews and armourers were challenged during the late afternoon and early evening of the 10th, preparing for battle a 75(NZ) Squadron record of twenty-three Lancasters for the night's operation against the marshalling yards at Courtrai in Belgium. This represented 28% of the 3 Group effort of eighty Lancasters, and while this operation was in progress, similar attacks would be in progress at Dieppe, Ghent, Lens and Lille. The Mepal element took off between 21.55 and 22.15 with S/Ls Climie and Drummond the senior pilots on duty and F/O Berney undertaking his first sortie with the squadron. Three other captains were making their debut, F/Sgt James Kenneth McRae RNZAF, F/O Francis Charles Fox RNZAF and F/Sgt Keith Owen Whitehouse RNZAF. A Master Bomber was on hand at the target to direct the bombing, which took place from between 9,000 and 11,000 feet in clear visibility and appeared to be highly accurate and concentrated. There was little opposition, but S/L Drummond's aircraft, ND914 AA-H, picked up a little flak damage, and S/L Drummond was slightly wounded.

All three flights were now fully equipped with Lancasters, and on the following night the squadron set a new record, when making ready twenty-four of them as part of a 3 Group force of sixty-eight for a joint effort with elements of 8 Group for a raid on the marshalling yards at Louvain (Leuven), situated ten miles east of Brussels in Belgium. There was one crew on debut, that of F/Sgt William Robert White RNZAF, as the 75(NZ) Squadron element departed Mepal between 22.40 and 23.07 with F/Ls Clark, Fauvel, Warren and Witting the senior pilots on duty and made their way towards the target in the face of a stronger-than-forecast headwind, which delayed their arrival for the two-phase attack. By the time the second-phase crews turned up, the Path Finder markers were all-but extinguished and the bombing, which was carried out from between 9,000 and 11,000 feet, became scattered, some of it falling up to ten miles from the aiming point. On return, F/L Clark and crew in ND917 JN-O claimed a Ju88 as destroyed following a combat over the North Sea, but their own aircraft had also sustained significant damage from cannon shells and the subsequent fire, which would see it declared Category AC. ND919 AA-D was one of four Lancasters missing from the operation, after exploding and crashing near Aardenburg at the south-western-most point of Holland, right on the border with Belgium. The fact that the Lancaster exploded suggests that it was outbound at the time with its bombs still on board, and there were no survivors from the highly experienced crew of F/L Derek Warren RAFVR. The presence of this crew would be missed at Mepal, and it seems likely that F/L Warren had been under consideration for the vacant B Flight commander's post.

W/C Max DFC was posted to 3 Group HQ on the 15th at the conclusion of his tour, and he was succeeded as commanding officer by the newly-promoted W/C Leslie AFC. Following a week without operations, twenty-four crews were called to briefing on the 19th to be told that their target for that night was the marshalling yards at Le Mans in company with seventy-six other 3 Group Lancasters and a dozen plus four Mosquitos of 8 Group. They departed Mepal between 22.10 and 22.35 with S/L Climie the senior pilot on duty and the newly-elevated F/L Berney in support. This was another two-phase operation, which began well enough with bombing taking place from between 9,000 and 11,000 feet through ten-tenths cloud under the instructions of the Master Bomber, W/C Fraser Barron DSO & Bar, DFC, DFM, RNZAF. However, according to the 3 Group ORB, the second phase aircraft were unable to hear him because of jamming, when in fact, he and his deputy, S/L Dennis DSO, DFC, also from 7 Squadron, had been shot down by flak, an event which led to the bombing becoming scattered. There were no survivors from the fifteen men in the two Lancasters, and a huge amount of experience was thus lost to the Command. W/C Barron had seventy-nine sorties to his credit, and the other member of the RNZAF in his crew, F/O Jack William Walters DFC, was a fifty-sortie veteran, most of which had been undertaken with 75(NZ) Squadron as a wireless operator with the McLachlan crew between January and August 1942. It emerged later that the attack had destroyed the locomotive sheds, blown up some loaded ammunition wagons, cut two main lines and blocked all of the others, while causing minimal collateral damage that cost just nine lives.

Preparations were put in hand on the 21st for the first visit for a year to the Ruhr city of Duisburg. 510 Lancasters and twenty-two Mosquitos of 1, 3, 5 and 8 Groups were made ready, 75(NZ) Squadron managing a new record of twenty-five Lancasters. They departed Mepal either side of 23.00 with F/Ls Berney, Burton and Fox the senior pilots on duty. The plan called for the first of the 3 Group aircraft to gain height as they flew in a north-westerly direction over Sleaford, and thereby avoid crossing the enemy radar cover, which penetrated the English east coast airspace. The entire 3 Group force of one hundred Lancasters was then to meet the 1 Group element over the North Sea at 03.00° east at 18,000 feet, before crossing the enemy coast at 20,000 feet. They were instructed to continue climbing at 155 indicated air speed (i.a.s.) until reaching 22,000 to 23,000 feet, increasing speed then to 200 i.a.s. for the run across the target and the withdrawal, and cross the enemy coast homebound at a height no lower than 12,000 feet. F/L Fox and crew were the first of three to return early for various technical reasons, and they were followed by F/Sgt Whitehouse and P/O Burke and their crews. The remainder pressed on to find the target cloaked in ten-tenths cloud with tops at 20,000 feet, which swallowed up the Oboe-aimed skymarkers almost before the bomb-aimers could take a bead on them. The impression from above was of a scattered attack, but local reports suggested a degree of concentration over southern districts, where a thousand buildings were hit and almost a third of them destroyed. Night-fighters were again active, and just as at Düsseldorf a month earlier, twenty-nine Lancasters failed to return. Among them and lost without trace was ND804 JN-K with the crew of P/O William Jarvis Willis RNZAF, which contained three other members of the RNZAF. LL865 AA-V was attacked by a night-fighter and F/Sgt Arthur Hill RAFVR, the navigator in P/O Humphrey's crew, was wounded, but despite significant damage to the aircraft, including the loss of the starboard-inner engine and the consequent shedding of height, they made it over the Channel to reach home.

Twenty-four hours later it was the turn of Dortmund to host its first major raid for a year, and the 1, 3, 6 and 8 Group Lancaster stations made ready 361 aircraft, which would be accompanied by eighteen Path Finder Mosquitos. The twenty-three-strong 75(NZ) Squadron contingent departed Mepal between 22.39 and 23.00 with F/Ls Berney and Fox the senior pilots on duty and climbed out into ice-bearing cloud, that would cause twenty-three of the eighty-four 3 Group aircraft to turn back before reaching enemy territory. F/Sgt McRea and P/Os McCardle and Stott were the 75(NZ) Squadron representatives among these, leaving the others to push on to the target, where the skies were all but clear and P/O Wainwright and crew in ND904 JN-P, "Target for Tomorrow Night", had an inconclusive combat with a Ju88. The bombing was concentrated around the well-placed Oboe-laid TIs, which had fallen into the south-eastern, predominantly residential districts, where 852 houses and six industrial buildings were destroyed and a further 788 houses severely damaged. The success cost eighteen Lancasters, two of which were from Mepal, both with RNZAF captains. ME690 AA-Z was shot down by a night-fighter over Belgium and crashed a few miles from Lommel, close to the frontier with Holland, and ND768 AA-F "Freddie" was hit by flak over the target, which detonated the bomb load. There were no survivors from the crews of P/O Edgar Burke and P/O "Snow" Armstrong respectively, the latter containing a RNZAF bomb-aimer.

The first of two raids on Aachen's pair of marshalling yards was scheduled for the night of the 24/25th, for which a mixed force of 442 aircraft was put together from all but 5 Group and included a contribution from 3 Group of forty-three Lancasters. 75(NZ) Squadron made ready thirteen Lancasters for the main event and eleven others for a raid on a coastal battery, probably one of the two at Le Portel on the southern outskirts of Boulogne. The France-bound element, including the two RNZAF freshmen crews of F/Sgt John Devon Lethbridge and F/O Noel Alfred Deal Stokes, departed first between 00.10 and 00.25, and they were followed into the air immediately by the others led by F/Ls Berney, Clark, Fauvel, Fox and Witting. There were no early returns, and all reached their respective targets to find clear skies with some ground haze at Aachen, where the marking was accurate and the bombs were delivered from 20,000 feet at 180 i.a.s. in the face of weak opposition from the ground. Returning crews were confident of a successful raid, which was confirmed by post-raid reconnaissance and local reports, the latter claiming that 10% of the high explosive bombs had been duds. *(It should be pointed out that bomb loads frequently included delayed-action bombs, and one wonders if the report was written before they went boom!)* The operation cost twenty-five aircraft, eighteen of them Halifaxes mostly to night-fighters, but all from Mepal returned safely, F/L Berney and crew in ND915, AA-L to claim the destruction of a night-fighter, and P/O Buckley and crew in ME754, AA-A to report damaging a FW190, in exchange for significant damage to their own aircraft. The attack at Boulogne was delivered from between 7,000 and 9,000 feet without opposition and was also declared to be successful.

On the 25th a film crew from the Strand Film Unit arrived at Mepal to make a documentary movie about the squadron for Spectator Short Films. It would be based around a typical night operation over Germany and star F/L Eric Witting, his crew, and their faithful Lancaster, ND752 AA-O "Oboe", as the main actors, although as the crew was about to be declared tour-expired, some flying sequences were completed by others. Even the new commanding officer, W/C Jack Leslie, made a cameo appearance. The finished film was titled "Maximum Effort", and it captured a realistic record of Mepal in June 1944. That night twenty-two crews were ready to go to Mannheim when a late cancellation came through.

It had been decided that the Rothe Erde marshalling yards to the east of Aachen required further attention, and a force of 162 Lancasters and eight Mosquitos of 1, 3 and 8 Groups was assembled on the 27th to provide it. The 3 Group ORB makes no mention of this operation and records only mining activity off the Biscay ports and further north off Dunkerque and Ijmuiden. 75(NZ) Squadron contributed eighteen Lancasters to the operation, including that of debutant, F/O Ralph William Brumwell RAFVR, and they departed Mepal between 00.32 and 00.50 led by the usual gang of flight lieutenant pilots and each Lancaster carrying a load that included some delayed-action bombs. Only F/Sgt Brown and crew were forced to return early, while the remainder from Mepal pressed on to the target, at least fifteen of them arriving to bomb under clear skies and inflict severe damage upon the yards, sufficient to halt all through-traffic. Sadly, for its residents, the adjacent suburb of Forst was razed to the ground. Night-fighters were again active over Holland and Belgium and F/L Berney in ND915 AA-L returned to report five successive inconclusive combats with a Me410 in the Hasselt area of Belgium. Flak at the coast and also over the target claimed a number of aircraft and had probably been alerted by a simultaneous large-scale predominantly Halifax attack on a military camp at Bourg-Leopold in north-eastern Belgium. Twelve Lancasters failed to return from Aachen and among them were two from Mepal. ND802 JN-D "The Flying Scotsmen" and ND908 JN-M were both carrying a second pilot, and the former crashed near the night-fighter airfield at Gilze-Rijen in southern Holland, killing Sgt Francis Scott RNZAF, who was on his twenty-fifth operation, and two others, including the RNZAF bomb-aimer. The remaining five crewmen survived to be taken into captivity, the navigator also a member of the RNZAF. The latter came down at Poelkapelle in Belgium, a couple of miles to the north-east of the famous WWI town of Ypres (Ieper) and within sight of what were once the poppy fields of Passchendaele. There were no survivors from the highly-experienced crew of F/L Fauvel RNZAF, of which three others were also members of the RNZAF. They had been together for thirty operations and their loss would be a body-blow to their friends and colleagues at Mepal and result in two more 'headless' crews. While this operation was in progress, F/Sgts Burtt and White and their crews carried out successful mining sorties in the Cinnamon garden off La Rochelle.

The target for the night of the 28/29th was to be the marshalling yards at Angers in north-western France. While returning to Mepal from an air-test in preparation, ND914 AA-H swung off the runway in the hands of F/Sgt Howell and crew at 15.25 and wrecked its undercarriage, before finishing up on the Mill House site. The crew walked away but would not take part in the operation and were not destined to survive their tour. 3 Group detailed eighty-four Lancasters in a joint endeavour with thirty-eight Lancasters and eight Mosquitos of 8 Group. 75(NZ) squadron made ready sixteen Lancasters at short notice and could have prepared a larger number had the armourers been given more time. The Mepal contingent included one debutant, F/Sgt John Dudley Perfrement RAAF and took off between 18.35 and 18.55 with W/C Leslie the senior pilot on duty for the first time. They headed in daylight for Land's End, before flying at 2,000 feet to a point over the Atlantic, about seventy-five miles west of La Rochelle, by which time F/L Fox had turned back with engine trouble and darkness had fallen. They gained height to cross the French coast at between 8,000 and 10,000 feet and maintained that altitude for the run across the target. The bombing was concentrated and accurate, and the crews reduced height thereafter to exit France at 3,500 feet. The only casualty was a 622 Squadron Lancaster, which flew too low and too close to Nantes on the way to the sea and was brought down by light flak. The crew survived, and a number evaded capture.

On the 30th, the squadron contributed ten Lancasters to a 3 Group main force of fifty for an attack on a coastal battery at Boulogne, which was again probably either Religion or Andante, situated at either end of Le Portel. The 75(NZ) Squadron element departed Mepal at 23.00 with F/Os Brumwell, Myers and Stokes the senior pilots on duty and would arrive at the target as the 4 Oboe Mosquitos were delivering the TIs or spotfires. F/O John William Anthony Myers RNZAF was one of two debutants, and the other was F/Sgt Raoul John Wisker RNZAF. The attack was carried out in excellent conditions with no effective opposition, and all returned safely home.

The final operation of a busy month was directed at the marshalling yards at Trappes on the night of the 31st, for which the squadron made ready twenty-three Lancasters as part of an overall force of 219 aircraft from all but 5 Group. This is another operation that the 3 Group ORB failed to record. Departures took place at Mepal either side of midnight with acting S/L Berney the senior pilot on duty and now confirmed as the new A Flight commander. F/Sgt Gray returned early with engine trouble, leaving the others to push on to the target, where the two-phase attack was carried out accurately in good visibility. F/O Bonisch and crew in ME702 AA-Q were involved in an engagement with an enemy night-fighter, which another crew observed to be shot down. During the course of the month the squadron took part in fifteen operations and dispatched a record 233 sorties for the loss of eight Lancasters and seven crews.

June 1944

June was to be a hectic month, which would make great demands on the crews and the first week was dominated by unsettled weather, which caused concerns for the impending launch of Operation Overlord. Despite being one of the most recent recipients of the Lancaster, the squadron now had thirty-one on charge as D-Day approached, and that was second only to 1 Group's 101 Squadron, which needed more aircraft than others in order to provide RCM cover for most major operations. The final preparations for D-Day brought the focus of operations upon coastal defences in the Pas-de-Calais and 75(NZ) Squadron detailed fifteen Lancasters on the 2nd for such an operation that night at Wissant, situated between Calais and Cap Gris Nez. Three RNZAF pilots were on debut, those of F/Sgt Thomas Rodgers Donaghy, F/Sgt Benjamin William Bateson and F/Sgt Edward Howell, and they took off with the others between 01.00 and 01.20 with F/Os Brumwell, Myers and Stokes the senior pilots on duty. Ten-tenths cloud over the target rendered the marking ineffective and twelve crews brought their bombs home, which was not operationally significant as long as the deception was maintained. Events a few days hence would demonstrate this to be the case.

The weather had improved on the following night, when ten of the Squadron's Lancasters took off from 00.30 led by F/Os Baker and Myers, with the debutant crew F/Sgt Colin George Nairne RNZAF also in attendance. Their target was a coastal battery near Calais, probably at Sangatte, where clear skies allowed concentrated marking and accurate bombing in the face of only slight opposition. There were just three gardening sorties by the squadron on the night of the 4/5th, by the crews of F/Sgt Gray, F/Sgt Perfrement and F/O Stokes in the Iris II, Iris V and Cypress Tree II gardens, each of which had been recently introduced and were off the occupied coast, it is believed, covering the deception area between Dunkerque and Calais. They took off either side of 02.30 and were back within two hours after successfully delivering their vegetables by H2S through ten-tenths cloud cover.

Operation Overlord and already been put back by twenty-four hours when the decision was taken to launch it during the early hours of the 6th. It was with trepidation in view of the anticipated choppy sea conditions that the executive order was issued, and 1,211 crews across Bomber Command were called to briefings late on the 5th to learn of their part in attacks on coastal defences and in support and diversionary operations. No mention was made of the impending invasion, but strict guidelines were put in place which probably alerted them to the fact that a momentous night lay ahead. They were told that more than a thousand aircraft would be operating throughout the night, and that they must adhere to assigned flight levels and not jettison bombs over the Channel. The 3 Group Stirling squadrons had important roles to play in deception and diversionary operations, while 107 of its Lancasters attacked the coastal battery at Ouistreham, situated on the Normandy coast at the eastern end of the invasion area, where Sword and Juno Beaches would be the scene of the Anglo-Canadian landings. 75(NZ) Squadron made ready a record twenty-six Lancasters, and they took off either side of 03.30 with W/C Leslie the senior pilot on duty. They were timed to reach the target at first light, and on arrival found a layer of cloud at 7,000 feet with occasional gaps, through which some crews were able to see the markers. The bombing appeared to be fairly concentrated, no opposition was met, and all aircraft returned safely to Mepal after a round-trip of under four hours. This was one of ten coastal defences targeted during the night by 1,012 aircraft and the total of more than five thousand tons of bombs delivered was a record for a single night. Some of the crews returning in the grey light of dawn caught a glimpse through breaks in the cloud of the largest armada in history, as it ploughed its way sedately towards the Normandy beaches at about eight knots.

Another thousand aircraft were aloft on D-Day Night to attack road and railway communications leading to the beachhead, for which 3 Group detailed a hundred Lancasters, including twenty-four at Mepal. Their target was a railway junction in the town of Lisieux, some twenty miles to the east of Caen, and all took off safely either side of midnight with F/L Clark the senior pilot on duty. They reached the target to find a thin layer of cloud at 5,000 feet, which obscured the aiming point, but the Oboe TIs could be seen clearly, and the bombing was accurate and concentrated. Post-raid reconnaissance confirmed the success of the attack in cutting the railway lines, but also revealed heavy damage within the town itself.

Just six of the squadron's crews were briefed for operations on the night of the 7/8th as part of a sixty-six strong 3 Group Lancaster force assigned to a railway junction at Massy-Palaiseau, south-south-west of Paris, and a road junction at Chevreuse further to the west. *(Chevreuse is not referred to in either the 3 Group or 75(NZ) Squadron ORBs but is mentioned by Bill Chorley in Bomber Command Losses for 1944 as the target for the six 115 Squadron Lancasters shot down by night-fighters on this night).* There was just one first-time captain operating with the squadron on this night, F/O Charles Gordon Washer RNZAF, who departed Mepal with the others between 00.35 and 00.50 with no senior pilots on duty, and after F/Sgt Nairne turned back with instrument failure, the rest pressed on to find the target covered by ten-tenths cloud at between 5,000 and 7,000 feet. The Master Bomber ordered the crews to descend to below the cloud base, where they came under fire from accurate light flak, despite which the attack developed well and an excellent concentration of bombing was achieved. Night-fighters were very much in evidence, particularly during the outward flight, and eight Lancasters were lost from this target, although none from 75(NZ) Squadron. F/Sgt Perfrement and crew in ND756 AA-M reported a brief engagement with a Me210, which they claimed as damaged.

Communications continued to provide the main focus for operations on the night of the 8/9th, when 3 Group was assigned to the town of Fougeres, situated some twenty miles south-east of St-Malo in the American sector. 75(NZ) Squadron made ready twenty Lancasters, which took off either side of 22.00 with F/L Clark the senior pilot on duty, and all reached the target area, where the conditions were good with a little patchy cloud. One aircraft failed to release its bomb load because of a faulty bomb sight, but the others carried out their attacks from between 5,000 and 8,000 feet under the instructions of a Master Bomber, whose contribution was praised by returning crews, two of which reported inconclusive combats. The operation appeared to be successful, and the main problems were faced at home, where poor weather conditions made landing something of a challenge.

The squadron made ready twenty-four Lancasters on the following day for an operation that night against the marshalling yards at Dreux, some twenty-five miles west of Paris, one of four similar targets earmarked for destruction. They took off between 23.00 and 23.25 with F/L Clark once more the senior pilot on duty and F/Sgt Richard Stockdale Barker RNZAF and crew as the sole debutants. They climbed out over Mepal to eventually join up with sixty-six other 3 Group Lancasters heading for the Channel coast, on the French side of which, the weather conditions were favourable and crews were able to identify the aiming point visually until smoke began to drift across it. The bombing took place from between 7,000 and 9,000 feet and was initially scattered but became more concentrated as the raid progressed and all seemed satisfied with the results. Night-fighters began to arrive during the attack and F/Sgt Howell in ND753 AA-D had an inconclusive skirmish with a Ju88. The fighters continued to harry the returning bombers until they reached the Channel Islands, and five Lancasters failed to return. Among them were HK553 AA-S and ME702 AA-Q from Mepal, the former crashing at Tillieres-sur-Avre, fifteen miles west of the target and the latter just short of the coast near Bayeux. The mid-upper gunner from each of the crews of F/Sgt Thomas Donaghy RNZAF and P/O Lester Bonisch RNZAF were the only survivors, one to evade capture and the other to be taken prisoner. There were two other members of the RNZAF in the latter crew, which had been around long enough to be considered experienced.

75(NZ) Squadron made ready seventeen Lancasters on the 11th while their crews were being briefed for a 3 Group raid on a railway junction at Nantes involving fifty aircraft. A late take-off had them climbing out over their stations by midnight, with S/L Berney the senior pilot on duty among the Kiwis. They reached the target area to find unfavourable conditions in the form of cloud layers between 2,000 and 7,000 feet, which prompted the Master Bomber to issue an instruction to them to come down to clear air. Those hearing the order complied but found difficulty in bombing from such a low level even though the TIs were well-placed. Many crews failed to pick up the Master Bomber's broadcast and bombed on the glow of the TIs through the cloud from 7,000 feet, as a result of which, the bombing was somewhat scattered and those attacking from low level became vulnerable to intense light flak. As ME751 AA-B was leaving the target area, a shell exploded in the cockpit, severely wounding the pilot, P/O McCardle, and slightly wounding the flight engineer. The bomb-aimer, W/O Alexander William Hurse RAAF, took over the controls and with the assistance of the navigator, F/O Albert Hart Robertson Zillwood RNZAF, brought the aircraft back to a perfect landing at Boscombe Down. For their magnificent efforts they received the immediate awards of a CGM and DFC respectively.

Bomber Command's workload was about to increase substantially as new responsibilities were added to its already busy schedule. Immersed in the campaign against the enemy's transportation system, and on hand to support the breakout of the invasion forces, two new offensives against oil and V-Weapons were introduced, beginning with the former at Gelsenkirchen on the night of the 12/13th. It was to be a hectic night generally for the stations, those of 4, 5 and 6 Groups concentrating on preparing more than six hundred Halifaxes and Lancasters for attacks on communications targets, while 1 and 3 Groups put together a force of Lancasters to attack the Bergius-process Gelsenkirchener Bergwerke A G oil plant, known to the bomber crews as Nordstern and to the Germans as the Gelsenberg A G. (A.G is Aktien Gesellschaft or production company). Path Finder Mosquitos and Lancasters were on hand to provide the marking at all seven sites to be targeted, and together with the minor operations taking place, 1,083 aircraft would take to the air on this night.

75(NZ) Squadron made ready fifteen Lancasters, which departed Mepal either side of 23.30 with W/C Leslie the senior pilot on duty. They set course for the east coast to rendezvous with the rest of the 286-strong heavy force at the midpoint of the North Sea at 18,000 feet, before climbing to 20,000 to 22,000 feet for the run to the target. and then shedding height during the final approach to bomb from 18,000 feet. The skies over the Ruhr were clear, but the first TIs, which were estimated to be eight miles south of the target, attracted thirty-five bomb loads, before the main Path Finder effort marked out the intended aiming point. The bombing became concentrated around the TIs and large fires were soon emitting copious amounts of black smoke. The ground defences were not as troublesome as had been anticipated, but night-fighters chased the bombers home and scored steadily, particularly over Holland's Ijsselmeer. Seventeen Lancasters were lost, but the Mepal brigade all made it back safely from what was later established to have been a highly destructive operation, which halted all production at the plant for several weeks at a cost to the German war effort of one thousand tons of aviation fuel per day.

This was the day on which the first V-1 flying bombs fell on London, an event which would prompt a response from Bomber Command within a matter of days. In the meantime, the heavy squadrons enjoyed a rare night off, which the 75(NZ) Squadron crews, no doubt, took advantage of in the local watering holes of Cambridge, Huntingdon or the much nearer Chatteris. The first major daylight operation since the departure from Bomber Command of 2 Group a year earlier was mounted against Le Havre on the evening of the 14th in a two-phase attack involving 221 Lancasters and thirteen Mosquitos of 1, 3, 5 and 8 Groups. The targets were destroyers, U-Boots, minesweepers and the fast light surface vessels (E-Boots) that posed a threat to the Allied shipping supplying the Normandy beachhead. A predominantly 1 Group force was to take the first of the evening shifts, with 3 Group following up later after nightfall, and elements of 617 Squadron were also on hand with their Barnes Wallis-designed 12,000lb Tallboy earthquake bombs, if required. Twenty-six Lancasters were made ready at Mepal and they were all safely airborne just before midnight with S/L Berney the senior pilot on duty. Six RNZAF skippers were on debut, those of F/Sgt David John Moriarty, F/Sgt Eldrid Duke O'Callaghan, F/O John Keillor Aitken, F/O James Allan Fleming, F/Sgt Roland Desmond Ernest Betley and F/Sgt Victor Arnold Adolph. Only F/Sgt Gray had to turn back early with engine trouble, leaving the others to continue on to find the target under clear skies and on fire from the earlier assault. They bombed with the rest of the group from 12,000 to 14,000 feet, achieving in the process great concentration and contributing to a highly successful raid from which few enemy vessels escaped intact.

A similar operation was mounted on the following evening against enemy craft at Boulogne, also with highly satisfying results, but 3 Group did not take part. It had been assigned to attack the marshalling yards at Valenciennes in north-eastern France, and Lens, twenty-five miles away to the west. The latter was a Stirling affair, while a force of ninety-nine Lancasters was made ready for the former, of which twenty-four represented 75(NZ) Squadron. Two carried first-time captains, F/Sgt Hoturoa Arnel Dean Meyer RNZAF and F/Sgt Harold Whittington RNZAF. The Kiwi element took off between 23.00 and 23.28 with F/Ls Fox and Washer the senior pilots on duty and were greeted over the target by a cloud base at 7,000 feet and an invitation from the Master Bomber to descend to that level. The initial markers were scattered, and he delayed the start of the bombing until the aiming point had been remarked. However, the second set of TIs undershot slightly, causing the Master Bomber to call for the bomb-aimers to allow a two second overshoot, which caused a degree of confusion, partly as a result of aircraft running in on a variety of headings. As a result, the operation was only moderately effective and cost five Lancasters, among them LL888 JN-X, which crashed five miles east-north-east of Cambrai with no survivors from the crew of F/Sgt Roland Betley RNZAF. There were three other members of the RNZAF on board, and the crew were on just their second operation together. P/O Crawford landed at Manston with a badly damaged Lancaster ND904 JN-P, resulting from a combat with a night-fighter, which was claimed as damaged.

A new station commander took over RAF Mepal on the 16th, G/C A.P. Campbell, CBE replacing G/C K.M.M. Wasse, DFC. The second new campaign of the month, a renewed effort against flying-bomb storage and launching sites in the Pas-de-Calais, began on the night of the 16/17th, but did not include 3 Group. Four sites were bombed effectively after accurate marking by Oboe Mosquitos, while another large force attended to the synthetic oil plant at Sterkrade/Holten on the outskirts of Oberhausen in the Ruhr. The latter operation was conducted through cloud, was less successful and cost thirty-one aircraft, twenty-two of them Halifaxes.

Three railway targets were selected for attention on the night of the 17/18th and fourteen 75(NZ) Squadron crews were briefed for one at Montdidier in north-eastern France. They took off between 01.13 and 01.30 with F/L Washer the senior pilot on duty and reached the target to find ten-tenths cloud at between 1,500 and 8,000 feet, conditions which were not conducive to accurate bombing. This situation would not have impeded an attack on a German target, but with collateral damage in mind and possible French civilian casualties, the Master Bomber called a halt after just twelve aircraft had bombed. All but one of the Mepal element returned their bombs to store, the exception, F/Sgt Whittington and crew in ND756 AA-M, having jettisoned theirs over the Channel during a combat with a FW190, which was claimed as possibly destroyed.

S/L Neilson Arnold Williamson RNZAF was posted in from 1651 Conversion Unit on the 21st to succeed S/L Climie as C Flight commander on the 21st, and he would soon be leading from the front. Williamson had already flown a tour on Stirlings with 214 Squadron and now picked up what would have been the Lukey crew, but for the tragic loss of their skipper on his 'second-dicky' trip. Three flying bomb sites were assigned to elements of 3, 6 and 8 Groups on the evening of the 21st, and as the squadron ORB pointed out, this was to be the squadron's first full daylight operation since 1941. The target for a hundred 3 Group Lancasters, including twenty-one from 75(NZ) Squadron, was a V-Weapon storage site at Domleger, situated east of Abbeville in the Pas-de-Calais. The large concrete storage and supply sites springing up in the Pas-de-Calais region of north-eastern France were in various stages of construction and were referred to in operational orders and ORBs as "constructional works". The plan called for aircraft to form into loose pairs in squadron order as they headed south to rendezvous with the leader at 9,000 feet over Braintree in Essex. They departed Mepal between 18.00 and 18.25 with W/C Leslie the senior pilot on duty and once in contact with the rest of the force, gained height to 14,000 feet over the Channel with the intention of bombing from between 12,000 and 14,000 feet. Unfortunately, ten-tenths cloud in the target area prevented even a faint glow from the TIs and the Master Bomber was forced to send the force home with its bombs. Despite this setback, valuable experience had been gained in formation flying in daylight, which would prove to be useful from the autumn onwards. Later on, during this night, 5 Group entered the oil campaign with attacks on the refineries at Wesseling, near Cologne, and Scholven-Buer in the Ruhr. Cloud at both targets rendered the low-level marking system unworkable, and night-fighters got amongst the Wesseling force to contribute to the loss of thirty-seven Lancasters, or 27.8%.

Twenty Lancasters were made ready at Mepal on the 23rd for a 3 Group raid that night on another constructional works at L'Hey, situated some fifteen miles south of Dunkerque. They took off between 23.00 and 23.28 with S/Ls Berney and Drummond the senior pilots on duty and reached the target a little ahead of schedule, which led to some congestion. However, conditions were good, if cloudy, and the well-placed markers allowed the main force crews to bomb on their glow under the instructions of the Master Bomber. The attack appeared to be successful and was concluded for the loss of a single Lancaster, which probably fell victim to coastal flak.

The squadron detailed twenty-five Lancasters for operations on the 24th, the crews learning at briefing that a constructional works at Rimeux (probably Brimeux) was to be their target. This was just one of seven such sites to be attacked on this night, for which 739 Lancasters, Halifaxes and Mosquitos were made ready. The 75(NZ) Squadron participants, including debutant F/Sgt Gerald Brian Roche RNZAF, took off either side of 23.30 with F/L Fox the senior pilot on duty and arrived at the target in clear skies and under bright moonlight to contribute to an accurate attack by the 100-strong force on well-placed markers. A considerable night-fighter presence in the target area and on the route home led to the loss of twenty-two Lancasters, among which was ND920 AA-P, which crashed near Fruges, killing F/Sgt Ben Bateson RNZAF and his crew, which included a RNZAF rear gunner.

On both the 25th and 26th the squadron was put on standby to provide aircraft for an attack on constructional works at Zudausques in the northern area of the Pas-de-Calais, but the weather prevented any operation from taking place. The same fifteen crews, including that of newcomer F/O Victor John Andrew RNZAF, were briefed again on the 27th, this time for a "constructional works" supply site at Biennais, situated twenty miles south of Dieppe, for which they took off shortly before midnight with S/Ls Berney and Drummond the senior pilots on duty. They joined up with eighty-five other Lancasters from the group as they headed for the Channel coast and reached the target to find it hidden by ten-tenths cloud, through which the glow of the TIs was just visible. A large explosion suggested that the bombing had found the mark, and then the crews had to fight their way through considerable night-fighter activity on the return journey, during which one of the squadron's crews was engaged in an inconclusive combat.

There was another cancellation on the 29th but New Zealand personnel enjoyed a visit from AVM Leonard Isitt, Chief of the Air Staff of the RNZAF, who lunched in the officers' mess before returning to London. The residents of Mepal and the surrounding communities were roused from their sleep at 04.20 on the 30th, when LL942 JN-C blew up on an A Flight dispersal pan with a full bomb load on board. Fortunately, no personnel were nearby, and damage was restricted to five other Lancasters, some adjacent civilian housing, a few station buildings and an AEC aero petrol tanker, which was holed by a piece of shrapnel and lost about 1,000 gallons of fuel. The aircraft had been one of a record twenty-eight bombed up for an operation against marshalling yards at Vaires near Paris, which had been cancelled because of the weather.

The incident meant that only twenty-four Lancasters were available later for a daylight attack on a road junction at Villers-Bocage, a village perched across a main road on the western approaches to Caen, through which two German Panzer divisions were planning to pass that night on their way to the beachhead. Twenty-four Lancasters were made ready at Mepal, but two were subsequently withdrawn because of technical faults. This left the remainder, including that occupied by newcomers F/L Garth Reginald Gunn RNZAF and crew, to begin their take-offs shortly after 18.00, with the newly arrived S/L Williamson the senior pilot on duty for the first time. The 127-strong 3 Group contingent formed into loose pairs as it flew south to rendezvous with the 4 and 8 Group elements and reached the target under the protection of a Spitfire escort provided by 11 Group. They intended to carry out the attack from between 12,000 and 14,000 feet, until the presence of some broken cloud persuaded many crews to descend to 4,000 feet, and a highly successful attack ensued, which entirely achieved its purpose and elicited messages of congratulations from the American and British army commanders. There was moderate flak to contend with, some of which hit S/L Williamson's ND917 JN-O and tore off his flight engineer's kneecap, causing rapid loss of blood. This prompted an unscheduled landing at the beachhead fighter strip, B10, which had been constructed on the 18th of June on the site of a former landing strip in the village of Plumetot, within two miles of the sea west of Ouistreham. A medical centre had already been set up there, which attended to Sgt McDevitt, and ND917 thus became the first Lancaster to land in liberated territory. It was a particularly notable piece of airmanship given that it was S/L Williamson's first time piloting a Lancaster! Two other aircraft suffered flak damage, one putting down at Woodbridge, and the other making it safely home to Base.

During the course of the month the squadron participated in twenty operations, including mining by single aircraft at three locations, and dispatched 327 sorties for the loss of five Lancasters and four crews.

July 1944

The first week of the new month was dominated by the campaign against flying-bomb sites, and elements of 4, 6 and 8 Groups opened proceedings in daylight on the 1st. On the following afternoon 1, 3 and 8 Groups were assigned to three sites, 3 Group contributing 119 Lancasters to a raid on a site at Beauvais, situated between Paris and the coast. The twenty-three aircraft provided by 75(NZ) Squadron, including those occupied by RNZAF newcomers F/Sgt Gerald Michael Francis Moore, F/Sgt Kenneth McIndoe Mackay and F/O Nelson Hastings Bright, took off either side of 13.00 with S/L Berney the senior pilot on duty. They met up with a fighter escort from 11 Group as they approached the Channel and reached the target area to find good conditions with three to four-tenths cloud, through which the markers were clearly visible. The bombing was carried out entirely without opposition from the ground or in the air, and the bombing appeared to be concentrated and effective.

The squadron put twenty-four crews on standby from the early hours of the 5th and right throughout the day for an attack on the "constructional works" at Biennais, but poor weather conditions prevented the operation from taking place. Eventually the target was changed to another "constructional works", the rocket launching site at Watten, situated a dozen miles south-east of Calais. The same twenty-four crews, including freshman F/Sgt Frank Maxwell Timms RNZAF, took off either side of 23.00 with F/Ls Fox, Gunn, Stokes and Washer the senior pilots on duty and joined up with fifty-six others from the group, while a second, smaller 3 Group element headed for Wizernes a few miles to the south. In all, 542 aircraft from 3, 4, 6 and 8 Groups were involved in these attacks on two launching sites and two supply sites, and by the time that they reached their respective target areas, the skies over north-eastern France had cleared to leave bright moonlight but also some ground haze. All four operations were concluded successfully, but each site would require further attention over the ensuing two months.

A major assault on enemy positions in fortified villages north of Caen was carried out by 460 aircraft on the evening of the 7th in support of British and Canadian ground forces. The two locations were well-plastered under the control of Master Bombers, but the choice of aiming points was flawed, rendering the operation ineffective, and the resultant damage to the outskirts of Caen would prove to be a hindrance rather than a help in the effort to break out. A proposed attack on the marshalling yards at Vaires, east of Paris, on the night of the 6/7th, which had been cancelled because of adverse weather conditions, was reinstated on this night, and twenty-one 75(NZ) Lancasters departed Mepal between 22.35 and 23.03 with F/Ls Fox and Myers the senior pilots on duty. They were part of a 100-strong 3 Group element, which was reduced by seven early returns, three of which were by Mepal crews. The others found the target under clear skies and bombed it from 12,000 feet with excellent results and no losses. This was in stark contrast to a simultaneous 5 Group attack on flying-bomb storage caves at St-Leu-d'Esserent, north of Paris, where night-fighters got amongst the bombers and shot down twenty-nine Lancasters and two Mosquitos, a massive 14% of the force.

Six flying-bomb launching sites were earmarked for attention by daylight on the 9th, for which 347 aircraft from 3, 4, 6 and 8 Groups were made ready. 3 Group detailed fifty Lancasters for the site at Lisieux, of which half were provided by 75(NZ) Squadron, including ME751 AA-B, skippered by newcomer P/O Gordon Lindsay Kennedy RNZAF. They took off either side of 13.00 with S/Ls Berney and Williamson the senior pilots on duty and found the target hidden beneath ten-tenths cloud. The markers proved to be difficult to see and most crews bombed on either a Gee-fix or DR, which led to a scattered and unsuccessful raid. HK554 JN-F, containing F/Sgt Wisker & crew, suffered substantial flak damage over the target.

It was a similar story on the following day, when a new 75(NZ) Squadron record of twenty-seven Lancasters took off at dawn to attack the "constructional works" at Nucourt, some twenty-five miles north-west of Paris. S/L Drummond was the senior pilot on duty as he and the other squadron participants encountered complete cloud cover over the target, which again led to bombing by navigational aids and another scattered and ineffective outcome. The unfavourable weather continued on the 12th, when 153 Lancasters and six Mosquitos from 1, 3 and 8 Groups attempted once more to hit the marshalling yards at Vaires. 110 of the Lancasters were provided by 3 Group and twenty-five of these took off from Mepal between 18.05 and 18.20 with S/Ls Berney, Drummond and Williamson all on the order of battle. All reached the target area, but only two from the squadron were able to identify the aiming point and they bombed with ten others before the Master Bomber called a halt and sent the remaining aircraft home with their bomb loads intact.

The weather caused planned daylight attacks on the marshalling yards at Villeneuve-St-Georges to be cancelled on the 13th, and Vaires on the 14th and 15th, on the last occasion after the squadron had broken all of its former records to make ready thirty Lancasters. Finally, on the night of the 15/16th, the squadron was able to set a new record, when dispatching twenty-eight Lancasters, eighteen between 21.55 and 22.18 to attack the marshalling yards at Chalons-sur-Marne in the Champagne region east of Paris, including debutant F/Sgt Neil Douglas Davidson RNZAF, and a further ten either side of 23.30 bound for the V-1 launching site at Bois-des-Jardins. S/L Drummond led the first element, and all arrived in the target area in conditions favourable enough for most crews to be able to identify the aiming point visually. The markers were accurate and were bombed by the main force crews from below 8,000 feet to cause severe damage to the yards. There was no flak opposition but two inconclusive combats with fighters took place, with F/Sgt Perfrement's LL866 (originally AA-W but by now re-coded AA-S) damaged in the engagement. F/L Gunn was the senior pilot on duty in the second element, which encountered eight to ten-tenths cloud in the target area, and although returning crews reported bombing the markers, the raid was scattered and probably ineffective.

The squadron detailed twenty-seven Lancasters on the 16th for another crack at the Vaires marshalling yards, but the raid was cancelled, only to be rescheduled for the morning of the 17th. Seven Lancasters were recorded as taking off at 11.00, to be followed by the remaining twenty between 12.10 and 12.29 with S/Ls Berney and Williamson the senior pilots on duty. Shortly after take-off they were recalled and landed back at Mepal between 13.20 and 15.15, whereupon they were refuelled and told to stand-by for a tactical target, which, in the event, did not materialize until the following dawn.

The tactical target turned out to be five enemy strongholds in the villages of Colombelles, Mondeville, Sannerville, Cagny and Manneville, all situated to the east of Caen and standing in the path of the advancing British 2nd Army, which was about to attack under Operation Goodwood. This was Montgomery's plan for a decisive breakout into wider France as a prelude to the march towards the German frontier. A force of 942 Bomber Command aircraft was made ready and American bombers were also drafted in to add weight to the attacks. Twenty-eight Lancasters stood ready at Mepal on the 18th as the first streaks of light appeared in the eastern skies, and they took off between 04.25 and 04.50 with W/C Leslie the senior pilot on duty supported by S/Ls Berney and Williamson. 3 Group provided 129 Lancasters for three aiming points, with the Mepal element assigned to the village of Cagny, situated five miles south-east of the centre of Caen. All attacks were marked by Oboe and carefully controlled by Master Bombers and were delivered from between 5,000 and 9,000 feet. Two German divisions, the 16th Luftwaffe Field Division and the 21st Panzer (armoured) Division were hit particularly hard, and Bomber Command was responsible for 5,000 of the 6,800 tons of bombs dropped at the five locations. The ground defences were soon overwhelmed, but

HK568 AA-K had a light flak shell explode in the cockpit, causing eye and head wounds to the pilot, F/Sgt David John Moriarty RNZAF. Despite this, the crew completed the attack and the badly injured pilot was able to remain at the controls and bring the Lancaster home to a safe landing. F/Sgt Moriarty was awarded a CGM.

The day's work was not yet done, as more than nine hundred aircraft were involved that night in attacks against synthetic oil refineries at Wesseling and Scholven-Buer, while others went for railway centres at Revigny and Aulnoye. The Revigny raid had already been attempted twice by 1 Group but abandoned because of unfavourable weather conditions in the target area. The Luftwaffe had intercepted both raids and shot down a combined total of seventeen Lancasters. On this night it was left to 5 Group to complete the job, which was accomplished, but at the high price of twenty-four Lancasters, 22% of the force. Meanwhile, 3 Group dispatched 127 Lancasters to the Aulnoye marshalling yards, situated close to the Belgian frontier. 75(NZ) Squadron was represented by twenty-eight Lancasters, which took off between 22.35 and 23.10 with S/Ls Drummond and Williamson the senior pilots on duty. The number included the debutant crews of F/Sgt Cyril Desmond Mulcahy RNZAF and P/O Ian Edward Blance RNZAF. They crossed the French coast at 17,000 feet before descending to between 8,500 and 9,500 feet for the bombing run and aimed their bombs at the well-placed markers under the clear and concise instructions of the Master Bomber. There was little flak activity, but night-fighters were present over the target and on the route home, and on their return, the crew of P/O Kennedy RNZAF in ME751 AA-B reported engagements and claimed to have shot down two unidentified twin-engine night-fighters. LL921 AA-E failed to reappear at Mepal, and it was learned later that it had collided with an attacking night-fighter and crashed four miles south-south-east of Mons in Belgium at 01.20. F/L John Myers RNZAF lost his life, but his crew all baled out and survived, three, including one member of the RNZAF, to evade capture, while three, including another member of the RNZAF, were taken into captivity. This was the first loss of the month from 256 sorties, but sadly, matters were about to turn sour for the Kiwis.

The pressure on Bomber Command was demonstrated on the night of the 20/21st, when more than nine hundred aircraft were involved in attacks associated with three of the four on-going campaigns. Three hundred aircraft were made ready to attack a triangular railway junction at Courtrai, a further three hundred for oil refineries at Bottrop and Homberg in the Ruhr and yet more for V-Weapon sites at Ardouval and Wizernes, while support and minor operations accounted for over two hundred other sorties. 3 Group made ready 128 Lancasters to target the Rheinpreussen (Meerbeck) Bergius process oil refinery on the west bank of the Rhine at Moers/Homberg, opposite Duisburg. 75(NZ) Squadron dispatched twenty-six Lancasters between 23.20 and 23.46 with S/L Drummond the senior pilot on duty and there were no early returns. The force was still intact as it approached the target area in conditions of good visibility, and it was at this point that the first night-fighters arrived on the scene and would then remain in contact all the way to the Dutch coast on the way home. The markers were clearly visible, and the ensuing concentrated bombing fell in and around the refinery, causing at least two large explosions and a column of black smoke that increased in density and altitude as the raid developed. Eight combats were reported, including one by S/L Drummond and crew in HK568 AA-K, whose rear and mid-upper gunners claimed a Me410 as damaged. On return to Mepal, crews were confident of a successful operation, but shocked at the realisation that seven of their number, a total of forty-nine of their colleagues, would not be coming home.

Post-raid reconnaissance and local reports confirmed the effects of the raid, which had caused massive damage to a plant, which, only weeks earlier, had been producing six thousand tons of aviation fuel per day, but was now fluctuating between 120 and 970 tons.

News gradually began to filter through concerning the fate of the missing crews, but there was little to celebrate after it became clear that only eight men had survived. Six of the Lancasters had been shot down over Holland, three on the way out and, perhaps, four on the way home, although this is difficult to confirm. The fate of ND800 AA-J and the crew of F/Sgt Ken Mackay RNZAF, which included three other members of the RNZAF, has never been established. The likelihood is that the Lancaster crashed either into the Ijsselmeer or the North Sea when homebound, and three Luftwaffe night-fighter claims may have been associated with this loss. Two claims refer simply to a four-engine aircraft, one shot down north of Rotterdam from 11,500 feet at 01.50, and the second south-west of Rotterdam at 02.09 when flying at 3,000 feet. The positive claim of a Lancaster kill was of one flying at 10,500 feet near Katwijk-aan-Zee at 02.16, and any one of these could have been ND800. The first from the squadron to go down was PA967 AA-D, which had just crossed the Belgian/Dutch frontier and was approaching Nederweert when it crashed at about 01.12 in open country a couple of miles to the north of the town, south-east of Eindhoven. Oberfähnrich (flight cadet) Gerhard Wartenberger of 4./NJG3 claimed his first ever kill, a Lancaster flying at 17,000 feet south-west of Eindhoven at 01.09, and it seems likely that this was PA967. There were no survivors from the crew of F/Sgt Edward Howell RNZAF, two others of which were members of the RNZAF.

ME752 AA-E was about seven miles beyond Nederweert heading east to the target, when it crashed at Heythuysenat 01.15, killing F/Sgt Gerald Roche RNZAF and four of his crew including two other New Zealanders. Two Kiwis, the bomb-aimer and mid-upper gunner, were the only survivors, the latter ultimately evading capture. The flight engineer, Sgt Joseph Armstrong RAFVR, was forty years of age and among the oldest to be lost on a Bomber Command operation. The details of the crash suggest that the Lancaster had been shot down by Uffz Bruno Rupp of 4./NJG3, who claimed his ninth kill near that location at 17,000 feet at 01.14. HK569 AA-Q crashed into the River Maas near Kessel at 01.25, it is believed while outbound, and just one man survived as a PoW from the crew of F/Sgt Neil Davidson RNZAF, the only Kiwi on board. Oblt Dietrich Schmidt of 8./NJG1 claimed this as his twenty-ninth career victory, after shooting it down from 20,000 feet at 01.16. At 01.33 ME691 AA-R crashed onto farmland clipping the farmhouse, near Veghel further to the north, while making for the Dutch coast, and only the flight engineer survived as a PoW from the crew of W/O Harold Whittington RNZAF, four others of whom were members of the RNZAF. The Lancaster had been shot down by Lt Walter Briegleb of 10./NJG3 when at 11,500 feet near Tilburg and was his thirteenth kill. Just five minutes after this, ND915, now re-coded AA-A, fell two miles away to the south-east, and was probably the victim of Hptm Hermann Greiner of 11./NJG1, who claimed his thirty-sixth kill in the Hertogenbosch/Tilburg area from 15,500 feet at 01.37. W/O Hugh Edward Gilmour RAAF and four of his crew perished, while the two survivors from this predominantly Australian crew joined their colleagues in enemy hands. The rear gunner, Sgt John Leonard Stephenson RAFVR, was just eighteen years old, and in contrast to Sgt Armstrong mentioned above, was one of the youngest to lose his life in service with Bomber Command. Finally, ND752 AA-O "Oboe" crashed at around 01.40 about four miles north of Tilburg when in sight of the Scheldt estuary, killing F/O Henry John Burtt

RNZAF and four of his mixed Commonwealth crew, which contained another Kiwi, an Australian, a Canadian and three members of the RAF. The Australian navigator and Canadian bomb-aimer both survived to be taken prisoner. It was possibly the third career victim of Lt Joseph Förster of 8./NJG2, who claimed a kill at 01.45 in that area at 10,500 feet. *(The details of the Luftwaffe claims come from Theo Boiten's epic book The Nachtjagd War Diaries).*

Even a disaster of this magnitude could not be allowed to disrupt operations, and nineteen crews were put on stand-by for a daylight raid later on the 21st, although nothing came of it. Six crews were sent mining in one of the Silverthorn gardens in the Kattegat on the night of the 22/23rd, departing Mepal shortly after 21.00 and returning safely either side of 05.00 to report successful sorties.

There were no operations for most of the Command on the 22nd, but the 23rd would be busy and generate 1,188 sorties, the bulk of which would be involved in night-time activity. After a two-month break from city busting, Harris had sanctioned a major raid on the naval and ship-building port of Kiel on the 23rd, for which a force of 629 aircraft was made ready. 3 Group put up one hundred Lancasters of which twenty took off from Mepal between 22.39 and 22.50 with S/Ls Berney and Drummond the senior pilots on duty. Imaginative routing and changes of height helped to keep the night-fighters at bay, and a large RCM effort by 100 Group enabled the force to appear suddenly and with total surprise from behind a "Mandrel" screen. There was complete cloud cover over the target, forcing crews to bomb on skymarkers and their own navigational aids, but the attack found the mark anyway, causing damage in all parts of the town, with particular focus in the port area, where the Krupp-Germania and Deutsche Werke ship and U-Boot construction yards and naval facilities were hit. Returning crews reported seeing the glow of fires from the west coast of Denmark as they flew home.

The first of a three-raid series on Stuttgart took place on the night of the 24/25th, for which a force of 614 aircraft had been prepared. 75(NZ) Squadron dispatched twenty-one Lancasters between 21.40 and 22.07 with W/C Leslie the senior pilot on duty and the debutant crews of P/O Terence Cecil May RNZAF and F/Sgt Murray Smith RNZAF on the order of battle. S/L Williamson in HK574 JN-P was forced to turn back with engine trouble and was back on the ground an hour after leaving it. The others pushed on across France and into south-western Germany and arrived in the target area over ten-tenths cloud with tops at 5,000 feet, into which the ground markers disappeared to leave only a dim glow. This compelled the main force crews to bomb on e.t.a., H2S and drifting green skymarkers with yellow stars in accordance with the Master Bomber's instructions. No local report came out of Stuttgart for this night, but it was clearly a successful and destructive raid, although gained at a cost of seventeen Lancasters and four Halifaxes. Some explosions and fires were observed, and it seemed likely that a good proportion of the bombs had found the city. There was no post-raid reconnaissance, and the local report would combine the results from all three attacks. Enemy night-fighters made their presence felt south-east of Paris and contributed to the failure to return of twenty-one aircraft. Mepal was missing two Lancasters, HK568 AA-K, which crashed near Strasbourg, and HK575 AA-O, which, was on its first operation with the squadron and came to earth at around 02.50 in an area of wooded country between Burlioncourt and Chateau-Voue further to the north-west. The timing of the latter suggests that both aircraft were homebound, and there were no survivors from the crews of P/O Keith Whitehouse RNZAF and P/O James McRea RNZAF, which each contained one other member of the RNZAF.

A force of 550 aircraft was made ready for a return to Stuttgart on the following night, and fourteen of the Lancasters belonged to 75(NZ) Squadron. They took off between 21.25 and 21.50 with S/Ls Berney and Drummond the senior pilots on duty and set course for the Channel, where ice-bearing cloud between 7,000 and 15,000 feet contributed to twenty-three early returns, two of them to Mepal. A third Kiwi Lancaster, F/Sgt Smith's HK554 JN-F, became involved in a combat with an enemy night-fighter and jettisoned its bombs after the starboard-inner engine caught fire. The others pressed on to the target through the layer cloud, which provided excellent protection from night-fighters, but this dispersed to leave clear skies over Stuttgart. Most crews were able to identify the target visually, with the TIs clearly evident through the ground haze, but F/L Fox and crew in ND911 JN-V failed to see any markers and brought their bombs home. On the homeward leg, P/O Stott's bomb aimer, F/O Archer, flying as rear gunner in ND917 JN-O, fired at and claimed a Ju88 as damaged. Two aircraft landed at Ford on the south coast, F/O Megson's ND801 JN-X as a result of engine trouble and ND753 (re-coded AA-G) with the crew of F/Sgt Adolph on board, with flak damage to a fuel tank and rear turret. F/Sgt Smith and crew returned to claim a FW190 as destroyed. There was no post-raid reconnaissance, but returning crews reported explosions and large fires in central districts and local reports emerged eventually to confirm that this had been a highly destructive raid, which had devastated the city centre and destroyed most of its remaining cultural and public buildings.

The last of the Stuttgart series was mounted on the night of the 28/29th and involved an all-Lancaster heavy force of 494 aircraft drawn from 1, 3, 5 and 8 Groups, while 307 Halifaxes, Lancasters and Mosquitos from 1, 6 and 8 Groups targeted Hamburg. 75(NZ) Squadron made ready twenty-two Lancasters for the former, which took off between 21.50 and 22.07 with S/L Drummond the senior pilot on duty. In contrast to the previous trip to this location, there was bright moonlight to assist the enemy night-fighters to infiltrate the bomber stream and many bomber crews took advantage of a layer of cloud between 5,000 and 7,000 feet over France to hide themselves. This exposed them to light flak from the ground, which proved to be troublesome, particularly in the area around Orleans as the outward route passed well to the west of Paris. It was near Brou, some fifty miles south-west of Paris, that NE148 AA-H "Howzat!" was shot down, killing F/L Noel Stokes RNZAF and his rear gunner. The remaining members of this highly experienced crew, all but one of whom were members of the RNZAF, survived and evaded capture, and this included second pilot, F/O John Moore Morris RNZAF, who was on board to gain experience. The bombers turned sharply to port at this point to adopt a course slightly north of east to the frontier, and night-fighters began to score heavily all the way from there to the target. S/L Drummond was attacked five times by a Ju88, which failed to cause any damage, and when a second unidentified enemy aircraft attacked, it was shot down in flames and claimed as destroyed, along with another Ju88 that was claimed as damaged.

A thin layer of ten-tenths cloud lay over the target at 8,000 feet, through which the TIs were clearly visible and two distinct areas appeared to be marked about three miles apart. One had undershot the aiming point, while the other one was in the right place, and both attracted bombs from 15,000 feet. Thirty-nine Lancasters failed to return, and 75(NZ) Squadron's second missing aircraft was ND756 AA-M, which crashed at about 01.25 on the eastern bank of the Moselle, some eight miles north-north-west of Nancy, with still eighty miles to go to the German frontier near Strasbourg. P/O Ian Blance RNZAF died with three of his crew including two other members of the RNZAF, while the RNZAF navigator fell into enemy hands and the RAF flight engineer and RNZAF rear gunner evaded a similar fate. They were on only their second operation with the squadron. The Hamburg force had run into heavy night-fighter activity on the way home, and twenty-two aircraft were lost, making this a very expensive night for the Command.

692 crews were roused from their beds early on the 30th for daylight operations against six enemy positions facing mainly American forces in the Villers-Bocage-Caumont area south-west of Caen. Seventeen 75(NZ) Squadron crews were briefed for a target at Amaye-sur-Seulles and took off between 06.00 and 06.20 with F/L Washer the senior pilot on duty. Three were newcomers, P/O Colin Glossop RNZAF, F/O Sam Wilson RAAF and P/O Wilson Orchard Hadley RNZAF. Cloud interfered with four of the attacks, which were based on Oboe ground marking, but it seems that all went according to plan at the 3 Group aiming point, where the bombing was carried out from low level under the precise instructions of a Master Bomber. The attack appeared to achieve concentration, and as intended, crept southwards as the attack developed, but crews saw nothing of the results other than clouds of smoke. Fewer than four hundred aircraft released their bombs because of the conditions, the remainder returning theirs to store, and just four Lancasters failed to return. One of these was HK558 JN-D, which is thought to have collided with another Lancaster over the Channel and was lost without trace with the experienced crew of F/Sgt Colin Nairne RNZAF, whose navigator and rear gunner were also members of the RNZAF. Nairne's commission and promotion to pilot officer rank came through the day after he was lost. The remaining sixteen aircraft were all diverted to Woodbridge due to extremely bad weather conditions at Mepal.

During the course of this busy month, the squadron carried out seventeen operations, dispatching a record 362 sorties for the loss of thirteen Lancasters and crews, the last statistic occurring in the space of just twelve days.

August 1944

The first week of the new month was dominated by operations against flying-bomb sites and targets associated with oil production and storage. 777 aircraft took off on the 1st to attack numerous flying bomb sites, but weather conditions proved to be unhelpful and only seventy-nine aircraft were able to carry out an attack. Sixteen 75(NZ) Squadron Lancasters departed Mepal between 19.00 and 19.13 as part of a 3 Group force assigned to an attack on the constructional works at Le Nieppe five miles to the east of St-Omer. P/O Maurice Edward Dare RNZAF was the debutant and S/L Drummond was the senior pilot on duty as they flew out across the Channel, only to encounter ten-tenths cloud in the target area. The first ten from the squadron to arrive were able to bomb on the smoke trails, before the Master Bomber called a halt to proceedings and sent the rest of the force home.

A similar target at Noyelle-en-Chausee was scheduled for the squadron's attention on the 2nd, but the raid was called off. The weather in the Paris area had improved sufficiently on the 3rd to provide clear skies for an attack on the flying bomb supply dump at L'Isle Adam (Bois-de-Cassan) to the north of the French capital. Twenty Lancasters took off from Mepal as part of a 115-strong 3 Group force, with F/Ls Gunn and Washer the senior pilots on duty, and they contributed to a concentrated and accurate raid. P/O John Rees Layton RNZAF and P/O James Johnson RAFVR and crews flew their first operation with the squadron.

Twenty 75(NZ) Squadron Lancasters were detailed for an operation against another flying bomb site in the Foret-de-Nieppe on the 4th, but this was cancelled in favour of an oil storage facility at Bec d'Ambes, situated on the west bank of the Dordogne River near its separation from the Gironde estuary ten miles north of Bordeaux. A second force of 1 Group Lancasters was assigned to a similar target at Pauillac, on the west bank of the Gironde Estuary, ten miles further north, and both targets were to be marked by 8 Group Lancasters. The plan routed the two forces out over Land's End to fly at 1,000 feet to a point at 06.00°W, continuing south before turning towards the French coast and climbing from 02.00°W to a bombing height of 7,000 to 9,000 feet. The Mepal section took off between 13.20 and 13.50 with F/L Washer the senior pilot on duty and flew out in clear conditions, which persisted all the way to the target. One unidentified crew found itself flying in the 1 Group stream, and went on to bomb at Pauillac, while the others carried out their attacks as briefed, describing on their return many fires and explosions with smoke rising to 10,000 feet. The presence of a fighter escort, provided for the first time by "Serrate" Mosquitos of 100 Group, ensured that the bombers went about their tasks unmolested, while 11 Group Spitfires provided cover for the return trip across the Brest peninsula. All crews arrived safely home between 21.05 and 21.36, highly satisfied with their day's work.

The following day brought a return by eighteen of the Squadron's Lancasters to within five miles of the centre of Bordeaux to attack oil storage facilities at Bassens to the north-east. 1 and 8 Groups were also to be active at Blaye and Pauillac, and this meant a total of 306 Lancasters heading out and adopting a similar route and tactics as twenty-four hours earlier. 100 Group again provided the escorting Mosquitos, while two squadrons of Mustangs patrolled the target area and Spitfires covered the return route over the Brest peninsula. The Mepal element including freshmen F/O Godfree Arnold Brunton RAFVR, F/O Francis Colin Wood RNZAF, F/O Hubert Rees RAFVR, F/Sgt Kenneth William Cooper RAFVR and F/O Thomas Christie Waugh RAFVR, took off between 14.15 and 14.35 with W/C Leslie the senior pilot on duty, and the only departure from the previous day's tactics was a climb to between 15,000 and 17,000 feet for bombing because of the expected heavy flak so close to the port of Bordeaux. Weather conditions were good with five-tenths cloud over the target, and this allowed the crews to identify the aiming point visually. On return they reported a concentrated raid which caused several large explosions and much smoke and commented on there being less flak than had been anticipated.

More than a thousand aircraft were detailed on the 7th for operations in support of ground forces still trying to break out of the Caen area. Seventeen Lancasters were made ready at Mepal as part of a 100-strong 3 Group element and they took off either side of 22.00 with S/L Williamson the senior pilot on duty. Their aiming point was a troop concentration and road communications at Mare-de-Magne (untraced), which was just one of five enemy strongpoints to be attacked. The marking was assisted by a pre-arranged use of searchlight coning, star shells and Bofors tracer to provide a reference for the Path Finder element, and the attack went ahead in clear conditions onto a well-defined target. All of the attacks were closely controlled by a Master Bomber and 360 aircraft brought their bombs home because of uncertainty as to the accuracy of the marking. One of the Mepal contingent had an inconclusive combat, while ten Lancasters were lost, four of them from 3 Group, and among them was HK567 AA-C, which crashed in the target area, almost certainly as the result of an encounter with a night-fighter. On only their second operation with the squadron, F/O Godfree Brunton and all four others in the front of the aircraft, three of whom were members of the RNZAF, parachuted to safety and evaded capture, but both gunners, who were just nineteen years of age, lost their lives.

The target for twenty 75(NZ) Squadron Lancasters on the night of the 8/9th was an oil storage facility behind enemy lines at Lucheux in north-eastern France. This was one of two similar targets assigned to elements of 1 and 3 Groups, both with 8 Group support, for which the Mepal element took off between 22.00 and 22.20 with W/C Leslie and S/L Williamson the senior pilots on duty. They flew out in good conditions to cross the French coast at 17,000 feet, before shedding height quickly and passing through a forest of searchlights to bomb from 12,000 feet. The bombing was concentrated and accurate, and left many fires burning and columns of smoke rising to 9,000 feet as the bombers turned away. There was little flak, but night-fighters were active, three inconclusive combats took place and two Lancasters returned to Mepal bearing minor battle scars. One of those was ND801 JN-X "Get Sum Inn", which had its starboard rudder almost demolished in a collision over the target, F/O Waugh and his mid-upper gunner having exchanged bullets and various other pieces of metal with a Ju88.

More than three hundred Lancasters, Halifaxes and Mosquitos of 1, 3, 6 and 8 Groups were detailed to attack five flying bomb sites on the night of the 9/10th. Four of them were launching sites, while the one at Fort-d'Englos, situated four miles west-south-west of Lille, was described in the group and squadron ORBs respectively as a petrol storage site and army fuel depot. The details mattered little to the seventeen crews departing Mepal between 22.00 and 22.10 with no pilots on duty above flying officer rank. Making their debut were F/O Henry Charles 'Harry' Yates RAFVR and crew. Many years later, Yates would write one of the definitive accounts of life on operations at Mepal, "Luck and a Lancaster". The attack was carried out in clear conditions, but the marking was scattered and the instructions from the Master Bomber confusing, which led to poor early bombing. Matters improved somewhat later, and returning crews were able to report a large conflagration, which suggested that the target had been hit.

Railway targets dominated the 11th, for which 459 Lancasters, Halifaxes and Mosquitos of 1, 3, 4 and 8 Groups were assigned to three marshalling yards and a bridge. Twenty-two Lancasters were made ready at Mepal, one piloted by debutant F/Sgt Douglas Arthur Severn King RAFVR, and they took off between 14.15 and 14.31 as part of a 120-strong 3 Group force bound for the yards at Lens in north-eastern France. S/Ls Drummond and Williamson were the senior pilots on duty as they flew out in good weather conditions under a fighter escort and contributed to an accurate and concentrated attack with negligible opposition from the ground and none from the air.

A major night of operations on the 12th would involve more than 1,150 sorties at widely dispersed locations in Germany and France, the largest of which was an experiment to gauge the ability of main force crews to locate and attack an urban target on the strength of their own H2S equipment in the absence of a Path Finder element. The huge volume of operations generated by the four concurrent campaigns, each of which called upon the finite resources of

8 Group, compelled it, in the short term at least, to spread itself more and more thinly. The conclusion of the flying-bomb campaign at the end of the month, together with the end of tactical support for the ground forces, would remove the pressure, and the planned independence of 3 Group through the G-H bombing system from the autumn would solve the problem altogether. In the meantime, however, no one knew what demands might be made of the Command, and it would be useful to see what main force crews could do when left to their own devices and H2S. The target was to be the northern and historic city of Braunschweig (Brunswick), for which a force of 379 aircraft was assembled from all but 8 Group, while a second large operation over Germany involved 297 aircraft to target the Opel motor factory at Rüsselsheim situated two hundred miles south of Braunschweig. The factory had been building heavy trucks for the Wehrmacht until production switched to tanks and aircraft parts in 1942 and was one of Nazi Germany's most important production facilities, despite being a subsidiary of America's General Motors. 75(NZ) Squadron detailed six crews for Braunschweig and a further ten for the Opel works and the two elements took off together between 21.44 and 22.03, with all pilots bound for northern Germany of flying officer rank and F/L Gunn the senior pilot on duty for the southern element. They were well on their way to their respective targets before six other crews departed Mepal to lay mines in the Deodar garden in the Gironde estuary, S/L Drummond leading them away in a seventeen-minute slot from 22.40.

While the above operations were in progress, a "rush job" after midnight called upon the services of 144 crews to attack German troop concentrations and a road junction north of Falaise and south of Caen. S/L Williamson took off at 00.47 as the lone squadron representative and returned safely to report that the bombing appeared to be concentrated around the markers. Post-raid reconnaissance confirmed that the area around the junction was heavily cratered and the roads leading from it mostly blocked. The gardening element also returned safely from uneventful sorties.

The Braunschweig force made landfall on Germany's north-western coast over the Ems estuary and arrived at the target to find ten-tenths cloud with tops at 7,000 feet but good visibility. They established their positions by H2S before delivering their bombs from 16,000 to 19,000 feet from around 00.10 and observed what appeared to be a concentrated attack that caused explosions and fires. In fact, the bombing had been scattered with no point of concentration, and even though extensive damage occurred in central and southern districts, much fell onto outlying communities up to twenty miles to the south. The local flak defence were moderate in intensity, but night-fighters were much in evidence, and their efforts would complete an expensive night for the Command and take a toll of seventeen Lancasters and ten Halifaxes. The performance, generally, confirmed that main force crews were not yet able to perform to the highest standard without a Path Finder presence, although, previous raids on this city during 1944 had also failed to deliver a telling blow.

The Rüsselsheim force crossed France to arrive at the target at the same time as the above raid and found a small amount of thin cloud with haze below. The attack opened punctually with illuminating flares and green TIs, the former rendered more or less ineffective by the haze, while a visual identification of the aiming-point was hindered by the diffused glow from early incendiaries. Green TIs were scattered initially to the north and south until a degree of concentration was eventually achieved and a number of fires developed covering a circular area approximately one-and-a-half miles in diameter. The main force bombing was carried out from around 16,000 to 19,000 feet either side of 00.20, but a detailed assessment was not possible, and the force headed home uncertain as to the outcome and harried by enemy night-fighters. It was left to post-raid reconnaissance to ascertain that a number of buildings had been damaged within the Opel factory complex, but nothing vital to production, and fires had spread through a wood three miles away and adjacent housing estates to the south-east. There were also many bomb craters in open country, confirming that the target would need further attention, and this was a disappointment compounded by the loss of twenty aircraft. One Kiwi Lancaster survived an inconclusive combat with a Ju88, but the squadron's HK564 AA-P did not and crashed at Ouren on the Belgian border with Germany and Luxembourg with no survivors from the crew of P/O Cyril Mulcahy, all of whom, apart from the RAF flight engineer, were members of the RNZAF.

The 14th was devoted to supporting British and Canadian Divisions as they closed in on German forces in the Falaise area. 805 aircraft were made ready and divided among seven aiming points, with the 3 Group element of one hundred Lancasters assigned to Hamel. Twenty-two Lancasters of 75(NZ) Squadron took off either side of 14.00, with P/O John Harold Scott RNZAF and P/O Leslie Arthur Martyn RNZAF on debut and S/L Drummond the senior pilot on duty. All arrived in the target area to find clear weather conditions, which aided the Master Bomber at each aiming point to carefully control proceedings. The Master Bomber at Hamel was described as particularly good, directing the bombing skilfully and with concise instructions. Bombing took place from between 8,000 and 9,000 feet and was seen to be accurate, but smoke and dust from other aiming points began to drift across the target in the later stages, denying three of the Kiwi crews a clear view and they brought their bombs home. Some confusion arose at another aiming point, resulting in bombs falling into a large quarry occupied by Canadian troops. This "friendly fire" incident cost thirteen lives, while a further fifty-three soldiers were wounded, and many guns and vehicles were hit.

With his primary responsibility to SHAEF now fulfilled, Harris could start directing more of his resources towards industrial Germany, whilst remaining on hand to support the ground forces as required, particularly in their quest to recapture the German-held ports of France and Belgium. In preparation for his new night offensive against Germany, Harris dispatched a thousand aircraft during daylight on the 15th to bomb nine night-fighter airfields in Holland and Belgium. 3 Group contributed one hundred Lancasters to the attack on St Trond in Belgium and nineteen of them departed Mepal either side of 10.00 with S/Ls Drummond and Williamson the senior pilots on duty. The weather conditions were ideal as the bombing took place from 17,000 feet in a perfectly executed, unopposed attack, and all 3 Group aircraft returned safely to their home stations, where their crews reported observing the bombs to impact the runways. The other aiming points were also bombed accurately, and it remained to be seen what effect this effort would have on night-fighter operations over the ensuing weeks.

F/Ls Roy Earl and Garth Gunn were installed on the 16th as A and B Flight commanders respectively, and the latter had acting squadron leader rank bestowed upon him immediately. For whatever reason, F/L Earl's acting promotion would not be officially recognised until the 10th of November, and he would continue until then in the rank of flight lieutenant. However, for the purpose of this account and to confirm in the mind of the reader his status as A Flight commander, he will be referred to as S/L Earl.

The new assault on Germany began that night, when Stettin and Kiel were posted as the targets for forces of 461 and 348 aircraft respectively. 3 Group detailed ninety-seven Lancasters for the former, of which twenty-three were made ready at Mepal. They took off between 21.00 and 21.17 with S/Ls Earl and Gunn the senior pilots on duty, but F/O White was forced to return early as a victim of icing. The others continued on at around 1,000 feet to remain under the enemy radar and reached the target area, situated on the main waterway some thirty miles south of the Baltic coast at Swinemünde, to find seven-tenths cloud between 15,000 and 20,000 feet. This impaired the marking to some extent, causing the TIs to become scattered, and the Master Bomber's performance was criticised for failing to communicate clearly his order to the crews to bomb from 14,000 feet. On the way back, F/O Layton and crew in ND782 AA-U were attacked by a Ju88 from the starboard beam, but took evasive action and opened fire, the rear gunner claiming the attacker as damaged. Three areas of fire were reported by returning crews, who were unaware initially of the extent of the damage that they had inflicted on this port-city, which never seemed to escape heavy punishment at the hands of Bomber Command. Fifteen hundred houses and twenty-nine factories were destroyed, and a thousand houses and twenty-six factories seriously damaged. In the port area five ships were sunk and a further eight damaged, and 1,150 people lost their lives. The raid on Kiel was moderately successful, and inflicted severe damage in the port area, but much of the bombing also fell outside of the town.

Bremen was posted as the target on the 18th, for which a relatively small heavy force of 281 Lancasters and Halifaxes was made ready, with seven Mosquitos to deliver the initial markers. 3 Group provided 120 of the Lancasters with twenty-five taking off from Mepal between 21.28 and 21.58, led by S/L Williamson. F/Sgt Moore and crew were back in the circuit shortly after midnight for an unspecified reason, leaving the others to press on to a city, which, for the first three years of war, had been one of the Command's most frequently-visited destinations, but had been left in peace by the heavy brigade for a considerable time. The attack took place in clear conditions, which the main force crews exploited to leave the city burning fiercely and smoke rising to 13,000 feet. One inconclusive combat was reported by a Kiwi crew, but the most effective opposition came from flak between the German coast and the target, and three aircraft returned to Mepal bearing the scars. A reconnaissance Mosquito over Bremen at 01.05 reported an area of intense and unbroken fire covering 4 x 1½ miles with black smoke rising through 23,000 feet. It was confirmed later that the 1,100 tons of bombs had devastated central and north-western districts, including the docks, destroying 8,635 "dwelling houses", mostly in the form of apartment blocks and too many industrial units to count, while sinking eighteen ships in the harbour. The death toll probably exceeded eleven hundred people, and this was the start of a torrid time for Germany's cities, which would last until war's end, as Bomber Command grew in strength and Germany's ability to defend itself waned.

It was on this day, that G/C John "Speedy" Powell DSO DFC OBE, whose association with 75(NZ) Squadron is well documented, lost his life while flying in a Beaufighter of 19 Squadron SAAF in the Balkan theatre.

The heavy squadrons spent the greater part of the ensuing week away from the operational scene, as a number of attacks on Stettin were posted then cancelled because of the weather. Major operations resumed on the 25th, when preparations were put in hand to make ready more than nine hundred aircraft to launch against three major targets, while four hundred others would be engaged in a variety of smaller endeavours. The largest operation was to be the all-Lancaster affair involving 412 aircraft from 1, 3, 6 and 8 Groups in a return to the Opel tank works at Rüsselsheim, while 334 others attended to eight coastal batteries between Brest and the islands to the south of Lorient, leaving 5 Group to focus on Darmstadt, a university city renowned as a centre of scientific research and development, and one of a few almost virgin targets considered to be worthy of attention. 75(NZ) Squadron contributed twenty-eight of 3 Group's 130 Lancasters and they departed Mepal between 20.22 and 20.57 with S/L Williamson the senior pilot on duty and F/O Jack Plummer RNZAF and crew operating for the first time. They adopted the familiar route across France and clear conditions awaited them as they ran in on the TIs from 20,000 feet. One of the squadron's crews was unable to identify the target and jettisoned their bombs, while HK554 JN-F was caught in searchlights, and not only dumped its bomb load during violent evasive action, but also had both ailerons fly off into the night. F/Sgt O'Callaghan maintained control, and the navigator managed to keep the Lancaster on track for the return journey, despite the failure of his instruments and having lost his charts. The others contributed to a successful attack based on accurate marking, and returning crews reported many fires and oily smoke rising through 14,000 feet as they turned away.

It was established later that the forge and gearbox assembly shop had been put out of action for several weeks, but the assembly line was operating again within days, and production was barely affected because of a stockpile of ready-made components. Enemy fighters were in evidence and F/Sgt Moore and crew in HK593 AA-H were involved in an inconclusive combat on the way to the target, during which the rear and mid-upper gunners drove off a single-engine aircraft that had attacked twice. Fifteen Lancasters failed to return and two from Mepal were conspicuous by their absence. LL866 AA-S crashed somewhere near the target, killing P/O Richard Barker RNZAF and his crew, which included two other members of the RNZAF. F/O James Fleming RNZAF and his crew also failed to survive, and their burial in the Reichswald Cemetery may indicate that LM593 AA-N came down much further north, but this is speculation. The navigator was the only other member of the RNZAF on board.

Kiel was the target for 372 Lancasters and ten Mosquitos of 1, 3 and 8 Groups on the following night, for which 75(NZ) Squadron made ready twenty aircraft as part of a 3 Group contribution of 124. The crew of F/Sgt Patrick Leo McCartin RAAF was on debut as the Mepal element took off between 20.01 and 20.30 with W/C Leslie the senior pilot on duty and flew out over the North Sea at below 2,000 feet until reaching 05.00ºE, where they began to climb in the clear skies to between 17,000 and 19,000 feet for the passage across the Schleswig-Holstein peninsula. The ground in the target area was concealed by haze, but the markers stood out clearly and a concentrated attack ensued in the face of a moderate heavy flak barrage. Over the target, F/L Andrew's LM544 JN-Y was hit in the fuselage and mid-upper turret, causing serious leg injuries to the occupant, Sgt Molony RAF, but this was the only damage sustained by the squadron. Night-fighter activity was not mentioned particularly, but F/Sgt Smith in PB418 AA-C was involved in an inconclusive combat with a FW190. Returning crews reported witnessing accurate bombing, which hit the town centre and surrounding districts, where a strong wind helped to spread the fires.

The final operations against V-1 launching and storage sites were mounted on the 28th, when 150 aircraft carried out twelve small-scale attacks in the absence of a 3 Group participation. The Pas-de-Calais region would return to Allied hands within a matter of days.

Stettin was earmarked for its second visit of the month on the 29th, for which a force of 402 Lancasters and a single Mosquito of 1, 3, 6 and 8 Groups was assembled. 3 Group put up eighty-eight Lancasters, including fourteen representing 75(NZ) Squadron, while a further six Lancasters at Mepal were loaded with mines to deliver into the Privet and Spinach gardens in the Gulf of Danzig under cover of the main operation. The gardeners took off at 20.15 led by S/L Williamson, and it was fifty-five minutes later before the bombers began to take to the air in a twenty-minute slot with S/Ls Earl and Gunn the senior pilots on duty. They flew out over cloud for most of the way to the target, and the presence of night-fighters was felt by three of the squadron's crews, two of which were involved in inconclusive encounters, while F/O Scott and crew in HK601 JN-D would claim a Ju88 as probably destroyed, after it had carried out four attacks against them. The skies were clear by the time the target hove into view and the TIs were bombed visually from between 15,000 and 18,000 feet. It was another highly successful operation which destroyed 1,569 houses and thirty-two industrial premises, sank a 2,000-ton vessel in the harbour and damaged seven others. The death toll was again high and amounted to 1,033 people. Twenty-three Lancasters failed to return, and among them was HK594 AA-G containing the crew of F/Sgt Douglas King, in which the navigator and bomb-aimer were members of the RNZAF. The rear gunner had been killed in an attack by a night-fighter, and damage to the tail rendered the aircraft uncontrollable, compelling the pilot to order the rest of the crew to bale out. All five landed in the Baltic Sea and failed to survive, but by the time that F/Sgt King left the aircraft, he was over land. He came to earth on Swedish territory in a badly injured state and was eventually repatriated by the Swedish authorities.

Although the V-1 threat had been largely nullified, the V-2 menace was very much in the minds of the British authorities and a force of 601 aircraft was assembled on the 31st to attack nine sites in Northern France, where the Germans were believed to be storing the weapon. 3 Group made available a hundred Lancasters, eighteen of them at Mepal, to attack a site at Pont-Remy, situated four miles south-east of Abbeville. Three were debutant crews, those of F/O Terrence Arthur Ford RAFVR, F/O J. H. Winter RAFVR and F/Sgt Donald Francis Atkin RAFVR, and they took off with the others between 16.09 and 16.30 with S/Ls Earl, Gunn and Williamson the senior pilots on duty. They reached the target area to find cloud partially obscuring the markers and most crews had to orbit the aiming point two or three times before drawing a bead on it, and this led to scattered bombing. On the run up to the target, F/O Aitken's PB427 AA-U was hit eight times by flak and tiny shards of Perspex inflicted serious facial injuries on the bomb-aimer, F/O Ronald Desmond Mayhill RNZAF, and left him temporarily blinded in one eye. Mayhill insisted that the bombing run continue, and after dropping their load successfully, they returned safely to base, where Mayhill was hospitalised and awarded an immediate DFC. Years later Ron Mayhill would write a brilliant account of the squadron's Lancaster era, "Bombs on Target". The expectation of success was not high among returning crews, but there were reports of a large explosion followed by a column of black smoke.

During the course of the month the squadron carried out twenty-one operations and dispatched 348 sorties for the loss of five Lancasters and crews.

September 1944

The destructive power of the Command was now almost beyond belief with each of its heavy bomber groups capable of laying waste to a German city at one go, and from now until the end of the war, this would be demonstrated in awesome and horrific fashion. Much of the Command's effort during the new month, however, would be directed towards the liberation of the three French ports remaining in enemy hands, Le Havre, Boulogne and Calais. However, oil and railways would continue to occupy elements of the Command, and when the opportunities presented themselves, urban targets in Germany also. Seventeen Lancasters stood ready at Mepal on the 1st for an operation against Dieppe, but this was cancelled when news came through that Canadian forces had entered the town. Operations against six airfields in southern Holland, which had been cancelled because of the weather on the 2nd, were mounted on the 3rd by 675 aircraft. 75(NZ) Squadron contributed ten of fifty 3 Group Lancasters assigned to Eindhoven, and they departed Mepal between 15.35 and 15.50 with no pilots above flying officer rank and two crews on debut, those of F/O Louis Thomas Friedrich RNZAF and F/Sgt Leonard Boyer RAFVR. The attack took place from 6,000 feet through five-tenths cloud onto well-placed markers and returning crews reported a successful outcome, although three came back with minor flak damage.

A concerted effort was made between the 5th and the 11th to dislodge the enemy from strongpoints around Le Havre, and twenty-five Lancasters were made ready at Mepal on the 5th, after eighteen crews had been briefed initially for a raid on Dortmund for the opening round of a new Ruhr offensive. Four were debutants, F/Sgt Alan Russell Galletly RNZAF, F/L Alan Cheyne Baxter RNZAF, F/O David Antill Gawith RNZAF and F/Sgt Ronald Gordon RAFVR. They took off between 17.10 and 17.45 as part of an overall force of 348 aircraft with S/L Earl the senior pilot on duty and all reached the target to find excellent weather conditions, which enabled the crews to bomb visually. There was little opposition and a great concentration of bombs, estimated to be 90% of those dropped, fell onto the aiming point.

On the following day, twenty-four Lancasters were made ready at Mepal to return to Le Havre as part of a 3 Group attack on the German Army HQ. A further four of this number were newcomers, all RNZAF, F/Sgt William John Farr, F/O Edmund Frederick Robertson, F/O Robert Gordon Cuming and F/O Keith Southward. They took off between 15.38 and 16.04 with F/Ls Baxter and Brumwell the senior pilots on duty and reached the target area to find fires still burning in the town from the previous day. In contrast to the clear conditions then, they encountered a layer of rain cloud between 7,000 and 8,000 feet and came below it on the instructions of the Master Bomber to carry out the bombing, which was highly accurate and unopposed.

The final four Stirlings to perform as bombers in Bomber Command service belonged to 149 Squadron and were among 120 aircraft made ready on 3 Group stations on the 8th, while their crews were roused early from their beds to participate in a two-wave attack on enemy defensive positions at Doudeville, situated some thirty miles to the north-east of Le Havre. Twenty-three Lancasters departed Mepal between 06.05 and 06.30 with F/Ls Andrew, Baxter, Brown and Kennedy the senior pilots on duty and those in the first wave found cloud with a base at 3,000 feet. This created considerable difficulty in identifying the aiming point, and with the close proximity of Allied troops in mind, it was decided to abandon this part of the attack. The second wave found more favourable conditions and in the early stages at least, delivered their bombs from 4,000 feet onto easily-identified markers. As the bombing began to overshoot late on, however, the Master Bomber called a halt and thirteen 75(NZ) Squadron crews brought their bombs home. At debriefing they reported that considerable light flak and machine gun fire had been encountered in the target area.

3 Group was not involved in the operations against Le Havre on the 9th, which were abandoned by the Master Bomber because of poor visibility. On the 10th, the squadron was briefed for an attack on a position at Montivilliers, situated five miles to the north-east of the port, and this was just one of eight German strong-points occupying the attention of 992 aircraft during the afternoon and evening. The aiming-points were given the names of car manufacturers, Buick 1 and 2, Alvis 1, 2, 3 and 4 and Bentley 1 and 2. Twenty-seven Lancasters were dispatched from Mepal between 15.16 and 15.37 with F/Ls Andrew, Baxter, Kennedy and Waugh the senior pilots on duty and they found ideal bombing conditions in the target area with negligible opposition. A highly concentrated attack was delivered, and there was not a single missing aircraft from any of the sites attacked. The final operations in this campaign were carried out on the following day and shortly afterwards the German garrison surrendered to the two advancing British divisions.

3 Group did not take part in the final act at Le Havre on the 11th but made ready one hundred Lancasters to join 279 other aircraft to attack synthetic oil plants at Castrop-Rauxel, Bergkamen and Gelsenkirchen in the Ruhr. 75(NZ) Squadron contributed fifteen Lancasters to the Chemwerke-Steinkohle refinery at Bergkamen on the north-eastern rim of the Ruhr and they took off between 15.58 and 16.40 with S/L Gunn the senior pilot on duty. They flew out in formation to join up with the others, shepherded all the way to the target by a fighter escort of twenty Spitfire, three Mustang and three Tempest squadrons. They found the target in excellent weather conditions and many crews were able to pick out ground detail as they approached in pairs, line astern. The markers were well-placed and clearly visible and the highly successful attack, carried out in accordance with the Master Bomber's instructions, left clouds of black smoke rising to 15,000 feet as the bombers withdrew. Two crew members required medical treatment on return, pilot, F/O Harry Yates, with injuries to his right eye from Perspex splinters, and navigator, F/O Topping (Brown crew), with a compound fracture to the forearm from a flak splinter. After a flak burst had sent splinters through his cockpit, F/O Yates had been forced to fly his aircraft back to base with most of its nose and front cockpit windscreen missing, which necessitated two hours with a freezing gale blasting his bloody face.

That night, while 5 Group was laying waste to Darmstadt, killing in excess of twelve thousand people and rendering seventy thousand others homeless, an extensive mining operation was mounted in the Silverthorn gardens in the Kattegat, for which the squadron made ready eight Lancasters. They took off shortly after 19.30 with all pilots of flying officer rank and reached the target area to deliver their mines in good conditions and completely unopposed. There was some night-fighter activity as they headed home and F/O Winter in ND747 AA-T reported an encounter with a Ju88. LM268 AA-D failed to arrive back at Mepal with the crew of F/O Wilson Hadley RNZAF and it was established later that they had crashed at 00.15 at Ørslev on the south-western corner of Denmark's Zealand Island. Two men had survived, the RAF flight engineer and the bomb-aimer, who like the rest of the crew, was a member of the RNZAF. The former evaded capture, while the latter fell into enemy hands and became a PoW. Sadly, five members of a family were killed when the Lancaster crashed onto a farmhouse.

On the following night the southern cities of Frankfurt and Stuttgart were posted as the targets for forces of 378 and 204 aircraft respectively, the former of 1, 3 and 8 Groups and the latter predominantly of 5 Group. 3 Group put up 119 Lancasters, of which twenty represented 75(NZ) Squadron and took off between 18.37 and 18.55 with F/Ls Baxter, Kennedy and Waugh the senior pilots on duty. They all reached the target area, where good conditions prevailed, but they had run the gauntlet of night-fighters from 6°E and would do so again on the return journey. There were many searchlights around the target, supported by heavy flak, but this was not overly troublesome as the crews picked out ground detail such as the River Main and the railway yards as they crossed the aiming point at 17,000 feet. The first markers had fallen towards the south-west, but this was soon corrected by the Master Bomber and the main weight of bombs then fell into the more-industrialized western districts. Fires began to spread rapidly and it was clear to the crews that a successful raid had taken place. This would be the last major raid of the war on Frankfurt, and it cost seventeen Lancasters, although none from Mepal. F/O Bateman and crew in LM266 AA-A "Seven Sinners" claimed a twin-engine enemy night-fighter as destroyed, and F/O Winter flying ND747 AA-T reported an inconclusive combat.

There were no operations on the 13th, but Mepal held its inaugural Sports Day, a great success, which raised money for the PoW Fund and G/C Campbell presented prizes at the conclusion. The outstanding performance of the day was a long jump by F/Sgt Bill Kereama (wireless operator in the Baxter crew) of 19 feet and 2 inches! Among those attending were AVM Harrison, A-O-C 3 Group and G/C Heard, Station Commander at RAF Waterbeach.

Ten crews were called to the Mepal briefing room on the morning of the 14th, where they learned that they were to attack a suspected V-2 storage site at Wassenaar near the Dutch capital, The Hague. 3 Group provided the thirty-strong main force and 8 Group the ten Mosquito markers and the Kiwi element set off either side of 13.00 for the relatively short trip across the North Sea. There were no senior pilots taking part as they arrived in the target area in good conditions and bombed the markers, and there was little for returning crews to report.

With Operation Market Garden about to be launched, Bomber Command prepared to support it with attacks against communications targets during the night of the 16/17th. A dozen Lancasters were made ready at Mepal to join others from 3 and 8 Groups to target the railway bridge across the Hollandsch Diep at Moerdijk in southern Holland. They took off either side of 21.30 with S/L Gunn the senior pilot on duty and found the precision target in favourable weather conditions. They released their bombs from 9,000 feet and photographic reconnaissance revealed later that the bridge had been hit and severed.

The entry in the squadron ORB for the 17th stated that "We celebrated Battle of Britain Sunday by carrying out two operations." With Le Havre safely back in Allied hands and the work to make it useable progressing, attention turned upon Boulogne, for which a force of 762 aircraft was made ready on the 17th. 75(NZ) Squadron contributed fourteen Lancasters, which began taking off shortly after 10.00 with S/L Gunn the senior pilot on duty. The one hundred 3 Group aircraft were divided between two aiming points, the first of which was attacked from below the cloud base at 3,500 feet and was called off by the Master Bomber as the initial bombing became scattered. It is assumed that the second aiming point was also attacked from low level, as the light flak was described as troublesome. Returning crews reported that they had been able to identify landmarks and described the bombing as accurate. PB430 AA-P was severely damaged by light flak and struggled back across the Channel with both starboard engines feathered. S/L Gunn put it down at 11.45 on the fighter airfield at Hawkinge, three miles inland from Folkestone, but the Lancaster soon ran off the end of the short runway and crashed. The RAF flight engineer, Sgt John Henry Bruce RAFVR was killed on impact, while S/L Garth Gunn RNZAF and his bomb-aimer, F/O Angus Moorcroft Millar RNZAF, were taken to Kent and Canterbury hospital with life-threatening injuries, to which S/L Gunn succumbed four days later. The attacks on German positions around Boulogne, during which three thousand tons of bombs were dropped, had the desired effect and the garrison surrendered shortly afterwards.

That night, 3 Group contributed forty Lancasters to diversionary operations in support of Operation Market Garden and ten were provided by Mepal. They took off between 19.23 and 19.37 with S/L Earl the senior pilot on duty and Emmerich, situated on the German bank of the Rhine, as their destination. All reached and bombed the target, which, because of its oil storage facilities, was well-defended by light flak, and all returned safely with little to report.

Acting F/L John Robert "Bob" Rodgers was posted in from Waterbeach to succeed S/L Gunn as B Flight commander and had acting squadron leader rank bestowed upon him immediately. He brought with him an outstanding reputation as an operational pilot and captain, his skill and devotion to duty having seen him rise quickly through the ranks. He had arrived in the UK from New Zealand in March 1942 and after completing his training, joined 115 Squadron at Mildenhall, where he undertook twenty-two sorties on Wellingtons, before being seconded in late February 1943 to 105 Squadron to instruct its crews on the Gee navigation system. By the time he returned to 115 Squadron, it had moved to East Wretham and converted to Mk II Lancasters, enabling him to carry out his twenty-third sortie, an attack on Berlin at the end of March, as a Lancaster captain for the first time. His first tour ended on the 12th of May after completing thirty sorties, upon which he was posted to a Lancaster Conversion Unit at Waterbeach.

S/L Rodgers arrived at Mepal in time to participate in the campaign to liberate the port of Calais, and his name was on the order of battle along with that of S/L Williamson for the opening salvo, which was mounted on the afternoon of the 20th. The battle order included five other debutants, F/Sgt Henry Tweed RAFVR, F/Sgt Norman McLeod McRitchie RNZAF, F/O Charles Thomas Spain RAFVR, F/Sgt Roy Alvin Osborne RAFVR and F/O James Alexander McIntosh RNZAF. Twenty-seven Lancasters were made ready at Mepal as part of an overall force of 646 aircraft, which were assigned to five aiming points, three of them to receive two visits. The Kiwi element took off between 14.29 and 14.52 with the 3 Group squadrons, and presumably, those from the other groups also, flying out in formation in excellent weather conditions. The bombing was carried out entirely according to plan from 2,500 feet and suffered the loss of a single Lancaster belonging to 514 Squadron.

Before the next attack was mounted against Calais, a major operation was scheduled for the night of the 23/24th to the city of Neuss, which faced Düsseldorf across the Rhine in the southern Ruhr. 75(NZ) Squadron made ready twenty-six Lancasters in a 3 Group contingent of 159, whose crews were briefed to bomb the marshalling yards, while others in the 549-strong 1, 3, 4 and 8 Group overall force went for the industrial and inland docks areas. The Mepal element took off between 19.20 and 19.45 with S/Ls Earl and Rodgers the senior pilots on duty and all but one reached the target area to encounter ten-tenths cloud with tops at between 10,000 and 12,000 feet. The group ORB states that crews bombed from 20,000 feet, aiming at the glow of TIs through the cloud, but the squadron Form 540 describes most crews as bombing from below the cloud base, where explosions and flashes were observed but no detailed assessment could be made. F/L Brown had been forced to turn back after the electrical system in his Lancaster failed completely, and another crew suffered a technical failure on the way home and landed at Woodbridge in Suffolk as a precaution.

The attacks on Calais resumed on the 24th as the poor weather continued, but 75(NZ) Squadron was not involved on this day. The campaign intensified on the 25th, when 872 aircraft were made ready for a morning assault on enemy positions, for which the squadron bombed up twenty-seven Lancasters, including LM266 AA-A "Seven Sinners", piloted by debutant W/O Jeffery Baines RNZAF. They departed Mepal between 08.15 and 08.33 with F/Ls Andrew, Baxter and Brown the senior pilots on duty and encountered a layer of cloud at between 1,000 and 2,000 feet, which made it impossible to bomb from above because of an inability to see the ground, or from below because of the danger from the lethal light flak batteries. The Master Bomber had no option but to abandon the attack and all bombs were brought home. The following day brought the coastal batteries further down the coast at Cap Gris Nez into the bomb sights of a proportion of the 722 aircraft involved, while others went for enemy strongpoints closer to Calais. The squadron made ready eighteen Lancasters, which took off for the former between 11.40 and 12.06, with no pilots on duty above flying officer rank. They all reached the target area to deliver their attacks from low-level without opposition and returned safely to report a successful excursion.

1, 3, 4 and 8 Groups joined forces to put together a force of 341 Lancasters and Halifaxes on the 27th, 120 of the former provided by 3 Group divided 40/80 between the two aiming points. The fourteen 75(NZ) Squadron Lancasters took off either side of 07.30 with S/L Rodgers the senior pilot on duty and all reached the target, where the Master Bomber brought them down to 5,000 feet. Crews were able to bomb visually under his instructions and the attacks at both aiming points were concluded successfully. The final operations against enemy positions around Calais took place on the 28th, when four were earmarked for attention, while six coastal batteries at Cap Gris Nez occupied the remainder of the 494 participating aircraft. 3 Group detailed eighty Lancasters split equally between the two aiming points, for which the Mepal element of twelve Lancasters took off between 07.47 and 08.02 with S/L Earl the senior pilot on duty. F/O McIntosh's HK601 JN-D developed a technical problem shortly after take-off and had to be put down on the emergency strip at Woodbridge, leaving the others to push on to the target area, where the weather continued to be unhelpful and just one crew managed to find a gap in the clouds through which to drop their bombs. The remainder circled the target for a considerable time before the Master Bomber sent them home with their bombs still on board. Canadian ground forces moved in shortly afterwards to accept the surrender of the German garrison, and thus all of the Channel ports were now back in Allied hands.

The station had a rude awakening at 05.30 on the morning of the 29th when a V1 flying bomb passed over the A Flight dispersals and exploded in the Fens at Sutton Galt about a mile away, without causing any damage. The squadron operated for the final time in this busy month on the night of the 29/30th, when sending five Lancasters to the Baltic to deliver mines into one of the Silverthorn gardens in the Kattegat. They took off between 23.39 and 23.46, all with pilots of flying officer rank and reached the target area to find challenging weather conditions, which four crews were able to overcome to complete their sorties as briefed, while one returned their mines to store.

During the course of the month the squadron operated on nineteen occasions, despatching 327 sorties for the loss of two Lancasters, one complete crew and one pilot and flight engineer. The month was also notable for the arrival of the squadron's first 12,000lb HC bombs. High explosive bombs were categorised medium capacity or high capacity according to the charge to case weight ratio. High capacity bombs, like the 4,000lb cookie and the 12,000 pounder that had been introduced to operations by 617 Squadron for canal-busting in September 1943, contained a maximum charge weight in a light casing to create a massive blast, while the Barnes Wallis designed 12,000lb Tallboy medium capacity earthquake bomb contained a smaller charge in a thick steel case that was able to withstand the impact as it penetrated earth and concrete.

October 1944

The squadron began the new month with ten crews on stand-by on the 1st and the 2nd to assist ground forces, but they were not required. During the previous month, preparations had been put in hand to capture the heavily-defended island of Walcheren in the Scheldt estuary, which was barring the approaches to the much-needed port of Antwerp. The coastal battery at Domburg had been the main target, but it had been decided now to attack the sea wall at Westkapelle, and allow the sea to inundate the land to make it difficult to defend when the ground forces went in. A force of 252 Lancasters and seven Mosquitos was made ready on the 3rd, and these included 120 of the former belonging to 3 Group and an element from 617 Squadron carrying Tallboys for use if necessary. The plan called for eight waves of thirty bombers each to attack the walls, and twenty-one Lancasters of 75(NZ) Squadron took off in two sections, the first departing shortly before 11.30 led by S/L Earl and the second thirty minutes later with S/Ls Rodgers and Williamson the senior pilots on duty. They found cloud in the target area with a base at 3,000 to 4,000 feet and some crews had to make several attempts before releasing their bombs from 5,000 feet under the instructions of a Master Bomber. The first breach occurred during the fifth wave and subsequent attacks widened it to more than a hundred yards to leave flood water encroaching into the town of Westkapelle as the last crews retreated westwards. One Kiwi crew was unable to release their bombs because of a technical fault and returned them to store.

The mining of northern waters continued on the night of the 4/5th, when the squadron contributed five Lancasters to gardening duties in the Kattegat. F/L Baxter was the senior pilot on duty as they departed Mepal at around 17.00 and all returned safely between midnight and 01.00 to report successful and uneventful sorties. Saarbrücken had been left in relative peace for two years until the advancing American Third Army requested it be attacked, with the aim of cutting the railway and blocking enemy supply routes. A heavy force of 531 Lancasters from 1, 3 and 8 Groups was assembled on the 5th and included a new record thirty-one Lancasters provided by 75(NZ) Squadron. They took off between 17.07 and 17.37 with W/C

Leslie the senior pilot on duty, supported by S/Ls Earl and Rodgers and were part of a 184-strong 3 Group element divided between the marshalling yards and the town on a 121/63 split. The Master Bomber and Deputy were unable to agree on which markers to aim for at the former, and that part of the operation was abandoned after only half of the force had bombed. The attack on the town, however, which took place through three-tenths cloud, went very much according to plan and the main town area north of the River Saar sustained massive damage. Fortunately, the railway lines passed through this area and were cut. Local reports gave a figure of 5,882 houses destroyed with a further 1,140 seriously damaged and 344 fatalities, a modest figure in view of the level of destruction, and the likelihood is that the town's close proximity to the Siegfried Line had already prompted most of the residents to evacuate. P/O Ford's crew in PB132 AA-Y had a brief, inconclusive combat, but ND904, by now re-coded as AA-B, failed to return with the crew of F/Sgt Alan Galletly RNZAF. It was established later that the Lancaster had collided with PD344 KO-M of 115 Squadron over Wolsfeld and both had crashed within sight of the Luxembourg border with total loss of life. By curious coincidence, ND904 had previously flown with 115 Squadron under the code KO-M. The navigator, F/Sgt Stuart Edwin Mosley, was the only other member of the RNZAF on board.

On the following day, F/L John Mathers Bailey DFC, RNZAF arrived from 31 Base as the successor to S/L Williamson as C Flight commander and he would be granted acting squadron leader rank. S/L "Jack" or "Paddy" Bailey's first tour with the squadron had been as a sergeant pilot between the 9th of September 1942 and the 9th of May 1943, operating first on Wellingtons before converting to Stirlings in November. His wireless operator at that time had been Sgt Bruce Hosie RNZAF, who was currently serving in the rank of flying officer with 617 Squadron at Woodhall Spa. Jack Bailey was commissioned in December 1942, and at the conclusion of his first tour was posted to 1665 Conversion unit for instructional duties, before the short spell at 31 Base preceded his posting to Mepal.

On the night of his arrival, Dortmund was selected to host the opening round of a new Ruhr campaign, which would prove to be even more devastating than the first. A heavy force of 495 Lancasters and Halifaxes representing 3, 6 and 8 Groups included 171 of the former provided by 3 Group, of which twenty-eight belonged to 75(NZ) Squadron. A simultaneous operation by 5 Group would be directed for the final time at Bremen, which had already endured thirty-one major raids. There was just one debutant crew, that of F/Sgt James Alexander Elmslie RNZAF among the Mepal gang as they took off between 16.20 and 17.10 with F/Ls Andrew, Baxter and Brown the senior pilots on duty. After F/O May in HK563 JN-W "Paper Doll" had returned early to Woodbridge with technical problems, the remainder reached the target to find clear weather conditions and well-placed markers, which were bombed in concentrated fashion from 18,000 feet to produce explosions and many fires. The flak was less intense than expected, with shells seen to explode well below the level of the bombers, and night-fighters were few, although F/Sgt Farr and crew in NF935 AA-P were attacked a number of times and claimed to have shot down one of their assailants. Farr was another pilot to suffer an eye injury from Perspex splinters, his left eye requiring specialist treatment and time off operations. Just five aircraft failed to return, and among them was the squadron's LM104 JN-K, which was hit by flak while passing through the well-known defensive belt south-west of Mönchengladbach. Flying at 22,000 feet it was unlucky to be brought down, but all except the pilot, F/O Keith Southward RNZAF, survived to fall into enemy hands. The navigator and bomb-aimer were the other two members of the RNZAF on board. Post-raid reconnaissance revealed heavy damage in industrial and residential districts and to transportation.

The history of 75(NZ) Squadron from this point is as much a history of the resurgence of 3 Group as a major force, having, at last, fully converted to the Lancaster. Each Group was now capable of finding and destroying a target independently and 3 Group would be employing the G-H blind bombing device to great effect, mostly by daylight, but also at night, and with particular emphasis on railway and oil related targets. Allied forces advancing on the Rhine near the Dutch frontier were under threat from enemy forces following the failure of Operation Market Garden. The towns of Cleves (Kleve) and Emmerich stood about four miles apart on opposite sides of the river on the approach routes and were earmarked for destruction by daylight on the 7th. 3 Group contributed 153 Lancasters to the two operations, eighty to join elements of 4 and 8 Groups at Cleves, and seventy-five as part of a 340-strong 1, 3 and 8 Group force assigned to Emmerich. The Mepal brigade of twenty-six Lancasters took off for the latter between 12.04 and 12.30 with S/Ls Rodgers and Williamson the senior pilots on duty, and all reached the target area, where clear conditions prevailed and offered good visibility. The bombers ran the gauntlet of heavy flak, particularly over Emmerich, and three were brought down, but nothing could prevent the bombs from raining down from 10,000 feet to leave the town devastated and covered by smoke. More than 2,400 buildings were destroyed, and similar destruction was visited upon Cleves.

Meanwhile, at Woodhall Spa, thirteen Lancasters took off to carry out a daylight attack on the Kembs barrage, a structure across the River Rhine deep in southern Germany at the point where Germany, France and Switzerland meet. Flying as wireless operator in the crew of S/L Drew "Duke" Wyness was the above-mentioned F/O Bruce Hosie, who had won his seat on the toss of a coin. As they attacked with a Tallboy bomb from 600 feet, their Lancaster was hit by flak and ditched in the Rhine, whereupon two crew members ran along the wing and jumped onto the French bank, soon to be joined by another, who had decided to abandon the dinghy and swim to safety. None of the three was seen again and it must be concluded that they were arrested and murdered by the French Gendarmery. Wyness and the others, including Hosie, were paddling towards the Swiss bank, but were apprehended by the pursuing Germans and were shot soon afterwards by the German civilian authorities and their bodies dumped in the river. *(For a full and detailed account, see Chris Ward's Dambusters. The complete WWII History of 617 Squadron, published by Mention the War Publications in 2018.)*

After Emmerich, the squadron was put on stand-by to support ground forces but was not called upon and an entire week passed without operations. The 14th brought the opening salvoes of Operation Hurricane, a terrifying demonstration to the enemy of the overwhelming superiority of the Allied air forces ranged against it. Bomber Command ordered a maximum effort from all but 5 Group to attack Duisburg, for which 1,013 Lancasters, Halifaxes and Mosquitos answered the call. The American 8th Air Force would also be in business on this day, targeting the Cologne area further south with 1,250 bombers escorted by 749 fighters. 3 Group briefed 196 crews, thirty-one of them at Mepal, which took off either side of 07.00 with S/Ls Earl and Williamson the senior pilots on duty and the crew of F/L Alan Roy Bidwell Barton RNZAF on debut. F/O Glossop and crew were forced to turn back with technical problems, leaving the others to press on to the Ruhr, where the Path Finder spearhead arrived over the western edge to find drifting cloud in layers at between 8,000 and 14,000 feet. This created challenges for the Master Bombers, who had five aiming points to control, not all of which could be identified, and instructions were issued to main force crews to bomb the built-up area generally. Some of the 3 Group crews observed the ground through gaps in the cloud, while others tried to use G-H, but found the release pulse to be weak. Bombing took place from around 18,000 to 21,000 feet from shortly after 09.00 and a total of 4,500 tons of high-explosives and incendiaries fell into the city to cause unimaginable destruction at a cost to the Command of thirteen Lancasters and a single Halifax. It was clear that most of the bombing had fallen within the city, particularly around the inland docks, and massive damage resulted. F/O O'Callaghan brought ND917 JN-O home with damage to the bomb bay and landed on the emergency strip at Woodbridge as a precaution.

That night 1,005 aircraft set off in two waves, two hours apart, to return to Duisburg to press home the point about superiority. Such was the efficiency of the ground crews at Mepal that the squadron was able to send twenty-six Lancasters on this second raid, taking off between 22.34 and 23.04 with S/Ls Earl and Williamson once more the senior pilots on duty. The night did not start well, with two Lancasters colliding while taxying around the perimeter, and then a third catching a wheel in the grass on take-off and performing a ground loop, which resulted in injury to the rear gunner. This last accident was too much for W/C Leslie, who immediately cut the pilot's tour short, (it was to have been his third operation), sent him back to Lancaster Finishing School and his crew to RAF Gamston to find a new skipper. F/O Wilson and crew in HK601 JN-D "Snifter" returned early with an unserviceable rear turret, while the others pressed on to find the target this time under clear skies with excellent visibility. As the first wave crews, including those from Mepal, approached the target, they found the city to be still burning from the morning raid and experienced little difficulty in finding somewhere for their hardware. The burning city stood out even more clearly for the second wave main force crews, who aimed their bombs at red and green TIs from 17,000 to 21,000 feet either side of 03.30 in accordance with the instructions of the Master Bomber. The glow from the tortured city was still visible from the Dutch coast as the bombers reached the safety of the North Sea, and this time five Lancasters and two Halifaxes failed to return.

F/Sgt McCartin and crew were in HK563 JN-W "Paper Doll" and reported an inconclusive combat, while the crew of P/O Plummer endured a terrifying experience, which won him an immediate DFC and was widely reported in the newspapers back in New Zealand. Just after bombing, the nose of his Lancaster ME753 AA-N was effectively blown off by a flak burst, along with all the Perspex in the front sections of the cockpit. The bomb-aimer and engineer were immediately blown back down the fuselage and navigational equipment was lost. The Lancaster was at 22,500 ft, where the temperature was 25 degrees below zero, so Plummer dived 20,000ft to get to warmer air, by which time his gloveless left hand was frozen to the control column and could not be moved. He was faced with more than two hours of freezing open cockpit flying to bring his machine home, but fortunately, the flight engineer and bomb aimer managed to work their way forward against the wind to assist him with the controls, and eventually they made a perfect landing. The ground crew had to dismantle the column with his hands still attached, so he could be taken to the medical section for treatment. Plummer reportedly said to W/C Leslie, "My hands are a bit cold sir, but I am going to fly tomorrow." In fact, treatment for frostbite meant he would not return to operations for another three months. More than 4,000 tons of bombs fell into the city with greater concentration than earlier in the day and Duisburg ceased to exist as a functioning city. The commitment of 2,018 aircraft to Duisburg in under twenty-four hours was a massive achievement by the Command, and this figure did not include the 233 Lancasters and seven Mosquitos sent by 5 Group to Brunswick while the evening raid was in progress. After surviving previous attempts to deliver a crushing blow, Brunswick's heart was finally torn out as the old town was reduced to rubble.

3 Group was now ready to conduct daylight operations using G-H, a system based on the original Gee principle, which required bombers to fly to the target in a loose formation called a gaggle, and within that, were smaller sub-formations of three or four aircraft each, as designated by the squadron. The gaggle had an appointed leader and within each vic or box, there was a G-H leader, who carried the G-H equipment and was able to locate the aiming point by a radio signal and a beam arc, similar to Oboe. As the gaggle neared the target, formations tightened up, then as each G-H leader detected the trigger pulse and dropped his bombs, the two or three accompanying aircraft would release theirs also. The approach was similar to the system used by the Americans, but unlike that, G-H could be used at night. In order to make them stand out in a gaggle, the Lancasters of G-H leaders had their tailfins painted with clearly-identified designs, twin yellow bands in the case of 75 (NZ) Squadron, to enable those following to attach themselves.

It was necessary to carry out a large-scale trial of the method, for which the virtually virgin city of Bonn was selected on the 18th, so that assessment of the results would not be compromised by previous damage. 3 Group prepared a force of 128 aircraft, of which sixteen were provided by 75(NZ) Squadron. The crews had actually been briefed on the 17th and were close to take-off when the cancellation order came through, and so it was the same sixteen which now departed Mepal between 08.21 and 08.42 with W/C Leslie the senior pilot on duty. It proved harder than expected to form up into the planned vics of three aircraft, each with a G-H leader, and some leaders found themselves alone, while others had four of five in their section. The meteorological brains had promised ten-tenths cloud over the target, but crews were greeted by three to five tenths cloud and a heavier than anticipated flak defence, which broke up the formations. An additional problem was a fading of the G-H release pulse, and some crews decided to bomb visually rather than wait for their leaders. Those persevering with G-H produced good results, however, and the operation was surprisingly successful given the difficulties. The heart of the city was left devastated with seven hundred buildings destroyed and a further one thousand seriously damaged, and it was achieved for the loss of a single Lancaster.

When orders came through on 1, 3, 6 and 8 Group stations on the 19th for an all-Lancaster attack that night on Stuttgart, 3 Group detailed 176 aircraft, twenty-eight of them representing 75(NZ) Squadron. They were part of an overall force of 565 aircraft, which would form two waves separated by four-and-a-half hours with thirteen of the Mepal crews, including RNZAF debutants F/O Raymond Arthur Cumberpatch and F/O Eric Frank Butler, assigned to the first wave and fifteen to the second. The former took off between 17.29 and 17.47 with S/L Earl the senior pilot on duty and reached the target to find nine-tenths cloud and both sky and ground marking in progress. Most bombed from between 15,000 and 17,000 feet on the "Wanganui" skymarkers, but some picked up the glow of TIs through the cloud and aimed for these. They were well on their way home as the second-phase aircraft began to take to the Cambridgeshire skies between 22.05 and 22.21 led by F/Ls Andrew and Baxter. By the time they arrived over southern Germany, the cloud had increased, and bombing took place on skymarkers and the glow of fires burning from the earlier attack. Four crews returned to report inconclusive combats. It was impossible to assess the outcome, but it was established later that central and eastern districts had sustained substantial damage, as had a number of outlying towns, and the important Bosch factory had been hit.

The assault on the island of Walcheren continued on the 21st, when three coastal batteries at Flushing (Vlissingen) were targeted by seventy-five 3 Group Lancasters divided equally among them. The 75(NZ) Squadron element of twenty-five began taking-off shortly before 11.00 with F/Sgt Donald Percy Leadley RNZAF and crew operating for the first time and S/L Earl the senior pilot on duty, and all reached the target to bomb visually from 8,000 feet without the benefit of Path Finder marking. For this operation W/C Leslie acted as Master Bomber for the squadron's aircraft, calling instructions via his wireless operator, Sgt Crabtree RAF. The only opposition came in the form of a moderate amount of heavy flak, and this accounted for the squadron's HK596 AA-O, which was seen at around 12.32 to have at least one engine on fire. Seven minutes later the Lancaster crashed in the target area after five parachutes had been seen to deploy, despite which, there were no survivors from the crew of F/O James Johnson RAFVR and his crew, of which only the bomb-aimer was a member of the RNZAF. The conclusion has to be that the pilot and one other died in the crash, while the others became victims of the bombing.

An operation to Essen on the 22nd was cancelled and a G-H attack on Neuss substituted for the 3 Group element of one hundred Lancasters. The contribution of twenty-seven Kiwi Lancasters detailed for the former was reduced to nine, and they took off between 13.12 and 13.30 with F/Ls Andrew, Barton and Waugh the senior pilots on duty. Forming up again proved to be difficult, which caused one unspecified Mepal aircraft to become delayed on the way out, and realising they would not reach the target in time, the crew dropped their bombs on Mönchengladbach. The others found Neuss to be completely concealed by cloud, but G-H worked well, and the bombing took place from between 17,000 and 18,000 feet. Post-raid reconnaissance revealed the attack to have been accurate and concentrated and the operation was considered to be another success for the G-H system.

The Essen raid was rescheduled for the 23rd, for which a record force of 1,055 aircraft was assembled, which would carry 4,538 tons of bombs, more than 90% of which was high explosive, and once again this massive force would be achieved without the involvement of 5 Group. 171 of the Lancasters were provided by 3 Group, twenty-seven of them belonging to 75(NZ) Squadron, which departed Mepal between 16.37 and 17.07 with S/L Rodgers the senior pilot on duty on an evening of heavy cloud over the Continent. They climbed into scattered cloud on their way south to exit England over the Sussex coast at Beachy Head and set course for the French coast and a southerly approach to the target. This would take them through the narrow corridor between Cologne and Mönchengladbach and up into the central Ruhr, and by the time that the target hove into view, the cloud had become ten-tenths up to 14,000 feet. The Path Finders had prepared a ground and skymarking plan to cover this precise eventuality, and once the Oboe TIs had been swallowed up by the cloud, red skymarker flares were released at 19.28 to be followed by greens three minutes later. Bombing took place from between 10,000 and 20,000 feet onto what was left of the built-up area, and although it proved impossible to observe the fall of the bombs, an intense glow on the cloud told its own story that there was still plenty of combustible material in the tortured city. Local reports confirmed the destruction of 607 buildings with a further eight hundred seriously damaged and a death toll of 667 people.

Not yet finished with Essen, the command dispatched a reduced force to it of 771 aircraft on the 25th, for which 3 Group detailed 170 Lancasters and 75(NZ) Squadron twenty-six, including one for the debutant crew of F/O Alexander Dunbar Simpson RNZAF. F/Ls Andrew, Barton, Baxter, Martin and Waugh were the senior pilots on duty as they departed Mepal between 12.58 and 13.34, but F/O Cooper and F/Sgt Osborne were forced back early with technical problems, and another crew would bring its bombs back after they failed to release over the target. They adopted a route that took them across Belgium to enter Germany near Aachen, and proceeded to the target in cloudy, but quite favourable weather conditions. They encountered ten-tenths cloud with tops at between 6,000 and 12,000 feet during the run-up to the target, but isolated breaks appeared, which allowed crews to assess the accuracy of the red and yellow TIs in relation to the Krupp complex or simply to bomb visually or on skymarkers. The master Bomber ordered the red TIs to be ignored in favour of the yellows, which appeared to be a little to the north of the aiming-point, before a massive explosion close by at 15.29 created a pall of smoke, which the Master Bomber was then able to employ as the focus for the rest of the bombing. The Master Bomber performed well, and post-raid reconnaissance revealed a more concentrated attack than that achieved by the larger force thirty-six hours earlier. 1,163 buildings had been destroyed and the Krupp steel works badly damaged, but most of the city's industry had been moved out, meaning that this one-time powerhouse of war production ceased to be so.

Leverkusen was posted as the target for a 3 Group G-H attack on the 26th, for which 104 Lancasters were made ready. Mepal dispatched ten Lancasters either side of 13.00 led by S/L Rodgers, and the forming up procedure went well, as did the attack through ten-tenths cloud, which was centred upon the chemicals factory of the notorious I G Farben company. It was not possible to assess the results, but the operation was believed to be successful, and no aircraft were lost.

Cologne's turn to face a Hurricane-style force came on the 28th, for which a two-wave force of 733 aircraft was assembled, which included eighty-four 3 Group Lancasters. First, however, seventy-six 3 Group Lancasters were detailed to bomb three coastal batteries at Flushing on Walcheren, for which thirteen 75(NZ) Squadron crews were briefed and departed Mepal shortly after 09.00 with F/Ls Baxter, Dawes and Wylie James Wakelin RNZAF, the last-mentioned on debut, the senior pilots on duty. All reached the target in good weather conditions to deliver accurate bombing from between 6,000 and 7,000 feet in the face of accurate light flak, which probably accounted for the loss of a 90 Squadron Lancaster. A large explosion was witnessed towards the end of the raid, and the expectation was of a successful outcome.

It was 13.15 when S/L Bailey, who was also on debut, took off at the head of the squadron's seven-strong contribution to the attack on Cologne, which included freshman, F/O Martin Adam Kilpatrick. The operation was to be conducted in two phases, with one aiming-point in the district of Müllheim, to the north-east of the city centre, and the other in Zollstock to the south-west. They encountered a weather front over the North Sea on their way to making landfall on the French coast in the Dunkerque region, and a dozen Halifaxes turned back as a result, it is believed, of icing that affected engines and prevented them from climbing. The others pressed on to the target, where five to ten-tenths cloud prevailed, through which red TIs were glimpsed by some on the ground at aiming point G, which is believed to be the Müllheim district. The bombing was carried out visually or on red skymarkers from 18,000 to 20,000 feet from around 16.00 onwards and extensive fires were observed that remained visible for a hundred miles into the return journey. A large explosion was reported at 16.04 in the Zollstock district following a direct hit on a factory, and smoke was rising through 15,000 feet from Müllheim as the force retreated. Despite reservations about the quality of the bombing of aiming-point H, both aiming-points had been devastated, local reports confirming the destruction of 2,239 blocks of flats and fifteen industrial premises, along with many other buildings of a public nature. Severe damage had also been inflicted upon power stations, transportation and railway and river docks installations.

1, 3, 4 and 8 Groups put together a force of 358 aircraft on the 29th to attack eleven German positions resisting the Allied advance across Walcheren. 3 Group sent seventy-five Lancasters back to Flushing to attend to the three coastal batteries, and the Mepal element of fourteen Lancasters included newcomers, P/O Douglas Ross Sadgrove RNZAF and F/Sgt Donald James Williams RNZAF. They took off at 10.00 with F/Ls Barton, Wakelin and Waugh the senior pilots on duty and encountered favourable weather conditions over the Scheldt estuary with large gaps in the cloud, and two of the sites were bombed with great accuracy. The markers at the third aiming point, near Westkapelle, to which the Kiwi crews were assigned, were not as well-placed, however, and attracted a proportion of the bombing, although some crews ignored the markers and bombed visually under the instructions of the Master Bomber.

The next G-H operation by 3 Group was mounted on the morning of the 30th against the Union Rheinische Braunkohlen-Kraftstoff A G oil refinery at Wesseling near Cologne. 102 Lancasters were prepared, of which six represented 75(NZ) Squadron and took off at 09.00 with S/L Bailey the senior pilot on duty. As they approached the target over a layer of ten-tenths cloud, some crews picked up a false release pulse, which was discovered later to have come from a new G-H station testing its equipment. Their bombs fell five miles short of the intended aiming point, but the others pushed on and carried out what was believed to be an accurate attack, during which one aircraft was damaged.

Later that evening, the squadron made ready twenty-one Lancasters as part of an overall "Hurricane"-sized force of 905 aircraft, the destination for which was Cologne. They took off between 17.46 and 18.02 with S/L Rodgers the senior pilot on duty and climbed away into ten-tenths cloud, with a full moon shining brightly above to reveal the presence of the vast armada of bombers. Over the Channel the cloud tops reached 20,000 feet, but this had lowered to 10,000 to 15,000 feet as the target drew near, and main force crews were greeted by red and white marker flares delivered by nine of the Oboe Mosquitos. They drifted in concentrated fashion into the cloud tops, and main force crews confirmed their accuracy by Gee and H2S before carrying out their attacks. Fortunately, the Luftwaffe Nachtjagd failed to appear and missed a golden opportunity provided by the conditions to score heavily. Apart from the glow of fires lighting up the cloud, it was impossible to assess what was happening on the ground and the expectation at Bomber Command HQ was of a scattered attack with light damage. The reality, however, was destruction on a massive scale, particularly in the suburbs, where civilian housing suffered most, but railways and public utilities were also hit, plunging the tortured city into a deeper state of chaos. The operation was concluded without loss to further demonstrate the overwhelming superiority of the Allied air power.

3 Group detailed 101 Lancasters on the 31st for a G-H raid on a Fischer-Tropsch process coal liquefaction oil plant located in the Welheim district of Bottrop, situated on the northern edge of the Ruhr, for which 75(NZ) Squadron made ready six Lancasters. They took off shortly before noon with F/Ls Andrew, Baxter and Waugh the senior pilots on duty and flew out in vics of three behind a G-H leader. The leaders were carrying flares, which were released with the bombs and any crews not able to bomb with the leader were instructed to aim for the flares on a given heading. The operation seemed to progress according to plan in the face of an intense flak barrage, despite which, only one Lancaster failed to make it home and all from Mepal returned safely without damage.

Cologne's torment was not yet over, as a force of 493 aircraft was prepared for another attack on it that night. 75(NZ) Squadron briefed eighteen crews as part of a 3 Group contribution of seventy-one Lancasters and they took off between 17.55 and 18.31 with F/Ls Barton and Brown the senior pilots on duty. They reached the Rhineland capital to be greeted by ten-tenths thick cloud with tops at 6,000 to 10,000 feet, by which time proceedings had begun with red and white flares delivered by Oboe Mosquitos at 20.56. These were backed up in what appeared to be concentrated fashion by greens from the Path Finder heavy marker element, and the main force crews established their positions by Gee and H2S-fix. The bombing was concentrated around the markers as they sank slowly towards the cloud tops and the main weight of the attack fell into southern districts. It was difficult for post-raid reconnaissance to determine how much additional damage had been caused and returning crews could only report on the glow of fires in the clouds and the lack of opposition.

During the course of this very busy month the squadron participated in twenty-one operations, more than half of them by daylight and dispatched a record 394 sorties for the loss of three Lancasters and crews.

November 1944

The preceding two months had seen only four of the squadron's aircraft fail to return from operations, but November would have a sting in its tail. Operations began for the squadron on the 2nd, with participation in a 3 Group G-H attack on the Rheinpreussen (Meerbeck) oil refinery at Moers/Homberg opposite Duisburg, the scene of the squadron's blackest night back in July. It was mounted to follow up on an unsuccessful attempt by 5 Group on the previous day, and that, in itself, was sufficient to produce a warm glow of satisfaction in the 3 Group briefing rooms. The fact that the much-vaunted 5 Group, highly successful as it was, and with the "glamour boys" of 617 Squadron grabbing all the headlines, had been shown to be fallible, and that 3 Group had been chosen to rectify its failure, was a matter of great pride. 184 Lancasters were detailed, drawn from all ten of the group's "squadrons of the line", with twenty of them representing 75(NZ) Squadron, and the crews were further cheered by the news that two hundred Spitfires would shepherd them to and from the target. They departed Mepal between 11.30 and 11.45 with a time-on-target of 14.00 and forecast conditions of scattered light cloud with minimal ground haze. W/C Leslie demonstrated the highest quality of leadership by being the senior pilot on duty for this most sensitive of operations, and this was much appreciated by the other participants. Seven of the Lancasters were carrying an 8,000 pounder, while the others had a cookie on board, and all bomb bays contained a mixture of 1,000 and 500 pounders to complete their loads. The plan called for a bombing height of 20,000 feet and the usual G-H method to be employed, but not all aircraft were assigned to a G-H Leader, and these additional crews were instructed to bomb on "Wanganui" flares dropped by the leaders at the same time as their bombs. This last point suited all self-respecting bomb-aimers, who would much prefer to bomb on their own equipment, rather than watch the bomb bays of their G-H leaders. The cloud in the target area turned out to be five-tenths as the attack began, and, although the bombing would be described by returning crews as scattered, large fires and a thick column of black smoke were observed as the bombers turned away. Flak opposition was moderate to intense, and eight aircraft picked up minor damage, while F/L Andrew's NF981 JN-Y was hit by heavy flak, resulting in a difficult-to-extinguish starboard engine fire. The damage was sufficient for her to be returned to A.V. Roe for two weeks for repairs.

That night 992 aircraft took off to attack Düsseldorf in the absence of a contribution from 3 Group, and those reaching the target destroyed or seriously damaged five thousand houses in predominantly northern districts, while reducing further the city's capacity to produce war materials.

The medium sized town of Solingen, situated on the south-eastern edge of the Ruhr, was posted on the 4th as the target for a G-H raid by 177 Lancasters of 3 Group, of which twenty-one were made ready at Mepal. They took off between 11.29 and 11.54 with W/C Leslie again leading from the front and found seven to ten-tenths cloud in the target area, which allowed some crews a sight of the built-up area. The attack seemed to go well with little flak opposition, but four aircraft failed to return, which, in the absence of flak and fighters, perplexed the planners at 3 Group HQ. Curiously, three of the missing Lancasters belonged to 195 Squadron at Witchford, and a number of reports suggested that "friendly" bombs may have been responsible for their demise. The fact that two of these exploded with great force over the target seems to support that conclusion. 75(NZ) Squadron's ND917 JN-O was the other failure to return, and there were no survivors from the experienced crew of F/O John Scott RNZAF, which contained three other members of the RNZAF. That night more than seven hundred aircraft from 1, 4, 6 and 8 Groups attacked Bochum and destroyed or seriously damaged four thousand buildings. The Luftwaffe chose this night to make its presence felt, and twenty-three Halifaxes and five Lancasters failed to return.

The raid on Solingen was repeated on the following day at the hands of a 3 Group G-H force of 172 Lancasters, of which eighteen belonged to 75(NZ) Squadron. They took off between 10.10 and 10.55 with F/Ls Martyn and Wakelin the senior pilots on duty, reaching the target with their 8,000 or 4,000 pounders to encounter ten-tenths cloud and little opposition from the ground. The attack appeared to be concentrated and was described by returning crews as the best G-H performance yet. It was impossible to assess what was happening beneath the cloud, but local sources listed 1,300 houses destroyed along with eighteen industrial premises, while sixteen hundred other buildings had been seriously damaged and up to eighteen hundred people killed. Just one Lancaster failed to return, and this XV Squadron aircraft was seen to be hit by falling bombs.

738 aircraft took off for Gelsenkirchen at around noon on the 6th, the crews having been briefed that the Nordstern synthetic oil plant was the specific aiming point. The raid became somewhat scattered, but more than five hundred aircraft had bombed the approximate area of the refinery before smoke obscured the ground. It was difficult to assess the outcome, but local reports suggested extensive damage to the town in general. 3 Group participated in this operation, but 75(NZ) Squadron was not called into action until later in the day, when sixteen crews were briefed at Mepal for a G-H raid by 128 aircraft on Koblenz, an old city nestling in the confluence of the Rivers Rhine and Mosel some forty miles south-east of Cologne. The force should have been larger but bombing-up problems at Methwold led to the cancellation of twenty-one aircraft. The 75(NZ) Squadron crews were all safely airborne by 17.02 with S/L Rodgers the senior pilot on duty and carrying either an 8,000 or 4,000 pounder with No 14 and 17 Cluster bombs and 4lb incendiaries. F/O Winter was forced back early with engine problems in ME751, now recoded AA-M, leaving the remainder to press on in good weather conditions with excellent visibility, which enabled them to identify the target visually. The TIs that dropped with the leaders' bombs were tightly bunched as they fell towards the built-up area, and the pattern of streets and the rivers was plain to see in their light. In fact, only seventeen of an intended forty-five aircraft had delivered TIs, but the operation was hugely destructive and left half of the town in ruins, with the glow from the extensive fires visible for seventy miles into the return journey. P/O Leadley in HK593 AA-H and F/O Kilpatrick in HK562 AA-L each had short inconclusive encounters with Ju88s.

The second attack of the month on the Meerbeck oil refinery at Homberg was mounted on the 8th by a 3 Group G-H force of 136 Lancasters. A dozen of them began departing Mepal shortly before 08.00 with S/L Bailey the senior pilot on duty and the main difficulty in the early stages was forming up in the cloudy conditions. All from Mepal reached the target with their loads of an 8,000 or 4,000 pounder supplemented by 1,000 and 500 pounders and a large gap in the clouds over the north-western corner of the Ruhr allowed crews to confirm that their bombs were on the mark. The flak was heavy and accurate, and some aircraft sustained damage, although there were no such reports from the returning Kiwi crews. They described many fires and copious amounts of black smoke covering the target area before the attack had concluded, and it was not possible to make an accurate assessment of the results.

Crews were up early on the 11th as preparations were put in hand for an attack on the town of Heinsberg, which, together with Düren and Jülich, stand in an arc north to east of Aachen, where American forces were about to break through. Twenty-five Lancasters had been made ready at Mepal when the cancellation came through, and the ordeal facing the residents of these towns would ultimately be postponed for five days. Nineteen crews were stood-down, leaving six to be briefed as part of a 122-strong 3 Group G-H raid on the Klöckner Werke A G synthetic oil plant at Castrop-Rauxel in the north-eastern Ruhr. They took off at 08.30 with F/L Martyn the senior pilot on duty and all reached the cloud-covered target to release their bomb loads on their G-H equipment. Returning crews reported that the flares were concentrated as they drifted into the cloud-tops at 8,000 to 9,000 feet, but others claimed a degree of chaos as aircraft bombed on a variety of headings and an accurate assessment was not possible. That afternoon, four of the squadron's Lancasters took off either side of 15.30 to join others mining in the waters in the Onion garden off Horten in Oslo Fjord with F/L Baxter the senior pilot on duty. All were successful and returned safely between 22.47 and 23.20, diverting to Tain in Scotland due to doubtful weather conditions at Mepal.

After operations against a variety of intended targets were cancelled on the 13th, 14th and 15th, twenty-five of the squadron's Lancasters finally got away at lunchtime on the 15th as part of a 177-strong 3 Group G-H raid on the Hoesch-Benzin oil plant in the Wambel district of Dortmund. S/L Rodgers was the senior pilot on duty and Keith Joshua Jones RNZAF was on debut as captain as they headed out to form up, a procedure which went well on this occasion, and at the target, the concentration of flares and bombing by the G-H leaders was described as very good. Intense flak in the early stages of the attack diminished somewhat towards the end but was responsible for the loss of two Lancasters. Returning crews were unable to offer an assessment of the raid because of the ten-tenths cloud with tops at 10,000 feet, but it was believed to have been successful.

The destruction of the small towns of Düren, Jülich and Heinsberg had been rescheduled for the 16th, which was probably a late decision as twenty-five Mepal crews had already been briefed to attack the Ruhr-Chemie oil refinery at Sterkrade-Holten in the Ruhr. The same twenty-five took off either side of 13.30 with S/L Earl the senior pilot on duty and joined up with 157 other Lancasters heading for Heinsberg, the most northerly of the towns, situated no more than five miles from the Dutch frontier south-east of Roermond. This was an exclusively 3 Group G-H target, while Düren and Jülich were to face much larger forces from 1, 5 and 8 Groups and 4, 6 and 8 Groups respectively. The Master Bomber at Heinsberg was W/C Watkins DSO, DFC, DFM, the commanding officer of XV Squadron, who had completed more than fifty operations as a navigator, some of them, as already documented, with the Feltwell station commander at the time, the late G/C John "Speedy" Powell. His Lancaster was shot down on approach to the target, and he alone of the eight occupants survived to fall into enemy hands, suggesting that the aircraft had broken up and thrown him clear with his parachute attached. The Deputy Master Bomber took over his duties and rescued the operation from failure after the G-H release co-ordinates were found to be inaccurate. The town was all-but erased from the map, but fortunately, only 110 civilians were still resident in the town and half of these lost their lives. This was in contrast to more than three thousand fatalities at Düren, and no report was available from Jülich. In the event, the American advance was thwarted by wet ground and proceeded very slowly and with great difficulty. Two Mepal Lancasters received minor damage.

On the 20th, twenty-eight 75(NZ) Squadron Lancasters were made ready to return to the Meerbeck oil plant at Homberg for the third time in the month and were part of a 3 Group G-H force of 185 aircraft. *(In the book, Luck and a Lancaster by Harry Yates, published in 2001 by Airlife Classic, pages 184 to 187 appear to deal with this operation, and one passage refers to a cheer from the assembled crews as W/C Leslie announced that he would be accompanying them on this operation. The ORB does not list him for this one, and the author has clearly confused this operation with that of the 2nd of November to the same target and involving a similar number of aircraft.)* They took off between 12.36 and 12.58 with F/Ls Barton, Baxter and Martyn the senior pilots on duty and F/O John Henry McDonald RNZAF and crew making their operational debut. F/O Dare in LM544, now re-coded AA-J, returned early because of severe icing, while two others would bomb last-resort targets at Duisburg and Hamborn probably for the same reason. The outward flight proved difficult for all crews because of the towering ice-bearing clouds with tops at 23,000 feet, and some climbed to 25,000 feet to break free of ice. Others found a clear lane at 20,000 feet and managed to formate on a number of G-

H leaders and deliver their bombs, but the operation was a failure, and this target again exacted a heavy toll from the squadron.

Of five missing Lancasters, three were from Mepal, and there were widely differing fortunes for the crews involved. PB689 AA-X was hit by flak from Baerl on the western bank of the Rhine in north-western Duisburg and exploded, killing F/O Ronald Gordon and his RAF crew. Only the rear gunner survived from the crew of F/O Patrick Leo McCartin RAAF in ND911 JN-V, which broke up after being hit, either by flak or possibly by the falling PB689. It came down in the general target area, and he was taken into captivity. In contrast, F/O Hubert Rees RAFVR and crew, who were approaching the end of their tour, all survived as PoWs from PB520 AA-G. The bomb-aimer was the only member of the RNZAF on board, and the only Kiwi to go missing on this day. F/L William French Morison Naismith RAFVR, the squadron's signals leader, had been a member of S/L Gunn's crew at the time of its crash in mid-September.

There may have been a sharp intake of breath inside the Mepal briefing room on the following morning, when twenty-one crews were told to return to Homberg that afternoon. W/C Leslie demonstrated strength of leadership by putting himself on the order of battle for what would be a difficult operation, and he was supported by S/L Rodgers as they took off between 12.26 and 13.15. They were part of a 3 Group G-H force of 159 aircraft, which this time found clear conditions over the target, enabling crews to identify ground detail. The problem on this occasion, however, was unserviceability of G-H equipment and heavy, accurate flak, which upset the run of those leaders with functioning sets. 3 Group HQ judged this to be a not particularly effective attack, yet a Bomber Command report mentioned that a vast sheet of yellow flame had been witnessed, followed by black smoke rising to a great height, and it must be assumed from this that it was, therefore, a successful raid. Later that afternoon, three of the squadron's crews took off independently to mine the waters of the Onion garden in Oslo Fjord, and only two returned eight hours later to report successful sorties in clear weather conditions. NN745 AA-A failed to make it back with the highly-experienced mixed Commonwealth crew of F/L Leslie Martyn RNZAF, which contained one other member of the RNZAF, three members of the RAF, including wireless operator, Sgt John Calverley Crabtree, who had flown with W/C Leslie, and one each of the RAAF and RCAF, and no trace of them has ever been found.

A day away from the operational scene on the 22nd was followed on the 23rd by the briefing of twenty-five crews for an attack on the Nordstern synthetic oil plant at Gelsenkirchen. They were to be part of a 3 Group G-H force of 168 Lancasters and took off between 12.38 and 12.57 with S/L Earl the senior pilot on duty. They were carrying a cookie each and fifteen 500 pounders and all reached the target area, where ten-tenths cloud was present with tops at 12,000 feet according to the 3 Group ORB, and 8,000 feet as recorded by the squadron ORB. The G-H formations were good, the equipment worked well and black smoke inside the cloud suggested a successful raid, although the outcome could not be accurately assessed.

A few more days away from the war preceded an operation on the 27th against the Kalk-Nord marshalling yards situated on the eastern edge of Cologne. 3 Group assembled a G-H force of 169 Lancasters, of which twenty-three represented 75(NZ) Squadron, one of them containing the freshman crew of F/O Ernest Joseph Abraham RNZAF. They departed Mepal between

12.11 and 12.28 with F/Ls Barton, Baxter and Yates the senior pilots on duty and each Lancaster carrying a 4,000lb cookie and sixteen 500 pounders. They arrived at the target to be greeted by moderate, accurate flak and the 3 Group ORB complained that the navigator at the tip of the spearhead seemed to lead the formation through most of the Ruhr defences on the way. Those following his leadership were believed to have overshot the yards by a quarter of a mile, while others chose a more direct route, and their bombs were concentrated within the yards with apparently good results. F/O Leadley's Lancaster HK593 AA-H was damaged by flak and he landed at Manston.

F/L John Leonard "Jack" Wright DSO, DFC, RNZAF arrived from 31 Base on the 28th to begin his third tour of operations and he would be handed the acting rank of squadron leader to succeed S/L Earl as A Flight commander. Jack Wright had flown his first tour with 75(NZ) Squadron between May and October 1942, and had gone on to lead the famous and much-decorated "Thomas Fredrick Duck" 156 Squadron Path Finder crew, largely made up of ex-75ers. By the time he arrived at Mepal he had already completed fifty-nine operations.

Briefings took place later that day for a rare night attack, which was to be hosted by the Ruhr city of Neuss, located on the Rhine opposite Düsseldorf. Twenty-one Lancasters were made ready at Mepal and twenty of them were loaded with a cookie, six 1,000 and six 500 pounders. In a first for the squadron, W/C Leslie's HK600 JN-K "Kiwi" had a 12,000-pounder light case "blockbuster" winched into its bomb bay, a bomb first used by 617 Squadron against the Dortmund-Ems Canal in September 1943 and employed on other occasions by that squadron against flying-bomb sites and factories later in the year and in early 1944. *(This should not be confused with the 12,000lb Wallis-designed Tallboy earthquake bomb employed by 617 Squadron from June 1944 and later by 9 Squadron.)* They took off between 02.50 and 03.14 as part of a 3 Group G-H force of 145 Lancasters accompanied by eight ABC Lancasters from 1 Group and flew out at the same time as more than three hundred aircraft from 1, 4 and 8 Groups bound for Essen. They reached the target area, where W/C Leslie found himself in the wrong stream of bombers, and considering it too dangerous to cross three streams, ended up dropping his 12,000 pounder and two 500 pounders on Essen. The attack on Neuss went ahead over ten-tenths cloud on G-H and "Wanganui" skymarkers and local reports described modest damage predominantly in residential districts.

3 Group mobilized 120 Lancasters on the 30th, which were to be divided equally between two targets in the Ruhr, the coking plant at Bottrop-Welheim and a benzin plant at Osterfeld, a district of Oberhausen. 75(NZ) Squadron supported the latter with eighteen Lancasters, which took off between 10.46 and 11.01 with F/Ls Barton and Yates the senior pilots on duty. F/Sgt John O'Malley RNZAF was on debut, and F/O Osborne in HK562 AA-L lost his starboard-inner engine on take-off, but elected to carry on to the target, "cutting corners" while still lagging behind the others. They reached the target area to find a blanket of cloud with tops at 10,000 feet and delivered their loads of a cookie and sixteen 500 pounders in what appeared to be an accurate and concentrated attack. The squadron's NF980 JN-F was hit by flak over the target and was believed to have had its tail shot away. The same flak burst damaged nearby NN747 JN-O "Dogsbody Again" flown by F/O McDonald and crew, who watched as NF980 and another Lancaster both exploded and fell away. NF980 crashed a mile south of the town's railway station, where the bodies of F/O James McIntosh RNZAF and five of his crew, two of whom were also members of the RNZAF, were recovered for burial. The rear gunner, Sgt

Edward Roy Cooper RAFVR, was found to be alive and was taken to a hospital in Oberhausen, where he succumbed to his injuries a month later. G-H was now being installed across the squadron's Lancaster fleet and by the 30th of the month nine aircraft had been equipped.

During the course of the month the squadron operated on sixteen occasions, dispatching 286 sorties for the loss of six Lancasters and crews.

December 1944

December would follow a similar pattern, and it began for 3 Group with a raid on the Zeche-Hansa benzol plant at Dortmund on the 2nd. The force of ninety-three Lancasters included seventeen from Mepal, including that of newcomer F/O Kenneth William Roland McMillan RNZAF. They took off in good weather conditions between 12.36 and 12.52 with S/Ls Bailey and Rodgers the senior pilots on duty and bomb loads consisting either of a cookie and nine 1,000 pounders or thirteen 1,000 pounders. They flew out in bright sunshine above the thick cloud with tops at around 13,000 feet and found the ground in the target area to be obscured, but these were ideal conditions for a G-H attack, and for the first time, all G-H aircraft detailed to employ the system did so, which the 3 Group ORB described as "a fine achievement, from the manipulation by the crews to the servicing of the equipment by the radar tradesmen". The flak defence was moderate and erratic and the operation appeared to be successful with no damage incurred by the Mepal participants.

Twenty 75(NZ) Squadron Lancasters were made ready for operations on the 4th, when Oberhausen was revealed to the crews as the target. They were to be part of a 160-strong 3 Group G-H raid using an oil plant as the nominal aiming point, but this was an area raid as made clear by the high capacity "blockbuster" bombs that were loaded into the bomb bays. There was one 12,000 pounder in F/O Robertson's HK563 JN-W "Paper Doll", while five 8,000 pounders and fourteen 4,000 pounders and incendiaries accounted for the remaining loads, and these were lifted into the air between 12.11 and 12.27 with F/L Barton the senior pilot on duty. Two RNZAF pilots were on debut, F/O Douglas St.Clair Clement and F/O Leonard Walter Hannan. The winds were lighter than forecast, and this caused the G-H leaders to fly at too great a speed for satisfactory formation-keeping, which elongated the stream, although F/O Hannan in HK601 JN-D could not keep up with the gaggle anyway, due to an issue with his engines. They all reached the target area to find the expected nine to ten-tenths cloud with tops at 10,000 feet and 87% of the G-H crews bombed on their equipment. NN710 AA-Q was hit by flak and F/O Atkin and crew bombed Gelsenkirchen as an alternative, before returning safely home with the others. It was not possible to assess the results, but a local report mentioned 472 houses destroyed and a similar number seriously damaged.

That night, 5 Group attacked the southern city of Heilbronn, which had the misfortune to sit astride a north-south railway line. In a short orgy of destruction, 82% of the built-up area was destroyed and seven thousand people lost their lives.

3 Group detailed ninety-four Lancasters on the 5th to attack the highly important marshalling yards at Hamm to the north-east of the Ruhr, and fifty-six others to attempt to destroy the Schwammenauel Dam in Germany's Eifel region close to the Belgian frontier, where American forces were advancing. Twenty-one Lancasters were made ready at Mepal, and they

took off between 09.00 and 09.23 with S/L Bailey the senior pilot on duty. The operation began in promising fashion with a good formation and concentrated flares dropping into the ten-tenths cloud cover with the G-H leaders' bomb loads. F/O Gawith in NN710 AA-Q was taken five to six miles off track by his leader with the rest of the bomber stream clearly on track, and a Gee-fix suggested his bombs may have fallen into the north-eastern rim of the town. S/L Bailey in NE181 JN-M "The Captain's Fancy" was also led astray and overshot Hamm by six miles. Believing he had no chance of getting back on track, he bombed the first built-up area that presented itself, and that was Heintrop, to the east of Hamm. Some crews caught sight of the ground through small breaks in the cloud and noted the bombing to be scattered, some of it falling into a wooded area. F/L Hannan in HK601 JN-D "Snifter" was unable to locate his assigned G-H leader, and formated on another one, who weaved violently with his bomb doors open and scattered the formation. Despite the presence of a fighter escort, the Luftwaffe Tagjagd mounted a concerted effort against this raid, and it was the first time since daylight operations began in June, that a 3 Group force was intercepted. In the event only one straggling Lancaster was damaged and that landed safely on an Allied airfield in Holland. Mixed opinions were offered by returning crews as to the effectiveness of the raid, but the consensus was favourable. It would be established after the war that 140 acres of Hamm, or 39% of its built-up area, had been laid waste in this attack.

A 1, 3 and 8 Group heavy force of 475 Lancasters was assembled on the 6th for an attack on the synthetic oil plant at Leuna near Merseburg, one of many refineries located in an arc from north to south to the west of Leipzig in eastern Germany. The I G Farben-owned plant was the second largest in Germany and was the one employed to develop the Bergius process of producing oil from bituminous coal. 75(NZ) Squadron briefed a dozen crews to add to the 123 others representing 3 Group, and they departed Mepal shortly after 17.00 with F/Ls Barton and Waugh the senior pilots on duty. The weather outbound was poor and caused a few early returns, although none from the 75(NZ) Squadron element. A ground marking (Newhaven) plan had been prepared, but the presence of ten-tenths cloud over the target with tops at 14,000 feet forced a change to "Wanganui" flares, which fell plentifully and continuously with good concentration throughout the raid. Returning crews would report the glow of fires beneath the cloud and a spirited flak barrage, but none from Mepal sustained damage. F/O Atkin and crew were on their way home at 14,000 feet at 21.33 when HK574's starboard-outer engine suddenly developed a runaway propeller that could not be feathered. They were approaching Giessen at the time, south of the Ruhr and heading for the Belgian frontier with a long flight still ahead of them. The engine caught fire, and although the flames were extinguished, it continued to glow and give off sparks. During the North Sea crossing the starboard-inner engine also failed and the Lancaster began to sink at the rate of a hundred feet per minute. Everything moveable was thrown out to save weight and the Lancaster, (now re-coded AA-R and named "Rio Rita"), finally ran out of altitude over the River Orwell between Ipswich and Felixstowe, where it was ditched without injury to the occupants at 01.30. Fog and darkness led the crew to believe that they had ditched in the Channel, and after some time sitting in a dinghy in strangely calm water beside a Lancaster that refused to sink, it was the mooing of a cow on the riverbank that finally gave away their true location! Post-raid reconnaissance confirmed that the one thousand-mile round-trip had been worthwhile and had inflicted extensive damage upon the oil refinery.

It was early in December that the first references were made in the squadron ORB to "Munro" bombs, which were not explosive, but canisters tightly-packed with propaganda leaflets, the concept having been developed from the American Monroe Leaflet Bomb. Some of these "weapons" were loaded into the bomb bays of the twenty-one Lancasters prepared for a 3 Group G-H attack on the marshalling yards at Duisburg on the 8th, which departed Mepal between 08.30 and 08.51 with S/Ls Bailey and Rodgers the senior pilots on duty. Three Lancasters contained skippers on debut, F/Sgt George Stanley Davies RNZAF, P/O Eric George Parsons RAFVR and F/Sgt John Henry Thomas Wood RNZAF. Their first task was to rendezvous with the rest of the 163-strong force, a process made highly challenging by the presence of cloud in thick layers up to 25,000 feet, which stretched all the way to the German frontier and prevented the stream from forming up into a G-H configuration. Once again, HK601 JN-D was left behind, as F/Sgt Wood struggled to climb to a respectable height. However, the navigation was so good, that on emerging from the cloud, the aircraft were in close enough contact to be able to form up. The target remained covered by nine to ten-tenths cloud, but the flares and the bombing were concentrated, and one Kiwi crew reported black smoke rising through the cloud-tops at 15,000 feet as they turned away. Having arrived and bombed after the main force had left, F/Sgt Wood made for home and landed at Woodbridge as a precaution.

W/C Raymond John Newton, a former flight commander with the squadron in 1942, returned to its bosom on the 11th to succeed W/C Leslie as squadron commander. Newton was a comparatively reserved character and brought a more relaxed leadership style in contrast to his predecessor. Sadly, however, his tenure would be brief. The departure of W/C Leslie, it is believed to 3 LFS, in the short term at least was not mourned, for although he had inspired his men by leading from the front, particularly on difficult operations, he had also shown himself to be a strict disciplinarian, given to extreme levels of punishment for minor infractions.

That morning Osterfeld had been posted as the target for 150 Lancasters of 3 Group, ninety-eight of them to attack the marshalling yards and fifty-two the coking plant. Seventeen Lancasters were made ready at Mepal, including one to be occupied by debutant skipper F/Sgt Robert Jaspar Pearson RNZAF and his crew, but the ORB does not identify the aiming point to which they were assigned and for which they took off between 08.40 and 08.53 with S/L Bailey the senior pilot on duty. Forming up and climbing to bombing height became a challenge because of cloud over the bases, where the tops were at 15,000 feet. At the targets the cloud tops reached 19,000 feet and this forced the attack to be delivered from higher than intended. The G-H flares disappeared quickly into the cloud, and this led to scattered bombing at both aiming points.

On the following day 3 Group detailed 140 Lancasters for a raid on Witten, a large mining town tucked in a pocket of the Ruhr south-west of Dortmund and south-east of Bochum. Sixteen Lancasters took off from Mepal between 11.06 and 11.21 with S/L Rodgers the senior pilot on duty, ten of them carrying a 4,000lb cookie and fourteen 500 pounders. Of the others, five had an 8,000 pounder and eight small bomb cases (SBCs) of 4lb cluster bombs in their bomb bays, while F/O Abraham in HK576 AA-G was responsible for the 12,000lb blockbuster and three Munro T238s. There were four debutants, all members of the RNZAF, F/Sgt Vernon John Zinzan, F/O Terence Douglas Blewett, F/O Herbert Wilfred Hooper and F/Sgt Ronald Christie Flamank. On the run into the target the stream divided into two parts, a small bunch from 31 Base (Stradishall, Chedburgh and Wratting Common) and Methwold positioning itself about seven miles ahead of the main concentration. The bulk of the fighter escort remained with the rear section, but the fighter leader had the foresight to send one squadron ahead to cover the lead group, which was fortuitous, as the Luftwaffe was waiting for them over the Ruhr, having chosen this day to mount its largest effort since daylight bombing operations began in June. A strong force of BF109s managed to break up the forward section of bombers, shooting down, among others, four 195 Squadron Lancasters, and this led to a scattered start to the attack. However, on observing the events ahead, the main section tightened its formation, which helped to create very concentrated bombing and forty of the forty-six G-H leaders were able to use their equipment effectively. F/L Hannan's NE181 JN-M "The Captain's Fancy" was involved in a collision with another aircraft during the bombing run, badly damaging the starboard outer engine, but was able to carry on to deliver an attack before returning home safely. HK562 AA-L was damaged when it made a heavy landing on return, and the bomb-aimer in F/Sgt Zinzan's crew, F/O Mesure, sustained a broken leg.

F/L Wakelin was the senior pilot of four Mepal crews sent to mine the waters of one of the Silverthorn gardens off Kullen Point in the Kattegat on the 14th, taking off either side of 15.00 and returning to report successful sorties after landing at Lossiemouth more than seven hours later. The squadron dispatched thirteen Lancasters on the 15th as part of a 3 Group G-H force assigned to the marshalling yards at Siegen, situated fifty miles east of Cologne, but they were recalled after the fighter escort was unable to take-off in the prevailing weather conditions. The operation was rescheduled for the following day, when a force of 108 Lancasters was made ready, of which eighteen were provided by 75(NZ) Squadron. They took off between 11.13 and 11.27 with S/L Bailey the senior pilot on duty and encountered icing-bearing cloud between base and 06°E with tops at 20,000 feet. This led to sixteen early returns, three of which involved Mepal crews. One of these, captained by F/Sgt Flamank, had a terrifying experience over the Channel, when he tried to counter ice build-up on HK554 JN-Z at 14,000 feet by coming down to 4,000 feet, only to have the aircraft continue to drop like a stone. Unable to jettison his load against the G forces, he finally regained control just above the wave tops, and no doubt with great relief, headed off to the jettison area. When the cloud began to break up at the fighter rendezvous point at 03°E, the bomber stream found itself to be about fifteen minutes ahead of schedule and orbited before forming up into a recognisable gaggle, which was maintained for the remainder of the outward flight. The target was covered by nine-tenths cloud, but the flares were concentrated and the bombing appeared to be accurate, while the USAAF 8th Air Force escort kept enemy fighters at arm's length. The bombing did hit Siegen and the neighbouring town of Weidenau, but destroyed many public buildings and houses rather than the railway yards.

It was on the 16th that the German counter attack began against American forces in the Ardennes in what became known as the Battle of the Bulge. The Americans were taken completely by surprise as the German armoured divisions forced their way through the Allied lines in an attempt to recapture Brussels and the port of Antwerp. On the night of the 17/18th a 1 Group main force took off to attack the city of Ulm, situated on the Danube to the south-east of Stuttgart and west of Augsburg in southern Germany. It was similar in nature to the recently-bombed Heilbronn, and as a result of the catastrophic raid there, the local Gauleiter had urged the women and children to evacuate the inner city urgently. Plans were put in place to begin evacuation on Monday the 18th, so that Advent could be observed on the Sunday, but something caused a change of plan and loudspeaker vans toured the city on Sunday urging the population to leave at once, which proved to be a fortuitous move. Unlike Heilbronn, Ulm contained industry, including the important Magirus-Deutz and Kässbohrer lorry factories, and there were also military barracks and depots. One square kilometre of the city became engulfed in flames, affecting in some way 82% of the built-up area and even though the evacuation saved many lives, seven hundred fatalities were recorded.

Other virtually virgin urban areas would find themselves similarly in the firing line as the Command sought fresh targets to keep its bombers busy now that the major towns and cities had been reduced to rubble. On the 19th seventeen 75(NZ) Squadron Lancasters were made ready for a 3 Group G-H raid on the railway yards at Trier, through which the enemy could bring reinforcements to the battle front. In the event, poor weather at Mepal prevented them from taking off, leaving only thirty-two Lancasters to carry out the attack and cause substantial damage within the town. Four Lancasters did manage to get off the ground at Mepal either side of 15.30 bound for an undisclosed garden in the Baltic to lay mines, and all successfully completed their brief before returning safely to Lossiemouth more than seven hours later.

Trier was the target again on the 21st, when a 3 Group force of 145 Lancasters was made ready for a two-phase attack. Thirty-two aircraft, mostly from 31 Base, were unable to take-off in the prevailing weather conditions, leaving 113, including 75(NZ) Squadron's twenty Lancasters, to do the job. They departed Mepal between 12.14 and 12.37 with S/L Rodgers the senior pilot on duty and reached the target to find it concealed beneath a layer of low cloud, which had not been forecast. Originally intended as a visual attack controlled by a Master Bomber and Deputy, it was changed to G-H at the last minute and fourteen of the Mepal crews bombed with their leaders, while six others were unable to do so as their leader, F/L McDonald in NF981 JN-Y, was prevented from releasing his load, apparently because of an electrical failure. Four of these crews jettisoned instead. As the bombers turned away, a circle of thick, black smoke began to drift up through the cloud tops and the consensus among returning crews was of a concentrated and successful raid, although no genuine assessment was possible. A local report mentioned heavy casualties as a result of the second phase attack. F/L Hannan landed at Mendlesham on return but flew back to Mepal that evening.

That night, other groups attacked railway targets at Cologne and Bonn while 5 Group attended to an oil refinery at Politz. There was to be no rest for Trier as a third 3 Group raid was sent against it on the 23rd, this this time involving a force of 153 Lancasters, among them twenty-one from 75(NZ) Squadron, whose crews had been briefed for this operation on the previous day and had been on stand-by waiting in vain for a break in the weather. This might have been a nervous wait for F/O Haddon Shaw Miles RNZAF, who was about to undertake his maiden operation. They departed Mepal between 11.44 and 12.00 with S/L Bailey the senior pilot on duty and benefitted from the much-improved weather conditions as they formed up and headed south-eastwards. They ran the gauntlet of intense, predicted flak as they traversed the battle front shortly after crossing the Luxembourg/Germany frontier, and it was here that a 90 Squadron Lancaster exploded with great force and spread itself far and wide to become the single Bomber Command casualty of the operation. The others continued on to cover the short distance to the target, which they found beneath clear skies, and the planned visual attack took place under the excellent control of the Master Bomber, S/L Scott of 90 Squadron. He cancelled the one errant TI, and the town was soon enveloped in smoke and dust.

The target for an early-evening attack on the 24th was Hangelar airfield near Bonn, for which the squadron made ready twenty-one Lancasters. Mepal had been shrouded in fog all day and was one of a number of stations unable to launch its aircraft. The operation went ahead with 104 Lancasters from 31 and 32 Bases and Methwold, but crews were unable to offer an assessment of results. Thick fog reduced visibility to no more than a hundred yards on the 25th, ensuring that, once the day's planned operation had been cancelled during morning briefing, the final wartime Christmas could be celebrated in traditional style at Mepal. The Airmen's Christmas Dinner began at 12.30, followed by a film show at 15.00 and an all-Ranks dance at 20.00.

The weather had greatly improved by Boxing Day, and aircraft from all groups combined to support the Allied ground forces in the Ardennes as the German advance ran out of steam around St Vith in Belgium. 75(NZ) Squadron was not called into action but made ready twenty-six Lancasters on the 27th for an attack on Cologne, which was cancelled in favour of the nearby Rheydt marshalling yards. G-H leaders and inexperienced crews were scrubbed from the order of battle at Mepal and twenty Lancasters ultimately took off between 12.10 and 13.00 with S/L Bailey the senior pilot on duty. They joined up with 180 others drawn from 1, 3, 5 and 8 Groups for a visual attack controlled by a Master Bomber, which took place under clear skies and produced accurate and concentrated bombing. Clouds of smoke were seen to rise over the target and post-raid reconnaissance revealed severe damage in the southern half of the yards and widespread destruction in the town to the east. Several crews reported the considerable danger posed by bombs cascading from aircraft above at 23,000 feet, in some cases forcing them into violent evasive action. The single missing aircraft was the 75(NZ) Squadron Lancaster, NN710 AA-Q, which was struck by bombs from above and was seen to spiral down to crash in the target area. This was a particularly tragic way for F/O Haddon Miles RNZAF and all but one of his crew to lose their lives, on only their second operation together. The wireless operator was also a member of the RNZAF, and the sole survivor was the bomb-aimer, who fell into enemy hands. F/O "Stan" Davies had suffered a starboard-outer engine fire in HK573 AA-H not long after take-off, but feathered it and carried on to bomb, despite being unable to climb above 11,000 feet on three engines. A hung-up bomb had to be manually released, and then a FW190 approached, forcing evasive action and the firing of a red Verey distress flare. Luckily for them, two USAAF P38 Lightnings arrived on the scene and were happy to escort Stan and the boys back to friendly territory. The incident is mentioned in F/O Davies' DFC citation.

On the following day twenty-one crews were briefed at Mepal for a raid on the Gremberg marshalling yards situated south-east of Cologne city centre. It was a 3 Group show involving 167 Lancasters, for which the Mepal element took off between 12.00 and 12.19 with W/C Newton leading the squadron into battle for the first time. Two other pilots were also on debut, both RNZAF, F/O Roderick Bruce Crawford and P/O Valentine Richard Egglestone. F/O Sadgrove in LM276 AA-S "Sugar" lost his starboard-inner engine immediately after take-off, but carried on until his starboard-outer also began to lose power and he found himself unable to keep up with the stream. He jettisoned his cookie and four of his 250 pounders live over the Channel from 6,000 feet at 14.51, when some forty miles short of Dieppe and brought the remaining bombs home. The others pressed on in favourable conditions towards the target, where the approach to bomb was beset with a great deal of jockeying for position as crews attempted to attach themselves to a G-H leader. Some aircraft were observed to be well above the main bunch, as high as 21,000 feet and this put others in danger of being hit by falling bombs. W/C Newton in NF935 AA-P dropped his bombs four miles short of the release point because of a technical fault and F/O Davies in PB418 AA-C released fifteen seconds early when bombs from above fell dangerously close to his Lancaster. F/O McMillan complained that crews were releasing "window" without breaking the string holding the bundles together, and F/O Osborne's beef was that he was wedged in by other aircraft flying between 500 and 2,000 feet above and he and his crew were forced to watch as bombs passed within feet of them. Despite this organised chaos, the bombing was concentrated, and a mushroom of smoke was seen to rise through the low cloud to reach 9,000 feet as the force retreated.

The railway theme continued at Koblenz on the 29th, a main centre serving the Ardennes battle front. Attacks were briefed for the Mosel marshalling yards near the city centre, previously attacked by 1 and 8 Groups a week earlier, and the Lützel yards in a northern suburb and eighty-five Lancasters of 3 Group were made ready for the latter. Nine of these represented 75(NZ) Squadron and took off between 12.00 and 12.09 with S/Ls Rodgers and Wright the senior pilots on duty. All reached the target area to find good visibility and the 4 Group attack in progress, and the 3 Group attack began as planned at H+8. Mixed opinions were offered by returning crews as to the effectiveness of the raid, F/L Barton calling it scattered and inaccurate, while others reported concentrated bombing with explosions and black smoke. 3 Group leaned towards the former, blaming a poor G-H signal, clear skies allowing the flak gunners to be more accurate, and the tail-end of the 4 Group raid becoming mixed up with the lead aircraft from 3 Group. A local report spoke of the bombing completing the destruction begun by the Americans on the previous day and reported the railway to be blocked and the Koblenz-Lützel bridge to be out of action for the rest of the war.

Four crews were sent mining in the Rosemary garden in the Heligoland Bight on the 30th, using "special equipment", which usually referred to H2S, and they departed Mepal between 16.35 and 16.55. All successfully planted their mines in the allotted areas, three of them noting enemy night-fighters in the vicinity, but only F/O Parsons and crew in LM544 AA-J became involved in a combat, which they survived and claimed the assailant, a Ju88, as damaged. F/Sgt Pearson and crew in LM740 AA-B watched an enemy aircraft drop flares half a mile away, which the Lancaster gunners shot out, before the pilot corkscrewed the bomber down into cloud for a safe return.

The final operation of the year launched from Mepal was against the railway yards at Vohwinkel, situated on the south-eastern edge of the Ruhr between Düsseldorf and Wuppertal. 75(NZ) Squadron contributed seventeen Lancasters to a 3 Group G-H force of 155 aircraft, and they took off between 11.30 and 11.46 with F/Ls Barton, Hannan, McDonald and Yates the senior pilots on duty. They had to pass through accurate heavy flak on the way to the target and found themselves driven on by a wind forty m.p.h faster than had been forecast. On return to Mepal the crews reported a scattered attack, for which the wind appeared to be responsible. Two aircraft failed to return, both from 218 Squadron, and they had been observed to be hit by falling bombs.

During the course of the month the squadron carried out eighteen operations including the recall and dispatched 275 sorties for the loss of two Lancasters and one crew. It had been another uncompromising year for the crews of 75(NZ) Squadron since its return to the forefront of operations with the advent of the Lancaster, but the end was in sight as the scent of victory wafted in from the Continent. Much remained to be done, however, before the proud and tenacious enemy finally laid down his arms, and more crews would be sacrificed in the remaining months of the war.

Above and below: Stirling EH948, AA-Q, "Queenie" piloted by F/Sgt Cecil "Snow" Armstrong, formation flying, January 1944.
EH948 was lost in Kiel Bay with the Bruhns crew on the 24th of February.
(Both photos from the Dennis Jones collection, via Glynis Bakker)

F/Sgt Harold Henry Bruhns RNZAF, lost with all his crew on the 24th of February 1944 flying EH948, AA-Q, "Queenie". (AWMM)

*Right: Stirlings and "erks" at dispersal, Mepal.
(Gerry Newey collection, courtesy of Phil and Bruce Newey)*

"C" Flight Inst Sect Mepal. Mac, Doherty, Burley, Frost, Ansell and Dave Smith." From the collection of Joe Tomlin, Instrument Repairer. (NZ Bomber Command Assn. archives, Tomlin collection)

Staged "crew" photos, Mepal, February-March 1944, above (L-R): P/O Glen Marshall (wireless operator, Witting crew), Sgt Reg Gunn (flight engineer, Witting crew), Sgt Alf Newnham (rear gunner, S/L Max's crew), F/Sgt Alan Bromley (wireless operator, Burke crew), F/O Henry Murray (pilot), Sgt John McFarland (navigator, Murray crew). (Both photos thanks to Elizabeth McFarland, via David and Helen McFarland)

Above and below: W/C Roy Max (far right) briefing crews for an operation, 10 March 1944. (NZ Bomber Command Assn. archives, Fearon collection))

Crews at briefing before an operation, 10 March 1944. F/O Murray Fearon (navigator, F.H. Turner crew) left of centre, wearing glasses. (NZ Bomber Command Assn. archives, Fearon collection)

After briefing for "Special Operations" over France, airmen head to their aircraft, 10 March 1944. Includes members of the Herron, Baker and F. Turner crews. 7th from right is Sgt Kenneth Hook. (Air Force Museum of New Zealand)

The Herron crew de-briefing after "Special Operations" over France on the night of 10-11 March 1944. W/C Roy Max rear, leaning over the Intelligence Officer. (NZ Bomber Command Assn. archives)

After de-briefing; the standard meal of eggs and bacon, washed down by hot tea laced with rum. Members of the Baker crew at the left table, including F/Sgt Kenneth Hook (mid-upper gunner), 2nd from left. (Iain Hook)

P/O Colin McKenzie and his crew flew Stirling EF233 AA-L on a mining operation off La Rochelle, 13 March 1944. (NZ Bomber Command Assn archives, Ward collection)

The Colin McKenzie crew, October 1943 - June 1944 (L-R): Back - P/O Drummond Livingstone (navigator), unknown, W/O Jack Jones (wireless operator), P/O Gilbert Ward (air bomber). Front - unknown, P/O Colin McKenzie (skipper), unknown. (NZ Bomber Command Assn archives, Ward collection)

*"EH955 JN-K. Lost 19 April 1944 shot down by nightfighter over Denmark.
Due to "C" Flight re-equipping with Lanc's in March 44 this a/c re-lettered "AA-K" just before being lost."
From the collection of Joe Tomlin, Instrument Repairs Section, C Flight.
(NZ Bomber Command Assn. archives, Tomlin collection)*

*F/O Robert Weir Herron RNZAF, lost with
all his crew on 27th April 1944.
(AWMM)*

*S/L Euan Wilfred Sachtler RNZAF, lost with
all his crew on the night of the 1st/2nd of
May 1944, crashing at St Arnault in France.
(AWMM)*

C Flight ground crew with one of the new Lancasters, LL888 JN-X, March, 1944.
FME LAC Dennis Jones 4th from left, front.
(Air Force Museum of New Zealand)

"Danger! Erks at work!" C Flight armourers with a 4,000 lb 'Cookie', Mepal, May 1944.
(Dennis Jones collection, via Glynis Bakker)

The Megson crew (L-R): Back - Sgt John Overfield-Collins (flight engineer), F/Sgt Thomas Rowe (rear gunner), Sgt Frank Ball (mid-upper gunner), F/Sgt Albert Fagg (air bomber). Front - F/O Stanley Walton (navigator), P/O Colin "Lucky" Megson (skipper), Sgt T. Hamilton (wireless operator). (Dennis Jones collection, via Glynis Bakker)

F/L Derek Warren RAFVR and his crew were lost on the 11/12th of May 1944, their Lancaster exploding and crashing near Aardenburg. (AWMM)

F/O Jack William Walters DFC, RNZAF ex-75 (NZ) Squadron wireless operator lost on 19/20th May 1944 flying with W/C Fraser Barron DSO & Bar, DFC, DFM, RNZAF. (AWMM)

The Berney crew, mid-1944 (L-R): Back- F/S Roy Young (air bomber), Sgt W.J. Todd (flight engineer), Sgt Frederick Hulbert (mid-upper gunner), Sgt S. Bellis (rear gunner). Front - P/O Eric McNamara (wireless operator), S/L Richard Berney (skipper and flight commander), F/O Murray Fearon (navigator). S/L Berney took over the crew after their original skipper, F/Sgt Francis Turner, was hospitalised with pneumonia in March.
(NZ Bomber Command Assn archives, Fearon collection)

"D-Dog refuelling"
(NZ Bomber Command Assn. archives, Mayhill collection)

On their first operation with the squadron, S/L Berney's bomb aimer F/Sgt Roy Young took this photo from Lancaster ME690 AA-Z over the target, Courtrai, 10/11th May 1944. The photo flash flare (lower right) has illuminated falling bombs, centre and left. (NZ Bomber Command Assn archives, Fearon collection)

75 (NZ) Squadron Operations block and briefing room, Mepal, seen from B Flight dispersal. (NZ Bomber Command Assn. archives, Mayhill collection)

The Burke crew, all lost when shot down by a night fighter over Belgium on the night of the 22nd/23rd of May 1944. P/O Edgar Lawrence Burke RNZAF 4th from left.
(Simon Sommerville, 75nzsquadron.com)

P/O William Jarvis Willis RNZAF lost with all his crew on the night of the 21st/22nd of May 1944. (AWMM)

P/O Cecil Ernest "Snow" Armstrong RNZAF and his crew were also lost on the night of the 22nd/23rd May. (AWMM)

75 (NZ) Squadron RAF, Mepal, May 1944. Above, aircrew, W/C Roy Max seated front (5th chair from left). Below, B Flight aircrew (Acting Flight Commander F/L Eric Witting centre) and Ground crew. (NZ Bomber Command Assn. archives)

The Witting crew 1944 (L-R): Sgt Reg Gunn (flight engineer), F/Sgt Joe Collins (rear gunner), F/O Ted Anderson (navigator), F/L Eric Witting (skipper), P/O Jack Thomas (air bomber), F/Sgt William Campbell (mid-upper gunner), P/O Glen Marshall (wireless operator). (NZ Bomber Command Assn. archives)

F/L Eric Witting and W/C Jack Leslie at dispersal as they appear in the film "Maximum Effort", June 1944. ("Maximum Effort")

The Scott crew (L-R): Back – F/Sgt Stephen Cook (air bomber), F/Sgt Ron Howson (wireless operator). Front – F/Sgt "Red" Hill (navigator), F/Sgt Alan Mantle (mid-upper gunner), Sgt Frank Scott RNZAF (skipper), F/Sgt Reg Dale (rear gunner), Sgt Max Harris (flight engineer). Sgt Scott, F/Sgt Cook and F/Sgt Howson were killed when their Lancaster ND802 JN-D "The Flying Scottsmen" was shot down in southern Holland on the 27/28th of May 1944. (Jan Dodgson)

F/L Spencer Francis Fauvel RNZAF and seven crewmates were lost on the 27/28th of May shot down at Poelkapelle in Belgium. (AWMM)

F/Sgt Thomas Rodgers Donaghy RNZAF and all but one of his crew were lost on the 10/11th June 1944. (AWMM)

*F/Sgt Roland Desmond Ernest Betley RNZAF – there were no survivors when his Lancaster was shot down returning from Valenciennes on the 15/16th of June 1944.
(AWMM)*

*F/Sgt Benjamin William Bateson RNZAF and all his crew were killed on the 24th June 1944, shot down near Fruges.
(AWMM)*

*Lancaster ND914, AA-H swung on landing after an air test, 28th of May 1944.
(NZ Bomber Command Assn. archives, Tomlin collection)*

The Meyer crew June-October 1944 (L-R): Back – Sgt Bill Brown (rear gunner), Sgt George Payne (mid-upper gunner), F/O David Mercier (navigator), unknown, F/Sgt Arnel Meyer (skipper), unknown. Front – Sgt Glass (flight engineer), F/O Simon Snowden (bomb aimer). (NZ Bomber Command Assn. archives, Meyer collection)

"Our ground crew at Mepal. Spinney, Ginger and the two Bills". The team who maintained F/Sgt Arnel Meyer's Lancaster ND747 AA-T "Tommy". (NZ Bomber Command Assn. archives, Meyer collection)

*Left: S/L Neilson Arnold "Nick" Williamson RNZAF.
(Robyn Williamson-Omer)*

*Below: S/L Nick Williamson in the cockpit of Lancaster NE181, JN-M, "The Captain's Fancy".
(Robyn Williamson-Omer)*

*S/L Williamson crew's bomb aimer F/O Graham Coull (centre) receives camembert cheeses on the occasion of his 22nd birthday, Martragny, France, 2 July 1944. S/L Nick Williamson at right. Lancaster ND917, JN-O in the background. Williamson's emergency landing of a Lancaster on a fighter air strip in Normandy within shooting distance of the frontline made the news in England and back home. It was the first time he had flown a Lancaster.
(NZ Bomber Command Assn. archives)*

"1,000lb bombs loaded. Sqdn Ldr Williamson ("Nick") and some of the boys in a Lancaster bomb bay. L-R: "Brummie" Brown, Colin Pascall, S/L Nick Williamson. In front Cpl Pilkinton, at rear Sgt Reg Gay, Arthur Dean, & "Blondie"? Nick's dog at his feet." C Flight ground crew with Williamson and his Black Labrador Rex. The Lancaster is thought to be HK563, JN-S (later re-coded JN-W) "Paper Doll".
(Dennis Jones collection, via Glynis Bakker)

A fully-bombed-up LL942 JN-C "Charlie" was destroyed when it blew up at dispersal at 4.20am on the 30th of June 1944, damaging several other Lancasters. (NZ Bomber Command Assn. archives Mayhill collection)

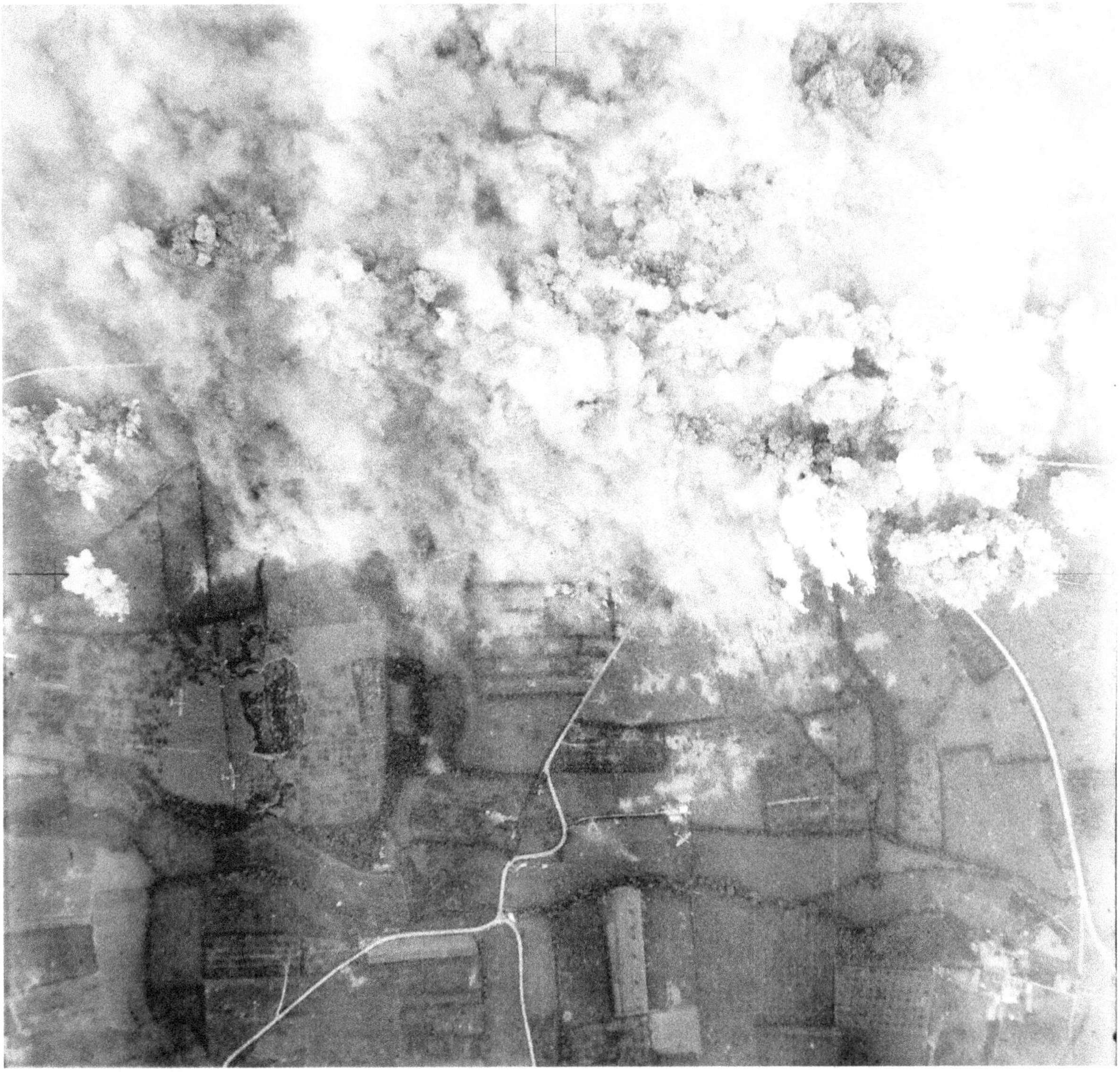

Bombing photo of the attack on Villers-Bocage (near Caen) on 30th of June 1944, taken by F/O Ron Mayhill, air bomber with the Aitken crew. Three Lancasters can be seen far below, two of them probably those of the Master Bomber and his deputy. It was the first time that massed heavy bombers had been used as 'artillery' before a ground attack. (NZ Bomber Command Assn. archives, Mayhill collection)

P/O Henry Burtt and crew flying Lancaster ND752 AA-O "Oboe" home from Cagny, on 18th of July 1944, photo taken by one of the Aitken crew. The Burtt crew were lost in this aircraft just two days later. (NZ Bomber Command Assn. archives, Mayhill collection)

The Whittington crew (L-R): Back - F/Sgt Andrew Fletcher (rear gunner), F/O Philip Tompkins (wireless operator), Sgt Desmond Wallace Gore (flight engineer,) Sgt Alfred Simpson (air bomber). Front - F/Lt Joseph Stevens (navigator), P/O Harold "Dick" Whittington (pilot), Sgt Ronald Batty (mid-upper gunner). All but Sgt Gore were killed when they were one of seven 75 (NZ) Squadron Lancasters shot down on the night of 20/21 July 1944. (Graham Nicholson)

*Lancaster ME691 crash site at Maria-Heide near Veghel, with the Vissers family and their damaged farmhouse, Sunday 23 July 1944. A piece of the Lancaster wreckage is visible at left, marked "Organ Grinder's Swing", a reference to a popular song of the 30's and 40's, and probably to the aircraft's previous 'owners', the Horgan crew.
(Mr H.F. du Maine, via his daughter Mrs Willie Bloks-du Maine, courtesy of Adrian van Zantvoort)*

F/Sgt Gerald Brian "Rocky" Roche RNZAF was killed with four of his crew on the disastrous Homberg operation, 20/21st of July 1944, shot down by a night fighter. Two managed to bale out; one was captured as a PoW and one successfully evaded.
(NZ Herald)

F/L Noel Alfred Deal Stokes RNZAF and his rear gunner died when their Lancaster NE148 AA-H was shot down on the night of 28/29th July 1944.
(AWMM)

P/O Colin George Nairne RNZAF and his crew were all lost in a collision over the Channel, returning from Amaye-sur-Seulles on 30th of July 1944.
(Keith Springer)

The Blance crew (L-R): Back – W/O Ronald "Oscar" Spencer (air bomber) Sgt Bill Hyde (flight engineer), F/Sgt Colin Greig (navigator) F/Sgt Frank Jenkins (mid-upper gunner). Front – F/Sgt Jim "Winkie" Kirk (rear gunner), P/O Ian Blance (skipper), F/Sgt Fred Climo (wireless operator). A night fighter shot down their Lancaster ND756 AA-M on the night of 28/29th of July 1944 near Millery village, killing P/O Blance, W/O Spencer, F/Sgts Jenkins and Climo. It was only their second operation. F/Sgt Greig was captured, but Kirk and Hyde evaded and made it back to England. (NZ Bomber Command Assn. archives, Kirk collection)

Lancaster ND756 AA-M, shot down with the Balance crew, 29th of July 1944. A very rare colour slide from the collection of P/O Ralph Barker, wireless operator in the Menzies crew. (Air Force Museum of New Zealand)

Incredibly, 1,500 people from Millery village turned out for the funeral of the four members of the Blance crew who died on 29th of July, creating an impressive floral tribute.
(Both photos this page NZ Bomber Command Assn. archives, Kirk collection)

F/O Wilson Orchard Hadley RNZAF killed with four of his crew on the night of 11/12th September 1944 on a mining operation in the Baltic Sea.
(AWMM)

S/L Garth Reginald Gunn RNZAF died as a result of injuries received from a crash landing at Hawkinge on the 17th of September 1944, in which his flight engineer was killed.
(AWMM)

Lancaster ND904 "Target For Tomorrow Night" was lost with the Galletly crew on 5th of October. Shown here with S/L Lin Drummond and crew, 15 August after a raid on St. Trond.
(Harry Holmes)

F/Sgt Alan Russell Galletly RNZAF.
(Alan Galletly via 75nzsquadron.com)

*75 (NZ) Squadron Lancasters flying in a "gaggle" to a daylight target.
(NZ Bomber Command Assn. archives, Jack Meehan collection)*

*Below: The 15th of August attack on the night fighter airfield at St Trond Belgium clearly showing the crossed runways. Taken by F/Sgt Clive Estcourt, bomb aimer in the Layton crew, flying HK600 "AA-J".
(NZ Bomber Command Assn. archives, Estcourt collection)*

The Layton crew (L-R): F/Sgt Clive Estcourt (bomb aimer), F/Sgt David Light (mid-upper gunner), P/O John "Aussie" Layton (skipper), F/Sgt John Christie (navigator), F/Sgt Leslie Moore (rear gunner), Sgt F. Samuel (flight engineer), F/Sgt Ta Tio Tuaine Nicholas (wireless operator). On the night of 16/17th August, returning from Stettin, F/Sgt Moore claimed a JU88 as damaged. (NZ Bomber Command Assn. archives, Estcourt collection)

*Off duty and enjoying some sun. F/Sgt Jack Meehan 4th from left.
(NZ Bomber Command Assn. archives, Meehan collection)*

Above left and right: The starboard rudder of Lancaster ND801 after colliding with a German night fighter on the 8th August 1944. (Robert McAdam, via 75nzsquadron.com)

Left: 75 (NZ) Squadron Lancasters fly over Mepal in formation on return from a daylight attack on Le Havre, September 1944. (NZ Bomber Command Assn. archives Tomlin collection)

Lancaster ND782 AA-U "Uncle" with F/O John "Jake" Aitken in the cockpit, August 1944. (NZ Bomber Command Assn. archives, Mayhill collection)

Looking from under the bomb bay of ND782 AA-U "Uncle" loaded with 500lb HEs, towards the Meyer crew's Lancaster ND747 AA-T "Tommy", August 1944. (NZ Bomber Command Assn. archives, Mayhill collection)

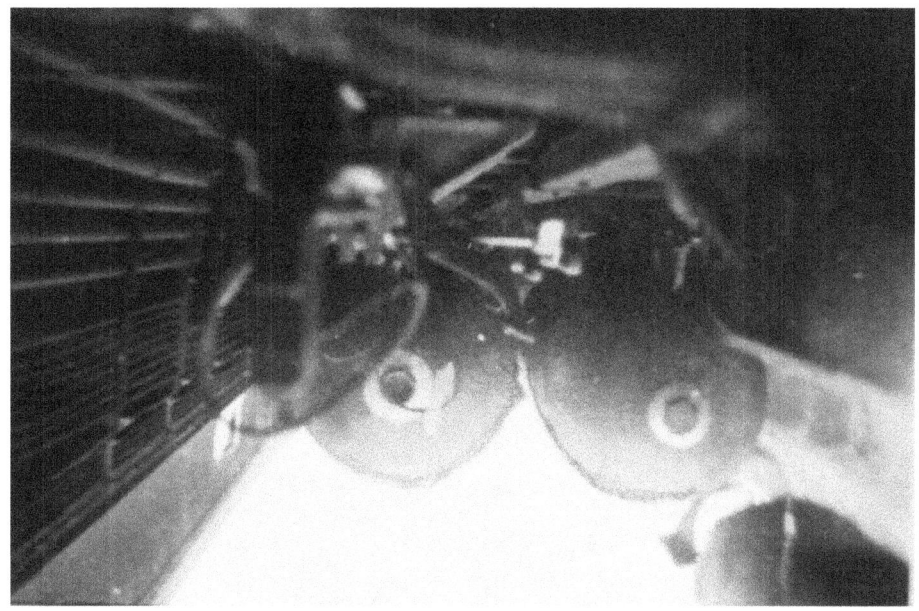

*Bomb aimer F/O Ron Mayhill's view of the bomb bay in flight.
(NZ Bomber Command Assn. archives, Mayhill collection)*

Ron Mayhill's spectacular bombing photo, 4th August attack on the oil storage facility at Bec d'Ambes. The Aitken crew were flying ND782 AA-U "Uncle" at 7000 feet. (NZ Bomber Command Assn. archives, Mayhill collection)

Formating on Mepal lanes on the return from Hamel, 14th August 1944. In the foreground, Lancaster HK562 AA-L 'Lucy', piloted by Des Brown, and behind is HK574 AA-R 'Rio Rita', piloted by Harry Yates.
(NZ Bomber Command Assn. archives, Mayhill collection)

In the circuit - Mepal base from the air.
(NZ Bomber Command Assn. archives, Mayhill collection)

*Members of the Glossop crew with Lancaster, 1944. F/Sgt Jack Meehan 4th from left.
(NZ Bomber Command Assn. archives, Meehan collection)*

*Glossop crew members on top of their Lancaster, 1944. F/Sgt Jack Meehan centre top.
(NZ Bomber Command Assn. archives, Meehan collection)*

F/O Vic Adolph and his crew with Lancaster PB520 AA-G.
(NZ Bomber Command Assn. archives, Adolph collection)

On the 11th of September F/O Vic Adolph and his crew took Lancaster PB520 AA-G to Kamen.
(NZ Bomber Command Assn. archives, Adolph collection)

Bombing photo showing the attack on the Kamen oil refinery, 11th of September 1944. Taken by the Adolph crew's bomb aimer F/O Richard Hodgson from Lancaster PB520 AA-G.
(NZ Bomber Command Assn. archives, Adolph collection)

Members of the Jim Elmslie crew with Lancaster LM266 AA-A "The Seven Sinners", probably 7 October 1944.
(NZ Bomber Command Assn. archives, Wiltshire collection)

No. 75 (NZ) Squadron R.A.F. — Battle Order – 14th October 1944 (DUISBURG)

A/C	Captain	Navigator	A/Bomber	W/O Air	F/Eng	MU/Gnr	R/Gnr
A	F/O Bateman	F/S Monoghan	F/O Ward	F/S Teverson	Sgt Scott	Sgt. Williams	F/S Fox
B	F/O Bright	F/L Dawes	F/O Laing	F/S Kemp	Sgt Funnell	Sgt Woods	Sgt Newman
C	S/L Earl	F/O Lovejoy	F/O Rich	F/O Finnegan	W/O Howells	W/O Brown	F/O Goodridge
D	F/O Martyn	F/O Elliot	P/O Dunkerley	P/O Abrahams	F/S Golombeck	Sgt Lindsay-	P/O Wright
E	F/O Glossip	F/S McNeil	F/S Mace	F/S Meehan	Sgt Harvey	Sgt Killick	Sgt Howarth
F	F/O McRitchie	Sgt Purdy	F/S Jolliffe	Sgt Crabtree	Sgt Starkey	Sgt Bolland	F/S Whitehead
G	P/O Freidrich	Sgt Grant	F/S Moore	F/S Jenkins	Sgt Johnstone	Sgt Bates	Sgt Howell
H	F/S Elmslie	F/S Wiltshire	F/S McKenzie	Sgt Dear	Sgt Futter	F/S Burbury	Sgt Vallender
J	F/O Dare	F/O Warren	F/S McDonald	F/S Neville	Sgt Dunbar	F/S Bannan	F/S Lawton
K	F/L Baxter	P/O Birch	F/S Higgins	F/S Kereama	Sgt Haig Brown	Sgt Kelsey	Sgt Whitlam
T	F/S Tweed	F/S Long	F/S John	F/S Pollard	Sgt Neil	Sgt Bangar	Sgt Bishop
M	F/L Brown	F/S Wood	F/S Harkness	F/S Billing	Sgt Rattle	F/S De Lungo	Sgt Fitzpatrick
N	F/O Plummer	F/S Humphreys	F/O Holloway	W/O Chambers	Sgt Fell	F/O Scott	F/S McDonald
S	F/O Winter	F/O Parsons	F/S Muir	F/O Calloway	Sgt Oades	Sgt Crome	Sgt Cooks
O	F/O Ford	F/O Weeden	F/O Chapman	F/S Tredinnick	Sgt Muller	Sgt Glover	Sgt Fitzwater
Q	F/O Gawith	F/O Baker	F/O Taylor	F/O Piesse	Sgt Jones	Sgt Caldwell	Sgt Beeston
P	F/S Gordon	P/O Bell	F/S Weston	F/S Otway	Sgt Freeman	Sgt Hone	Sgt Forrester
R	F/O Atkin	F/S Coulson	F/S Thurston	F/S Curtis	Sgt Jones	Sgt Madden	Sgt Johnstone
L	F/S Osbourne	F/S McCarthy	F/S Harris	F/S Mason	Sgt Smulovitch	Sgt Pretty	Sgt Pryce
U	F/O Spain	F/S Renner	F/S James	F/S Bergman	Sgt McNeil	Sgt Dickinson	Sgt Chamberlain
M JN	S/L Williamson	P/S Woonton	F/S Mathers	F/S Witchard	F/O Moss	P/O Ellis	F/L Tugwell
W JN	F/O May z	F/S Carrington	W/O Tuck	F/S Lewis	Sgt Hutton	F/S Calnon	F/S McDowell
P JN	F/O Wood @	F/S Johnson	F/O Hurcombe	F/S Taylor	Sgt Gibbs	Sgt Woolley	Sgt Mahoney
F JN	F/O Scott	F/S Scott	F/S Anderson	F/S Howard	Sgt Thomas	Sgt Beardmore	Sgt Bayes
V JN	P/S McCartin	Sgt Miles	F/O Martin	F/S Smith	Sgt Warlow	Sgt Bryer	Sgt Gray
O JN	F/O O'Callaghan	F/S Hartley	F/S Mitchell	F/S' Matheson	Sgt Simpson	Sgt Baines	Sgt Sheperd
D JN	F/O Wilson	F/S Morris	F/O Fitch	P/O Buckworth	Sgt Watkins	F/S Jones	F/S Pettet
K JN	F/O Smith	F/S Lynch	F/S Willetts	W/O Cocks	Sgt Flynn	Sgt Jones	Sgt Johnson
Z JN	F/O Boyer	F/S Mendes	F/S Couper	F/S Blue	Sgt Burkell	Sgt Adlard	Sgt Davies
Y JN	F/O Cumming	F/S Scott	F/S Sewell	F/S Cristie	Sgt Lambert	Sgt Scott	Sgt McElligott
X AA	F/L Waugh	F/S Morgan	F/S Newman	F/S Beag	Sgt Graves	Sgt Brewer	Sgt Cooper

2nd Pilots:- x F/O Cumberpatch   x F/L Barton
z F/O Simpson   @ F/O Butler

Officer i/c Flying:- W/C Leslie, A.F.C.

DUTY PERSONNEL
Eng. Officer:- F/L Fuller Sigs. Officer:- F/S Hancock A,C.P. Sgt Foote W/Mechs:- Cpl Allen, Lac Nixon I/Reprs:- Cpl Tomlin
Lac Roback Photo:- AC Edwards Stores:- Lac Bellamy Compass Adjstr:- Sgt Dalby Radar:- P/O Anthony Elect. Officer:- P/O Lang
Elects.: - Cpl Smart Lac Boulton Armt.Officer:- Sgt Conner Armr:- Cpl Walton Sgt Holdsworth Lac Stride.

Signed ....
for Wing Commander, Commanding, No. 75 (NZ) Squadron, R.A.F.

75 (NZ) Squadron Battle Order for the Duisburg operation, 14th October 1944, as posted on the Operations noticeboard. W/C Leslie Officer in Charge of Flying. Crews and their allocated aircraft were listed under A, B and C Flights, with designated 2nd Pilots and duty personnel listed below. Usually a reserve aircraft and crew were also nominated. Cpl Joe Tomlin listed as in charge of Instrument Repairs.
(NZ Bomber Command Assn. archives, Tomlin collection)

P/O Jack Plummer won an Immediate DFC on the night of 14/15th October 1944 when he flew his Lancaster back to England and landed safely, despite having most of the nose and windshield blown away over Duisburg and suffering frostbite to his hands.
(Humphries collection)

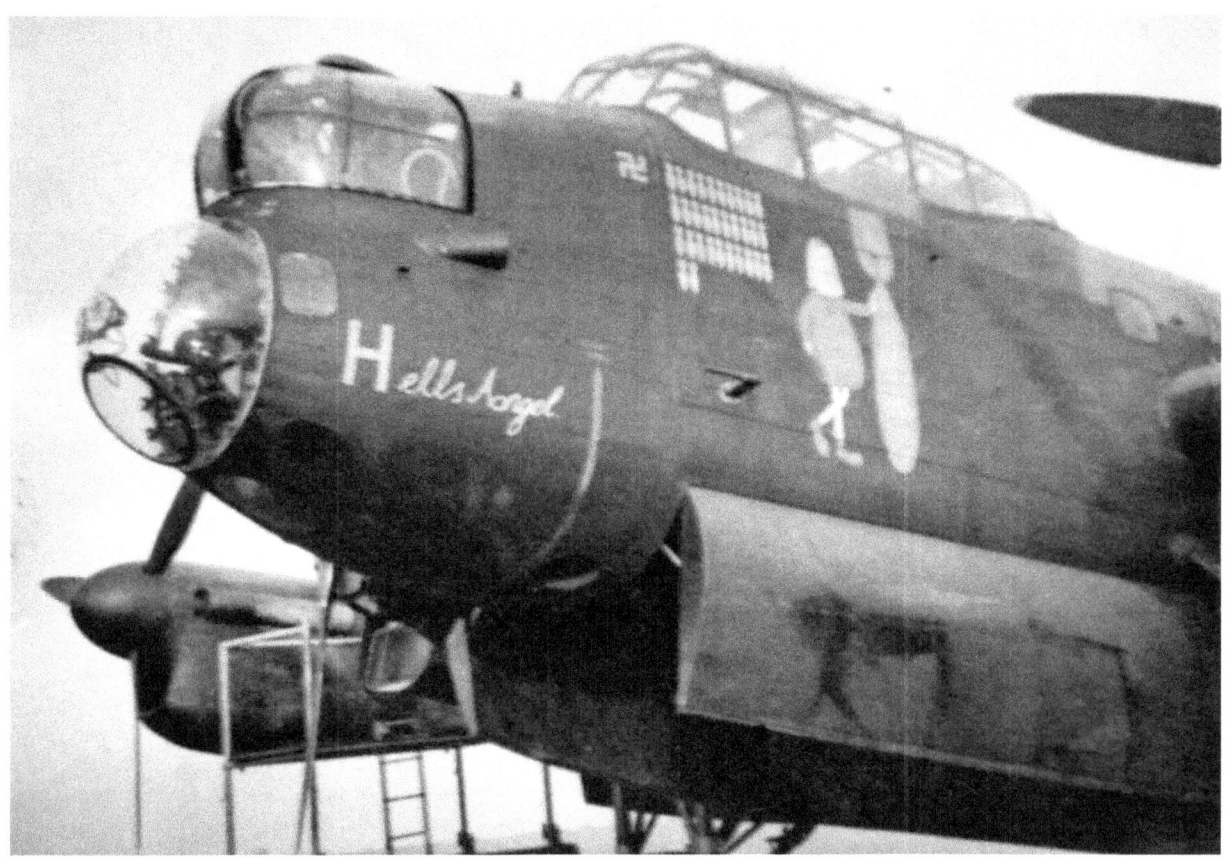

*"Hells Angel", Lancaster HK593 AA-H, showing 32 op's marked, so probably taken 1-2 November 1944. HK593 was re-coded JN-X in February 1945 and the "Hell's Angel" nickname disappeared.
(NZ Bomber Command Assn. archives, Tomlin collection)*

*Bombing up a C Flight Lancaster at dispersal. A "Cookie" (under the bomb bay), 500 pounders and incendiaries.
(NZ Bomber Command Assn. archives)*

F/O Patrick Leo McCartin RAAF and all but one of his crew were lost over Homberg on the 20th of November 1944. Photo thought to be taken in the cockpit of their regular Lancaster ND911 JN-V with 70 op's marked – it was lost on its 72nd op'. (Australian War Memorial)

The McCartin crew, six lost and one PoW, 20 November 1944. (Harry Holmes)

The Sam Wilson crew after they were tour expired on 21 November 1944, in front of their regular "kite" Lancaster HK601 JN-D "Dog" or "Snifter", celebrating with their ground crew (L-R): Back – F/Sgt William Morris (navigator), Sgt Leonard Watkins (flight engineer), F/O Sam Wilson (skipper), Cpl Ron Schoefield (ground crew), F/O Alan Fitch (air bomber), P/O G. Buckworth (wireless operator). Front - Unknown ground crew, F/Sgt "Shorty" Pettet (rear gunner), LAC Dennis Jones (Flight Mechanic Engines, ground crew), F/Sgt Clarie Jones (mid-upper gunner), Sgt Alan Rowe (ground crew). Dog's wheelblock in front. (Dennis Jones collection, via Glynis Bakker)

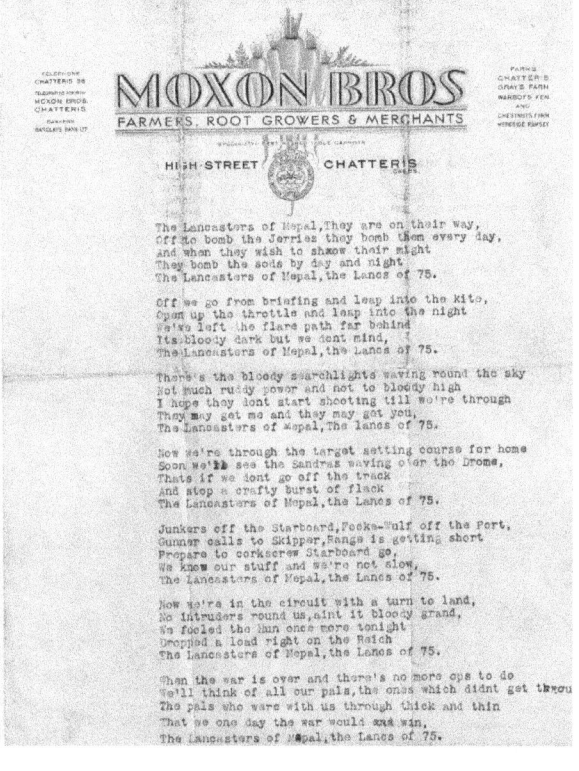

A popular squadron sing-a-long, "The Lancs of Mepal", sung to the tune of "Lili Marlene". Lyrics typed up on the letterhead of Moxon Bro's, carrot growers and merchants, Chatteris (about 5 miles away from Mepal). (NZ Bomber Command Assn. archives, Meehan collection)

The three Flight Commanders, late 1944. L-R: S/L Bob Rodgers, B Flight, S/L Jack Wright, A Flight, S/L Jack Bailey, C Flight. (NZ Bomber Command Assn. archives, Baker collection)

Bombing Leader F/L "Russ" Russell used a motorbike with side car to get around the Mepal dispersals. (From G.A. Russell's "Dying for Democracy")

The Hubert Rees crew all survived as PoWs after being shot down over Homberg on the 20th of November 1944. *(David Layne, via Rootschat)*

F/O John Harold Scott RNZAF and his crew were all lost on the Solingen op', 4th of November 1944. *(AWMM)*

A group of C Flight ground crew, including several whose autographs appear in the Christmas Day menu (L-R): Peter Rainbow, Cyril Stone, Colin Penfold, Gerry Tiller, Victor Smith. Sitting: Tom McGibbon, Bob Pirie. Front: Ron Stroud. *(Dennis Jones collection, via Glynis Bakker)*

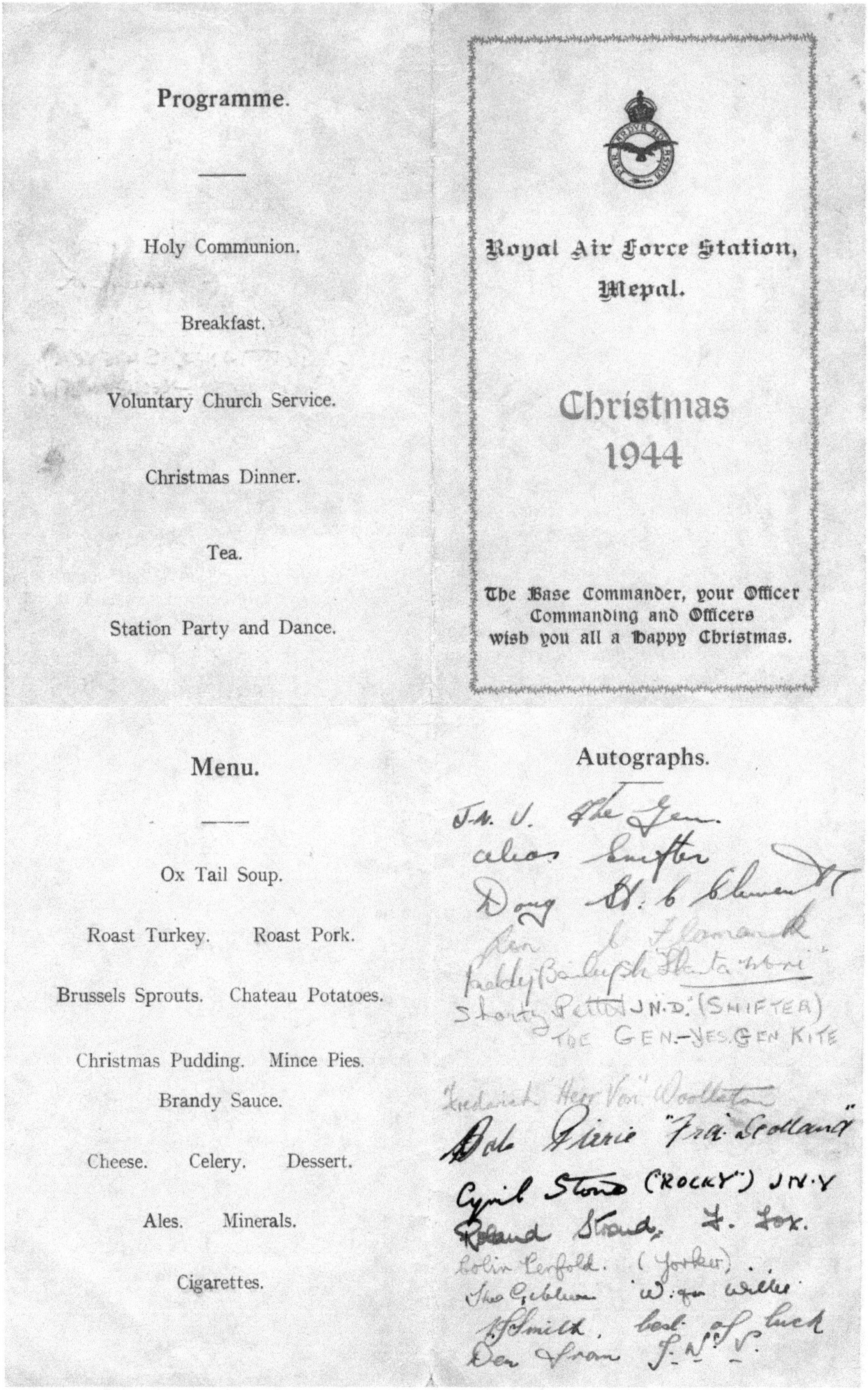

Programme.

Holy Communion.

Breakfast.

Voluntary Church Service.

Christmas Dinner.

Tea.

Station Party and Dance.

Royal Air Force Station,
Mepal.

Christmas
1944

The Base Commander, your Officer
Commanding and Officers
wish you all a Happy Christmas.

Menu.

Ox Tail Soup.

Roast Turkey. Roast Pork.

Brussels Sprouts. Chateau Potatoes.

Christmas Pudding. Mince Pies.
Brandy Sauce.

Cheese. Celery. Dessert.

Ales. Minerals.

Cigarettes.

Autographs.

J.N. V. The Gen.
alias Snifter
Doug St. C Clement
Ron J Flamank
Shorty Pettit J.N.D. (SNIFTER)
THE GEN.–YES. GEN KITE
Frederick "Herr Von" Woolterton
Bob Pirie "Fra Scotland"
Cyril Stone ("ROCKY") J.N.Y
Roland Stroud, T. Fox.
Colin Penfold. (Yorker)
V. Smith, best of luck
Den from J.N.V.

1944 RAF Mepal Christmas Day programme and Christmas Dinner menu card. Signatures collected by LAC Dennis Jones, FME for Lancaster HK601, JN-D "Dog" aka. "Snifter", include pilots Doug StClair Clement and Ron Flamank, C Flight Commander S/L "Paddy" Bailey, "Shorty" Pettit (rear gunner, tour-expired Wilson crew), and C Flight ground crew – Fred Woolterton, Bob Pirie, Cyril Stone, Ron Stroud, Colin Penfold, Tom McGibbon and Victor Smith. (Dennis Jones collection, via Glynis Bakker)

*Lancaster ND801 JN-X "Get Sum Inn" skipper F/L Tom Waugh and his flight engineer Sgt N. Southgate. Probably taken before the crew's last op' to Merseburg on the 6th of December.
(Robert McAdam, via Harry Holmes)*

*Below, the Osborne crew (L-R): Back – F/Sgt Derek Mason (wireless operator), F/O Bill Osborne (pilot), Sgt Henry Smulovitch (fight engineer) and Sgt Jack Pryce (rear gunner). Front – Sgt Sid Petty (mid-upper gunner, F/Sgt Pat McCarthy (navigator) and F/Sgt Len Harris (air bomber). Standing in front of HK562 AA-L "Lucy", probably 28 December 1944, before her 64th operation to Gremberg marshalling yards, Cologne.
(Gerry Newey collection, thanks to Phil & Bruce Newey)*

January 1945

The year in which victory would finally be achieved brought no let-up in the pace of operations, although worthwhile targets were becoming increasingly difficult to find. The defences, while stretched beyond their limit to protect all corners of the Reich, were still capable of hitting back and many more crews would go down before the end finally came. The New Year began in hectic fashion as the Luftwaffe launched its ill-conceived and ultimately ill-fated Operation Bodenplatte (Baseplate) at first light on the 1st. Designed to catch Allied aircraft on the ground at the liberated airfields in France, Belgium and Holland, it succeeded only modestly and cost the enemy day fighter squadrons 250 aircraft and around 150 pilots killed, wounded or captured, a setback from which it would never recover, while the Allies could make good their losses within hours from their enormous stockpiles..

3 Group's 1945 campaign began with a return to the railway yards at Vohwinkel on the 1st, for which 75(NZ) Squadron made ready nineteen Lancasters as part of an overall force of 146. They took off between 15.45 and 16.05 with W/C Newton and S/L Wright the senior pilots on duty, each aircraft carrying a cookie, a selection of 500 pounders and some Munro bombs. Newton was flying "Nan", the Lancaster that had belonged to F/L Harry Yates, who had finished his tour the day before. In his book "Luck and a Lancaster", Yates described his sentimental decision to excuse himself from farewell drinks at the "Three Pickerels" so he could see his old kite off that evening. It is believed that ME321 AA-N "Nan" was the victim of a Ju88 night-fighter and came down in flames to crash near Maastricht, exploding with such force that only one body of the eight on board was recovered for burial. It is understood that W/C Newton DFC, MiD, RNZAF was undertaking the fiftieth operation of a distinguished career, and his loss would be keenly felt by the squadron and station communities at Mepal. The second pilot, P/O Richard Justin Aitchison, was the only other member of the RNZAF among the crew. F/O McMillan in NF935 AA-P, meanwhile, had become separated from the bomber stream, and realising that re-joining it would result in an overshoot, he attacked an unspecified last-resort target instead. The others were able to pick out ground detail in the light of the markers and produced a concentrated attack in the face of a strong wind, which had made it difficult to maintain formations. Returning crews reported bomb bursts and a red glow, and the consensus was of a concentrated raid, which was confirmed by post-raid photographs. An unfortunate outcome of this operation was the "reporting" of F/O Ron Flamank to 3 Group HQ for flying above the briefed height of 4,000 feet on the way out to the English coast. F/O Flamank's written explanation of the need to fly higher, at 8,000 feet to avoid unexpectedly thick cloud and icing conditions, was 'not considered sufficient" to justify breaking the rule, which was particularly ironic given his near-disastrous experience with icing two weeks earlier. He was sent on an aircrew refresher course at Sheffield.

A consequence of Operation Bodenplatte was a bunch of very twitchy and trigger-happy American anti-aircraft gunners in Belgium, who shot first and asked questions later and two 3 Group Lancasters were hit, one of them crashing with fatal consequences for the crew.

More than nine hundred aircraft made their way to southern Germany on the 2nd, 514 of them Lancasters belonging to 1, 3, 6 and 8 Groups bound for Nuremberg, while 389 mostly Halifaxes from 4, 6 and 8 Groups were assigned to Ludwigshafen. Nine Lancasters took off from Mepal between 15.11 and 15.39 with S/L Wright the senior pilot on duty and the Mepal station commander, G/C Campbell, flying as second pilot with F/L Barton. The newly-promoted F/L McMillan was forced to return early with engine trouble in PB427 AA-U, leaving the others to press on to reach the target, which lay under clear skies with a rising full moon to aid visibility. The Path Finders had prepared a ground marking plan and the TIs were seen clearly burning in the city centre, which sustained massive damage during the concentrated attack. Residential districts in the north-east and the south were also devastated, a local report detailing 4,640 houses as destroyed and more than four hundred industrial buildings were also wrecked along with railway installations. The death toll was also high, at 1,838, with others still missing at the time of the local report, and this was undoubtedly the most effective raid of the war on this great symbol of Nazism. Returning crews reported the glow of fires visible from 150 miles into the homeward flight and a very modest four Lancasters and three crews were lost over enemy territory.

On the 3rd, 3 Group put together a force of ninety-nine Lancasters, fifty to attack the Zeche-Hansa benzol plant at Dortmund and forty-nine to target the Klöckner Werke A G refinery at Castrop-Rauxel, a short distance to the north-west. Fourteen crews were briefed at Mepal and their Lancasters loaded with a cookie each along with fifteen 500 pounders and a Munro bomb. They took off between 12.27 and 12.41 with F/L Hannan the senior pilot on duty and headed for Dortmund's north-western district of Huckarde, wherein lay their target. F/O Pearson was unable to climb above 15,000 feet, and in order to catch up with the rest of the formation, reduced altitude and cut the final turning point. Conditions for a G-H raid were perfect, with ten-tenths cloud up to 12,000 feet and clear skies above. Flak was intense and accurate as the attack began shortly after 15.30, and a 622 Squadron Lancaster was seen to explode over the target, the only loss from the two operations. Returning crews offered mixed opinions as to the effectiveness of the raid, some complaining that the stream had been too spread out and the bombing not concentrated, while others reported black smoke rising through the clouds as they turned away. P/O Sadgrove in LM276 AA-S "Sugar" came home on three engines, and F/L Hannan in NE181 JN-M flew into a snowstorm and nearly collided with another aircraft. He called "Darky" unsuccessfully three times to obtain an emergency radio bearing and eventually landed at Mendlesham.

The group's next target was the marshalling yards at Ludwigshafen, which required a deep penetration into southern Germany under a fighter escort. 75(NZ) Squadron contributed twenty-one Lancasters to the 160-strong 3 Group force, and they departed Mepal between 11.21 and 11.43 with S/L Rodgers the senior pilot on duty. The G-H tracking pulse proved to be weak, which led to a poor bombing run and the clear skies over the target allowed the flak gunners to draw a bead on the attackers and break up the stream. F/O Sadgrove's LM544 AA-J had an engine damaged by flak and dropped below the stream firing red flares to attract a fighter escort, which was ignored. The opinions of returning crews were again divided between a "good prang" and a scattered attack and a number of references were made to the raid leader disappearing off track and taking others with him. F/Sgt Noel Humphrey Thorpe RNZAF and crew were on their maiden operation and thought it was "a bit hot" for a first one, their Lancaster, LM276 AA-S "Sugar", suffering significant flak damage. The other debutants, F/Sgt Ronald Wynn Russell, RNZAF and crew flying in HK576 AA-G described the lead-in as "rough", while F/Sgt Davies found forty holes in HK573 AA-H's wing on return and she was sent off to a maintenance unit for repairs. Enemy fighters turned up and accounted for a

90 Squadron Lancaster, but the escort performed heroically and just two aircraft failed to return. Post-raid reconnaissance confirmed that the railway yards had been hit, but the northern suburbs and outlying communities had also found themselves in the firing line and 535 houses and eighty-seven industrial building had been destroyed or seriously damaged.

W/C Cyril Henry Baigent DFC, RNZAF was posted in from 3 Group HQ on the 6th and would be the squadron's last wartime commanding officer. "Mac" Baigent was already on his third tour, having completed fifty-five operations with XV and 115 Squadrons, and took over ten days short of his twenty-second birthday, making him the youngest squadron commander in Bomber Command. He was extremely capable and would prove to be very popular with his men. His arrival coincided with a visit to the squadron by New Zealand High Commissioner Bill Jordan, and the New Zealand Deputy Prime Minister, Mr Sullivan.

The targets for that night were railway installations at Hanau, to the east of Frankfurt, and Neuss in the Ruhr, and the latter was to be a joint effort between 1 and 3 Groups, which provided thirty and 117 Lancasters respectively. The Mepal element of fifteen was about to take-off when the operation was cancelled, only to be re-instated later in the day, and they eventually became airborne between 15.46 and 16.01 with S/L Bailey the senior pilot on duty and two RNZAF newcomers in the persons of F/Sgt Charles Mackenzie Stevens and F/L Sidney Lewis Spillman. It proved to be a bad day for the squadron in terms of serviceability, and half of the eight early returns involved Lancasters from Mepal. F/O Cumberbatch's starboard-outer engine on LM266 "Seven Sinners", which had been re-coded AA-F, developed a coolant leak on take-off and he jettisoned his bombs in the Wash. F/Sgt Russell and crew in LM740 AA-B had to deal with an engine fire as they made their way out and also jettisoned their load, while F/O Crawford and crew in PB761 AA-Y had reached 15,000 feet and were thirty miles south-east of Arras when defective turrets persuaded them to turn back. F/L Hannan in NF981 JN-Y was approaching the Belgian frontier when his port-outer engine seized up and put an end to his chances of reaching the target, leaving the remainder to press on to find nine-tenths thin cloud over the target, which was marked by G-H-laid TIs with additional skymarkers as a back-up. The attack became somewhat scattered, and although the marshalling yards were hit, most of the bombing fell into adjacent areas, where 1,749 houses, nineteen industrial and twenty public buildings were destroyed or seriously damaged.

While this operation was in progress, a further four crews from Mepal joined a small 3 Group mining party in the Privet garden off Danzig on the Baltic coast, from which all returned safely from successful and uneventful sorties of up to ten hours duration. F/O Clement in NE181 JN-M "The Captain's Fancy" reported several Ju88s, although none approached and it was simple mechanical failure on the way home that left them with only three engines.

The final heavy raid of the war on Munich by Bomber Command was briefed out on the 7th to 645 Lancaster crews, of which ninety-six represented 3 Group. Of these just eight took off from Mepal between 19.00 and 19.12 with F/Ls Hannan, McDonald and McMillan the senior pilots on duty. It was a two-phase operation with a two-hour gap between waves, and the 3 Group participants formed part of the second wave. F/O Flamank's rear gunner found his electrically-heated flying suit to be defective, so he swapped places with the bomb-aimer in an attempt to keep the sortie going. However, the Gee system in HK597 JN-P "Bad Penny IV" then failed to provide the necessary navigational assistance and they were about eighty miles south-east of Paris flying at 16,000 feet when they decided to turn back at 21.00. The rest of the force pressed on to the target to find thick cloud over the aiming point, which all-but obscured the TIs, while variable winds upset the timings. Most crews bombed on the glow of fires resulting from the earlier attack and a large mushroom explosion was observed by some, followed by a red glow. Many returning crews had nothing to report and it was left to post-raid reconnaissance to establish that severe damage had been inflicted upon central and industrial districts. This completed a busy first week of the year.

Nineteen crews were briefed at Mepal on the morning of the 11th in preparation for an attack on the railway yards in the Uerdingen district of Krefeld on the western edge of the Ruhr. They were part of a 3 Group G-H force of 152 Lancasters and took off between 11.30 and 11.58 with S/L Bailey the senior pilot on duty. The target area was covered by ten-tenths cloud, and this caused F/Sgt Russell in PB418 AA-C to lose contact with his G-H leader. He glimpsed a river and built-up area through a patch of thin cloud and let his bombs go before turning back. F/L Hannan in HK597 JN-P "Bad Penny IV" had already feathered his port-outer engine and was within twenty miles of the target, having just crossed over the frontier into Germany, when the port-inner began to overheat, and he too, dropped his bombs onto whatever was underneath at the time. The others continued on to the target in what seemed to be a general state of disorder, and F/Sgt O'Malley in PB421 AA-K complained of being cut up by a 622 Squadron Lancaster ten minutes from the aiming point, which almost caused a collision. This was by no means the first accusation of dangerous flying by a 622 Squadron crew. A number of other crews complained that the briefed bombing height was ignored by some and they were put in danger by bombs falling around them from above. Despite the difficulties, the main weight of the attack fell into the eastern districts containing the railway yards and enormous damage resulted.

3 Group was invited on the 13th to prepare a force of Lancasters to attack the railway yards at Saarbrücken and 158 answered the call, nineteen of them loaded at Mepal with a cookie and a Munro bomb each along with a selection of 500 and 250 pounders. They took off between 11.25 and 11.53 with W/C Baigent the senior pilot on duty and all reached the target to find good visibility. Crews were able to pick out ground detail, including the marshalling yards, and the G-H-laid blue smoke-puff markers proved to be very effective against the background of snow. As W/C Baigent's bomb-aimer attempted to release the bombs, the master switch in PB763 AA-A was found to be broken and the entire load had to be brought back. F/L Spilman in PB761 AA-Y was forced to take evasive action after an unattached 514 Squadron Lancaster dropped its load from just fifty feet above, clearly after failing to check on what was underneath. All crews were diverted to Portreath on return, where they unanimously reported a concentrated and successful raid, although perhaps with an element of overshooting. As a result of the doubt, a follow-up operation was scheduled for the next day, for which a force of 134 Lancasters was made ready, although none from 75(NZ) Squadron. The operation took place in good visibility and was concluded successfully without loss.

Two targets occupied the group on the 15th, both benzol plants, one in the coal-mining town of Erkenschwick near Recklinghausen on the north-eastern edge of the Ruhr and the other, the Robert Muser refinery at Langendreer, situated between Bochum and Dortmund. Forces of eighty-two and sixty-three Lancasters respectively were made ready, the Mepal element of eighteen taking off for the latter between 11.28 and 11.44 with F/Ls McDonald, McMillan and

Spilman the senior pilots on duty. F/O Leadley in NG113 AA-D was forced to turn back from south-east of Namur in Belgium with a failing starboard-inner engine, leaving the others to press on to find the target hidden beneath ten-tenths cloud with tops at 6,000 feet. The formation was poor at the outset, but improved as the bombing progressed and the blue and green smoke-puffs again proved to be effective, the blue ones more so than the greens as they remained visible for longer. The flak proved to be light over the target but troublesome in the Mönchengladbach area, and F/L Spilman's aircraft was among those picking up damage. Returning crews were unable to provide an assessment of the results and it seems that no report was made available.

Seventeen crews were briefed at Mepal on the 16th in preparation for an attack on the Nordstern oil refinery at Gelsenkirchen, which was subsequently cancelled. However, the crews were briefed again later, this time for a night attack on the Krupp Treibstoffwerke benzol plant at Wanne-Eickel, a little further to the north-east towards Herne, and they took off between 23.15 and 23.39 with S/L Bailey the senior pilot on duty. They joined up with the rest of the 138-strong G-H force and flew out over low cloud, which was ten-tenths over the target with tops up to 7,000 feet. Bombing was carried out on G-H and skymarkers, but there was never a chance of observing any results. A red glow seen through the clouds was the only indication that the bombing had found the mark and no post-raid reconnaissance took place. F/Sgt Wood and crew in HK597 JN-P "Bad Penny IV" were attacked by a FW190 on the way home, prompting rear gunner F/Sgt Sparrow RCAF to give the order to "corkscrew port" and open fire, getting off three hundred rounds. The attacker broke off and no damage was sustained. While approaching base to land, PB761 AA-Y crashed at 04.20 near Woodditton, some thirteen miles south-east of Cambridge, killing the pilot, F/L "Tim" Blewett RNZAF and his bomb-aimer, F/O John Stanley Wilson RNZAF, who were the only two Kiwis on board. The navigator, F/Sgt Bryant Thomas Cornell RAFVR, sustained critical injuries, to which he succumbed on the following day. The other crew members were badly injured and taken to hospital. An official accident report cited pilot error, which is harsh in view of the stresses of operations, particularly by a pilot who had already flown fourteen operations. That day the crews had been briefed and geared up twice for this operation, both attempts abandoned due to the weather. Their third briefing had been at 21.45 with take-off at 23.30 followed by five hours of intense night flying. Speculation at the time was that the pilot had fallen asleep at the controls and extreme fatigue seems a fairer explanation of the cause than "pilot error".

A few days away from operations preceded a call to arms on the 22nd, when Duisburg was revealed to be the target for 286 Lancasters and sixteen Mosquitos from 1, 3 and 8 Groups. Fifteen crews attended the briefing at Mepal, and they took off between 17.10 and 17.23 with S/L Wright the senior pilot on duty. They reached the target to find clear conditions with moonlight, which enabled them to identify the Rhine and observe the TIs falling onto the aiming point. Many explosions and fires were witnessed in a compact area and thick, black smoke was observed to climb skywards as the bombers retreated to the west. The raid was concluded successfully and almost totally unopposed and it was established later that five hundred bombs had hit the Thyssen steelworks, which the local authorities assumed to have been the specific target.

The Gremberg marshalling yards in the south-east of Cologne was offered as the target for 153 Lancasters of 3 Group on the 28th. It was probably something of a relief to the twenty crews detailed at Mepal, most if not all of whom had attended briefings almost daily since the last operation but had been left frustrated by cancellations. It is difficult to comprehend how men with the most dangerous jobs in the war became listless and agitated when deprived of the opportunity to put themselves at further risk. Three crews were on debut, those of P/O Wallace Bassett Martin RAAF, P/O Kenneth James Rothwell RAAF and F/L Donald Winter Thomson RNZAF. W/C Baigent was the senior pilot on duty as they departed Mepal between 10.07 and 10.37 and headed out over cloud, which broke in the target area to leave clear skies and excellent visibility. The main problem was the formation of condensation trails, which made formation-keeping and the run-in to the target somewhat challenging. Despite this, returning crews reported many explosions in the yards, although some noted a degree of overshooting in the early stages. F/L McDonald's NF981 JN-Y suffered flak damage to the rear turret and wireless aerial.

A large raid on the Stuttgart area was mounted that night by more than six hundred aircraft from 1, 4, 6 and 8 Groups, which attacked specific targets two hours apart. The railway yards in the town of Kornwestheim to the north and Stuttgart's north-eastern suburb of Zuffenhausen, containing the Hirth aero-engine factory, were both hit, but many stray bombs fell into other northern districts of the city, where a Bosch plant sustained damage. This was the last major raid of the war on this much-bombed industrial city.

The group operated for the final time in the month on the 29th, when the railway yards at Uerdingen in Krefeld was posted as the target. A force of 148 Lancasters was made ready, of which nineteen took off from Mepal between 10.00 and 10.21 with S/L Bailey the senior pilot on duty, backed up by no less than eight pilots of flight lieutenant rank. This was the maiden operation as crew captain for F/Sgt Wi Rangiuaia, RNZAF. It was a momentous day for NE181 JN-M "Mike", aka. "The Captain's Fancy", which was undertaking its one-hundredth operation of a career stretching back to April and on this occasion was in the hands of S/L Jack Bailey and crew. The forming up process was accomplished without difficulty and was maintained all the way to the target, which was covered by eight to ten-tenths cloud. Crews reported problems with another squadron cutting across, disrupting the formation and raining down bombs from above, and in the case of F/L Kilpatrick in NF935 AA-P, damage to his front turret was caused by a falling bundle of "window". Having been troubled in the past by wrongly forecast winds, a Master Windfinder system was tried out on this operation and proved to be effective. The bombing appeared to be concentrated and a large white mushroom of smoke was seen to rise through the clouds as the bombers turned for home.

During the course of the month the squadron operated fourteen times and dispatched 217 sorties for the loss of two Lancasters and one-and-a-half crews. With the European war moving into the final phase and plans in the pipeline for a contribution by Bomber Command to the war in the Pacific, a new 3 Group G-H Training Flight was established at RAF Feltwell to train crews in the use of the new radar navigational aids. This replaced 3 Group's Lancaster Finishing School, which closed down at the end of January. The first G-H Course was held on the 22nd of January and from then until the end of the war, most 75(NZ) Squadron crews attended, spending five days at Feltwell, their logbooks displaying the requisite two G-H training flights of between ninety minutes and three hours duration in one of eight Lancasters with a "MU" coding.

February 1945

Weather conditions over the Continent would prove challenging for the bombers during the first week of the new month, which began operationally with a daylight 3 Group G-H raid on Mönchengladbach on the 1st, an operation originally briefed out but cancelled on the previous day. A force of 160 Lancasters was made ready to attack the marshalling yards, of which seventeen were provided by 75(NZ) Squadron. They took off between 12.36 and 13.02 with S/Ls Rodgers and Wright the senior pilots on duty, and just behind them, A/C Kirkpatrick DFC, Senior Air Staff Officer 3 Group HQ, departed in HK563 JN-W "Paper Doll" to observe the squadron forming up. With W/C Baigent along for the ride, Kirkpatrick followed them across the Channel before turning back for Mepal, satisfied with what he had seen. All reached the target area to find six to nine-tenths cloud and little opposition and some crews from other squadrons observed bombs apparently bursting on the aiming point. On return, there would be mixed opinions concerning the effectiveness of the raid, most from Mepal having observed nothing. The consensus was of a scattered attack, which was confirmed by post-raid photographs that suggested the main weight of bombs to have fallen to starboard of the railway yards.

The first and only attack of the war on Wiesbaden, a city situated twenty miles west of Frankfurt, was planned for the night of the 2/3rd and the job handed to 1, 3, 6 and 8 Groups, which put together a force of 495 Lancasters and a dozen Mosquitos. 3 Group's contribution amounted to 160 of the former with 75(NZ) Squadron responsible for eighteen of them, including one containing the freshman crew of F/O Matthew Watson RAFVR. Two of the Mepal brigade, F/L Davies and F/Sgt Thorpe, became bogged down after leaving their dispersals and had their sorties scrubbed. On a bad night for the group, 90 Squadron lost its recently-appointed commanding officer to a collision with another 90 Squadron Lancaster during the climb-out, while 149 Squadron's similarly newly-appointed commander would fail to return. The remaining sixteen Kiwi aircraft took off between 20.46 and 21.10 with W/C Baigent the senior pilot on duty supported by S/L Bailey, and all reached the target area, which was covered by cloud with tops in places at 21,000 feet. Skymarkers were employed by the Path Finder element and some crews observed dummy flares deployed by the enemy that attracted an occasional bomb load. Most crews bombed on a Gee-fix, H2S or DR and it was impossible to assess the outcome, but local reports suggested an effective attack, mentioning the destruction of over five hundred houses with a slightly lower number seriously damaged and a death toll of approximately a thousand people. NF981 JN-Y was damaged by flak over the target, but F/L Hannan landed her safely on the emergency landing strip at Woodbridge.

Sixteen crews were briefed at Mepal on the 3rd and learned that they were to be part of a 149-strong 3 Group attack on the Zeche-Hansa benzol plant situated in the Huckarde district of Dortmund to the north-west of the city centre. Two RNZAF pilots were on their first operations as skippers, and they were F/Sgt Leslie George Scott and W/O Esmond Edgar Delwyn Ware. The squadron took off between 16.25 and 16.43 with S/Ls Rodgers and Wright the senior pilots on duty and found clear conditions over the target, along with searchlight activity for the first time in months. Flak was also quite intense at the outset, but diminished quickly, giving rise to the speculation that ammunition must be in short supply. The marking was carried out by G-H and returning crews described accurate bombing accompanied by one particularly large explosion, and fires were observed to be taking hold as they turned away. Enemy night-fighters made their presence felt and S/L Wright in ME751 AA-M was involved in three combats, one of which resulted in a claim for the destruction of a Me110. Having lost its port-outer engine prior to bombing, ND801 JN-X "Get Sum Inn - Astra" overran the end of the runway at Mepal on return at 22.23 and crashed into a bakery, which resulted in injury to F/O Bruce Crawford RNZAF and three of his crew. F/L Hannan and crew in HK554 JN-Z also came home on three engines. Post-raid reconnaissance revealed that the operation had not been successful, after hitting areas north and north-west of the aiming point.

Eighteen Lancasters were detailed at Mepal on the 7th to take part in a 3 Group G-H raid on the Krupp Treibstoffwerke synthetic oil plant at Wanne-Eickel, but the squadron's participation was cancelled, and the raid went ahead without it. Difficult weather conditions led to 25% of the force failing to bomb, and the results were inconclusive. That evening heavy raids were carried out on the frontier towns of Goch and Cleves (Kleve) ahead of the advancing British XXX Corps, and involved aircraft from 1, 4, 6 and 8 Groups.

Briefings took place on the morning of the 8th for a planned attack on an oil refinery at Lützkendorf, a location which no longer appears on a map and is now known as Mücheln or Krumpa and was one of the many such sites close to Leipzig. The site actually contained a small Wintershall refinery, a Bergius hydrogenation plant and a Fischer-Tropsch processing plant, but it is believed that the first-mentioned was the specific target for this operation. However, this raid was cancelled during the afternoon and replaced by one against the Hohenbudberg railway yards at Krefeld, for which the squadron made ready twenty-one Lancasters as part of a 3 Group force of 151. Departures from Mepal took place between 03.38 and 04.14 on the 9th with W/C Baigent the senior pilot on duty. They formed up as they headed south, passing over Reading at altitudes ranging from 7,000 to 15,000 feet, and all reached the target to find eight-tenths cloud with tops at 10,000 feet, little flak, but effective searchlights. Opinions were again divided at debriefing between a concentrated and a scattered raid, some crews claiming to have seen the glow of TIs through the cloud, but no accurate assessment could be made while the attack was ongoing. Post-raid reconnaissance revealed eventually that the bombing had fallen to the north-west of the aiming point and that no new damage could be detected.

No further major operations were undertaken until the first round of the Churchill inspired Operation Thunderclap series against Germany's eastern cities, which was devised partly to act in support of the advancing Russian ground forces and also as a demonstration to Stalin of RAF air power, should he turn against the Allies after the war. The historic and culturally significant city of Dresden was selected to open the offensive in another two-phase affair, with a 5 Group force of 246 Lancasters and nine Mosquitos leading the way, to be followed three hours later by 529 Lancasters of 1, 3, 6 and 8 Groups. It had proved to be a successful tactic thus far, with the 5 Group low-level marking system and main force attacks providing a beacon for the second force, and should it be required on this night, 8 Group would provide any necessary marking for phase two from high level. This would become the most controversial Bomber Command operation of the war and would define Bomber Command's entire war effort. It would also unjustly blight the reputation of ACM Sir Arthur Harris, while calling into question the legitimacy of the part played by every member of aircrew throughout the conflict.

The briefing at Mepal that evening included a contribution from the squadron's bombing leader, F/L Grant Alan Russell RNZAF, who presented reconnaissance photos of the railway marshalling yards, nominated as their aiming point. Russell then joined the operation as a replacement for F/L Don Thompson's sick bomb aimer. Twenty Lancasters of 75(NZ) Squadron, including that of debutant F/O Maurice James Adamson RNZAF, departed Mepal between 21.52 and 22.20 with W/C Baigent the senior pilot on duty as part of a 3 Group contingent of 162 Lancasters. The 5 Group first phase attack delivered eight hundred tons of bombs through a thin layer of cloud after the aiming point had been marked from low-level by Mosquitos of 627 Squadron. This opening phase of the operation was moderately successful and created fires that were concentrated south of the River Elbe between the marshalling yards and the second phase aiming point. They had three hours to develop and become a beacon visible from a hundred miles away, and as the second force approached the target area, the cloud dispersed to leave clear skies. The existing fires provided the anticipated reference for the Path Finder element and although the bombing was a little scattered at first, the Master Bomber soon corrected it and the remainder of the 1,800 tons of bombs carried by this force fell in great concentration, causing a firestorm of terrifying proportions along the lines of that experienced in parts of Hamburg in July 1943. It devoured large parts of the city, the population of which had been swelled by an influx of refugees from the eastern front, and returning crews reported the glow of fires still visible a hundred miles into the return flight, expressing confidence in the success of the operation.

A few hours later, a daylight raid by 311 American B17s delivered a further 771 tons of bombs, intended ostensibly for the railway yards, and some of the escort fighters descended to rooftop height to strafe open spaces and traffic on the roads around the city and increase the level of chaos. There is a mistaken belief in Dresden even today, that the RAF was responsible for the strafing. Initial propaganda-inspired reports from the Office of the Propaganda Minister, Joseph Göbbels, falsely claimed a death toll of 250,000 people, but an accurate figure of twenty-five thousand has been settled upon since.

The destruction of Dresden has been used in Germany and also by some elements in this country as a weapon with which to condemn Bomber Command and Harris and label them as war criminals. Curiously, no similar accusations have been levelled at the Americans. It should also be understood that Harris had no interest in attacking Dresden and had to be nagged by Chief-of-the-Air-Staff Portal to fulfil Churchill's wishes. Dresden was Germany's seventh largest city and its largest predominantly intact built-up area, which, according to American sources, contained more than a hundred factories and fifty thousand workers contributing to the war effort. It was also an important railway hub, to the extent that the marshalling yards had been attacked twice in late 1944 by the USAAF. The aircrew simply did the job asked of them and Dresden was no different from any other attack on a city. The death toll at Hamburg was much higher, and yet there has been no similar outcry. The legacy of this operation served to deny Harris and the men under his Command their due recognition for the massive part they played in the ultimate victory, and only in recent times has a monument been erected in Green Park in London and a campaign clasp awarded, sadly, far too late for the majority. Churchill, with his eyes set on a peacetime election, betrayed Harris and the Command in a typical politically motivated U-turn, in which he accused Harris of bombing solely for the purpose of inflicting terror. In the post-war honours, Harris was the only commander in the field to be omitted and was vilified for the rest of his life.

The following night brought round two of Operation Thunderclap, when Chemnitz was posted as the target for 717 Lancasters and Halifaxes of 1, 3, 4, 6 and 8 Groups, which would be divided into two waves separated by three-and-a-half hours. 5 Group would also be in the area with 224 Lancasters and eight Mosquitos to target an oil refinery in the small town of Rositz, situated twenty-five miles due south of Leipzig and thirty miles north-west of Chemnitz. Located about thirty miles west-south-west of Dresden, the city produced military hardware and was home to the Astra-Werke A G oil refinery, which was supplied with labour from the nearby Flossenburg female forced labour camp. Twenty-one Lancasters were fuelled up at Mepal for the long round-trip and loaded with a cookie each, 500 pounders and cases of cluster bombs. They took off between 20.20 and 20.44 with S/L Rodgers the senior pilot on duty, F/L Russell Ashley Banks RNZAF and crew on debut and W/O Ware the only non-commissioned captain. F/O Pearson and crew flying RA510 AA-J were deep inside enemy territory when engine failure forced them to turn back and they shed 2,000 feet of altitude, coming home at 15,000 feet to land safely at 03.10 with nothing to show for six-and-a-half hours aloft.

The remainder of the force flew out in clear skies until about fifty miles from the target, when they encountered two thin layers of ten-tenths stratus cloud with tops at 10,000 and 18,000 feet. The blind illuminators opened the attack at 20.52, but as the cloud precluded identification of the aiming-point, the Master Bomber called for skymarking from 20.59 onwards. Salvoes of green/red flares were released by seven aircraft but proved to be scattered over a wide area with no point of concentration. However, with nothing else to aim at, the Master Bomber instructed crews to bomb on DR or navigational aids (H2S), and some managed to aim at the brief glow of flares falling through the clouds. Returning crews suspected that the raid had been scattered and ineffective, and post-raid reconnaissance largely confirmed that view, revealing that many parts of the city had been hit, while the majority of bombs had fallen into open country. Among the thirteen failures to return was the squadron's NG113 AA-D, which came down somewhere in Germany after the crew of F/L George Stanley Davies RNZAF had saved themselves and fallen into enemy hands. F/L Stan Davies had borrowed NG113 for this operation, as his own 'kite' HK573 was not fitted with H2S. North of Karlsruhe a fire had developed in the starboard wing, possibly from a broken oil line, and unable to feather the prop or put out the fire, the crew all baled out successfully. Sadly, three weeks later, when three of them were on their way to a PoW camp, their train was strafed by an Allied fighter. A flak carriage attached to the train fired back and a second fighter attacked, it's cone of fire hitting one of the PoW carriages and killing twenty-five RAF and USAAF prisoners, including bomb aimer F/Sgt Henry Edward Chalmers RAFVR. F/L Davies and his navigator, F/Sgt Claude Cuthbert Greenhough RNZAF, in the adjacent carriage, were unharmed.

The town of Wesel, which nestled on the east bank of the Rhine, north of Duisburg, found itself directly in the path of the advancing Canadian 1st Army, and a series of raids over the ensuing days would see it effectively wiped off the map. The first one was mounted on the 16th by a 3 Group force of one hundred Lancasters with a single Path Finder Mosquito to provide the initial markers by Oboe. 75(NZ) Squadron made ready twenty-one aircraft, which departed Mepal between 12.29 and 12.51 led by S/L Bailey. Three crews were on debut, those of F/L Laurence Douglas McKenna RNZAF, F/Sgt Louis Eldon Bernhardt Klitscher RNZAF and W/O Eric Morton Ohlson RNZAF. The intention of the attack was to hit all road and railway communications to prevent enemy reinforcements from passing through, and clear skies aided the bombers to find the mark and put most of the bombs in the right area. Smoke and dust began to obscure the ground towards the end of the attack, but all aircraft returned safely home for their crews to report that the town and the railway installations had been smothered by bomb bursts.

Elements of 4, 6 and 8 Groups returned on the following day, when thick cloud was present, and the Master Bomber called a halt to proceedings after just a handful of aircraft had bombed. Similar conditions prevailed on the 18th, when 3 Group sent 160 Lancasters back to the town to carry out a G-H raid, to which cloud offered no impediment. 75(NZ) Squadron had dispatched twenty Lancasters either side of noon with no flight commanders in action, and after F/Sgt Scott in LM733 AA-R had turned back with a technical issue, the others, including newcomer F/Sgt Bernard Lincoln Lukins RAFVR, reached the target to find ten-tenths cloud with tops at 10,000 feet. G-H worked well and although returning crews could offer no assessment of the outcome, confidence was high that a successful raid had taken place. The final attack of the series took place on the 19th, for which the squadron made ready twenty-one Lancasters in a 3 Group force of 168. Three captains were on debut, F/O Trevor Cyril Cox RNZAF, F/L Ian Taylor RAFVR and P/O James Shaw RAFVR and they departed Mepal with the others between 13.15 and 13.33, again leaving the senior officer pilots at home. F/Sgt Lukins and crew in RA510 AA-J missed out when engine problems forced them to turn back, leaving the remainder to encounter seven-tenths cloud, through which they were able to identify the river and the town and deliver their bombs accurately into what remained of the built-up area and the railway yards to the east.

The pace of operations did not slacken, and ten crews attended briefing at Mepal on the 20th to learn that the southern half of Dortmund was to be their target that night as part of a heavy force of 514 Lancasters drawn from 1, 3, 6 and 8 Groups. They took off either side of 22.00 with F/Ls Abraham and Simpson the senior pilots on duty, but the former, flying PB741 AA-E, was forced to turn back when over north-eastern France after his starboard-inner engine failed. The others pressed on to find nine to ten-tenths thin cloud with tops at around 6,000 feet, through which the TIs on the ground were visible. Returning crews reported some scattered bombing, but generally a successful attack which left fires burning.

The group divided its resources on the 22nd between the Hydrierwerke-Scholven synthetic oil refinery in the Buer district in the north-west of Gelsenkirchen and the extensive marshalling yards at Osterfeld in Oberhausen, dispatching eighty-six and eighty-two Lancasters respectively. The Mepal brigade of twenty-one took off between 12.35 and 13.00 with W/C Baigent the senior pilot on duty and headed for Osterfeld with the other participants from 33 Base and Methwold. Three were freshman crews, captained by F/Sgt Derek Singleton Barr RAFVR, P/O Duncan Matthew Stevenson RNZAF and P/O Alan Frederick Woodcock RAFVR. F/L Jones and crew in NN747 JN-O "Dogsbody Again" were thirty miles south-east of Antwerp outbound when their starboard-inner engine failed and put an end to their involvement in the operation, but the others made it all the way to the target to find it under clear skies but partially hidden by ground haze. To this was soon added smoke, which made it difficult for the crews to identify the aiming point visually, a situation exacerbated by accurate flak, which did its best to break up the formation. Leading the squadron in on the bombing run, S/L Bailey's HK554 JN-Z was hit by flak, causing him to shut down one engine, and the same burst also damaged the three Lancasters behind him, those of W/C Baigent, F/L Sadgrove and

F/O Pearson. Bailey carried on to the target and would be awarded a Bar to his DFC for his actions. The Lancasters of W/O Ohlsen, F/Os Cox and Russell and F/L Sadgrove all sustained flak damage to engines but made it home to tell their stories of concentrated bombing on the aiming point accompanied by many explosions and smoke.

The pressure on the enemy's oil industry was maintained on the 23rd, when 3 Group sent 133 Lancasters to carry out a G-H raid on the Alma Pluto benzol plant at Gelsenkirchen. 75(NZ) Squadron dispatched sixteen aircraft between 11.39 and 11.58 with one debutant crew captained by F/Sgt Thomas Wagner Good RAFVR and no pilots above the rank of flight lieutenant. According to the squadron ORB they found a layer of ten-tenths thin cloud over the target with poor horizontal visibility of between five hundred and a thousand yards. This differed somewhat from the 3 Group ORB, which described cloud tops ranging from 16,000 to 24,000 feet and horizontal visibility down to two hundred yards at times. These conditions made it difficult to maintain the formation and after bombing with their G-H leaders, many crews confirmed their precise position by Gee-fix. Weather conditions for landing were also very poor and it was an achievement that all got down without an accident, F/Sgt Barr and crew landing at Warboys. At debriefing they were unable to offer a clue as to the results of their efforts.

In an indication of the destructive power of the Command, on the night of the 23/24th a force of 360 aircraft from 1, 6 and 8 Groups delivered 1,825 tons of bombs from 8,000 feet onto the southern city of Pforzheim in a twenty-two-minute orgy of destruction that created a firestorm and left 17,000 fatalities in its wake. This was the third highest death toll to result from a single attack on a German city after Hamburg (40,000) and Dresden (25,000). It was during this operation that the final Victoria Cross was earned by a member of RAF Bomber Command. It went posthumously to the Master Bomber from 582 Squadron, Captain Ed Swales SAAF, who continued to control the attack in a Lancaster severely damaged by a night-fighter, before sacrificing his life to allow his crew to abandon the stricken aircraft.

The group's participation in a raid on the oil refinery at Bergkamen in the Ruhr was cancelled on the 24th, and it went ahead anyway with a predominantly Halifax main force provided by 4 and 6 Groups. That evening F/L McKenna and F/O Rangiuaia took off shortly after 17.00 to lay mines in the Onion garden in Oslo Fjord and fulfilled their brief through eight-tenths cloud, before returning safely after midnight, the former to report an uneventful trip and the latter an interesting one.

The above-mentioned raid on the synthetic Chemwerke-Steinkohle oil refinery at Bergkamen on the north-eastern fringe of the Ruhr had caused extensive damage to the nearby town of Kamen but not the refinery, which thus became the target for a 3 Group G-H force of 153 Lancasters on the 25th. Eighteen Lancasters departed Mepal between 09.30 and 09.48 with a handful of flight lieutenant pilots leading the way, and all reached the target to find it hidden beneath layers of thin stratus cloud. However, some crews were able to make out the target, and on return reported large amounts of white smoke, followed by thick, black smoke rising to a considerable height. F/O Watson was reported to have been injured by a flak hit on LM276 AA-S "Sugar". LM740 AA-B did not arrive back at Mepal and was the only casualty of the operation. The Lancaster was hit by flak near Wesel while outbound and was seen to turn towards home with its port-inner engine feathered. It seems that F/Sgt "Ben" Klitscher RNZAF and his RAF crew abandoned the Lancaster soon afterwards and drifted down into the arms of their captors.

On the following day, 149 Lancasters of 3 Group were made ready for a G-H attack on the Hoesch-Benzin benzol plant in the Wambel district of Dortmund, 75(NZ) Squadron providing eighteen of them, which took off between 10.38 and 10.58 led by S/L Bailey and with F/L Jack Colin Parker RNZAF flying with the squadron for the first time. They found the target to be covered by ten-tenths low cloud with tops up to 6,000 feet and there was also a strong wind, which dispersed the skymarkers very quickly. The main problem for the Mepal crews was another formation no more than five hundred feet above them, the bombs from which were falling too close for comfort, persuading some of the Kiwis to break away. Despite this, G-H worked well and returning crews believed the attack to have been concentrated. ME450 AA-W was seen to pass over Mepal in formation, but did not land and news was soon received that it had crashed near Chatteris, a handful of miles to the north-west. F/O Noel Humphrey Thorpe RNZAF and three of his crew had been killed outright, while a fifth member of the crew lingered for two days before succumbing to his injuries. According to eyewitness testimony, the aircraft lost power in both starboard engines just after it broke formation.

Briefings took place on 3 Group stations on the 27th for a return to the Alma Pluto benzol plant at Gelsenkirchen. Eighteen 75(NZ) Squadron Lancasters departed Mepal between 11.15 and 11.33 with no pilots on duty above flight lieutenant rank and one of these, F/L Sadgrove in HK562 AA-L, lost his hydraulics system shortly after take-off and turned back when at 7,000 feet over Hertfordshire. F/O Adamson and crew in PB421 AA-K reached a point near the Belgian frontier with France, south-west of Charleroi, before one dead engine and an overheating second one forced them to turn back also. The others encountered ten-tenths thick cloud over the target, which hid the results of their efforts and flak claimed one Lancaster from 186 Squadron, which was seen to go down during the bombing run.

Gelsenkirchen was the destination again on the 28th, this time for a 3 Group G-H force of 156 Lancasters targeting the Nordstern synthetic oil refinery. Fifteen took off from Mepal between 09.03 and 09.19 with no fewer than nine pilots of flight lieutenant rank on duty, and they all reached the target area to find the expected blanket of thick, low cloud. Bombing began ahead of the planned 12.00 H-Hour, which was somewhat fortuitous, as G-H station 114 became unserviceable between 12.04 and 12.09 and could not send out a pulse. As no comment was made by the crews at debriefing, it was concluded that the attack had been completed before the malfunction occurred. Some crews reported signs of black smoke emerging through the cloud tops as they turned away and assumed from that that the attack had been accurate.

During the course of the month the squadron undertook seventeen operations and dispatched 291 sorties for the loss of four Lancasters and three crews.

March 1945

March was to be a massively demanding month for the Command as it attempted to eradicate the last pockets of enemy war-production, particularly oil, and cut all remaining communications by road and rail. The weather over Germany remained as it had been, and ten-tenths cloud greeted the 151 Lancasters of 3 Group as they headed for the oil refinery at

Bergkamen on the 1st. Seventeen 75(NZ) Squadron aircraft had departed Mepal either side of noon, including one containing the newcomer crew of W/O Cyril Vernon Opie RAAF, but F/O Barr in PB418 AA-C "Charlie" had lost an engine while climbing out over base and jettisoned his bombs into the Wash. The lead squadron seemed to overshoot the final turning point after failing to pick up the tracking pulse and orbited to converge on the main stream from a variety of angles. This had the effect of breaking up the formation and some of the Kiwi crews had their bombing runs compromised, while others described a good formation, concentrated bombing on plentiful blue smoke-puffs and a generally uneventful trip. F/L Simpson in NN747 JN-O "Dogsbody Again" reported returning at 10,000 feet over France after the oxygen feed to the rear turret had failed. F/Sgt Good lost both starboard engines on HK561 AA-Y "Liefy" on the way home and was ordered to land at Woodbridge. The main operation on this day was the final heavy raid of the war on Mannheim, which was already a broken city after being bombed dozens of times. Its neighbour across the Rhine, Ludwigshafen, also sustained severe damage in the attack, as did outlying communities.

The final raid of the war on Cologne, which now lay on the front line, was mounted on the following day in two phases, the first in the morning involving a force of 703 aircraft and the second in the afternoon by 155 Lancasters from 3 Group. The cloud that had sat over western Germany for weeks had finally cleared by the time the main raid took place, and further massive damage was inflicted on what was left of the city's built-up area. Twenty Lancasters departed Mepal between 12.59 and 13.20 led by S/L Wright, and among them was the crew of F/Sgt Harold James Dean Treewheela RNZAF on debut. Three of them sustained damage to engines courtesy of the flak near Mönchengladbach, which persuaded them to jettison all or part of their loads and turn back. HK554 JN-Z lost two engines but made it home. The others reached the target area and waited for the G-H leaders to drop their bombs, but the G-H releasing station in England was not working properly and only fifteen aircraft released their bombs on the eastern bank of the Rhine. F/O Woodcock in HK600 JN-K "Kiwi" was wounded in the neck, his flight engineer, F/Sgt Gibb, in the legs and an engine was hit by heavy flak, but they made it home safely. Most crews brought their full bomb loads back as instructed and were frustrated when the operation was classed as abortive (DNC) and would not count towards the completion of a tour, despite the fact that it had involved a full round trip and bombing run over the target, with associated flak damage and injuries. Four days later this once-proud capital of the Rhineland fell to American forces.

The cloud had returned to German skies by the time that the Krupp-Treibstoffwerke synthetic oil refinery at Wanne-Eickel and the nearby marshalling yards were posted as the target on the 4th. A 3 Group G-H force of 128 Lancasters was prepared, of which eighteen represented 75(NZ) Squadron and took off between 09.45 and 10.03 with no senior officers present. F/O Barr and crew in NG448 JN-P soon found themselves once more over the Wash jettisoning their bomb load after another engine failure, leaving the others to press on to the target area, where ten-tenths cloud with tops at 12,000 feet presented ideal bombing conditions for G-H. Blue smoke-puff markers were dropped for any aircraft failing to formate on a G-H leader, and the operation proceeded according to plan, although without any chance of assessing the outcome.

Twenty Lancasters took off from Mepal between 10.33 and 10.53 on the 5th led by S/L Bailey and set course to form up at 8,000 feet with the rest of the 170-strong 3 Group G-H force bound for the Consolidated benzol plant in the Schalke district of Gelsenkirchen. Three crews were on debut, those of F/Sgt William Evenden RAFVR, F/O Owen Joseph Cook RAAF and F/O Gordon Foster Cleminson RAFVR. F/L Parker got as far as Beachy Head on the Sussex coast in RF127 AA-W, before his starboard-outer engine blew up and forced him to turn back. According to the squadron ORB, F/O Cleminson in HK593, recently re-coded JN-X, was just past the mid-point between Great Yarmouth and the Dutch coast when he decided to abandon his sortie after losing his starboard-inner engine on take-off. Why he would be outbound eastwards over the North Sea, while F/L Parkers' route was to take him over the south coast and the English Channel suggests that the squadron scribe made the entries while somewhat confused, and it is uncertain which is correct. The others found the target under ten-tenths cloud with tops at 15,000 feet, which happened to be the briefed bombing height, and either bombed with their G-H leader or on H2S if they were in cloud. Flak damaged the rear turret of PB421 AA-K and F/L Parsons' rear gunner, W/O Holdaway RAFVR, was wounded. The attack appeared to be concentrated, but no results were seen.

That night, Operation Thunderclap set off to return to Chemnitz with 760 aircraft drawn from 1, 4, 6 and 8 Groups and nine 6 Group aircraft crashed close to home after climbing into severe icing conditions. Those reaching the target left central and southern districts engulfed in flames and lost twenty-two of their number in the process.

The Wintershall synthetic oil refinery at Salzbergen, situated in the flat Münsterland region of Germany close to the Dutch border north of the Ruhr, was the oldest oil plant in Germany and had been founded in 1860. 119 Lancasters of 3 Group were made ready on the 6th to carry out a G-H attack upon it, and the sixteen participants from Mepal, including the freshman crew of W/O Frederick Robert Bader RNZAF, took off between 08.30 and 08.46 with W/C Baigent and S/Ls Rodgers and Wright the senior pilots on duty. S/L Rodgers was flying as one of the G-H leaders, and this would be his fifty-sixth and final operation. Conditions were again ideal for a G-H attack, with ten-tenths cloud and tops between 9,000 and 12,000 feet. This allowed for a good and tight formation, which delivered its bombs in concentrated fashion and the crews were rewarded with the sight of black smoke billowing up through the clouds.

That night, two attacks were carried out on Wesel by elements of 3 Group to follow up on another by 8 Group Mosquitos earlier in the day. It was believed that many German troops and vehicles were holed up in the ruins of the town as they retreated to the east and needed to be flushed out, while the town's bridge across the Rhine was the only one still intact north of Cologne. The squadron ORB is confusing again and describes five aircraft taking part in the first attack and three in the second, and yet the take-off times recorded show F/O O'Malley and F/Ls Hannan and Spilman departing shortly after 18.20, and five, led by F/L McMillan, taking off at around 03.00. They were all carrying a cookie and eleven 500 pounders, which they delivered accurately onto the target and despite the area being covered by cloud during both operations, explosions and the glow of fires were visible through it.

A force of 526 aircraft from 1, 3, 6 and 8 Groups was assembled on the 7th and their crews briefed for the first attack of the war on Dessau, situated some two hundred miles east of the Ruhr and a hundred miles south-west of Berlin. 3 Group put up 124 Lancasters, of which thirteen were provided by 75(NZ) Squadron, and they departed Mepal between 17.22 and 17.36 with S/L Wright the senior pilot on duty. On the way over Germany, near Kassel, F/L

Spilman's mid-upper gunner, F/Sgt Clouston, spotted and fired at a FW190 attacking from the port quarter and claimed it as damaged. There was no damage to LM276 AA-S "Sugar". The target area was almost completely concealed by haze and a layer of thin cloud, in the face of which the Master Bomber instructed crews to bomb on the skymarkers. However, it was standard practice for the Path Finders to prepare for both sky and ground-marking, and some crews were able to see TIs, while two crews from the squadron identified streets. With an abundance of markers to aim at and barely any defence from the ground, the force produced accurate and concentrated bombing and many fires were burning across the city as the bombers retreated. Why this centre of learning and culture was targeted is unclear, as it had no obvious strategic significance, but it appears to have been almost completely destroyed in this attack.

An hour after the above element had taken off from Mepal, F/L Parsons and crew also took to the air in LM266 AA-F "The Seven Sinners" to join a handful of 3 Group Lancasters laying mines in the Melon garden in Eckernförde Bay, an inlet in the Baltic north of Kiel. He and his crew returned safely after a round trip of six hours and five minutes and reported delivering six assorted mines into the briefed locations.

3 Group remained at home on the following night, when elements from other groups attacked Hamburg and Kassel, but 159 Lancasters were made ready on the 9th to target two Emscher-Lippe benzol plants in the town of Datteln, situated on the north-eastern edge of the Ruhr. They were divided between the two aiming points, north and south, seventy-eight on A and eighty-one on B, for which 75(NZ) Squadron provided twenty-one aircraft taking-off between 10.32 and 10.52 with no senior pilots present. Five crews were on debut, all with RNZAF pilots, and they were F/Sgt Robin James Hamilton, F/Sgt John Somers McLernon, F/Sgt Albert George Bone, F/Sgt William Mallon and W/O Donald Babington Shearer. They encountered ten-tenths cloud but no opposition and the bombing at aiming point B was described in the 3 Group ORB as "excellent", while that at aiming point A was scattered. It is not specified which attack involved the Mepal element, but returning crews reported observing blue smoke-puffs, a good formation at bomb-release time, and a simultaneous dropping of bombs in a well-co-ordinated G-H attack, followed by a mushroom of smoke rising through the cloud tops as they turned away. Post-raid reconnaissance confirmed the effectiveness of the attack on aiming point B, and also revealed that the nearby Dortmund-Ems Canal, a vital component in the enemy's communications network, had been breached and rendered 100% unnavigable, presumably by stray bombs.

Twenty-four hours later 155 Lancasters from 3 Group retraced the steps of the previous day, to within ten miles of Datteln, to target the Scholven-Buer synthetic oil refinery in Gelsenkirchen. Twenty-one 75(NZ) Squadron crews made the trip, departing Mepal between 12.20 and 12.40, again with no senior pilots on duty, but with S/L "Slim" Ormerod, the squadron's navigation leader, the most senior officer on duty, filling in for the regular navigator in the crew of F/O Rothwell. F/O Leslie Gordon Sinclair RNZAF and crew were on debut. They approached in tight formation above ten-tenths cloud and all bombed together in another example of a well-co-ordinated G-H attack, the accuracy and effectiveness of which was confirmed by photo-reconnaissance.

A new record was set on the following morning, when 1,079 aircraft took off to deliver the final raid of the war on Essen. 3 Group put up 143 Lancasters, of which twenty-one represented

75(NZ) Squadron. They took off between 11.40 and 12.00 led by W/C Baigent, and all reached the target to find it covered by ten-tenths cloud with tops at 6,000 feet, which required the Path Finder element to employ skymarkers in the form of blue and later red smoke puffs, and the first of these went down at 14.59 to be backed up throughout the course of the raid. The Wood crew's wireless operator, Gerry Newey, described the awe-inspiring sight as a gigantic armada, "the sky was filled with kites from horizon to horizon". The Path Finders provided the marking for the main force, while 3 Group employed G-H, and the Kiwi formation was tight, which allowed for concentrated bombing. The clouds were seen to take on a brown tinge as the attack developed, before black smoke was observed by some to billow through the cloud-tops. It was impossible to assess what was happening on the ground, but the 4,661 tons of bombs delivered in this attack left the city paralyzed and nine hundred people dead.

The record set on the 11th lasted barely twenty-four hours and was exceeded on the 12th when a force of 1,108 aircraft took off to deliver the final heavy raid of the war on Dortmund. Twenty-one Lancasters departed Mepal between 13.00 and 13.19 with S/L Wright the senior pilot on duty, and they were part of a 3 Group contribution to the operation of 159 aircraft. Two were newcomers, F/Sgt Douglas Fairbairn RNZAF and P/O Kiwi Ernest Amohanga RNZAF. They arrived over the Ruhr to find it still under a blanket of ten-tenths cloud with tops at 6,000 feet, conditions for which the Path Finders had prepared a skymarking plan based on green and blue smoke puffs. The first Oboe-aimed greens appeared at 16.26 to be followed a minute later by blues from the blind primary markers, and the Master Bomber directed the main force crews to aim for the blues. It was not long before brown smoke was climbing through the clouds to 8,000 feet from the northern end of the city, and crews also reported a ring of smoke encircling the entire area so dense, that it remained visible for 120 miles into the return flight. The 3 Group attack was to be delivered on the same lines as the previous day, on G-H after approaching in tight formation with F/L Plummer in NG449 AA-T the designated G-H leader for the vics at the front of the squadron. When he lost the G-H tracking pulse, F/L Watson in RF157 AA-X moved up to take the lead. A new record of 4,851 tons of bombs was dropped on central and southern districts to end all hope of further war production, and the loss of just two Lancasters spoke volumes about the enemy's inability to defend itself.

It was back to the Ruhr again for 3 Group on the 14th, to target coking plants at Datteln and Hattingen, the latter located just south of Bochum. It was for the Heinrich Hutte plant at Hattingen that twenty crews were briefed at Mepal and took off between 13.30 and 13.49 with no senior pilots on duty, before joining up with sixty-nine other Lancasters as they made their way to the target area. For once the skies over the Ruhr were free of cloud, according to the 3 Group ORB at least, and this created problems for the Datteln element in particular, which came under accurate fire from flak batteries that broke up the formation. The Hattingen element also came under heavy ground fire, but maintained formation throughout and was able to deliver a concentrated attack. F/O Zinzan in RF127 AA-W was forced into a four-second overshoot, through trying to avoid dropping his bombs on a damaged Lancaster which had fallen behind its formation directly underneath, and this may have been PB741 AA-E, which was seen to be hit by flak in the port-inner engine at 16.35, and shortly after was observed to have both port engines feathered. The final sighting was of the port wing on fire, and breaking off as the stricken Lancaster entered the cloud-tops. F/L Eric Parsons RAFVR had undertaken thirty operations, and he and his crew were amongst the most experienced and respected on the squadron. Sadly, all lost their lives when so tantalisingly close to completing their tour and surviving the war. Flak damage was widespread, including to LM266 AA-F, which F/Sgt McClernon brought back safely to Woodbridge, before returning to Mepal the next day.

3 Group was handed two targets on the 17th, a coking plant at Dortmund and the Auguste Viktoria benzol plant at Marl/Hüls, situated on the north-eastern edge of the Ruhr north-west of Recklinghausen. Nineteen Lancasters departed Mepal between 11.51 and 12.11 and set course for the latter with F/L McMillan the senior pilot on duty as the more junior captains among them were given a chance. F/O Robert Sinclair Milsom RNZAF was making his debut. There was cloud in the target area at bombing height, which, along with the forming of condensation trails, created visibility problems and made it difficult for aircraft to maintain close contact with each other. They managed to remain in loose formation with visibility at times down to fifty feet and the bombs were dropped together to give hope of concentration. No results were observed, but the consensus was of an effective raid.

The oil offensive continued on the 18th, when 3 Group was again handed two assignments for which it detailed fifty Lancasters each. The targets were the coking ovens and benzol plants at Hattingen and Bruchstrasse, the latter a north-western district of Duisburg, situated barely a mile from the Homberg oil refinery that had caused the squadron so much pain in the previous summer. 75(NZ) Squadron made ready seventeen Lancasters, four of them for the debutant crews captained by F/Sgt Ivan Silvester Carroll, F/Sgt Ronald Thomas Clarkson, F/L William Edward Robert Alexander and P/O Aeneas Hendry McLeod, all members of the RNZAF. They took off between 11.40 and 12.02 led by pilots of flight lieutenant rank and mostly carrying a cookie and fourteen 500 pounders, with a number of other small variations, but F/O Sinclair in HK601 JN-D "Snifter" had a 12,000lb blockbuster in his bomb bay. They arrived in the target area to find ten-tenths cloud with tops at around 7,000 feet and moderate to heavy flak, which was very accurate for height. Returning crews reported that a good formation had been achieved and that all bombs had fallen away together, but they had been unable to observe any results.

At Mepal, the 19th was spent training and carrying out air-tests, while other elements of the group targeted the Consolidated coking plant in the Schalke district of Gelsenkirchen. Twenty-one crews were called to briefing on the 20th to learn that, for the first time in the month, the target was not oil-related or an area attack, but the marshalling yards at Hamm, which promised to be a hot one because of its importance to the enemy's communications system. P/O Alfred Errol Brown RNZAF was on debut as crew captain. They took off in a twenty-minute slot from 10.00, with W/C Baigent the senior pilot on duty and supported by S/L Bailey, joining up with the rest of the ninety-nine-strong G-H force as they made their way across the North Sea. They arrived at their destination to find six to seven-tenths cloud with tops at 10,000 feet and perhaps less flak than might have been expected and no enemy fighters. The squadron directly ahead deviated from track and took the Mepal element with it, which scattered the formation and caused confusion as they tried to get back together. Some semblance of order was regained and the bombing achieved a degree of concentration. The target could be seen through gaps in the cloud, and it appeared that the main weight of bombing fell to the south-east of the aiming point, although some bomb bursts were observed to be within the boundary of the yards.

With the war so close to the end and the enemy's defensive capabilities so depleted, it must have seemed that the days of multiple losses were behind the squadron. The 21st brought a stark reminder that it wasn't over until it was over, but this would not have been in the minds of the twenty-one crews preparing for battle at Mepal, including the first-time crew of F/Sgt Allan Francis Thompson RNZAF. They had learned at briefing that 3 Group was sending 160 Lancasters to Münster to bomb the railway yards and a nearby railway viaduct. The Kiwi element had been assigned to the viaduct and took off between 09.36 and 10.02 with S/L Wright the senior pilot on duty. What was not known, was that the G-H co-ordinates had been reversed inadvertently, and this would lead to the main weight of the attack falling on the secondary aiming point. They arrived in the target area under clear skies and in good visibility to face a moderate amount of very accurate flak. The navigation error resulted in an overshoot, meaning that the squadron had to turn and run back over the target from the wrong direction, exposing it to aircraft bombing from higher altitudes, which caused the formation to break up just before bombing. A reasonable concentration was achieved, however, but three Lancasters were seen to go down in the target area and all belonged to 75(NZ) Squadron.

NG449 AA-T was hit by flak in two engines before breaking up. It contained five members of the RNZAF, including the pilot, F/L Jack Plummer DFC, along with the bomb-aimer, F/O Edgar John Holloway and mid-upper gunner F/O Russell James Scott, who all lost their lives. Of the four survivors, the RNZAF rear gunner managed to evade capture, while his colleagues would have to endure a short term in captivity. There were no survivors from the crew of F/O Derek Barr RAFVR in RA564 JN-P, which was hit by a bomb falling from another aircraft and was blown apart. The navigator, F/Sgt Arthur Leslie Archibald Oakey, was the only member of the RNZAF on board, while the others were all RAFVR, the air bomber, F/Sgt Dryden Stewart, wireless operator, P/O Robert William West, flight engineer, F/Sgt Clifford Isaac Stocker, mid-upper gunner, Sgt Bruce Henry Nichol and rear gunner, W/O Alwyn Amos. LM733 AA-R was hit by falling bombs, one of which took the nose off and the bomb-aimer with it. It possibly also received flak damage and was seen to break into two sections as it plummeted to earth. F/O Alfred Errol Brown RNZAF and his Kiwi bomb-aimer, F/Sgt James Haswell Wood, were found in its wreckage, but five members of the crew, including two other members of the RNZAF, managed to save themselves and join their squadron colleagues in enemy hands. It must have been a shock to all at Mepal when three crews failed to return, but thankfully, this was the last occasion on which the squadron would post missing one of its own.

Mepal was not involved in a 3 Group attack on the town of Bocholt on the 22nd, the day on which elements of 1, 6 and 8 Groups devastated the culturally significant city of Hildesheim, situated twenty miles south-east of Hannover, destroying 70% of its built-up area and killing more than sixteen hundred people. It was decided that Wesel required further softening-up before the Allied crossing of the Rhine and the taking of the town went ahead, and 3 Group was invited to send a force of eighty Lancasters to flush out any remaining enemy units. Eight 75(NZ) Squadron crews were briefed and took off between 15.08 and 15.13 with no senior pilots present, each carrying a dozen 1,000 pounders and two Munro bombs. The skies over the target were clear, the aiming point was identified visually and all aircraft bombed together on G-H with excellent results. On the following morning the British 2nd Army crossed the Rhine and took the town with just thirty-six casualties, finding some of their German prisoners to be so traumatized that they could not be interrogated for forty-eight hours. A message of congratulations was received from General Montgomery and his American counterpart, General Dempsey.

During a rare lull in operations, F/L Herbert Wilfred Hooper RNZAF and crew took off from Mepal at 20.40 on the 25th on a unique mission that would see F/L Hooper awarded the DFC. Earlier, he had been called to the briefing room by W/C Baigent, just the two of them present, "Mac" and "Wilf", the youngest and oldest pilots in the squadron who shared a friendship and mutual respect. F/L Hooper was asked if he would carry out a special operation, and after agreeing, was detailed to undertake a lone, high-level G-H-guided nickeling (leaflet) raid on the Scheveningen district in The Hague, the Dutch Capital. Three weeks earlier, on the 3rd of March, fifty-five Mitchells and Bostons of the RAF's 2nd Tactical Air Force had carried out a highly risky bombing of German V-2 rocket launching sites in the Haagse Bos, a forest park within the city, adjacent to civilian housing. Cloud cover, winds, and a mix-up in coordinates had resulted in many bombs falling outside the designated 500 yard 'safety margin'. Houses in the Bezuidenhout residential area had suffered heavy damage, with over 500 civilians killed, 340 seriously injured, and 12,000 made homeless. The Dutch government in exile had protested to the British ("The temper of the civilian population has become violently anti-Allies as a result of this bombardment."), and Prime Minister Churchill had become involved.

Bomber Command had been given the job of delivering an apology from the British government to the people of the Bezuidenhout district and 75(NZ) Squadron had been nominated to carry it out. F/L Hooper later spoke of the honour and responsibility that he and his crew felt at being chosen from the whole of Bomber Command to help defuse an international incident. In the event, it was a trouble-free trip, F/L Hooper and crew in PB424 JN-O dropping twelve Munro bombs full of leaflets over The Hague and returning at 23.21 to report completing their sortie according to brief. After the war, back on his family's South Taranaki dairy farm, Wilf Hooper was visited by a young Dutch couple who came to buy eggs. The conversation turned to Holland and the leaflet operation, and incredibly, the couple had kept one of the leaflets that he had dropped. He met other survivors of what became known as the Bezuidenhout Bombardment in later life, including a woman who had been a sixteen-year-old at the time, and he gave her a copy of the leaflet, which she had never seen. He said it was quite gratifying to talk to the people for whom he had dropped the leaflets and learn what it meant to them at the time.

On the 27th the group detailed 150 Lancasters to attack benzol plants at Konigsborn and Sachsen in the Hamm area, for which 75(NZ) Squadron made ready twenty-one aircraft. They departed Mepal between 10.20 and 10.48 with no senior pilots on duty and one aircraft carrying a 12,000 pounder, while the other bomb bays contained a cookie and up to fifteen 500 pounders. They found ten-tenths cloud in the target area with tops at 10,000 feet and held a tight formation as they bombed with concentration and precision by G-H. No results could be seen, but thick, black smoke rose through the cloud tops at both locations and the crews went home happy with their day's work. The only hiccough was a 500 pounder that had hung up in F/L Parker's bomb bay and needed to be jettisoned. On the following day twenty-one crews were on their way to the dispersals having been briefed to attack Weimar, but the operation was cancelled before they reached their aircraft.

No doubt it was the same twenty-one crews that made their way out to their Lancasters for the final time during the month on the 29th, three of them debutants captained by F/Sgt Charles Raymond Wagstaff, F/Sgt Richard John Urlich and F/Sgt Eric Lloyd Kennedy Meharry, all members of the RNZAF. This time there was no cancellation and they took off between 12.29 and 12.48 with no senior pilots present, bound for the Hermann Goering benzol plant at Salzgitter, located to the south-west of Braunschweig (Brunswick). They were part of a 3 Group G-H force of 130 aircraft, which found the target area covered by cloud with tops at 19,000 feet and thin cloud and contrails above to 23,000 feet, which reduced visibility to five hundred yards and made formation-keeping a challenge. This operation marked the introduction of G-H/H2S Mk III as a marking device, but the tracking pulse was found by some to be intermittent and back-up blue smoke-puff markers quickly disappeared into the cloud, all of which probably caused the bombing to be scattered.

Thus ended the penultimate month of the bombing war, which had been busy in the extreme, and during the course of which the squadron had operated on twenty-two occasions, dispatching 346 sorties for the loss of four Lancasters and crews.

April 1945

In contrast to the hectic schedule during March, operations in early April would be sparse, and it was not until the 4th that the first crews were called to briefing at Mepal. The target was the I G Farben-owned oil refinery at Leuna (Merseburg) near Leipzig, for which a 3, 6 and 8 Group heavy force of 327 Lancasters was prepared. The twenty-one 75(NZ) Squadron participants, including newcomer F/L Stanley Maurice George Peryer RNZAF, took off between 18.32 and 18.45 with W/C Baigent leading from the front on this potentially difficult deep-penetration raid. F/O Stevens in LM728 AA-R lost his intercom ten minutes after take-off but continued on hoping to be able to communicate with his crew sufficiently to be able to carry out an attack. Sadly, shortly after crossing the French coast south of Boulogne, he decided it was futile and turned back. HK601 JN-D "Snifter" was hit by flak at 19,000 feet when some forty miles short of the target, having just passed close to the V-Weapons production site in caves at Nordhausen, which had been attacked for the second time earlier in the day, and was probably protected by trigger-happy flak gunners. Shrapnel pierced the de-icing tank, causing a fire that burned through a number of electrical leads and inflicting slight burns on the pilot, F/O John Henry Thomas Wood RNZAF, and more serious burns to his bomb-aimer, F/Sgt Noel Ridley Hooper RAF. Navigator F/Sgt John Austin White Pauling RNZAF managed to extinguish the fire and bomb-aimer's clothing, earning an immediate DFM for his efforts, while his skipper received an immediate DFC. The flight engineer, Sgt Douglas Bannerman Williamson RAF, could not be found and was initially believed to have fallen to his death through the mid-under gun position, but an entry in the ORB records his safe return home by the end of April, after three days of evading and a brief stay in German police cells. The bombs were jettisoned shortly afterwards at 22.30, and the charred Lancaster made it back to a landing at Manston at 02.02. Those reaching the target found a layer of low cloud with tops up to 5,000 feet, through which the Path Finder TIs were barely visible and the skymarkers of little help. The bombing was scattered, and little damage resulted to the refinery. F/L Peryer's starboard-inner engine caught fire on his bombing run and he was unable to feather it, but managed to bring NG322 JN-F and his crew home safely.

The above-mentioned site at Nordhausen was actually a pair of enormous parallel tunnels under the Kohnstein Hill, which had been developed originally by the BASF Company to mine gypsum between 1917 and 1934. Following the destruction of Peenemünde, smaller tunnels had been created as a link between them to form a horizontal ladder effect, and the site turned over to the Mittelwerk GmbH (Gesellschaft mit beschrenkter Haftung, or Limited Company) for the manufacture of V-2 rockets and other secret projects. The "barracks" were part of the Mittelwerk-Dora forced workers camp, where inmates existed under the most horrendous conditions and brutal treatment, while they were starved, worked to death or simply executed by an increasingly desperate regime seeking to change the course of the war.

3 Group remained off the order of battle for the first eight days, and missed, therefore, the final heavy raid of the war on Hamburg, which was delivered by over four hundred aircraft from 4, 6 and 8 Groups on the night of the 8/9th. A force of 591 aircraft was assembled from 1, 3 and 8 Groups on the 9th for a two-pronged attack on the harbour district of Kiel, where the Germania Werft and Deutsche Werke shipyards were located. This was a big night for 3 Group, which put up a record 241 Lancasters, of which nineteen belonged to 75(NZ) Squadron. Two were captained by newcomers, F/L James Colin Westbrooke RNZAF and F/O Peter Lloyd Trevarthen RNZAF and all took off between 19.43 and 19.58 with W/C Baigent and S/L Bailey the senior pilots on duty. They reached the target to find ground haze but clear skies and a Master Bomber on hand to assess the Path Finder marking and direct the main force bombing, which was delivered accurately and caused extensive damage to the Deutsche Werke U-Boot yards, sank the pocket battleship Admiral Scheer and damaged the cruisers Emden and Admiral Hipper. Three other shipyards were also hit and adjacent residential districts found themselves under the bombs, which inflicted severe damage, all at a cost to the Command of three Lancasters and their crews.

While this operation was in progress, seven of the Squadron's Lancasters joined in a large mining effort in the Forget-me-not garden in Kiel Bay. They had taken off at the same time as those for the main event and followed the same route to the target area. However, when about 150 miles out from the Yorkshire coast, having observed excessive petrol consumption, F/O Ohlsen in PB427 AA-U turned back with a suspected fuel leak in the port No 1 tank, which had lost about a hundred gallons and left insufficient reserves to complete the operation. The others found little cloud to bother them and delivered their stores into the briefed location, before returning safely from largely uneventful sorties. The one exception was F/L Watson and crew in RF157 AA-X, who were fired upon from the mid-upper turret of another Lancaster. "With friends like that………". S/L Jack Bailey concluded his tour with the above operation and was succeeded as C Flight commander by another Jack, the newly promoted S/L Jack Colin Parker DFC, RNZAF. S/L Jack Wright also stepped down as A Flight commander and was succeeded by the newly promoted S/L Laurence McKenna RNZAF.

The next time the squadron appeared on the order of battle, it was for a return to Kiel on the night of the 13/14th, for which twenty-one Lancasters were made ready as part of a 3 Group element of 199 Lancasters in an overall 3, 6 and 8 Group heavy force of 377 Lancasters and 105 Halifaxes. The Mepal element took off between 20.30 and 20.53 with W/C Baigent taking the lead and S/L Parker operating for the first time as a flight commander. F/O Morgan and crew in ME531 AA-K were some one hundred miles short of the west coast of the Schleswig-Holstein peninsula outbound when they were forced to turn back by the failure of the navigational aids. The compass took them away from the stream, and although they made efforts to catch up, they found themselves far enough behind it to lose contact in the darkness. The others reached the target to find ten-tenths thin stratus cloud with tops up to 5,000 feet, and Path Finder ground marking in progress. A Master Bomber was on hand to control the bombing, which as far as the Mepal crews were concerned, was concentrated and the glow of fires could be seen. The Master Bomber instructed crews to aim for the glow, and two large explosions were witnessed, one of them resulting from a hit on an ammunition dump at the northern end of the harbour district. Generally, however, the bombing was scattered, and focussed largely on the suburb of Elmschenhagen two miles from the harbour. W/O Evenden and crew in LM728 AA-R had to make two passes over the target, having arrived ahead of the first markers and bombed the glow of fires in accordance with instructions. On return at 02.25, this crew ended up in a heap after the undercarriage of LM728 collapsed on touch-down at Mepal. The crew was able to walk away, but it proved to be the end of the line for the unfortunate Lancaster.

Harris's heavy bombers had left Berlin in peace for more than a year when orders came through on the 14th for an attack that night on Potsdam, situated some fifteen miles south-west from the centre of the German capital. This would be the first incursion into the Berlin defence zone for the heavy brigade since March 1944 and would prove to be the last major raid of the war on a German city. A force of five hundred Lancasters from 1, 3 and 8 Groups was assembled, a figure that included a 3 Group contribution of 198 aircraft. Twenty-five Lancasters at Mepal were loaded with mixed calibre HE bombs, mostly amounting to under 7,000lbs total weight, and they took off between 18.11 and 18.45 with no senior pilots on duty but the station commander, G/C Campbell, flying as second pilot with F/O Pearson. Five RNZAF captains were on debut, F/O Robert Elliot, F/O Allan Ralph Baynes, F/O Charles Harold Lumsden, F/Sgt William George Reay and F/Sgt Ivan Edgar Reddish. They found clear skies over north-eastern Germany and good visibility, which helped them to pick out the lakes on approach to the target. The Path Finders were responsible for the marking and a Master Bomber for keeping the raid on track, and he ordered crews to aim for bunches of red and green TIs, which were right on the aiming point. W/O Bone and crew were late on target after a port-inner engine malfunction, and they observed many fires already burning well and a good concentration of bombing. About fifty searchlights were operating and proved to be bothersome to a number of crews, but the flak was non-existent, while a few night-fighters made their presence felt and PB132, now re-coded AA-T, was attacked by two Ju88s when homebound at 15,000 feet twenty miles south-west of Potsdam at 23.07. The first attacked from head-on and below, while the second aircraft stood off as a decoy. A cannon shell caused damage to the nose and the cockpit and killed the flight engineer, Sgt Allan Melrose Sliman RAFVR, a prominent professional footballer in civilian life. The rear gunner managed a long burst before the attacker broke away and disappeared. Ten minutes later, however, two Ju88s appeared again, one attacking from dead astern and slightly damaging the rear turret, which was by now out of action due to loss of hydraulics. It was a terrible maiden operation for F/O Baynes and his crew, taking them off the front line for a month, but the Lancaster made it home to a safe landing at 03.11. The operation succeeded in causing severe and widespread damage in Potsdam, where some five thousand people lost their lives, and stray bombs also hit northern and eastern districts of Berlin.

The 18th brought a massive assault on the island of Heligoland, situated in the North Sea some thirty miles out from the west coast of Schleswig-Holstein. It had been a fortress throughout the war, with a seaplane base, an airfield, U-Boot bunkers and coastal batteries and contained an air-raid shelter with an extensive tunnel system. It had attracted British attention during the early war years, but interest waned, although the waters around it in the Rosemary garden had been mined frequently. With the end of the war in sight and the Kriegsmarine running out of safe havens for its U-Boots and other craft, the island began to take on a greater significance. A force of 969 aircraft was assembled, of which 254 were provided by 3 Group. Twenty-five Lancasters were loaded at Mepal with five 1,000, eight 500 pounders and a 350lb Munro bomb and took off between 10.10 and 10.37 with W/C Baigent and S/L Parker the senior pilots on duty. When they arrived in the target area, which lay under clear skies, only the northern tip and western fringe of the island could be identified. The rest was concealed beneath smoke and dust as the surface of the island was reduced to, what in reconnaissance photographs, would resemble a cratered moonscape. The 3 Group crews bombed on the instructions of the Master Bomber, and although some bombs were seen to fall into the sea, the majority hit the island, killing 285 people, most of them members of the flak crews and naval support staff. Thirty-six Lancasters of 9 and 617 Squadrons followed up on the 19th with Tallboy and Grand Slam earthquake bombs, and after being hit by 7,000 tons of bombs, the island was rendered uninhabitable and was abandoned.

The squadron sat out a small 3 Group G-H raid on the Pasing railway yards at Munich on the 19th but made ready twenty Lancasters on the 20th as part of a hundred-strong 3 Group force briefed to attack petrol and oil-storage tanks in Regensburg, a medieval city deep in south-eastern Germany, which was home to an oil refinery and a Messerschmitt aircraft factory producing BF109s. In actual fact, what had been the Bayerische Flugzeugwerke in Augsburg became Messerschmitt A G in 1938 and relocated to Haunstetten, some forty miles north-east of Augsburg and twenty-five miles west of Regensburg. A new housing settlement sprang up to accommodate the huge increase in the work force, which would reach a peak of 18,000 in 1944, 47% of which were either foreigners or slaves drafted in from satellite camps of Dachau. However, as far as the RAF and USAAF were concerned, for operational purposes the factory was referred to as located in Regensburg.

Three RNZAF skippers were on debut for this operation, F/Sgt Ronald Norman Drummond, F/O William Roy Brinsden and F/Sgt Barry Leonard David Anderson. They took off between 19.40 and 19.58 with S/L McKenna the senior pilot on duty and flew out under clear skies that held all the way to the target. F/O Ohlsen in PB427 AA-U was forced to turn back from a position twenty miles south-east of Namur in Belgium after a problem developed in two engines, but the others reached the target area, where the visibility was excellent and allowed crews to identify the river, the docks and the aiming point visually. This was a G-H attack approaching from the north, and the system worked well, although the lead squadron dropped short and there was some overshooting onto the marshalling yards later on. In between, the aiming point was plastered and a crew on the right-hand edge of the formation claimed a direct hit on a railway bridge. F/Sgt Hamilton in HK806 AA-B had to break away during the camera run to avoid being hit by falling bombs, and F/O Elliot in NN747 "Dogsbody Again", now re-coded AA-D, shut down his starboard-outer engine as it began to smoke after leaving the target.

3 Group provided 195 Lancasters in a combined force of 767 aircraft detailed on the 22nd to attack the south-eastern suburbs of Bremen ahead of the approaching British XXX Corps. 75(NZ) Squadron contributed twenty-one aircraft, which departed Mepal between 15.16 and 15.38, led away by W/C Baigent and with S/L Parker also on the order of battle. They approached the target on a south-easterly heading, passing over Wilhelmshaven at 17,500 feet

at 18.30, where they were greeted by accurate flak. A number of aircraft sustained damage, among them S/L Parker's NF935 AA-P, as a result of which the flight engineer, Sgt Roy Stanley Clarke RAFVR, was fatally wounded. F/Sgt Fairbairn's NN773 AA-G was hit in the mid-upper turret and a hole appeared in the starboard fin, while P/O Lukins in PB418 AA-C lost his starboard-outer engine. They pressed on to reach the target area, where according to squadron records, two to five-tenths cloud prevailed, although the 3 Group account states up to nine-tenths cloud with tops as high as 9,000 feet. The attack proceeded well with the bombing falling within the built-up area, despite a little under and overshooting. The 75(NZ) Squadron formation followed in the wake of another unit, which delivered its bombs right onto the aiming point, leaving the Kiwis to watch their bombs fall into smoke. W/C Mac Baigent led them over the city in HK806 AA-B with a 12,000 pounder under his feet. He wrote in his diary: "One of the pilots at the rear of the Squadron said it was an unforgettable sight. Twenty-one Lancasters in tight formation, all with bomb doors open, cruising steadily up to Bremen, flak puffs all round, bombs poised, waiting for the leading aircraft to give the bombing signal. As our 12,000lb 'Cookie' fell away a further twenty bomb loads of about 11,000 pounds each started their journey to the Bremen docks. The noise when the whole load landed must have been terrific." The operation was successful, and the city would become the first German port to fall into Allied hands five days later.

To prevent German reinforcements from reaching Bremen, 3 Group was ordered to attack the marshalling yards at Bad Oldesloe, a town to the north-east midway between Hamburg and Lübeck. A G-H force of 110 Lancasters included twenty from Mepal, which took off between 07.06 and 07.27 with F/Ls Adamson, Taylor and Watson the senior pilots on duty. F/Sgt Reay and crew in HK561 AA-Y "Liefy" were halfway into the North Sea crossing when engine failure forced them to turn back, leaving the others to push on to the target, which they found under three-tenths cloud with tops at around 4,000 feet. The visibility was good and crews were able to identify the target visually as they ran in in a good formation of five G-H boxes of four aircraft each to deliver their bombs. Some bombs were seen to fall to port of the aiming point, but the majority were on the mark and produced the hoped-for results, returning crews reporting many explosions and fires. The town was not expecting an attack and its air-raid precautions were slack, which led to a death toll of an estimated seven hundred people. It was perhaps fitting that No 5 G-H formation on this last operation was led by NE181 JN-M, "The Captain's Fancy", the squadron's most famous Lancaster. Supposedly retired, and listed in the ORB as its replacement, RF129, skipper F/O Ed Ware and his crew were, nonetheless, adamant that it was "The Captain's Fancy" that they flew that day, claiming it as NE181's 104th operation, and they had a photograph taken to commemorate the occasion. The squadron stood-by in preparation for further operations, but none came that involved 3 Group, and two days later, the main force ceased offensive operations.

After years of carrying bombs and death to Continental Europe, the squadron was among those handed the heart-warming, humanitarian task of delivering much-needed food supplies to the starving Dutch people still under enemy occupation. A deal had been struck under Operation Manna to allow unarmed Bomber Command aircraft to fly to designated drop zones and drop the supplies from low level. As nine 75(NZ) Squadron Lancasters arrived over the Delft area in the early afternoon of the 29th with five panniers each, they were greeted by crowds of deliriously happy Dutch people standing in the streets and on rooftops, waving flags and anything else they could lay their hands on. W/C Baigent and S/L McKenna were the senior pilots on duty as they located the poorly-defined drop sites only at the last minute, and, sadly, a total of ten of the forty-five panniers hung-up, for which the packing was blamed. The squadron continued to participate in these operations until peace was declared on the 8th of May, when a station parade was held at 14.30 to celebrate the event. From the 9th the squadron took part in Operation Exodus, the repatriation of Allied prisoners of war, which would continue on into the summer.

75(NZ) Squadron served magnificently for five long years of war and was only prevented from taking a full part in all the major campaigns by the restricted performance of the Stirling. Much of its wartime career was spent as a three-flight unit and consequently it was able to launch a higher-than-average number of sorties. The squadron's record of service places it at or near the top of all performance tables and because of its prolific activity, it suffered particularly heavy numerical losses. However, in percentage terms, which provides a more accurate picture of casualties, the squadron fared better than many and contributed much to the overall success of the Command. Dominion aircrew in Bomber Command died in their thousands, fighting a war which, strictly speaking, wasn't theirs, and their contribution to victory was massive and decisive and should forever stand as a testimony to their national characters. A total of 1,679 members of the RNZAF lost their lives in Bomber Command service, 3% of those who served. The squadron ended the war with the highest number of sorties in Bomber Command, the second highest number of overall operations in Bomber Command, the second highest number of aircraft operational losses in Bomber Command, the fifth highest number of bombing operations in Bomber Command and the third highest number of mining sorties in Bomber Command. It also registered the highest number of overall operations and sorties in 3 Group and the third highest number of Wellington operations and second highest number of Wellington sorties in Bomber Command.

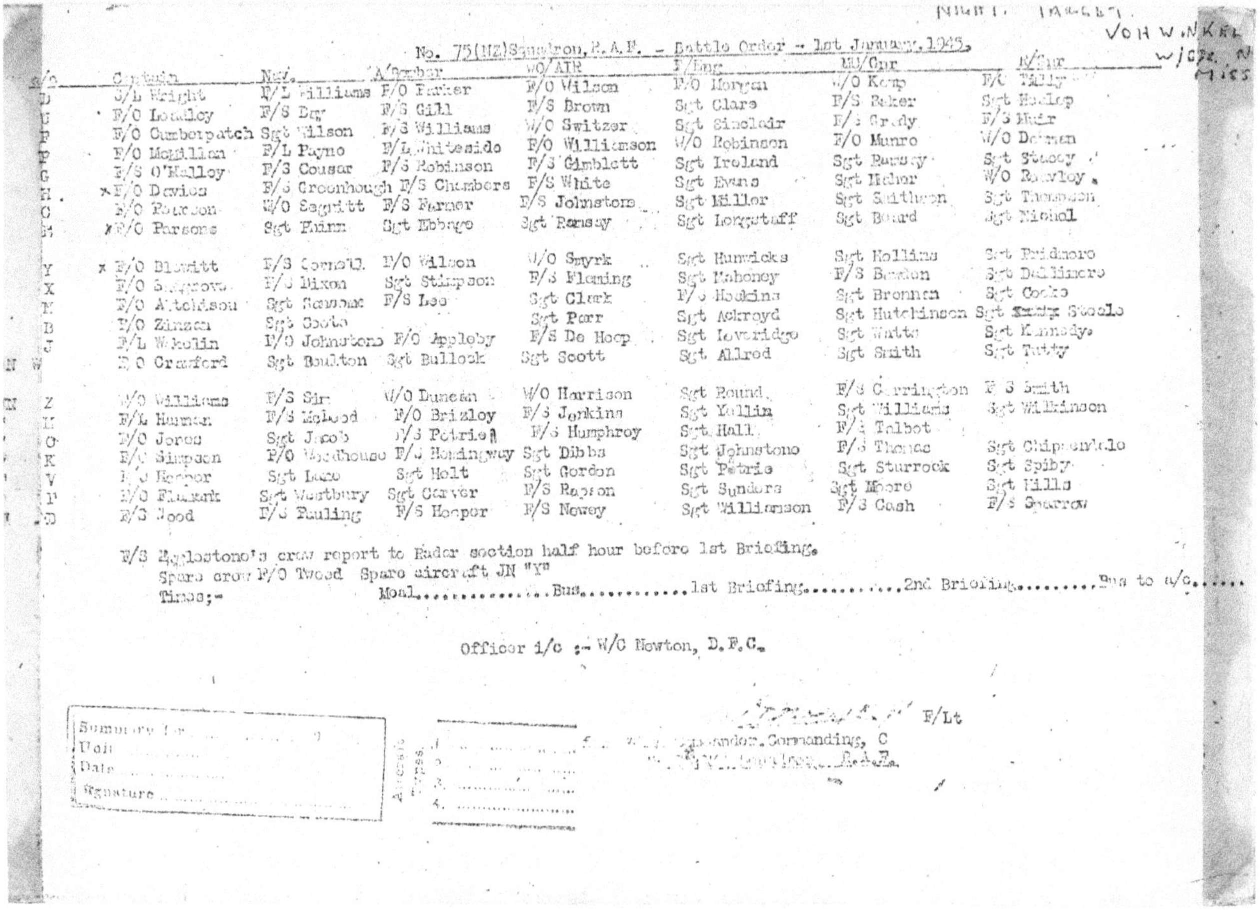
NIGHT. TARGET. VOHWINKEL
W/CDR. N MISS

No. 75(NZ)Squadron, R.A.F. – Battle Order – 1st January, 1945.

A/C	Captain	Nav.	A/Bomber	WO/AIR	F/Eng	MU/Gnr	R/Gnr
D	S/L Wright	F/L Williams	F/O Parker	F/O Wilson	F/O Morgan	W/O Kemp	F/O Tilly
U	F/O Lomalley	F/S Day	F/S Gill	F/S Brown	Sgt Clare	F/S Baker	Sgt Heslop
F	F/O Cumberpatch	Sgt Wilson	F/S Williams	W/O Switzer	Sgt Sinclair	F/S Grady	F/S Muir
P	F/O McMillan	F/L Payne	F/L Whiteside	F/O Williamson	W/O Robinson	F/O Munro	W/O Dorman
G	F/S O'Malley	F/S Cousar	F/S Robinson	F/S Gimblett	Sgt Ireland	Sgt Ramsay	Sgt Stacey
H	× F/O Davies	F/S Greenhough	F/S Chambers	F/S White	Sgt Evans	Sgt Maher	W/O Rawley
C	F/O Pearson	W/O Seggitt	F/S Farmer	F/S Johnstone	Sgt Miller	Sgt Smithson	Sgt Thompson
[illegible]	× F/O Parsons	Sgt Fairn	Sgt Ebbage	Sgt Ramsay	Sgt Longstaff	Sgt Board	Sgt Nichol
Y	× F/O Blewitt	F/S Cornell	F/O Wilson	W/O Smyrk	Sgt Hunwicks	Sgt Hollins	Sgt Pridmore
X	F/O Sagrove	F/S Dixon	Sgt Stimpson	F/S Fleming	Sgt Mahoney	F/S Bowden	Sgt Dallimore
M	F/O Aitchison	Sgt Sansome	F/S Lee	Sgt Clark	F/S Hoskins	Sgt Brennan	Sgt Cooke
B	F/O Zinzan	Sgt Scott		Sgt Parr	Sgt Ackroyd	Sgt Hutchinson	Sgt ~~[illegible]~~ Steele
J	F/L Wakelin	F/O Johnstone	F/O Appleby	F/S De Hoop	Sgt Loveridge	Sgt Watts	Sgt Kennedy
W	F/O Crawford	Sgt Boulton	Sgt Bullock	Sgt Scott	Sgt Allred	Sgt Smith	Sgt Tutty
Z	W/O Williams	F/S Sim	W/O Duncan	W/O Harrison	Sgt Round	F/S Carrington	F/S Smith
L	F/L Harman	F/S Mcleod	F/O Brizley	F/S Jenkins	Sgt Yellin	Sgt Williams	Sgt Wilkinson
O	F/O Jones	Sgt Jacob	F/S Petrie	F/S Humphrey	Sgt Hall	F/S Talbot	
K	F/O Simpson	P/O Woodhouse	F/S Hemingway	Sgt Dibbs	Sgt Johnstone	F/S Thomas	Sgt Chippendale
V	F/O Hooper	Sgt Lace	Sgt Holt	Sgt Gordon	Sgt Petrie	Sgt Sturrock	Sgt Spiby
P	F/O Flu[illegible]	Sgt Westbury	Sgt Carver	F/S Rapson	Sgt Sanders	Sgt Moore	Sgt Mills
D	F/S Wood	F/S Pauling	F/S Hooper	F/S Newey	Sgt Williamson	F/S Cash	F/S Sparrow

F/S Egglestone's crew report to Radar section half hour before 1st Briefing.
Spare crew F/O Tweed Spare aircraft JN "Y"
Times;- Meal.............. Bus............ 1st Briefing.......... 2nd Briefing......... Bus to a/c......

Officer i/c :- W/C Newton, D.F.C.

F/Lt
for Wing Commander, Commanding, [illegible]
[illegible] R.A.F.

Summary for [illegible]
Unit
Date
Signature

The Battle Order for the Vohwinkel operation, 1 January 1945. "W/Cdr Newton missing" noted in the top corner. (NZ Bomber Command Assn. archives)

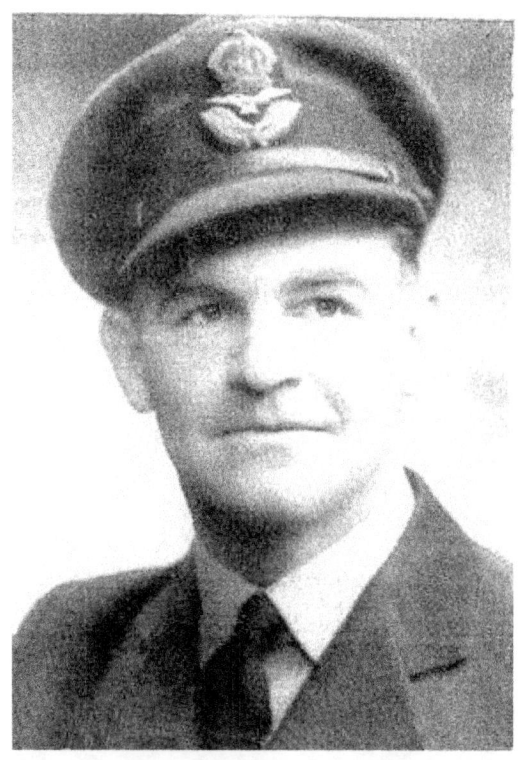

W/C Raymond John "Ray" Newton DFC, MiD, RNZAF, killed with all his crew on the Vohwinkel operation 1 January 1945. (Bernard Kingsbury)

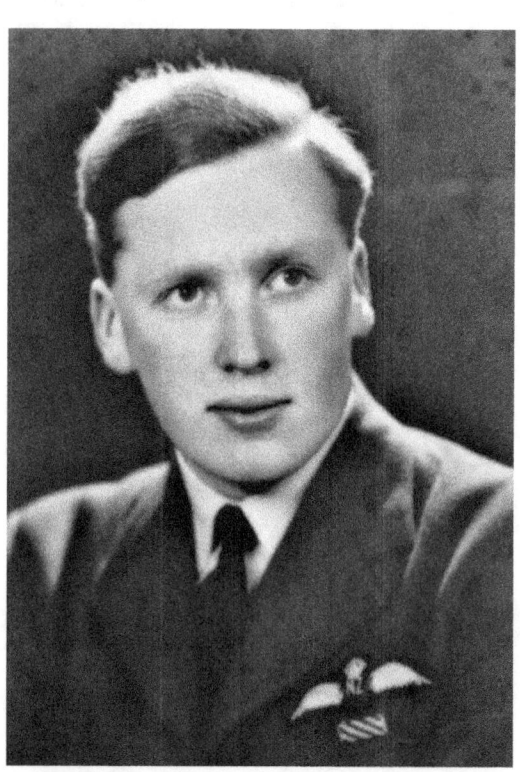

W/C Cyril Henry "Mac" Baigent DFC, commanding officer of the squadron from 6 January until disbandment on 15 October 1945. (NZ Bomber Command Assn. archives, Baigent collection)

Staff from the Mepal Officers Mess. WAAF Marjorie Rowland, 2nd from right, later married mid-under gunner F/O Charles Green DFC. (From G.A. Russell's "Dying For Democracy")

The Spilman crew (L-R): Back - Sgt Gerry Abrahams (wireless operator), F/Sgt Tom Corlett (bomb aimer), Sgt Norm Holbrook (navigator), Sgt Harry Thorne (flight engineer). Front - F/Sgt Vern Clouston (mid-upper gunner), F/L Sidney "Buzz" Spilman (pilot), F/Sgt Pat Burke (rear gunner). (NZ Bomber Command Assn. archives, Spilman collection)

Lancaster PB132 AA-X refuelling (Baigent collection).

Ground crews refuelling and bombing up a Lancaster at Mepal for a night raid on Krefeld, Germany. The bomb load consists of a 4,000-lb HC 'cookie' and mixed 1,000-lb and 500-lb MC bombs. (IWM)

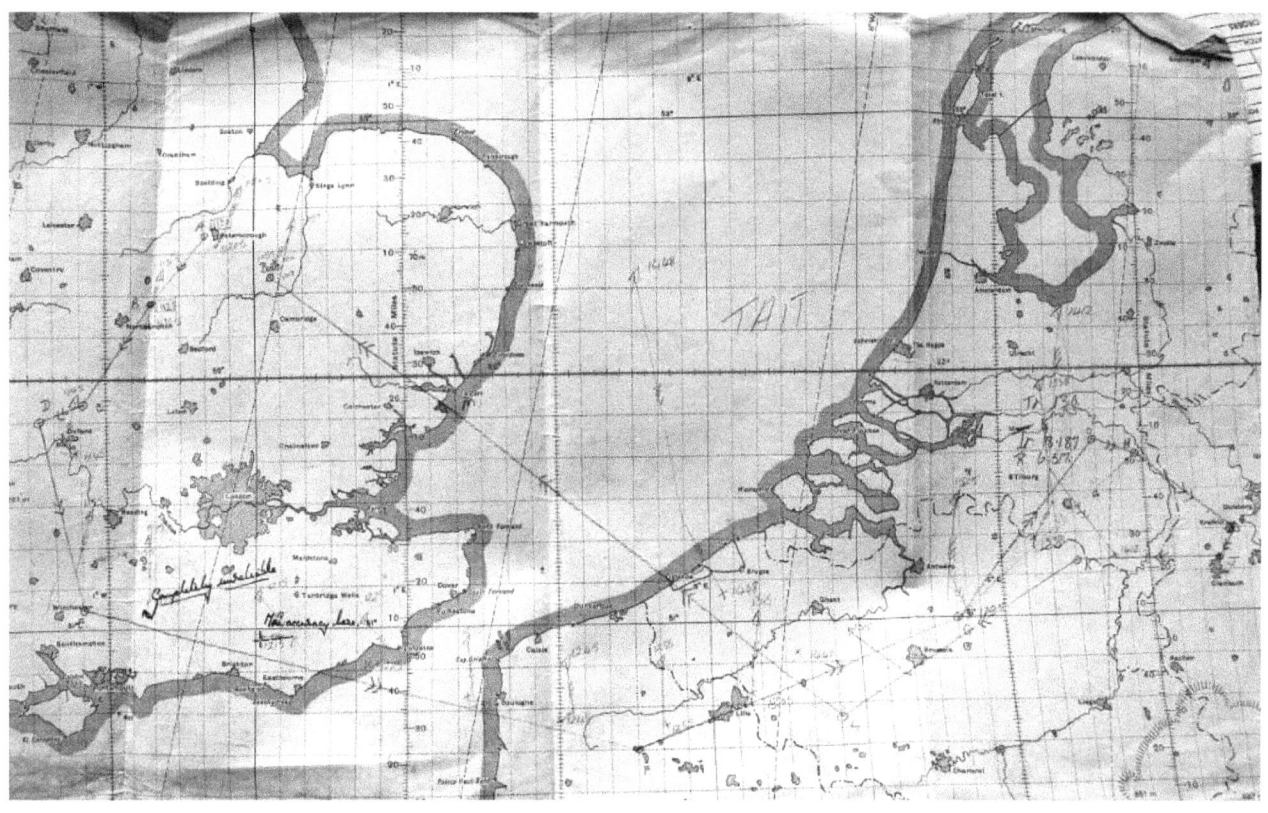

*Kilpatrick crew navigator P/O Ray Tait's plot for the Krefeld operation, 29 January 1945.
(NZ Bomber Command Assn. archives, Tait collection)*

*Lancasters taxying around the Mepal perimeter.
(NZ Bomber Command Assn. archives, Ware collection)*

Crews relax on the grass by the perimeter track after take-off is delayed for an hour.
(Air Force Museum of NZ, Russell Brothers collection)

Bombs cascade from a 75 (NZ) Squadron Lancaster.
(NZ Bomber Command Assn. archives, Estcourt collection)

The Bailey crew in front of NE181 JN-M "Mike" aka 'The Captains Fancy' (99 op's marked), ready to depart for the Krefeld operation on the 29th of January 1945 (L-R): Back – F/L Jack Brewster (navigator), F/O Norman Bartlett (flight engineer), S/L Jack Bailey (skipper), F/O Jack Wall (bob aimer), Sgt Dick Pickup (wireless operator). Front - W/O Roy Corfield (rear gunner), P/O Tony Gregory (mid-upper gunner). This was the aircraft's 100th bombing sortie, and she was the squadron's first and only Lancaster to achieve this milestone. Below – with ground crew, 2nd from left kneeling, LAC Thompson, right LAC Fred Woolterton.
(Both photos Richard Pickup collection, thanks to Tony Pickup, via 75nzsquadron.com)

A cold snowy day at Mepal as the Bailey crew board Lancaster NE181 JN-M 'The Captains Fancy' to take her on the aircraft's 100th bombing operation, 29th January 1945.
Below, taxying out to take off.
(Both photos NZ Bomber Command Assn. archives, Scott collection)

NE181's ground crew apply the 101st op' bomb marking, as S/L Jack Bailey watches on. As well as her 100th, S/L Bailey and his crew took 'The Captains Fancy' on the 101st, to Wiesbaden on the 2nd of February. L-R: Sgt Grantham, LAC Fred Woolterton, LAC Taylor, LAC Thompson, S/L Bailey, unknown ground crew.
(Ron Baker collection, via Don Simms)

Below: S/L Jack Bailey in the cockpit of his regular "kite", NE181, JN-M 'Mike', 'The Captain's Fancy'. (Ron Baker collection, via Don Simms)

The Amohanga crew (L-R): Back – F/O Alf Woolcock (bomb aimer), F/Sgt Ken Dalzell (navigator), P/O Kiwi Amohanga (skipper), F/O Jack Richardson (mid-upper gunner). Front – Sgt Steven Fletcher (flight engineer), F/Sgt Sandy Strachan (rear gunner), F/Sgt Max Spooner (wireless operator).
(NZ Bomber Command Assn. archives, Dalzell collection)

The Robertson crew with Lancaster HK563 JN-W "Paper Doll", skipper Eddie Robertson centre front.
(NZ Bomber Command Assn. archives, Robertson collection)

On her 86th op' to Dortmund on 3rd February 1945, ND801 JN-X "Get Sum Inn" suffered a port outer engine failure, and on return she overshot the runway and crashed into a chicken shed and bakers van (below) in Sutton Village. Pilot F/O Bruce Crawford and four of his crew were injured and taken to hospital.
(Both photos from the Baigent collection)

Mechanics working on the port-outer Merlin engine of C Flight Lancaster HK593 JN-X at Mepal, 9 February 1945. Previously coded AA-H, HK593 was re-coded JN-X to replace ND801 which had overshot the Mepal runway only 6 days before this photo was taken. (IWM)

The Flamank crew with HK593, JN-X, F/O Ron Flamank kneeling second from right. (Harry Holmes)

A Lancaster being refuelled from an AEC Matador bowser, "Baby Dumbo".
(NZ Bomber Command Assn. archives, Ware collection)

75 (NZ) Squadron C Flight Lancaster HK601 JN-D "Snifter" flying over Europe, early 1945. The white streak at the bottom of the photo is thought to be the River Rhine.
(Air Force Museum of NZ, R.W. Russell collection)

F/L George Stanley Davies RNZAF and crew baled out of NG113 AA-D after a fire developed in the starboard wing on the Chemnitz op', 14/15th February 1945.
(From "Still Vivid", thanks to the Davies family)

F/O Noel Humphrey Thorpe RNZAF and three of his crew died returning from Dortmund on the 26th of February 1945, when their Lancaster appeared to lose power in both starboard engines and crashed near Chatteris.
(Kete Horowhenua)

75 (NZ) Squadron Lancasters on their way to Wesel, early 1945, as seen from F/O Ed Ware's cockpit.
(NZ Bomber Command Assn. archives, Ware collection.)

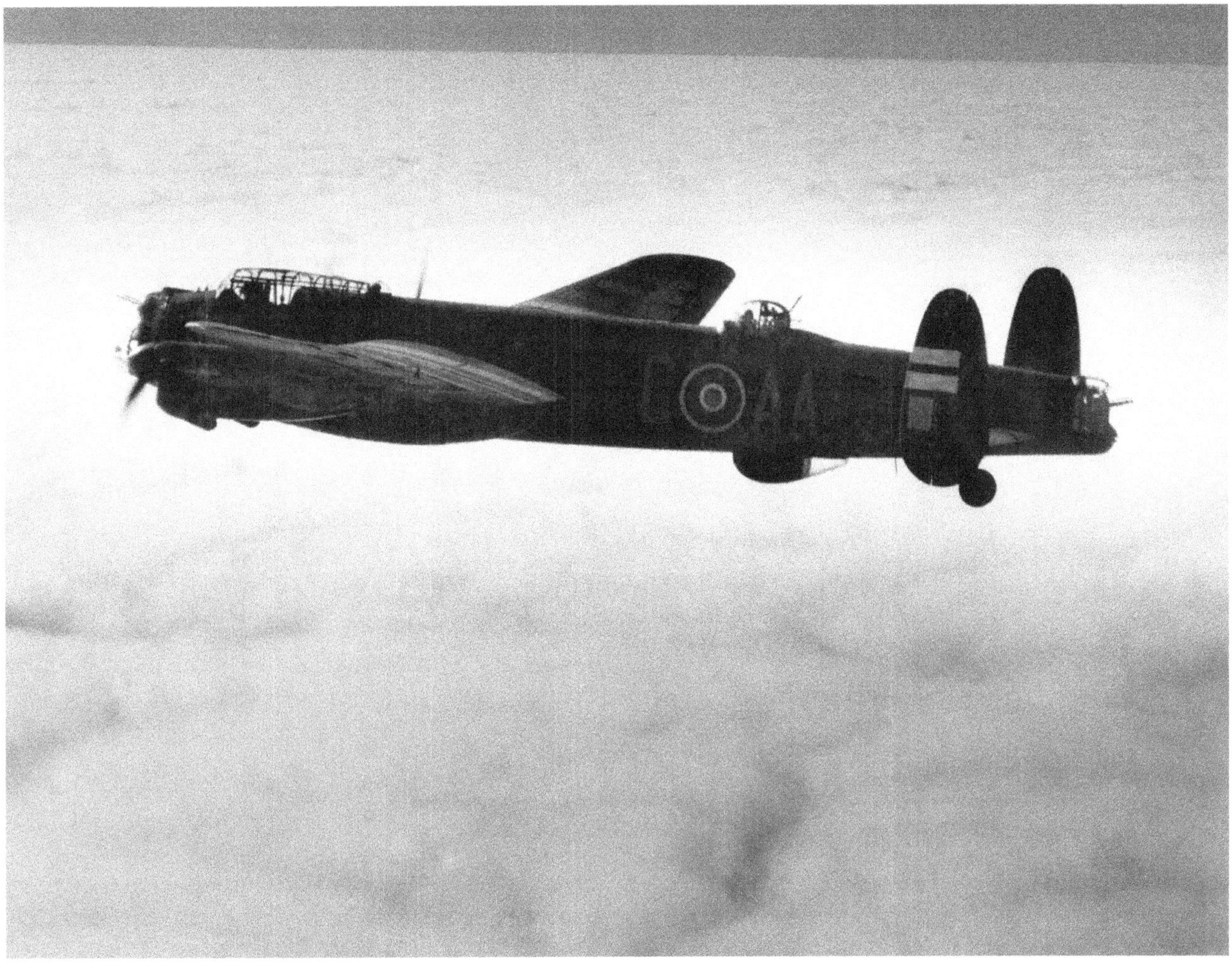

Lancaster PB418 AA-C "Charlie" on its way to the target, February 1945.
(Air Force Museum of New Zealand)

F/O Mart Kilpatrick's NF935 AA-P lost its port outer engine with flak damage on the run in to Osterfeld on 22 February 1945, and starboard inner not long after bombing. Struggling to maintain height, F/O Kilpatrick nursed the Lancaster home safely and was awarded an Immediate DFC. (NZ Bomber Command Assn. archives, Tait collection)

Boarding the Dodge crew bus to be taken out to dispersal, Mepal, February 1945. Far left, F/Sgt Ben Klitscher, his navigator P/O David King (carrying bag) and members of the Russell crew – bomb aimer F/O Vic Hendry, pilot F/O Wynne Russell (centre, looking straight at camera), navigator F/O Neville Selwood, W/Op F/Sgt Fred Jillions, rear gunner Sgt George Robson, and flight engineer Sgt John Hunt (far right). Flak damage forced the Klitscher crew to abandon LM740 AA-B near Wesel on the 25th of February, all surviving as PoWs.
(NZ Bomber Command Assn. archives, Mayhill collection)

Lancasters of C Flight queue up for take-off, Mepal, March 1945. Nearest is PB820, JN-V.
(NZ Bomber Command Assn. archives, Ware collection)

*75 (NZ) Squadron, Mepal, near Ely, Cambridgeshire, 15 March 1945. W/C "Mac" Baigent, O/C, centre front, seated.
(NZ Bomber Command Assn. archives)*

W/C "Mac" Baigent DFC and Squadron Adjutant, F/L Charles Bewsher RAF.
(NZ Bomber Command Assn. archives, Baker collection)*

*The squadron Bombing Leader's door plaque.
(From G.A. Russell's "Dying For Democracy")*

W/C "Mac" Baigent DFC* and B Flight commander S/L Bob Rodgers DFC.
(NZ Bomber Command Assn. archives, Baigent collection)

S/L Bob Rodgers DFC, F/L Doug Sadgrove and F/L Jack Plummer DFC, Mepal, March 1945.
(NZ Bomber Command Assn. archives, Baigent collection)

*W/O Harold Trewheela in the cockpit of Lancaster NG322 JN-F, March 1945.
(NZ Bomber Command Assn. archives, Putwain collection)*

*The Trewheela crew carrying out a D.I. (Daily Inspection) on NG322 JN-F.
(NZ Bomber Command Assn. archives, Putwain collection)*

The Banks crew in front of LM276 AA-S (L-R): Back – John "Ted" Smith, Jimmy Wood, Russell Banks, Maurice Wiggins. Front – Norman 'Paddy' Allen, John Mossman, Harry 'Jock' Fraser. (Harry Holmes)

The Sinclair crew (L-R): Back - George Painting (flight engineer), Bill Sinclair (pilot), Alexander 'Sandy' Sommerville (navigator), Ian Foster (wireless operator), Ian Rowe (bomb aimer). Front - Bill Glover (rear gunner), Alan McRobert (mid-upper gunner). (Brian Foster, via 75nzsquadron.com)

"Waiting to start up". F/L Jack Plummer DFC (right), navigator F/Sgt "Tiny" Humphries (2nd from right) and crew, with their regular Lancaster NG449 AA-T. F/L Plummer, bomb-aimer F/O Edgar Holloway and mid-upper gunner F/O Russell Scott were killed in the attack on the Münster Viaduct, 21st of March 1945.
(NZ Bomber Command Assn. archives, Baker collection)

F/S Thomas Good landing Lancaster HK561 AA-Y safely at Woodbridge "prang drome" after losing both starboard engines during a daylight attack on Kamen, 1 March 1945. (IWM)

Sgt Allan Melrose "Jack" Sliman RAFVR, flight engineer in the Baynes crew, was killed by cannon fire on his first operation, Potsdam, 14 April 1945.
(Chelmsford War Memorial)

Right: 75 (NZ) Squadron Lancasters break formation over Mepal on returning from operations. (Dennis Jones collection, via Glynis Bakker)

The Hooper crew (L-R): Back - W/O A. Gordon (wireless operator), Sgt Royston Lane (navigator), F/Sgt E. Holt (bomb aimer), Sgt J Petrie (flight engineer). Front - Sgt Robert Sturrock (mid-upper gunner), F/L H. "Wilf" Hooper (pilot), Sgt J. Spiby (rear gunner). Flight engineer Sgt Petrie was sick on the 25th of March, so his place on the nickeling raid on The Hague was taken by F/Sgt John Palmer, from the Adamson crew. (Bruce Hooper)

```
NO. 75(NZ)SQUADRON - BATTLE ORDER - 25th/26th MARCH,1945

A/C     CAPTAIN     NAVIGATOR   A/BOMBER    WO/AIR      F/ENG       MU/GNR      R/GNR

JN O    F/L HOOPER  SGT LANE    F/S HOLT    W/O GORDON  SGT PALMER  SGT STURROCK SGT SPIBY

        TIMES:-     MEAL........BUS.........1st BRIEFING........2nd BRIEFING.........BUS TO AIRCRAFT.........

                        OFFICER I/C FLYING:- W/C. BAIGENT, D.F.C.

                                                        F/LT
                                            for WING COMMANDER, COMMANDING,
                                                NO. 75(NZ)SQUADRON, R.A.F.
```

The Battle Order for the single-aircraft nickeling raid on The Hague, F/L Hooper and crew, 25th of March 1945. (Bruce Hooper)

BOODSCHAP AAN DE BEVOLKING VAN DEN HAAG

In antwoord op een verzoek om opheldering van het bombardement op Den Haag op 3 Maart j.l. heeft de Britsche Regeering de volgende verklaring afgelegd, die reeds uitgezonden is door de B.B.C. en Radio Oranje.

In den morgen van den derden Maart hebben vliegtuigen van de Tweede Tactische luchtmacht van de R.A.F. een aanval gedaan op rocket-doelen in Den Haag. De bommen zijn zeer ongelukkig ver van het doel terecht gekomen en dientengevolge is een groot aantal slachtoffers gevallen onder de burgerbevolking en werd groote schade aangericht in woonwijken.

Terstond nadat men zich had rekenschap gegeven van hetgeen was, gebeurd werd een onderzoek gelast om de oorzaak van deze betreurenswaardige ramp vast te stellen. Uit een voorloopig rapport is gebleken, dat het ongeluk toe te schrijven is aan een foutieve uitvoering. Een nauwgezet onderzoek is nog gaande en disciplinaire maatregelen zullen genomen worden tegen allen, die zullen blijken schuld te hebben gehad.

Het Britsche volk en in het bijzonder de Royal Air Force spreken hun diepste leedwezen uit over dit vreeselijke ongeluk en zij betuigen hun warme deelneming met allen, die geleden hebben van de gevolgen van een ramp, die zoozeer de ellende, die zij reeds te verduren hebben, heeft verhoogd. Het Nederlandsche volk kent maar al te goed de risico's, welke de oorlogvoering medebrengt en zij zullen beseffen, dat het niet steeds mogelijk is ongelukken van dezen aard te voorkomen.

De R.A.F. zal echter haar uiterste best doen om ervoor te waken, dat een dergelijke fout niet weer gemaakt zal worden. Zij zal in haar aanvallen op dit onmenschelijke rocketwapen, waartoe de vijand den Nederlandschen bodem gebruikt, alles doen wat in haar vermogen is om gevaren voor het Nederlandsche volk te vermijden.

The leaflet in which His Majesty's Government apologised to the people of the Bezuidenhout district for the RAF's tragic accidental bombing of a residential area on the 3rd of March 1945. (Bruce Hooper)

Translation: *In reply to the request of why The Hague was bombarded on the 3rd of March, the British Government has sent the following explanation, which was already sent via the BBC and Radio Orange.*
On the morning of the 3rd of March, the war planes of the Second Tactical Airforce of the R.A.F. attacked the rocket centre in The Hague. The bombs landed quite a distance from the target and because of that a lot of civilians died. There was also much damage to the city.
When they realised afterwards what had happened, an inquiry was held to establish the cause of the catastrophe. The report showed that this disaster happened because of a faulty execution. A painstaking investigation is in progress and disciplinary action will be taken against those who are guilty.
The British nation, and in particular the R.A.F., express their deepest sympathy with the suffering of the people as result of that disaster. The Dutch nation knows only too well what risks a war brings and they realise that it is not always possible to avoid these catastrophes.
However the R.A.F. will do anything in their power to avoid a similar mistake in the future. They will, in their air raids on these inhuman rocket weapons, for which the enemy uses Dutch territory, do everything in their endeavour to avoid further danger for the Dutch population.

On the first Sunday after the 3rd of March every year a memorial service is held in The Hague to commemorate those who lost their lives on that day, in March 1945.

F/Sgt Tapua Heperi, wireless operator in the Clement crew, on return from the daylight raid on Essen, 11th April 1945. LAC Dennis Jones behind. (Air Force Museum of NZ)

LM728 AA-R suffered an undercarriage collapse on landing, returning from Kiel with the Evenden crew, 14 April 1945. (NZ Bomber Command Assn. archives, Williams collection)

*The Trevarthen crew, Mepal, March-April 1945 (L-R): Back - F/Sgt Doug Birnie (wireless operator), Sgt Les Powell (rear gunner), Sgt Dave Dunmore (mid-upper gunner) and F/Sgt Brian Waugh (flight engineer). Front - F/O Buster Bancroft (navigator), F/O Pete Trevarthen (skipper) and F/O Tony Hewitson (bomb aimer).
(NZ Bomber Command Assn. archives, Trevarthen collection)*

*Lancaster PB427/G, AA-U on the way to the target. The "G" signifies that special equipment is installed.
(NZ Bomber Command Assn. archives, Tait collection)*

*75 (NZ) Squadron Lancasters en route to Regensburg, 20 April 1945.
(NZ Bomber Command Assn. archives, Scott collection)*

*Bombing photo of the attack on Regensburg, 20 April 1945, as taken by bomb aimer F/Sgt Stan Heald. Although the ORB records RF129 JN-M, crew members say they were flying NE181, JN-M, "The Captain's Fancy" that day.
(NZ Bomber Command Assn. archives, Ware collection)*

The Anderson crew (L-R): Back - LAC Tom McGibbon (ground crew), F/Sgt Bert Hitch (navigator), F/Sgt Bruce Scott (flight engineer), F/Sgt "Binks" Anderson (skipper), (next three are unknown ground crew). Front - F/Sgt Alan Scott (wireless operator), F/Sgt Wally Perry (bomb aimer), F/Sgt Tom Harvey (mid-upper gunner), F/Sgt Patrick Atkins (rear gunner). (NZ Bomber Command Assn. archives, Scott collection)

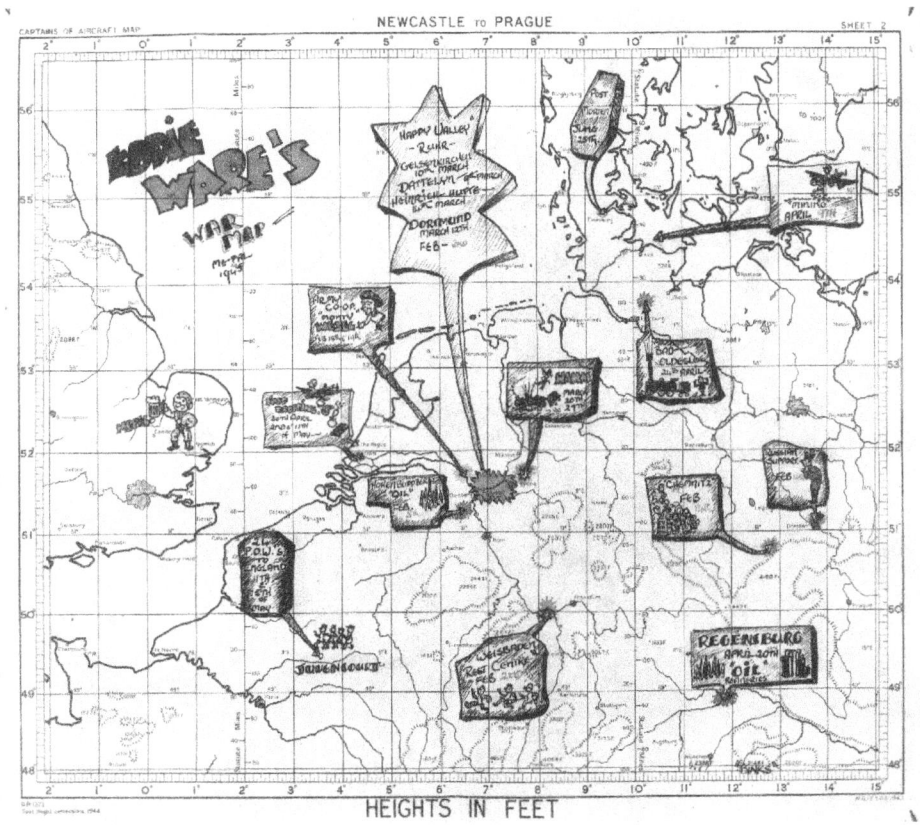

"Eddie Ware's War Map, Mepal, 1945" – the Ware crew's operational tour summarised in a series of cartoons, signed "Binks". (NZ Bomber Command Assn. archives, Heald collection)

Lancaster RF127 AA-W "Willie" on the way to Bad Oldesloe on 24 April 1945, as seen by F/O Ware and crew flying NE181, JN-M. "Willie" was being flown by F/Sgt Bill Mallon and his crew. (NZ Bomber Command Assn. archives, Ware collection)

F/O Ed Ware and his crew with NE181, JN-M, "The Captain's Fancy", "Sortie No. 104, 24 April 1945" (L-R): F/Sgt J White RCAF (mid-upper gunner). F/Sgt Stan Heald (bomb aimer), Sgt R Wright (rear gunner), F/O Ed Ware (pilot), F/Sgt Wilf Cairns (wireless operator), Sgt D Carter (flight engineer), F/O Colin Emslie (navigator). The Ware crew flew NE181 to Bad Oldesloe on the squadron's final bombing operation of the war, which they believed was NE181's 104th op'. (NZ Bomber Command Assn. archives, Emslie collection)

Lancasters approach Delft on the squadron's first Operation Manna supply drop, 29th of April 1945. From the personal collection of W/C "Mac" Baigent who led the nine aircraft sent from Mepal that day.
(NZ Bomber Command Assn. archives, Baigent collection)

F/O Wynn Russell and navigator F/O Neville Selwood with Lancaster PB418 AA-C "Charlie", on the occasion of the aircraft's 100th op', the Operation Manna supply drop to Delft on 7 May 1945.
(NZ Bomber Command Assn. archives, Selwood collection)

Roll of Honour

Sgt	ABBOTT	Clifford	21	29.04.43.
F/O	ADAMSON	David Maurice	27	28.09.43
Sgt	ADDIS	John Henry	26	25.03.42
Sgt	AINSLIE	Tom Dale	21	26.02.41
F/Sgt	AITCHISON	Campbell Ewen Justin	22	12.03.42.
P/O	AITCHISON	Hugh MacLachlan	28	15.09.41
P/O	AITCHISON	Richard Justin	28	01.01.45.
F/O	ALBISTON	Kenneth	24	23.09.43
Sgt	ALCOCK	Frank Kitchener	28	24.08.43
F/Sgt	ALFRED	Joseph McKenzie	23	26.02.45
Sgt	ALLEN	Francis Frederick	23	03.02.43
Sgt	ALLEN	Ronald Gillam	20	29.03.42
F/Sgt	ALLEN	William Morton	23	14.01.44
W/O	AMOS	Alwyn	24	21.03.45.
Sgt	AMSTEL	Raymond Henry	20	07.08.43
W/O	ANDERSEN	Eliner Knud Alfred	23	20.08.42
F/Sgt	ANDERSEN	Kenneth Peder Christian	28	04.11.44
Sgt	ANDERSON	Charles Norman	22	10.09.42.
Sgt	ANDERSON	Lindsay Douglas	20	20.09.40
F/Sgt	ANDERSON	Ronald Alexander John	26	20.07.40
Sgt	ANDERSON	William	20	03.09.42
Sgt	ANDREWS	James Samuel	23	13.05.43
Sgt	ANDREWS	Reginald Frederick	22	16.08.43
Sgt	ANNAN	William Douglas Francis	20	26 07.40
Sgt	ANTHONY	Daniel Thomas	21	11.04.43
S/L	APPLETON	Edward Robert Myddleton	23	31.08.43
Sgt	ARCHER	George Walter Matthew	25	29.06.42
W/OII	ARLEN	Anthony	30	08.03.43.
Sgt	ARMITAGE	Douglas	19	25.06.43
P/O	ARMSTRONG	Cecil Ernest	27	23.05.44
Sgt	ARMSTRONG	Joseph	40	21.07.44
Sgt	ASHDOWN	Michael Henry Charles	20	26.07.43
Sgt	ASHLEY	John Richard	29	12.10.41
Sgt	ASHWIN	Eric Lumley Durham	22	17.12.42
Sgt	ASHWORTH	Alan	21	03.08.43
Sgt	ASKEW	Raymond	21	16.12.43
Sgt	AUSTIN	Francis Edward	27	12.10.41
F/L	BABER	Thomas James Edward	23	12.03.42
W/O	BAGNALL	Trevor Horace	26	17.12.42
F/Sgt	BAILEY	Martin	27	28.08.43
F/Sgt	BAILEY	Robert	20	23.04.44

P/O	BAILIE	Cyril Philip	21	03 08.43
Sgt	BAIN	Andrew	27	24.08.43
F/Sgt	BAITTLE	Horace David	19	29.08.42
Sgt	BAKER	Henry George	19	26.08.44
F/Sgt	BAKER	James Guthrie	27	01.09.43
Sgt	BAKER	Robert Charles	21	25.07.44
F/O	BAKER	Thomas Henry William	26	11 08.42
F/Sgt	BANDY	Frederick Alexander	23	30.05.43
Sgt	BANGS	Archibald Robert	19	27.09.43.
F/Sgt	BARCLAY	Thomas Smith	22	12.08.42
Sgt	BARKER	Richard Charlwood	20	15.10.41
P/O	BARKER	Richard Stockdale	28	26.08.44
Sgt	BARKER	William John	33	06.09.41
Sgt	BARKHOUSE	Donald Frederick	20	15.10.41
W/OII	BARNES	Raymond James	26	16.04.43
F/O	BARR	Derek Singleton	29	21.03.45
Sgt	BARSON	Jack Frank MacDonald	21	21.07.44
F/Sgt	BARTON	Arthur James Douglas	23	05.02.43
F/Sgt	BATESON	Benjamin William	22	25.06.44
F/L	BATTEN	Hector Austin Charles	23	31.05.42
Sgt	BATTY	Ronald John Morton	26	21.07.44
P/O	BAYES	Joseph Thomas	35	04.11.44
Sgt	BEARD	John Lawrence	19	14.03.45
Sgt	BEARDMORE	John Thomas	19	04.11.44
Sgt	BEARNE	Wilfred	22	06.09.41
Sgt	BEAVEN	James Wilfred	31	22.05.42
Sgt	BEECH	Cyril	20	05.03.44
F/O	BELL	John Robson	34	20.11.44
P/O	BELL	Maurice Perrott	26	29.03.42
Sgt	BELL	Ronald	22	24.05.43
Sgt	BENEY	David Levick	19	15.10.41
P/O	BENNETT	Raymond Frederick	29	30.05.43
Sgt	BENNETTON	Frederick Horace	20	05.05.43
F/Sgt	BENTLEY	Loch Lomond	28	23.12.41
P/O	BENTLEY	Robert Henry Waldron	23	05.05.43
Sgt	BERESFORD	John Bosworth	20	28.09.43.
F/Sgt	BERNARD	Arthur George	22	22.11.43
Sgt	BERRY	Eric	20	23.01.43.
P/O	BERTRAM	Robert	26	29.06.42
F/Sgt	BETLEY	Ronald Desmond Ernest	22	16.06.44
Sgt	BEYER	Edwin Harry	25	03.09.42
F/O	BICKHAM	Charles John	24	28.04.43.
F/Sgt	BIGGAR	John Matthew	22	12.09.44

Sgt	BISHOP	Arthur John	22	01.09.43.
Sgt	BISHOP	Sidney Thomas	22	14.03.44
F/Sgt	BISSET	Stuart Richard	20	23.06.43.
Sgt	BLACK	Charles Thomas	30	07.11.41
F/Sgt	BLACK	John William	27	07.11.41
Sgt	BLACKMAN	George Joseph	23	22.11.43
P/O	BLANCE	Ian Edward	21	29.07.44
F/Sgt	BLANK	John Frederick	20	23.06.43
F/L	BLEWETT	Terence Douglas	26	17.01.45.
P/O	BLINCOE	Kenneth Howard	33	03.02.43
Sgt	BLOXHAM	Malcolm Victor	21	23.09.43
P/O	BLUCK	Norman Bradford	22	24.06.43
Sgt	BLUNDELL	John James	19	21.07.44
F/Sgt	BOAG	Robert James	24	30.11.44.
Sgt	BODE	John William	22	22.05.42
Sgt	BOESE	Frank Arthur	22	03.02.43
P/O	BONISCH	Lester Lascelles	21	11.06.44
Sgt	BOOTH	Clifford	23	25.07.44
Sgt	BOOTH	Ronald	21	07.08.43
Sgt	BOSWELL	John McLaren	26	05.05.43
Sgt	BOTTOMLEY	Jack Wilson	24	07.08.41.
Sgt	BOXALL	Charles Henry George	19	28.04.43.
F/Sgt	BOYD	William James Victor	20	12.09.44
P/O	BRADEY	George Edward Francis	25	11.08.42
Sgt	BRAILEY	Clifton Robert	23	21.06.42
Sgt	BRAMWELL	Walter	22	30.05.43.
P/O	BRAUN	Michael Ryves	19	20.09.40
Sgt	BRENNAN	Martin	21	01.01.45
Sgt	BREWER	Cyril	22	30.11.44.
Sgt	BREWSTER	James Edward	21	23.01.43
F/Sgt	BRIAN	William Leslie Fred	23	28.04.43.
F/Sgt	BRIDGER	Cyril Jack	26	28.08.43
P/O	BRIDGMAN	Arthur Mervyn	26	03.03.43.
Sgt	BRISCO	Robert Hylton	26	29.07.42
Sgt	BROADLEY	Ronald	22	26.07.43.
Sgt	BROADY	Raymond Herbert John	28	28.11.42
Sgt	BRODIE	Andrew Moore	25	21.02.41
P/O	BRODIE	Ian James Duncan	27	08.03.43.
F/Sgt	BROMLEY	Alan Stevens	23	23.05.44.
F/O	BROTHWELL	Jack	24	22.11.43.
P/O	BROUN	Alan Stewart	32	09.07.42
F/O	BROWN	Alfred Errol	25	21.03.45
F/Sgt	BROWN	John Lukies	22	12.03.42

Rank	Surname	Given Names	Age	Date
Sgt	BROWN	Norman Wilson	24	26.07.40
F/Sgt	BROWN	Russell Howard	24	22.05.44
Sgt	BRUCE	John Henry	23	17.09.44.
P/O	BRUHNS	Harold Henry	22	24.02.44.
Sgt	BRYER	Dennis George Albert	19	20.11.44.
F/Sgt	BRYSON	Norman Albert	26	26.07.42.
Sgt	BUCKBY	Peter	21	30.11.41
F/Sgt	BUCKLEY	Ross Cameron	29	28.04.43
P/O	BUCKLEY	Wallace Edward	28	21.06.42.
P/O	BUDGE	William Finlay	24	06.04.42.
F/Sgt	BURBIDGE	Kenneth Alfred	22	23.06.43
Sgt	BURBRIDGE	Eric James	21	16.12.42.
P/O	BURKE	Edgar Lawrence	26	23.05.44
F/Sgt	BURRILL	Frank	20	10.09.42
Sgt	BURTON	Clarence Sydney	22	03.03.43.
F/O	BURTT	Henry John	31	21.07.44.
F/Sgt	BUTLER	Laurie Licence	22	24.02.44.
Sgt	BUTLER	Patrick Frederick	21	23.04.44.
Sgt	BUTT	Raymond George	20	12.10.41
Sgt	BUZZA	Reginald Ernest	24	21.07.44.
F/Sgt	BYRNE	Martin John	32	29.07.42.
F/Sgt	CAIRNS	Louvain Trevor	25	26.07.42
Sgt	CAITCHEON	Gordon Edwin	28	29.07.42
Sgt	CALLAN	John Patrick	22	30.08.44.
F/O	CALLOW	Horace	27	21.07.44
P/O	CAMERON	Edward Colin Joseph	19	20.07.40
Sgt	CAMERON	Gibson	23	23.06.43.
Sgt	CAMERON	Leslie Charles	23	17.04.43.
F/Sgt	CAMPBELL	Alan	22	29.07.42
Sgt	CANT	Leslie Ronald	20	24.06.43
Sgt	CARDOO	Alexander Rodger	20	30.05.43
F/Sgt	CAREY	John Henry Roy	27	30.05.43.
Sgt	CARLING	Rodney Patrick	22	24.07.41.
P/O	CARNCROSS	Murray Ellis	19	29.07.42.
Sgt	CARTER	Tony Kevin	20	12.03.42.
Sgt	CARTER	Walter Frederick	21	21.07.44.
Sgt	CAUSLEY	Herbert William	22	30.08.44.
F/Sgt	CHALMERS	Henry Edward	22	03.03.45.
F/Sgt	CHAMBERLAIN	Lloyd Montgomery	28	12.03.42.
S/L	CHAMBERLAIN	Paul Burton	25	12.10.41
P/O	CHAMPION	William James	25	04.11.43.
Sgt	CHANDLER	James John	19	30.05.43.
F/Sgt	CHARLTON	Ronald	22	04.11.43.

Rank	Surname	Names	Age	Date
Sgt	CHESSON	Frederick John Charles	21	28.09.43.
F/O	CHILMAN	Peter Ernest	25	28.04.44
F/Sgt	CHRISTIE	Arthur Stafford	21	21.06.42.
Sgt	CHURCH	David	29	28.04.43.
F/O	CLARE	Frederick William	25	28.05.44
P/O	CLARK	Mervyn Oliver	20	17.12.42.
Sgt	CLARK	Roy Stanley	22	22.04.45.
Sgt	CLARK	Victor James	20	01.01.45
Sgt	CLARK	William Graham	29	09.06.42.
Sgt	CLARKE	Albert	24	28.08.43.
Sgt	CLARKSON	Henry Paul	22	14.07.41.
P/O	CLEAK	Frederick Bernard	30	24.10.40.
Sgt	CLEARWATER	Desmond	24	03.02.43.
Sgt	CLEGHORN	Alan Hall	32	23.09.43.
W/OII	CLEVELAND	Archie	24	26.07.43.
Sgt	CLEZY	William	21	12.03.42.
F/Sgt	CLIMO	Frederick Walter Percival	22	29.07.44.
Sgt	CLINCH	Kenneth	23	28.05.44.
F/Sgt	CLOUGH	David	21	12.05.44.
F/O	CLUBB	Selwyn James	20	13.05.43.
Sgt	COATES	Dudley Dobson	33	26.05.43
F/Sgt	COBB	Cyril Thomas	30	21.04.43.
F/O	COLEMAN	William Harcourt	23	26.07.40.
Sgt	COLES	Thomas Edward	28	07.09.42.
S/L	COLLETT	Wilfred Ira	28	04.08.40.
F/L	COLLINS	John Noel	23	21.05.40
Sgt	CONIBEAR	David Henry	32	17.07.41.
Sgt	COLYER	Gordon William	19	25.06.43.
F/Sgt	CONNER	Josiah Robert	22	31.05.42.
Sgt	CONNETT	Ernest Lewis	21	25.06.44.
Sgt	COOK	Ernest Desmond	19	15.04.43.
Sgt	COOK	George Wood	24	03.02.43
F/Sgt	COOK	Peter Jackson	21	16.06.44
F/Sgt	COOK	Stephen Astley	21	28.05.44.
Sgt	COOKE	John Peter	22	05.10.44.
Sgt	COOKE	Leonard James	19	01.01.45
F/Sgt	COOKSEY	James Brett	23	24.06.43.
F/Sgt	COOMBRIDGE	Trevor Walter	21	27.12.44.
Sgt	COOPER	Edward Roy	20	28.12.44.
Sgt	COOPER	James Henry	33	23.05.44.
Sgt	COPELAND	Arthur Alfred	23	04.11.43.
Sgt	COPPERSMITH	Raymond Patrick	21	26.07.42.
Sgt	COPSEY	Leonard George	20	01.12.43.

Rank	Surname	Given Names	Age	Date
Sgt	CORIN	Henry George	34	28.04.43.
F/Sgt	CORLETT	Geoffrey Scott	20	03.08.43.
F/Sgt	CORNELL	Bryant Thomas	22	18.01.45.
Sgt	CORNISH	Vernon Charles	20	21.07.44.
Sgt	CORRIS	Douglas	21	21.07.44.
F/Sgt	COSTELLO	Michael	32	16.08.43.
Sgt	COULTER	Barry Herbert	19	09.06.42.
F/Sgt	COUPER	James Arthur	31	03.08.43.
Sgt	COUSINS	Frank William	22	11.06.44
F/Sgt	COWIE	James Lindis	22	22.11.43.
F/Sgt	CRABTREE	John Calverley	35	21.11.44.
Sgt	CRAIG	Robert Gerald	20	22.09.41.
Sgt	CRAIG	Robert Samuel Carson	26	24.07.41
Sgt	CRAN	Franklyn Bertram	21	29.03.42.
Sgt	CRARER	Thomas Eric	21	29.07.42.
Sgt	CRAWFORD	Henry Varley Gibb	28	07.09.42.
F/Sgt	CRAWFORD-WATSON	Lewis Stanley	21	04.11.43.
Sgt	CRISP	Basil George	22	16.08.43.
Sgt	CROSS	Thomas Richard	35	29.03.42.
Sgt	CROWTHER	Frederick Edward William	20	03.10.43.
Sgt	CROXON	Kenneth Eric	31	24.08.44.
Sgt	CULLEN	Herbert Sidney George	22	12.03.42.
Sgt	CULSHAW	John Richard	21	28.08.43.
Sgt	CUMMING	Gordon Murry	27	20.07.40.
P/O	CUMPSTY	Frederick William Raukawa	25	31.07.43.
Sgt	CUNNINGHAM	George	30	25.07.44.
Sgt	CUNNINGHAM	Leonard Roy	23	11.04.43.
Sgt	CURLEWIS	Raymond Fullerton	25	11.10.41.
Sgt	CURTIS	Stanley Arthur	28	09.04.43.
F/O	DALE	James Atkinson	27	25.08.44.
P/O	DALZELL	Errol Thomas Paterson	22	28.08.42.
F/O	DANCE	Alfred Thomas	25	04.11.43.
F/Sgt	DARNEY	Jack Neville	22	31.07.43.
Sgt	DARTNALL	John Victor	19	30.05.43.
F/Sgt	DARTON	Thomas William	22	26.05.43.
Sgt	DAVEY	Charles Raglan	21	08.03.43.
F/Sgt	DAVIDSON	Alexander	19	24.08.43.
P/O	DAVIDSON	Neil Douglas	21	21.07.44.
Sgt	DAVIES	George Chamberlain	31	31.07.43.
Sgt	DAVIES	Ronald	23	06.09.41.
Sgt	DAVIES	Raymond David	21	14.03.44.
Sgt	DAVIES	Roy Joseph	21	23.05.44.
W/O	DAVIES	William John	25	21.07.44.

Sgt	DAVIS	Jim Jack	26	16.04.43.
F/Sgt	DAVIS	Ronald Fraser	22	29.07.42.
F/Sgt	DAVIS	Sydney Bernard Thomas	20	29.08.42.
Sgt	DAWSON	Harold Clyde	21	26.07.43.
Sgt	DAY	Michael Irvine Ryder	19	19.11.43.
Sgt	DAY	Maurice Ronald	20	13.10.41.
P/O	DEBENHAM	Kevin Frederick	26	16.04.43.
P/O	DE LABOUCHERE-SPARLING	Francis Albert Gabrial Ferdinand Joseph	20	21.05.40.
Sgt	DENNIS	Harry	31	05.02.43.
Sgt	DENYER	Ernest Claude	34	26.07.43.
P/O	DEVLIN	Kevin John	26	11.09.42.
Sgt	DEW	Norman Hylton	29	11.06.44.
Sgt	DEWHURST	Harold	23	12.05.44.
Sgt	DIBBEN	Ronald Oswald	22	28.11.42.
Sgt	DIMOCK	Vallance Albert Oliver	22	25.10.42.
F/L	DIVE-ROBINSON	Leonard Charles	23	31.07.43.
F/Sgt	DOBBIN	Laurence St.George	29	12.08.42.
F/Sgt	DOBSON	Peter Gerald	28	08.09.43.
F/Sgt	DONAGHY	Thomas Rodgers	33	11.06.44.
F/O	DOWDING	Michael McLoughlin	20	27.12.44.
Sgt	DOWDS	John	19	26.07.40
F/O	DOWNING	John Wallace	33	23.05.44.
F/Sgt	DROMGOOLE	Sydney Houston	28	22.04.42.
W/O	DUDDING	Keat	25	25.07.44.
Sgt	DUKE	John Lawrence	19	28.02.45.
Sgt	DUNDAS	Richard	23	08.11.41.
P/O	DUNKERLEY	Allan Roy Frank	33	21.11.44.
Sgt	DUNLOP	Derek Frederick	29	12.09.41.
Sgt	DUNN	Leslie Joseph	19	12.03.42.
Sgt	DUNN	William Joseph	23	21.07.44.
Sgt	DYER	Sydney Allan	19	16.07.41
Sgt	EARLE	Frederick Joseph	22	21.04.43.
P/O	EARLE	John	29	12.03.42.
F/Sgt	EAST	Patton Mason	29	24.10.43.
S/O	EASTON	Joan Marjorie	26	08.09.43.
F/Sgt	EBBAGE	Francis Henry	21	14.03.45.
Sgt	EDWARDS	Allan Clifford	19	11.10.41.
F/O	EDWARDS	John Lloyd	29	15.06.43.
Sgt	ELLINS	Charles Percival	22	23.09.43.
F/O	ELLIOT	Thomas Isaac	24	21.11.44.
Sgt	ELLIOTT	Richard Booth	19	10.01.41.
F/Sgt	ELLIOTT	Thomas Edison	20	08.11.41.
F/Sgt	ELLIS	Arden Ivan	28	11.08.42.

Rank	Surname	Given Names	Age	Date
Sgt	ELLIS	Ronald	33	29.07.42.
F/Sgt	ELLIS	William Henry	31	21.04.43.
P/O	ELVIN	William	21	12.08.44.
Sgt	ELWELL	Bertram	26	15.04.43.
Sgt	EMERY	Ronald Harry	24	06.04.42.
F/Sgt	EMMERSON	Ronald Harry	24	16.12.43.
P/O	ERIKSON	Mervyn Arthur	26	24.08.43.
Sgt	EVENS	Ronald Charles George	22	31.07.43.
Sgt	EVERDEN	Leslie Leonard	23	17.04.43.
Sgt	EYRE	Kenneth Cedric	21	03.03.43.
P/O	FALCONER	Arthur James	23	21.02.41.
F/Sgt	FALKINER	Philip	21	30.07.44.
F/Sgt	FARNWORTH	John	23	26.08.44.
F/L	FAUVEL	Spencer Francis	21	28.05.44.
F/Sgt	FAWCETT	Arnold Goodrick	31	04.11.43.
Sgt	FAWCETT	Derek Richard	21	15.09.41.
WO	FEAR	Trevor	21	24.08.43.
Sgt	FEENAN	Andrew James	24	08.03.43.
F/Sgt	FELLOWS	John	23	17.12.42.
F/Sgt	FERGUSSON	Allister Archibald	22	22.05.44.
P/O	FINLAYSON	William John	23	24.10.40.
Sgt	FIRTH	Ellison George	19	13.10.42.
W/O	FIRTH	Raymond	28	26.08.44.
F/Sgt	FISK	Joseph George Arkless	28	01.09.43.
F/Sgt	FITZGERALD	John	23	30.08.44.
P/O	FITZGERALD	Maurice Isidore Joseph	20	28.05.44
F/O	FLEMING	James Allan	27	25.08.44.
F/Sgt	FLETCHER	Andrew Crawford	24	21.07.44.
Sgt	FORBES	John	21	06.10.42.
F/Sgt	FORMAN	John	21	06.10.42.
Sgt	FORRESTER	James Leonard	19	20.11.44.
P/O	FOSTER	Ralph Owen	29	08.11.41.
Sgt	FOTHERINGHAM	Robert Ewen Ernest	29	16.07.41.
Sgt	FOULKES	John Gifford	20	15.09.41.
P/O	FOUNTAIN	Cedric Niel	23	23.04.42.
Sgt	FOWLER	Peter Douglas	19	23.01.43.
Sgt	FOX	Ernest	20	14.07.41.
Sgt	FRAMPTON	Laurie Albert	20	29.07.42.
Sgt	FRANCIS	Alan John	19	17.05.43.
Sgt	FRANKLIN	Benjamin Allan	21	16.12.42.
F/O	FRASER	Allan Armistice	23	21.06.42.
F/Sgt	FRASER	Myles Frederick Gordon	22	16.05.42.
Sgt	FREEMAN	Carl Robert	33	20.11.44.

Rank	Surname	Names	Age	Date
Sgt	FREEMAN	Frank Morris	33	24.08.43.
Sgt	FREEMAN	Patrick Paul Deane	22	05.02.43.
P/O	GAGE	Donald Irwin	24	12.05.44.
Sgt	GALE	John William	23	31.07.43.
F/O	GALE	Norman Hathway	30	08.09.43.
P/O	GALLETLY	Alan Russell	33	05.10.44.
Sgt	GANNAWAY	Eric Francis	21	12.05.41.
Sgt	GARDE	Fred	21	11.10.41.
Sgt	GARFORTH	Eric	21	25.08.44.
Sgt	GARVIN	William Henry	20	25.07.43.
Sgt	GASKINS	Leonard Charles	21	04.11.43.
P/O	GAVEGAN	Jack Ralph	30	09.07.42.
Sgt	GERMING	John William	22	28.04.44.
Sgt	GIBBS	Jack	19	24.10.40.
Sgt	GIBSON	John Cuthbert McKechnie	29	07.11.41.
F/Sgt	GILBERTSON	John Edward	22	29.07.42.
P/O	GILES	John Cecil	19	31.08.43.
F/Sgt	GILES	John Patrick Arthur	21	12.09.44.
Sgt	GILFILLAN	William	20	19.11.43.
Sgt	GILL	John Trevor Vivian	27	04.09.42
W/O	GILLAN	Gottfred Lyall	21	21.07.44.
Sgt	GILLARD	John William	24	24.06.43.
Sgt	GILLIATT	Edward George	22	16.06.44.
Sgt	GILMORE	Daniel	25	19.03.41.
W/O	GILMOUR	Hugh Edward	24	21.07.44.
F/Sgt	GITTINS	Thomas Henry	24	07.08.43.
Sgt	GLENDINNING	John Thomas	31	29.04.43.
Sgt	GODDARD	Arthur Ernest John	22	21.07.44.
Sgt	GODFREY	Joseph Henry	29	12.03.42.
Sgt	GOFF	Stuart John	20	17.12.42.
Sgr	GOING	Raymond Cyril	21	03.03.43.
Sgt	GOLDIE	Harry Edward	21	03.09.42.
Sgt	GOLDSACK	Henry Edward	28	13.10.42.
F/O	GORDEN	Ronald	22	20.11.44.
F/Sgt	GORMAN	Ralph Ernest	24	10.09.42.
Sgt	GOULD	James Douglas	21	11.07.42.
F/Sgt	GOWER	Kenneth Wilfred	28	28.05.44.
Sgt	GRAHAM	Andrew	21	28.04.43.
Sgt	GRAINGER	Eric	21	23.06.43.
P/O	GRAINGER	James Kennedy	21	15.04.43.
Sgt	GRANGE	Terence	22	01.09.43.
Sgt	GRANT	Donald Cameron Kitchener	29	23.05.44.
Sgt	GRANT	Horace Llewellyn	27	04.09.42.

Rank	Surname	Name	Age	Date
Sgt	GRATTON	John James	22	24.08.43.
Sgt	GRAY	Trevor Hedley	27	07.11.41.
Sgt	GREEN	Alfred Joseph	31	20.09.40.
F/Sgt	GREEN	Cyril Vincent	21	11.08.42.
F/Sgt	GREEN	Leslie Cyril	21	07.11.41.
Sgt	GREEN	Reginald Thomas Charles	27	15.04.43.
P/O	GREENING	Joseph Wesley	27	03.07.41.
Sgt	GRENFELL	Richard John	22	29.06.42.
Sgt	GRIFFITHS	Basil	22	16.06.44.
Sgt	GRIMES	Harold Dawson	26	15.10.41.
Sgt	GRIMWOOD	Leslie	20	04.11.43.
Sgt	GROVE	Richard Frederick	22	31.08.43.
F/Sgt	GROVES	Alpheus Leslie	30	07.09.42.
P/O	GROVES	Kelvin Havelock Green	30	17.04.43.
P/O	GUDGEON	John Bernard	23	12.09.44.
S/L	GUNN	Garth Reginald	26	21.09.44.
Sgt	GUPPY	Frederick Richard	26	10.09.42.
F/Sgt	HADFIELD	Graham Stanley	23	14.03.44.
F/O	HADLEY	William Orchard	30	12.09.44.
Sgt	HAINSWORTH	Edwin	28	06.04.42.
F/Sgt	HALE	Lawrence Eastmure	26	16.06.44.
Sgt	HALL	John	20	07.05.41.
Sgt	HALL	Robert Ewen	35	24.02.44.
Sgt	HALL	Thomas John	19	08.08.44.
Sgt	HALLIBURTON	Keith	23	28.04.43.
P/O	HAMER	Douglas Vincent	24	28.04.43.
F/Sgt	HANCOCK	Stanley Albert	23	22.05.44.
P/O	HARDING-SMITH	Dudley	24	13.02.43.
Sgt	HARE	Philip Edgar	19	16.07.41.
P/O	HARKNESS	Charles	28	29.07.42.
Sgt	HARKNESS	William	21	05.05.43.
Sgt	HARRIS	Claude Joseph	31	29.03.42.
Sgt	HARRIS	Richard James	24	23.04.42.
F/Sgt	HARRISON	Alfred Herbert	25	08.11.41.
Sgt	HARRISON	William Frederick	21	23.04.44.
F/Sgt	HARRISON-SMITH	Francis Charles	20	30.11.41.
Sgt	HARROLD	Ronald Kenneth	22	26.07.43.
Sgt	HARRY	James William	20	24.02.44.
Sgt	HART	Robert	28	17.12.42.
Sgt	HARTSTONE	Roydon Horatio	29	03.07.41.
Sgt	HARVEY	Edgar William	27	16.12.42.
Sgt	HARVEY	Robert Frederick	23	13.05.43.
Sgt	HASELDEN	Howard Clive McLeish	22	18.09.41.

Rank	Surname	Name	Age	Date
Sgt	HASLAM	George Frederick	35	27.12.44.
F/Sgt	HAUB	Darcy Leslie Conrad	23	31.08.43.
Sgt	HAWKINS	Anthony Henry Ryder	20	15.09.41.
Sgt	HAWKINS	Frederick John	22	12.06.43.
Sgt	HAYCOCK	Richard Edward	28	03.07.41.
Sgt	HAYLER	Edwin John	19	08.08.44.
Sgt	HAYTON	Cyril	22	22.05.42.
Sgt	HAYWARD	Desmond David	20	03.02.43.
F/O	HAZARD	Whelan Fallon	20	12.08.44.
Sgt	HEGAN	John Gordon George	23	30.06.42.
Sgt	HEGARTY	Terence James	22	23.09.43.
Sgt	HELLIER	Harry Thomas	22	21.02.41.
P/O	HELM	George Vincent	23	01.09.43.
Sgt	HEMMINGS	Cyril Benjamin	21	23.06.43.
F/O	HENDERSON	Hugh William	24	05.03.44.
F/Sgt	HENDERSON	Matthew Ronald	25	28.04.44.
P/O	HENLEY	Douglas Charles	23	01.09.43.
W/OII	HENRY	Ernest Frank	26	30.07.43.
F/O	HERON	Allan Gleave	22	02.05.44.
F/O	HERRON	Robert Weir	23	28.04.44.
F/Sgt	HEWETT	Harold Max	21	12.05.44.
F/Sgt	HICKFORD	Leonard Charles	21	21.07.44.
Sgt	HIGGINS	Eric Vincent Keiran	27	16.07.41.
F/Sgt	HIGHAM	Frank Douglas	24	28.08.43.
Sgt	HILDITCH	William Webster	23	25.06.43.
Sgt	HILL	Charles Burton	26	30.08.44.
F/Sgt	HILTZ	Lawrence Donald	20	29.08.42.
Sgt	HINTON	James William	24	29.03.42.
Sgt	HIRST	Raymond John Finlay	22	11.07.42.
F/Sgt	HISCOX	Henry John	35	21.07.44.
Sgt	HITCHMOUGH	William Grice	19	24.08.40.
Sgt	HOBBS	Frederick Johns	19	23.06.43.
F/Sgt	HODGES	Ronald George Renauf	22	12.08.42.
Sgt	HOEY	Joseph Edwards	32	23.09.43.
Sgt	HOGAN	Denis Patrick	23	28.08.42.
Sgt	HOLBROOK	Ivor George	23	22.11.43.
Sgt	HOLLEY	Douglas Cecil	19	12.10.41.
F/O	HOLLOWAY	Edgar John	29	21.03.45.
Sgt	HOLME	Harry Pears	35	28.04.43.
Sgt	HOLMES	Joseph Andre Cletus	21	24.08.43.
F/Sgt	HOLT	Derek Arthur	20	01.12.43.
Sgt	HOND	Reginald Samuel	23	05.10.44.
Sgt	HONE	Sidney George	35	20.11.44.

Rank	Surname	Given Names	Age	Date
Sgt	HOOPER	Frederick George	21	30.05.43.
W/O	HOPE	Lawrence Beresford Hamilton	29	19.04.45.
F/Sgt	HOPKINS	Talfryn Barton	22	12.09.41.
Sgt	HORNER	Arthur William	24	14.03.44.
Sgt	HORRIGAN	William Hadley	29	31.08.43.
F/Sgt	HORSFORD	Ray Steele	28	25.07.44
F/Sgt	HOSKINS	John Stanley	23	01.01.45.
F/Sgt	HOWARD	Edward John Francis	24	04.11.44.
Sgt	HOWE	Ronald	28	16.06.44.
Sgt	HOWELL	Alexander Clunie	22	28.04.43.
P/O	HOWELL	Edward	21	21.07.44.
Cpl	HOWES	Kenneth John	27	28.02.42.
Sgt	HOWES	Victor Charles	20	28.04.43.
Sgt	HOWES	Walter John	29	06.10.42.
F/O	HOWLETT	Arthur Douglas	32	23.09.43.
Sgt	HOWLETT	Arthur Edgar	26	08.03.43.
F/Sgt	HOWSON	Ronald Edward	21	28.05.44.
Sgt	HUDSON	Eric Francis	21	04.10.43.
Sgt	HUGHES	Victor Stanley	19	22.11.43.
Sgt	HUGHILL	Howard James	21	25.10.42.
Sgt	HUNTER	Patrick Torre	29	28.04.43.
Sgt	HUNTING	Eric Francis	22	03.08.43.
F/Sgt	HUNTING	Eric Raymond	21	03.09.42.
F/Sgt	HURDLE	Walter	28	04.11.43.
F/Sgt	HUTT	George Alister	25	29.07.42.
F/Sgt	IMRIE	George Burns	22	04.11.43
F/O	INGHAM	John Paul	21	23.09.43.
Sgt	INGLIS	James Robertson	23	11.04.43.
Sgt	INGLIS	William Gordon Lloyd	27	12.08.42.
Sgt	INNES	Owen Alfred	22	30.05.43.
F/Sgt	IRVINE	Walter Harrison	25	29.08.42.
F/O	IRVING	Arnold Earle	23	12.05.44.
Sgt	ISHERWOOD	Joseph	31	03.08.43.
F/Sgt	JACKSON	Kensington Campbell	23	31.08.43.
F/0	JACOBSON	Gerald Howard	27	17.12.42.
W/O	JAMBOR	Oldrich	29	31.05.42.
F/Sgt	JAMES	Charles James	34	04.11.43.
Sgt	JARVIS	Claude Joseph Frederick	22	07.09.42.
F/Sgt	JARVIS	William Louis	25	23.09.43.
P/O	JELLEY	Edward Arthur	33	30.09.40.
F/O	JENKIN	Ralph Francis	23	16.12.43.
W/O	JENKINS	Ernest Roy	25	29.04.43.
F/Sgt	JENKINS	Frederick Francis Arthur	30	29.07.44.

Sgt	JENNINGS	Harold	19	28.08.43.
Sgt	JOBLIN	Frederick John Leigh	25	24.05.43.
Sgt	JOBSON	George Trueman	20	28.11.42.
F/Sgt	JOHNS	Arthur Grahame	20	29.07.42.
P/O	JOHNSON	David Malcolm	21	31.05.42.
F/O	JOHNSON	James	26	21.10.44.
P/O	JOHNSON	James Edward	21	06.09.41.
F/Sgt	JOHNSTON	Haig Douglas	27	12.08.44.
F/O	JOHNSTON	John	28	13.05.43.
Sgt	JOHNSTON	Peter Simpson Dickson	28	06.09.41.
F/Sgt	JONES	Arthur Stanley	28	05.03.44
Sgt	JONES	Daniel Vernon	20	11.04.43.
Sgt	JONES	Gordon Baden	19	26.08.44.
Sgt	JONES	Harold	21	03.07.41.
Sgt	JONES	Henry Edward	19	09.06.42.
F/O	JONES	Roy King	26	21.07.44.
Sgt	JOYCE	David Campbell	21	16.07.41.
Sgt	JUDD	Douglas Howard	26	10.09.42.
Sgt	JURY	Jack Leslie	20	12.08.42.
Sgt	KAHLER	Hyman Chaim Mordecai	21	19.04.44.
W/O	KAVANAGH	Stanley Leo	24	30.05.43.
F/Sgt	KAY	Alan Lister	35	22.05.44.
Sgt	KELCHER	Walter Foch	23	11.09.42.
P/O	KELL	William Robert	23	19.11.43.
Sgt	KELLY	Reginald Joseph Stephen	24	22.04.42.
Sgt	KENDAL	Christopher James	21	17.12.42.
Sgt	KENDLAN	Michael	23	24.06.43.
Sgt	KENNEDY	Raymond Anthony	28	23.06.43.
W/O	KERR	George John Stewart	22	01.12.43.
W/O	KIDBY	Dennis Alfred	22	30.07.44.
F/Sgt	KILBY	William Adam	40	01.09.43.
S/L	KIMBER	Ronald Ernest	31	11.08.42.
P/O	KINROSS	Colin John	30	16.12.43.
F/O	KIRKPATRICK	Laurence John	20	23.09.43.
S/L	KITCHIN	Peter James Robert	24	12.03.42.
Sgt	KITCHING	Stephen Tom	22	07.08.43.
F/Sgt	KNAPTON	Ronald	22	21.07.44.
Sgt	KNIGHT	Leon Gaston	22	09.06.42.
Sgt	KRALJEVICH	Mark	25	29.07.42.
Sgt	LACKENBY	Andrew	32	06.07.43.
Sgt	LACKENBY	Thomas	19	04.10.43.
Sgt	LAMB	Erwin Henry Reubin	29	05.05.43.
P/O	LAMMAS	Manson	30	23.04.44.

Sgt	LANG	Raymond Stanley	32	21.07.44
Sgt	LARKIN	Cyril Walter	23	30.05.43.
Sgt	LARSON	Ivar	33	23.04.44.
S/L	LAUD	Ronald Hugh	27	12.06.43
F/Sgt	LAVERS	William Wilfred Henry	23	10.09.42.
Sgt	LAW	James	21	04.09.42
Sgt	LAWRENCE	William Joseph	22	16.12.42.
Sgt	LEA	Jack Vernon	22	11.06.44.
P/O	LEACOCK	John Trelawney	24	14.07.41.
F/Sgt	LEE	Arthur	25	01.01.45.
Sgt	LEE	Reginald George Arthur	20	29.08.42.
Sgt	LEES	Eric	21	10.09.42.
P/O	LEES	Reginald Sidney	26	27.07.42
Sgt	LEFT	Edward	35	27.12.44
Sgt	LEGGE	Robert Colin	22	05.02.43.
Sgt	LEIGHTON	Bernard	34	25.07.44.
Sgt	LENNOX	George Len	25	28.04.43.
P/O	LENS	Aubrey	22	24.08.43.
Sgt	LETHERBARROW	Edward John	21	11.04.43.
Sgt	LEVACK	Sidney Joseph Lawrence	23	22.10.41.
Sgt	LEVY	George Arthur	39	21.07.44.
Sgt	LEWINGTON	Leslie Owen	28	06.07.43.
F/Sgt	LEWIS	Alfred Edward	25	28.04.43.
Sgt	LINDSAY	George	21	21.11.44.
P/O	LLOYD	Eric	28	07.11.41.
Sgt	LOCK	Alexander John	22	11.09.42
Sgt	LOCKEY	George	21	23.06.43.
F/O	LODGE	Tom	35	04.11.43.
F/O	LOGAN	Clifford Charles Pownall	28	23.09.43.
P/O	LOMBARD	Michael Ferdinand	29	02.05.44.
Sgt	LONGSTAFF	Charles Albert	31	14.03.45.
F/O	LOVELOCK	James Benjamin	26	01.09.43.
Sgt	LOVEWELL	Jack Edmond	21	16.08.43.
F/O	LOWE	Harold	23	03.02.43.
F/O	LOWE	William	22	25.07.44
F/Sgt	LOWTHER	Peter Desmond	22	11.07.42.
Sgt	LOWTHER	Richard William	21	11.04.43.
Sgt	LUCAS	Charles	21	17.12.42.
Sgt	LUCAS	George William Thomas	22	01.12.43.
F/O	LUKEY	Francis Henry Clark	23	28.05.44.
F/Sgt	LUNDON	Francis Patrick	25	24.08.43.
Sgt	McADAM	Robert Douglas	21	21.07.44.
P/O	McALPINE	Walter Duncan	30	17.12.42.

Rank	Surname	Given Names	Age	Date
F/Sgt	McARTER	Glenville	29	03.09.42.
F/O	McCARTIN	Patrick Leo	28	20.11.44.
P/O	McCASKILL	Donald Gordon	19	15.04.43.
Sgt	McCONNELL	James Allison	21	25.10.42.
Sgt	McCOO	Oliver	31	01.09.43.
Sgt	McCORMICK	Joseph Edward	25	20.09.40
Sgt	McCREADY	Daniel	25	30.11.41.
F/L	McCRORIE	Thomas Fraser	27	23.06.43.
P/O	McCULLOUGH	John	30	03.02.43.
F/Sgt	McDERMOTT	Edward	19	03.02.43.
Sgt	McDONALD	Murray Alexander	23	12.03.42.
Sgt	MacDONALD	Norman	24	20.09.40.
F/Sgt	McDONOGH	Athol Ian	27	20.08.42.
F/Sgt	McEWIN	Andrew James	25	23.06.43.
F/O	McGEORGE	John Ronald	22	21.07.44.
Sgt	McGIBBON	Robert	26	12.03.42.
Sgt	MacGILLIVARY	John David Robert	24	29.08.42.
Sgt	McGLOIN	Thomas	23	22.11.43.
F/Sgt	McGREGOR	Keith Alexander	21	01.09.43.
Sgt	McGREGOR	Murdoch Gordon	23	30.06.42.
Sgt	McGREGOR	Roderick	20	28.08.42.
F/O	McINTOSH	James Alexander	26	30.11.44.
Sgt	McINTYRE	Francis Cassidy	25	25.06.44.
Sgt	McISAAC	Alexander	24	28.11.42.
P/O	MacKAY	Andrew Donald	22	22.05.42.
F/Sgt	McKAY	Daniel Archibald	31	29.08.42.
P/O	MacKAY	Kenneth McIndoe	27	21.07.44.
F/Sgt	MACKENZIE	Douglas John	27	02.05.44.
Sgt	McKENZIE	Frank Edwin	22	09.07.42.
P/O	McKENZIE	Francis Max	26	23.06.43.
F/Sgt	McKENZIE	James Murdoch Thomas	27	11.06.44.
F/O	MACKENZIE	Stanley Henry	23	22.11.43.
Sgt	MacKINNON	Douglas Malcolm	20	16.07.41.
F/O	McLACHLAN	Euen Wilfred	22	28.04.44.
F/Sgt	McLEAN	John McKenzie	22	31.05.42.
F/Sgt	MacLEOD	Norman Alexander	26	30.05.43.
Sgt	McLINDEN	John Frederick	24	22.04.42.
Sgt	McLOUGHLIN	John Bernard	29	06.07.43.
Sgt	McMAHON	Henry Thomas Owen	27	22.04.42.
Sgt	McMANUS	George William	35	26.02.45.
Sgt	McMORRINE	Alexander Watson	22	03.12.42.
Sgt	McMURCHY	James Gordon	31	29.07.42.
P/O	McNAMARA	Brian Patrick	26	10.01.41.

Rank	Surname	Given Names	Age	Date
Sgt	MacPHAIL	Allan Corson Anderson	30	30.05.43.
F/Sgt	McPHERSON	Colin Valentine	21	26.07.42.
Sgt	McQUADE	Hugh Steel	21	12.06.43.
Sgt	McQUATER	Alick	21	26.05.43.
F/Sgt	McRAE	Christopher Frederick (Bud)	26	23.09.43.
F/O	McRAE	James Kenneth	27	25.07.44.
Sgt	McVETY	Maurice Wyndham Stuart	20	12.09.41.
Sgt	McVICAR	Angus	20	15.04.43.
Sgt	McWILLIAM	Allan	20	30.05.43.
Sgt	McWILLIAM	Robert James	20	28.11.42.
F/Sgt	MAHOOD	Thomas Stanley	25	22.04.42.
Sgt	MAPPIN	Sir Charles Thomas Hewitt	32	08.11.41.
Sgt	MARFIL	Lorenzo	23	21.10.44.
F/Sgt	MARGETTS	John Edward Stanley	25	22.11.43.
Sgt	MARLOW	John Leslie	22	16.04.43.
F/O	MARSH	Henry Herbert	23	11.06.44.
F/Sgt	MARSHALL	Eric William Elliott	31	23.05.44.
F/Sgt	MARTIN	Donald Ernest	26	23.06.43.
F/O	MARTIN	Leonard Arthur	31	20.11.44.
F/L	MARTYN	Leslie Arthur	35	21.11.44.
P/O	MARVIN	Douglas William James	21	28.05.44.
Sgt	MASON	Frederick David	21	16.08.43.
F/Sgt	MASON	James Rooker	27	28.05.44.
Sgt	MASSEY	William	33	08.11.41.
Sgt	MASSIE	Charles John	23	04.10.43.
P/O	MASTERS	William Stuart	21	04.11.43.
Sgt	MATETICH	John Anthony	28	15.10.41.
F/Sgt	MAYO	John Russell	21	07.08.43.
Sgt	MEAGHER	Brian Dominic	20	30.11.41.
Sgt	MEE	Alexander Coutts	23	07.05.41.
Sgt	MELLON	William Neill Kennedy	27	07.08.41.
Sgt	MELLOR	Albert Leslie	30	08.09.43.
F/Sgt	MELVILLE	Robert James Ian	26	05.03.44.
F/O	MENZIES	Ian Robert	21	08.09.43.
Sgt	MEPHAM	Denis Norman	23	27.12.44.
Sgt	METCALFE	Thomas Otto	19	11.09.42.
Sgt	MIDDLETON	Harvey Johnson	24	04.10.43.
F/O	MILES	Haddon Shaw	27	27.12.44.
P/O	MILES	John	35	20.11.44.
F/Sgt	MILLER	James Stuart	33	11.06.44.
P/O	MILLINER	Jack Thomas	22	25.07.44.
P/O	MILLS	George William Alfred	27	07.09.42.
F/Sgt	MILLS	Samuel	32	21.07.44.

Rank	Surname	Name	Age	Date
Sgt	MILLWARD	Eddie	20	03.08.43.
F/Sgt	MILNE	Bruce	21	25.06.44.
Sgt	MINCHIN	Robert Michael	22	06.09.41.
F/O	MITCHELL	George Eric	40	06.04.42.
Sgt	MITCHELL	Gilbert Frank	36	23.01.43.
Sgt	MITCHELL	Harry Douglas	21	11.06.44.
Sgt	MITCHELL	Norman	25	29.06.42.
W/C	MITCHELL	Victor	27	17.12.42.
Sgt	MOCOCK	Reginald Crosby	20	17.12.42.
F/Sgt	MOFFATT	Bertram Augustus	25	09.04.43.
Sgt	MONCRIEF	Eric Francis Sydney	25	30.06.42.
P/O	MONK	Walter Jack	24	30.06.42.
Sgt	MOON	Derrick Leonard Desmond	21	30.08.44.
Sgt	MOORE	Bernard Arthur Riley	25	12.05.43.
Sgt	MOORE	Cyril James	25	06.07.43.
Sgt	MORE	Robert McLeod	19	22.11.43
Sgt	MORGAN	Maurice Frederick	23	25.06.44.
F/Sgt	MORGAN	Robert Carhampton	26	30.11.44.
Sgt	MORRIS	John Lewis	21	09.06.42.
Sgt	MORRISON	William Donald	24	21.02.41.
Sgt	MORTON	William Wilson	23	17.12.42.
F/Sgt	MOSLEY	Stuart Edwin	29	05.10.44.
P/O	MOSS	Douglas Hamilton	23	24.08.43
Sgt	MOULD	Charles Cyril	29	25.06.43.
Sgt	MOULTON	Frederick Arthur	23	28.04.43.
P/O	MUIR	Anthony Vincent	29	21.02.41.
P/O	MULCAHY	Cyril Desmond	21	12.08.44.
Sgt	MULHOLLAND	Henry Stephen	20	12.06.43.
Sgt	MULLIGAN	John	20	19.04.44.
Sgt	MUNN	Hugh	22	28.09.43.
Sgt	MUNRO	Charles	20	24.08.43.
P/O	MURDOCH	Graham Edward	26	09.06.42.
W/O	MURDOCH	Thomas Talbot	22	21.10.44.
Sgt	MURPHY	Terence Austin	30	03.02.43.
Sgt	MURPHY	Timothy Rowley	20	11.10.41.
F/O	MURRAY	Henry James	26	19.04.44.
F/L	MYERS	John William Anthony	25	19.07.44.
Sgt	MYHILL	William Raymond	21	24.10.43.
P/O	NAIRNE	Colin George	22	30.07.44.
Sgt	NASH	Clifford George	21	26.08.44.
Sgt	NATION	John Ross	22	03.07.41.
Sgt	NEVILL	William Eric	23	26.07.40.
Sgt	NEWMAN	Richard Alfred William	24	04.09.42.

F/Sgt	NEWMAN	Robert Wynne	29	30.11.44.
Sgt	NEWNHAM	Alfred	24	14.03.44.
W/C	NEWTON	Raymond John	28	01.01.45.
Sgt	NICHOL	John	28	14.03.45.
Sgt	NICHOLL	Bruce Henry	26	21.03.45.
Sgt	NICHOLS	John Owen Henry	20	16.05.42.
Sgt	NICHOLSON	Jack Ernest	22	24.08.43.
W/O	NICOL	Henry	23	25.07.43.
P/O	NICOL	Trafford McRae	21	23.04.42.
Sgt	NOLA	David Leo	26	07.05.41.
F/Sgt	NORMAN	Raymond Fraser	23	30.05.43.
Sgt	NORRINGTON	Harold Sidney	23	25.07.43.
F/Sgt	NORTON	William George	28	26.08.44.
Sgt	NUNN	Geoffrey Sidney	20	08.11.41.
F/Sgt	OAKEY	Arthur Leslie Archibald	33	21.03.45.
Sgt	OATEN	Percy	24	29.08.42.
Sgt	O'DOWD	Albert William	25	09.06.42.
Sgt	O'FARRELL	John Herbert	19	31.07.43.
Sgt	OGDEN	George	19	24.08.43.
Sgt	OLIVE	John	23	10.01.41
W/O	O'LOUGHLIN	Vincent John	26	21.10.44.
Sgt	ORR	Albert Cyril	21	13.10.42
F/L	OSBORN	Andrew Francis Atterbury	25	28.08.42.
F/Sgt	OSBORNE	John Edward	23	21.07.44.
Sgt	O'SHEA	William Clerken	28	29.07.42.
Sgt	OWEN	John Lewis	24	20.07.40
Sgt	OWEN	William	19	24.07.41
F/Sgt	OWENS	William Alfred	21	30.05.43.
Sgt	PADDEN	Gerald Thomas	20	17.12.42.
P/O	PAGE	Clifford Frederick	22	07.05.41.
W/O	PAGE	Frank Albert	29	23.05.44.
F/O	PAGETT	William George Simpson	27	22.11.43.
Sgt	PAINTER	Eric Henry James	26	30.11.41.
Sgt	PARISH	Cecil Reginald	22	24.08.43.
F/Sgt	PARKER	Albert Charles William	22	17.12.42.
Sgt	PARKER	Robert Ronald Smithie	20	12.08.44.
F/Sgt	PARKES	William Ronald	31	07.09.42.
Sgt	PARKIN	Richard	22	11.06.44.
F/Sgt	PARKIN	Victor Trevor	21	31.08.43.
Sgt	PARKINSON	Lewis Harry	20	13.10.42.
Sgt	PARNHAM	John Frederick Massey	21	12.03.42.
Sgt	PARSONS	Algernon	22	11.10.42.
F/L	PARSONS	Eric George	23	14.03.45.

P/O	PARTON	William James	20	12.03.42.
Sgt	PASCOE	Tom	21	16.12.42.
Sgt	PATTEN	Frederick Hubert	22	25.07.44.
F/Sgt	PAYNE	Douglas Beardsley	22	23.05.44.
Sgt	PEARSON	Peter Braithwaite	22	16.04.43.
W/O	PEARSON	Reginald William	27	17.12.42.
F/Sgt	PEEVERS	Thomas Alexander	29	02.05.44.
F/O	PENMAN	Alexander Mitchell	23	21.10.44.
F/Sgt	PENNYCOOK	Charles	20	04.10.43.
F/Sgt	PEPPER	James	23	23.05.44.
Sgt	PERCIVAL	Walter Reginald	22	28.04.44.
F/Sgt	PERKS	Eric	29	29.08.42.
F/O	PERROTT	William Rosser	21	25.06.43.
P/O	PERRY	Lyndon Clifford	21	30.07.44.
Sgt	PETE	Edmund John	20	25.10.42.
Sgt	PETTIFER	John Gilbert	38	02.05.44.
Sgt	PHILLIPS	Cyril George	29	05.02.43.
Sgt	PHILLIPS	George	28	29.04.43.
F/Sgt	PHINN	William	22	14.03.45
Sgt	PICKERING	Walter	22	23.05.44.
Sgt	PIERSON	Rodney Leslie	28	17.04.43.
F/Sgt	PIRIE	James Allan	22	30.05.43.
F/L	PLUMMER	Jack	29	21.03.45
P/O	POOLE	Frank Twain	24	26.07.40.
Sgt	POOLE	Jack	22	24.08.43.
Sgt	POSNER	Sydney	22	11.10.42.
P/O	POTTS	Donald Norman	25	09.07.42
F/Sgt	POTTS	Thomas Christopher	27	25.07.44.
Sgt	POW	Leslie	33	04.10.43
W/O	PRESTON	Robert Edward	22	10.04.45.
Sgt	PRICE	Frederick Joseph Edward	24	14.07.41.
F.Sgt	PRICE	Henry John	25	12.03.42
Sgt	PULLAR	Henry Welsh	25	17.12.42.
Sgt	PURDIE	Thomas	27	03.08.43.
F/Sgt	PURVES	James John	35	25.10.43.
Sgt	QUIN	Joseph Guy	25	29.06.42.
Sgt	QUINN	Arthur	21	25.10.42.
F/Sgt	QUINN	Eric James	20	21.07.44.
Sgt	RADFORD	Charles Edward	20	25.07.43.
F/O	RAINFORD	Robert Gorman	28	31.08.43.
F/Sgt	RAMSAY	Eric	20	14.03.45.
W/OI	RAMSAY	James Alexander	26	29.03.43.
Sgt	RAMSAY	William Robertson	25	09.06.42.

Sgt	RANDLE	Douglas Haig	24	30.06.42.
F/Sgt	RANDLE	James Robert	21	24.10.43.
P/O	RANKIN	Andrew	21	24.08.43.
Sgt	READER	Edgar Henry	21	23.06.43.
Sgt	REAVELEY	William Thomas	39	11.06.44.
Sgt	REDDICLIFFE	Francis Henry	28	09.04.43.
Sgt	REDDING	Randolph Ernest	30	05.02.43.
Sgt	REDHEAD	John Brewick	25	19.10.42.
Sgt	REDPATH	Stephen	19	26.05.43.
F/Sgt	REDWOOD	Gerard Henry	34	21.07.44.
F/Sgt	REEVES	Sydney Cecil Oliver	21	03.08.43.
Sgt	REID	Alexander	25	21.10.44.
Sgt	REID	Ian Laurie	23	03.07.41.
Sgt	REID	James Henry	21	08.11.41
Sgt	REID	Jeffrey Walter	23	29.12.41.
P/O	REID	William Ferguson	21	22.05.44.
Sgt	RENFREW	Robert	24	28.08.43.
Sgt	RENTON	Rupert Ernest	22	04.09.42.
Sgt	RHODES	George William	20	06.10.42.
F/Sgt	RICHARDS	James Leonard	25	23.06.43.
F/O	RIDDLE	Charles Hudson	21	30.05.43.
Sgt	RIDDLER	Stanley Winston	22	03.10.43.
Sgt	RIDER	Arthur Henry	31	17.12.42
Sgt	RILEY	Francis Christopher	21	12.05.44.
Sgt	RIMMER	Donald	20	22.05.44.
Sgt	RIORDAN	John Milton Patrick	32	26.05.43.
Sgt	RITCHIE	Alfred Henry	22	22.12.40.
Sgt	RITCHIE	Matthew Roy	19	10.01.41.
F/Sgt	ROBERTS	Eric John	25	31.08.43.
Sgt	ROBERTS	James	20	22.10.41.
Sgt	ROBERTS	Joseph Harold Campbell	24	16.07.41.
P/O	ROBERTSON	Norman Bruce	25	27.07.42.
P.O	ROBERTSON	Trevor Bernard	26	15.10.41.
P/O	ROBINSON	Joseph Allan	23	12.10.41.
F/Sgt	ROBITAILLE	Arthur Hector	19	20.08.42.
F/Sgt	ROCHE	Gerald Brian	21	21.07.44.
Sgt	ROE	Keith Vernon Dudley	19	12.09.41.
Sgt	ROFF	Leonard Arthur	28	17.12.42.
Sgt	ROFFEY	Douglas Archibald Thomas	19	25.07.44.
Sgt	ROGERS	Brian Arthur	22	27.04.43.
Sgt	ROGERS	Charles Thomas	20	30.11.42.
Sgt	ROGERS	Gilbert Humphreys	27	05.05.43.
Sgt	ROSE	George Herbert	30	07.09.42

Rank	Surname	Name	Age	Date
Sgt	ROSS	Desmond Ray	23	28.04.43
F/Sgt	ROSS	Stanley David	25	26.07.42.
F/Sgt	ROTHSTEIN	Irvine Sydney	20	07.08.43.
F/Sgt	ROUSSEAU	Henry Edwin	23	17.12.42.
P/O	ROWBERRY	Geoffrey Warren	24	14.03.44
Sgt	RUDDY	Brian Hartley	21	24.08.43.
Sgt	RUGG	Raymond James	21	15.11.41
Sgt	RUOCCO	Domenico	20	30.05.43.
Sgt	RUSSELL	John Herbert	21	12.06.43.
Sgt	RUSSELL	Walter	23	07.05.41.
P/O	RYAN	Alexander James	25	10.01.41
P/O	RYDER	Robert Leslie Owen	25	08.11.41.
S/L	SACHTLER	Euan Wilfred	24	02.05.44.
Sgt	SAFFILL	Frederick Henry	29	26.02.45.
F/O	ST.LEDGER	Peter Sylvester Anthony	21	30.07.43.
F/Sgt	ST.LOUIS	Michael Bertram	27	10.09.42.
F/Sgt	SALT	Ian Charles	20	21.04.43
F/Sgt	SAMSON	George King	27	23.06.43.
P/O	SAMPSON	Louis David	28	20.11.44.
P/O	SANDERSON	Rex Martyn	24	24.10.40
F/O	SANDS	Hugh Powell	26	23.09.43.
F/O	SANDYS	John Frederick Kelly	25	12.03.42.
Sgt	SANSOME	Harry	21	01.01.45.
Sgt	SAUL	Nothan Priestley	30	07.09.42
Sgt	SAUNDERS	Anthony Francis	20	31.08.43.
Sgt	SAUNDERS	Eric	20	31.08.43.
Sgt	SAVAGE	John Henry	33	29.07.42.
P/O	SAVAGE	Kenneth Edward Algar	20	18.09.41.
Sgt	SAVAGE	Willis Arthur	20	16.12.43.
W/C	SAWREY-COOKSON	Reginald	27	06.04.42.
F/Sgt	SAWTELL	Arthur Hartley	19	24.02.44.
Sgt	SCARFE	Leslie Thomas	21	28.04.43.
Sgt	SCHOFIELD	James William	33	23.01.43.
Sgt	SCOTT	Alexander	20	03.12.42.
F/Sgt	SCOTT	Alistair Henry	27	04.11.44.
P/O	SCOTT	Andrew James Newell	21	03.02.43.
Sgt	SCOTT	Francis Alexander Jack	28	28.05.44.
F/O	SCOTT	John Harold	29	04.11.44.
Sgt	SCOTT	Roy Harold	20	11.10.42.
F/O	SCOTT	Russell James	23	21.03.45.
Sgt	SCUDDER	John William	22	09.04.43.
P/O	SEDUNARY	Alan Joseph Lyall	20	24.08.43.
Sgt	SERVICE	Arthur	22	15.10.41.

Rank	Surname	Names	Age	Date
Sgt	SHALFOON	Charles John	22	11.10.42.
Sgt	SHARMAN	George William	27	07.09.42.
Sgt	SHARP	Richard Edwin	23	11.07.42.
Sgt	SHAW	Kenneth Fazackerley	22	23.06.43.
Sgt	SHAW	Stanley Alfred George	21	16.05.42.
Sgt	SHELNUTT	Barney Walker	23	26.10.41.
P/O	SHEPHERD	Ian James	26	27.07.42.
Sgt	SHERGOLD	Tom Graham	21	17.04.43.
Sgt	SHOGREN	Malcolm Edward John	29	28.04.43.
W/O	SHONE	George Ernest	29	29.07.42.
Sgt	SIDHU	Devinder Singh	24	28.04.43.
Sgt	SILCOCK	Trevor	20	31.08.43.
Sgt	SIMNETT	Brian	22	14.03.44.
Sgt	SIMONSEN	Horace Dean	31	17.04.41.
F/Sgt	SIMPSON	Alfred Alexander	28	21.07.44.
F/Sgt	SINGLE	Alan Roy	26	22.11.43.
Sgt	SIZMUR	Douglas Victor	19	30.11.41.
Sgt	SLATER	Colin Harry	20	25.06.44.
Sgt	SLATER	Edwin	20	25.08.44.
Sgt	SLATER	Geoffrey	22	06.10.42.
Sgt	SLEIGHTHOLM	David	22	23.05.44.
Sgt	SLIMAN	Allan Melrose	39	14.04.45.
Sgt	SLOMAN	Horace George	21	15.09.41.
Sgt	SLOMAN	Robert Gerald	24	21.07.44.
P/O	SMART	Randolph Cruickshank	25	10.09.42.
Sgt	SMEATON	Wilfred Herbert	28	23.05.42.
F/Sgt	SMITH	Albert Ivan	27	16.05.42.
Sgt	SMITH	Charles Arthur	36	08.04.41.
F/Sgt	SMITH	Ian Hector Ross	34	01.09.43.
Sgt	SMITH	James	21	21.10.44.
W/O	SMITH	Keith Alfred	23	28.04.44.
F/Sgt	SMITH	Keith Emmett	21	21.07.44.
F/Sgt	SMITH	Phillip Francis	20	20.11.44.
Sgt	SMITH	Ronald	20	01.12.43.
Sgt	SMITH	Ronald Alexander	21	15.04.43.
Sgt	SMITH	Raymond Charles	22	30.07.44.
P/O	SMITH	Rupert John	26	09.06.42.
Sgt	SMITH	Selwyn Clarence	29	25.10.42.
P/O	SMITH	Trevor Harry	24	09.07.42.
Sgt	SMYTH	William Bennett Megarry	23	18.09.41.
Sgt	SNEDDON	James Wilson	31	03.08.43.
S/L	SOLBE	Edward Urlic Guerin	30	21.02.41.
F/O	SOUTHWARD	Keith	28	06.10.44.

Rank	Surname	Given Names	Age	Date
F/Sgt	SOWERBY	Geoffrey Phillips	22	23.09.43.
Sgt	SPARK	Frederick Alexander	26	22.09.41.
W/O	SPENCER	Ronald Howard	21	29.07.44.
P/O	SPITTAL	Phillip Charles	26	26.07.42.
Sgt	SQUIRE	Harry	31	26.06.43.
Sgt	STANNARD	Alfred Richard	22	30.07.44.
Sgt	STARKEY	Charles Ronald	20	21.11.44.
Sgt	STARTIN	Geoffrey Leonard	20	25.06.44.
Sgt	STEAD	George	21	20.08.42.
Sgt	STEELE	William Reid	21	22.10.41.
Sgt	STEPHENSON	John Leonard	18	21.07.44.
F/L	STEVENS	Joseph	32	21.07.44.
Sgt	STEVENS	Piers Trevor	23	02.05.44.
Sgt	STEWART	Alan Raymond Bryce	23	25.08.44.
F/Sgt	STEWART	Dryden	22	21.03.45.
F/Sgt	STEWART	Donald MacKay	29	01.09.43.
Sgt	STEWART	Francis Barkhouse	23	03.03.43.
Sgt	STEWART	Ian Gordon	20	29.07.42.
Sgt	STEWART	Leslie Ian	25	29.07.42.
Sgt	STEWART	Thomas	21	23.09.43.
Sgt	STOBBS	William Edward	21	06.07.43.
Sgt	STOCK	Donald Percival	20	06.04.42.
F/Sgt	STOCKER	Clifford Isaac	30	21.03.45.
F/L	STOKES	Noel Alfred Deal	25	29.07.44.
Sgt	STOKES	Wallace Frederick	27	17.12.42.
Sgt	STONE	Leighton Mansel	20	08.03.43.
Sgt	STONE	Ronald Charles	26	17.04.43.
F/Sgt	STONE	Robert James	20	31.07.43
Sgt	STOREY	Derrick George Amos	19	24.05.43.
Sgt	STRATTON	Raymond Walter John	23	04.11.43.
Sgt	STREETER	Donald Frederick	24	24.07.41.
F/Sgt	STRONG	Geoffrey Walter	31	24.06.43.
Sgt	STUART	Phillip Gordon	30	09.04.43.
F/Sgt	STUART	Richard Charles	23	20.08.42.
P/O	STUCKEY	William	29	23.06.43.
Sgt	SUMMERS	Woolf Jack	22	24.02.44.
F/Sgt	SUTHERLAND	Alexander George	23	29.07.42.
Sgt	SUTTON	Arthur Kitchener	29	05.10.44.
Sgt	TABOR	Adrian Oscar	25	29.07.42.
Sgt	TARRANT	Alfred Bertram	20	08.03.43.
Sgt	TASKER	Robert Holtby	27	22.10.41.
F/Sgt	TAVERNER	George Alfred Badge	21	25.07.44.
Sgt	TAYLER	Douglas Arthur Allen	21	06.07.43.

Rank	Surname	Given Names	Age	Date
Sgt	TAYLOR	Cyril	21	22.10.41.
Sgt	TAYLOR	Richard Thomas	21	30.11.44.
Sgt	THAIN	George McAra	20	08.11.41
P/O	THIRD	James	34	24.08.43.
P/O	THOMAS	Alfred John	25	31.07.43.
Sgt	THOMAS	Edwin Henry	35	23.04.44.
Sgt	THOMAS	Howard Mansel	26	04.11.44.
F/Sgt	THOMAS	Raymond	22	06.07.43.
Sgt	THOMAS	Reginald James	21	04.11.43.
Sgt	THOMPSON	Colin Maurice	23	11.10.41.
P/O	THOMPSON	Desmond Lewis	21	29.04.43.
Sgt	THOMPSON	Jack Dennis	21	07.11.41.
Sgt	THOMPSON	William Howard	21	03.08.43.
F/Sgt	THOMSON	Edward Leonard	20	12.08.44.
F/Sgt	THOMSON	Gordon Douglas	22	25.06.43.
F/Sgt	THOMSON	Jack	26	03.08.43.
Sgt	THOMSON	John Smith	22	23.09.43.
F/Sgt	THORNLEY	Sydney Russell	25	30.05.43.
Sgt	THORPE	Ernest	20	04.10.43.
F/O	THORPE	Noel Humphrey	21	26.02.45.
F/Sgt	THORSTENSEN	Frederick William	26	24.08.43.
Sgt	THREADGOLD	Ronald Walter	21	26.07.43.
Sgt	TIETJENS	Stephen Muir	26	24.05.43.
Sgt	TITCOMB	William Arthur	21	29.07.42.
W/OII	TOD	Richard Douglas	23	23.06.43
W/OII	TOD	Robert Ernest	23	23.06.43
Sgt	TOLLER	Robert William	20	15.09.41.
P/O	TOLLEY	Alan Gray	21	21.04.43.
Sgt	TOMLINSON	Kenneth Aubyn	21	12.09.41.
F/O	TOMPKINS	Phillip Edwin	21	21.07.44.
Sgt	TOMPSETT	Stanley Charles	27	15.06.41.
F/O	TONG	Harold	34	30.05.43
Sgt	TONKIN	Douglas Noel	22	25.10.42.
W/OII	TOOHEY	Edward Wallace	22	16.06.44.
Sgt	TOOTHILL	Kenneth Hutley	29	15.09.41.
Sgt	TORRANCE	Bernard	19	23.01.43.
Sgt	TOWN	Gerald Albert Raymond	20	21.04.43.
P/O	TRENGROVE	Raymond Wickliffe John	20	21.06.42.
Sgt	TREVAYNE	Paul Rodney	19	03.02.43.
Sgt	TUNBRIDGE	Victor Arthur	28	28.08.42.
Sgt	TURNBULL	George Watson	24	24.05.43.
F/O	TURNBULL	John George	33	16.08.43.
Sgt	TURNER	Albert Edward	20	07.08.43.

Rank	Surname	Given Names	Age	Date
F/L	TURNER	Geoffrey	30	23.12.43.
F/Sgt	TURNER	John Cecil	21	22.11.43.
Sgt	TURNER	Reginald James	28	24.07.41.
F/O	TURNER	William	22	03.08.43.
Sgt	TUTHILL	Peter Eric	21	05.10.44.
Sgt	TWEEDIE	Norman	25	12.09.41.
F/Sgt	UPTON	Frank Wakefield	28	21.04.43.
F/Sgt	VAUGHAN	Douglas William	28	23.04.44.
F/Sgt	VERCOE	Terrance James	27	31.07.43.
F/O	VERNAZONI	Richard Barry	20	30.05.43.
Sgt	VICCARS	Eric Clifford	22	14.07.43.
F/Sgt	VICKERS	Charles Henry	22	29.08.42.
F/Sgt	VINCENT	Frank Arthur	21	25.08.44.
Sgt	WADESON	Thomas Edward	21	03.08.43.
P/O	WAEREA	Tame Hawaikirangi	29	28.09.43.
Sgt	WAITE	Aubrey Reginald	20	12.06.43.
Sgt	WALKER	George Albert	21	03.08.43.
Sgt	WALKER	Graham Stuart	25	24.07.41.
W/O	WALSH	John Arthur Ernest	27	09.04.43.
Sgt	WALSHE	Desmond James	25	11.09.42.
Sgt	WANSTALL	Richard Fleury	29	17.04.43.
Sgt	WARBURTON	Carl Arthur	11	23.05.44.
Sgt	WARBURTON	Robert Lee	21	11.10.41.
Sgt	WARD	James Allen	22	15.09.41.
Sgt	WARLOW	William John	30	20.11.44.
Sgt	WARNER	John Albert	19	16.12.43.
F/L	WARREN	Derek	20	12.05.44.
Sgt	WARRING	Robert John	21	12.08.42.
Sgt	WATERMAN	Jeffery James	21	06.09.43.
Sgt	WATKINS	Stanley	26	19.11.43.
F/O	WATSON	Clifford Arnold	34	01.09.43.
S/L	WATSON	Raymond Johnson	27	05.03.44.
F/O	WATSON	Samuel Miles Mackenzie	27	20.07.44.
F/Sgt	WATSON	Walter Davis	30	30.08.44.
F/Sgt	WATTERS	Terrence	21	31.08.43.
Sgt	WATTERS	Ventry	22	13.10.42.
Sgt	WATTS	David Michael Turner	26	16.04.43.
W/OII	WAY	James Oscar	26	17.04.43.
Sgt	WAYMAN	Stanley John	21	24.05.43.
Sgt	WEAVER	Emrys Herbert	20	03.03.43.
Sgt	WEBB	John	23	11.04.43.
Sgt	WEBB	Stanley Lawrence	33	23.06.43.
Sgt	WELCH	Harold Rangi	23	16.12.42.

Rank	Surname	Name	Age	Date
Sgt	WELLS	Roy Albert	21	05.10.44.
F/Sgt	WELSH	Neville Henry	20	15.10.41.
P/O	WEST	Robert William	22	21.03.45.
F/Sgt	WESTERMAN	Victor Kenneth	24	29.07.42.
F/Sgt	WESTON	Albert John	29	20.11.44.
P/O	WESTON	Robert	34	09.06.42.
P/O	WESTWOOD	Reginald Francis	20	05.05.43.
Sgt	WHATLEY	Timothy	22	06.09.43.
F/Sgt	WHATMOUGH	Thomas	30	12.06.43.
Sgt	WHITCOMBE	William Henry	32	16.12.42.
Sgt	WHITE	Lewis Alan	20	20.09.40
Sgt	WHITE	Reginald William Bryant	20	24.10.40.
Sgt	WHITE	William George Henry	27	17.12.42.
Sgt	WHITEHART	John Herbert	23	28.04.43.
F/O	WHITEHOUSE	Keith Owen	23	25.07.44.
F/Sgt	WHITELAW	Clifford James	22	25.06.43.
Sgt	WHITEMAN	John Charles Lawrence	21	26.05.43.
Sgt	WHITING	Norman Edward	27	16.05.42.
P/O	WHITMORE	Richard Charles	22	28.09.43.
F/Sgt	WHITTA	Neville Bruce	20	16.08.43.
F/Sgt	WHITTINGTON	Eric Raymond	22	22.11.43.
P/O	WHITTINGTON	Harold	26	21.07.44
F/Sgt	WILCOCKSON	Walter Frederick	34	23.06.43.
Sgt	WILDING	Norman Vaughan	19	29.07.44.
Sgt	WILKES	Eric Arthur	22	24.02.44.
P/O	WILKINSON	Ernest Stanley	25	06.09.43.
F/Sgt	WILKINSON	George Stanley	27	06.09.43.
F/Sgt	WILKINSON	Richard John	21	21.07.44.
Sgt	WILKS	Ronald	21	23.09.43.
F/Sgt	WILLIAMS	John Muir	23	29.04.43
P/O	WILLIAMS	Roy Arthur	21	13.02.43.
Sgt	WILLIAMS	William Iorwerth	23	11.06.44.
F/Sgt	WILLIS	Frederick Arthur William	26	03.03.43.
P/O	WILLIS	William Jarvis	33	22.05.44.
Sgt	WILLSHER	Frederick Phillip	25	26.05.43.
Sgt	WILMSHURST	John Charles	25	11.07.42.
F/Sgt	WILSON	Eric Glover	27	07.09.42.
F/O	WILSON	John Stanley	34	17.01.45.
Sgt	WILSON	John Stephen	27	08.11.41.
F/O	WILSON	Norman Clarence Bruce	23	04.11.43.
F/L	WILSON	Peter John	22	29.07.42.
F/Sgt	WILSON	Wesley William	20	05.02.43.
Sgt	WINSTANLEY	James Francis	20	27.07.42.

Rank	Surname	Name	Age	Date
Sgt	WOLFENDEN	Harold	32	11.10.42.
F/Sgt	WOOD	Benjamin Brinley	24	23.06.43.
Sgt	WOOD	Frederick Lionel Roy	23	15.10.41.
F/Sgt	WOOD	James Haswell	29	21.03.45.
Sgt	WOODCOCK	Roy Joffre Desmond	26	12.03.42.
Sgt	WOODFORD	Stanley Alfred George	29	30.07.44.
Sgt	WOODHAM	Henry William	27	28.02.42.
F/Sgt	WOODS	Ralph Morley	29	05.03.44.
Sgt	WOOLCOTT	Douglas George	23	24.08.43.
Sgt	WOOLAM	Peter	19	19.04.44.
Sgt	WORLLEDGE	Frederick Harry	22	15.10.41.
Sgt	WORT	Donald Frank	20	01.12.43.
F/Sgt	WORTH	Jim	24	21.07.44.
Sgt	WORTHINGTON	Jack Herbert	19	09.04.43.
P/O	WRIGHT	Andrew Roy	21	21.11.44.
F/Sgt	WRIGHT	John Herbert	26	12.08.44.
Sgt	WRIGHT	Leslie Charles	22	17.05.43.
Sgt	WRIGHTSON	Cyril Charles	22	22.04.42.
Sgt	WYKES	Joseph	22	13.05.43.
Sgt	WYLLIE	Thomas Young	25	08.11.41.
Sgt	YOUNG	George Anthony	21	09.07.42.
Sgt	YOUNG	Peter Anthony	28	10.09.42.

With grateful thanks to Kevin King and John Tyler for their work in compiling this Roll of Honour, and for allowing it to be included in this book.

75(NZ) Squadron.

MOTTO **Ake ake kia kaha.**   Codes **AA JN**
    (For ever and ever be strong).

Stations
As New Zealand Squadron

MARHAM	01.06.39. to 28.09.39.
HARWELL	28.09.39. to 15.01.40.
STRADISHALL	15.01.40. to 16.02.40.
FELTWELL	16.02.40. to 04.04.40.

As 75(NZ) Squadron

FELTWELL	04.04.40. to 15.08.42.
MILDENHALL	15.08.42. to 01.11.42.
OAKINGTON (Detachment)	15.10.42. to 06.12.42.
NEWMARKET	01.11.42. to 28.06.43.
MEPAL	28.06.43. to 21.07.45.

Commanding Officers

WING COMMANDER M W BUCKLEY	04.04.40. to 24.11.40.
WING COMMANDER C E KAY	24.11.40. to 27.08.41.
WING COMMANDER R SAWREY-COOKSON	01.09.41. to 06.04.42.
WING COMMANDER E G OLSON	06.04.42. to 31.07.42.
WING COMMANDER V MITCHELL	31.07.42. to 18.12.42.
SQUADRON LEADER G E FOWLER (temp)	18.12.42. to 31.01.43.
WING COMMANDER G A LANE	31.01.43. to 03.05.43.
WING COMMANDER M WYATT	03.05.43. to 19.08.43.
WING COMMANDER R D MAX	19.08.43. to 15.05.44.
WING COMMANDER R J A LESLIE	15.05.44. to 11.12.44.
WING COMMANDER R J NEWTON	11.12.44. to 02.01.45.
WING COMMANDER C H BAIGENT	02.01.45. to 10.45.

Flight Commanders
A Flight

S/L Cyril Eyton Kay	04.04.40. to 23.09.40.
S/L Francis George Levett Bain	23.09.40. to 24.01.41.
S/L Edward Ulric Guerin Solbe	28.01.41. to 21.02.41.
S/L John McKenzie Southwell	07.03.41. to 26.05.41.
S/L Frederick John Lucas	26.05.41. to 29.01.42.
S/L Raymond John Newton	30.01.42. to 27.07.42.
S/L Arthur Ashworth	27.07.42. to 28.08.42.

S/L Robert Stanway Crawford	25.09.42. to 09.12.42.
S/L Gilbert Meston Allcock	18.01.43. to 10.05.43.
S/L Ronald Hugh Laud	11.05.43. to 12.06.43.
S/L Jack Joll	12.06.43. to 01.11.43.
S/L Raymond Johnson Watson	04.12.43. to 04.03.44.
S/L Lindsay Johnson Drummond	09.03.44. to 31.05.44.
S/L Richard Bruce Berney	31.05.44. to 16.08.44.
S/L Roy Campbell Earl	16.08.44. to 28.11.44.
S/L John Leonard Wright	28.11.44. to 05.04.45.
S/L Laurence Douglas McKenna	10.04.45. to .

B Flight

S/L Wilfred Ira Collett	21.05.40. to 04.08.40.
S/L Aubrey Arthur Ninnis Breckon	05.08.40. to 08.09.40.
S/L Norman Maxwell Boffee	08.09.40. to 18.12.40.
S/L Garry Carlton Kain	18.12.40. to 22.03.41.
S/L Reuben Pears Widdowson	22.03.41. to 20.09.41.
S/L Paul Burton Chamberlain	20.09.41. to 12.10.41.
S/L Peter James Robert Kitchin	28.10.41. to 12.03.42.
S/L Cecil McKenzie Hill	13.03.42. to 04.05.42.
S/L Frank Henderson Denton	29.04.42. to 20.07.42.
S/L Edgar Bernard Richard Lockwood	22.08.42. to 20.10.42.
S/L George Eric Fowler	02.11.42. to 18.12.42.
F/L Charles Woodbine Parish (Temp)	18.12.42. to 31.01.43.
S/L George Eric Fowler	31.01.43. to 07.05.43.
S/L Edward Robert Myddleton Appleton	07.05.43. to 12.05.43.
S/L Frank Albert Andrews	13.05.43. to 14.11.43.
S/L David Stewart Gibb	15.11.43. to 04.04.44.
S/L Euan Wilfred Sachtler	04.04.44. to 02.05.44.
S/L Garth Reginald Gunn	16.08.44. to 20.09.44.
S/L John Robert Rodgers	20.09.44. to 28.03.45.
S/L Stanley Maurice George Peryer	28.03.45. to.

C Flight

S/L Richard Broadbent	18.04.43. to 19.10.43.
S/L James Kenneth Climie	19.10.43. to 21.06.44.
S/L Neilson Arnold Williamson	21.06.44. to 05.10.44.
S/L John Mathers Bailey	06.10.44. to 09.04.45.
S/L Jack Colin Parker	09.04.45. to

Aircraft

WELLINGTON I	07.39. to 04.40.
WELLINGTON IA	04.40. to 09.40.
WELLINGTON IC	04.40. to 01.42.
WELLINGTON III	01.42. to 10.42.
STIRLING I	10.42. to 08.43.
STIRLING III	02.43. to 04.44.
LANCASTER I/III	03.44. to 10.45.

Operational Record

OPERATIONS	SORTIES	AIRCRAFT LOSSES	% LOSSES
739	8017	193	2.4

CATEGORY OF OPERATIONS

BOMBING	MINING	OTHER
584	149	6

WELLINGTONS

OPERATIONS	SORTIES	AIRCRAFT LOSSES	% LOSSES
320	2540	74	2.9

CATEGORY OF OPERATIONS

BOMBING	MINING	OTHER
291	24	5

STIRLINGS

OPERATIONS	SORTIES	AIRCRAFT LOSSES	% LOSSES
210	1736	72	4.1

CATEGORY OF OPERATIONS

BOMBING	MINING	OTHER
103	107	0

LANCASTER

OPERATIONS	SORTIES	AIRCRAFT LOSSES	% LOSSES
209	3741	47	1.3

CATEGORY OF OPERATIONS

BOMBING	MINING	OTHER
190	18	1

Aircraft Histories

WELLINGTON. **To October 1942.**

L4330	From NZ Flight. To 3 BAT Flight.
L4340	From NZ Flight. To 15 Operational Training Unit.
L4355	From NZ Flight. To 11 Operational Training Unit.
L7784 AA-D	From 37 Squadron. To Central Gunnery School.
L7797 AA-F	To XV Squadron.
L7806	From 37 Squadron. To 149 Squadron.
L7818 AA-R	To 15 Operational Training Unit.
L7847	From 214 Squadron. To 99 Squadron.
L7848 AA-V	To 21 Operational Training Unit.
L7857 AA-C	Abandoned over Cumberland on return from Kiel 17.10.40.
N2747 AA-J	To 214 Squadron.
N2777	To 37 Squadron.
N2854 AA-U	FTR Brest 24.7.41.
N2877	From 115 Squadron. To 15 Operational Training Unit.
N2894	On loan from Central Gunnery School. FTR Cologne 30/31.5.42.
N2895 AA-L	From 9 Squadron. To 15 Operational Training Unit.
N2901	From 115 Squadron. To 15 Operational Training Unit.
N2913	From 99 Squadron. To 15 Operational Training Unit.
N2937	From 37 Squadron. To 218 Squadron.
N2982	From 9 Squadron. To 15 Operational Training Unit.
N2985	From 99 Squadron. To 15 Operational Training Unit.
N3014	From 9 Squadron. To 215 Squadron.
P9205	From NZ Flight. To 9 Squadron.
P9206 AA-A	From NZ Flight. To 20 Operational Training Unit.
P9207 AA-C	From NZ Flight. To 38 Squadron.
P9209 AA-B	From NZ Flight. To 311 Squadron.
P9210 AA-A/Y	From NZ Flight. To Royal Aircraft Establishment.
P9212 AA-F/C	From NZ Flight. To 311 Squadron.
P9280 AA-Z	From 99 Squadron. To 40 Squadron.
P9292 AA-C	From 115 Squadron. FTR Berlin 23/24.10.40.
R1020	From 37 Squadron. Crashed on landing at Feltwell during training 18.11.40.
R1038 AA-H	FTR Kiel 11/12.9.41.
R1095	To 37 Squadron.
R1161 AA-W	To 311 Squadron.
R1162 AA-Y	To 27 Operational Training Unit.
R1163 AA-L	From 15 Squadron. To 103 Squadron.
R1177 AA-F/C/K	Abandoned over Essex on return from Frankfurt 29.9.41.
R1237 AA-G/X	To 21 Operational Training Unit.
R1409 AA-N	From 15 Operational Training Unit. To 1505 BAT Flight.
R1457 AA-P/Y	To 156 Squadron.
R1458 AA-E	Crashed on landing at Ternhill on return from Berlin 18.4.41. To 311 Squadron and back. To 101 Squadron.

R1466 AA-E	From 311 Squadron. To 15 Operational Training Unit.
R1518 AA-X	Abandoned over Norfolk on return from Berlin 21.9.41.
R1589	To 57 Squadron.
R1648 AA-K	FTR Mannheim 6/7.8.41.
R1771 AA-R/T	To 311Squadron.
R1792	To 57 Squadron.
R3156 AA-G	From 115 Squadron. Became ground instruction machine.
R3157 AA-H	From 115 Squadron. FTR Dinant 21/22.5.40.
R3158 AA-J	From 115 Squadron. Crashed on landing at Manston on return from Eindhoven 22.10.40.
R3159 AA-K	From 115 Squadron. Crashed on approach to East Wretham on return from Hanover 2.9.40.
R3160	From 115 Squadron and back.
R3165 AA-L	From 149 Squadron. FTR Horst 20/21.7.40.
R3166 AA-M	To 311 Squadron.
R3167 AA-N	To 99 Squadron.
R3168 AA-O	Force-landed in Devon on return from Leipzig 30.9.40.
R3169 AA-P/O from	To 57 Squadron and back. Crashed in the Humber River on return from Hamburg 6/7.5.41.
R3171 AA-Q/E	From 148 Squadron. FTR Duisburg 15/16.7.41.
R3172	From 214 Squadron. To 11 Operational Training Unit.
R3176	Force-landed in Suffolk on return from Horst 4.8.40.
R3194 AA-S	
R3195	From 37 Squadron. To 57 Squadron.
R3211 AA-J	From 37 Squadron. FTR Hamm 29/30.12.40.
R3212 AA-G	
R3216	To 9 Squadron.
R3218 AA-T	To 311Squadron.
R3224 AA-H	From 37 Squadron. To 22 Operational Training Unit.
R3231	From 37 Squadron. To 57 Squadron.
R3235	FTR Kassel 25/26.7.40.
R3239	From 37 Squadron. Returned to 37 Squadron.
R3275 AA-K	From 37 Squadron. To 57 Squadron.
R3277 AA-Y	From 311 Squadron. To 12 Operational Training Unit.
R3284 AA-O	From 37 Squadron. To 11 Operational Training Unit.
R3297 AA-S	To 57 Squadron.
T2463 AA-T/E	FTR from attack on invasion ports 20/21.9.40.
T2464	To 9 Squadron.
T2468	To 9 Squadron.
T2471	To Sywell.
T2474 AA-W	FTR Mannheim 22/23.12.40.
T2503 AA-P	From 37 Squadron. FTR Wilhelmshaven 21/22.2.41.
T2504	From 37 Squadron. To 57 Squadron.
T2508	From 37 Squadron. Returned to 37 Squadron.
T2525 AA-M	
T2547 AA-D F	From 37 Squadron. Crashed on landing at Feltwell on return from Wilhelmshaven 22.2.41.

T2550 AA-L		Crashed in Cambridgeshire during air-test 10.1.41.
T2575		To 37 Squadron.
T2736 AA-A		Abandoned over Yorkshire on return from Kiel 19.3.41.
T2741 AA-V		To 15 Operational Training Unit.
T2747 AA-D/J		
T2805 AA-E/D		From 115 Squadron. Force-landed in Norfolk on return from Berlin 21.9.41.
T2820 AA-B		Force-landed near Methwold on return from Hamburg 21.10.40.
T2821 AA-A		To 37 Squadron.
T2822		To 37 Squadron.
T2835 AA-C		To 1503 BAT Flight.
T2837		To 37 Squadron.
T2854 AA-U		
T2881		Damaged Cat R, to Weybridge.
W5618 AA-F		From OADF. To 21 Operational Training Unit.
W5621 AA-D/E		FTR Essen 3/4.7.41.
W5663 AA-O		FTR Cologne 15/16.10.41.
W5718		From 149 Squadron. To 99 Squadron.
X3176 AA-E		From 149 Squadron. To 1504 Flight.
X3194 AA-S		SOC 26.3.42.
X3205 AA-L		FTR Hamburg 15/16.9.41.
X3282 AA-F		From A&AEE. FTR Kiel 12/13.3.42.
X3285		From 57 Squadron. Returned to 57 Squadron.
X3339		To 9 Squadron.
X3355 AA-Y		Crashed in Norfolk during air-test 28.2.42.
X3359 AA-H		To 419 (Moose) Squadron RCAF.
X3367		To 9 Squadron.
X3389		From 9 Squadron. FTR Nuremberg 28/29.8.42.
X3390 AA-W/S		From 9 Squadron. To 419 (Moose) Squadron RCAF.
X3396 AA-S		FTR Emden 3/4.9.42.
X3397		From 9 Squadron. To 115 Squadron.
X3402		From 57 Squadron. Returned to 57 Squadron.
X3403 AA-S		To 1418 Flight.
X3408 AA-Q		From 115 Squadron. To 1418 Flight and back. FTR Essen 2/3.6.42.
X3416		From 9 Squadron. To 115 Squadron.
X3420 AA-O		To 419 (Moose) Squadron RCAF.
X3451 AA-G		From 9 Squadron. To 150 Squadron and back via 419 (Moose) Squadron RCAF. To 150 Squadron.
X3452 AA-A		From 9 Squadron. FTR Hamburg 28/29.7.42.
X3459 AA-T		To 150 Squadron.
X3461		To 466 Squadron RAAF.
X3462 AA-D		FTR Lübeck 28/29.3.42.
X3464		To 101 Squadron.
X3468 AA-H		From 115 Squadron. To 23 Operational Training Unit.
X3475 AA-L		To 156 Squadron.
X3476		To A&AEE.
X3477		To 419 (Moose) Squadron RCAF.

X3478		
X3479 AA-B	To 156 Squadron.	
X3480	To 429 (Bison) Squadron RCAF.	
X3482 AA-J	FTR from mining sortie 15/16.5.42.	
X3487 AA-O	Crash-landed at Feltwell on return from Cologne 22/23.4.42.	
X3488	From 115 Squadron. To 419 (Moose) Squadron RCAF.	
X3489 AA-P	FTR Cologne 5/6.4.42.	
X3538 AA-N	Crashed on approach to Mildenhall during training 27.8.42.	
X3539 AA-T	To 115 Squadron and back. FTR Bremen 29/30.6.42.	
X3540 AA-H	To 115 Squadron and back. To 115 Squadron.	
X3541 AA-H/G	To 101 Squadron.	
X3557 AA-X	FTR Wilhelmshaven 8/9.7.42.	
X3558 AA-Z	From 57 Squadron. FTR Hamburg 28/29.7.42.	
X3584	To 115 Squadron and back via 57 Squadron. To 57 Squadron.	
X3585 AA-V	FTR Kiel 12/13.3.42.	
X3586 AA-A/J	To 23 Operational Training Unit.	
X3587 AA-P/S	FTR Essen 8/9.6.42.	
X3588 AA-U	FTR Kiel 12/13.3.42.	
X3595 AA-K	To Manufacturers for conversion.	
X3597 AA-C/Y/C	To 115 Squadron.	
X3636 AA-R	To 1483 Flight.	
X3637	To 9 Squadron.	
X3646 AA-M	FTR Mainz 11/12.8.42.	
X3652 AA-O	FTR Essen 25/26.3.42.	
X3661 AA-A/Q	FTR Cologne 5/6.4.42.	
X3664 AA-X/Q/V/Y	FTR Hamburg 28/29.7.42.	
X3667 AA-D	FTR Le Havre 22/23.4.42.	
X3705 AA-F	To 29 Operational Training Unit.	
X3714 AA-W	FTR Hamburg 26/27.7.42.	
X3720 AA-U	FTR Düsseldorf 10.7.42.	
X3747	From 57 Squadron. To 12 Operational Training Unit.	
X3751 AA-P	To 23 Operational Training Unit.	
X3755	From 57 Squadron. To 150 Squadron.	
X3756	From 57 Squadron and back.	
X3760 AA-L	FTR Emden 20/21.6.42.	
X3794	From 9 Squadron. FTR Emden 3/4.9.42.	
X3867 AA-P	FTR Duisburg 6/7.9.42.	
X3931	To 1483 Flight.	
X3936 AA-T	To 156 Squadron.	
X3946	From 57 Squadron. To 115 Squadron.	
X3954	FTR Kiel 13/14.10.42.	
X3959	To 156 Squadron.	
X9628 AA-A	FTR Essen 8/9.11.41.	
X9634 AA-F	Ditched off Suffolk coast when bound for Bremen 13/14.7.41.	
X9742 AA-Q	From 311 Squadron. To 115 Squadron.	
X9757 AA-S	To 419 (Moose) Squadron RCAF.	
X9759 AA-R	FTR Hamburg 15/16.9.41.	

X9760 AA-P		To 57 Squadron.
X9764 AA-V		To 304 Squadron.
X9767 AA-S		FTR Hüls 6/7.9.41.
X9806 AA-R		From 101 Squadron. To 311 Squadron.
X9825 AA-V		To 1505 BAT Flight.
X9834 AA-O		FTR Karlsruhe 17/18.9.41.
X9914 AA-M		FTR Mannheim 22/23.10.41.
X9916		FTR Cologne 15/16.10.41.
X9918 AA-U		To 21 Operational Training Unit.
X9941 AA-W		To 1503 BAT Flight.
X9951 AA-L		FTR Berlin 7/8.11.41.
X9975 AA-U		To 156 Squadron.
X9976 AA-O		FTR Berlin 7/8.11.41.
X9977 AA-D		FTR Essen 8/9.11.41.
X9981 AA-X		FTR Nuremberg 12/13.10.41.
Z1053 AA-H		To 57 Squadron.
Z1068 AA-R		To 156 Squadron.
Z1077 AA-N		To 419 (Moose) Squadron RCAF.
Z1083 AA-K		From 40 Squadron. To 419 (Moose) Squadron RCAF.
Z1087		To 57 Squadron.
Z1091 AA-V		To 57 Squadron.
Z1093 AA-M		To 57 Squadron.
Z1096		To 57 Squadron.
Z1099 AA-M/S		FTR Emden 30.11/1.12.41.
Z1108 AA-X		To 156 Squadron.
Z1114 AA-C		To 156 Squadron.
Z1144		Abandoned over Lincolnshire on return from Emden 26.11.41.
Z1145		To 57 Squadron.
Z1149 AA-B		To 18 Operational Training Unit.
Z1153		Crashed 29.11.41. Details uncertain.
Z1168 AA-H		FTR Hamburg 26/27.10.41.
Z1566 AA-K		Crashed in Staffordshire while training 22.5.42.
Z1570 AA-B		FTR Hamburg 28/29.7.42.
Z1572 AA-M		From 115 Squadron. To 419 (Moose) Squadron RCAF.
Z1573 AA-T		FTR Essen 8/9.6.42.
Z1592 AA-O		To 18 Operational Training Unit.
Z1596 AA-K		FTR Hamburg 26/27.7.42.
Z1616 AA-D		Crashed soon after take-off from Feltwell bound for Bremen 29.6.42.
Z1652 AA-D		From 57 Squadron. FTR Milan 24/25.10.42.
Z1738		To 115 Squadron.
Z1747		From 57 Squadron. To 1483 Flight.
Z8429 AA-V		From 57 Squadron. To 158 Squadron.
Z8441 AA-T		To 158 Squadron.
Z8495		To 305 Squadron.
Z8834 AA-P		Crashed in Suffolk on return from Brest 23.12.41.
Z8854		From 101 Squadron. To 1429 Flight.
Z8858 AA-G		From 9 Squadron. To 214 Squadron.

Z8859		To 40 Squadron.
Z8868	AA-C	To 57 Squadron.
Z8904	AA-O	From 57 Squadron. To 40 Squadron.
Z8909		
Z8942	AA-J	FTR Essen 8/9.11.41.
Z8945	AA-O	FTR Cologne 15/16.10.41.
Z8961	AA-F	From 57 Squadron. To 25 Operational Training Unit.
Z8968	AA-D	From 57 Squadron. To 40 Squadron.
Z8969	AA-R	FTR Cologne 10/11.10.41.
Z8971	AA-A	Crashed in Devon on return from Brest 27/28.12.41.
Z8977	AA-N	From 57 Squadron. To 40 Squadron.
Z8978	AA-G	From 57 Squadron. To 156 Squadron.
BJ584	AA-C	To 115 Squadron.
BJ596		From 57 Squadron. FTR Frankfurt 8/9.9.42.
BJ599	AA-U	From 1483 Flight. FTR Hamburg 28/29.7.42.
BJ625	AA-T	FTR Mainz 11/12.8.42.
BJ661	AA-X	FTR Hamburg 28/29.7.42.
BJ707		From 57 Squadron. To 156 Squadron.
BJ708		FTR Kassel 27/28.8.42.
BJ721	AA-A	To 29 OTU.
BJ725	AA-H	From 9 Squadron. FTR Milan 24/25.10.42.
BJ756		To 115 Squadron.
BJ758		To 1483 Flight.
BJ765	AA-L	FTR Duisburg 6/7.9.42.
BJ766		To 150 Squadron.
BJ767	AA-V	FTR Mainz 11/12.8.42.
BJ772	AA-D	Destroyed on the ground at Mildenhall by exploding 88 Squadron Boston Z2285 28.9.42.
BJ773		Force-landed in Cambridgeshire while training 11.8.42.
BJ774	AA-X	FTR from mining sortie 20/21.8.42.
BJ790	AA-J	To 82 Operational Training Unit.
BJ828		FTR Düsseldorf 10/11.9.42.
BJ832	AA-Z	From 115 Squadron. Returned to 115 Squadron.
BJ837	AA-F	Crash-landed at Lakenheath on return from Kiel 13/14.10.42.
BJ898		To 115 Squadron.
BJ968	AA-W	FTR Düsseldorf 10/11.9.42.
BJ974		FTR Düsseldorf 10/11.9.42.
BK206		To 115Squadron.
BK207		To 18 Operational Training Unit.
BK274	AA-Y	To 115 Squadron.
BK275		To 115 Squadron.
BK341		FTR from mining sortie 11/12.10.42.
BK362		To 115 Squadron.
BK386		To 156 Squadron.
DF639		FTR Osnabrück 6/7.10.42.
DF673		FTR Nuremberg 28/29.8.42.
DV845	AA-Y	

DV865 AA-J
DV883 AA-F

STIRLING.　　　　　From October 1942 to April 1944.

N6123 AA-Q	From 1657 Conversion Unit. FTR from mining sortie 3/4.3.43.
N3683	From 1657 Conversion Unit. Returned to 1657 Conversion Unit.
N3704	From 15 Squadron. Returned to 15 Squadron.
R9200 AA-S	From 149 Squadron. SOC 19.7.45.
R9243 AA-C	To 1651 Conversion Unit.
R9245 AA-N	Crashed soon after take-off from Newmarket when bound for a mining sortie 16.12.42.
R9246 AA-S	Crash-landed in Huntingdonshire while training 24.11.42.
R9247 AA-W	FTR Fallersleben 17/18.12.42.
R9248 AA-H	FTR Lorient 23/24.1.43.
R9250 AA-C	FTR Hamburg 3/4.2.43.
R9290 AA-Y/X	FTR from mining sortie 28/29.4.43.
R9316 AA-K	From 214 Squadron. FTR Lorient 13/14.2.43.
W7469 AA-O	From 149 Squadron. FTR Mannheim 16/17.4.43.
W7513 AA-G	From 149 Squadron. FTR from mining sortie 28/29.4.43.
BF311	From 149 Squadron. To 15 Squadron.
BF321	To 1657 Conversion Unit.
BF377 AA-J	From CRD. To 1651 Conversion Unit.
BF396 AA-X	From 1657 Conversion Unit. FTR Fallersleben 17/18.12.42.
BF397	From 1657 Conversion Unit. To 1657 Conversion Unit.
BF398 AA-F/P	Partially abandoned over Staffordshire and crashed while training 17.5.43.
BF399 AA-O	Crashed near Oakington while training 28.11.42.
BF400 AA-G	FTR Fallersleben 17/18.12.42.
BF412 AA-Y	From 15 Squadron. To 1665 Conversion Unit.
BF434 AA-X/Y	To 1665 Conversion Unit.
BF437 AA-L	FTR Nuremberg 8/9.3.43.
BF443 AA-V	To 1651 Conversion Unit.
BF451 AA-Z	FTR Mannheim 16/17.4.43.
BF455 AA-Y	Ditched off Sussex coast on return from Frankfurt 11.4.43.
BF456 AA-J	FTR Frankfurt 10/11.4.43.
BF458 JN-P	FTR Remscheid 30/31.7.43.
BF459 JN-G	FTR Mannheim 23/24.9.43.
BF461 JN-B	FTR from mining sortie 4/5.11.43.
BF465 JN-K	From 15 Squadron. FTR Berlin 23/24.8.43.
BF467 AA-W	To 214 Squadron and back. FTR from mining sortie 28/29.4.43.
BF473	From 90 Squadron. To 199 Squadron.
BF506 AA-P	FTR Rostock 20/21.4.43.
BF513 JN-E	FTR Stuttgart 14/15.4.43.
BF516	To 214 Squadron.
BF517 AA-O	To 1657 Conversion Unit.
BF518 AA-E	Crashed on landing at West Malling during transit flight 1.9.43.

BF561 AA-O	FTR Wuppertal 29/30.5.43.
BF564 JN-W	FTR Berlin 23/24.8.43.
BF573	To 149 Squadron.
BF575 AA-H	To 295 Squadron.
BF577 JN-M	FTR Hamburg 2/3.8.43.
BK602 AA-R	From 7 Squadron. FTR Düsseldorf 25/26.5.43.
BK604 AA-S	From 1657 Conversion Unit. FTR Hamburg 3/4.2.43.
BK608 AA-T	Crashed on landing at Stradishall on return from Turin 29.11.42.
BK609 AA-R	Crashed on landing at Bradwell Bay on return from Turin 30.11.42.
BK614 JN-H/N	FTR from mining sortie 6/7.8.43.
BK615	To Royal Aircraft Establishment.
BK617 AA-D	Crashed in the sea off Cromer when bound for mining sortie 5.2.43.
BK618 AA-Q	FTR Frankfurt 2/3.12.42.
BK619 AA-O/X	To 1651 Conversion Unit.
BK620 AA-A	FTR Fallersleben 17/18.12.42.
BK624 AA-A	From 1651 Conversion Unit. Returned to 1651 Conversion Unit.
BK646 AA-N	FTR from mining sortie 14/15.6.43.
BK647 AA-M	Crash-landed soon after take-off from Newmarket when bound for Essen 5/6.3.43.
BK664 AA-M	Crashed on landing at Newmarket on return from Mannheim 16/17.4.43.
BK695 AA-X/N	From 15 Squadron. To 199 Squadron.
BK721 AA-Z Duisburg	Crashed soon after take-off from Newmarket when bound for 13.5.43.
BK768 AA-L	FTR Gelsenkirchen 25/26.6.43.
BK770 AA-L	Crashed in Norfolk on return from Duisburg 8/9.4.43.
BK776 AA-R	FTR Wuppertal 29/30.5.43.
BK777 AA-U/JN-F	To 1653 Conversion Unit.
BK778 JN-U	FTR from mining sortie 4/5.11.43.
BK783 AA-Q	FTR Dortmund 23/24.5.43.
BK807 AA-M	FTR from mining sortie 28/29.4.43.
BK809 JN-T	Crashed at Mepal on take-off for Boulogne 8.9.43.
BK810 AA-G	FTR Mülheim 22/23.6.43.
BK817 AA-B	FTR Düsseldorf 11/12.6.43.
EE878 AA-P/F	FTR Berlin 31.8/1.9.43.
EE881 JN-G	To 1657 Conversion Unit.
EE886 AA-L	Crashed on landing at Oakington on return from Aachen 14.7.43.
EE890 AA-L	FTR Hamburg 24/25.7.43.
EE891 AA-Q	FTR from mining sortie 15/16.8.43.
EE892 AA-F	Crashed off Suffolk coast on return from Essen 25/26.7.43.
EE893 JN-N	FTR Mannheim 5/6.9.43.
EE897 AA-G	FTR from mining sortie 4/5.11.43.
EE898 AA-D/N	To 1651 Conversion Unit.
EE915 AA-X	FTR Remscheid 30/31.7.43.
EE918 AA-D	FTR Berlin 31.8/1.9.43.
EE938 AA-X/F	FTR Berlin 23/24.8.43.
EE955 AA-D	FTR Nuremberg 27/28.8.43.

EE958 AA-V/A	To 513 Squadron and back. To 1653 Conversion Unit.
EF130 JN-M	FTR Frankfurt 4/5.10.43.
EF135 JN-W/AA-T	Crashed on landing at Mepal on return from Hanover 28.9.43.
EF137 JN-Y/AA-E	FTR from mining sortie 23/24.4.44.
EF142 AA-C	Crashed near Mepal on return from mining sortie 24/25.10.43.
EF148 AA-R	FTR Berlin 22/23.11.43.
EF152 JN-T/AA-T	To 1653 Conversion Unit.
EF163 JN-L	Crashed in Cambridgeshire on return from mining sortie 16/17.12.43.
EF181	To 218 Squadron.
EF200	To 513 Squadron.
EF201	To 513 Squadron.
EF205	To 513 Squadron.
EF206	To 513 Squadron.
EF207	To 218 Squadron.
EF211	To 513 Squadron.
EF215 AA-M	From 214 Squadron. FTR Special Operations 5/6.3.44.
EF217	From 622 Squadron. To 1653 Conversion Unit.
EF233	From 214 Squadron. To 218 Squadron.
EF236 AA-J	Crashed on landing on return from mining sortie 13/14.4.44
EF251	To 90 Squadron.
EF254	To 90 Squadron.
EF327	To 149 Squadron.
EF337	To 149 Squadron.
EF340 AA-Q	From 149 Squadron. FTR from mining sortie 5/6.5.43.
EF398 AA-A	FTR Wuppertal 29/30.5.43.
EF399 AA-O	From 15 Squadron. FTR Mülheim 22/23.6.43.
EF400	To 149 Squadron.
EF408 AA-P	FTR Mülheim 22/23.6.43.
EF435 JN-J/Y	SOC 5.6.47.
EF436 AA-A	FTR from mining sortie 5/6.7.43.
EF440	To 620 Squadron.
EF451	To 620 Squadron.
EF454 AA-A/C	To 1657 Conversion Unit.
EF456	To 620 Squadron.
EF458	To 90 Squadron.
EF462 AA-M	To 218 Squadron.
EF465 AA-H/K	To 513 Squadron.
EF466	From A&AEE. To 1653 Conversion Unit.
EF491 AA-O	Crash-landed at Coltishall on return from Berlin 31.8/1.9.43.
EF501 AA-K	FTR Berlin 31.8/1.9.43.
EF507 AA-P	To 1332 Conversion Unit.
EF512 AA-A	To 1661 Conversion Unit.
EF513 JN-E	To 1657 Conversion Unit.
EF514 AA-D	To 199 Squadron.
EF515 AA-F	FTR Hanover 27/28.9.43.
EH877 JN-C	FTR Hanover 27/28.9.43.

EH880 AA-D/J	Crashed in Northumberland during approach on return from mining sortie 1/2.12.43.	
EH881 AA-Z	FTR Wuppertal 29/30.5.43.	
EH889 AA-Z	FTR Mülheim 22/23.6.43.	
EH901 JN-O	To 1657 Conversion Unit.	
EH902 AA-K	FTR Wuppertal 24/25.6.43.	
EH905 AA-R	FTR Berlin 31.8/1.9.43.	
EH928 AA-A	FTR Hamburg 2/3.8.43.	
EH929	To 15 Squadron.	
EH930	To 15 Squadron.	
EH935 JN-K	FTR Mannheim 23/24.9.43.	
EH936 JN-W	FTR Mannheim 23/24.9.43.	
EH938 AA-F	FTR Mönchengladbach 30/31.8.43.	
EH939 JN-J	To 90 Squadron.	
EH946	To 620 Squadron.	
EH947	To 90 Squadron.	
EH948 AA-Q	FTR from mining sortie 24/25.2.44.	
EH949 JN-P	To 1651 Conversion Unit.	
EH955 JN-K/AA-K	FTR from mining sortie 18/19.4.44.	
EJ108 AA-O	To 1657 Conversion Unit.	
EJ901 JN-O		
LJ441	To 1653 Conversion Unit.	
LJ442 JN-F	FTR Leverkusen 19/20.11.43.	
LJ453 AA-K	From 15 Squadron. FTR Berlin 22/23.11.43.	
LJ457	To 1657 Conversion Unit.	
LJ462 AA-O	From 15 Squadron. FTR from mining sortie 13/14.3.44.	
LJ473 AA-R	Crash-landed at Mepal on return from mining sortie 4/5.1.44.	
LK378 JN-G	To 1657 Conversion Unit.	
LK384 JN-X	To 1653 Conversion Unit.	
LK389	To 1661 Conversion Unit.	
LK396	From 622 Squadron. To 218 Squadron.	
LK540	To 1651 Conversion Unit.	

LANCASTER. **From March 1944.**

R5692 JN-P	From 15 Squadron. To 90 Squadron.
R5846	From 622 Squadron. To 5 Lancaster Finishing School.
W4174	From 15 Squadron. To 1654 Conversion Unit.
ED310	From 15 Squadron. To 1 Lancaster Finishing School.
ED425	From 622 Squadron. To 5 Lancaster Finishing School.
HK541	From 300 Squadron. To 115 Squadron.
HK542	From 156 Squadron. To 115 Squadron.
HK544	From 626 Squadron. To 115 Squadron.
HK551 JN-E	To 115 Squadron.
HK553 AA-S	FTR Dreux 10/11.6.44.
HK554 JN-F/Z	
HK557	To 5 Maintenance Unit.

HK558 JN-D		FTR Amaye-sur-Seulles 30.7.44.
HK561 AA-Y		
HK562 JN-Y/L		
HK563 JN-W		
HK564 AA-P		From 115 Squadron. FTR Rüsselsheim 12/13.8.44.
HK565 JN-C		To 115 Squadron.
HK567 AA-C		FTR from tactical operation to Mare du Magne 7/8.8.44.
HK568 AA-K		FTR Stuttgart 24/25.7.44.
HK569 AA-Q		FTR Homburg 20/21.7.44.
HK573 AA-H		
HK574 JN-P/AA-R		Ditched in the River Orwell on return from Leuna (Merseburg) 6/7.12.44.
HK575 AA-O		FTR Stuttgart 24/25.7.44.
HK576 AA-G		
HK593 AA-H/JN-X		
HK594 AA-G		FTR Stettin 29/30.8.44.
HK596 AA-O		FTR Walcheren (Flushing) 21.10.44.
HK597 JN-P/N		To 46 Maintenance Unit
HK600 JN-K		
HK601 JN-D		To 10 Maintenance Unit.
HK697		To 195 Squadron.
HK751		To 1667 Conversion Unit. Conversion Unit.
HK792		From 138 Squadron.
HK806 AA-B		
JA903		From 44 (Rhodesia) Squadron.
LL864		To 115 Squadron.
LL865 AA-V		
LL866 AA-W/S		FTR Rüsselsheim 25/26.8.44.
LL867		To 115 Squadron.
LL880		To 115 Squadron.
LL888 JN-X		FTR Valenciennes 15/16.6.44.
LL921 AA-E		From 115 Squadron. FTR Aulnoye 19/20.7.44.
LL942 JN-C		Blew up at Mepal 30.6.44.
LL945		To 15 Squadron.
LM104 JN-K/Z AA-Z		FTR Dortmund 6/7.10.44.
LM265		To 514 Squadron.
LM266 AA-A/F/J		
LM268 AA-D		FTR from mining sortie 11/12.9.44.
LM276 AA-S		
LM510		To 115 Squadron.
LM544 JN-Y AA-J/O		From 115 Squadron. To 138 Squadron. Returned to 75(NZ) Squadron.
LM593 AA-N		To 622 Squadron and back. FTR Rüsselsheim 25/26.8.44.
LM728 AA-R		From 514 Squadron. Undercarriage collapsed on landing at Mepal 14.4.45.
LM733 AA-R		From 514 Squadron. FTR Münster 21.3.45.

LM740 AA-B		FTR Kamen 25.2.45.
ME321 AA-N		FTR Vohwinkel 1/2.1.45.
ME450 AA-W		Crashed in Cambridgeshire on return from Dortmund 26.2.45.
ME531 AA-K		
ME682 AA-E		From 625 Squadron. To 1662 Conversion Unit.
ME689 AA-Y		FTR Chambly 1/2.5.44.
ME690 AA-Z		FTR Dortmund 22/23.5.44.
ME691 AA-R		FTR Homburg 20/21.7.44.
ME692		To 115 Squadron.
ME702 AA-Q		FTR Dreux 10/11.6.44.
ME751 AA-B/M		From 115 Squadron. To 138 Squadron.
ME752 JN-Z/AA-E		From 115 Squadron. FTR Homberg 20/21.7.44.
ME753		From 115 Squadron. To 1651 Conversion Unit.
ME754 AA-A		From 115 Squadron. To 166 Squadron.
ME834		To 115 Squadron.
ND745		To 115 Squadron.
ND747 AA-T/O		To 5 Lancaster Finishing School.
ND752 AA-O		FTR Homberg 20/21.7.44.
ND753 AA-D/G		To 115 Squadron.
ND754		To 115 Squadron.
ND756 AA-M		FTR Stuttgart 28/29.7.44.
ND758		To 115 Squadron.
ND760		To 115 Squadron.
ND761		To 115 Squadron.
ND768 AA-F		FTR Dortmund 22/23.5.44.
ND782 AA-U		To 3 Lancaster Finishing School.
ND796 AA-J		FTR Friedrichshafen 27/28.4.44.
ND800 AA-J		From 115 Squadron. FTR Homberg 20/21.7.44.
ND801 JN-A/X		Crashed while landing at Mepal 3.2.45.
ND802 JN-D		FTR Aachen 27/28.5.44.
ND804 JN-K		FTR Duisburg 21/22.5.44.
ND904 JN-P/AA-B		From 115 Squadron. FTR Saarbrücken 5/6.10.44.
ND908 JN-M		FTR Aachen 27/28.5.44.
ND911 JN-V		FTR Homberg 20.11.44.
ND914 AA-H		Crashed during landing at Mepal 28.5.44.
ND915 AA-L/A		FTR Homberg 20/21.7.44.
ND917 JN-O		From 115 Squadron. FTR Solingen 4.11.44.
ND918 AA-Y		To 1654 Conversion Unit.
ND919 AA-D		FTR Louvain 11/12.5.44.
ND920 AA-P		From 115 Squadron. FTR Rimeux 24/25.6.44.
NE148 AA-H		From 115 Squadron. FTR Stuttgart 28/29.7.44.
NE181 JN-M		To 514 Squadron.
NF935 AA-P		
NF980 JN-F		FTR Osterfeld 30.11.44.
NF981 JN-Y/D		
NG113 AA-D		FTR Chemnitz 14/15.2.45.
NG322 JN-F		

NG448 JN-P/AA-A
NG449 AA-T   FTR Münster 21.3.45.
NN710 AA-Q   FTR Rheydt 27.12.44.
NN745 AA-A   FTR from mining sortie 21/22.11.44.
NN747 JN-O/AA-D
NN773 AA-G   From 514 Squadron.
PA967 AA-D   From 115 Squadron. FTR Homberg 20/21.7.44.
PB132 AA-Y/T
         JN-X
PB380 JN-V   From 44 (Rhodesia) Squadron.
PB418 AA-C
PB421 AA-U/K/JN-P
PB424 AA-O   From 44 (Rhodesia) Squadron.
PB427 AA-U
PB430 AA-P   Crashed while landing at Hawkinge on return from Boulogne 17.9.44.
PB520 AA-G   FTR Homberg 20.11.44.
PB689 AA-X   FTR Homberg 20.11.44.
PB741 AA-E   FTR Hattingen 14.3.45.
PB761 AA-Y   Crashed in Suffolk on return from Wanne-Eickel 16/17.1.45.
PB763 AA-A
PB767   To 514 Squadron.
PB820 AA-V
PD327   From 630 Squadron.
PD422   From 44 (Rhodesia) Squadron.
PP663
RA510 AA-J/E
RA541 AA-J   To 514 Squadron.
RA564 JN-P   FTR Münster 21.3.45.
RF127 AA-W
RF129 AA-M
RF157 AA-X
RF190 AA-F   From 115 Squadron.

HEAVIEST SINGLE LOSS.

20/21.7.44. Homberg. 7 Lancasters FTR.

Key to Abbreviations

A&AEE	Aeroplane and Armaments Experimental Establishment.
AA	Anti-Aircraft fire.
AACU	Anti-Aircraft Cooperation Unit.
AAS	Air Armament School.
AASF	Advance Air Striking Force.
AAU	Aircraft Assembly Unit.
ACM	Air Chief Marshal.
ACSEA	Air Command South-East Asia.
AFDU	Air Fighting Development Unit.
AFEE	Airborne Forces Experimental Unit.
AFTDU	Airborne Forces Tactical Development Unit.
AGS	Air Gunners School.
AMDP	Air Members for Development and Production.
AOC	Air Officer Commanding.
AOS	Air Observers School.
ASRTU	Air-Sea Rescue Training Unit.
ATTDU	Air Transport Tactical Development Unit.
AVM	Air Vice-Marshal.
BAT	Beam Approach Training.
BCBS	Bomber Command Bombing School.
BCDU	Bomber Command Development Unit.
BCFU	Bomber Command Film Unit.
BCIS	Bomber Command Instructors School.
BDU	Bombing Development Unit.
BSTU	Bomber Support Training Unit.
CF	Conversion Flight.
CFS	Central Flying School.
CGS	Central Gunnery School.
C-in-C	Commander in Chief.
CNS	Central Navigation School.
CO	Commanding Officer.
CRD	Controller of Research and Development.
CU	Conversion Unit.
DGRD	Director General for Research and Development.
EAAS	Empire Air Armament School.
EANS	Empire Air Navigation School.
ECDU	Electronic Countermeasures Development Unit.
ECFS	Empire Central Flying School.
ETPS	Empire Test Pilots School.
F/L	Flight Lieutenant.
Flt	Flight.
F/O	Flying Officer.
FPP	Ferry Pilots School.

F/S	Flight Sergeant.
FTR	Failed to Return.
FTU	Ferry Training Unit.
G/C	Group Captain.
Gp	Group.
HCU	Heavy Conversion Unit.
HGCU	Heavy Glider Conversion Unit.
LFS	Lancaster Finishing School.
MAC	Mediterranean Air Command.
MTU	Mosquito Training Unit.
MU	Maintenance Unit.
NTU	Navigation Training Unit.
OADU	Overseas Aircraft Delivery Unit.
OAPU	Overseas Aircraft Preparation Unit.
OTU	Operational Training Unit.
P/O	Pilot Officer.
PTS	Parachute Training School.
RAE	Royal Aircraft Establishment.
SGR	School of General Reconnaissance.
Sgt	Sergeant.
SHAEF	Supreme Headquarters Allied Expeditionary Force.
SIU	Signals Intelligence Unit.
S/L	Squadron Leader.
SOC	Struck off Charge.
SOE	Special Operations Executive.
Sqn	Squadron.
TF	Training Flight.
TFU	Telecommunications Flying Unit.
W/C	Wing Commander.
Wg	Wing.
WIDU	Wireless Intelligence Development Unit.
W/O	Warrant Officer.

www.ingramcontent.com/pod-product-compliance
Lightning Source LLC
Chambersburg PA
CBHW081206230426
43666CB00015B/2665